ZONE 4

Contents

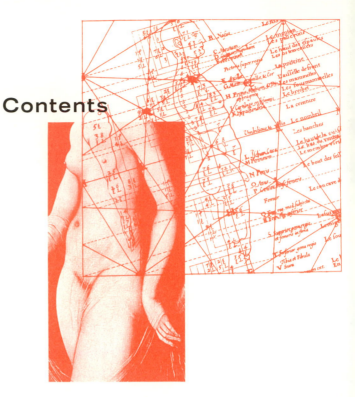

Fragments for a History of the Human Body

Part Two

Edited by Michel Feher

with Ramona Naddaff and Nadia Tazi

Editors: Jonathan Crary, Michel Feher, Hal Foster, Sanford Kwinter

Special Editor of this Issue: Michel Feher

Associate Editors of this Issue: Ramona Naddaff, Nadia Tazi

Managing Editor: Ramona Naddaff

Designer: Bruce Mau

Translation Editor: Siri Hustvedt

Translations: Anna Cancogni, Lydia Davis, Roger Friedman, Janet Lloyd, Ughetta Lubin, Ralph Manheim, Sarah Matthews, Ian Patterson, Alyson Waters.

Editorial Assistance: Judith Aminoff, Ted Byfield, Reynolds Childress, Barbara Czarnecki, Deborah Drier, Meighan Gale, Freya Godard, Astrid Hustvedt, Mike Taylor, Nancy Worman.

Production: Steven Bock, John Calvelli, Alison Hahn, Anita Matusevics, Damian McShane, Susan Meggs-Becker, Greg Van Alstyne, Dorothy Vreeker.

Picture Research: CLAM! (Christine de Coninck, Anne Mensior) and Marie-Hélène Agueros.

Special thanks to: Archie, Ron Date, Mark Elvin, Mickey Fear, Madeleine Feher, Albert Fuss, Marvin Green, Judith Gurewich, Krista Hinds, Jonathan Joaquin, Barbara Kerr, Gus Kiley, Kerri Kwinter, Rick Lambert, G.E.R. Lloyd, Janet Lloyd, Sandra Naddaff, Lisa Naftolin, Mary Picone, John Scinocco, Alice Sindzingre, Mike Tibre.

Typesetting by Canadian Composition.

Film Preparation by P.B.C. Lithoprep.

Printed in Canada by Provincial Graphics.

Distributed by The MIT Press, Cambridge, Massachusetts and London, England.

We gratefully acknowledge translation assistance provided for this volume by the French Ministry of Culture and Communication.

© 1989 Urzone, Inc.
ZONE 611 Broadway Suite 838
New York, NY 10012
All rights reserved.

First printing February, 1989
Second printing April, 1990

ISSN: 0887-0411
ISBN: 0-942299-26-4 (cloth)
ISBN: 0-942299-24-8 (paper)

Library of Congress Catalog Card Number: 88-051439

FRAGMENTS FOR A HISTORY OF THE HUMAN BODY   PART THREE

Foreword

The present volume forms the second part of *Fragments for a History of the Human Body*. As the notion of fragment implies, the texts collected here do not pretend either to form a complete survey or to define a compact portion of the history of the body. The fact that so many problems are addressed only indicates the extent of the field to be explored and marks the several approaches of the ongoing investigation. These fragments, therefore, find their consistency in a cross section in which the connections among different themes and disciplines — history, anthropology, philosophy, etc. — are highlighted rather than in a general overview or a strictly delimited schema. Each of the three volumes of this project corresponds to a specific research approach — though the articles in it complement and connect with one another in more than one way.

The first approach can be called vertical since what is explored here is the human body's relationship to the divine, to the bestial, and to the machines that imitate or simulate it. The second approach, represented by the present volume, covers the various junctures between the body's "outside" and "inside": it can therefore be called a "psychosomatic" approach, studying the manifestation — or production — of the soul and the expression of the emotions through the body's attitudes, and, on another level, the speculations inspired by cenesthesia, pain and death. Finally, the third approach brings into play the classical opposition between organ and function by showing how a certain organ or bodily substance can be used to justify or challenge the way human society functions and, reciprocally, how a certain political or social function tends to make the body of the person filling that function the organ of a larger body — the social body or the universe as a whole.

Michel Feher

11

Jacques Louis David, The Death of Socrates (New York, Metropolitan
Museum of Art, Wolfe Fund, 1931).

Therefore, Socrates is Immortal

Nicole Loraux

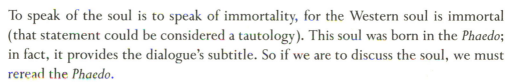

To speak of the soul is to speak of immortality, for the Western soul is immortal (that statement could be considered a tautology). This soul was born in the *Phaedo*; in fact, it provides the dialogue's subtitle. So if we are to discuss the soul, we must reread the *Phaedo*.

— Reread the *Phaedo*: Whatever for? It's such a bore and so spiritualistic.

— Reread the *Phaedo*? Maybe. But there is nothing left to say about it. Tradition — and what a tradition it is! — has already said it all.

Two reactions: on the one hand, an outright rejection of what is seen as an edifying text; on the other, a reverential reiteration of a long tradition of spiritualistic commentaries.[1] Both attitudes tend to distance us from this once much-read dialogue. But between the two extremes is there no other possible approach to the *Phaedo*?

One effect of this double warning might be to prompt us to look further, in the hope of devising a new strategy for coping with the enormous prestige of this dialogue, a prestige based, first, on its supposedly authentic account of Socrates' death; second on its purely philosophical speculation (some developments of which are dauntingly difficult); and third, of course, on the immortality of the soul — for which the *Phaedo* is said to contain more than one proof.

This study will attempt a new reading of the *Phaedo*, not by calling upon philology, philosophy or theology,[2] but by turning, for once, to history. However, there is no point in pondering the historicity of the account of Socrates' death: this question has been left behind by now, as it always has been for readers alive to the role that fiction plays in Plato's work. Rather, let us concentrate on the new departure that the *Phaedo* represents in Greek (and, more generally, Western) representations of immortality. To claim that in this dialogue the immortality of the soul made its official entry into Greek thought is not to forget all that the subject owes to the mysticism of the Orphic and Pythagorean sects, long before Plato:[3] that is something the text of the *Phaedo* itself acknowledges, frequently justifying its initiatory concept of philosophy with appeals to "ancient discourse" (*palaios logos*). But the important point is that with the *Phaedo* and the institutionalization of philosophy as a literary genre, a line of thinking, hitherto marginal to the life of the city, acquired a legitimacy that was never again disputed.

But to note this new departure is only half the battle: we must still find out what it is about this text that made such a turning point possible in the Greek representations of immortality. The *Phaedo* may be a seminal text, but in order to discover a reading of it that does more than just reiterate the tradition, let us try to analyze the discursive tactics adopted by this daring promotion of immortality. The aim of the present study will be to seize both on the ways in which the dialogue breaks new ground and on the features that established it as a tradition.

A Practice of Separation

From Homer down to the classical period, Greek man had a body (*sōma*) and a *psuchē* (a word that I shall not translate at this point for fear of identifying it prematurely with "soul"). This *psuchē* was liberated by death. Let us see what a Greek would make of these two notions in the three consecutive, or at times concurrent, figures with which he identified: the epic hero, the soldier-citizen of the classical period and the philosopher. As it happens, these three images correspond to three models of death, and this correspondence imbues them with their exemplary importance.

Consider the death of the Homeric hero: if the collectivity to which he belongs treats the inert corpse in the appropriate fashion, the deceased warrior will attain the social status of death, the bard will be able to sing of his undying glory (*kleos aphthiton*) for the edification of posterity, and his *psuchē* will join the dim, fleeting shades of the dead from the past, in Hades.[4] This last stage is certainly a crucial moment, and yet for Homer, the body seems infinitely more real than the insubstantial *psuchē* that upon death flees, weeping, from the warrior, at last to become a shade among other shades. Gently mocking Socrates' questioners, Plato recalls this:

"You seem to have a childish fear that the wind literally blows a soul to bits when it quits the body, and scatters it in all directions, more especially if one happens to die when it's blowing a full gale."[5]

Now let us consider the death in battle of the soldier-citizen of classical Athens. He has given his life (*bios*) for the city — but, equally, the texts sometimes say that he has given his body (*sōma*) or his *psuchē*, which was his breath of life. In exchange, the city gives him immortal glory beyond death and a place in the memory of the living. He may go to Hades (always supposing that something remains of him to make that journey, apart from his name, which now belongs to the collective memory of the living); but that is not the essential point. The civic tradition does not have much to say about what becomes of this glorious dead warrior, for the full meaning of his death now belongs to the city. The citizen's life was of scant importance: the collectivity bestowed it upon him. Nor did his body matter: already cremated on the field of battle, it has been reduced to bones, an abstract basis on which to construct the political ceremony of the public funeral rites. The official orator steps forward to celebrate the city through its dead; all that matters now are his words.[6]

Socrates is about to die, and as he awaits death, he speaks of immortality — the death of his body and the immortality of the soul (and since the essence of the Western soul lies in its immortality, we need no longer hesitate to translate that term, *psuchē*). In other words, according to Socrates, body and soul are already irrevocably separated, just as are the visible and the invisible, that which is destined to lose its identity and that which keeps it forever, the dissoluble and the indissoluble, the mortal and the divine. But he explains to his disciples that this dialectical division preexists whatever death will bring about: namely, *lusis kai chōrismos*, the detachment and separation of the soul, which death liberates from the body. Sentenced by the city to die, the model philosopher awaits his death. He does not anticipate it by suicide: he has already done so far better in his lifetime, since he knows that "to philosophize is to learn to die." He has trained himself to reject all the pleasures of the body so that, even in the here and now, his life resembles as closely as possible the existence of one who is dead. Socrates' disciples will have to part from him, bidding him that same farewell (*chairē*) that the funeral *stēlai* in the Athenian cemeteries repeat over and over again. And Socrates, for his part, bids a serene and seemingly joyful farewell to all that he is leaving, all that he has already left: the mass of

Helmeted man dying during a race, funerary stele, 6th-5th century B.C.
(Athens, National Museum).

Athenians, the life of a man and a citizen, the body. Hence, the series of exits — not
to say expulsions — and leave-takings, all rehearsals for the farewell to the body, that
punctuate the *Phaedo*.[7] Because all life is in the soul, the philosopher, at last liberated from his body, will know the bliss of Hades, the last abode of every soul delivered from its *sōma* but endowed with thought (*phronēsis*)[8] — indeed, assimilated into
the very activity of thinking. Socrates the *atopos*, disconcerting as he was in having
no place of his own in his lifetime, prepares himself for the only journey now con-
ceivable, for even the affirmation of immortality does not preclude the need to
"organize one's space in the beyond."[9] He will die so as to philosophize in the
underworld...meanwhile, the poison is already being prepared for him.

16

While the text of the *Phaedo* is well-known, this brief summary will at least have helped us grasp the full extent of Plato's innovations and to assess the consequences of his shifting the emphasis from the body to the soul, which is now regarded as immortal. From the age of the epic to the world of the city, death was a matter for the society of the living. In Plato the individual philosopher sets out to reappropriate it for himself, laying claim to the blessed status of death. Society dealt with the bodies of its members after the event; the individual is concerned about his soul in advance. For the Homeric hero and the citizen of Athens, death, the threshold of glory, came about in a last battle of warriors; the philosopher, in contrast, has rehearsed the annihilation of his *sōma* throughout his life, and because for him, the battle with the body began with his philosophical life, the battle with death is, neither a beginning nor an end. So if we speak of immortality in both cases, we must be clear about our terms: as used to qualify glory, immortality came after death; but in the *Phaedo*, the soul, immortal in its essence, must be prepared for its autonomy before death takes place. As for the body, its fate is of no concern.

Phaedo the narrator recalls the scene: his long locks tumbled about his neck and, as the discussion seemed to be grinding to a halt, Socrates stroked his head:

"Tomorrow, I daresay, Phaedo, you will clip these fair tresses."

"I suppose so, Socrates," I replied.

"But if you take my advice, you won't."

"Oh, why not?" I asked.

"Because this very day we will both of us clip our hair if our talk [*logos*] comes to a dead end and we can't bring it back to life!" (89b)

For the next of kin, mourning involved imitating with his own body the loss of life that the passing away of the dear one represented. Wailing and beating her breast, Socrates' wife, Xanthippe, has already anticipated her mourning for Socrates, and she has been firmly removed from the group of philosophers right at the beginning of the dialogue. Phaedo, overly faithful to the city's customs, intends to crop his hair in mourning for Socrates. But the philosopher teaches him the uselessness of such funerary rites: at this point all that counts is the *logos*, for it concerns the immortality of the soul.

The same goes for the way in which a corpse is treated. From the age of the epic to classical Athens, society exorcised death with rites of passage. Between dying and being dead, rituals took place, and no one had the right to be called dead unless the funerary rites had been performed in his honor, authorizing his *psuchē* to enter the misty kingdom of the underworld.[10] But the philosopher has telescoped the natural order of time, anticipating dying by practicing death:[11] he has no need of a transition managed by society; once liberated, his soul needs no authorization to move on to Hades without more ado. The complete philosopher, at least, is convinced of the inanity of the rites, even if his timorous disciples need his reassurance; for while they are certainly eager to believe in the immortality of the soul, they continue, swayed as they are by social practice, to attribute too much reality to "what is visible of man, the body, lying there for all to see — what we call the corpse." So Socrates has to comfort the Theban Cebes, who is afraid that the soul will be dispersed and annihilated as it leaves the body, and is overly impressed by how long a corpse lasts and even by the seeming "immortality" of some of its parts, such as the sinews and tendons.[12]

Once he has produced his arguments, Socrates proceeds to implement his conclusions: having convinced his disciples, Socrates can use his own body to subvert the funerary ritual. He draws on all the resources of his cunning intelligence. First, he undermines the canonical temporal sequence of the rites. Custom dictates that the body be bathed and prepared soon after death, after which the corpse is laid out (*prothesis*); then the funeral procession (*ekphora*) and burial take place. By dying already bathed[13] and reclining, Socrates completes the whole first stage of the ritual while still alive. To be sure, he has a ready justification to account for this bath which, in itself, is an anomaly: "I really think it is better to have a bath than to give the women the trouble of washing a dead body" (115a) — a creditable gesture of consideration that is somewhat disconcerting coming from one whom Aristophanes accused of never washing. But Socrates' words are unlikely to satisfy any thinking reader. Any number of interpretations have been suggested for this bath: the partisans of initiations have seen it as a ritual purification in the strictest orphic tradition, while philosophers have not failed to point out that by bathing, Socrates himself commences the funerary rituals, as if he were already dead. I would only add that, by acting in this way, Socrates is not only denying his dead body any influence over the future fate of his soul: by depriving the women of their traditional intervention with the corpse, which they consider to be their concern, he denies them their essential ritual role. In a similar fashion, Crito later takes the women's place when, on the philosopher's death, he hurries to close his mouth and eyes: the group of disciples replaces the dead man's kin; his companions in thought take the place of the women.[14]

Thus, transferring to friends what seemed due to his family is the second means of subversion that Socrates adopts, and it is altogether consistent with his overall attitude. His third and last ploy consists of proclaiming, not the basic pointlessness of funerary rituals, but the sage's indifference toward practices that are all equally worthless, since none of them has the slightest bearing on what is essential, and the choice of which he leaves to others. Socrates is no Diogenes: he does not arrange to have his corpse thrown to the dogs and birds of prey,[15] and to Crito's question, "How are we to bury you?" he simply replies, "However you like." Never mind if the illustrious Cynic, his over-zealous imitator, freezes Socratic indifference toward the body into a rigid code. Socrates himself, who is more truly detached from life – and probably less critical of the city – leaves everything to do with his funeral rites up to Crito. It is a good choice. Crito, the long-standing companion and orthodox double of the unorthodox Socrates, has, throughout the dialogue, held a special place in the little group gathered to attend the philosopher on the threshold of death. He is the only Athenian not confined to the role of a speechless interlocutor, although, locked in his distress and totally absorbed by his preoccupation with all that concerns the body and life of his friend, he has taken no part in the dialectical discussion. But as he quite rightly entrusts the care of his body to Crito, Socrates cannot resist teaching his undialectical companion a lesson on the immortality of the soul: "Bury me however you like," he says, then adds "provided you can catch me and prevent my escaping you." If Socrates, while alive, truly exists entirely in his *logos*, as he claims, Crito should understand that "Socrates" is nothing but his soul, a soul which, at the moment of death, will immediately flee the lifeless body: so the corpse that Crito will shortly see burned or buried no longer deserves the name "Socrates," and "he won't have to distress himself on my behalf, as though I were being outraged."[16] And "with a quiet laugh," the philosopher exhorts his friend (and through him, the rest of his sorrowful companions) to perform the funeral rites as no more than what Pascal was to call "an afterthought" (*une pensée de derrière*):

"And he won't have to say, at the funeral, that it is Socrates whom he is laying out or carrying to the grave or burying" (115c-e).

Socrates is leaving, going to "some happy land of the blessed" (115d): the philosopher's lot is that which Hesiod reserved for the elite of the heroes of the Trojan War, and which Pindar, in his second *Olympian*, kept for the favorites of the gods:[17] for his body, rites now rendered devoid of meaning; for the philosopher, identified with his soul, immortal life. It is up to his disciples to decipher the traces of the soul's immortality upon his inert, silent, opaque corpse. It is a difficult lesson and only Socrates' still-living voice can convey in the face of all the accepted ideas of the city. But if we are to gauge the full extent of the originality that the *Phaedo* introduces into Greek thought on death, we must examine how it is that, by assimilating Socrates to his soul, it thus immediately procures him a philosophic life among the Blessed in Hades.

The Philosopher's Courage

All men are mortal.
Socrates is a man.
Therefore, Socrates is mortal.

That well-known argument is a favorite scholastic illustration of an Aristotelian syllogism.[18] Whether or not it is truly demonstrative, the exemplary quality of this model demonstration is founded on the exemplary mortality of Socrates, and that fact is probably not without significance. But is the Socrates of the *Phaedo* a man (*anthrōpos*)? Or rather: is he *just* a man?

One point must be made immediately. In the *Phaedo*, Plato presents Socrates as being, in many respects, the model philosopher, and the text of his dialogue is a linguistic monument designed to celebrate Socrates the philosopher. Similarly, in archaic poetry, the prologue of the *Theogony* and Aesop's *Life* provided an identity and name for the model (or "generic") poet Hesiod or Aesop. That may seem a surprising comparison until one remembers that in the interval between his sentence and his execution, Socrates turned poet with an imitation of Aesop, who was, like him, both a servant of Apollo and a victim sacrificed to the god. It is with a mention of Aesop's name that Cebes opens the dialogue at the beginning of the *Phaedo*, and for just a moment the image of the *therapōn* of Apollo takes the place of that of the philosopher. Of course, the comparison between Socrates and Aesop goes no further: the poet may be presented as an alternative to the image of the philosopher, but Socrates the philosopher was never to be the object of a heroic cult as was the poet Aesop;[19] nevertheless, the text of the *Phaedo*, which condenses the life of Socrates into his last moments, is the founding text for a discourse on immortal glory, a discourse with many traditional features whose well-known themes provide a contrapuntal accompaniment to Plato's innovative theory of the immortality of the soul.

However, despite the fact that the poet is explicitly conjured up by the text, it is not in relation to him that I shall seek an answer to the question, "Is Socrates *just a man?*" Rather, let us turn to the warrior.

It is well known that Greek language and thought accommodate men of more than one kind: on the one hand, there is the human being (*anthrōpos*), and on the other, there is the virile man (*anēr*), endowed with great qualities and valor, whom the texts delight in distinguishing from the common run of passive human beings. The epic hero is an *anēr*; so too is the solder-citizen of the Athenian funeral speech, that bit of civic ideology. Now at the very heart of the *Phaedo*, we find an image of the virile man, the *anēr philosophos*, repeatedly set in opposition to the common run of mortals (*anthrōpoi*). This opposition is essential to the dialogue and is introduced at a crucial point in it (64a-65a): if we are to understand the meaning of this acclimatization to death that the philosophic life constitutes, we must dismiss the multitude from our minds (and along with it, its spokesman, the comic poet), that multitude which regards philosophers as "moribund"[20] because they entertain, in their lifetimes, a morbid love of death. "Philosophers desire death [*thanatōsi*]," declares the multitude, promptly offering them the fate to which they aspire. So it is that the Athenians condemn Socrates to death, emulating Aristophanes' Strepsiades who, in the *Clouds*, ends up by burning down the "thinking-house" of the intellectuals. Meanwhile, however, the philosopher calmly takes leave of the multitude and all its opinions; and only at this point does the text present the opposition between soul and body, an opposition beyond the comprehension of the Athenian multitude. It is also at this point that the soul is allowed to escape symbolically from the body, since it could not escape earlier from this human life from which no *anthrōpos* has the right to flee by means of suicide.

Wounded warrior from the Temple of Athena in Aegina,
6th century B.C. (Paris, Musée des Monuments).

And what of the *anēr philosophos*? He is not far away. If, from Achilles through to the hoplite, and from the hoplite through to the citizen, virile man has been char-acterized by the fact that he enters willingly upon the "paths that lead to his chosen death" ("les voies de la mort choisie"),[21] it is significant that throughout the *Phaedo* the philosopher's choice is defined as an acceptance of death. It is a deliberate accep-tance, the recognition of a law, rather than a quest for annihilation. And this rea-soned rather than impulsive desire is expressed by the verb *ethelein*. The word itself suggests the hoplite tradition behind the philosophy and behind Socrates' choice, the choice of the soldier-citizen who accepts (*ethelei*) death for the sake of the city.[22] The philosopher is an *anēr*, just as are the hoplite and the citizen and, like the hero and the soldier-citizen, he knows how to die. In other words, if Plato borrows his language from the civic tradition, it is because he intends to replace one model with another – the soldier-citizen with the *anēr philosophos*. The funeral speech views the Athenians as "true citizens" (*gnēsioi politai*); the *Phaedo* prefers true philosophers (*gnēsiōs philosophoi*: 66b2). With that twist of language Plato records something that he was largely responsible for bringing about: the fourth-century victory of the phi-losopher over the citizen as the model of the virile man.

All virile men confront danger, and the philosophic life is based on that fine risk (*kalos kindunos*) which consists in taking a chance on the immortality of the soul. This is just what the truly philosophic risk involves: believing in the immortality of the soul, conforming to that idea through one's actions and convincing reluctant questioners, whose objections may at any moment deal a "deathblow" to the *logos*. And it is a much graver risk than that faced by Socrates when he confronted his judges. The philosopher's *Apology* did not save his life because it did not win over the city; but it would have been far worse if he had failed to instill in his disciples the idea that the soul truly is immortal: that is why we should regard the *Phaedo* as Socrates' real "apology" (defense).

But both the beginning and the end of the *Phaedo* also contain something akin to a funeral speech for a philosopher who has known how to die nobly (*gennaiōs*), and who was acknowledged as the most courageous (*aristos*), wise and righteous man of his time. Really, a funeral speech?... Yes, really. The attentive reader will per-haps remember that Plato did, in fact, take an interest in the literary genre of the funeral speech, to which he even devoted a dialogue that is named, significantly enough, after one of the silent interlocutors of the *Phaedo*.[23] If the list of those friends gathered around Socrates is symbolic — and there is every reason to suppose that it is, considering both those who are present and those who are not, and those mentioned and those not mentioned[24] — then the fact that Menexenus is one of those present is probably no mere chance: Menexenus, whose name appeared last among all the Athenians present on that day, and for whom Socrates produced his brilliant parody of the civic funeral speech.

The *Menexenus* should be read alongside the *Phaedo*. It is an exercise all the more justifiable since the two dialogues appear to have been written around the same date. When we do so, we notice that the *Phaedo* stands in opposition to the collective funeral speech, a social pronouncement that is misguided (if not positively dangerous) in that it apportions to the good man (*agathos*) and the bad man an equal share of glory in the city. The *Phaedo* implicitly praises a man who did not wait for death to reveal his value/valor[25] and who will find bliss in an afterlife, where it is clearly known how to distinguish the good from the bad. We might also do well to ponder the hidden resemblance which relates the beginning of the critique of the funeral speech in the *Menexenus* to the formulation of the philosophical ideal of the fine risk. On the one hand, we find *kinduneues kalon* ("death in battle may be fine indeed"), on the other, *kalos kindunos*; on the one hand, an overtly expressed doubt about the value/valor of the "fine death" of the soldier-citizen, on the other, the calculated heroism of the philosophical life, with which Socrates closes his discussion. But we should also note another, even more important reversal of the *Menexenus* in the *Phaedo*, one that affects the philosopher as an individual. The *Menexenus* explores the effects of the civic discourse of glory on Socrates; the *Phaedo* creates its effect by presenting the *anēr philosophos* in all his glory. Spellbound by the funeral speech, Socrates revelled in his own immediate sensation of greater nobility (*gennaioteros*) and in appearing more admirable in the eyes of strangers. But it is a borrowed nobility that disappears as the memory of the orator's words fades away. In the *Phaedo*, in contrast, what we have is the force of the true conviction that emanates from the philosopher's person and that is felt by all, his close companions and the prison jailor alike. The admiration evinced by those around him reaches its peak when he rescues them from a dialectical rout and is able to inspire them with renewed ardor

(88e-89a). But it falls to the prison jailor to declare that the highest degree of true nobility (*gennaiotatos*) has been reached in Socrates (116c). There is every justification for admiring the Socrates of the *Phaedo*, for here he is preparing himself for the journey that will take him to the last abode of philosophers, the blessed place of bliss. We cannot help but recall the *Menexenus* and smile at the imaginary journey that Socrates, under the spell of civic eloquence, believed himself to have made to the Islands of the Blessed.

Of course, to appreciate the difference between the Socratic *logos* and the eloquence of the official civic speech, we must beware of the trap of resemblance. As Plato is always telling us, nothing looks more like the truth than that which is false — which is why he so often labels as "false" a thought whose language he nevertheless tries to twist to his own advantage. Thus, the reader's task is to detect in that very terminology a clash between alternative models. We should note with amusement that in the *Menexenus* the mention of courage (*andreia*) is accompanied by an astonishing juxtaposition of appearance and truth (247d8), but we should seriously take note when the *Phaedo* declares that "true friends of knowledge are virtuous and brave" (*andreioi*: 83e).

The philosopher thus appropriates *andreia*,[26] which is the word for both courage and virility and is also the password of the city's ideology. However, it is not only with reference to the *Menexenus* but also more generally that Plato marshalls his forces against the civic language of immortality by systematically dispossessing the funeral speech of its key words. Pericles, in his funeral speech, claims that the Athenians are in love (*erastai*) with the city; moving one step further, and passing from the city itself to what it considers to be immortality, Diotima in the *Symposium* regards glory as the object of love suitable for most people; finally, in the *Phaedo*, the only kind of love is love of thought (*erōs phronēseōs*). For the *anthrōpoi*, then, the city and its glory; for the *anēr philosophos*, the practice of reflection, which feeds the soul. The funeral speech makes no distinction between life, the soul and the body. Thus it says interchangeably of citizens that they have given their persons (*sōma*) for the city or that they have decided not to cherish life (*philopsuchein*); the philosopher cherishes life no more than the model citizen, but for Plato the word *philopsuchein* will not suffice to express philosophic detachment, since his entire purpose is to wrest the soul from the life of the body. Therefore he forges a new word and sets the philosopher in opposition to the *philosōmatos*, one who loves the body. With his "fine death," the citizen gave all that he had — his life — but according to Lysias in his funeral speech, that life did not belong to him (*psuchē allotria*) anyway. By dismissing all forms of prestige attached to the body, the philosopher of the *Phaedo* rejects them as alien (*allotrious*) to his being, but he retains what is essential, namely thought, which feeds his soul, is truly his own and will accompany him beyond death. The incalculable advantage of Plato's strategy is that while the words remain the same, an unbridgeable gap is created between glory, on the one hand, and immortality of the soul, on the other.[27] To return to the point that most interests us, it is small wonder that Plato, who classifies political virtue on the side of the body (82a-b), is anxious to put the civic mechanism of *andreia* out of action: in order to show that only philosophers are worthy enough to be called *andreioi*, all he need do is declare that "all men are brave out of fear, except philosophers." What the funeral speech is prone to mask is thereby brought to light, namely, the fashion in which civic virtue is treated as an item for barter: for the orators, the "fine death" involved the incommensurable exchange of a life in return for glory, but Socrates regards that as simply swapping one fear for another, albeit one of a different kind.[28]

Exit civic courage, enter the *andreia* of the philosopher, which involves not an exchange but a purification.

This is certainly a strange kind of *andreia* in comparison with the hoplite morality, whose values Socrates delights in subverting. He sets about doing so by incongruously praising flight — the noble flight of the soul — which, as death advances on a man, jubilantly abandons the field to it. A hoplite never takes to flight (that is precisely what defines him as such), but even in the *Laches*, Plato, reflecting on courage, had already set a value on retreat; and it was on the occasion of a retreat in the last stages of the battle of Delium that Socrates the hoplite showed the paradoxical courage that Alcibiades praises in the *Symposium*. And as Socrates repeatedly mixes up the vocabulary of war (in which one takes to flight) and that of slavery (in which one makes one's escape), we also sense that what he really intends to do is subvert civic courage.

Now we come to the most famous and most frequently discussed passage in the *Phaedo*. When Socrates declares, to justify the prohibition against suicide, that "we men are in a sort of *phroura*" from which we should not free ourselves or escape (62b), how should that word *phroura* be translated? Tradition has a ready reply: without worrying unduly about the fact that this is a noun denoting an action (generally that of "guarding") or that at this point in the dialogue the separation of man into a body and a soul has not yet been introduced or even suggested, it declares that Plato is simply alluding to the Orphico-Pythagorean theory of the body-prison. It is true that the *Gorgias* contains a passage in which it would be hard to avoid translating *phroura* as prison, but that is an exceptional meaning of the word — not that this is of much concern to the commentators. Of as little concern is the reversal that Plato introduces in the *Phaedo*, when what he assimilates into a prison is the world of the living and not the world of Hades, which is traditionally seen as one. There is little doubt that the idea of prison is contained in *phroura*; but if we pay closer attention to the passage where Socrates says that this expression "is not easy to get to the bottom of," we will not accept a univocal translation of the word. The fact is that *phroura* is connected not only with the idea of a prison but also with that of a jail or a "pen" for slaves, since the next image develops the idea that men are owned by the gods, who mount guard over them. But in the *Phaedo* the word *phroura* also has its most common meaning, the one that Plato gives it in the *Laws*, the one — above all — that his contemporaries gave it quite naturally: *phroura* also means garrison service, the guard that ephebes mounted along the frontiers of the civic territory, under the surveillance of magistrates. *Phroura* means surveillance under surveillance. Thus it must be recognized that the word condenses three separate images: first, the image of a prison; second, that of a pen in which slaves — in this case the whole human race — are confined, with the gods as their masters; and third, that of a garrison service that cannot be avoided by taking flight in suicide. Men, who are slaves under the guard set upon them, cannot escape from life. Moreover, being themselves guardians of this life over which the gods preside, they have no right to flee. Those unwilling to recognize the polysemy of the term have tried to exclude the military sense, without noticing that in the *Phaedo* warfare is constantly intertwined with slavery. Furthermore, the warfare in question is not of the standard type. *Phroura* is the correct word for the operations of ephebes or a siege garrison, while *taxis*, "order in the ranks," is the term used in the *Menexenus* for the discipline under which hoplites fight. Historians of philosophy tend to pay insufficient attention to the background of warfare in Plato (presumably because they do not consider warfare a philosophical subject worthy of the great Plato and his discourse on the soul). However, to do so is to miss the contrast, essential to the dialogue, between the general run of humanity and the philosopher: on the one hand, ordinary human beings are forbidden to escape from the *phroura* because men whose bodies and souls are tied together annihilate all that they are when they commit suicide; on the other, the *anēr philosophos*, subjected though he is to the human condition, is able to free his soul so that it can flee the body.[29] In our reading of the *Phaedo*, we shall clearly have to reflect on the virile courage of the philosopher.

Socrates, the model philosopher, faces death without a moment of fear, and that calm proves the soul to be immortal better than any dialectical argument could. He drinks the poison "quite calmly, without a tremor or any change of expression," a worthy descendant of the Homeric heroes among whom a brave man was recognized by the fact that he "never changes color at all and is not...perturbed."[30] But when his disciples can contain their grief no longer and burst into tears, lamenting for themselves even as they lament for their companion (as do the mourning women of the *Iliad*), Socrates' reaction is that of a citizen of Athens, where tears, which are essentially feminine, are forbidden to virile men, and it is as a hoplite that he speaks, as he recalls his friends to fortitude ("Do not give way!" *kartereite*: 117c-e).

In the first part of the dialogue, Socrates dispossessed the multitude of *andreia* by refuting or reversing its accepted values. He countered the funeral speech with his declaration that only philosophers are courageous; as for Aristophanes, who in the *Clouds* compared his pale, emaciated disciples to the Laconian prisoners from Pylos, Socrates refutes him by imprisoning the entire human race in a *phroura*. His calm in the face of death is manifest proof that he is the very embodiment of the philosophical nature to which books six and seven of the *Republic* attribute the essential quality of *andreia*. Philosophers in general are courageous because they do not give way (*karterein*) to their bodies or their desires (82c), but Socrates in particular is brave in that, in the dialectical discussion, he is a war leader to his disciples. I have already mentioned the admiration that he arouses in his companions when, acting both as a healer and as a good general, he is able to inspire his "routed and beaten" troops with new ardor: Asclepius, the god of medicine, will have truly deserved the cock (the emblem of victory) that Socrates, with his last words, dedicates to him on behalf of the group of philosophers (88e-89a, 118a). But to over-come the defeatism of his followers, he also has had to evoke the part-historic, part-legendary Thyreatid war, a ritual and initiatory battle,[31] and he has promised Phaedo assistance that, in the last analysis, closely resembles the strength of Heracles (89b-c). The point here is that the philosopher's courage is evident in his speech even more than in his life.

The edifying example of Socrates' serenity may be the ultimate proof of the immortality of the soul, but we must also follow the argument to the end. And there is every indication that courage is necessary for the practice of dialectical discussion. This is particularly the case when it concerns the effects of death upon the soul — for then childish fears of bogeys must be stilled among the disciples — or when, in the course of a discussion on the opposition of contraries, some hesitant speaker puts forward an objection that terrifies him. Furthermore, one must remain calm when some anonymous fighter from the ranks, bursting with an unthinking courage that smacks of foolhardiness, rekindles the debate (77e, 101a-d, 103a-b). In short, dialectical discussion is a battle, and although the *Phaedo* is not the only dialogue of Plato to make that point,[32] the language of warfare in it breaks through in an exceptionally coherent fashion. One can argue "in Homeric fashion," in other words, waste no time in coming into close quarters with one's adversary (in testing out a theory, that is: 95b); one can stand firm in what one takes to be a strong position (the verb *diischurizomai* is repeatedly used in this sense), but, in either case, one should always "manfully exert oneself" (90e) in tackling the *logos*, because even the process of reasoning out the arguments involves fierce fighting, which, when the ultimate is at stake — namely, the immortality of the soul — sometimes looks very much like a fight to the death (102d-104b).

Thus, whether as epic hero or new-style hoplite, the philosopher stands firm[33] in *logos* as in life, and the masterly dexterity that the philosopher Plato demonstrates throughout the dialogue as he undertakes to appropriate the current values of the city for his tutelary hero cannot fail to command the highest admiration. By irreversibly separating the soul from the body, Plato once and for all detaches the idea of immortality from the civic glory with which it has hitherto been associated. This is where the long Western history of the soul begins. But whether through philosophical cunning or as a result of the unconscious influence of the rich language bequeathed by a glorious past, the *logos* on immortality continues to be accompanied by a displaced and reversed discourse on courage and deliberate death. Perhaps this is one reason, the *Greek* reason, for the *Phaedo*'s brilliant reputation. After all, the innovations that proved successful were perhaps the very ones that on the face of it looked like repetitions.

Nevertheless, that is surely not the ultimate reason for the *Phaedo*'s astonishing success. For tradition, as well as for us, this dialogue surely owes its great force to the fact that the model philosopher is here given both a name and a body and claims to have a soul. Since the presence of Socrates animates the model figure of the philosopher, to ponder the originality of the *Phaedo* is almost to reflect on its subtly orchestrated effect of realism. Of course, it is all for the greater glory of the soul in general, but without the slightest doubt, it is also for the particular glory of this mortal Socrates, now immortalized forever.

On Socrates' *Logos* and His Memorable Body

Nothing is left to chance when it comes to authenticating the *Phaedo* as the "historical" account of the death of Socrates: the narrator was present in person (*autos* is the very first word of the dialogue), a fact which guarantees the accuracy of what he says and thereby validates it. This is probably also the function of the calculated vaguenesses (in the list of Socrates' friends, for example) and even of the memory lapse that causes Phaedo to forget the name of one speaker more zealous than enlightened. As for the famous "Plato was, I believe, not strong enough to attend,"[34] this initially takes the reader's breath away. Before he has had time to recover enough to realize that behind this narrator with the faulty memory stands Plato the writer (who certainly did know how things stood, on this score at least), he has already been carried deeper into the dialogue. But he will probably have to read further before it occurs to him to raise the problem of fiction itself and wonder how this account can possibly claim to be authentic, if Plato himself was absent.

However, as I have already suggested, it is Socrates himself who does the most to persuade us of the truth of the *Phaedo*: the truth of the philosopher's last moments, which this dialogue stages so imaginatively that the reader feels he is actually present; also, the truth of the arguments in favor of the immortality of the soul, which rather depend on Socrates' presence to carry conviction. Of course, one could set out to list the "proofs" of the immortality of the soul, as indeed all too many commentators have done (finding five, or seven, or eleven, or more or fewer such "proofs"). Or, like certain Anglo-Saxon scholars, one might embark on endless discussions of the validity of this or that proof. But to steer us in the right direction our reading must recognize that the long dialogue of the *Phaedo* is constructed around the process through which the person and the *logos* of Socrates mutually reinforce one another, in order to give credence to the idea that the soul is immortal.[35] Right from the beginning of the dialogue, we learn that "proof is not its primary object,"[36] and even toward the end we may still be in doubt as to the persuasive power of the *logos* since, to allay the last fears of his disciples, Socrates has to resort to no less than a wager on moral life, following it up with a myth (107a-114c). There can be no doubt that, were it not for the active presence of Socrates, the discourse would be in danger of foundering, much to the consternation of the apprentice philosophers so anxious to confirm their wavering beliefs. On the other hand, Socrates needs the *logos* to convince his companions that his serenity is well-founded: the discussion must not "die," because the philosopher is in need of its aid. That is why Socrates is bent on "rescuing the *logos*, breathing new life into it [*eboēthei tōi logōi, anabiōsasthai*]" (88c-89c), after which, with the philosopher's and the argument's combined victory over death assured, it is only fitting to give thanks to Asclepius.[37] In the meantime, the solidarity established between the man and the argument that is proclaimed in the passage on "misology" (89d-90d) is so closely maintained throughout the dialogue that particular key words are interchangeable between the two, applying now to Socrates, now to the *logos*.[38]

But one question can be put off no longer, for it is one that the *Phaedo* asks forthrightly: who is Socrates? The answer seems obvious if we do not look beyond the text's explicit message, which elaborates what appears to be a theory of individuality:[39] Socrates is, of course, his soul. In any event, we first learn that, generally speaking, the personality of a philosopher must be identified with his *psuchē*. We pick this up from the phrases in which, in order to avoid any association with the body, the generic "we" of philosophers in general is used, instead of *psuchē*, as the subject of the action (67a). And the reason why Socrates, having defined Hades as the dwelling-place of souls, ends up by installing "the dead" there, is that it is at the moment of death that the essence of a man ideally passes into his soul: the dead man no longer has a body, but then again the body is no longer anything at all.... This general lesson may lead clearly enough to the personality who is Socrates. But for Crito, who is not much of a philosopher, it needs to be spelled out. So, when his friend suggests that he should put off the moment of drinking the hemlock, like condemned men who seize one last chance to eat, drink and make love — those very activities that, at the beginning of the discussion, have been defined as plea-sures suitable only for a soul too much attached to its body (81b, 116e) — Socrates explains that he is already on his way and that this Socrates who is leaving is a soul that no longer has anything to do with the visible individual thing that Socrates' body used to be.

All the same, it is important to note that this lesson comes very late in the day, after (and only after) Socrates has upheld his *logos* with all the living force of his physical presence. Until his discourse had won the day, Socrates still needed to be that mixture of body and soul that constitutes a man.[40] Thus, during a pause in the discussion, the text says: "Socrates himself [*autos*] was entirely given over to pondering the argument that had just been set out" ("Socrate était tout entier à l'argument qui venait d'être exposé") (84b-c). Léon Robin translates this as "You could see at a glance that Socrates' *mind was entirely preoccupied* by the argument that had just been set out" ("*Socrate, cela se voyait à le regarder*, avait l'esprit tout entier *à l'argument qui venait d'etre exposé*"). But this anticipates the direction that the dialogue is about to take. *Autos ho Sōkratēs*: Socrates himself, the person of Socrates, is not yet just a soul, is not just a mind but an entity there to be seen — and we know how keenly his disciples watched him — despite the fact that, in the earlier stages of the discussion, he has concentrated on attacking whatever is visible and all its misleading charms.

Who is Socrates? His soul, according to him. In the flesh-and-blood discussion, however, Socrates' self has a lot to do with his body, that Silenus-like body which Alcibiades describes in the *Symposium*, a body that masks the internal man and the beauty of his soul, yet is indisputably charged with an emotive attraction that his disciples connect with the philosopher's personality. So, despite the authority of the *Phaedo* and the lesson it teaches, not just to Crito but to the reader too, we must go against the grain of the text, or at least its apparent content, and return to the body of Socrates. At another level, to do so comes down to paying due attention to the flesh-and-blood discussion and the language it uses.

In the opening pages of *Psyche*, Erwin Rohde points out that, generally speaking, the *psuchē* is mentioned only when its separation from the living man is either imminent or has already taken place. In the *Phaedo*, Socrates is on the point of taking leave of life and much is said about the *psuchē*, his *psuchē*. But his body, too, by no means goes unmentioned, that very body from which his soul must frequently have detached itself if he has himself engaged in the *meletē thanatou*, that practice of death which Socrates recommends to philosophers. (And if we have read the *Symposium*, in which he falls into a catalepsy several times, we know that he did indeed engage in it, and often.) Therefore, we must make a detour to take in this *meletē thanatou*, the ascetic practice whose aim, from the archaic shamans down to the philosopher of the *Phaedo*, has always been to separate the soul from the body.

According to Socrates, the practice involves anticipating the state of death, which is first defined here as "the body having been parted from the soul and come to be by itself; and ... the soul having been parted from the body, and being by itself" (64c). The order adopted here is a strange one: the separation is first envisaged from the point of view of the body, and only then from the soul's point of view. To be sure it is no sooner suggested than rejected, for from then on, nothing more is said of the body's role in this separation: henceforth, only the soul is entitled to isolate itself. However, it would be reasonable for anyone reading the text attentively to suppose that the body does not allow itself to be abandoned in this fashion, since it is to the language of the body that Plato the writer turns to describe the soul engaged in the process of separation.

The soul certainly appears to be alive, which means that, like the body, it needs nurturing (*trophē*, 81d, 84b, 107d). The fact remains that one cannot but be struck by the physicality of the soul's movements as it seeks to leave the body, making an effort to "gather itself together from every region of the body" (67c). In a word, the soul does exactly what the chorus in the *Clouds* orders Strepsiades to bring about within himself by concentrating, or to be more precise, by "densifying himself" (*puknōsas*) in order to think better. Nor should we seek to justify such language by recalling the soul which is too attached to the body, with the result that it "wanders in a sort of dizzy, drunken confusion" or, following death, roams about tombs as a ghostly phantom, an image both visible yet illusory (*eidōlon*).[41] Rather, it is the soul of the sage that concerns us here, a soul striving, in all the purity of its philosophical motivation, to effect its separation. Of course Plato has been at pains to forestall the reader's astonishment by underlining the "terrible power" of the enclosure represented by the body to which the soul is shackled and, as it were, adheres in such a way that the philosopher is obliged to undertake a kind of education of the senses in reverse, teaching the soul to shed every dimension of the body, one by one, in order to concentrate itself within itself.[42] Nevertheless, it is by means of this "technical" vocabulary (which is used throughout the *Phaedo* to convey the soul's efforts at concentration) that Plato manages better than anyone to underline the paradoxical fact that, at the very moment of separation, "it is at the level of the body that the being appears to experience its identity."[43] But now we must return to Socrates, to his soul and his body, to Socrates who has passed beyond the need to practice being dead and now faces death itself, a death clearly no longer in any sense metaphorical — unless, that is, in these last moments of the philosopher's life his body has become a metaphor for his soul, whose liberation it makes manifest just as, at the beginning of the dialogue, Socrates' unshackled body looked forward to the deliverance of his *psuchē*.

So let us return to Socrates and his symbolic or, at the very least, extremely significant body, to this *sōma* that is the clearest indicator provided by the dialogue of how to read it, which makes us consider the importance of the body in a text totally devoted to getting rid of it.

Throughout most of the dialogue Socrates is seated. Until his disciples arrive he has been lying down, but he sits up as soon as he sees Xanthippe's back and, at first in a hunched position, lowers his feet to the ground. Thus, Socrates is seated and will rise to his feet only to go to take a bath. He will be seated as he drinks the poison, after which, heeding the instructions given to him, he will take no more than a few steps before lying down again, this time for good. Socrates is seated and his position is eminently symbolic, being both that of a man under sentence of death and that of an initiate,[44] as the philosopher himself points out: refuting the analyses of materialist thinkers who, obsessed by physical causes, would think they were explaining the position by describing the interaction of bones and flesh, muscles, nerves and tendons, he declares that the reason why he is seated is that he has accepted the judgment of the Athenians (98c-99b). Socrates is seated, and the few movements he makes in the course of the dialectical conversation serve to redirect the discussion from time to time. He took his body as the starting point for the dialogue, when his remarks about pleasure and pain were prompted by the painful numbness of his leg, but this soon led on to reflections on the interrelations of contraries.

When Crito, as instructed by the man responsible for administering the hemlock, advises him to speak (actually, to dialogue: *dialegesthai*) as little as possible so as not to become heated — for this would counteract the action of the poison, which achieves its effect through coldness — the philosopher rejects such a mundane consideration. The fact is that it is absolutely necessary for the hot and the cold, like pleasure and pain, to clash within Socrates' body, since this body is a mirror for the dialectical discussion, particularly the part about the clash of contraries.[45] Only when the discussion is completed and the day comes to an end will Socrates drink the poison. At that point, Plato will turn the inquiry that is suited to dialectical argument (*skopein*: 64d) toward Socrates' body, which must now be examined by the man responsible for administering the poison. The purpose of that examination is to determine the progress made by the hemlock. In this way, Plato suggests to the reader an inverted image of the withdrawal of the soul.[46]

In conclusion, I offer a few words on the action of the hemlock as it affects the philosopher's body, since it is a process into which Plato seeks to condense the entire meaning of the dialogue. In calling this poison "hemlock," I am following a convention that postdates the *Phaedo* (but is historically well-founded), but I am not unaware that in referring to this death draft simply as a *pharmakon*, Plato's intention was to turn it into a drink of immortality.[47] Hemlock, a *pharmakon* of immortality? How can that be? But that is certainly how Socrates regards it since, when the time comes, the philosopher decides to drink it of his own accord, without having to be told to do so.[48] In fact, it is the hemlock, seen by Aristophanes as the shortest path (*atrapos*) to death, that gives material form to what is described in the *Phaedo* as the *atrapos* of the philosopher — that practice of death by which one frees oneself, while still alive, from the constraints of the body. The hemlock, as the material counterpart of the *logos* on the liberation of the soul, effects what Socrates has already virtually accomplished.[49] The hemlock liberates, all the more so since it gives Socrates the chance for an exemplary death in which he can display that calm serenity that generations of readers have so admired. Now, it is precisely with this serene death that the realism of the dialogue — that is to say, the effectiveness of the fiction — reaches its peak. And Plato is certainly counting on the persuasiveness of the description to make the reader forget to wonder what death by hemlock must really be like.

But let us once again shatter the paralyzing spell of that sublime moment and see what other ancient authors (not only Aristophanes and Theophrastus, but also Nicander, the doctor) have to say about hemlock. All of them speak of sensations of cold and numbness (and they also agree about the speed with which this poison causes death). But Nicander mentions further details that are at considerable variance with what is suggested in the *Phaedo*. According to him, not only does the subject who has drunk the hemlock become agitated as well as numb but, with his mind wandering, his intelligence and consciousness appear to be affected first. Now the reader must look again at the *Phaedo*. A prudent conclusion would be that Plato simply chose one version in preference to another — that of the poison's gentle effects rather than that of its violence. But one might press on further and accept the consequences of a less reverential inquiry, in which case the death of Socrates, which seems so very genuine, becomes a pure and simple philosophical construction.[50] In fact, the dispersion of the hemlock through the philosopher's body must be symbolic: his head is never affected. It is true that, in the *Timaeus*, the head is where whatever is divine in man is rooted, and the philosopher, of all men, is the most capable of cultivating those divine roots. The poison spreads upward, from the feet that have trampled the earth to the heart, whose heat is extinguished by the cold of the hemlock. But for Socrates, the battle is over once his feet and legs are paralyzed and the cold grips his abdomen — the seat of the desires that the philosopher has managed to overcome. The rest is silence, silence concerning the nobler part of the body and the liberation of the soul, which the reader must try to imagine for him- or herself.

In freeing Socrates from the body forever, the *Phaedo* thus concentrates on the very thing from which, it seems, Socrates must be liberated: the mortal body of

Socrates that, by rooting the man to the ground, makes him an earthly plant. But is it that easy to get rid of Socrates' body? In the last lines of the dialogue, the body — cold and petrified as it is, the body of that Socrates who has already left it — continues effectively enough to sustain the role of an archaic *kolossos*, the dead man's double and a memorial to him.[51] The force of Plato's text is such that it turns his stiffened corpse into a statue. It is reasonable to suppose that Crito will find it very difficult not to seek Socrates in that frozen presence, that he will hardly believe that the Socrates lying there is no longer anything at all, since Socrates-the-soul has already reached the Islands of the Blessed. The *Gorgias*, in orphic fashion, declared the body to be a *sēma*. But for this tomb-body, which throughout the dialogue has been first and foremost a sign-body, the *Phaedo* itself stands as a *sēma*, in the sense of a commemorative *stēlē*.

The strategy that Plato adopts in the *Phaedo* is truly astonishing: he sets out to expunge the city from the dialogue, even as he borrows civic language and values; to banish the body, even as he uses the language of the body itself. The first of those two operations must have taken the Greek reader by surprise, for without realizing it he found himself won over to a new thinking expressed in traditional words. The second may well have disturbed Plato's contemporaries, but it has most certainly fascinated generations of later readers (and after all, that is what tradition means in the case of a text, so it truly was a tradition that was inaugurated by the account of Socrates' death).

To use the body to banish the body is not as unjustifiable as it may appear. The body, it could be said, is simply an image used to speak of the soul; and how can one possibly speak of the soul without resorting to imagery? In the dialogue itself, Cebes begs pardon for resorting to a "comparison." But to win over his readers at any price, those readers whom Plato needs to be tractable, Plato is a master at manipulating images and their own reflections.[52]

In this inquiry we have tried not to be too easily swayed by the text's suggestiveness, to be attentive but not mesmerized readers. We have tried to be readers who must be won over. The only hope of coming close to the immortality of the soul seemed to lie in exploring all the paths that led to it in this text, which for a long tradition has provided a veritable storehouse of arguments favoring that immortality. But if we have thereby been led to the paradox of a body rejected, depreciated and banished, yet more present than ever, how should we now speak of the immortality brought about in the *Phaedo*? If it is Socrates' memorable body that also constitutes a memorial, that makes us believe in the survival of his soul (just as, in the *Symposium*, it was his Silenus-like ugliness that vouched for his internal beauty), what are we to do with that body of Socrates? Now that we have rashly committed ourselves to reflecting on the effectiveness of the dialogue, let us risk the following hypothesis: the *Phaedo* owes its success not only to the brilliance with which it supplants one immortality by another, replacing words of glory with the survival of the soul; but that success also has much to do with the immense unconscious impact made by the play of double meanings. Clearly, Plato is simultaneously playing on two levels when he proclaims that the body is nothing, yet he uses the language of the body to speak of the soul.

Plato resorts to many cunning ploys: he outlaws *mimēsis* from the city in a dialogue where the writing depends on a masterly use of that very *mimēsis*; he condemns cunning intelligence even as he manipulates the techniques of *mētis* with marvelous skill; he argues the annihilation of the body in a language where the body dominates. Furthermore, Plato expects the reader to accept these exclusions — and the reader is all the more prepared to do so since, without realizing it, whatever is excluded (*mimēsis*, the city or the body, as the case may be) then bounces back to the reader. Like a perverse child, Plato's reader continues to enjoy the very things that philosophy is repressing: the text is full of hints of them, and these work (silently, secretly and, as it were, innocuously) on the irreproachable champion of knowledge that he believes himself to be. And this is how the tradition of a spiritualistic reading of the *Phaedo* has quietly established itself.[53]

We have tried to read Plato's dialogue on immortality as an argument playing on two levels: the soul is immortal, but that immortality is upheld chiefly by the memorial that was Socrates' unforgettable body.

NOTES

1. In this study I shall be considering the *Phaedo* insofar as it established a new tradition. I am, of course, well aware that, set in the context of the evolution of Platonic thought as a whole, this text simply marks a particular stage in Plato's treatment of the subject of the soul. Nevertheless, in this

paper I shall be considering only the new departures that it introduced. The history of the tradition from mid to Neoplatonism has already been studied: see, for example, P. Courcelle, "L'âme fixée au corps," in *Connais-toi toi-même: De Socrate à Saint Bernard* (Paris, 1975), vol. 2, ch. 3, pp. 325-414. The history of the *Phaedo* in university circles during the nineteenth and twentieth centuries essentially remains to be tackled.

2. These are the three disciplines sanctioned as means of approaching the dialogue by R. Schaerer in his much-quoted article, "La composition du *Phédon*," *Revue des Etudes Grecques* (1940), p. 7.

3. On the prehistory of the immortality of the soul: see, for example, M. Detienne, *La notion de Daimon dans le pythogarisme ancien* (Paris, 1963), pp. 69-85 [Pythagoreanism]; J.C.G. Strachan, *Classical Quarterly* 20 (1970), pp. 216-220 [Orphism]; also, more generally, E. Rohde, *Psyche* (New York, 1966); F. Sarri, *Socrate e la genesi storica dell'idea occidentale di anima* (Rome, 1975); and J. Bremmer, *The Early Greek Concept of the Soul* (Princeton, 1983).

4. On funerary ritual in epic literature, see J.-P. Vernant, "La belle mort et le cadavre outragé," in *La mort, les morts dans les sociétés anciennes*, eds. G. Gnoli and J.-P. Vernant (Cambridge-Paris, 1982), pp. 45-76, and also the summary of Vernant's 1976-77 lectures in *L'Annuaire du Collège de France* (1977), pp. 423-41; also, more generally, E. Vermeule, *Aspects of Death in Early Greek Art and Poetry* (Berkeley, 1979), esp. ch. 3, pp. 83-116.

5. Plato, *Phaedo*, trans. with intro. and commentary by R. Hackforth (Cambridge, 1955), 77d-e. On the reality of the body in Homer, see E. Vermeule, *Aspects of Death*, p. 97; in Homer, *psuchē* is the vehicle of a man's identity but does not in itself constitute that identity: G. Nagy, "Paroklos, Concepts of Afterlife and the Indic Triple Fire," *Arethusa* 13 (1980), p. 162.

6. See N. Loraux, *The Invention of Athens: The Funeral Oration in the Classical City* (Cambridge, Mass. and London, 1986); also, "Mourir devant Troie, tomber pour Athènes," in *La mort, les morts*, pp. 27-43.

7. Xanthippe taken home: Plato, *Phaedo* 60a; Crito told to pay no attention to the servant and his advice: 63e; the multitude dismissed by philosophers: 64c; the soul takes leave of the body: 81e; discourse on material things left behind: 100d, 101c-d; the man who bids farewell to the pleasures of the body: 114e; the servant to the Eleven bids farewell to Socrates, who reciprocates: 116c-d; why the women were sent away: 117d.

8. In that he locates souls in Hades, Plato is faithful to the orthodox Greek representations; but when he ascribes *phronēsis* to those who philosophize, he takes a decisive step forward. What he thereby does is extend to philosophers in general the fate that, in Homer, was reserved for Tiresias alone: in the *Odyssey* 10.492-95, the diviner preserved his consciousness (*phrenes*) and his reason (*nous*) in Hades. On *phrēn* (clearly connected with *phronēsis*) and *nous*, see Nagy, "Patroklos," p. 165.

Phronēsis, which in the fifth century meant the activity of thought, seems to have been a key word in Socrates' thought, to judge from Aristophanes' *Clouds*: E.A. Havelock, "The Socratic Self as Parodied in Aristophanes' *Clouds*," *Yale Classical Studies* 22 (1972), pp. 1-18.

9. I have borrowed this expression from J. Le Goff, *La Naissance de Purgatoire* (The Birth of Purgatory) (Paris, 1981), p. 14. The question of place pervades the *Phaedo*, culminating in the mythical geography of the underworld, because what is at stake is the posthumous existence of the soul: to exist means to exist somewhere. Epicurus was to be the first Greek philosopher to conceive of the destiny of the soul in terms of time rather than space: see D. Lanza, "La massima epicurea 'Nulla è per noi la morte,' " in *Democrito e l'atomismo antico*, ed. I. Romano (Catania, 1980), pp. 357-65.

10. J.-P. Vernant, "La belle mort," p. 65 and "Mort grecque, mort à deux faces," *Le débat* 12 (May 1981), p. 52; E. Vermeule, *Aspects of Death*, p. 12; S. Humphreys, "Death and Time," in *Mortality and Immortality: The Anthropology and Archaeology of Death*, eds. S.C. Humphreys and H. King (London, 1981), p. 263.

11. In this respect, the philosopher's behavior has some analogies to that of the renouncers of ancient India: see C. Malamoud, "Les morts sans visage: Remarques sur l'idéologie funéraire dans le Brahmanisme," in *La mort, les morts*, pp. 447-49.

12. Plato, *Phaedo* 80c-d. It is interesting to note that what Plato does in the interests of his demonstration is cut short the ritual, immobilizing the body at the point when it is put on show, at the *prothesis* (the laying out); as he sums up Cebes's thoughts, Socrates "forgets" the cremation that brings the ritual to a close and essentially annihilates the body: it is a typically Platonic ploy.

13. In agreement with W.J. Verdenius ("Notes on Plato's *Phaedo*," *Mnemosyne* 11 [1958], p. 242) and against L. Robin (the Belles-Lettres edition), I think the perfect participle *leloumenos* should be restored at 116b7, for it makes an important point.

14. Orphism: D.J. Stewart, "Socrates' Last Bath," *Journal of the History of Philosophy* 10 (1972), pp. 253-59; Socrates already dead: P. Trotignon, "Sur la mort de Socrate," *Revue de métaphysique et de morale* 81 (1976), pp. 1-10; the women and their care of the dead body: E. Vermeule, *Aspects of Death*, p. 14.

15. See M. Daraki, "Les fils de la mort: la nécrophagie cynique et stoïcienne," in *La mort, les morts*, pp. 155-76, esp. pp. 159-60.

16. In *De rerum natura* 3.870-93, Lucretius was to introduce a similar argument concerning the idea that the soul *is not* immortal: since there is no life after death, why lament over the destiny of one's own body?

17. Hesiod, *Works and Days* 164-73, and Pindar, *2nd Olympian* 66-89.

18. On the authentic Aristotelian view of death, see D. Lanza, "La morte esclusa," *Quaderni di storia* 11 (1980), pp. 157-72.

19. Socrates as a poet, and Aesop: 60b-61c; Socrates as the servant of Apollo: 84a-85b. On Aesop, Apollo and the heroic cult of the poet, see G. Nagy, *The Best of the Achaeans: Concepts of the Hero in the Archaic Greek Poetry* (Baltimore and London, 1979), pp. 315-16. I have also borrowed from G. Nagy the idea of the model or "generic poet" as the epitomy of a poet (by which it is not necessarily intended to suggest that Hesiod and Aesop are themselves fictitious figures).

20. Or even ghosts, according to E.A. Havelock's commentary on line 94 of *Clouds* (*psuchōn sophōn*: "The Socratic Self," pp. 15-16), where he detects a play on words involving, on the one hand, the Homeric meaning, on the other the truly Socratic meaning of *psuchē*.

21. M. Daraki's expression ("Les fils de la mort," pp. 164-65).

22. See N. Loraux, *The Invention of Athens*, pp. 101-04.

23. On the *Menexenes*, see N. Loraux, *The Invention of Athens*, pp. 265-70 and 311-27.

24. A whole study would be needed for a detailed commentary on this list. We should, for example, note with K. Dorter ("The Dramatic Aspect of Plato's *Phaedo*," *Dialogue* 8 [1969-70], pp. 564-80) that the number of individuals named tallies with that of Theseus's companions on his Cretan expedition: it is a way of reminding us that the initiatory myth of Theseus mentioned at 58a-b gives the *Phaedo* its meaning.

25. Translator's note: the French word "valeur" has both meanings.

26. For another modality of the same process of appropriating *andreia*, see N. Loraux, "Socrate, Platon, Heraklès: Sur un paradigme héroïque du philosophe," in *Histoire et structure: A la mémoire de Victor Goldschmidt*, eds. J. Brunschwig, C. Imbert and A. Roger (Paris, 1985), pp. 93-105.

27. A series of comparisons have been made: *Phaedo* 68a1-2 and 6; Thucydides 2.43.1 and *Symposium* 208c; *Phaedo* 68b 9c 1 and Lysias, *Funeral Speech* 25; *Phaedo* 114c and Lysias, *Funeral Speech* 24.

28. *Phaedo* 68b-69b; on the exchange involved in a fine death, see O. Longo, "La morte per la patria," *Studi Italiani di Filologia Classica* 49 (1977), pp. 5-36.

29. *Phroura*, a noun denoting an action: F. Bader, *Revue de philologie* 46 (1972), p. 202; the body as a prison: P. Courcelle, "La prison de l'âme," in *Connais-toi toi-même* 2, pp. 345-80, and P. Bovancé, *Revue de philologie* 20 (1963), pp. 7-11; the Platonic reversal of the traditional representation of Hades as a prison: see also the *Cratylus* 403a-404b; the jail, the animal compound: P. Chantraine, *Revue de philologie* 20 (1946), pp. 5-11; the guard post: J. Roux and G. Roux, *Revue de philologie* 35 (1961), pp. 207-11. We should also note that there may well be an ironic reference to the military sense of this word in *Clouds*: at 716-21, Strepsiades, the ordinary man who tries to become initiated to phi-

losophy, finds himself worn out "from mounting guard and singing [*phrouras aidōn*]": yet another (particularly bold) example of the systematic reversal of *Clouds* in the *Phaedo*.

30. Plato, *Phaedo* 117b3-5, which may be compared to the *Iliad*, trans. E.V. Rieu (Harmondsworth, 1950) 13.278-86.

31. See A. Brelich, *Guerre, agoni e culti nella Grecia arcaica* (Bonn, 1961), pp. 22-34.

32. Cf. P. Louis, *Les métaphores de Platon* (Rennes, 1945), pp. 57-63.

33. It is significant that *menein*, a verb associated with hoplites, and its compounds appear over and over again in the *Phaedo* (see, esp., 62a-e, 98e, 102e-07e2 and 115a-16a).

34. Rather than "Plato was unwell," might this "weakness" have something to do with the human weakness referred to in 107b (which is characterized by insufficient faith in the immortality of the soul)?

35. On the importance of the theme of persuasion in the *Phaedo*, see Dorter, "The Dramatic Aspect," p. 574.

36. J. Moreau, "La leçon du *Phédon*," *Archives de philosophie* 41 (1978), pp. 81-92, notes (p. 82) that this point does not emerge until after the early passage devoted to Socrates' attitude to death; in a famous article ("La méditation de l'âme dans le *Phédon*," *Revue de métaphysique et de morale* 33 (1926), pp. 469-91), M. Gueroult tries to show that one should get over one's first impression that "the entire conversation is aimed solely at persuading us to share a *belief*..." (p. 471).

37. Among the countless interpretations of the dedication of a cock to Asclepius, it is worth noting that of R. Minadeo (*Classical Journal* 66 [1971], pp. 293-97), who compares 118a with 89a-b, regarding it as "an expression of gratitude for the success of the dialectical discussion." That success matters as much to the disciples as to Socrates, hence the "we" ("we owe a cock..."). Asclepius, the doctor-god, was believed to have brought human beings back to life: in the *Phaedo*, saving the life of the *logos* — even ensuring its immortality — is of even greater importance.

38. *Misologia* (hatred of discourse) is coined by analogy with *misanthrōpia* and is based on the idea that "there is a similarity between *logoi* and human beings." Instances where Socrates and the *logos* are treated as interchangeable: at 102, the verbs *hupomenenein* and *ethelein*, which serve to describe the behavior of a hoplite, are transferred from Socrates to the *logos*, then applied once again to Socrates.

39. M. Detienne points out that in passing from Homer (*Odyssey* 11.602) to Plato (*Laws* 12.959b), we move on from the body, which is the basis of Heracles' personality, to the soul, which constitutes the self in any person ("Ebauches de la personne dans la Grèce archaïque," in *Problèmes de la personne*, ed. I. Meyerson (Paris, 1973), pp. 46-52).

40. See V. Goldschmidt, "La religion de Platon," in *Platonisme et pensée contemporaine* (Paris, 1970), esp. pp. 68-71.

41. Plato, *Phaedo* 79c, 81d. The soul too much attached to the body evokes the *psuchē* of the Homeric poems and lyric poetry. There, it is an *eidōlon* which, as E. Vermeule points out (*Aspects of Death*, p. 29), cannot really be separated from the body.

42. Plato, *Phaedo* 82d-83a: see J.-P. Vernant, "The River of Ameles and the *Meletē Thanatou*," in *Myth and Thought among the Greeks* (London, 1983), pp. 106-23; also M. Daraki, "Les fils de la mort," pp. 161-65.

43. M. Detienne, "Ebauches de la personne," p. 49; see also, on 67e, 70a, 80e, 81b-c and 83a, M. Detienne, *La notion de Daimon*, pp. 71-85.

44. Cf. L. Gernet, *The Anthropology of Ancient Greece* (Baltimore and London, 1981), in particular pp. 244-47.

45. *Thermos* and its derivatives occur sixteen times in the dialogue; in interpreting Socrates' reaction to the advice "not to become heated," we should bear in mind that *thermos* can also mean "courageous": Crito is inadvertently advising his friend to forswear his dialectical courage.

46. It is still perfectly possible for a recalcitrant reader on the contrary to use this description to attack the thesis of the immortality of the soul, as does Lucretius who, without actually naming Socrates, certainly appears to be thinking of the *Phaedo* in lines 526-32 of the *De rerum natura* 3.

47. J. Derrida, *Dissemination* (Chicago, 1983), ch. 1.

48. This acceptance of death is in line with the theme of the dialogue, and we should not seek to make it out to be suicide even if, in the institutional practice of the Athenians, the hemlock, used as the penalty for political crimes, seems to introduce an element of suicide into the execution (cf. L. Gernet, *Anthropology*, pp. 254-55).

49. The Platonic tradition regards the *atrapos* of the *Phaedo* (66b) as the straight and narrow path of virtue, as mentioned by Hesiod and Pythagoras; cf. A. Festugière, *Les trois protreptiques de Platon* (Paris, 1973), pp. 79-80, and P. Courcelle, *Connais-toi toi-même*, vol. 3, pp. 625-45. Without seeking to contradict the tradition that consistently adopts this particular view, I would compare this passage to line 123 of Aristophanes' *Frogs* (where the effects of hemlock are described in the same terms as those used by Plato); it is furthermore worth noting that *atrapos* is not a common word in Plato's works (only one other occurrence). Yet again, Plato here twists Aristophanes' words, or turns them around, in order to make a serious point.

50. This point has already been made, for example by C. Gill, "The Death of Socrates," *Classical Quarterly* 23 (1973), pp. 25-28. On hemlock, see Aristophanes, *Frogs* 123-26; Theophrastus, *Historia plantarum* 9.8.3, 16.8-9; Nicander, *Alexipharmaka* 186-94 (hemlock and madness: see also Galen, *Quod animi mores corporis temperamenta sequantur* 3.775-77 and *Etym. Magnum*, s.v. *kōneion*). Of the many

Greek euphemisms for hemlock, it is worth drawing attention to the term *aphrōn* (the "mad" drink, the drink that destroys *phronēsis*): cf. A. Carnoy, "Les noms grecs de la ciguë," *Les études classiques* 28 (1960), pp. 369-74.

51. I owe this idea to a suggestion made by J.-P. Vernant (see his article "The Representation of the Invisible and the Psychological Category of the Double: The Colossos," *Myth and Thought among the Greeks* (London, 1983), pp. 305-20. On the interplay between the sign and the tomb in the word *sēma*, see G. Nagy, "*Sēma* and *Noēsis*: Some illustrations," *Arethusa* 16 (1983), pp. 35-55.

52. See Plato, *Phaedo* 99d-100a, an impressive passage on imagery.

53. From the Church Fathers onward. Perhaps the reason for this is that the *Phaedo* frees the pure soul definitively from the body, delivering it forever from the cycle of reincarnation. In any event, Gregory of Nazianzus and Saint Ambrose develop the metaphor of the body-prison at considerable length, which is all the more remarkable in view of the fact that, by proclaiming the resurrection of the body, Christian thought from the outset avoids the pitfalls of the spiritualistic approach.

From *Le temps de la réflexion*, vol. 3, Paris, Gallimard, 1982.
Translated by Janet Lloyd.

Reflections of a Soul

Eric Alliez and Michel Feher

"Plotinus, the philosopher of our times, seemed ashamed of being in a body." When his disciple, Amelius, "asked him to allow his portrait to be painted, his reply was: 'Why, really, is it not enough to have to carry the image in which nature has encased us, without your requesting me to agree to leave behind me a longer-lasting image of the image, as if it was something genuinely worth looking at?' "[1] If what Porphyry, Plotinus's biographer and disciple, tells us is true, it may seem somewhat paradoxical to choose Plotinus's thought as the basis for an essay on the body. More than any other philosopher, Plotinus tried to distance himself from his own body, and as far as we know, he succeeded. Such disdain was doubtless in tune with the Platonic tradition to which Plotinus claimed to belong, and it was part of a style of life[2] much in vogue in the third century A.D. in the intellectual circles of the Empire — both in Rome and in Alexandria, among pagans and Christians alike. But Plotinus was not just trying to perpetuate Platonism by exploiting a fashion that would favor its influence. Nor did he attempt to distort Platonism to make it tally with the disgust for the sensible world that was fashionable among many of his contemporaries. Plotinus regarded the human body as a degradation of the soul but also as a reflection of it; and his philosophy was not so much the occasion of a synthesis as a crossroad between two different worlds. Theoretically, it was a philosophy based on a notion of spiritual light — a noology — that did not correspond either to its heritage of Greek cosmology or to the Christian eschatology that it conditioned, but to which it remained uncommitted. In practice, it manifested a detachment at once radical and serene. It broke away from the exaltation of graceful bodies that characterized classical Antiquity and that even Plato could never quite shake off. Yet it was equally antipathetic to the fascinated horror of the flesh manifested at the time by the Gnostic movements and the early Church Fathers.

Plotinus was certainly not the only writer to see the body as a reflection of the soul.[3] But he added crucial theoretical depth to that image. On the one hand, the psychology that he founded distanced itself from the classical Greek tradition to the extent that it no longer located its reference points in an immutable heaven. Though it was not bound up with a promise of final redemption, it rested on a construct that was also destined to enjoy lasting popularity. Following Pierre Hadot and Julia Kristeva, we shall call that construct Narcissian[4] — even if the ethic it refers to is devoted to the condemnation of Narcissism. On the other hand, Plotinian psychology encompassed an aesthetic based on the sublime that was the inspiration behind certain tendencies in the art of the late Roman period[5] but that was above all responsible for changing the athlete of classical sculpture into the ascetic of the Byzantine icons.

The Civic Way and the Mystic Way

To understand the importance of Plotinus's Neoplatonism in the history of the soul–body relationship, we must first pause to reflect upon the original Platonism. It is well known that Plato's point of view regarding the relationship between the human soul and the body allotted to it is not the same in all his dialogues. His thought oscillates between two models: that of a soul of celestial origin imprisoned — or even entombed — in the body (this is expressed in the famous *sōma–sēma* formula);[6] and that of a soul as the source of motion that dominates the body that it moves. Thus Plato, too, stands at the crossroad of two traditions: the one, which goes back to the Orphic and Pythagorean sects, emphasizes that the body and the soul are different by nature and that the immortal soul's residence within the corruptible body is an exile. The other, which inspired the moral view and also the aesthetic attitude of Plato's Athenian compatriots, ranks the soul's control over the body as a cardinal virtue but also celebrates the grace (*charis*) engendered by the union of the two. Sometimes Plato embarks upon the mystic way that he believes to lead to the fulfillment of the philosophical life; sometimes he takes the civic path, intent on reforming it. When he engages in the first of these two courses, he is more inclined to draw attention to the deformations that the body inflicts on the soul. When he is pursuing the civic path, he tends to stress the influence that the soul exerts on the body. The coexistence of the two tendencies does not introduce a fatal contradiction into Platonic thought, for it is possible to span the divide even between the *Phaedo*, the dialogue most committed to the mystic way, and the *Timaeus*, which associates the civic path with cosmological necessity.

Thus the term *phroura* that Socrates applies to the body in the *Phaedo* means not only "prison" but also "military service, the manning of a garrison."[7] The philosopher may accordingly rejoice at the idea of his imminent death, since it will deliver his soul from its material chains. At the same time he is duty-bound not to precipitate his death, because the life of the body is an onerous task that must be executed scrupulously. Conversely, in the *Timaeus*, even if the association between the soul and the human body is seen as part of the design of a Craftsman who has created a universe in conformity with the intelligible world and its absolute perfection, the soul experiences its descent into the body as the most traumatic of ordeals. It is submerged by the affections of the body that are conditioned in their turn by the ebb and flow of nourishment. "Hence it comes about that now...as in the beginning, so often as the Soul is bound within a mortal body it becomes at first irrational."[8] Only by growing up and by receiving the right education can the soul recover reason and take control of the body.

These two texts represent extreme positions on the separation between the soul and the body and on their union, but each makes concessions to the opposite point of view. Besides, the variations in Plato's thought can also be explained by the fact that he always adapts what he has to say to the particular subject of the dialogue (whether it is a description of the philosophical life or a plan for political reform) and also to the type of man under consideration. In the case of a philosopher, domination of the body gives hope of deliverance for the soul; for statesmen, such as the Guardians of the *Republic*, mastery over one's own body is both a condition for governing other men and the proof of one's capacity to do so. Furthermore, the functional difference between these two categories of citizen manifests and reflects the difference that, in the case of a human soul, distinguishes between one that is rational and one that is spirited.[9] The rational soul is characterized by its ability to contemplate intelligible realities, the spirited one by its power to direct the appetitive soul — together with the corporeal affections that it echoes. So in Plato's writings as a whole, it *is* possible to link the "civic line," which is that of the male adult

citizen, and the "mystic line," which is presented as the royal way of the philosopher. Nevertheless, it is only by grasping the opposition between the two that we
can follow the path that leads from Platonism to Neoplatonism.

The civic way, which assigns control over the body to the soul, corresponds to
the dominant values of the classical culture. It revolves around two principles: first,
the domination of the passive by the active; and second, the quest for the golden
mean. If man is considered a mixed substance, the soul that gives movement to the
body represents the active part, while the body, which receives that impulse and
responds to it, represents the passive part. Now, given that in the last analysis a passive element is bound to be dominated by an active one, every human body will
necessarily be governed by a soul. If that soul is the one to which the body is connected, the human being composed of that body and soul will be free. On the other
hand, a person whose soul proves incapable of ruling the behavior of the body and
who, as a result, gives free rein to that body's passions immediately becomes subject to the activity of other souls and will always live in a state of dependence on
things external to him. In other words, a person in thrall to his body, a depraved or
violent individual, is certainly doomed – not so much because he is evil, but because
he is weak and passive. Such a person is not active but "agitated," that is to say moved
by external forces. In contrast, a free individual whose soul controls his body manifests not only his independence but also moderation; and the combination of the
two qualifies him to exercise authority over others. To put this another way, he is
capable of wielding authority over his household and assuming political responsi-
bilities within the framework of the city.[10] For, once this relationship of domination is recognized, the next question that arises is how to recognize an individual
whose soul has mastered his body. This is where the second great principle of classical thought comes in: the quest for the golden mean. It finds expression in the
idealization of moderation (sōphrosunē) in the moral field and proportion (summetria)
in the aesthetic one. On the one hand, the soul's government of the body must
eschew all excesses: there must be no anarchy but no tyranny either, in order to
avoid falling into either license (akolasia) or insensibility (anaisthēsia).[11] The needs
of the body must therefore be recognized, as must the balance upon which its health
depends. On the other hand, the belief that the body must be subjected to a strict
discipline that restrains its impulses without inhibiting its powers is the corollary

to the notion of grace held by a free and active citizen of classical Athens.[12] The correctness of the proportions of a body and the measured poise of its gait and movements were considered as so many aesthetic criteria that reflected the ethical excellence of the individual who possessed them. It was as if the impression of harmony conveyed by a man's graceful body was a sign of his temperance.

Finally, the classical view of man is marked by a third characteristic. The notion of grace (*charis*), which in man is a combination of moral temperance and physical elegance, is constantly justified by an astronomical paradigm. The circular arrangement of the celestial bodies and their cyclical movements are considered the sensible manifestation of an ideal of symmetry and regularity that is embodied by the heavens, a harmonious whole that integrates and moves the parts that compose it. Observation of the Universe thus provides the aspiring citizen with a model of both ethical and aesthetic equilibrium that he should strive to reproduce at the level of his own personal life. By absorbing the universal harmony, he cultivates his own "charisma," which will enable him to influence his peers and win a place in the memory of his descendants.

Plato never totally abandons the civic way. In fact, he even helps to consolidate it. But, as he follows it, he steers it in a direction that enables him to develop a radical dualism. In the first place, he remains faithful to the cosmological model, for he regards the heavenly sphere as the most exact image of the intelligible essences: the regular movements of the stars stand in contrast to the corruption of the sublunary bodies — that is to say, the agitation that undermines them — and provide a sensible representation of the eternity that is a property of the intelligible world. In the *Timaeus*, the Craftsman who builds the Universe contemplates Intellect and communicates it to the Universal Soul, which thereupon converts it into movement. But unlike human bodies and in spite of their material existence, the celestial bodies that execute those movements do not cause any degradation for the Universal Soul that presides over their revolutions. Therefore, Plato can only invite the man who wishes to perfect himself to seek inspiration in the cosmic order. Furthermore — still according to the *Timaeus* — contemplation of the heavens revives in a man's soul the divine imprint that it bears but that was initially effaced by its fall into a mortal body. All the same, even though Plato confers the role of model upon the Universe, he also attributes such a role to the "impression" of intelligence that — thanks to the work of the Craftsman who literally imprinted intelligible reality upon the sensible world — is inherent in the Universe and may be transmitted to the human soul in quest of authentic knowledge. Thus, in Platonic thought, observation of the cosmos and its organization is merely a — no doubt necessary — stage or means of mediation leading to the goal of every soul committed to wisdom, namely the "immediate" contemplation of Ideas. In other words, an ideal model — the intelligible world — transcends the exemplary model provided by "our" Universe. Platonic psychology aspires to direct knowledge of the intelligible world, whereas classical cosmology — of which Plato makes use, adapting it to his own needs — permits only an indirect knowledge of that world, mediated through "our Universe."

Second, while Plato appropriates the virtue of temperance, stressing the asceticism that it involves, as author not only of the *Timaeus* and the *Laws* but also of the *Phaedo* and the *Phaedrus*, he remains ambivalent regarding the purpose of controlling the body. Should the soul govern the body in order to make it more perfect or dominate it in order to free itself from it? Should the soul overcome the body it inhabits in order to live apart from it or so that the compound formed by the two may correspond to the norms of ideal beauty? Plato's determination to distinguish between true wisdom and the all too "worldly" ploys of the sophists, combined with his own inclinations and admiration for the Orphic and Pythagorean traditions, leads him to adopt the *sōma–sēma* formula of the latter and, whenever he has the chance, to emphasize the soul's aspiration to separate from the body in which it is embedded. As prisoner of the body, the soul is constantly threatened by two forms of irrationality: on the one hand, the ignorance in which it is kept by the misleading messages transmitted by the senses, and on the other, the madness that results from the violent passions that can take over the body and contaminate the soul by blinding it.[13] But it is on the level of aesthetics that Plato, without breaking explicitly with the civic way followed by his fellow citizens, distances himself from the values with which they identified.

In the first place, he declares his deep distrust for any exaggerated cultivation of the body. He does not deny the importance of physical exercise but regards it as no more than a means, necessary but not sufficient, by which an individual may gain control of himself. The practice of gymnastics and the observance of dietary rules should be prompted by a desire for independence on the part of the soul rather than by a yearning for strength and physical beauty.[14] Yet Plato certainly does not treat a graceful body as a misleading appearance. Indeed, he considers that the attraction one feels toward physical beauty may be the best preliminary training for the quest for true beauty. The trouble is, though, that the civic line of thought, in particular the sophistic trend, regards grace as an *effect* produced by a graceful body — or a well-turned speech or a work of art, as the case may be — whereas for Plato intelligible beauty is the *cause* of the beauty that one recognizes in a human body. Similarly, it is dangerous to regard an individual's strength and physical elegance as the manifestation of his moral excellence, for they are no more than an indication of it. In short, the cultivation of the body and the cult of charisma that predominate among his contemporaries seem to Plato to represent an alarming obsession with the impression of beauty that floats on the surface of the world and captivates its inhabitants, obscuring the essence that it can only hint at.

Hence Plato's skepticism toward art, particularly the plastic arts, the second issue on which he distances himself from the civic values. The painter's and the sculptor's representation of the human body may no doubt be considered salutary so long as the artist strives to imitate nature by selecting elements in it that correspond to the cosmic order — axes of symmetry, proportionality in the various parts, regularity in the features — and also to the intelligible beauty of which the heavenly sphere conveys the most exact impression. Provided the artist does so, art, no less than a love of beautiful bodies, may be preliminary training for the discovery of true beauty. In fact, however, Plato has noticed that artists are concerned less with the exaltation of ideal forms than with the simulation of empirical reality, that is to say appearances.[15] It is worth pointing out that at the time he was writing, a "hyperrealist" school of sculptors and painters existed in Athens. These artists' works were full of effects of perspective and trompe l'oeil: for instance, the grapes painted by Zeuxis were said to be so lifelike that even the birds mistook them for real fruit.[16] Clearly, Plato is extremely hostile to this school whose artifices remind him of those of the sophists, who favored effects rather than causes to the point of obscuring all distinctions between them.[17] But quite apart from the encouragement thus given to disorder and confusion, Plato's particular reproach to art lovers and physical culture enthusiasts alike is that, by concentrating on what is modeled, they lose sight of the intelligible model to which any material copy owes all the grace bestowed upon it.

From a theoretical point of view, Plato does not break with the "impressionism" of classical thinking – that is to say the notion according to which forms are branded onto matter and movements are imprinted upon bodies. But he stresses the distinction between the apparent imprint and the reality that is imprinted, defining the progress made from one to the other as the specifically philosophical movement of the human soul. For Plato, the soul is divided between contemplating Ideas and motivating the body, that is, imparting movement and shape to it. Moreover, by giving precedence to the former function over the latter, Plato takes a step toward emancipating human psychology from its dependence on cosmology. After Plato but within a framework of thought of Platonic inspiration, this emancipation was to lead to the elaboration of a mystic way.

Plato's disciples and the successive tendencies within the Academy were inclined chiefly to explore the most radically dualist of the themes developed in the Socratic dialogues. They favored in particular those that made it possible to identify the philosopher with his soul and that consequently emphasized the efforts that the human soul must be prepared to make to extricate itself from the alien body in which it is embedded. It was a trend characteristic of the philosophical climate prevailing in the Greco-Roman world (or *oikoumenē*) from the end of the Republic down to the beginning of the late Empire. Not that the climate manifested itself in a general mystic fervor, for even the Platonists were far more concerned with combining the elevation of their souls with a social life and public duties. Rather, the period witnessed rival schools of wisdom competing to outdo one another in both ascetic rigor and "pathetic" tone.

The orientation of ancient thought between the first century B.C. and the second century A.D., which was reflected in middle Platonism, stemmed from the adoption of what Michel Foucault calls "the care of the self" as the principal object of philosophical research.[18] While that research became more than ever concerned with the human soul's control over the body it inhabits, the role assigned to the soul was changing as a result of the increasing importance ascribed to "pathos," that is, the somatic afflictions and psychic affections against which every respectable individual spends his life struggling. In this anxiety-ridden, even slightly hypochondriac atmosphere, the control of the self that an individual exercised was not so much directed toward forming a healthy body whose grace would impress the minds of his peers with the memory of the soul that had modeled it. Rather, it aimed to maintain a fragile body that was constantly in danger and so constituted a threat to the soul that it held.[19] As for the principal virtue claimed by such an ethics, although it might still be said to be self-control, it consisted not so much in promoting activity in the individual as in guiding him toward an ever greater impassivity. Admittedly, the new ideal varied slightly from one doctrine to another: thus, among the Epicureans, it meant the state of relaxation in which a wise man can enjoy the true pleasures, those that are constant by virtue of their simplicity; for the Stoics, on the other hand, impassivity meant maximum vigilance on the part of the soul that was unfailingly on the qui vive.[20] All the same, whatever the school of thought, internal liberty (*autarkeia*) became the aim of every fine and wise life — attainable only by dint of a long, hard struggle, whereas in classical culture, it had been considered above all as a precondition for the judicious exercise of civic authority. Similarly, impassivity, tranquility of soul (*ataraxia*), was now seen as the crowning achievement of asceticism, the expression of self-sufficiency finally attained, whereas the classical form of self-control (*sōphrosunē*) had been valued chiefly as a training for political activity, and its ensuing effect, which the citizen so much desired, was charisma rather than serenity.

We must remember, however, that this reinforcement of austerity did not mean that those who practiced philosophy turned away from politics. Contrary to an idea once widely held, the emphasis on and idealization of self-shaping that are such a feature of this period do not reflect the introspection of a degenerate kind of citizen whom the collapse first of Greek democracy, then of the Roman Republic, condemned to a purely internal liberty, as if to house arrest. For these "men of the world" who were won over by philosophy, the problem was, on the contrary, to maintain and apply the principles they were committed to but — except in the case of the cynics — to do so without ever breaking totally with their community, where some of them (such as Cicero and Marcus Aurelius) held the highest of offices. Nevertheless, it is fair to say that during the Hellenistic period and under the early Empire, the tendency was to reverse the priorities of the ancient ethos: internal self-sufficiency was no longer the necessary condition for leading a memorable life but, rather, it became an objective to be attained throughout — and frequently despite — the ups and downs of social and political life.

A lover of wisdom was no longer preoccupied with the charismatic effects that classical culture had associated with the life of the soul, but now concentrated far more on the quality of his psychic life per se; and such a development inevitably encouraged the most austere and radically dualist interpretations of Plato's work among the middle Platonists. For them, the impassivity pursued by other schools of thought in some cases even took the form of a detachment that prepared for the definitive separation of the soul from the body. So the Platonists may well have been a match for their Epicurean, Stoic and Aristotelian rivals on the score of ascetic rigor. On the other hand, by judging the soul's aspiration to free itself from the flesh that enveloped it to be more important than its functions as the moving force of the body, they were bound to deepen the endemic rift between the cosmology inherited from the *Timaeus* and the mystic way opened up by the *Phaedo* and the *Phaedrus*. As for Stoicism and Epicureanism, they certainly encouraged their disciples to break with the agitation of daily life, in which the soul is guided by its passions, the body by its appetites. But they also urged them, in doing so, to raise themselves morally "up to the level" of the Universe and its laws,[21] rather than to turn away from the world in order to accede to an immediate vision of the Intelligible. For the Platonists, however, there was an abiding tension between, on the one hand, the moving force that the soul must display with regard to its body — in conformity with the cosmological model — and the desire to rise even higher, to which they wished the soul to be totally devoted. And this tension confronted the Platonists with a daunting choice: either they could renounce the doctrine of the necessity and beauty of the sensible world (some did indeed adopt this "gnostic" solution); or they could opt for a form of syncretism that more or less successfully combined the ethic of Socrates in his mystic moments with an attitude toward the physical world inspired by the Stoics and Aristotelians.

Not until the third century did the mystic way stemming from Plato take real shape. Now the Neoplatonism of Plotinus and his disciples succeeded in combining an original and rigorous cosmogony with an authentically mystic impulse. But it was able to do so only by substituting a truly psychological model, centered on the human soul and its speculative capacities, for the cosmological model of universal harmony that had operated as an "interface" between the world of essences and that of appearances.

The Audacity of the Human Soul

Plotinus resolves the tension between action and contemplation that is inherent in Platonic thought by making contemplation fully active, indeed turning it into the only activity that is truly productive. For Plotinus, everything starts with the One, a supreme principle, in the mold of the Platonic Good, but one that encompasses a whole new world. The One contemplates itself unceasingly, and this self-contemplation produces all that is. From the One that is nothing, since "all things come from it,"[22] proceeds "Intellect" (*nous*), which encompasses the totality of Being and emanates from the contemplation of the One by itself, just as light emanates from a luminous source. The Ideas that fill the intelligible world imply the One, which is their common origin, and each one plays its part in explicating it. Conversely, the One manifests itself through Intellect and is expressed in Ideas.[23] This movement of procession or emanation provoked by the self-contemplation of the One then leads to a second movement, namely the conversion of Intelligible Realities into their origin. To put this another way, the Ideas, too, are immersed in permanent contemplation, not of themselves but of the One from which they emanate. And this contemplation, too, is productive, in the sense that it projects the radiance from the One and gives rise to a second movement of reflection or, to use the Plotinian term, a second hypostasis: Soul (*psuchē*). First there is the Soul of the Universe, which envelops the whole of *life*, just as Intellect encompassed the whole of *being*. Next there are the individual souls, those of the stars and also those of men, animals and even plants. Immaterial as they are, these souls are "intensively" distinct from one another, that is, like so many degrees of intensity, but without being separated spatially, that is, by extension as the inhabitants of the material world are. Furthermore, this interpenetration of the individual souls within the Universal Soul depends upon their communion in a second movement of conversion: in this, the souls are converted to the Intellect from which they proceed and, through Intellect, to the One that finds expression in the intelligible world and of which the Soul of the World is a second manifestation. Finally, the contemplation of Intellect by the souls that proceed from it produces a further movement of procession, hence a new hypostasis:

Nature (*kosmos*), with all its animated bodies. These bodies capture only the most remote reflections of the spiritual light because they are formed on the surface of dark, absorbent Matter — Matter that corresponds to nonbeing as Intellect is identified with being.

Plotinus's cosmogony thus results from or is the extension of the fall of light, emanating from the One, on the material world: a fall that is not a fall from grace but the very process through which the One radiates its brilliance. The diffusion of this light engenders reflections that are more and more subdued the farther they are from the source of light, although, whatever their level, these reflections remain, thanks to their conversion, focal points of intellectual diffusion. At every level this philosophy of spiritual light, this noology, is based solely upon the notion of contemplation (*theōria*) that subsumes the twofold movement of procession from the One and conversion to the One. One reason is that ancient optical science, which Neoplatonic thought draws upon, identified rays of light with rays of vision. The One and its series of hypostases can thus be seen both as a contemplating eye and as a source of radiant light.[24]

However, Plotinus is not content with this theory bearing the stamp of necessity. Between the soul that is converted to the spiritual source that it expresses and the body that is illuminated by the reflection proceeding from that conversion but is, for its part, incapable of converting itself, Plotinus introduces a strictly human drama. According to him, the human soul may suddenly tire of contemplating the intelligible realities and allow itself to be captivated by its own reflection in the silvered mirror of matter, in other words, its own body. We should note that only the *human* soul is affected by such curiosity. The Universal Soul and the souls of the heavenly bodies never tire of contemplating the Intellect from which they proceed. And if, by so doing, they animate bodies that thereupon reflect them, they remain perfectly indifferent to this effect of their conversion, paying no attention to the evolution of their sensible reflections. In contrast, the human soul, not content simply to animate the body that it illuminates, may become so infatuated with it that it turns away from the contemplation of Intellect and thereby from the souls within the Universal Soul, which continue to commune together in their conversion to their common origin. Human souls

as if they were tired of being together...each go to their own. Now, when a soul does this for a long time, flying from the All and standing apart in distinctness, and does not look toward the Intelligible, it has become a part and is isolated and weak...and it embarks on one single thing and flies from everything else; it comes to and turns to that one thing...and is present and sinks deep into the individual part. Here, the "molting," as it is called, happens to it and the being in the fetters of the body, since it has missed the immunity which it had when it was with the universal soul....[25]

The fall of radiant light that originates in the One and encompasses the procession of the hypostases is followed by the human soul's fall into degradation when it becomes fascinated by its own reflection in matter. The human soul abandons itself to this fatal decline as soon as it inclines toward its material image: "If it declined, it was obviously because it had forgotten the intelligible realities."[26] The soul's error, which Plotinus calls its audacity (*tolma*), is now envisaged as a mirror: "But the souls of men see their images as if in the mirror of Dionysus and come to be on that level with a leap from above."[27]

We can now appreciate how far Plotinus's thought is from Gnosticism, despite the fact that both doctrines consider that this mirror-gazing is what constitutes human error, in fact that such error is narcissism. For the Gnostics, archetypal man, the *Kadmon* Adam, who is still pure soul, is tricked by the *Archōn*, the evil Craftsman who created the material world. This *Archōn* captures the image of primordial man as it is reflected in the water of the oceans, together with his shadow, which is projected across the surface of the Earth. Captivated by this reflection and this shadow, the *Kadmon* Adam rushes toward them and sinks into the degraded human condition in which the soul is the body's prisoner, submerged by matter and constantly troubled by the passions by which matter is disturbed. In other words, in Gnostic thought the reflection of the human soul in matter, the constitution of man as an association of soul and body and, more generally, the whole cosmogony that culminates with this anthropogony – this whole process is presented as a drama. For the Gnostics, the sensible universe is not, as it is for Plotinus, a natural reflection of the contemplative action of souls, a reflection produced by their conversion to Intellect. Instead, the creation of the sensible world is the work of a malevolent god with evil designs. As for the reflection of the soul in the body that it illuminates, this is not regarded as the soul's necessary sensible manifestation, but as a trap set by the evil Craftsman. In short, for the Gnostics there is but one fall that, in a single dramatic movement, determines both the cosmic order and the fall of man.[28]

Plotinus, in contrast, constantly emphasizes the difference between the radiation of spiritual light that produces the Universe on which it falls — a fall that is necessary and in no way baneful — and the fall or degradation that is peculiar to man and that is the consequence of the audacity shown by his soul. This degradation diminishes the brilliance of the human soul, whereas the fall that consists in a radiation of light produces reflections that may be dimmer in relation to the intensity of light at the source from which they emanate, yet that in no way obscure that source. Plotinus thus makes a distinction between cosmogonic necessity (namely, the constitution of the body as a reflection of the soul) and psychological audacity (the decline of the soul — and its inclination — as it is captivated by its own reflection). However, a human soul that is in love with wisdom rather than a prey to audacity still possesses a body, and it neither can nor should prevent itself from illuminating "what is below," for this "is not a sin, just as casting a shadow is not a sin."[29] But its reflection leaves it unaffected, not in the sense that it cuts itself off from that reflection, but in that it is no longer there, where the reflection is; and the soul is no longer there because "the whole soul is looking to the intelligible world."[30] The audacious soul, in contrast, turns away from Ideas and in that same movement detaches itself from the other souls and is absorbed into the body it animates. Captivated by the body, it lives in isolation, whereas when it was contemplating Intellect, it lived in communion with the souls of the celestial bodies and the Soul of the Universe. As we have noted (and this is a point we shall return to in our discussion of aesthetics), the effect of matter is to separate living creatures into discrete entities that are dispersed throughout the world, whereas souls that are converted to Intellect are not distinguishable except in degree of intensity, which can vary from one soul to another depending on the quality of each one's conversion.

The audacity of the human soul is certainly akin to the "strange infatuation" that Ovid attributed to Narcissus.[31] His error was not really a matter of intrinsic malevolence: rather, it was an optical illusion. The audacious soul only inclines toward the body because it does not realize that this body to which it is subjecting itself is none other than its own reflection in the mirror of matter. When it inclines in this way, it behaves "as if someone looking at his image and not knowing where it came from should pursue it."[32] And in *On the Beautiful*, the first treatise he ever wrote, Plotinus makes his reference to the myth of Narcissus quite explicit:

> For a man runs to the image and wants to seize it as if it were the reality (like a beautiful reflection playing on the water, which some story somewhere, I think, said riddlingly a man wanted to catch and sank down into the stream and disappeared); then this man who clings to beautiful bodies and will not let them go will, like the man in the story, but in soul, not in body, sink down into the dark depths, where intellect has no delight, and stay blind in Hades, consorting with shadows both there and here.[33]

Narcissism thus expresses the tragic fall, which for the Gnostics and for Plato himself stemmed from the constitution of the world, but for Plotinus comes later, resulting from a folly that is all too human.[34] Does this mean that, for Plotinus, Evil itself is situated in the human soul? Such a notion would contradict Plotinus's *theōria* as a whole since, for him, the human soul is a particle or, to be more precise, a spark from the Universal Soul, which is an emanation from the One, that is to say from the Good. Evil must assuredly be attributed in the first instance to matter. It accounts for its darkness just as the Good accounts for the light emanating from the One. And the psychological error that the human soul commits, despite the fact that it itself proceeds solely from the light, is that it tarnishes its own brilliance by becoming fixated with the portion of matter that reflects it. In other words, by embedding itself in matter, the narcissistic soul causes darkness to increase and light to decrease and thereby becomes associated with Evil. So it is necessary to distinguish between Evil itself, which is material, and the soul's error, which lies in inclining toward it. But as we have seen, that error is also a misunderstanding, like an optical illusion. The narcissistic soul, in love with its own body, wishes to become united with it. The desire for union, *erōs*, is unquestionably a good impulse, but in this case it was misguided and ill-conceived. Misguided it certainly was, since it was directed downward toward matter and what is particular: the audacious soul desires to fuse only with its own body and, by extension, with the other bodies that its body desires; whereas that same soul *should* have launched itself upward, toward the Intellect from which it emanated. Above all, though, the narcissistic desire for union was ill-conceived: first, because the human soul seized by it did not realize that what it loved in the body it wished to belong to was none other than its own reflection; second, because, as a result of this mistake, it did not understand that the unity it was really seeking could not be a union of heterogeneous elements, that is to say, union between the soul and the body. The only true unity to which the soul can aspire is the fulfillment of a process of simplification or purification. From an aesthetic point of view, as we shall see, the demands of Plotinus's philosophy are answered better by the procedures of painting than by those of sculpture. Nevertheless, the ethical problem raised by the audacity of the soul suggests to Plotinus a metaphor that exalts the work of the sculptor over that of the painter. The sculptor operates by cutting away, hollowing out the stone or marble, whereas the painter pursues beauty by adding more and more features and colors. What Plotinus says is:

> Go back into yourself and look; and if you do not yet see yourself beautiful, then, just as someone making a statue that has to be beautiful [cuts away here and polishes there and makes one part smooth and clears another, until he has given his statue a beautiful face], so too, you must cut away excess...and clear the dark...until the divine glory of virtue shines out on you.... If you are at home with yourself in purity, with nothing hindering you from becoming in this way one, with no inward mixture of anything else, but wholly yourself...concentrate your gaze and see. This alone is the eye that sees the great Beauty.[35]

Plotinus's reasoning is complex and may seem contradictory. First, he preserves the necessary beauty of the human soul that, basically, wants only to find unity but that makes a mistake, thinking that it has found that unity in the autonomy of the pair that it forms in conjunction with the body. Entirely given over to an irresistible impulse, it does not perceive that the fusion of soul and body is in reality nothing but a movement of dispersion, since matter disperses into space that which is distinguishable at the level of the Universal Soul only in terms of intensity. Furthermore, this desire for fusion between soul and body truly produces an act of obscurantism since, even if the body does not totally absorb the light of the mind or soul (for the face, in particular, does to some extent reflect some of the soul's ardor), the human soul can preserve the purity of its brilliance only by turning away from it. The true union that the soul ought to seek should thus be achieved by withdrawing into itself instead of uniting with this other entity that is the body. However, this process of purification or simplification, which ought to inspire the soul and counter its guilty audaciousness, is far from being an end in itself. Plotinus sees it as just a first stage that may allow the human soul to convert itself to intelligible reality and to commune with other souls. But does this not immediately degenerate into the very idea that Plotinus condemns: namely, the notion of achieving unity through union with one other than oneself, rather than by withdrawing into oneself? In reality, this objection is no more than superficially valid. We must remember that the Universal Soul and the individual souls it encompasses are, in the same way as the Intellect and the Ideas that compose it, all manifestations or expressions of the One. And even if there is a strict hierarchy to the successive hypostases, the diffusion of the noetic light that constitutes them never at any time interrupts the continuity that exists between them. For Plato, the *influence* that the Good exerts upon Ideas and that the Ideas exert upon souls does not prevent them from all being separate entities.[36] But the *effluence* that, for Plotinus, leads from the One to the souls makes each emanation different in degree from the rest without it ever being a separate entity on its own. Thus, when a human soul turns away from its body to convert itself to the Intellect from which it proceeds, it is launching itself not toward something other than itself – even something superior – but toward the very Spirit that shines brightly within it. In short, the man who is rightly inspired by his desire for unity and who does not mistake gleaming reflections for the burning source of light is not projecting his soul in the Platonic manner, up toward the sky and beyond to the realm of Ideas, the most perfect impression of which is conveyed by the heavenly sphere. Instead, he is devoting himself to exploring his own psychic space, his own internal life deep within which he discovers radiant Intellect and, even deeper, the One of which Intellect is already a reflection. The internal coherence of Plotinus's theory can thus not be faulted, since the only otherness that it attributes to the human soul is the matter of which the body that the soul illuminates is composed.

Plotinus's theory, it is true, condemns the narcissistic venture, that is, the soul's love for this body that conveys no more than a weak reflection of itself. However, the Narcissian structure underpins the whole process of the soul's conversion. In other words, it is important to distinguish between the specular (or mirror-gazing) form of narcissism and the speculative variety in which eroticism is correctly directed toward the inside of the soul and the internal light that constitutes it. Thus, the psychological error of misplaced audacity that drags the soul downward contains the condition of its own repair: to reverse the dramatic course of events, all the soul needs to do is realize that what it loves in that body with which it initially desires to be united is nothing other than its own reflection. It is the soul itself that makes the face graceful and imparts that captivating depth to the eyes. Thus, as soon as the human soul perceives that it is moved by its own ardor and not by the body, which does no more than reflect it imperfectly, it turns not simply away from this dark mirror but right around and converts itself to the source of light from which it proceeds and which it now discovers deep inside itself.

Human audacity certainly introduced drama, confusion and obscurantism into the cosmogonic necessity, which is itself the result of the pure radiation of the Intellect. But perhaps that very error was also necessary in its own way, to the extent that it involved instruments of repair and salvation (especially the face and, even more, the brilliance of its gaze, those visible manifestations of the depth of the soul) and in that it suggested the form that the process of conversion should take: what had to be done was re-identify the effect/reflection with its cause/source. Even though the body is rejected as a legitimate partner for the soul, the mirror-gazing or specular relationship between the two and the movement that this inspires constitute the model for the Plotinian speculation; and that speculation leads to the human soul making the ultimate effort by which it finds itself, for a moment of ecstasy, alone with the One: "seeing with one's self alone That alone."[37]

The adventures of the audacious soul bestow an ambiguous status upon the human body since it is the body's feeble yet real capacity to reflect the noetic light that causes not only the soul's fall but also its "reconversion." It is because the soul sees its reflection illuminating its body that it turns away from contemplation of the intelligible realities and from the company of the other souls. But then, it is because it perceives that it is no more than its own reflection that it turns right around again and discovers the beauty inside itself.

The question that now arises is to what extent plastic representations of the human body have the power to counterbalance the Evil indissociable from its material nature and to evoke the spiritual ardor manifested through it. This is the problem for Plotinus's aesthetics. At no point does he address this study systematically, but he approaches it, in line with the "optical" paradigm that underpins his work, from the angle of "reflection":

> The wise men of old, who made temples and statues in the wish that the gods should
> be present to them, looking to the nature of the All, had in mind that the nature of

Soul is everywhere easy to attract, but that if someone were to construct something sympathetic to it and able to receive a part of it, it would of all things receive soul most easily. That which is sympathetic to it is what imitates it in some way, like a mirror able to catch [the reflections of] a form.[38]

The Ambivalence of Depth

Plotinus thus requires a work of art to mirror reality as faithfully as possible. However, he attributes authentic reality only to that which is intelligible, which projects no more than an uncertain reflection onto the sensible world. The Soul of the Universe is the intermediary power thanks to which a little intellect still exists on the surface of bodies. It operates as a focal point that captures the spiritual light, then itself emits rays of light and thereby animates the sensible world, outlining every part of it. How then should the "realistic" artist set about seizing upon the radiance of the soul that penetrates the bodies he is trying to represent? First, says Plotinus, by respecting the "true" sizes and the "true" colors of things.[39] He contrasts this truth not so much to artistic fantasy and license, but to the distortions to which the depth of space subjects material bodies. For distance blurs colors and deforms objects. What Plotinus condemns above all is geometric perspective, in fact three-dimensional representation in general.[40] The reason for his hostility toward depth (*bathos*) is that, to his mind, it constitutes par excellence the dimension of matter; it is the density of the world that is responsible for absorbing the intelligible light reflected by the Universal Soul. But Plotinus counterbalances his condemnation of the third dimension by appealing to another kind of depth: a fourth dimension, which is not the thickness of matter but the inwardness of the mind or, to be more precise, the mind as internal light that reveals itself once the darkness produced by material depth is neutralized. In other words, true depth is to be found not in this extension of the sensible world but in the luminous intensity of which the One is the primordial source and from which proceed, as successive emanations, first being-intelligence, then soul and finally nature. These are the focal points that express light and propagate it.

Extension and the bodies that inhabit it can now be seen to be effects of the luminous radiance that emanates from the One and seems to well up from the depths of the soul. What the power of the mind thus effects is a necessary consequence and is in no way evil in itself. It must, however, be regarded as a diminution: for the very density of bodies and the distance that separates them cannot proceed from the light reflected by the Universal Soul without dimming its brilliance and dampening its ardor. The sensible world, which is a diminished expression of intelligible reality, is at fault not through malice but through lack of brightness. For Plotinus's contemporaries and rivals, the Gnostics, matter was the domain of the Prince of darkness; but Plotinus simply regards it as the zero-degree of intellect. Its fault is its darkness, but that is a consequence of its density, which absorbs the spiritual light; it is not the work of some malevolent usurper in the form of a demon or an *archōn* whose evil designs are embodied by matter. To put that another way, for Plotinus, nonbeing is simply a lack of being: it is not a challenge either to the intellect or to the Universal Soul (although, as we have seen, it does present a threat to a human soul that is infatuated with its body and allows itself to be captivated by the image reflected by the body).

Let us return for a moment to the artist who both loves reality and comes to grips with the bodies he perceives. His task is to celebrate the radiance of mind as he represents the bodies. In other words, he must make manifest the soul that reflects that radiance and dispel the matter that absorbs it. Now, as we have already noted, matter exists only in depth: the third dimension is not only where optical illusions occur (with the distortions and discolorations of figures); more "deeply," it also encompasses the volume and the separateness of bodies, the very obstacles with which matter blocks the propagation of light. An inspired artist should try to develop a "flattened" vision of the sensible world, in which the figures are brought to the foreground, avoiding hollows and relief, shadows and muted colors,[41] all of which are features of the third dimension. Such an artist will clearly be a painter rather than a sculptor. Once his work sloughs off that "bad" depth, the inner light can become manifest and be diffused without obstruction not only between the bodies but even through the figures that are now divested of all density. Now they appear not so much as an *imitation* of an empirical model or idea, but rather as an *emanation* of the spiritual light they reflect. What we are faced with is indeed a "transfiguration" since,, as soon as the solid bodies have lost their own volume, they present the artist with a substance capable of expressing the soul, instead of matter that is bound to dim its brilliance. Flattening the external world makes it possible for the

zone

painter to compose a translucent world in which the internal light passes through bodies and, as it propagates itself, can thereby abolish the distances that three-dimensional space creates between the bodies. The trouble with the sensible world is not only its opacity but also the fact that it is inhabited by discrete elements, all separate from one another. Such fragmentation and compartmentalization, both of which become increasingly marked as one turns away from the celestial sphere and plunges into the sublunary world, are opposed to the solidarity and interpenetration not only of the intelligible realities within the Intellect but also of the individual souls that are still enveloped in the Universal Soul — in other words, before the human soul has moved away from it. To make the Intellect manifest in his representation of nature, the artist must illuminate his composition from within and also dispel the state of dispersion in which physical bodies live. He must match the translucency of his painted figures with an evocation of the mutual transparency of their respective souls. What is more, the knowledge that art can sometimes convey depends upon that evocation since the separation that it is the artist's task to overcome is a lack of unity not simply between the various components of his picture but above all between that picture and whoever looks at it. For Plotinus, knowing something comes down to revealing the cause from which it emanates and that finds expression through it. Now, the light that bathes the painter's picture — and thereby dispels the state of dispersion of its sensible components — should seem to the dazzled observer to be the common cause that gives life to both the picture and himself and that, by eliciting his inner attention, invites him to melt into one with it. To bring about communion between souls that are distanced from one another in the evil dimension of material depth is thus also to help the spectator to enter into communion: he accedes to the knowledge conveyed by the work of art because in it he discovers reflections of a light from which not only the work of art but he himself proceeds. In this way he is truly plunged into contemplation of the spectacle.

This contemplative absorption is diametrically opposed to the absorption of light by matter and, in Plotinus's writing, this is no mere metaphor. For if "external" perception, namely perception of the body, amounts to no more than the impression left by an object in the eye of its beholder, the "internal" gaze that the "realistic" work of art stimulates, for its part, expresses the soul of the beholder. In other words, internal vision is not prompted by the influence of material things; on the contrary, it participates in the effluence of the Intellect that illuminates the sensible world. Internal vision is thus constituted not by the imprint of matter but by a diffusion of mind, and it does not reflect what is visible; rather, it is reflected in it, thereby making it visible. For Plotinus, it thus follows that true vision occurs not in the eye or soul of an individual, but in the place to which his internal gaze is directed, the place that it brings to life by shedding light upon it.[42] It is thus quite literally, not just metaphorically, that Plotinus ascribes to the inspired artist the ability to lead the spectator to allow himself to be absorbed by the spectacle before him. If a work of art is capable of prompting internal vision and if this is projected onto the object contemplated rather than located in the subject contemplating it, the spectator from whom the internal vision emanates is oblivious to his own situation and can become fused with what he sees. Then there is no longer a point at which one can fix the limits of oneself and say, "Up to this point, it is me."[43]

By way of a general summary of Plotinian aesthetics, it is fair to say first that a commitment to realism — a realism that may be described as "psychic" — leads the painter to produce a flattened image of the sensible world, in other words to dispel the depth that lurks there. That depth is deemed to be responsible not only for the separation and isolation of natural beings, but also for the darkness in which they live. The painter delivers bodies from their ballast of depth by reducing their world to a foreground; and by neutralizing material density, he makes manifest a quite different kind of depth: not the dark, heavy thickness of matter but the pure inwardness of mind, of which the soul is the focal point and which finds its true means of expression in light. As soon as represented figures are reduced to a two-dimensional surface, each one seems illuminated from within so that the corporeal appearance it represents reflects the soul from which it proceeds, instead of casting shadows upon it. But psychic realism also produces another effect: it wrests the motifs that the artist chooses to represent from the state of dispersion that reigns in three-dimensional nature. Encumbered with heavy, inflexible bodies, the psychic world cannot bring forth the power of the Universal Soul without separating individual souls and rendering them opaque to one another. However, according to Plotinus, the artist encourages their mutual transparency by capturing the radiance of that Universal Soul and making it possible for its beams to pervade his painting. In the physical world, bodies are distinct from one another and for that reason draw their respective souls into a life of darkness and exile. But in the pure light of the world's Soul individual souls live in perfect communion, distinguished from one another only by degrees of intensity. The work of art reverses the movement of dispersal that characterizes matter and thereby helps to convert the spectator to the spiritual incandescence from which, through the medium of his soul, he proceeds. With his internal eye he can now see the shining intensity from which he himself emanates, reflected in the surface of the painting he is contemplating. So by becoming absorbed in this vision, he is directing his soul toward its source.

Art that is governed by such a purpose has evolved a long way from the classical Greek aesthetic, the difference being most marked in the representation of the human figure. Alois Riegl makes the following observation: "The major achievement of Greek art is the way that it liberates figures from spatial relationships, together with all the consequences that that implies: molding and relief, the partial overlapping of figures, foreshortening and shadows."[44] Whereas in Egyptian art, and to a great extent in archaic Greek art, figures are always conceived with a backdrop — potential in sculpture, actual in painting — that surrounds them so as to protect them from the defilements of space and time, classical art tends to liberate figures from their background and plunge them into three-dimensional space where they can move freely.[45]

Like Plotinus, the Egyptian artists feared the corrupting effects of depth on the bodies they painted or sculpted. (But unlike him, they conferred on these figures the status of a material substratum or vehicle waiting to be inhabited by a mind.[46] That role was radically different from the one that Plotinus ascribed to the painted image: namely, that of a reflection of the soul.) Because of that fear, they opted for a two-dimensional art in which bodies were only seen from the front, from the side or horizontally: an art in which depth was dispelled by their refusal to adopt a point of view that would reveal it. They applied their figures onto a background divided into squares (eighteen or twenty-two, depending on the period; see Figure 1), a device that made it possible to give an absolute size to every part or gesture of the body, that is to say a size expressed in terms of the number of squares.[47] In contrast, a classical Greek artist depicts his figures according to a system of anthropometric proportions that are at once anthropometric (unaffected by techniques of representation) and organic (the size of each part of the body is calculated as a frac-

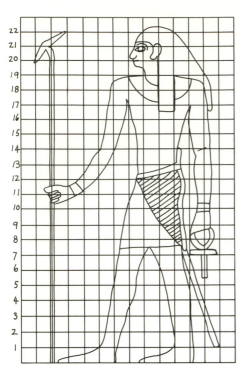

Figure 1: The "Later Canon" of Egyptian Art.
From Erwin Panofsky, *Meaning in the Visual Arts*
(Chicago: University of Chicago Press, 1982), p. 66.

tion of the size of the body as a whole). This canon of objective proportions is then adapted to the artist's subjective perspective, that is, to the point of view from which he decides to represent his subject. Such a method allows plenty of scope for harmonious adjustments, that is to say the optical distortions that may affect a body perceived in three-dimensional space.[48] The discovery of geometric perspective coincided with this taste for artistic illusion that constituted the "artistic intention" (*Kunstwollen*), although it remained approximative and was for the time being given no theoretical basis. Generally speaking, each figure corresponds to a particular point of view — an *aspectus* — and each body is constituted by the sum of its aspects. Such an artistic attitude truly does liberate figures from their background in that they not only are detached from it but furthermore do not appear to have emerged from it either. Greek art gave new value to a foreground that both implied and dictated the deployment of depth.[49] Three-dimensional space thus became the habitation of the artist's figures, the location for which the artist produced them and in which the spectator could take them in. The sculptor was clearly the artist par excellence to use these techniques (figure 2). His purpose now was not to create a substratum for the mind, but to imitate nature and at the same time embellish it. What he needed to protect his work from was not the corrosion of space and time but accidents of nature and the imprint of passion that can mask the traces of ideal beauty carried by sensible bodies. For in Platonic terms it could be said that sensible bodies display the imprint of intelligible beauty in the harmony of their features and the elegance of their proportions, that is, in the relationships of balance and symmetry that liken them to the cosmic order. As we have seen, classical thought confers upon the movements of the universe and the form of the stars a regularity and geometric perfection that are the foremost and most authentic incarnation of true beauty. There, beauty's reign is undivided, whereas in the sublunary world it leaves a blurred and imperfect impression: here, the eternal is mixed with what is mortal and — to use Aristotelian concepts — its form is engulfed in matter that is amorphous or even disturbed by deforming appetites. The task of the Greek artist was to restore a pure impression of beauty in the body of an athlete with supple muscles and a serene countenance, improving upon nature by retaining from it only what was symmetrical and ordered and so evoked eternity. What he aimed to jettison as corrupting agents were not time and space, but the excesses and sufferings that deform or even decompose the human figure *within* space and *within* time. In Platonic terms we may say that such an imitation/embellishment of nature presupposed that the artist found inspiration in an ideal rather than empirical model — the "ideal" being defined not exactly as an idea nor indeed as a particularly graceful individual, but as an "exact impression" of intelligible beauty.[50] That is the message of the words that Plato ascribes to Socrates when he has him declare that it would be wrong to question the talent or virtue of an artist who, "having drawn the model of the finest man and accurately rendered all his features in the drawing, might not be in a position to show that a man like this could exist."[51] The model for the artist thus oscillates between the sensible and the supersensible, the observation of things as they are and the contemplation of ideas. By imitating such a model, the artist is able to give new life to the impression of beauty that runs through nature, and he consequently has the power to reawaken the memory of it in the soul of the spectator.

Figure 2: Praxiteles Hermes, ca. 330-320 B.C.
(Greece, Olympia Museum).

According to Plato, the function of art is thus to evoke the intelligible world through representations of the human body. However, the intelligence that imbues the work of a classical sculptor belongs to one world; that from which the artist's painting should proceed according to Plotinus comes from quite another. For Plotinus, the value of art lies in its ability to reflect the light that is an expression of the soul rather than to imitate the cosmic harmony upon which the spirit is imprinted. In its evolution from the classical aesthetic (by which Plato is influenced despite his reticence vis-à-vis art in general) to the Neoplatonic aesthetic of Plotinus, the work of art, and also the body to which it is attached, has certainly assumed a different status: the work of art remains an image (rather than a substratum, as it was for the Egyptians), but it has become the reflection of a luminous source rather than a copy of an ideal model. In other words, the brightness of an emanation supplants the precision of an imitation. The rendering of the figure can no longer be regarded as a modeling of matter; instead, it corresponds to a modulation of light. And its beauty depends no longer on the harmonious composition in three-dimensional space of its various parts, but on the manifestation of the internal, undifferentiated power that precedes – and from which proceeds – its decomposition into physically distinct parts. The classical artist aimed for an overall unity, a totality. Plotinus replaces that aim with a quest for the simple, intense unity from which emanates the entire spatial composition of the figures involved in the picture.

The question that remains is whether an art that answered Plotinus's demands ever actually existed. André Grabar has pointed out that as early as the third century A.D., that is to say in Plotinus's own lifetime, certain tendencies can be noted in relief sculpture but above all in painting, in particular in the art of portrait painting, which was becoming increasingly popular – tendencies that do appear to correspond to the requirements of Plotinian doctrine.[52] Grabar emphasizes that this correspondence is all the more remarkable because it seems to have come about without the knowledge of either of the parties concerned.[53] There is no evidence that Plotinus directly influenced the artists of the late Empire, and there is every reason to believe that he knew nothing of their works.

Yet this art does seem committed to a respect for the true size and color of things: the painted figures are usually represented in a single plane, which means that they are sometimes depicted one above another or give the impression of floating in a

Figure 3: Christ and the Apostles, 5th century (Dijon, Musée des Beaux-Arts).

Figure 4: Miniature of Cosmas Indicopleustes, Alexandria, 9th-century reproduction after an original from the 6th century, Alexandria (Vatican City, Biblioteca Apostolica).

state of weightlessness. They are bathed in an even light that seems to be diffused simultaneously from a number of different points, with the result that shadows are eliminated and other effects of depth are neutralized. Little interest is shown in the plasticity of the bodies, which are now clothed. On the other hand, a halo of light surrounds their faces, seeming to emanate from the depths of their eyes. The faces are seen from the front and invite the spectator to merge with what he sees. But in some of these paintings the artist has gone beyond the single plane and rediscovered the strange techniques of reversed perspective and radiant perspective. When reversed perspective is used, the figures and objects increase in size the farther away they are from the foreground (see figure 3); in radiant perspective, their size decreases the farther they are from the central figure (see figure 4). Such techniques certainly correspond to Plotinus's notion of the internal eye, according to which vision takes place in the object that is beheld: to restore the normal appearance of things, all one has to do is imagine (for reversed perspective) a spectator located in the background or (in the case of radiant perspective) at the center of the spectacle being contemplated. So these techniques do seem to be attempts to incorporate the spectator in the object of his vision, in conformity with the internal vision that Plotinus valued so highly.[54]

These tendencies, still hesitant in the third and fourth centuries, were to come into their own later, as Byzantine art developed. Byzantine art has sometimes been described as the first truly metaphysical art. That is because it breaks with a selective imitation of nature and instead presents its works as so many emanations of the mind. This change is more or less in line with the categories defined by Alois Reigl, who sees it as a transition from an art devoted to embellishing nature to one that sought instead to spiritualize it.[55] But above all, it can be regarded as replacing the cosmology that dictated classical aesthetic with a psychology initiated by Plotinus.

In practical terms, this switch in the principle governing the "artistic intention" leaves its mark in at least three ways. First, the portrait painter replaces the sculptor as the artist par excellence; second, the ascetic replaces the athlete as the artist's subject; and third, harmony of form in the human body gives way to the internal light that is expressed in the human face as the particular quality of the represented figure that is exalted. Furthermore, the classical representation of harmony of form implies a downward movement in the sense that the Greek sculptor seeks "to bring the archetypes of an ideal beauty down into this world." Byzantine art, in contrast, implies an elevation, in the sense that the painter "seeks to exalt to heaven the spirituality conveyed by an individual's expression."[56] P.A. Michelis also points out:

> In order to represent the depth of man's internal life, art no longer needed to evoke the body's harmonious proportions; now it concentrated attention on the characteristic features of the face and its expressivity, on the eyes, the lips and the wrinkles of the faces of these ascetics whose dematerialized, stiff bodies remain suspended in space, as if they were "not of this world."[57]

From a Plotinian point of view, the first thing to notice is that Byzantine art satisfies the requirement that the sensible world be conveyed two-dimensionally in artistic representation. The style here is indeed "planate," not "planar" as in Egyptian art, for the Byzantine artist is not simply concerned with whether to depict figures full-face or in profile.[58] He is content to do without the impression of depth that is such a feature of classical art, although he may be perfectly well aware of it. Even when he represents his figures in three-quarter face, the Byzantine painter never bothers to create an impression of three-dimensionality. Abandoning "optically effective means of modeling the cast shadow," he uses foreshortening that no longer corresponds to the harmonious adjustments laid down by the Greco-Roman canons from Polyclitus down to Vitruvius. For that reason, his figures often look "distorted and weightless."[59] Second, the status of the depicted figure in relation to space, particularly that of the human figure, undergoes a change that is in keeping with the philosophy of light that constitutes Plotinian noology. If Riegl is right, the primary characteristic of classical Greek art is the manner in which it liberates spatial relationships, that is, it liberates its figures from their background. In contrast, the achievement of Byzantine art is to liberate light from three-dimensional space. The Greek sculptor uses light to delineate his figures:

> The more they are liberated from the background, the freer they become in the space in which the spectator apprehends them and takes them in. But that space is never the empty space that surrounds and passes through the spectator.... Forms are touched by light as a body is touched by a caress — a caress which is an "endless (asymptotic) approach" to the wholeness of flesh. "A beautiful individual" incorporates the light that surrounds it by subjecting it to human proportions.[60]

In contrast, Byzantine paintings and mosaics never manipulate light as if it came from one particular source. Instead, light is made manifest over the whole surface of the work of art, continually glinting from a myriad of points that contrast blacks with whites, shadows with brightness. It no longer surrounds the modeled outline of a figure, for the very good reason that the figure is not a modeling of matter but a modulation of light. Instead of forms manipulated from one point of view or another and figures defined by their outline in three-dimensional space, we are presented with a shower of light of which the rigid depicted figures are simply a consequence. To quote Maldiney again, who, in this instance, uses overtly Plotinian language: "Forms are born from a two-way movement of light along certain significant directions: first, its proceeding outward as it vibrates within them; second, its conversion, which returns them to the source of that light."[61]

As for colors, they cease to be apparel for the bodies represented and become degrees of intensity in the shower of light. Instead of precisely defined face colors we have pools of color that diffuse light in such a way that the shape of the figures seems to result from that diffusion: "An outline is to a figure what an edge is to a forest: the extreme fringe of its deployment.... Brilliant rays of color engender a figure whose existence preceded the definition of its outline."[62] In other words, the human figure is no longer an active form detached from a passive background (or *Grund*) of which it was never the product; now it proceeds from a farther background (or *Hintergrund*) or even from an infinitely deep luminosity of which it is an emanation, diminished but never really separated or distinct from it.[63]

Finally, instead of selecting ideal features from nature in order to copy them, this new art captures and mirrors reflections of the mind. The classical kind of physical beauty, which consisted in a harmony within a finite totality, is now replaced by a sublimity that manifests an internal infinity. The artist no longer strives to imitate the cosmic order, whose appearance is at once subordinated to and in conformity with the intelligible essence. Now he wishes to reveal the Intellect whose essence is radiating light and thus coincides with its own manifestation. An Intellect of this kind cannot be imprinted in the symmetry of a classically well-proportioned athlete's body; instead, it finds expression in the emaciated but radiant face of the ascetic (see figure 5). Byzantine art no doubt does still relate to an organic theory of proportion. But it is expressed not in common fractions but as multiples of a single unit. This is not the abstract and absolute entity of Egyptian art; rather, it is

Figure 5: Portrait of an old ascetic, Byzantine icon
(Athens, Byzantine Museum).

constituted by the length of a head, or rather a face. "This in itself is characteristic of the temper of the times. From the classical point of view, the metrical values of the face, the foot, the cubit, the hand, the finger, had been of equal interest; now the face, the seat of spiritual expression, is chosen as the unit of measurement."[64] Furthermore, the body must be subordinated to the face, it must be distorted and flattened so as not to impede the diffusion of light and the reflection of that light in the face that looms above the body yet no longer seems to belong to it. For the body is no more than a pale reflection of the procession of being; but the face is endowed with a greater dignity in that it expresses the conversion of the human soul to its own cause — so long, that is, as it dissociates itself from its body. Hence the lengthened face, the sunken cheeks and the hollow eyes of the ascetics depicted on Byzantine icons and mosaics. The artist is, to be sure, already working to banish the dark density of the world when he paints the translucent body, but it is with his rendering of the face that his art becomes truly metaphysical. That is because the face allows the internal light of the soul to shine out through it together with that depth of mind that is made manifest on the ceiling of some dark chapel through two great black eyes against a background of gold. "Such a gaze is not a spectacle, but another form of vision, ecstasy."[65]

Numerous arguments may, however, be adduced to challenge the legitimacy of a Neoplatonic view of Byzantine art, an art both imperial and Christian — indeed, according to some, the most authentic of all the arts of Christianity. André Grabar situates Plotinus at the origins of medieval aesthetics but admits freely that "a particular style in the time of Gallianus [the emperor who was Plotinus's contemporary] which some have believed to be inspired if not by the philosopher himself, at least by his followers, in the last years of his life, has not the slightest connection with the doctrine with which we are concerned here or with the New Art of late Antiquity."[66] He also points out that Plotinus's fourth-century disciples presented themselves as champions of the classical artistic tradition. So it is perfectly understandable that some prominent specialists in Byzantine art deny, or at least minimize, the Neoplatonic influence on the period that they study. Michelis, for instance, declares:

> Plotinian philosophy is inevitably misinterpreted when applied to explain early Christian art instead of the [pagan] art of its own age. Christian art, no matter the degree to which it may have been derived from Neo-platonic aesthetics, is inspired, not by the

Neoplatonist pagan mysticism which springs from the impersonal One, but by the divine revelation of the One and Only God. It is an art of the Sublime, not an art of the Beautiful.[67]

But if Christianity alone has the power to impart a sense of the sublime, one is entitled to wonder to what extent Christian art may have acknowledged a degree of dependence on Plotinian aesthetics. Moreover, it is surely correct to point out that the Neoplatonists, who were hostile to Christianity, would certainly not have wished to draw attention to "the connection that it is legitimate to establish between the ideas of their master and the art that served the cause of their enemies."[68]

In any event, quite apart from these questions of aesthetics, in our opinion, the entire Eastern current of Christian asceticism does seem marked by Plotinian philosophy. From Origen, Plotinus's fellow student, right down to the Desert Fathers, God is represented more as a Power of which man is the ultimate actualization than as a "personal" God whose most perfect creation is man. And these thinkers represent original sin in a form that is at least analogous to the audacity that the author of the *Enneads* attributes to the human soul. Furthermore, the salvation sought by a Christian anchorite depends upon a simplification and purification of his soul, a process that has much in common with the successive stages of Neoplatonic conversion. For, as Peter Brown points out, whatever terrible deprivations those absolute champions of asceticism inflicted upon their bodies, they still regarded the passions of the body as the least malignant of all the forms of turpitude to be overcome by a man in quest of saintliness.[69] A soul seeking purification certainly has to begin by quelling the temptations that stem from the flesh that envelops it; but that is just the first trial, no more than an introduction to the great "internal" reconquest of the Paradise lost. Far more dreadful are the intrinsic passions of the soul, such as pride or wrath. In the West, in contrast, from Augustine onward anyway, the battle against the flesh lasts as long as life on Earth.[70] Furthermore, this battle can be sustained only with the help of the Church (whereas the spiritual progress of the ascetics in the desert was a solitary affair) and won only by the intervention of providential grace. Without this, the struggle taking place within each individual between will and lust, *voluntas* and *voluptas*, is far too unequal. Now we can appreciate the difference in the status granted to the body and to its relationship with the soul. In the Christian East and for Plotinus, a man's body is a diminished and absorbent reflection of the soul, but also the starting point for its own reflection, in the sense of its reconversion, which soon leads the soul to turn away from its sensible image. In the West, on the other hand, and above all for Augustine himself, the body is the irreducible symptom of man's original fall but also the ultimate aim of his quest for salvation. In other words, for Western Catholicism, the aim of conversion is not for the human soul to achieve fusion in pure divine light. Instead, the aim is man's resurrection inside a spotless and glorious body.

This essay set out to do no more than suggest the crucial role played by Plotinus in the history of ethical and aesthetic conceptions of the psychosomatic link, and we have drawn extensively on the important studies on Plotinus by André Grabar, Pierre Hadot, Gilles Deleuze and Julia Kristeva. However, the great works that Michel Foucault and Peter Brown have devoted to ancient styles of life have encouraged us to surrender to the "audacity" of sketching a genealogy of the soul–body relation between the fourth century B.C. and the fourth century A.D. We cannot be sure that those authors would agree with our views, but from their findings it would appear that not only the relations of opposition between the soul and the body but also those of their conjunction have, each in turn, as if in a process of progressive shifts, been subsumed under four major pairs of concepts that correspond to four major trends in ancient thought. First, the opposition between activity and passivity seems to be the classical paradigm, which is best defined by the Aristotelian notion of form being impressed upon amorphous matter. Second, the opposition between impassivity and agitation seems to inspire a number of currents in Hellenistic wisdom, all of which stem from a notion of dynamic forces expanding through the Universe. Third, the tension between the reflection and absorption of intelligible or spiritual light is a dominant feature of Neoplatonic philosophy and equally of Christian mysticism from the Desert Fathers right down to the Renaissance. It originates in the idea of a source of light that finds expression through its emanations. Fourth and finally, the struggle between will and lust postulated by Augustine appears to be the paradigm adopted by the Western Church: it is based on the idea of incarnation of the spirit and equates it with the human condition. For many years to come, the faces of ascetics in Byzantine chapels continued to reflect the intensity that their souls received from an all-seeing and radiant God; in the West, meanwhile, Augustine's new message (*novitas*) turned the human body into an object of intentionality directed by the Passion and Resurrection of a God made visible — *imitatio Christi*.

Notes

1. Porphyry, *Life of Plotinus*, ch. 1.

2. On this idea of "style," see Peter Brown, *Genèse de l'Antiquité tardive* (Paris: Gallimard, 1983), the introduction to the French edition, p. 15.

3. The major currents of Gnostic thought share this concept. See esp., in *Zone 3: Fragments for a History of the Human Body*, the article by Michael Williams entitled "Divine Image, Prison of the Flesh: Perception of the Body in Ancient Gnosticism," pp. 128-57.

4. Pierre Hadot, "Le mythe de Narcisse et son interprétation par Plotin," *La nouvelle revue de psychanalyse* 13 (Spring 1976), pp. 81-109, and Julia Kristeva, *Histoires d'amour* (Paris: Denoël, 1983), pp. 103-17.

5. André Grabar, "Plotin et les origines de l'esthéthique médiévale" in *Cahiers archéologiques*, vol. 1: *Fin de l'Antiquité et Moyen Age* (Paris: Van Oest, 1945).

6. Plato, *Gorgias* 493a and *Cratylus* 400c.

7. Nicole Loraux, "Therefore, Socrates is Immortal," in the present volume, p. 28.

8. Plato, *Timaeus* 44a-b.

9. Plato, *Republic* 4.435-442 and 9.580d ff.

10. Michel Foucault, *The History of Sexuality*, vol. 2: *The Use of Pleasure*, trans. Robert Hurley (New York: Vintage Books, 1986).

11. *Ibid.*, pp. 69-70.

12. On the concept of *charis* or grace and its political importance, see Christian Meier, *La politique et la grâce* (Paris: Seuil, 1987), in the "Les Travaux" collection.

13. Plato, *Timaeus* 86b-87b.

14. On Plato's ambiguous relations with the plastic arts, see Pierre-Maxime Schuhl, *Platon et l'art de son temps* (Paris: Presses Universitaires de France, 1952).

15. P.-M. Schuhl, *Platon et l'art*, pp. 23 and 31-37.

16. *Ibid.*, Introduction, p. XVI.

17. Gilles Deleuze, *Logique du sens* (Paris: Minuit, 1969), pp. 292-307.

18. Michel Foucault, *The History of Sexuality*, vol. 3: *The Care of the Self*, trans. Robert Hurley

(New York: Pantheon Books, 1987).

19. Michel Foucault, *The Care of the Self*, chs. 2 and 4; and Jackie Pigeaud, *La maladie de l'âme* (Paris: Belles Lettres, 1981).

20. On this point, see Pierre Hadot, *Exercices spirituels et philosophie antique* (Paris: Etudes Augustiniennes, 1987), pp. 19-29.

21. *Ibid.*, pp. 119-33.

22. Plotinus, *Enneads* 5.2.1.

23. On the "expressionism" of Plotinian thought and its characterization as a philosophy of spiritual light, we are following Gilles Deleuze's analysis in *Spinoza et le problème de l'expression* (Paris: Minuit, 1968), pp. 153-69, and his exposition of this in his lecture course of 1985-86.

24. André Grabar, "Plotin et les origines," p. 21 and, more generally, Gérard Simon, *Le regard, l'être et l'apparence (dans l'optique de l'Antiquité)* (Paris: Seuil, 1988), in the "Les Travaux" collection.

25. Plotinus, *Enneads* 4.8.4.

26. *Ibid.* 2.9.4.

27. *Ibid.* 4.3.12.

28. Pierre Hadot, "Le mythe de Narcisse," pp. 100-01.

29. Plotinus, *Enneads* 1.1.2.

30. *Ibid.*

31. Ovid, *Metamorphoses* 3.350: "novitasque furoris."

32. Plotinus, *Enneads* 5.8.2.

33. *Ibid.* 1.6.8.

34. See P. Hadot, "Le mythe de Narcisse," p. 101.

35. Plotinus, *Enneads* 1.6.9.

36. G. Deleuze, *Spinoza*, p. 155 n.4.

37. Plotinus, *Enneads* 1.6.7; and Julia Kristeva, *Histoires d'amour*, pp. 110-11.

38. Plotinus, *Enneads* 4.3.11.

39. A. Grabar, "Plotin et les origines," pp. 18-19.

40. *Ibid.*, p. 19.

41. *Ibid.*

42. *Ibid.*, pp. 20-22.

43. Plotinus, *Enneads* 6.5.7.

44. Alois Riegl, *Spätrömische Kunstindustrie*, cited by Henri Maldiney, *Regard, parole, espace* (Paris: L'âge d'homme, 1973), p. 197.

45. Henri Maldiney, *ibid.*, p. 199.

46. Erwin Panofsky, *Meaning in the Visual Arts* (Chicago: University of Chicago Press, 1982), p. 61.

47. *Ibid.*, p. 59.

48. *Ibid.*, pp. 64-65.

49. H. Maldiney, *Regard, parole, espace*, p. 199.

50. Ernst Cassirer, *Eidos und Eidōlon* (Leipzig, 1924), cited by P.-M. Schuhl, *Platon et l'art*, p. 56.

51. Plato, *Republic* 5.472d.

52. A. Grabar, "Plotin et les origines," pp. 16-17.

53. *Ibid.*, pp. 16 and 30.

54. *Ibid.*, pp. 21-22.

55. Alois Riegl, *Grammaire historique des arts plastiques* (Paris: Klincksiek, 1978), pp. 8-21, 51-54, 78-94.

56. P.A. Michelis, *Esthétique de l'art byzantin* (Paris: Flammarion, 1959), pp. 155-56.

57. *Ibid.*, p. 45.

58. E. Panofsky, *Meaning in the Visual Arts*, p. 72.

59. *Ibid.*

60. H. Maldiney, *Regard, parole, espace*, p. 200.

61. *Ibid.*, p. 202.

62. *Ibid.*, pp. 204-05.

63. *Ibid.*, p. 206.

64. E. Panofsky, *Meaning in the Visual Arts*, p. 74 n.28.

65. Plotinus, *Enneads* 6.9.2.

66. A. Grabar, "Plotin et les origines," p. 30.

67. P.A. Michelis, "Neo-platonic Philosophy and Byzantine Art," in *The Journal of Aesthetics and Art Criticism* 2.1 (1952), p. 45.

68. A. Grabar, "Plotin et les origines," p. 31.

69. Peter Brown, "Late Antiquity," in *History of Private Life* (Cambridge: Harvard University Press, 1987), vol.1, pp. 299-300.

70. *Ibid.*, pp. 306-07; and Aline Rousselle, *Porneia: On Desire and the Body in Antiquity*, trans. Felicia Pheasant (New York: Basil Blackwell, 1988).

Translated by Janet Lloyd.

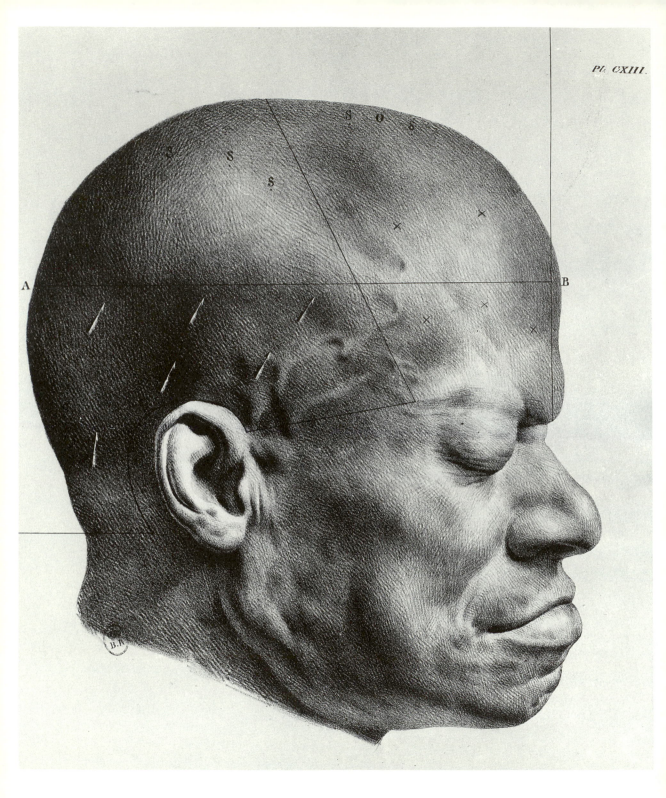

A "virtuous Negro"'s head. From Vimont, *Atlas de Phrénologie*, 1831.

The Face and the Soul

Patrizia Magli

Le visage humain est une force vide, un champ de mort.

— Artaud

Lacan describes the face as the most elusive of objects. Its rhythms and the various dynamics in its makeup all contribute to an unstable form. A *perpetuum mobile*. The roles of its individual actors, such as the nose, eyes, eyebrows, mouth, all belong to the indefinite time of their action, to a fluctuating and unstructured logic, one based on the genesis and the relationships between movement, stasis and variations in speed.

Yet, this same movement, which appears to defy any verbal description, and sometimes the abilities of memory itself, does not preclude the recognition of an identity, a physiognomy. There is a sort of perceptual perseverance that allows us to say, upon meeting a friend after a long time: "It is you," or "My God, how you have changed!" Western thought has been fascinated by this paradox, and has, from its origins, attempted to record and explain face recognition practices. Confronted with an ever-changing appearance, ancient physiognomists focused their investigations on an attempt to capture an immanent and univocal essence, and they did this by establishing norms through which to penetrate the secret behind a countenance.

Physiognomics — from *phusis* (nature) and *gnōmōn* (interpretation) — means "recognition, interpretation of nature." Giovanni Battista della Porta, however, points out that *gnōmōn* also means "rule, law," and thus physiognomics is also "rule of nature"; della Porta says that by following a particular rule, or norm, or order of nature, we can know "particular passions of the soul from the particular shape of the body [*ex tali corporis forma tales animae affectiones consequantur*]."[1]

As a science, or rather, pseudoscience, physiognomics is based on the assumption of a solidarity between body and soul, between inner and outer dimensions, as Aristotle remarks: "the soul's passions all seem to be linked with a body, as the body undergoes modifications in their presence" (*De anima* 1A.1.403a.15). It is a link of necessity between body and soul: Aristotle maintains that not just any soul penetrates a particular body: "rather, it is obvious that *each body has a form and countenance of its own*" (*ibid.* 1A.3.407b.15).

According to Aristotle, the soul is "figure" and "form." The body is "matter." Passions are forms immersed in matter. Let us take wrath, for example. This passion can be interpreted as a desire for vengeance or as a "boiling up of the blood around the heart." The former explains form or "notion," the second, matter: not two ways for the body to be, rather, two ways of perceiving the body. "Thus it is necessary for the soul to be a substance," says Aristotle, "as it is the form for the natural body and its potential life. Such a substance is entelechy: thus the soul is the entelechy of a body of that particular nature" (*ibid.* 2B.1.412.15). The entelechy of each thing is realized in that which such a thing is *in posse*, that is, its specific matter. The soul is the entelechy and the notion of that which it is potentially. The soul is the form (*eidos*) that determines the matter; it is the "quiddity of the body of a specific matter" (*ibid.* 412b.10).

Thus it is the cause and the beginning of the living body. It is the formal substance of living beings: "for the formal substance," says Aristotle, "is the cause of the existence of all things" (*ibid.* 2B.4.425b.10).

Vague Signs and Strict Certainties

But how to capture the soul within perceptible forms? How to capture these same perceptible forms when the body itself, and the face in particular, is that most elusive of objects? How to explain the gestaltic ineffability of an emotion or of a nuance in an expression that, at the very moment of its surfacing and almost becoming perceptible to the eye, is already gone, either too late or too soon, something fleeting and, at the same time, already vanished?

Identifying the body has always appeared to waver between two opposing approaches to interpretation: between what we might call *natural inferences*, on the one hand, and *arbitrary equivalences*, on the other. At times, facial traits are interpreted as symptoms, vague indications of something secret, or else as transparent symbols, a univocal text for those owning the key to its deciphering.

Physiognomic perception is a form of daily knowledge, a treasure belonging to all of us. It is based on subtleties which are hard to formalize, at times even untranslatable into words. The face of those near us presents itself as the space upon which it is possible to perceive infinitesimal traces which, in turn, sometimes allow us to glean a deeper reality, one hidden to most eyes. It is part of the local knowledge of which Carlo Ginzburg spoke. It is that type of knowledge without origin, memory or history, of which literary culture continues to attempt a precise verbal formulation, most often only succeeding in creating pale and impoverished formulas. "It should be sufficient to contemplate the abyss separating the rigid schematism of a physiognomics treatise from the flexible, yet precise, physiognomic penetration of a lover, a horse-dealer, or a card-player."[2]

The form of knowledge involved in understanding physiognomics is the result of concrete needs. Although tradition attributes to Pythagoras the founding of this science, Galen considers its true founder to be the "divine Hippocrates." As a pseudo-science, physiognomics was originally very closely linked with medicine. It probably originated around the fifth century B.C., and it shared the signs described by ancient physicians: *tekmērion*, "proof," "evidence," "symptom."

Hippocrates attributes to a symptom the function of a sign only at the moment of inference. Thus, physiognomics would appear to have been originally a science based on circumstantial evidence. The category of its signs appears to be characterized by the relation of *being about to*, based on an inference mechanism: *if* the body is too hot and feels cold chills, *then* it is feverish. It is the philonian implication mechanism, $p \supset q$.

Alongside such an inferential mechanism, based on relations of implication, there soon appeared a system of sign correlation, based on relations of equivalence of the type $p \equiv q$ (hooked nose=greed, fleshy lips=sensuality). This is a type of sign relationship established by convention.

Thus, we find, on the one hand, the uncertain conjectures rooted in everyday experience, not formalized by the powerful and fierce instrument of abstraction, and, on the other, a tendency to freeze the ineffable qualities of a face in a system of strictly codified equivalences. The human form becomes, then, an image and a symbol. The moral language code spreads over the entire surface of the body — over every detail, from man's head to his feet; over every shape, line or fold; over firm flesh as well as soft; over moist flesh as well as dry; over hair and nails; over the sound of one's voice, as well as over all parts covered with more or less thick hair. Such a code numbers each element as a lemma, defines it as a signifier, and attributes a precise meaning to it.

The Face as a Symbolic Form

Upon seeing a face, we immediately produce a symbolic framework that confronts us with a complex and ancient cultural experience. We would probably not be able to perceive, nor to recognize, those similar to us were we not able to grasp and separate that which is essential from that which is accidental. Perception seems always to require universal elements.

Physiognomic science talks of the recognition of forms through the isolation of the unchangeable elements peculiar to an individual. This abstraction process aims at isolating a sort of bottom layer that is presumed to remain unchanged despite the changes of expression linked with emotion. Thus, to isolate a face is to isolate a permanent form, one whose "unchanging traits" are to be perceived through a process that attempts to freeze the face's state of constant flux into a state of immutability.

Such a symbolizing process introduces us to a different time: no longer is it the non-time of an actual face, lost in the uninterrupted fluctuation of lights and shadows. Rather, it is the time of a "measure" that stills things, develops a formal image and locks it into an absolute fixity, wherein it then interprets proportions, defines outlines, and attempts to establish essential traits.

Della Porta maintains that it is not possible to surmise a person's true character from the signs of passions rushing over his face. He claims that "the face represents one's entire countenance, just as it does one's movements, and passions, and mores...So it is not unreasonable to be able to judge it at any time, but only after the soul's emotions and passions have cooled."[3]

Physiognomics thus appears to be based on a sort of apparent "neutral state" of passions, and, in this, it is distinct from pathognomics. For passions are of a temporal order; they are gradual and tense, above all when they surface on one's countenance. In this sense, they often appear inexpressible.

An odd coincidence exists between the stiff facial masks of ancient actors, which set expressions according to a few symbolic representations, recognizable even at a distance, and ancient physiognomics, with its interest in the stable and lasting traits of a face, as separate from the passions that might move it. In fact, passions, after brief mention in Aristotle's works, soon left the level of a manifest expression, and sunk, like a karst river, into philosophical reflections, to reappear on the surface of the face only in the seventeenth century, mainly due to their systematic treatment by the painter Charles Le Brun.

In physiognomics, the symbolic plan of a face is not a visual perception scheme as such; rather, it is a framework composed of cognitive traits. It is based on an abstract prejudicial principle that allows the appropriate selection of pertinent data for the identification of the so-called "dominant feature." Even in the everyday experience of perception, we make use of organizing principles that are capable of selecting relevant data from within a nebulous mass of feelings and stimuli.

Umberto Eco has stressed the fact that visual schemes often do not reflect the optical qualities of things, but, rather, what he calls the ontological relations: visual messages do not communicate the look of things, what we can see, but what we know about their immanent nature.[4] This holds true also for empathic phenomena such as lines, colors, rhythms and the sound of a voice, as they are points of a symbolic condensation around which the face's features become crystallized. If straight lines appear to us harsh and severe, while curved ones seem soft and tender, if some colors appear to us bright and lively, while others seem gloomy and melancholy, if particular sounds strike us as heartrending, while others seem irritating and even loathsome, we are always, at all times, dealing with a system of formal semantic correspondences affecting our own perception. These semantic categories, although they remain implicit, do, in fact, organize the syntax of perception and of gestaltic recognition as they encounter the world's great configurations. Even in the most innocent of perceptive experiences, we are always dealing with a system of values linked to a specific place, time and situation, and consequently some things will appear to us to be beautiful, others not, some things good, others bad.

That which occurs in a confused and ambiguous way every time we perceive, recognize or try to interpret a face is described by physiognomics in its innermost workings and with such precise delineations and emphasis as to even distort it through an excess of schematization.

The shape of a face as constructed with cultural rather than natural elements is seen principally in various works of artistic physiognomics. Leonardo da Vinci, for example, in his *Treatise on Painting*, suggested to the artist a system of classification based on dividing the face into four parts — forehead, nose, mouth and chin — and on studying the various shapes that they can assume. Once such components of the human physiognomy have been clearly established in the mind, according to Leonardo, we should be able to analyze and retain a face with a simple glance. Leonardo speaks of "relevant traits." So it is not just by chance that we owe him a series of grotesque variations on the face, not at all reflecting "live" observation, but which do tell us a lot about the way in which art can create symbolic forms and create a portrait as a symbol.

Let us take the example of deformation in caricature. Through a process of harsh schematization the caricature attempts to extract a dominant feature and then presses the representation of a desired content or idea to an excessive degree; in this it reveals some face recognition mechanisms and some figurative details in the creation of a face that probably belong also to other forms of representation of human physiognomy.

The division of a face into sections that Leonardo suggests leads in physiognomics to further subdivisions within each area. Each individual trait is subdivided into sections reflecting a stable typology of vices and virtues. The nose, for example, can be divided into root, spine and tip, and by the way in which its features combine — long/short, convex/straight, lean/fleshy — it is possible to identify up to eighty-one types, corresponding to an equal number of moral inclinations. This same method leads to the identification of fifty-eight types of forehead, forty-three types of eyes, fifty chins, and eighteen mouths.

The following can be read in an encyclopedic dictionary of physiognomics from the last century:

> Each trait, each line, each modification of the face does carry its own peculiar meaning, yet one must study them primarily together and in their reciprocal relationships. One must compare traits after taking them individually, and from such a juxtaposition one can derive precise interpretations. Before examining the face, we suggest examining the head.... After judging the head and the face, one should then proceed to examine the rest of the body, descending to the lower extremities with the same signs showing.[5]

92

However, this "harmony among all the parts of man [*harmonie entre toutes les parties de l'homme*]," of which Thoré speaks in this work of his, does not belong to the actual experience of the body. In fact, the total physiognomic sense of the person confronting us is not given by the sum of sense reactions to the individual components of the body as a whole. Rather, it is what Petrarch called "a face's air." Such a particular gestaltic experience results from an echo phenomenon among features, movements and appearance, between the sound of a voice and a distance, between shadings of color and the translucency resulting from a chance effect of light on the skin.

In the science of physiognomics, instead, the method in use is analytical and deductive. It loses itself in the obsessive process of dividing, subdividing, classifying, piece by piece, each fragment of the body. Recomposition seems to take place not in the context of a morphological analysis of the body seen as an organic whole, but rather within a Neoplatonic view of universal harmony.

"The strongest meanings are to be found in the parts close to the eyes," says della Porta, "the forehead, the face, the head...all of man is in his face, as therein lies the seat of reason; in second place is the chest, wherein lies the heart; in third place, the legs and the feet. Last is the abdomen, in which are located those natural parts which do nothing for knowledge."[6] But Aristotle had already said, in his *De partibus animalium,* that the natural parts of the body follow nature's order in such a way that "the upper part points in the direction of the upper part of the universe" (2B.10.656a.10). Thus, Aristotle maintains, "that which is superior and most noble, considering high and low, tends to be up high; considering front and back, front; considering right and left, right" (*ibid.* 3Y.3.4.665a.20-21). Aristotle bases his physiology on this typology, developing it into a true axiology, that is, a paradigmatic system of values: "Even the position of the heart," he says, "shows that it is located in an area appropriate to indicate a principle: it is in the center, rather higher than lower, rather forward than back: nature places that which is most noble in the most noble positions" (*ibid.* 665a.15-20).

Such subdivisions are to be found in all parts of the body, including the viscera, and all have a bipartite nature: some are to the right, some to the left. "In general," says Aristotle, "the parts on the left have a damper and colder nature. For each opposite is placed, by division, in the set with which it has the closest affinity: thus right is opposed to left, and cold is opposed to hot, and they form their own respective series" (*ibid.* 648a.25).

Such series of opposites are Pythagorean in origin, and they were used also in dichotomy tables, so as to form columns of the following type:

right	left
high	low
front	back
hot	cold
fire	earth
light	heavy
male	female

In Western culture, the terms of the left column are generally endowed with euphoric connotations, while the ones on the right are dysphoric. "Hence also the upper parts," says Aristotle, "show the same differences in relation to the lower ones, as also the male in relation to the female, and the parts on the right of the body in relation to those on the left" (*ibid.*).

Thus, according to Aristotle, nature has placed a sort of barrier between the nobler parts and the less noble ones, between the upper and the lower parts. For man is the only animal to stand erect, and his head points toward the highest part of the cosmos. All animals, he says, are less intelligent than man. The reason for this is that the essence of the soul is in many ways clumsy and physical. Should the heat which holds up the body decrease further, and the earthy elements increase, the animal bodies decrease in size, and the number of their feet grows; in the end, they become footless, and are flat on the ground. "Just one more small step," says Aristotle, "and their soul moves to their lower part, and the part which corresponds to the head becomes still and insensible: thus the animal has turned into a plant, and its upper part is now the lower, and its lower part the upper" (*ibid.* 686b.25).

We find the same cosmogonic structure, point by point, in the areas into which the face is divided: the upper ones are generally seen as revealing the more spiritual inclinations, while the lower ones represent the instinctuality which likens men to animals.

This approach can be found in physiognomics and phrenology, as well as in Lombroso's criminal anthropology.

We have seen how a topology of the face reveals, in fact, an underlying axiology that attributes to each area a particular ethical quality. The same holds for each active section of the face, as it appears to specialize in a particular passion: eyebrows for severity and haughtiness, teeth for vengeance, ill-feelings or menace, hair for whim and horror, the nose for shrewdness, even to the point of indiscretion, yet capable of disgust.[7] Each expressive trait consists of an element to which a particular meaning is assigned. "One must know first of all which parts are affected by which inclinations," says Charles Le Brun.[8]

In fact, physiognomic components are a pretext for the attribution of other meanings. Categories belonging to the level of expressive manifestations, such as the eidetic ones (straight/curved lines; broken/continuous lines), of the chromatic (light/dark), or the topological (high/low, before/after), are ratified by physiognomics into semantic categories of an evaluating order. Such ratifications generally rest upon more or less generalized cultural conventions, which generate types of odd microcodes. For in Western culture, the vertical line communicates an impression of elevation, the horizontal, one of stability; the circular, one of perfection; the oval, one of reduction; the broken, one of instability, of drama.

However, without going too far back in time, the symbolism of lines can occasionally be seen in its full visionary force even in our century, as in the theories of Ludwig Clauss (*Rasse und Seeles*, 1926), which divides men into spherical, parabolic, pyramidal and polygonal. Italians and Poles are spherical, with snub noses, round eyes, short legs and quick and flowing movements. Germans and Scandinavians are parabolic, with a long cranium, long face and neck, and a slow and imposing step. The hypertensive and extremely theatrical Jews are pyramidal; and finally, black people are polygonal, monstrously shaped, with an angular forehead, a shapeless nose, a long upper half of the face, and a wide lower half. At the deepest roots of racism, we find the outlines of a sort of symbolism which not only concerns lines, but mainly color.

Just as the theme of ascent is in opposition, point by point, in its symbolic development, to the theme of falling, in the same way dark symbols are in opposition to those of light. A kind of isomorphism appears universally to link ascent to light, while darkness appears to create a generally dysphoric impression. Darkness is always likened to chaos, to death, to the subterranean kingdom of silence.

The chromatic contrast between light and dark is not just a unit on the plane of expression, but is based on the semantic opposition of light and shade. On the basis of such semantic homologations, light and transparent colors are generally used, in physiognomics, as the chromatic symbols of truth, as opposed to the dark colors. Such color symbolism is at the roots of an odd racist theory which we find already expressed in the third century B.C. treatise *De physiognomonia* (also known as *The Secrets*, as tradition not only attributes it to Aristotle, but also interprets it as being a series of suggestions he gave to Alexander concerning his choice of counselors): "You should know, King Alexander," says the pseudo-Aristotle, "that the matrix, or embryo, is like a pot which is boiling and cooking over the fire. If the generating substance produces a man with light hair and a pale complexion, this indicates insufficient cooking. Thus, if such a lack occurs, his nature appears to be similarly diminished. So avoid the livid-looking man." Similarly, a "clear and sharp voice" indicates a diligent and peace-loving man, while red hair is the sign of a quick temper.

The impression of wrath that might be conveyed by a face's high blush does rely for this on a widely codified relationship between signal and emotion. The term "red" is often seen in association with "burning," while "blue" is seen as "cold." In this context, heat and cold are not simply thermal; instead, they contain a judgment value, for they signal an emotional or moral content. The relation of such moral and emotional symbolism of color to a face, although already present in pseudo-Aristotelian physiognomics, was treated in a systematic way only beginning in the sixteenth century, with della Porta, through Lomazzo and Goethe, to Humbert de Superville.

The moral and emotional effect of a color or of the softly curvilinear or sharply angular path of a line often has nothing to do with universal assumptions of human sensitivity. Consequently, despite a considerable stability, even these microcodes are liable to undergo variations over the course of time.

Della Porta, who diverges from pseudo-Aristotelian physiognomics, considers white to be a dysphoric color: "The moon is of a white color," he says, "and white is the color of lunatics, phlegmatics and shy individuals." He then adds: "Having said that red is a sign of a warm and sanguine disposition, and white of phlegm and coldness, together, the two add up to an excellent disposition."[9]

Thus, at the basis of physiognomic systems, we find homologations of the following type – red:blue :: "hot":"cold"; light:dark :: "cheerful":"sad"; and so on.

However, the demon of analogy is not limited to homologations inherent to a particular category; it also operates among different types of categories – between chromatic and eidetic ones, and between the latter and the topological ones. It establishes, on the same basis, homologations between primary forms and primary colors, as in the visual equations theorized by de Superville:

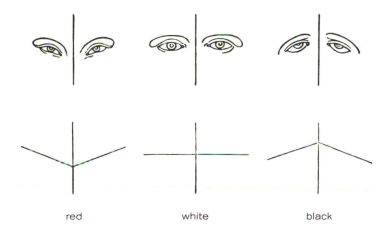

red   white   black

Zoological Physiognomics

The recognition of a face through a symbolic diagram relies not only upon a system of lines and colors, it refers even more frequently to other forms, which are considered simpler and more easily recognizable. Such references involve the animal world.

In his *Rhetoric*, Aristotle mentions a physiognomist, whose name he does not give, and who, in interpreting the human face, made reference to only two or three basic animals. Based on the assumption that the body structure of animals is simpler and more easily understandable, Aristotle considers the possible similarities between men and animals as a key to discovering "essential qualities." Whereas Aristotle often maintains that it is logically possible to infer a man's character from his facial traits, it is only in his writings on animal biology that he actually tries to demonstrate this. In *Analytica priora* (2.27.70.6-39) he claims that, if we assume that a single sign (*sēmeion*) refers to a single nature, and if, for a genus, we are able to establish its specific affection (*pathos*), as well as its specific sign, we should be able to judge an individual's nature on the basis of his body structure. Aristotle adopts the Greek term *physiognōmonein* to indicate "judging the nature of something based on its body structure." This is true semiotics, establishing, as it does, a system of correlations between *signs* and *affections*. "Each affection," says Aristotle, "has its own sign, given that it can, of necessity, only have one." This appears to be a term-to-term sign correlation but, in fact, it is a much more complex correlation mechanism, one which resorts to the mediation device of parallels between man and beast.

If a particular affection belongs to a particular genus, as in the case of the lion and courage, then, according to Aristotle, there must necessarily exist a sign of such an affection, given the reciprocal solidarity between body and soul. In the case of lions, its large extremities constitute such a visible sign. Where we find the same sign in other genera, such as the human, this means that they too are endowed with the same affection: they too are brave.

However, it can, and does, happen that a certain type of animal, as a whole, is endowed with two specific affections, as in the case of the lion, which has both courage and generosity. How then can we know which body sign refers to which affection? Aristotle resorts to a sort of comparative physiology between men and animals. Fixed as emblematic images, animals act as reversed mirrors through which it is possible to recognize the passions, vices and virtues of men. The human world, on the other hand, is not just the point of arrival of this semiotic process, but establishes itself as an interpreting device, and, in turn, initiates a further semiotic process, back to the animal.

Aristotle maintains that it might be possible to recognize the specific sign of each affection when both affections belong also to another genus, but without belonging to its entirety: that is, when each affection, separately, belongs to different individuals of the same genus. If a member of this genus is brave, but not generous, and if he clearly shows only one of the lion's bodily characteristics, that might also be the lion's sign of courage. "It is thus possible, in the first figure, to judge the nature of an object on the basis of its body structure, if we convert the middle part with the upper extremity, and if, on the other hand, it extends further than the third term, so that there is no conversion here. Let us call A, courage; B, large extremities; C, lion. In such a case, B belongs to all of the same things to which C belongs, although B belongs also to other objects. A, on the other hand, belongs to all that to which B belongs, and nothing else; here we have a conversion, for if it were not so, a single sign would not refer to one single nature" (*ibid.* 2.27.70b.30-31).

Aristotle uses his discussion of *physiognōmonein* as an illustration of the enthymeme. The enthymeme is the well known syllogism which, when based on precise signs, acquires demonstrative value.

In finding the signs that are specific to each affection, the physiognomic syllogism reproduces in the body, as a necessary and natural correlation, the signifier and the signified. Thus, it establishes the principle and the process itself by which this "science," through a complex mechanism of references between the human and the animal worlds, attributes to a somatic trait the expression of a moral meaning.

Only later, in the pseudo-Aristotelian treatise *De physiognomonia*, is the parallel between men and animals developed in a systematic way, although all of the theoretical principles are already present in Aristotle's works.

In the fourth book of the *De physiognomonia*, the entire animal world is divided into two parts: male and female. The male is symbolized by the lion, and the female by the panther. This work was extremely influential on later physiognomics, as later treatises only repeat the same principles in an obsessive and obstinate way, only adding to them occasional negligible variations.

Thus, a basically unified approach seems to pervade this entire science, from its origins to positivism, where, again, we find the same connection between body and soul, the distinction between man and woman, the influence of climate on character, the physiognomic syllogism, but especially the great problem of identifying the soul through the animal world.

As we have seen, the soul is assimilated with the form: the problem of attempting to identify it is based on the comparative method adopted by Aristotle. This approach to isolating a form is present not only throughout the classical world, in medieval bestiaries, in the sixteenth century, but even into the past century, when speculations concerning the face made even more obsessive reference to an analysis of animal nature. In Thoré's encyclopedic dictionary, we can still read: "For never was an animal created with the shape of one animal and the soul of another, but always with his own body and soul. Also, it is necessary for each body to be affected by a particular form."[10]

Animality is what allows us to identify man's form: the ways in which a human form approaches, or is removed from, an animal form; the way in which it resembles or is different from it. These seem to be the means to identify it. It is a paradoxical situation, for if man can recognize himself through the animal, the latter returns man to animality at the very moment in which its form surfaces in a recognizable way on a human face.

This identification mechanism is perverse in that it attempts to explain images through other images, and it juxtaposes mirror to mirror. It could also happen that the principle of this "science," which considers humanity and animality alongside each other, is fatally destined to elude the distances between the two. Zoomorphism, however, when used as a mechanism for defining the human form, appears to be indispensable to physiognomists. For it is the very artifice which allows the perception of what de Superville would call "some pure impressions [*quelques impressions pures*]," "the visible language of nature [*le langage visible de la nature*]," in which it is possible to identify "one or another of the basic directions of the game of physiognomics."[11]

Such a mechanism allows us to recognize a complex form by means of a more simple and elementary one, thanks mainly to a common agreement concerning the meaning to be attributed to a particular form. Della Porta says, in his *De humana physiognomia*, "so that, if we describe the form of each animal, and to such form we attribute a quality, a passion, a behavior, one can then tell from his appearance."[12] In this late sixteenth-century work, the mechanism is expressed with exemplary clarity. For della Porta was only taking Aristotle's physiognomic enthymeme and solving it. And in so doing he complicated it.

First of all, he took into consideration those animals to which the encyclopedia of the time attributed a particular passion, or a specific character. Then, he considered those animals that show this passion as their dominant one. Finally, he analyzed the physical characteristics shared by those animals. He discovered, for example, that all strong and vigorous animals were endowed with a "wide chest" and with "wide extremities," as in the case of bulls and horses. From this he concluded that all animals endowed with a certain particular characteristic were also endowed with the corresponding moral aspect, and that those without the latter were also lacking the former:

All animals endowed with *wide extremities* [B] are *strong* [A].

Lions [C] are endowed with *wide extremities* [B], therefore, *lions* [C] are *strong* [A].

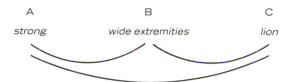

A
strong

B
wide extremities

C
lion

It is a common syllogism of the following type: all Bs are A, all Cs are B, all Cs are A, where the middle term B allows for the deduction plan, as its instrument of diagnostic forecasting. But, in this case, to solve the middle term B, involves deciding what must be explained. The middle term, "wide extremities," is the *sign* (*Sillogismi medium, silicet Signum*), says della Porta: it is there to set the rule. "All animals endowed with wide extremities are strong," in which the circumstance of "Lions are endowed with wide extremities," leads to the result: "All lions are strong." The middle term is the key to the entire inferential movement; it is the mechanism that releases sign correlations and cross-correlations. The middle term is the very cause of the strength.

Having solved the first syllogism, della Porta uses the result as a *premise*, that is, as a *rule*, for a second syllogism. It is an enthymeme, a persuasive syllogism, where, given the *premise* "All lions are strong," and the circumstance "Some men resemble lions," it then follows that "Such men are strong." This gives rise to a long list of character masks: Goat-Man, Lion-Man, Bird-Man, Monkey-Man.

In ancient times, man attempted to find moral qualities in the resemblances between men and animals. This was done by transferring to human individuals, by analogy, those attributes which fables had given to specific animals.

Thus, the lion is hot-tempered and strong. The leopard, despite its delicate features, is proud, deceitful, scheming and, at the same time, daring and fearful. The bear is deceitful, fierce and irascible. The wild boar is full of senseless rage, while the ox is simple and sincere. The horse likes pomp and craves honors. The fox is

G.B. della Porta. From *De humana physiognomia*, 1586. Private collection.

deceitful and scheming; the monkey likes joking and imitating. Sheep are self-assured; goats are lecherous; pigs are dirty and greedy. "Their appearance is appropriate for their behavior," says della Porta, "so that if a man appears similar to an animal in any of his features, let him be aware that he shall behave in a similar fashion."[13] So, man can be

> as brave as a lion, as timid as a hare, as bold as a rooster, as irritating and disagreeable as a dog, as severe as a deer, as compassionate as a turtledove, as malicious as a hyena, as pleasant as a dove, as deceitful as a fox, as gentle as a lamb, as fast as a roebuck, as cowardly and foolish as an ass, as obedient as a peacock, as chatty as a sparrow, as roving as a goat, as indomitable as a bull, as recalcitrant as a mule, as quiet as a fish, as reasonable as a lamb, as lecherous as a pig, as malicious as an owl, as useful as a horse, as harmful as a wolf.... Only man has all the qualities of animals.[14]

A complex taxonomy of permanent moral characteristics is involved here, one that is based on an analytical breakdown of the body into its individual parts: nose, forehead, mouth, wrinkles, hair, skin color, shoulders, legs, feet, abdomen. Each component of the body is then compared to the corresponding part in the animal body.

Such a juxtaposition is based on an analogy that, within the physiognomic enthymeme, becomes the very foundation of the correlation mechanism. Let us take the example of the Bird-Man. Birds are mobile, vain and loquacious, says della Porta. Birds have small heads. Thus, men with small heads will be as mobile, vain and loquacious as birds. To take a specific example, the ostrich is, among all birds, the one with the smallest head. And its stupidity is proverbial. For is it not the ostrich that hides its head among the bushes, under the illusion that it might thus escape its pursuers? This is attested to in the Bible, by Aristophanes and in many other ancient sources. Della Porta adds a physiological reason for such stupidity, by referring to what Galen had said about how a small and narrow space in the head does not allow the brain to function properly. Carried away by quotation fever, della Porta quotes Saint Thomas, who in turn was quoting Aristotle: "The head and the heart," says the famous Stagirite, "are placed in opposing locations, so that the coolness of the brain might temper the heat of the heart. So that men with small heads, given the disproportion between those parts, are irascible and violent, as the overwhelming heat of the heart is not tempered by the brain."

The character of an animal was explained in ancient times — as was also, by

G.B. della Porta. From *De humana physiognomia*, 1586. Private collection.

analogy, that of man — by organic reasons. The latter were rooted in the ancient theory of humors, which, beginning in the fifth century and extending all the way to Descartes, defined the system of passions. Thus, Hippocrates thought that joy was made easier by pure and sincere blood, while Aristotle maintained that fear was the consequence of a sudden cooling of the blood, as opposed to rage, which resides in animals endowed with earthy fibers, such as bulls and wild boars. Della Porta takes the classical tradition and adheres to it enthusiastically: "Hippocrates was correct in his writing that the reason for some to be happy and some melancholy is in their elements, as those with pure blood are always cheerful... while the deer and the hare are timid because their blood is cold... while these animals are brave because of their earthy and warm blood." And della Porta concludes, three centuries before the phrenologists, that, given that the character is defined by the physiological composition of the body, "the soul is turned from queen to slave of her own slave. So that, upon entering the body, she is ruled by it according to how it is put together."

Cosmic Physiognomy and Cosmogony of the Face

The theory of humors and elements appears often in the theories of Renaissance magicians, but it finds its true place within an organic view of the world in della Porta's *Magiae Naturalis*. For it is in this work that we find the most effective attempt at bringing together in a unified picture alchemy, magic, astrology and physiognomy. Astrology and physiognomics were already linked in the Middle Ages. We can read, both in Savonarola's *Speculum Physiognomiae* and in the *Calendries des Berges*, how star signs modify men's character and appearance. The four temperaments correspond not only to the four elements, but also to four animals: the man who is irascible not only has the nature of fire, but also that of the lion; the phlegmatic man has both the nature of water and that of the lamb; the sanguine man has both the nature of air and that of the monkey; the melancholic one has the nature of earth and that of the pig.

Della Porta crosses this esoteric tradition with a philosophical approach, showing the signs of Aristotle's deep influence. Natural substances, he states, are composed of matter and form. Matter consists of the "basic senses of nature, that is, its elements, its simple bodies." The latter are fire, air, water, earth. These elements are not inert: "Each element embraces another which is endowed with friendly qualities, and juxtaposes it to an unfriendly one." Nature has created mysterious correspondences between elements, so that there do exist among them not only relations of reciprocal attraction and rejection, but also a curious sort of circularity. "Through heat, fire slowly becomes air; air becomes water through dampness; water becomes earth because of the cold; and earth and fire are joined in drought. Thus, they are gradually changed into one another. They then change again to the opposite, and they become such that they can easily pass from one to the other."

This transformation process contains the great alchemic inspiration that postulates a circularity among the four elements, as they renounce their own nature in order to become one another during the course of the circle, to the point that, just as in the beginning there was only One, and everything originated in that One, by this process all reverts back to One. Within the circularity of the universe, each element is itself and, at the same time, other than itself. It makes one think of a raw material that, although unmodified, takes on all possible states and forms. The hidden operator who ensures such a circularity is cosmic sympathy and antipathy. As della Porta says: "Things are born of the friendship among elements, things are corrupted by their quarreling." The relationship between matter and form is the central aspect of this cosmological view.

Although matter is not inert, nor totally free of form in itself, it has, however, first place in the *Magiae Naturalis*. Even the elements and their qualities are "instruments" of form. Aristotle's material cause is, potentially, greatly inferior to his formal cause.

The dominant role of form in relation to matter is due to the provenance of form, as it originates in God himself: "Thus from the highest order, and next to this from the intelligent, and to these, finally, from God himself [*A suprema igitur vertigine proxime, huic ab intelligentiis, illis denique ab ipso Deo*]." God, the "Giver of Forms," is the source of an emanation process which reflects a Neoplatonic inspiration.

Just as matter and form are linked, so too are spirit and matter: there is no opposition, or split, between God and the world, between body and soul; rather, they are one and the same force operating through a continuity of relationships. In such a context, natural order and human order are not in opposition; instead, they are united: man's destiny finds a continuation in natural events, while the latter are, in turn, enriched with deep spiritual vibrations. In *Magiae Naturalis*, the chapter on

"Sympathy and Antipathy Among Things," which follows that on "Forms," explains how they must be conceived of and used. The idea of sympathy and antipathy among all things in the universe, although a philosophical concept, is at the heart of ancient medicine itself, as well as a large part of magic, and it is typical of Renaissance spirituality, from Giordano Bruno to Robert Fludd. In Latin, as in Greek, *sympathia* means to have the same feelings, to enjoy a moral affinity. Cosmic sympathy thus appears to be based on a relationship of conformity, which is not simply an analogy of form, but rather, a similarity of sentiment. The magical view of the universe sees it as a vast, passionate play of friendships and enmities, violent phobias and fatal attractions, sordid plots and tender allegiances between men and animals, animals and animals, animals and plants, plants and stones, stones and stars, and stars and men. It is the magician, as well as the physiognomist, who knows how to find the secret links within this cosmic theater.

With magic, similar forms involve similar behaviors, and mysterious relationships and alliances. A similarity in form is linked to a similarity in behavior: "Selenite is a stone which bears engraved in it the image of the moon, which makes it wax and wane as the days follow each other." Or the sunflower, which is shaped like the sun, and follows the sun with its corolla.

Within this view, the world appears to be interpreted in a symptomatic way, wherein things are signs for other things only when there is some resemblance between the two. Thanks to this harmony of interrelations, an object can signify another one and, in contemplating a visible object, we can glimpse the invisible world, and even the soul. The question of sympathy becomes thus inscribed in that of resemblance: a similarity of sentiment strictly linked to a similarity of form. The assumption of an analogy of formal relationships thus establishes an ethical and passional similarity among all things within a cosmic physiognomics.

The cosmic system of correspondences belongs to an organicist view of the universe, which institutes a system of equivalences between macrocosm and microcosm. The Stoics conceived of the cosmos as a living organism, endowed with reason and capable of generating reasoning microcosms, linked in turn to the macrocosm by universal sympathy. The *pneuma*, as psychic spirit, resides in the heart and rules the human body, just as the pneuma as universal spirit resides in the sun and rules the world.

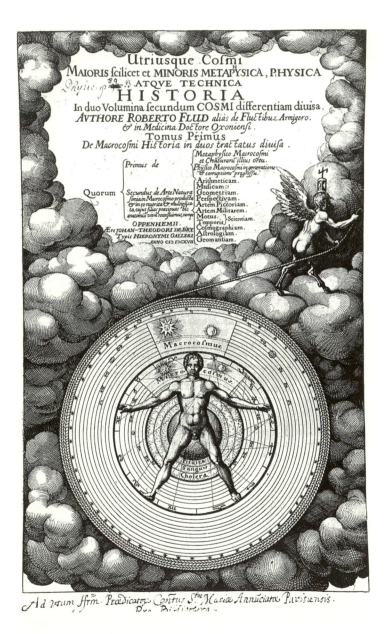

Cover of one of Fludd's most important works (Paris, Bibliothèque de l'ancienne Faculté de Médecine).

"The individual parts of this world," says della Porta, "are like the limbs of an animal, which are all...linked together by nature.... Thus, all parts of this large animal, that is, all parts of the world joined together, lend each other and are lent their natures, and from this kinship springs a reciprocal love and attraction.... And it is thus that a magnet attracts iron, yellow amber [attracts] straw...the moon, water."[15] This *concordia mundi* (world harmony) has the appearance of a polycentric, rhizomatic structure, composed of correspondences and crossed relations: "The philosophers," says della Porta, "discovered magic by observing certain links between natural things, and a reciprocal connection between them, that is, between visible things and hidden forces. We see celestial nature in earthly things, and earthly things in heavenly ones."[16] "The magician shall be the discoverer of the science of hidden secrets by contemplating and considering the countenance of this World," says della Porta. His competence lies primarily in his ability to read the face of the world, in knowing which are the rules governing the sign correlations between form and feeling within this cosmic physiognomics.

The correspondences between macrocosm and microcosm derived from the ancient medical science of the fifth century, blending, as they do, the theory of elements, qualities and humors, from the *Corpus Hyppocraticum* of Polybius (which was later given philosophical consecration in Plato's *Timaeus*), and resulted later, as is well known, in the theory of temperaments, in which the theory of humors was merged with the astrological one.

The physics of the *Timaeus*, with its ideal of a cosmic harmony, was, until the beginning of modern times, the source of some grand and fascinating views of the world, as we see in the *Corpus Hermeticum*, in which the sympathetic link uniting man, God and the world, is founded on resemblance. A typical correlation of this type is that between man's body and the world, based on a diagram in which, for example, the head corresponds to the sky, a place inhabited by the spirit and by higher intelligences, while man's lower half – "The genital parts, the origin of generation, are in the lower part [*Sunt in parte postrema genitalia membra, principium generationis*]," says Pico della Mirandola – corresponds to that part of the universe which is located under the Moon, an area where, "as everyone knows," says Pico, "generation and corruption are born."

Such an approach appears to remain implicit in the entire representation of the human body. For example, when de Superville tries to endow the vertical, horizontal or oblique directions with an ethical content, he refers to the human body and to the position it occupies in the cosmic space. Man is erect and tends toward the direction of the sky because the vertical axis of his body is a continuation of the radius of our globe, which is perpendicular to the axis of the horizon. He says: "Thus it is as if man were rising from the center of the earth to the heavenly vault, and filling the space in between those two extremes.... His physical strength and dignity, the result of his erect stance, become almost warrantors of his moral strength and dignity." The vertical direction and the erect position of the body feed on a sort of reciprocal ethical exploitation. Man is thus comprised in the "*expression of his own axis, the one and only original and absolute vertical direction.*"[17]

This topology of the body is ethically axiologized, and has nothing to do with any presumed "similarity" among things but, rather, is entirely based on the ancient symbolic associationism we found in Aristotle, linking man's body to the rest of the cosmos.

The feeling of sympathy linking all of creation in a common destiny is, according to de Superville, "that common feeling, the earliest in living matter, evolving through innumerable organisms, ever-higher, finally reaching the human race." For de Superville, man, who is placed at the center of this large arsenal of symbolic analogies, of correspondences and influences, of the reciprocal echoings of the small and the large cosmos, "subdues them and applies them all to himself *as measurement and as sole interpreter.*"[18]

Man sets himself up as the measure of all things, and as the rule for an ethical judgment of the rest of creation. He is the interpreter of those revelatory signs that, seen in the bodily shapes of all beings, indicate secret allegiances, mysterious sympathies, hidden relationships. Thus, man as interpreter, that is, as physiognomist.

In 1603, della Porta published in Venice the six books of his *Caelestis Physiognomonia* in which he analyzed the influences of bodies, movements and astral junctions on the appearance, the character and even on the destinies of men.

But even before that, another volume had acquired considerable importance in the history of physiognomics. In *Metoscopia* (1558), Girolamo Cardano, that great master of the occult, analyzed the various parts of the body on the basis of zodiacal localizations. The universe was organized in a hierarchy comprising three orders of decreasing value: the intellectual or divine order; the celestial or astral order; the earthly or elementary order – all mutually interdependent and constantly interacting. The human microcosm, and in particular the face, shows a synopsis of the correspondences and influences of the three macrocosmic orders. Each part of the forehead has its astral ascendant.

Jean Belot, master of divine and celestial sciences, ascribes some planetary and zodiacal affinity to all parts of the face, not only to the forehead. Thus, after Belot's work of 1628, *Familières instructions pour apprendre les sciences de chiromancie et physionomie* (Simple Instructions for Learning the Sciences of Chiromancy and Physiognomy), the forehead corresponded to Mars, the right eye to the Sun, the left to Venus, the right ear to Jupiter, the left to Saturn, the nose to the Moon, the mouth to Mercury. As for the signs of the zodiac, Cancer rules the forehead, Leo the right eyebrow, Virgo the left cheek, Scorpio the nose, and so on. This management of the body is bureaucratized to an obsessive degree, down to the last toe. Just as there is a medicine of signs, so there is a physiognomics of signs: the relationship between the hidden virtues of things and the celestial bodies that are responsible for them, is expressed by those formal aspects of things that correspond to the formal aspects of the celestial bodies. As a sign of their influence, celestial bodies mark man from the time of his birth. Such a *signatum* is often expressed in the outer shape of the body. Saturn confers memory and patience; Jupiter, judgment and prudence; Mars, courage and rage; the Sun, wisdom, moderation and magnificence; Mercury, imagination and memory.

To such celestial influence one should add the arrangement of the lines, their number, length, width, depth, color, path, which may be tortuous, ramified, broken, ascending or descending, right or left, as well as the value of the signs.

The seventeenth century also saw the publication of Fuchsius's metoposcopy, George de Raguse's two books of metoposcopic and chiromantic divination, Finella's works, as well as an entire chapter by Robert Fludd. Even more important, however, was Cureau de la Chambre's vast and unlucky opus, which, because of the length of time needed to print such an enormous work, was already surpassed, at the time of its publication, by Descartes's treatise on passion.

Cureau de la Chambre tried to shorten again the distance between physiognomics and a "healthy understanding" of astrology, as well as the observation of physio-

Mesoposcopy, 17th-century manuscript
(Paris, Bibliothèque de l'Ancienne Faculté de Médecine).

logical sympathies. He dedicates the forehead to Saturn, the right eye to the Sun, the left eye to the Moon, the nose to Venus, the cheeks to Jupiter, the ears to Mercury, the lips to Mars: all are confirmed, according to the illustrious royal physician, by the sympathy linking the markings on the face to those of the other parts. The forehead can only be ruled by the planet that rules the chest, since the bony parts are governed by Saturn; the cheeks, which are fleshy and sanguine, and which mirror the alterations of the liver and the blood, are ruled by Jupiter, which governs the liver. The lips can only be dependent on Mars, ruler of the abdomen, as they suffer from ulcers and excoriations during gall fever attacks.

This entire scholastic-occultist phantasmagory did not at all vanish in the whirlwind of the Cartesian revolution. It remained very active, although below the surface, reemerging periodically, as in the surgeon J.J. Sue's 1797 work, *Essai sur la physiognomie des corps vivants considerée depuis l'homme jusqu'à la plante* (Essay on the Physiognomy of Living Bodies, from Men to Plants). In this work, he analyzed physiognomic analogies among the different creatures of creation, and succeeded in finding in the stag beetle "something hard and fierce," in intestinal worms "a determined... countenance"[19]; and as to plants, "What an expression of goodness in fruit trees!... Kindly vegetables await being picked to provide us with healthy and pleasing food."[20]

Apart from some avowed drivel, which viewed the world as divine script, a tangle of markings or an organic labyrinth of similar meanings, the great cosmogonies of hermetic thought secretly continued to nourish even some of the positivistic interpretations of the human face and body. There existed in the nineteenth century a topological view of the brain, which quite closely mirrored ancient ethical cosmogony.

In his treatise on phrenology (1853), de la Corbière states: "Instincts, which men and animals share, and which are the essential foundation for the organic pyramid, occupy only the lower parts, while intelligence, which follows, is located in the upper front; and, third, there are emotions, which occupy the upper regions of the brain; and that assumes that the physical or topological position corresponds to the nature of the manifestations, and thus instincts have acquired the epithet of low, and feelings, that of high." He then adds, "Morals are based on an organic condition."[21]

The Line of Animality

The treatise of de la Chambre, who was the king's personal physician, and who wrote about man's moral being as reflected in his physical appearance, was mainly dictated by reasons of state, as was also another work from that century, Chiaromonti's *De congetturandis* (On Conjecturing), in which the body is seen as revealing the most intimate secrets hidden behind words.

During the seventeenth century, both at court and in the proceedings of the Inquisition, we can see how the body and its behavior emerge as a place for the truth. Physiognomics became, then, a method based on circumstantial evidence, a search for the truth, for what was hidden. This taxonomic vocation reflected the spirit of the times, which was obsessed with classifying and cataloging, an obsession that turned into real paranoia during the nineteenth century.

"Society and the State need animal characteristics to use for classifying people; natural history and science need characteristics in order to classify the animals themselves," say Deleuze and Guattari.[22] Such a mechanism of cross-referenced identifications, which remained active not only in physiognomics but also within physiology in general, took on a more scientifically rigorous character during the seventeenth century. On a deeper level, however, the theoretical assumptions seem to remain intact. As Deleuze and Guattari comment: "Many compromises are reached between the archetypal series and their symbolic structures."[23]

Such is the case with Le Brun, who drew a lion and a horse with human eyes. Human faces, on the other hand, are endowed with the eyes and eyebrows of their corresponding animals. In carrying out such transpositions, Le Brun proceeds in a methodical fashion, by studying the individual forms separately. A few scattered pages illustrating eyes form a sort of catalog in which one may make a first choice. Eyes and eyebrows of men, monkeys, camels, tigers, lynx, cats, foxes, pigs, rams, are all arranged on various lines. Open eyes, closed ones, heavy lids, wrinkled ones, as well as protruding, wide open or lowered ones. It is an inventory of diverse elements, which are already in themselves endowed with an expression, and are ready to be joined in odd and peculiar ways in order to create monstrous depictions in which the fragile threshold separating humanity from animality is revealed in an unsettling way.

Such a precise and methodical transfiguration generates both an ambiguous human-

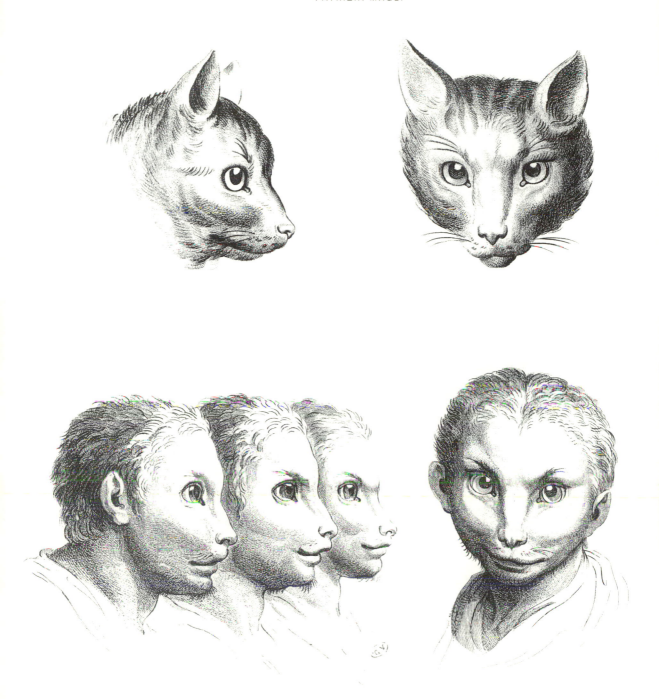

Charles Le Brun, Cat and Man: Similarities between Human and Animal Physiognomies (Paris, Bibliothèque des Arts Décoratifs).

Charles Le Brun, Eagle and Man: Similarities between Human and
Animal Physiognomies (Paris, Bibliothèque des Arts Décoratifs).

Charles Le Brun, Fox and Man: Similarities between Human and
Animal Physiognomies (Paris, Bibliothèque des Arts Décoratifs).

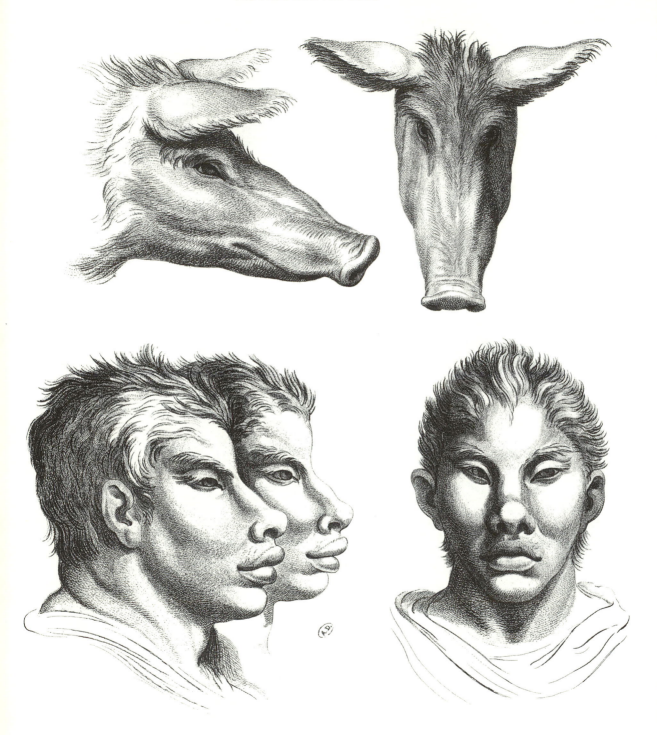

Charles Le Brun, Boar and Man: Similarities between Human and Animal Physiognomies (Paris, Bibliothèque des Arts Décoratifs).

ity and an ambiguous animality, remote yet familiar. Paradoxically, the Cartesian anatomy of passions contributed in itself to the reappearance of a mythical humanity by attributing to it a troubling vitality and casting upon it unsettling glances.

Imaginary forms are reflected upon and reconstructed in light of the positive sciences that interpret thousand-year-old signs in accordance with the zeitgeist. Physiognomics thus presents itself as a set of theorems, with a proposition and a demonstration. The geometric procedure which Le Brun uses to analyze the ancient parallels between men and animals is an example of this.

The character of a man and the nature of an animal, says Le Brun, can be measured on the basis of the angle formed by the straight line and the eyes' axis. If it rests on the nose, the individual is stirred by noble passions; if it is higher up, on the forehead, the impulses are shameful. A long demonstration of measurements follows, containing as its figurative representation some of the most beautiful illustrations in physiognomics.

In his links with ancient traditions, and in his merging them with more innovative trends, Le Brun both fell behind and preceded his own times. His theories were the point of departure for research carried out during the second half of the eighteenth century by the Dutch naturalist Camper (1722-89), who propounded the geometric method for measuring intelligence. The skeletons of man, dog, eagle and penguin, says Camper, show surprising analogies in their corresponding elements. Although diverse, the animal world is unitary. Camper describes a transformation system by which he can change a horse into a girl, a cow into a stork and a stork into a carp. In order to transform a cow into a bird, for example, it suffices to straighten the body of the cow, to change the front legs into wings, and to lengthen the neck. Nothing more. Such a game of metamorphoses reveals mysterious affinities among beings. However, the break in the continuity between man and animal is revealed even more clearly by the theory of the facial inclination. The increase in the angle of the line leading from the forehead to the upper lip shows the metamorphosis of one face into another, and this series of profiles of creatures that are so different shows us the entire evolutionary scale. The geometric method is connected to that of Le Brun, with additional observations based on the study of corpses and skulls which Camper received from African and Asian shores, as well as from casts of ancient statues.

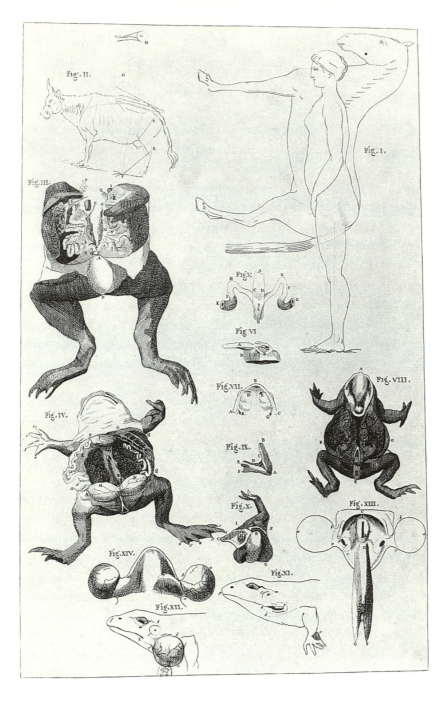

Petrus Camper, Metamorphosis of a Cow into a Bird and of a Horse
into a Human, 1791. From *Oeuvres de Petrus Camper qui ont pour
objet l'histoire naturelle, la physionomie et l'anatomie comparée*, 1803
(Paris, Bibliothèque nationale).

In order to carry out the measurements and to establish with the utmost precision the skull bones, Camper invented a special device, formed by a horizontal plane, and by a loom with stretched twine. His research revealed that the facial angle increases from forty-two degrees (a monkey with a tail) to fifty-eight in an orangutan, to seventy in a black man, to eighty or ninety in a European man, to ninety in Roman glyptics, to one hundred in ancient Greece. Beyond these limits a head becomes deformed. On the other hand, even Fichte was to say: "Where the individual, or... the race, remains an animal, and only knows his own interest, there is a prominent mouth; as the race becomes nobler, the mouth retreats under the arch of the thinking brow."[24] The hypothesis of facial angles was further explored by J.K. Lavater (1741-1801), in whose works the chapters on the "lines of animality" occupy an important position.

In the French edition of the Hague (1803), all the zoological essays are gathered in the ninth fragment of the second volume of *Physiognomische Fragmente* (1775-78). Those chapters revolve almost exclusively around animal physiognomics: the latter, however, is approached following anthropomorphic procedures and criteria. Man's image, the moral even more than the physical, is superimposed on the animal's, to reveal the latter's character.

Thus, the elephant's head is a "monument of prudence, energy and gentleness"; the beaver's teeth show "goodness and weakness." Lavater also analyzed the "vindictive" gaze of the wild fox, as well as the "good-naturedness" of pigeons. The most interesting section is that dedicated to crania, both human and animal. It was the result of the famous collaborative effort by Goethe and Lavater in which the visionary theory of the macrocosm resurfaced, although in a muted fashion. Lavater was convinced that each grain of sand and each leaf contain infinity, that there exist subtle harmonies between the body and the soul, as well as mysterious moral affinities among similar forms, whether they be animal or human, and consequently he placed man, both in body and in the position he occupies in space, within a cosmic view of the universe. Thus, man's cranium is held up by his spine as a cupola is held up by a pillar, and it mirrors the heavens, while the heads of animals are bowed, and their brains are a mere continuation of the spinal marrow.

The last volume of the *Fragmente* shows the gradual changes in the species. Lavater, however, proceeds in a fashion opposite to that of Camper, as he gradually straight-

J.-J. Grandville after Camper,
Transformation of Apollo into a Frog, 1844
(Paris, Bibliothèque nationale).

ens the line of the facial angle, from the frog through the entire evolutionary ladder, to the *Apollo Belvedere*.

The line of animality propounded by Lavater goes through twenty-four stages,
instead of eight: the creatures who follow each other after the initial frog are not
recognizable species, as they were for Camper. This is not a series of variations in
state, but, rather, a slow metamorphosis that evolves according to a continuous process of gradual humanization. These are monsters that have lost a recognizable animal form, but that have not yet reached a fully formed human shape, not even that
of a primate or of a black man.

The lowliest beast, as well as the gods of classical Antiquity, involute human
beings, monstrous hybrids, no longer animals and not yet men — are all included in
this uninterrupted line of contiguity. There is no opposition between the categories of man and animal, rather, a gradual and directional path. Animality is inscribed
in the human body; it cannot be gotten rid of, excluded or exorcised.

One and the same corporeality can be manifested in different forms. The underlying principle is the soul, through which the individual obtains the appropriate
body. The soul that has completely forgotten its spiritual origins is an animal.
One can then understand the shape of the dividing line in the realm of the soul's
spirituality, across which the values of humanity oppose those of bestiality; reason
opposes desire.

Animality is conceived of as a particular type of bodily corporality, and, consequently, corporeality is, in turn, seen as the material and spatial expression of spiritual and moral determinations. The body is not only the outward packaging of the
spirit, but also its symbol, and thus it is nothing more than the animalization of the
soul, its sensible image, its signifier. On the other hand, the animal's actions are
not a somatic figuration, but rather, the soul type, the morphology of the psyche.
Plato's semantics of animal forms returned in the nineteenth-century's physiognomic
theories: animality is expressed in a bodily morphology which is physically determined from above.

Such semantics, which completely mix man and animal, show how the line of
demarcation between humanity and animality passes through man himself. Animal
is in man. It is his unsettling double, his phylogenetic mirror. During the nineteenth
century, naturalists and physiologists tried to explain man's functions on the basis

Bust of Gall with cerebral mappings, side and frontal views
(Paris, Bibliothèque Charcot).

of those of animals, by establishing analogies between the functions of human and animal organs.

Gall, the founder of phrenology, set the principle of the impossibility of knowing human anatomy and physiology without resorting to comparative anatomy. In his work of 1810, *Anatomie et physiologie du système nerveux en général et du cerveau en particulier, avec des observations sur la possibilité de reconnaître plusieurs dispositions intellectuelles et morales de l'homme et des animaux par la configuration de leurs têtes* [Anatomy and Physiology of the Nervous System in General, and of the Brain in Particular, with Observations on the Possibility of Recognizing Various Intellectual and Moral Tendencies of Animal and Man by the Shape of Their Heads], Gall begins by stating that man is the "true complement to creation," and in this sense he does not differ from other organic beings except in possessing a greater number of organs without which he would inevitably be similar to all other animals. An animal's brain is still a man's brain, minus this and that part.

Animals differ one from the other only in the number of their parts. Thus, the difference is quantitative rather than qualitative: an interruption or an excess in development. Man's brain is more highly developed as it has a greater number of convolutions, and as a consequence of the placement of his thinking faculties.

It is interesting to note that Gall who, on the one hand, proclaims the autocracy of the brain, on the other hand, attributes to it a sort of federalism. The brain seems to consist of a departmentalized administration, in which the executive offices are, as in any proper administration, on the upper floors. Of course, that area is much larger in man than in animals.

Gall's theories met with considerable success, first in intellectual salons and among positivist philosophers, then among concierges and policemen. The success of such theories belongs, in fact, to that vast attempt at deciphering the body which appeared at the end of the last century, and which was deeply connected with the rise of bureaucratic societies. It is founded on the discovery of the "other," on the fear of the ever-increasing and uncontrollable size of the masses moving to the cities, on the fear of individuals losing their uniqueness. It confronts everyone's individuality; it elaborates typologies.

The passion for observing, discovering, classifying, filing faces and bodies is seen in the vast proliferation of treatises on physiognomics, phrenology and physiology during that period. Exploring the inner man through the outer man sets the foundations for a sort of physiology, whose parameters do not significantly differ from those once adopted by ancient people. Animality emerges again in an unsettling way in those beings which are at once man and beast: lunatics, women, primates, children. Phylogenesis becomes ontogenesis.

Doctor Morel, for example, in speaking of degenerative phenomena such as criminals and lunatics, and of their psychophysical deformations, which are seen as anomalies or interruptions in the development of the inner structure of their organs, examined the question of atavism. He maintained that such degenerations indicate the tendency, which is present in all species, to return to their origins. Similarly, Cesare Lombroso, the founder of criminal anthropology, saw the "atavistic phenomenon as forming almost the entire nucleus of the criminal type, as crime," he says, "is primarily a reawakening of primitive man."[25]

The question of degeneration, as a tendency for the human species to "return to

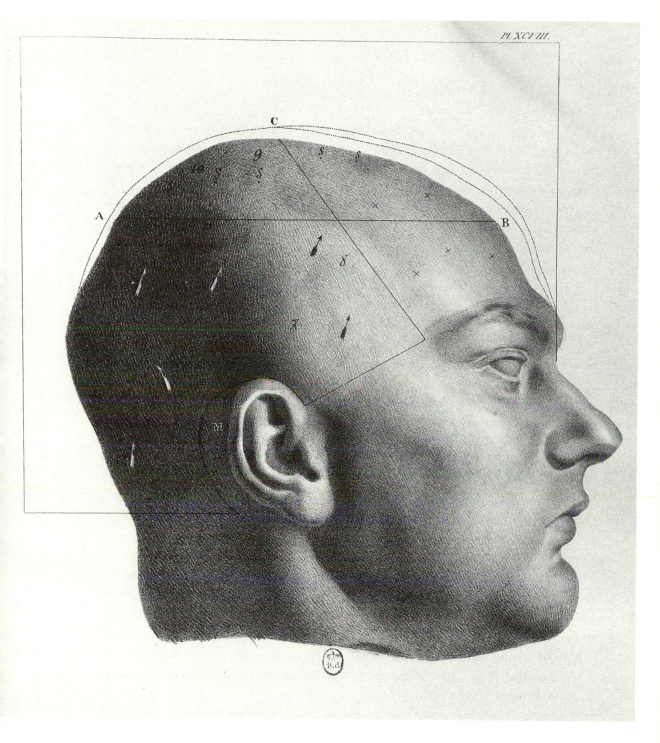

Head of the parricide Martin executed at Paris. From Vimont, *Atlas de Phrénologie*, 1831.

animality," was of interest both to anthropology and to the newly born psychiatry. When psychiatry first appeared and, as a medical and natural science, attempted to find within the body the organic source and the anatomical basis for the problems that concerned it, it began to use physiognomics as a diagnostic tool. The organic nature of passions, as manifested in physiognomic configurations, suggested a circular relationship of reciprocal causality between physical and moral elements, and asserted itself as a privileged moment in the contract between body and soul. "In order to fully appreciate the physiognomic features of the insane," maintained Esquirol, one of the founding fathers of psychiatry, "it would be necessary to draw the heads of a great number of them, and maintain for each its physiognomic character during availability."[26]

The above passage, which comes shortly after a reference to Lavater, not only inaugurated the inclusion of physiognomics in the epistemology of the newly developing psychiatry, but it also signalled, on a pragmatic level, the birth of asylum iconography, seen as an integral part of the therapeutic process.

Thus, physiognomics would appear to return to its ancient origins, to its point of departure, that is, to medicine. However, it remains far from La Bruyère's words in his *Caractères* (1688): "Physiognomics are not a rule given to us for the purpose of judging men: it can be useful for speculation." Physiognomics continues to rely, instead, on an inductive method that attempts to reduce the infinite variety of individuals and of facial configurations to a standardized state through drastic schematization and abstraction processes. This may lead to identifying a face through surveying and identifying shapes, colors and sounds belonging to the animal, the plant or the mineral worlds, as well as to other celestial universes. Although by different methods and approaches, anthropologists and psychiatrists, writers and policemen, suspicious lovers and amateur painters, are all taking up and developing anew the ancient idea of a close intermingling of forms, characters, abilities and passions within the living world.

As Baltrusaitis says, the old doctrine of the occult is reborn in positive research without, however, betraying its old spirit. The science of the unknown always clashes with the insoluble. The more closely it analyzes and purifies its notions, the more it tries to establish a solid foundation for itself, the more it loses itself in fantasy.

NOTES

1. G.B. della Porta, *De humana physiognomia* (Naples, 1586), p. 58.

2. C. Ginzburg, "Spie, radici di un paradigma indiziario," in *Crisi della ragione*, ed. A. Gargani (Turin: Einaudi, 1979), p. 81.

3. *De humana physiognomia*, p. 57.

4. U. Eco, *A Theory of Semiotics* (Bloomington, Ind.: University Press, 1976).

5. T. Thoré, *Dictionnaire de phrénologie et physiognomie, à l'usage des artistes, des gens du monde, des instituteurs, des pères de famille, des jurés* (Paris, 1836), pp. 276-77.

6. *De humana physiognomia*, p. 254.

7. P. Fabbri, "Le passioni del volto," in AA.VV., *Effetto Arcimboldo* (Milan: Bompiani, 1987).

8. C. Le Brun, *Conférence sur l'expression générale et particulière des passions* (Paris, 1698), p. 105.

9. *De humana physiognomia*, p. 105.

10. *Dictionnaire de phrénologie*, p. 33.

11. Humbert de Superville, D.P.G.H.D.S., *Essai sur les signes inconditionnels dans l'art* (Leyden, 1827), pp. 12-13.

12. *De humana physiognomia*, p. 21.

13. *Ibid.*, pp. 22-23.

14. *Ibid.*

15. G.B. della Porta, *Magiae Naturalis Libri XX* (Naples, 1589), pp. 17-18.

16. *Ibid.*, p. 22.

17. *Essai sur les signes inconditionnels*, p. 3.

18. *Ibid.*, p. 22.

19. J.J. Sue, *Essai sur la physiognomie* (Paris, 1797), p. 277.

20. *Ibid.*, p. 275.

21. C.S. de la Corbière, *De l'influence qui doit excercer la phrénologie* (1853), pp. 78-79.

22. G. Deleuze and F. Guattari, *A Thousand Plateaus*, trans. Brian Massumi (Minneapolis: University of Minnesota, 1987), p. 239.

23. *Ibid.*, p. 237.

24. J.G. Fichte, *Grundlage des Naturrechts nach Principien der Wissenschaftslehre* (1796-97).

25. C. Lombroso, *La donna delinquente, la prostituta e la donna normale* (Rome, 1893), p. 212.

26. E.D. Esquirol, *Des maladies mentales* (Bruxelles, 1838), vol. 1, p. 27.

Translated by Ughetta Lubin.

Detail of the tympanum, Autun.

The Ethics of Gesture

Jean-Claude Schmitt

In the years since the publication of Marcel Mauss's famous article "Body Techniques,"[1] it has come to be accepted that gesture, attitude and comportment are social acquisitions, the purposive or unconscious products of processes of learning or imitation. They only seem "natural" because they are common to a whole society, the shared property of an entire culture which has to be set at a distance for their relativity to be seen (this was the starting point of Mauss's investigation); in addition to which, they change so slowly that the changes are almost imperceptible, so that the history of gesture is paradigmatically a "longue durée." This continuity — at least as it appears at the general level — derives, of course, from the power of educational patterns and, beyond that, from the stability of the schemas that structure cultures and ideologies, and from the resilience of the principles in which codes and norms are rooted. Rules of this sort are, admittedly, found in every culture, but only rarely is their continuity as visible as it is in Western culture, where ethics and education have been written down for at least twenty-five centuries. It is a fragment of that history, from Roman Stoic ethics to the dawn of scholasticism, that I want to trace here, paying particular attention to the notion of gesture and the ethical values that originally inspired the establishment of ideal gestural models.[2] In this way I shall be able to show their practically immutable nature, but at the same time, by more detailed analysis, to reveal the changes they do undergo, which are always related to historical change at a more general level.

The most general characteristics of this long tradition of reflection on gesture are the following. Essentially it is an ethical tradition, and as such seeks to define normative rules governing gesture, to indicate which gestures are good and which are bad in the light of universal values which, depending on the period, may be

129

human reason or the gaze of God. Second, gesture is regarded as the outward (*foris*) physical *expression* of the inward (*intus*) soul. This conception of the expressivity of gesture (whether its referent is philosophical, religious or psychological), and the dual idea of the person that underlies it, are patterns constitutive of Western culture, even today.[3] Third, the relationship between the body and the soul which, in the ethical tradition, is sealed by gesture, can also imply a manner of acting upon the body, a discipline of gesture — the gesture of prayer or else more ordinary behavior — as influencing the soul to conform to moral norms; but this possibility is invoked more rarely, and only at times when reflection on gesture becomes more intense.[4]

Thinking about gesture has varied over the centuries, in intensity if not in its basic themes. In this connection, as often in the study of history, tracing the changes in vocabulary seems a particularly instructive way of following these fluctuations. The Latin word *gestus*, for example, meaning the movements and attitudes of the body in general rather than any specific gestures in particular, varies widely in the frequency with which it was used between classical Rome and the mid-Middle Ages, most noticeably by being almost totally eclipsed in the early Middle Ages. It seems that for the word to be used, gesture needed to be "objectified" and regarded as an appropriate subject for reflection. In descriptions of actions or in narrative it does not seem to be nearly as prominent as in ethical or philosophical treatises in which the observer is distanced from the gesture. This detachment was clearly absent in the early Middle Ages when a marked decline in classical scholarship was responsible for the loss of part of the intellectual equipment which had allowed for the thought about gesture in the classical period. To begin with, however, I want to look at another word, *modestia*, generally associated with *gestus* and sharing the same historical fluctuations, because it appears to be a central concept in the ethics of gesture from Roman Antiquity onward. Moreover, because it signifies the moderation that guarantees the golden mean, it is a notion which is still current today in the conventions that govern good manners and acceptable behavior. Avoid excess — *ne quid nimis* — "nothing too much": the old Delphic precept,[5] cited by Juvenal and, more importantly, by Terence, bequeathed to the Middle Ages by Macrobius,[6] taken up again by Saint Augustine, then by Alcuin, took a new lease on life after the twelfth century,[7] and has been with us ever since.

Gesture and "Duties" from Cicero to Saint Ambrose

In the classical and medieval lexicon *modestia* did not, or not solely, mean modesty in the modern sense. The etymology of the word is important: the root is *modus*, meaning, among other things, moderation, the correct proportion, scrupulous respect for which a virtue was called, precisely, *modestia*. Both for classical and Christian authors *modestia* was synonymous with *temperantia*, when it did not constitute one of its subcategories. Aristotle mentions it as a virtue alongside courage and justice, though in his work this enumeration does not take the form of a list.[8] In Cicero, however, the virtues, four in all, are presented as a real system.[9] In *De officiis* Cicero sets out to inculcate the principles of Stoic ethics into his rebellious son. The young man needs to become aware of the "duties" befitting his age and position in order to achieve the aim of the ethical life, which is *honestum* or "moral goodness." This means that his conduct must be appropriate, decent (*decus*), which consists of following, in society, the promptings of his natural reason. This ethic involves nothing transcendental: it is entirely social, defined by and for a class of noble male citizens, in the context of the management of the affairs of State.[10] Cicero explains that "moral goodness" is composed of four "virtues": *scientia*, the discernment of truth, prudence and wisdom; *beneficientia* or *liberalitas*, the ideal of justice which impels us to render to everyone what is due them and to respect contracts to protect social relations; *fortitudo*, strength and greatness of spirit which inspires contempt for human things; and *temperantia* or *modestia*, which consists in "orderliness and moderation in everything that is said and done." We are not dealing here with "agitation of the mind" (*mentis agitatio*): this is the realm of "action" (*actio*) in the social life of the "free man" whose "constancy" and "reserve" (*constantia, verecundia*, the two words have the same meaning) manifest moral and political excellence. And it is "every movement and attitude of the body," "in standing or walking, in sitting or reclining, in our expression, our eyes or the movement of our hands," "in gesture and action,"[11] which translate each Roman's excellence of mind and nobility of outward form, to be seen and judged by others. Aspects of gesture such as gait must not be "too animated" nor yet "overly-nice" or "effeminate"; the only rule is the golden mean: there virtue resides; "*mediocritas optima est*."[12]

This is a major text, fundamental in a number of ways, and not merely for Roman civilization. Seneca uses comparable expressions, and although he takes the ideal of Stoic conduct as far as sacrificing one's life, that ideal is to be expressed by "a modest gait, a calm and honest countenance, and a bearing that suits the man of wisdom." "All virtues are founded in moderation [*Omnis in modo est virtus*]."[13]

The system of the four virtues is also used by the late pagan authors, who played an important cultural role by creating the synthesis of classical learning which Latin Christianity inherited. Macrobius, for example, commenting on Cicero's account of the dream of Scipio in *De republica* and comparing it to the myth of Er with which Plato's *Republic* closes, notes that both authors shared the belief that noble souls, those who served the State "prudently, justly, courageously and temperately"[14] were destined to attain immortality and its mysteries. Earlier than that, however, the Church Fathers — Lactantius, Clement of Alexandria, Origen, Jerome — had adopted the system of the four virtues which Ambrose was the first to call "cardinal."[15] It is the coming together of these four virtues derived from pagan thought and the three specifically Christian virtues mentioned by Saint Paul, the "theological" virtues of faith, hope and charity,[16] that forms the basis of the moral theology of the Church as it takes its final form in the twelfth century. And *modestia*, too, either as a virtue itself or as a subcategory of the virtue of *temperantia*, enjoyed a new lease on life within that system in the works of the Church Fathers.[17] At the beginning of the third century, Tertullian commends this virtue, which he associates with *pudicitia*,[18] to Christian women in particular. It was, however, unquestionably Saint Ambrose in 389-90 who, by explicitly lifting both title and whole passages from Cicero's *De officiis* for his treatise *De officiis ministrorum*, defined the Christian virtue of Christian gesture, under the headings of *modestia, temperantia* and most importantly *verecundia*.[19]

In many of its features Ambrose's work is an adaptation of Cicero, as for instance when he recommends following nature to discover the rules of "discipline" and "propriety."[20] There are, however, at least two significant differences: the ethics that Saint Ambrose elaborates is thoroughly Christian, despite its classical vocabulary, and only makes sense in the context of the redemption of man's first disobedience, the avoidance of sin in the present and the earning of future salvation. Nature, therefore, which "gives movement its form," now has to be seen separately from reason and a self-justifying political order. For ontologically sinful man, natural reason does not in itself provide any guarantee of moral rectitude: "if there is some vice in nature, 'industry' should amend it; when art is at fault, at least let correction not be wanting."[21] The concept of *verecundia* is also very significant, appearing here in the sense of shame associated with the flesh and sexual sin: the example given is that of the shame felt by Noah when he discovered that his sons had laughed at his nakedness while he lay in a drunken sleep. So with Ambrose and Augustine the idea is established that the greatest sin, the original sin, is sexual.[22] Conversely the state of grace is virginity, and in its ideal model, the Virgin Mary, Ambrose finds not only the mirror of all virtues but also the supreme exemplar of gesture.[23]

Ambrose's intention, moreover, was not, like Cicero's, to prescribe the proper conduct of a Roman aristocrat, but to train young priests, the bishops of the future, for their ecclesiastical ministry. Here, too, it is *verecundia* that the young cleric needs "in his movements, gestures and gait." His spiritual quality will be gauged from the state of his body: "the movement of the body is the voice of the spirit."[24] Drawing directly on his experience as a bishop, Ambrose recalls how he refused to admit a friend into the clergy because his "gestures did not have the necessary propriety," and how he had forbidden a cleric ever to walk in front of him because his gait "wounded his eyes"; neither judgment was mistaken, as things turned out, as one succumbed to the Aryan heresy and the other fell prey to the temptations of money. A "praiseworthy gait," by contrast, bears within itself "the reflection of legitimate authority, the weight of dignity, the mark of serenity";[25] as social model, as well as power-holder, the senator had been replaced by the bishop. A century and a half later, the same tale was told by the Bishop of Pavia, Ennodius (d. 521). Celebrating the holy Bishop of Milan's memory in his poems, he praised him for having instructed his flock "by his gesture, his probity and his modesty."[26]

The Early Middle Ages: Gesture Is No Longer the Subject of Serious Thought

After Ambrose's death, however, the history of the ethics of gesture changes noticeably. Works of the *De officiis* sort undergo a change, becoming liturgical texts, in which the connection with gesture, while still important, is no longer contemplative in kind. The word *gestus* gradually disappears from the vocabulary, a sign that the attention once accorded specifically to gesture is on the wane. My sense is also

that *gesta*, the acts performed by God through men, replaces *gestus*, the latter imply-
ing a relative autonomy for human action which the ecclesiastical culture of the
early Middle Ages — whether in historical accounts or liturgy — could not easily
envisage. Ambrose's immediate disciple, Saint Augustine, devoted much attention
to the four virtues, especially to temperance and moderation, but he scarcely mentions gesture, or not at least in that context.[27] With the *Cenobitic Institutions* and the
Conferences of Cassianus (c. 420-25), *De vita contemplativa* of Pomerius (d. c. 490) and
Moralia in Job of Gregory the Great (c. 579-85), we move unmistakably into a monastic literature of a very different ascetic tonality. Its most notable characteristic is
the elevation of vices to set against the virtues, though as yet without any attempt —
as there would be in the twelfth century — to match the two lists word-for-word.
The central task in the sixth century was the enumeration of the many and insidi-
ous forms of demonic temptation and sin: Cassianus brought back a list of eight vices
from his twenty-year sojourn among the anchorites of Egypt, but this was soon overshadowed by the rival list of Saint Gregory which, in fact, was more of an outline of
the way the seven vices are engendered by the "mother," *superbia*, perfectly adapted
to Christian introspection and penitential practice.[28] What place, then, is given to
the movements of the body in this context?

Significantly, all of these authors mention the use of the body in connection with
vices — greed in Pomerius, fornication in Cassianus, pride in Gregory — rather than
virtues such as moderation, temperance or even modesty, as in earlier authors. The
suspicion with which the body was regarded had increased during the intervening
years.[29] When Cassianus, for example, speaks of "movements of the body" (*motus
corporis*), he does so in the sense of *commotio carnis*, "emotion of the flesh," in cases
of nocturnal emission during sleep.[30]

To this distrust of the body as the occasion and site of sin may also be added the
negation, pure and simple, of its concrete reality: the allegorization of the body sub-
limated into an image of the "body of the Church" is perhaps just another form of
denial of the real body. Although Gregory enumerates the separate but complementary "offices" of the "members of the body," he sees the eyes and the feet only as
metaphors of contemplation and action, both present and necessary in the life of
the Church.[31] In the same period another Italian, Cassiodorus (468-562), employed
and in fact extended the original Pauline schema,[32] but without being able to endow

it with the relevance of an organic description of society as a whole, as would be done in the mid-Middle Ages.[33]

The development is clear: along with the vocabulary of gesture, a good part of the sort of reflection on gesture that had been practiced from Cicero to Saint Ambrose disappeared during the early Middle Ages. Similar claims to the ones made here for the literature of ethics could also be made for other areas, such as rhetoric, which is characterized at this point by a lack of interest in *actio* and *pronunciatio*, the fifth and final part of the art of eloquence, and the one precisely concerned with the gestural and vocal performance of the orator.

There is, though, one area of what we may for convenience call "ethical litera-ture," in the early Middle Ages, where the eclipse of thought about gesture was less clear-cut, and that is in treatises written for the edification of sovereigns, the "mirrors for princes."[34] The earliest of these was written for King Miro of Galicia by Bishop Martin of Braga (d. 580).[35] The work is cast in the form of a treatise on the four car-dinal virtues: prudence, magnanimity or fortitude, continence and justice. In con-ception it is entirely classical, which is one of the reasons for its great success throughout the Middle Ages, when it was attributed to Seneca himself. The third section is concerned with *continentia*: it recommends moderation in eating, speak-ing, laughter and also in gait, which should be without "turmoil." The movements of the body, like those of the soul, should not be too uncontrolled: "be capable of change, but not fickle."[36] Observing the virtue of continence means keeping to "the line of the golden mean."[37] Also Spanish in origin, the treatise attributed to Isidore of Seville (d. 636) on the *Institutions of Discipline* recommends the noble young Visigoth to whom it is addressed to maintain "movements of the body full of con-stancy and gravity, with no vain fickleness or disorderliness, and a gait which does not by its extravagance imitate the contortions of actors and the gestures of clowns who run hither and thither."[38]

The real flowering of these works comes in the Carolingian period, as a result of a partial rediscovery of the classics, especially of rhetoric and edifying litera-ture; and also because of the *renovatio* of the Empire, based partly at least on the ancient model. Here again we find one of the principal figures of the "Carolingian renaissance," Alcuin, Charlemagne's close consultant and advisor, quoting pas-sages from Cicero's *De officiis* to explain the rules for "bodily moderation": "the head should be held up straight, the lips uncurled, the mouth not immoderately open, not looking behind one, or turning the eyes to the ground, neither bending the neck, nor raising or lowering the eyebrows." A little further on, Alcuin distinguishes three subcategories of "temperance" – continence, clemency and *modestia* – and defines temperance itself as the virtue that "ensures that in the quest for moral goodness one always and everywhere observes moderation of the body and of the spirit."[39] But this explicit return to the ideals and formulations of the Stoics was very short-lived; at the beginning of the ninth century, the *Via regia* by Smaragdus, Abbot of Saint-Mihiel,[40] and the two treatises by Bishop Jonas of Orleans, *De institutione laicali*, dedicated to Count Matfred, and *De institutione regia*, written for King Pepin,[41] recommend straightforwardness in action; on occasion they outline the correct way for a king to speak, but fail to describe his gestures or to specify rules for their use.

The Twelfth Century: The Flowering of the Ethics of Gesture

It was not, in fact, until the twelfth century that such thinking about gesture reappeared in the new intellectual setting of the reformed monasteries, then in the urban schools,[42] where a rediscovery of the ancients had once again, but this time more firmly than in the Carolingian period, given a new impetus to written culture. There are increased signs of renewed interest in gesture from the eleventh century onward. Taking vocabulary as an index of this, and looking at a variety of texts – chronicles, lives of saints, moral or didactic works and so on – the word *gestus*, often bearing a negative connotation but sometimes appearing in a positive sense, and *gesticulatio* (always in the bad sense) increase in frequency, after having almost completely vanished from the vocabulary of the early Middle Ages.[43] And in ethical literature *modestia*, the ideal of moderation and the golden mean, comes to be regarded as the virtue specifically relating to gesture, rarely appearing in texts without being accompanied by the word *gestus*.

In monastic culture the change was all the more noticeable because the long tradition of written rules and ordinaries (particularly the Rule of Saint Benedict) and the commentaries on them, had hitherto paid little or no attention either to the vocabulary or to the concepts. Yet they at once became part of the "intellectual equipment" of the new orders: reformed Benedictines and Cistercians, or new communities of regular canons following the more flexible rule said to be Augustine's, as at Prémontré or Saint-Victor de Paris. The part he plays in the history of monasticism and in the religious life of his century means that Saint Bernard (1091-1153) is the prime example here. He is able to come up with concise and memorable formulations in his definitions of the rules of ideal comportment: "Take your stand within yourself; you will not then sink beneath your level, nor rise above it, you will not go too far, nor spread out too wide. Keep to the middle if you wish to keep moderation. The midway is the safe way. Moderation abides in the mean and moderation is virtue."[44] In the *Liber de gradibus humilitatis et superbiae* he uses the device, very widespread at that time, of the spiritual ladder, in order to enumerate successively the twelve degrees or "steps" of humility, from the bottom upward, and then — from the top down — the twelve steps of pride. When he comes to the first step of pride, *curiositas*, he describes the "marks" (*indiciis*) that betray it: "If you shall see a monk, whom you formerly trusted confidently, beginning to roam with his eyes, hold his head erect, prick up his ears, wherever he is standing, walking, sitting; you may know the changed inner man from the movements of the outer." And he goes on to cite one of the commonplaces of the twelfth-century literature on gesture: "a wicked man winketh with his eyes, speaketh with his feet, teacheth with his fingers,"[45] and comments "the strange movement of the body reveals a new disease in the soul...." The third step of pride is devoted to "foolish mirth" (*De inepta laetitia*), particularly suspect in monasteries where tears of compunction should reign and laughter be banished:

> Facetiousness appears in his gestures, merriment in his face, vanity in his stride. He likes to make jokes; he is easily and quickly moved to laughter.... For just as a windbag with a small vent, if compressed when it is distended with air, will whistle as it deflates, and the escaping air, not leaking out but shot out, keeps making a noise, so the monk who has filled his heart with silly and ludicrous thoughts, finding no outlet for the blasphemous blast because of the rule of silence, lets it escape from his throat in snorts. He keeps covering his face from shame, he compresses his lips, he grinds his teeth; he laughs without wanting to, he guffaws involuntarily. And when he blocks his mouth with his fists, you can hear him chortle through his nose.[46]

This description is remarkable for the liveliness and exactness of its observation; it

Hell, detail of the tympanum, Autun.

also conveys a considerable subtlety in its psychological analysis and its recognition of repression as an effect of monastic education.

In his sermons on the *Song of Songs*, Saint Bernard returns to the question of laughter, but here his judgment is more nuanced. Having said that the body should shine with the radiance of internal spiritual love (*caritas*) he adds: "the body receives the light of the spirit and diffuses it by its members and senses; it shines out in each action, each word, each look, each step, each laugh – if, that is, there is laughter [*si tamen risus*] – tinged with gravity and infused with propriety." But when "the movements of these and other members, and the movements of the sense, gestures and habits (*gestus et usus*), appear serious, pure, modest, totally untouched by extravagance and lasciviousness, rather governed by piety and equality, then the beauty of the soul is manifest, so long at least as this is not a trick of the spirit's."[47] Laughter is thus not always hateful: Saint Bernard avoids using the word *cachinnatio*, which has a strong diabolical connotation (being used in particular to designate the derisive laugh of the devil). *Cachinnatio* is to *risus* as *gesticulatio* is to *gestus*: they are the negative poles of notions and behavior that in certain conditions may take on a positive value. In this passage Saint Bernard has lost none of his psychological perspicuity: at the very center of the monastery he has encountered fraud (*dolus*) and hypocritical dissimulation.

The most innovative scientific and philosophical culture of the twelfth century did not, however, develop in the Cistercian precincts but in the urban schools, notably at Chartres with Bernardus Sylvestris, whose pupil, William of Conches (1080-1145), deeply influenced by *De beneficiis* of Seneca and *De officiis* of Cicero,[48]

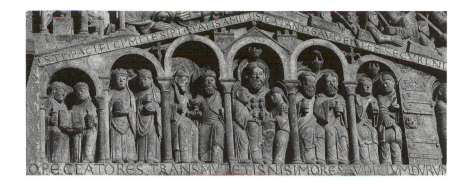

The Saints and the Elect, left side of the tympanum
(Conques, Church of Saint Foy).

wrote a vast moral treatise modeled on Boethius's *Consolation of Philosophy*, entitled *Moralis philosophia de honesto et utili*. This begins with a dream in which Cicero and Seneca appear to the author and inspire his reflections, and goes on to deal successively, on the classical model, with the four virtues of prudence, justice, fortitude and temperance. The latter is subdivided, not into three subcategories as in Cicero (*continentia, clementia* and *modestia*) but into eight (*modestia, verecundia, abstinentia, honestas, moderantia, parcitas, sobrietas, pudicitia*). *Modestia* is defined as "the virtue which keeps manners, movements and all our activity above insufficiency but below excess." After three sentences taken from Horace, Cicero and Seneca, a whole passage from *De officiis* is quoted word-for-word as a reminder that the body's movements express the internal movements of the soul. He does the same thing a little further on in relation to *verecundia*, which he defines as "the service of moral good [*honestas*] in gesture, speech and facial expression."[49]

The frame of reference is thus fixed, and will scarcely change until at least the second half of the thirteenth century. Hugh of Saint-Victor, in Paris (d. 1141), an exact contemporary of William of Conches, also recommends "modest and humble" gesture: "a speaker must have moderation [*modestiam*] in his gestures, such that, while he is speaking, his members do not move in a disordered, or immodest or extravagant fashion, and he does not diminish the peaceful nature of his speech by winks or by the changing expression of his face."[50]

In Paris at the end of the century the cathedral school of Notre-Dame was dominated by the unusual figure of Peter the Chanter (d. 1197). A major theologian, author of a *Summa de sacramentis*, he also wrote a very important ethical treatise, the *Verbum abbreviatum*. It demonstrates a mind resolutely turned toward the external world, toward the city – indeed toward Paris, a capital city – and anxious, in the 153 chapters which it comprises despite its title, to solve the numerous problems encountered by the Church and the Christian religion as it adapted to new political, social and economic conditions.[51] The work opens with an examination of scholarly *disputatio*, then of preaching, both clerical activities which were very much on the rise at the time. He also examines other contentious problems, all of a sort raised by a changing society in need of new ideological justifications, and resolves them as well as he can: these include simony, modes of dress, the building trade, almsgiving and so on. But what is significant is the way he tries to produce a new ethic using the still traditional vocabulary, concepts and "authorities." Once again, the works cited are Cicero's *De officiis* and Martin of Braga's *De quattuor virtutibus*, which he attributes, as usual, to Seneca; they govern the whole of his exegesis of temperance, its eight subdivisions and the moderation to be applied to movements "whether they are of the body or the soul."[52] None of this is any different from what William of Conches, for example, had written before him.

The ethical literature of the twelfth-century clerics culminates in the multi-faceted work of Alan of Lille, in which all the tendencies seem to come together. Heir to the Platonism of Chartres, he ended his days at Cîteaux in 1203. But he also inaugurates a new period: by his sermons and his manuals for preachers and confessors, and by his concern with the progress of heresy, which he refutes in the *De fide Catholica*, he laid the groundwork for the originality and success of the Mendicants. In addition, he left his mark on the allegorical poetic tradition, and in his *Liber de planctu naturae* (inspired by Boethius) and his *Anticlaudianus* (in which he argues against the poet Claudian), he anticipates Jean de Meun's *Roman de la rose*.[53] In *De planctu naturae*, which he wrote in prose, there is a meeting between the two allegorical figures of Nature and Temperance which provides us with a description of what are regarded as perfect bearing, dress and gesture: "Now while Nature was warmly welcoming her with glad conversation, behold, a matron, with moderate and measured gait, was seen to be directing her way toward us.... On her garments a picture showed with faithful characters what circumscription ought to be in the words of man, what circumspection in his deeds, what moderation in dress, what gravity in bearing, what bridling of the mouth in eating, what reproof of the throat in drink...." After *Temperantia* the superb female figure of *Largitas* approaches. "Her head did not bow humbly to the ground or bear a face cast down, but, with neck straight, fixed its gaze on things above, and kept the shaft of its vision for the heights.... The singular distinction of her beauty, the elegance of her unusual apparel, the individuality of her bearing [*gestus individualitas*] spoke openly of her arrival [*adventum*]."[54] Into a vocabulary that is frequently recondite and deliberately Hellenistic, Alan of Lille has slipped this strange word *individualitas*, the only time, so far as I am aware, that it is used in connection with gesture; the word carries none of the later connotations of individuality, but has to do with the theological and scientific debates of the period about the indivisibility of the atom: in this context it seems to specify the aesthetic quality of a physical movement so harmonious that it cannot be split up in any way.

In the *Anticlaudianus* the gifts of *modestia* are also described, this time in verse. "Even in giving she does not forget due measure"; "to the whole man she gives his bearing, tempers his actions, measures his speech, weighs his silences, balances his gestures [*gestus ponderat*], dresses him with propriety, curbs his senses.... She outlines the correct gestures of the head [*describit gestum capitis*], and gives the proper balance to the face, lest with face aloft, turning toward the beings above, he seems to spurn our mortal race and disdain to look upon our type of life, or with face turned overmuch to earth, show the signs of an inactive and vacant mind. It is raised, then, to a somewhat moderately controlled position and neither rises nor falls beyond due measure. She forbids buffoonish gestures [*scurriles gestus*], rejects an excessively grave gait lest wantonness betray the buffoon or excessive rigidness exhibit habitual pride, or lest scope is given to degenerate muscles, like those of buffoons, or some shameful gesture [*turpi gestu*] wound his arm."[55]

It may be that Alan of Lille allowed himself to be carried away by the poetry he was writing as he created these perfectly harmonious imaginary women, paragons of all the virtues; but the moral values they embody also informed and stimulated him to a quite different discourse, that of the preacher concerned to reform the habits of the faithful. Thus, he uses comparable language in his sermons to denounce pride which creates "close-fitting clothes, extravagant gestures [*exorbitat gestus*], exuberant language and lifted eyebrows."[56] In the *Summa de arte praedicatoria*, he contrasts the "monstrosity" of lust with the "perfume" of chastity, the sweet scent of which is composed of "purity of spirit, innocence of body, spotless gesture [*munditia in gestu*], modesty in clothing, abstinence in nourishment and deference in speech. It is a salve to combat lust, which sullies the spirit, soils the whole body and loosens gesture [*laxat gestum*].[57]

There is enough supporting evidence to remove all doubt that at the dawn of the thirteenth century the different currents of ethical literature, in the idea of *modestia*, are extolling a true virtue of ideal gesture, as the expression of internal harmony.[58] But these texts are too short or too scattered for us to be able to regard them as a complete *system* for the representation of gesture. We do find this, however, in the encounter between this literature and another, more specifically pedagogic, tradition: its high point is the *Institution of Novices* of Hugh of Saint-Victor (d. 1141).[59] It is not possible to embark here on an examination of this extremely interesting and, I think, historically crucial text; but there are nevertheless some concluding comments to be made about the circumstances surrounding the ethics of gesture at this particular moment of the twelfth century.

The "intellectual renaissance of the twelfth century," the renewal of familiarity with major classical authors such as Cicero and Seneca, is certainly an essential element in the explanation of the rediscovery of gesture as an object of thought and ethical consideration. But the history of ideas cannot be understood by reference to those ideas alone. The availability of this rediscovered intellectual equipment was itself the effect of critical social changes which occurred during the period. I shall content myself with listing a few of these factors, as follows: the resurgence of the city; the unprecedented opposition of clergy and laymen; the intensification of differences in status, function, social position and behavior (including among the clergy, i.e., between seculars and regulars, black friars and white friars, canons and so on); the disappearance of oblates, brought up within the monasteries from childhood, in favor of the recruitment of older novices who brought with them into the cloister a "worldly" use of gesture which was regarded a priori as sinful, and to be trimmed in the light of the clerical ideal of the golden mean; and also a new degree of attention paid to the body, which is no longer seen merely as the "prison-house of the soul," but regarded by moralists as capable, if well-governed, of becoming both the locus and a means of man's salvation. It seems, therefore, that a point of equilibrium was attained in the second half of the twelfth century. It was not long, however, before it was upset; after 1250, the rediscovery of Aristotle's *Ethics* somewhat changed the basis of learned interpretation of gesture. In addition, after the end of the twelfth century, lay and courtly milieus started to develop new codes of comportment which differed in form, but more often, perhaps, in the ideological issues that underlay them. Yet even there, for a long time to come, the discourse of gesture was principally an ethical one. To put it another way, the justification of "bearing" and "manners," like that of clerical *disciplina*, cannot but be external to the code itself, whether God, the soul, reason or chivalric virtue are invoked as its foundation. Just as, in fact, it could not be seriously argued today that the only reason for social conventions is that they exist.

NOTES

1. M. Mauss, "Body Techniques," in *Sociology and Psychology*, trans. B. Brewster (London, 1979), pp. 97-123.

2. These thoughts constitute the substance of one of the chapters of my forthcoming book on the history of Western medieval thought on gesture.

3. See esp. the contributions and introduction to *Gestures*, ed. J.-C. Schmitt, *History and Anthropology series* 1.1 (Nov. 1984), pp. 2-5. (This collection also contains the fundamental bibliography for the study of gesture in the social sciences.)

4. As in St. Augustine, in relation to prayer, and particularly in Hugh of Saint-Victor on the whole range of gesture (see below, nn.7 and 50).

5. P. Courcelle, *Connais-toi toi-même: De Socrate à Saint Bernard*, 3 vols. (Paris: Etudes Augustiniennes, 1974-75), vol. 1, p. 12. This precept and the two others ("Know thyself" and "Don't think yourself God") seem to have been first brought together in Euripides.

6. Juvenal, *Satires* 11.27. Terence, *Andria* 1.1. Macrobius, *Commentary on the Dream of Scipio*, trans. with introduction and notes by W.H. Stahl (New York, 1952).

7. Augustine, *De beata vita*, PL 32.975. Alcuin, *De rhetorica et virtutibus*, PL 101.943C.

8. Aristotle, *Nichomachean Ethics* 3.5.

9. Cicero, *De officiis* 1.5.15.

10. See J. Hellegouarc'h, *Le vocabulaire latin des relations et des partis politiques sous la République* (Paris, 1972), pp. 259-65.

11. Cicero, *De officiis* 1.5.35-36.

12. *Ibid.*

13. Seneca, *Lettres à Lucilius* 66.5, ed. F. Préchac & H. Noblot (Paris, 1947), pp. 116-17. Seneca adds that moderation (*modus*) implies proper proportions (*mensura*). Translator's note: The standard English translations are based on a text which varies from the one Schmitt uses here. I have therefore only referenced the French edition cited.

14. Macrobius, *Commentary* 1.8: "qui republicam cum prudentia, justitia, fortitudine ac moderentia tractaverunt." See also 8.7.

15. R. Thamin, *Saint Ambroise et la morale chrétienne au IVe siècle: Etude comparée des traités 'Des devoirs' de Cicéron et de Saint Ambroise* (Paris, 1895), p. 227. The expression "cardinal virtues" makes its first appearance in the *Expositio in Ev. sec. Lucam* 5.49 and 62; *PL* 15.1649, 1653.

16. 1 Cor. 13.13.

17. W. Hermanns, *Über den Begriff der Mässigung in der patristisch-scholastischen Ethik von Clemens von Alexandrien bis Albertus Magnus*, dissertation, Bonn, 1913.

18. Tertullian, *De cultu feminarum* (c. 202), translated as *La toilette des femmes*, ed. M. Turcan (Paris: Sources chrétiennes 173, 1971), pp. 138-39.

19. St. Ambrose, *De officiis ministrorum libri tres* 1.18-20 and 63; *PL* 16.46-53, 86-87.

20. *Ibid.*, 46B: "Nonne igitur ipsa natura est magistra verecundiae?"

21. *Ibid.*, 45B: "Motum natura informet. Si quid sane in natura vitii est, industria emendet; ut ars desit, non desit correctio."

22. J. Bugge, *Virginitas: An Essay in the History of a Medieval Ideal* (The Hague, 1975).

23. St. Ambrose, *De virginibus* 2.2.7; *PL* 16.209: "Virgo erat non solum corpore, sed etiam mente.... Nihil torvum in oculis, nihil in verbis procax, nihil in actu inverecundum: non gestus fractior, non incessus solutior, non vox petulantior; ut ipsa corporis species simulacrum fuerit mentis, figura probitatis." For an identical exposition, on the *verecundia* of women, see *De penitentia* 1.14.69, ed. R. Gryson (Paris: Sources chrétiennes 179, 1971), p. 110.

24. *Ibid.*, 48-49.

25. *Ibid.*, 49C: "Est etiam gressus probabilis, in quo sit species auctoritatis, gravitasque pondus, tranquillitatis vestigium."

26. Ennodius, "De vita et actibus S. Ambrosii ep.," *Carmina* 67: "...instituit populos gestu, probitate, pudore...."

27. See n.4.

28. St. Gregory, *Morales sur Job* 31.87, ed. R. Gillet and A. de Gaudemaris (Paris: Sources chré-

144

tiennes 32, 1952), p. 90. On the origins and history of these lists, see M.W. Bloomfield, *The Seven Deadly Sins* (Michigan, 1952).

29.   A. Rousselle, *Porneia: On Desire and the Body in Antiquity*, trans. Felicia Pheasant (New York: Basil Blackwell, 1988).

30.   Cassianus, *Collationes* 12; *De castitate* 9; *Interrogatio an corporis motus etiam dormientes possimus evadere*, *PL* 49.887-88.

31.   St. Gregory, *Moralia in Job* 19.25 and 32.5; *PL* 76.125-126 and 637-39.

32.   1 Cor. 12.30.

33.   See esp. M.C. Pouchelle, *Corps et chirurgie à l'apogée du Moyen Age: Savoir et imaginaire du corps chez Henri de Mondeville, chirurgien de Philippe le Bel* (Paris, 1983), pp. 181-83.

34.   On these treatises see H.H. Anton, *Fürstenspiegel und Herrscherethos in der Karolingerzeit* (Bonn: Bonner Historischer Forschungen 32, 1968), and P. Riche, *Ecoles et enseignement dans le Haut Moyen Age, de la fin du Ve siècle au milieu du IXe siècle* (Paris, 1979), p. 288.

35.   Martin of Braga, "Formula honestae vitae," in *Opera omnia*, ed. C.W. Barlow (New Haven, 1960), pp. 205-50.

36.   *Ibid.*, pp. 243-45: "Mobilis esto, non levis."

37.   *Ibid.*, p. 249: "Hac ergo mediocritatis linea continentiam observabis, ut nec voluptati deditus, prodigus aut luxuriosus appareas, nec avara tenacitate sordidus aut obscurus existas." Here too there is a noticeable "sexual" bias.

38.   P. Pascal, "The 'Institutionum Disciplinae' of Isidore of Seville," *Traditio* 13 (1957), pp. 425-31; and P. Riche, *Ecoles et enseignement*, pp. 390-91.

39.   Alcuin, *De rhetorica et virtutibus*, *PL* 101.942-45: "Dixi quia necessarie observandum est, ut recta sit facies, ne labra detorqueantur, ne immodicus hiatus distendat rictum, ne supinus vultus, ne dejecti in terram oculi, ne inclinata cervix, neque elata aut depressa supercilia.... Nam bonus modus est in loquendo, tamquam in ambulando, clementer ire, sine saltu, sine mora, quatenus omnia medii moderaminis temperantia fulgeant, quae est una de quatuor virtutibus.... Modestia est, per quam totius vitae modus seu animi seu corporis motibus ubique honesti cura servatur."

40.   *PL* 102.945-46.

41.   *PL* 106.258.

42.   J. Le Goff, *Les intellectuels au Moyen Age* (Paris, 1969).

43.   J.-C. Schmitt, "Gestus-gesticulatio: Contribution à l'étude du vocabulaire latin médiéval des gestes," in *La lexicographie du latin médiéval et ses rapports avec les recherches actuelles sur la civilisation du Moyen Age* (Paris: CNRS, 1981), pp. 377-90.

44. St. Bernard, "De consideratione ad Eugenium papam," in *Opera*, ed. J. Leclerc & H.M. Rochais (Rome, 1963), vol. 3, p. 426. Translated into English by G. Lewis as *On Consideration* (Oxford, 1908), pp. 58-59.

45. *Prov.* 6.12-13: "Perversus nuit oculo, terit pede, digito loquitur." The Vulgate has: "Homo apostata, vir inutilis...," and it is in the latter form that the verse is cited four times by Hugh of Saint-Victor in his *De institutione noviciorum*, *PL* 176.935C, 938C, 940C, 942D.

46. St. Bernard, "Liber de gradibus humilitatis et superbiae," in *Opera*, vol. 3. Translated into English by G.B. Burch as *The Steps of Humility* (Cambridge, 1940), pp. 181 and 201-03.

47. St. Bernard, *Sermones in Cantica Canticorum* 85.11; *PL* 176.935C, 938C, 940C, 942D.

48. P. Delhaye, "Une adaptation du *De officiis* au XIIe siècle," *Recherches de théologie ancienne et médiévale* 16 (1949), pp. 227-58.

49. William of Conches, *Moralis philosophia*, *PL* 171.1034-35, 1039.

50. Hugh of Saint-Victor, *De institutione noviciorum* 17; *Quomodo loquendum sit*, *PL* 176.948B. *Modestia* is also important in table manners: *ibid.*, 949C.

51. J.W. Baldwin, *Masters, Princes and Merchants: The Social Views of Peter the Chanter and his Circle*, 2 vols. (Princeton, 1970).

52. Peter the Chanter, *Verbum abbreviatum* 118; *De temperantia*, *PL* 205.501-02.

53. See esp. M.T. d'Alverny, *Alain de Lille: Textes inédits avec une introduction sur sa vie et ses oeuvres* (Paris, 1965); and Alain of Lille, *Liber poenitentialis*, ed. J. Longère (Louvain-Lille, 1965), vol. 1.

54. Alan of Lille, *De planctu naturae*, *PL* 210.473D-75A. Translated into English by D. Moffat as *The Complaint of Nature* (New York, 1908. Reprint: New Haven: *Yale Studies in English* 36, 1966), pp. 80-82, 176.

55. Alan of Lille, *Anticlaudianus*, *PL* 210.551-52. Translated into English and adapted by J. Sheridan, *Anticlaudianus* (Toronto, 1973), p. 177.

56. Alan of Lille, *Sermones diversi*, p. 260.

57. Alan of Lille, *Summa de arte praedicatoria* 5; *Contra luxuriam*, *PL* 210.122C; on *modestia*, see also 25.161-62.

58. There are a great number of other works which could be cited for the thirteenth and fourteen centuries: around 1230, for example, there is a long German poem, significantly entitled "Bescheidenheit" "Modesty": see Freidanks, *Bescheidenheit* (Leipzig, 1985). In the illuminations to a related manuscript, that of the *Welsche Gast* by Thomasin von Circlaere, Bescheidenheit is represented with Zucht (Discipline) kneeling before Recht (Law), (illus. 6). The baptistery sculptures at Parma, c.1200, show *prudentia* and *modestia* both associated with *spes*: see A. Katzenellenbogen, *Allegories of*

the Virtues and Vices in Medieval Art: From Early Christian Times to the Thirteenth Century (New York, 1964), p. 64 n.3.

59. On this, which I shall be dealing with in more detail, see my preliminary comments in Schmitt, "Le geste, la cathédrale et le roi," *L'Arc* 72 (1978), pp. 9-12.

From *Communications*, no. 46, Paris, Editions du Seuil, 1987.
Translated by Ian Patterson.

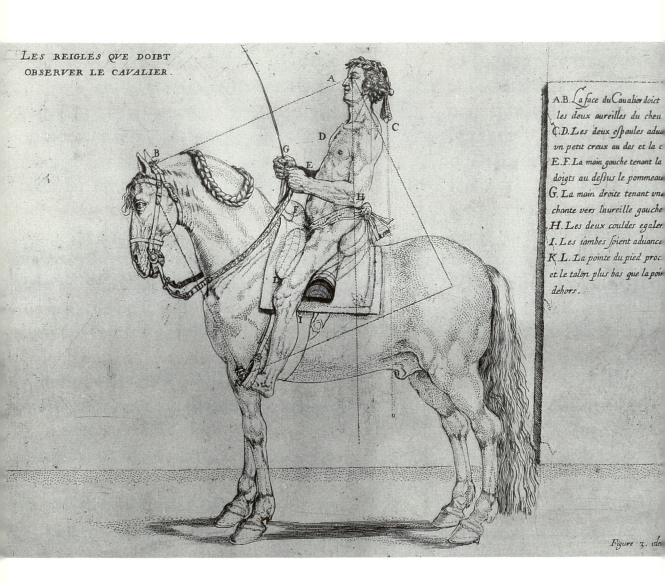

LES REIGLES QVE DOIBT
OBSERVER LE CAVALIER.

A.B. La face du Cavalier doict
les deux oureilles du cheu
C.D. Les deux espaules aduac
vn petit creux au dos et la c
E.F. La main gouche tenant la
doigts au dessus le pommeau
G. La main droite tenant vne
chante vers laureille gouche
H. Les deux couldes egaler
I. Les iambes soient aduance
K.L. La pointe du pied proc
et le talon plus bas que la poi
dehors.

Figure 3. ide

The rules that the rider should observe. From *Le manège royal de
M. Pluvinel*, Paris, 1623.

The Upward Training of the Body from the Age of Chivalry to Courtly Civility

Georges Vigarello

Civility and the Semiology of Rectitude

From the Middle Ages on, every failure of physical uprightness has been attributed to two main categories: the stigma of deformity, sanctioned by the attention given to strength and aesthetic qualities, and the lack of the proper deportment prescribed mainly by socialized ethics. In both cases, however, medieval comments were unpolished and hasty, even weak compared with those which would be made in the sixteenth century. The strongest and most valiant knight was lost if disabled — "he falls to the lowest level of public esteem"[1] — while a "straight neck"[2] was the sign of a physically sound individual. Nevertheless, more often than not descriptions were general, stressing overall strength: "generous, sincere, well-built, tall, strong, good-natured in his social relations...."[3] Strength was the first quality stressed: a powerful chest and shoulders were even more highly valued than beauty.[4] The soldier was to care for his body more than anyone else. He was expected to display intuitive and immediate stamina to a degree that became fixed in a stereotyped description. The representations of uprightness were conventional and nonanalytical. Strength and liveliness, even boisterousness, did not require detailed descriptions of all their component parts. The knights of Bertrand de Born, like legendary heroes, conformed to an ideal of strength that evoked, rather than dwelt on, the straight bearing of the body, suggesting overall images without analyzing them: descriptions did not linger on anatomical details; "an imposing stature"[5] said it all in a word.

Courtesy poems, which were quasi-pedagogical precepts for good manners, consider uprightness from another point of view, that of deportment. This literature was written for the upper levels of the aristocracy, those close to the great feudal lords. Only a few themes pertaining to posture are ever mentioned. Robert de Blois,

149

in *Le chastoiement des dames*, insists on the importance of walking with "straight" dignity, without scurrying or running.[6] Physical deportment, which is sketched hastily, is essentially moral in character. *Le Mesnagier de Paris* requires a lady to "walk without looking or turning her gaze toward any man or woman who might be to the right or to the left."[7] Uprightness seems to be mentioned here exclusively in relation to the eyes.

The many *Convenances de table* (table manners), which made up a large part of the courtesy books, condemn leaning on one's elbows as well as slumping on one's upper body: "Listen. Don't lean on your elbow."[8] In *Urbain le Courtois*, a poem which, in a series of well-crafted and easily memorized lines, summarizes the rules for living for young noblemen in the service of a great lord, an upright position at the table is, in fact, the only reference to posture: "Before his lord, at a meal, he should not lean on the table."[9]

When deportment is mentioned in these courtesy poems, it is as both a very general and a moral quality. It goes beyond simple physical posture: one's clothes must be proper, just like one's body: "Keep your mouth, hands, teeth and body clean, both inside and out."[10] One's posture as a whole must also show, together with a certain degree of self-possession, an attitude of humility. English texts, which were taken up in Furnival's *The Babees Book*, are written in the same style as their French equivalents:

Stand til you are told to sit

Keep your head, hands and feet quiet

Don't scratch yourself.[11]

To keep within bounds and avoid gesticulating are the main implications of the remarks concerning posture. The future knight must first be in control of his movements. His deportment has to reflect such an ability. The theme of uprightness is sketched, rather than drawn precisely; it is more implicit than explicit. It is suggested in a few words, blended into the image of a bearing that will leave humility as its main impression. The rule of Saint Augustine, as put forward by Hugh of Saint Victor, is an extreme example, in that it is also an ecclesiastical view of the same proper way of living. "Let there be nothing in your demeanor, your countenance, your attire, your gestures or your movements that might offend anyone."[12] The physical description remains rather vague, arrived at mainly through a moral evaluation.

One's bearing must be circumspect. Such admonitions are not really surprising, except for their rather naive simplicity. They were repeated faithfully in subsequent texts dedicated to the same subjects. They do, however, show a cultural trend away from the more brutal and triumphant images at which the descriptions of knights seemed to hint. The cleric was here to take the lead over the soldier, restraint over adventure, caution over impulsiveness. In fairness, both dimensions are present, each in its own simplification. Courtesy was imposing discipline on a caste whose ideal of physical violence had some parallels in its posture. It did it soberly, by dictating behavior and the position of the body.

In the sixteenth century this mechanism became more pronounced. New needs corresponded to a change in sensibility, whose reference point, while no longer necessarily that of the clergy, conformed to principles of moderation and reserve. The latter would continue to grow. Discussions on the subject were broadened to include matters previously unmentioned or expressed in other ways. A new court nobility was being established as the world of chivalry faded, and the emergence of a formal etiquette and a courtier class seemed to generate rules of deportment for the body. Whereas until then the straight back never went beyond a mere suggestion, a new awareness of it arose. This does not imply, of course, that the Middle Ages had no concerns about posture. It is simply that they appear generalized and imprecise compared with equivalent texts of later periods.

Beginning with the sixteenth century, a changed culture regulated the behavior of the nobility, which, in order to define itself, invented the idea of civility. Erasmus's treatise on civility[13] reflects the shift brought about by the courts of the sixteenth century in such rules for living. Similarly, Castiglione's *The Book of the Courtier*[14] was to be the much-published bible of a nobility that was introducing a detailed etiquette. These books of etiquette, soon to become textbooks, are still shocking in some of their remarks, which today are considered unseemly and crude.[15] But the mention of physical posture is an undeniable change from the courtly literature.

An entire chapter is dedicated to the "body's proper deportment," and it looks into each of the parts involved, with a view no longer cursory or general. The exhortation is still moral, but the requirements are more demanding: "The child is not to sink his head between his shoulders, as this shows arrogance; rather, he should hold himself upright effortlessly, as this shows grace. And he should not tilt his head to the side like a hypocrite except when necessary to express his meaning."[16] Outward appearance reflects a moral attitude. Civility obeys social rules. More than ever before, careful attention is given to posture and uprightness. The latter shows one's worth; its opposite indicates the traditional faults: hypocrisy, pride, laziness, etc. There was no list of postures in previous books, as if the body's positions could not yet be defined. It is difficult for the body to emerge in language when it is a matter of describing its behavior, the movements of its parts or the meaning of its deportment. In order to analyze this daily space, one must distance oneself from it. However, the body is often too involved in its immediate and unreflected actions to easily allow for an overview. For that reason the precision of this list and these descriptions is noteworthy.

Such categories also express the opinion, long considered trite, which holds that posture indirectly reveals a person's "inner depths." A familiar semiology quickly locates the place of the shoulders and of the head, and sets down the prerequisites for a typology. It states the flaw, and at the same time the "rectifying" precept. Education is summed up here in a reminder. Rectitude takes form through the errors conjured up. Despite the obvious sharper focus of the descriptions, it is still difficult to define a standardized learning progression. Saying is the same as doing. The latter consists of "holding oneself straight without effort."[17] Such a notion belongs to everyday life and is considered as intuitively given. The pupil is invited to obey, in order to comply with a morality of propriety. The precept becomes a rule to be applied immediately and directly, without any preliminary practice, without "working" on the positions. At most, it is accompanied by some justifications, but, apart from being new, these are sketchy: on the one hand, there are failings, things that shouldn't be done, and, on the other hand, there is a notion of "gracefulness,"[18] which must be respected.

The issue, however, is no longer just a moral one. There is now a threat that was not present in medieval texts. Books on manners in the sixteenth century attribute to posture a dimension that could already be classed as personal hygiene. A bad positioning of the torso, should it become habitual in a child, is considered physically dangerous. Bad posture results in the risk of a "hump":

> If neglected in boyhood, bodily habits of this sort become ingrained and deform the natural posture of the body. Accordingly, those who through laziness have acquired the habit

of hunching their bodies are ensuring for themselves a humpback which nature has not bestowed, and those who have become used to holding their heads to one side grow fixed in that habit, with the result that their efforts to alter it in later life are to no avail.[19] The "abnormal" curvature, when held for too long, becomes fixed, as if it were set in plaster. Without a doubt the stigma attached to the hunchback is even greater. The deformity here goes beyond cold pathology.[20] It is steeped in the fantasy of illness or deformation, an implicit threat which is considered edifying. Such a danger, which weighs on the future of the body of a child who neglects his posture, only reinforces the prescription.

Erasmus's book of manners, dedicated to the son of a prince, inspired many translations and texts which almost paraphrased it, until the end of the eighteenth century. Most of these inevitably mention bad postures that soon change in their nature, and deform and uglify the entire body beyond its nature.[21]

Thus, the sixteenth century appears to establish for the nobility a stricter control over posture and the right position. The great Italian treatises, which were also published in many French editions, when outlining the rules of behavior for the new nobility, dwell on these geometric and measured descriptions. "Moreover... you should know that men are wonderfully desirous of beauty, proportion and decorum. And, conversely, they avoid as much as possible that which is heavy, shapeless and deformed."[22] Posture must reflect this desire. Geometry and a mathematically constructed perspective have already transformed the painter's point of view. To the golden number are added a setting forth of plans, a division into simple forms. Marquetry, for example, and the way in which it organized a space which is orderly and precise, helped to spread the new models: "We see here a mathematical model specifically creating its own object. The plan for a perspective is a checkerboard: in the construction sketches we start with a regular grid pattern, and identical rectangles juxtaposed to each other generate, as they become more distant, similar triangles. Nothing is better suited to marquetry."[23] The sixteenth century was all the more ready to generalize such a view because there was a history of it during the preceding century.[24] The new insistence on a "well-proportioned" posture finds a theory. The distinctly Platonic reference occasions a translation of the stiffening rules concerning physical uprightness. Not only does "bad" posture pose a permanent threat to physical appearance, but the "good" one, because of the symbolism of the relations here at play, requires strengthening. The sixteenth century's enthusiastic belief in proportion is the justification for new requirements concerning physical bearing. The body's microcosm must evoke, by the subtleties and wealth of measures and relationships among its parts, those of the world at large. The new educational approach to posture and to a straight body broadens its references until it summons up a geometry of the universe, thus giving greater credibility to the new rules. But the treatises on the rules of civility did not go into the details of proportion, which appear as very generalized and accepted principles: the difference between elegance and deformity should be immediately apparent. Sixteenth-century pedagogy could not avoid the general tendency of that century's epistemology: duplication and similarity. In its proportions the body must evoke relationships which go beyond it. However, what appears possible in the creation of a perspective and in the development of the design of spatial depth becomes more formidable when applied to human or animal bodies. A structured visualization of their morphological architecture presupposes familiarity with mechanics and functional anatomy, which a mystical belief in proportion could not provide. There is no doubt that such tendencies relied more on speculation than on empirical proof.[25] Nonetheless, they are still referred to in the case of visible and tangible transformations.

When books of manners mention clothes, they no longer stress the neatness and modesty that clothes are supposed to reveal; instead, they are interested in form. The garment must be adaptable; it must "fall nicely on the body."[26] This effort to make the cloth structure match the body's evokes, in turn, "decorum and proportion."[27] Such remarks do not condemn all costumes of the fourteenth and fifteenth centuries as entirely inelegant. They simply fill a silence, for clothes are not referred to in their more formal aspects in courtly poetry. The fact that they are mentioned in treatises on behavior confirms that more attention was being paid to posture, since the fit of the cloth would allow any faults of posture to be noticed more easily. The sixteenth century saw the appearance for the first time of rigid corsets with whalebone stays, worn especially by women. These can be dated, because Rabelais, in describing the women of Thelemos, and taking his inspiration from the clothes worn at the court of Francis I, does not yet mention the rigid corset: "Over their smocks they wore a corset [*vasquine*] of pure silk camblet; and over this a farthingale [*verdugale*] of white, red, brown, gray or some other color, on top of which was a silver taffeta skirt embroidered with gold thread and close-patterned needlework...."[28] The coat was a bodice, certainly a tight-fitting one, but made of cloth, and imposing only a slight firmness. On the other hand, around the middle of the sixteenth century, this part of the attire gradually began to be made of more rigid materials, which molded the bust and back according to a set shape. Henry Estienne described the new practices: "The ladies call a whalebone (or something else, in the absence of the latter) their stay, which they put under their breast, right in the middle, in order to keep straighter."[29] An example can be seen in a sixteenth-century painting in the Museum of Rennes, *A Ball at the Court of Henry III*: the whalebone corset from the end of that century gives a very striking conical shape to the dancers' torsos. The attempt to impose a particular line, as well as proportion to the bust, leads finally to an inflexible mold. What began with adherence to lines of the body results eventually in the opposite: the imposition of a conventional shape. The garment no longer follows the outline of what it covers; on the contrary, it imposes its own shape. Rigid sheath dresses enclose torsos that are meant to be slender and straight. "To get a slim body, Spanish style, what torture do they not endure, tight-laced and braced, until they suffer great gashes in their sides, right to the live flesh — yes, sometimes even until they die of it."[30]

Sartorial culture changed in one way by granting privilege to rigidity and rectitude, as well as to geometric shape. It complements other indicators which show a new awareness of a straight body. The court nobility, whose example and influence, at least on the aristocracy, are not to be neglected, brought attention to the straightening of posture. Deportment has become more rigorous. To the social process is added a passionate discussion of the principles which revealed measures and proportions, even though they might be very theoretical and, in fact, more verbal than verifiable.

The Ambiguities of Physical Exercise

Pedagogical practice resorts to the formal precept of bodily uprightness and of a controlled deportment in spelling out various reasons for respecting them. It is a threat that demands an appropriate response. But this strong interest in improved appearance is not accompanied by well-developed and organized training. First, the position is simply mentioned much more often than it is actually shown in each of its components. And when pedagogical practice resorts to a series of exercises, their indirect influence on posture is more implicit than detailed: they are a preparation for "gracefulness." To say that the body must be held straight is never really sufficient if we do not add that it must be done "gracefully." The latter notion, which appeared in the sixteenth century, somewhat loosely encompasses that which has a noble bearing and which tends toward a measured balance. It is "nothing more than a certain light which emanates from a beautiful gathering of well-ordered things, well distributed with one another and as a whole. And, without such a proportion, that which is good would not be beautiful, nor beauty pleasant."[31] The terms "gracefulness" and "grace," through which the aristocracy was attempting to define itself even in its physical deportment, mean especially what achieves such "perfection" without appearing to, without a trace of artifice or perceptible effort. It is the opposite of affectation. It appears to have become second nature:

> Having already thought a great deal about how this grace is acquired, and leaving aside those who are endowed with it by their stars, I have discovered a universal rule which seems to apply more than any other in all human actions or words: namely, to steer away from affectation at all costs, as if it were a rough and dangerous reef.[32]

Excellence should in no way show the care which leads to it. It should truly become second nature. The nobleman should carry it as a sign of his breeding.

Certainly it is difficult for such texts, which attempt to demonstrate the prestige of a social class, to admit that aristocratic elegance can be learned. Bearing and presence should be hereditary, just like a title of nobility. They should suffice to confirm the name they symbolize. The body becomes a matter of lineage mainly when it is heavily laden with demonstrative value, in short, when one's breeding is evident in one's physical bearing. This is not, however, totally foreign to some exercise: "However, although it is almost proverbial that grace cannot be learned...I say that if anyone is to acquire grace as a sportsman or athlete (first assuming that he is not disqualified by Nature) he should start young and learn the principles from the best teachers."[33] Thus, teaching is possible, as a last resort, and it will make use of the "exercises" of the nobility: fencing, riding and dancing.

But the role of exercise, however well accepted, was to remain paradoxically imprecise. Although books on proper behavior do mention a few details about correct posture, they only describe gracefulness as a "halo" which should envelop a

person's bearing. To learn it was to learn a way of being. And the educational theory was based essentially on this. Thus, posture no longer receives any very specific
mention, but is blended into a larger picture. The language remains allusive. It refers
to what seems to be understood as normal behavior, using general terms that cover
implicit truths which only practice could uncover as accepted manifestations. The
body is only suggested, a vague place where a gesture says more than the words
attempting its definition. Ultimately, precision could appear to be superfluous: a
few banal words illustrate, and remind us of, familiar scenes where the body is lived
more than it is spoken: "Notice how ungraceful a rider is when he forces himself to
sit bolt upright in the saddle, as is said, in the Venetian way, in comparison with
another who sits on his horse as free and relaxed as if he were on the ground."[34]
Posture is shown in negative terms. The indicators envelop a whole, a reality that
stands up more to a glance than to an analysis. We are here referring, of course, to
general bearing. After being described in the texts on deportment, the upright stance
loses some of its precision in the texts that list the exercises.

Nor is the action of the good teacher described. The very empirical reporting
shows that exercise makes one more "adroit, light, healthy and full of energy,"[35]
and that it does affect the body's posture, which is the only thing being considered
here. The sphere of the body does not refer to those concepts which clarify the
details of the educational practices involved with it. The glance that "sees" the difference brought about by exercise is based on an immediate perception. And, most
of all, even though implicit, the mechanism behind the action of the latter does
not seem to constitute an indispensable precision. The evocation of this action
on posture is always indirect, that is, intuitive. One may even wonder, at times,
whether exercise does not require good physical proportions, as it encourages them:
"Dances are intended to show whether a lover is healthy and energetic, and at the
end he is allowed to kiss his mistress."[36] The relative precision in the description
of posture given in the manuals is not matched by an equal precision concerning
the effects of exercise.

The fact is that the body, just like its uprightness, is "caught" in a web of categories dominated by moral expectations. Deportment corresponds to the great
polarities in behavior, where respect for physical bearing has the same psychological basis as knowing how to be polite. Such implicit comparisons make physical

exercise, as well as the details of its actions, secondary. This is also because there are no mechanical categories that could make posture a precisely detailed construction, held up by a structure of bones and muscles where static and dynamic forces are joined. Deliberate muscular activity and its balancing function are unknown and unformulated.

The interpretation of the body within the framework of movement is illuminating. When Thibault,[37] in a sixteenth-century work on fencing, compares the physical proportions proposed by Leonardo with those proposed by Dürer, it is not really for the purpose of showing the morphological perfection which the practice of fencing aims to achieve. The ideal shape of the body is not a point of reference inspiring any transformations which might result from particular movements. It is not one of the guiding principles of the pedagogical approach. According to a logic which is foreign to that of mechanics, the controversy concerning proportions has as its sole purpose an abstract and Pythagorean establishment of displacements and guidelines to be followed by the limbs in order to ensure an efficient gestural technique:

> Just as the above-mentioned artists, architects, perspective draftsmen and others have tried to show the bases for their rules in the proportions of man's body, so have we kept the same course, but with a better aim, and we have found, to assist the same compass,[38] the true and proportional measurement of all movements, of all times and distances needing observation in our practice, as you will be shown very shortly in the declaration of our circle, where the measurements and proportions of man are applied to man himself and to the movements he makes with his own limbs, and where the proportion is found, without which it would be impossible for him to carry out the slightest action in the world.[39]

Speculation concerning the center of the body and the circles it might rule led to a hierarchy of circular movements from which attack and defense would be organized. The joints of the limbs are not taken into account in the theoretical calculation that aims to define such movements. Moreover, the dominant image is "roundness," reflecting what supposedly belongs to the universe and, consequently, imposing to excess, for each displacement, the outline of an arc of a circle:

> At present we shall say that it is also round and circular in the shape of its movements... which can be understood both with regard to natural actions and operations from within, and their secondary alterations, so reciprocal, and following one another, that one cannot find the beginning nor the end, except in the roundness of a circumference, and

with reference to the image of all localized movements going around in a circle which widens from the center of its force to the extreme circumference of its weakness.[40] Displacements cannot thus really be analyzed. They are ruled by an analogy which deforms the perception both of their direction and of their intensity.[41]

In short, exercise can affect the morphological structures even less insofar as these structures comprise ratios that are different in nature: those of relative bone length with those which can be linked with posture, such as the line of the hips and of the shoulders; in other words, proportions related to muscle development, and others that cannot be altered. Some very important points of reference are set on the surface of the body in places that have no relation to the skeletal structure or the muscular attachments (the navel, the breasts, etc.). They are chosen because of their visibility or because they relate to a number made absolute in advance: "the very perfect number ten is constantly set before his eyes, in its entirety, on his own fingers."[42] The body is thus surveyed according to relations established outside of it, or found on the limbs as a function of a "formulation" that is simply "striking" or even "troubling." It is a picture, or a wrapper, before being a structure struggling against weight. It displays the outline of a surface, not the lines of a structure. Markings are useful to the painter, who treats them as figures. Therefore, such a picture inspires an educational theory closer to that of drawing than of posture. The proportions that can be read on the grid where the body lies help the pencil to reproduce the human body with some accuracy, but they do not necessarily explain what causes it to be straight or to bend. One can understand why referring to them does not enable Thibault to specify more accurately any possible improvement in posture, or to visualize it clearly. One can also better understand how a Pythagorean view simply points to the formal indication of movement, detached from anything mechanical or practical.

Although more promising and better informed, some of Leonardo Da Vinci's intuitions suffer from the same limitations. He briefly mentions two different upright stances, distinguishing between those with an arched back and those with a straight back. But there are no indications showing such differences, except on the frontal surfaces, where they lose any element of interest relative to questions of posture: "The loins or backbone being bent, the breasts are always lower than the shoulder blades of the back. If the breast bone is arched the breasts are higher than the shoul-

From Girard Thibault, *Académie de l'espée où se démonstrent la théorie et la pratique du maniement des armes*, 1628 (Paris, Bibliothèque nationale).

E   F

G   H

N. 4
N. 3
N. 2
N. I

Tabula. III.

From Girard Thibault, *Académie de l'espée où se démonstrent la théorie et la pratique du maniement des armes*, 1628 (Paris, Bibliothèque nationale).

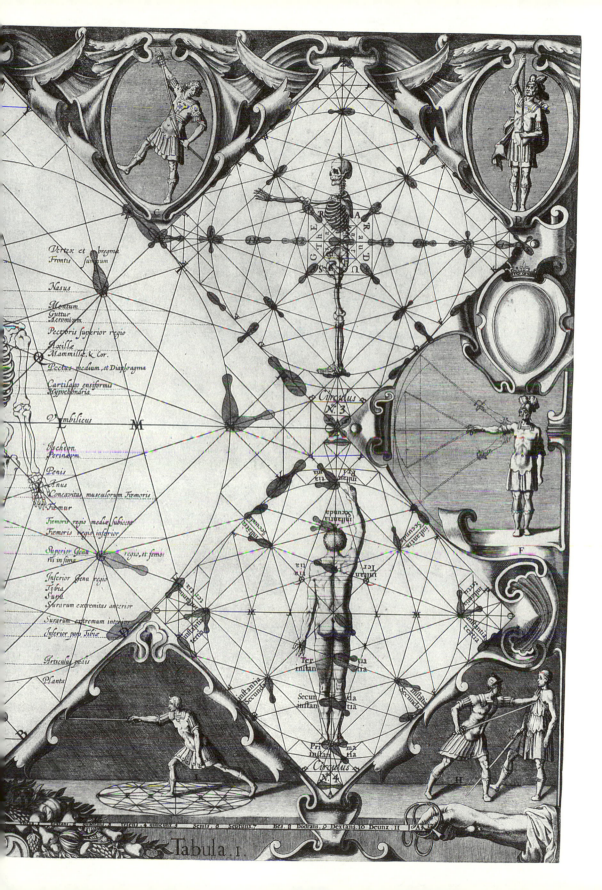

Vertex et bregma
Frontis summum

Nasus

Mentum
Guttur
Acromium

Pectoris superior regio
Axillæ
Mammillæ, & Cor.

Pectus medium, et Diaphragma

Cartilago ensiformis
Hypochondria

Umbilicus

Ischion
Perinæum

Penis

Anus
Concavitas musculorum Femoris

Femur

Femoris regio mediæ subiecta
Femoris regio inferior

Superior Genu
ris in sima regio, et femo:

Inferior Genu regio
Tibia
Sura
Surarum extremitas anterior

Surarum extremum interius
Inferior pars Tibiæ

Articulus pedis

Planta

Circulus N. 3

Circulus N. 4

Tabula I.

From Girard Thibault, *Académie de l'espée où se démonstrent la théorie et la pratique du maniement des armes*, 1628 (Paris, Bibliothèque nationale).

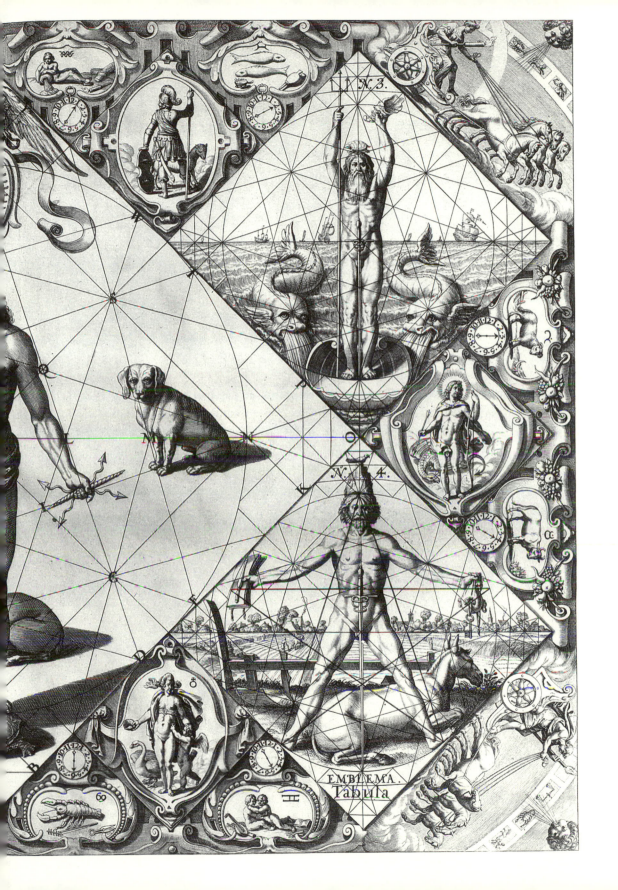

EMBLEMA.
Tabula

der blades. If the loins are upright the breast will always be found at the same level as the shoulder blades."[43]

One notices two types of positions, which is important at a time when there is very little differentiation among postures that are close to normal, but the superficial indicators conceal those that could explain the structure. The description speaks casually of peripheral outlines. Mention is made of the breasts which are visible at skin level, but their relationship to the morphological structure is in no way apparent.

Even when the back becomes associated with mechanical references in a world in which a "science of engineers"[44] is being established, these references are isolated and are more figurative than operational. According to a design that goes beyond simple metaphor, the muscles of the spine act like a brace to maintain one's uprightness.[45] But the design of these braces sets the upper parts in a position of privilege in comparison with the lower ones, and it does not show how the forces are layered in order to guarantee an upright position. Leonardo is also aware of certain dynamic aspects. His descriptions suggest the presence of precise forces; for example, muscles support the backbone so that it does not bend when a man lowers or lifts his heavy head.[46] Such a statement seems to suggest that the foundations are being laid for an anatomical analysis of movement and posture, as well as certain principles of straightening which have a modern air about them. However, practice does not yet correspond to those still uncertain descriptions. The latter are not retained in the strategy for straightening where more archaic descriptions replace them. Despite appearances, mechanical perspective is still incomplete and fragmented. It is largely secondary in the perceptions of the body, which is seen as a network of proportions that are more speculative than objectively verified, or which becomes, like any microcosm, "rocks, lakes and tides."[47] Galen had already mentioned exercises that would strengthen the spine:

> And so also when, approaching from the side another who bends toward him and throwing one's arms in a circle around his hips, one lifts him like a burden and holds him up and carries him forward; and the more, if one should bend forward and back while carrying him: for thus one would perfectly prepare the whole spine for strength.[48]

The author refers here to strengthening, not to straightening, which is never mentioned, but he does give organically localized details. Yet, however important such details might have been in inspiring a possible corrective work, they were without consequence for him. And during the sixteenth century the body is represented as a massive whole of "flesh" and bones, whose firmness and hardness are enhanced by exercise, rather than as an interplay of levers operated by muscles. Thus, the effects of an analytical and organized fragmentation as well as repetition of exercises, which would today be considered obvious, is not privileged. There is no investigation of muscular "work." The effective action of muscles is not immediately apparent to the eye that observes the moving body.

On the other hand, the role attributed to exercise is general rather than specific, diffuse rather than specialized. Exercise acts through a global process of purification of humors and strengthening by drying, where the more precise and directed dynamics of the muscles do not appear to be central. There is no prominence given to any very localized activity, limited to a particular and structured aspect of behavior. There are no special straightening exercises, but the figure can be strengthened by a subtle and very extensive purification. Exercise is not suggested as an analytical perfection of muscles, but rather as a code of hygiene: "The nature of his body... by means of strength and virtue of movement, which heated him and made him sweat and digest his food better by cleansing, without his realizing it, the excesses of his lazy body, began gradually to be well disposed, healthy and strong at the end of that summer."[49]

Lastly, there is no mention of muscle in a case in which this silence can be directly linked to the problem of straightening. City girls wear bandaging in order to perfect their figures; country girls, who are freer, grow differently. The former risk deformity by an excess of constriction, while among the latter "you never see one with a hunched back."[50] But the strength acquired by the latter through greater freedom of movement is not referred to by Paré, as it will be in the eighteenth century.[51] It is not the exercising of one's physical strength which is emphasized and discussed here, but rather the wrong placing of harmful bandages on city children. Country girls have taken advantage of the absence of constricting ties that attempt to mold the female body and that sometimes deform it through excessive tightness. The advantage is defined only in negative terms. The discussion takes on an apparent "Rousseauistic" form, although it does not have the same principles of application. The bandage deforms only because it is liable to become a bad mold, not because it weakens by limiting movement. Thus, movement is not seen as having a possibly corrective function. Once more the importance of exercise is not clearly emphasized.

We can understand that the prime element of the educational theory is still the repetition of essentially ethical rules of rectitude. It seems dedicated to docile imitation and nonverbal response. Exercise, whether too vague or too much ignored, is only mentioned discretely. The preceding example draws from it simply a renewed awareness: a vast field remains which one cannot call foreign to education, where an adult will manipulate a child's body in order to improve the shape of its figure and the firmness of its position, and where "city girls" must submit to the demanding pressures of tight clothing.

The Malleable Clay of the First Years

An adult's hand is still the best craftsman of straightness. The measure of good posture and of an assured stance seems rather linked to an early strengthening of positions. One must go back to the earliest moments of childhood in order to better solidify and set a shape, to impose correction as early as possible so as to impose the model more rigidly. Posture is among the precautions that surround the very young. Here, educational theory dreams of a force that can be directly applied to the body of an infant. Are not things of the body "material," and do not all actions pertaining to them resemble actions applied to an object?

Earliest childhood becomes the favored straightening time. It is the period during which the body seems to take its shape. The weakness of that age gives rise to the notion of a malleable body subjected to any correction or adjustment. This pedagogical approach rests on reductional and transformational manipulations performed upon a passive mass that seems as soft as clay. The clay body of the baby generates the vision of perfect straightening and on those same grounds justifies preventive diligence. More than others, it risks the metamorphoses of deformation. It is overflowing with humors. Hippocrates defines it as an excess of the hot and aqueous.[52] Thus, the bones threaten to slip out of their assigned places. A constant danger hangs over the articulations, which are described as saturated with dampness. Here, the sixteenth century is faithfully repeating its Hippocratic sources. In a certain sense, in fact, it rediscovers them and rationalizes their application.[53] Expert and repeated manipulation thus ensures the two goals which straightening aimed to achieve until now: to avoid all vertebral deformation or displacement and to guarantee the elegance of a controlled posture. The early application of this double precaution, in the materiality of its elementary and precise gestures, confirms in turn the aesthetic categories, just as it does, in the longer term, those of decorum and, most of all, those of the hygiene of a strong body.

Shapes will become the object of a true blending. Treatises on childhood diseases are the first to mention precepts concerning an upright posture. The precautions it requires and the gestures it calls for are all entrusted to texts that claim to be therapeutic but whose preventive and educational aims cannot be denied. They outline a picture of life whose daily habits are inculcated into the child. They draw up a list of attention which surrounds him and which should not only preserve the proper shape of the limbs and the body's upright posture, but should also refine them.

The fact that works on childhood diseases are now a separate group and that their advice is no longer dispersed among other writings indicates that a new place is being granted to childhood, and herein lies the importance, in this context, of the late fifteenth century and the sixteenth century.[54] In Hippocrates, the mention of the care of children is scattered among aphorisms and the work as a whole. Soranus of Ephesus,[55] whose remarks on the subject seem to be the most complete in the ancient world, only touches on it indirectly in reference to the care of women. Until the sixteenth century, the child appears as an inseparable physical dependent of its mother. Medical science does not really set children apart from adults. Texts specifically dedicated to the actions with which they were to be surrounded and cared for are a turning point. The very act of collecting written material on these indicates the desire to make a distinction. The material is limited, however, to the procedures and precautions dictated by ancient texts, and it concentrates on infants.

The texts point out, first of all, how malformed positions are stamped onto such unsettled shapes. The body becomes more solid as it grows, affected by awkward pressures. It registers in its waxy bones those contacts which exert too much pressure. All abruptness is said to be the cause of deformity. To allow a child to walk too early is to risk seeing his legs bend like bows. The same can be said of certain carrying habits: "Such a defect can occur when a wet-nurse habitually carries the child only on one arm, and presses its knees against her in a bowed fashion."[56] The shapes of infants and their future are threatened. Improper influences put an indelible stamp on them.

The proliferation of images evoked by a body immersed in a liquid environment generates, on the other hand, processes that impose their physical molding in order to imprint, or preserve, the shapes that are judged proper; this involves substituting some "abruptnesses" for others. The newborn child shall be carefully inspected, so that no deformity will escape the attention of the nurse. In the case of a deficiency, "modifying" action is required without delay. The strengthening of the joints, which is implied by this action, seems all the easier as the suppleness of the anatomical elements involved appears to be ideally suited to them. The gradual loss of the moisture of the bones will soon make that impossible. The period after birth is ideal for straightening. The power to correct this ductile clay which so passively submits to the mold appears boundless:

> Is there a time during which the bones are more obedient, whether one wishes to compress, or to bend, or to stretch them at will, than that incontinent period after birth; then they are soft and tender, but with the passing of time they will become hard and stiff, both for internal reasons, such as the natural heat which extracts humidity, and for external reasons, such as air and wind, which are very drying, as well as other things one encounters from the outside.[57]

All the analogies with hardening clay are present, suggesting a feeling of undeniable power over the subject. The child is "shaped" by the surgeon or even by the nurse. A sixteenth-century author goes so far as to call such manipulations "de facienda infante."[58] The treatise by Soranus contains a complete list, in which it is difficult to distinguish between shaping action and prevention. By "easily" repositioning vertebrae, the physician's hand "molds" the spine of the newborn: "One shall give a full hand massage, while the torso is kept in traction, in order to give it a proper shape."[59] But the straightening action is applied indiscriminately to all infants. It creates a shape, as well as guarantees against deviation:

> The index and the middle finger, when applied above the buttocks, dig a graceful depression, and the hands, when applied onto the upper parts of the cervical vertebrae, and when pressed forward act so that there will not be a forward curvature of the spine; and the same should be done in the dorsal region, opposite the diagram where hunching often occurs, so that all vertebrae are alike.[60]

The rules of physical appearance are directly applied by the physician's hands. Molding is a prerequisite for social recognition. The child enters an environment that appears to need to impress on him very concretely a predetermined model. In order to do so, it is necessary to have codified gestures. Straightening the body also means shaping it. Here again the body passively receives the "sign" of uprightness. Such manifestations are joined by others, always founded on the supposed quality of the body's substance.

The role of baths obeys, in turn, the pattern of representing a malleable form. The analogy with clay, although not formulated, is understood: the longer the drying of the earth is delayed, the longer it remains changeable. Bones can be straightened better when baths have increased their suppleness, by keeping their texture soaking in fluids. And the application of water dissolves all superficial agglomeration that might impede movement and favor dislocation. It is indirectly invested with correcting powers:

> As, in truth, there is nothing which so well and so gently cleanses the body of all its filth, nor so easily removes weariness, nor melts coagulated and bruised blood and prevents it from swelling[61] and from becoming purulent, nor which helps so much to straighten the position of the head and of the other limbs, while still preserving the softness of the bones.[62]

Swaddling clothes take the place of the hands in order to supply a firmly held straight bearing. They achieve the corrective action with a patient continuity. They fix the positions acquired: "After the child's limbs have been set straight, as they should be, and his skin strengthened, he must then be swaddled and wrapped."[63] The swaddling clothes themselves are endowed with corrective power. The soft matter on which they act can only submit to that power. This doughy mass, as the infant's body is seen to be, allows us to imagine, beyond a simple dislocation, deformations of the bones on which the constant pressure of well-applied bands should be able to exercise some power. The analogy with clay led inevitably to that of a corrective mold. Swaddling clothes, in their turn, impose the proper shape: "Concerning arms and legs, should they be poorly shaped, either bent or twisted, they shall be straightened with small strips and compresses, or else put right; similarly, in the case of a protruding spine or chest."[64]

Swaddling clothes, in the end, frustrate the forces that threaten the desired shape

of the body. The theory of humors, which attributed the constant possibility of deformity to the weakness of the child's bones, makes it impossible to dispute the use of
swaddling clothes. They must be applied to the limbs and to the torso of all infants.
This perseverance reinforces even the fragile substance of the child's body. By surrounding the flesh with constant pressure, the bands solidify it. The pressure gives
the limbs the lasting consistency of the ties, while avoiding forced positions. The
body is solidified, just like certain objects that we hold tightly: "The daily binding
of the limbs makes the nerves stronger, so that ankylosis cannot intervene."[65] Such
preventive vigilance is, however, accompanied by some precautions. Should the swaddling clothes be applied incorrectly, they could be counterproductive. Their role
itself is what demands a critical examination. A bad mold can only result in ques-
tionable replicas. Similarly, defective swaddling clothes could create deformities and
a curved spine. Soranus, as well as Galen, stressed such deficiencies as the reason
why a number of deformations become permanent. "Moreover, stenosis of the ducts
may arise from inflammation, or scirrhus, or obstruction or compression of the surrounding parts, or occlusion of their orifices."[66] Excessive compression can, by itself,
prevent food from reaching the body's organs, with results similar to those of a defective shape of the bands.

The precautions apply to both the material used and its position on the place that
is deformed or is to be "protected." Soranus's work refers to ancient texts (and to
their sixteenth-century copies) in his preoccupation with obeying this double need:

> Each part of the body has its particular shape, to which an appropriate binding must be
> adapted.... Clean woolen strips should be used, soft and not too worn, some having
> the width of three fingers, some of four fingers; they shall be made of wool because of
> its softness and because linen bands are too tight when they are damp with perspiration.[67]

In order to be well molded, the body must be wrapped well and constrained
with care.

The comparison with soft materials increases the number of analogies. The bands
are justified by certain authors because they resemble the stakes that support a young
tree. The spinal column could be understood, in fact, as a green wood branch which
the slightest of opposing forces dangerously bends: "We can see that a damp and
green twig can be easily bent."[68] This analogy with a stem, which increasingly came
to haunt the representations underlying straightening actions, is convincing.[69] It

evokes a corresponding answer: Is the stake not entrusted, very simply, with guiding the crooked young tree toward more "normal" paths? Rodion's book *Women's Childbirth*, the French translation of which dates from the middle of the sixteenth century, elaborates on this well-known image:

> A young tree, if it is kept straight and bent, keeps the same shape as it grows. The same happens with children, who, if they are well and properly bound in their little bands and swaddling clothes, will grow with straight body and limbs. On the other hand, if they are bound sideways and crookedly, they will remain the same way as they grow.[70]

Different analogies inspire an identical practice: the model of the mold, like that of the stake, is effected by the bands that compress the limbs and the torso of the newborn. The theory of humors encourages the representation of the vertebrae, all the more prone to the dangers of heaviness, as they are soaked in fluids: only an outside force can compensate for such a diffuse organic weakness. Even more, the body of the child appears at times to be a still "imprecise" matter, waiting to receive a definitive shape.

The infant is entirely subjected to an outside force. He acquires an importance which is at once very real and very potential. He is the object of special treatises, which take a particular interest in his age, but his own being is erased before the anonymous pressure of the bands. The "pedagogical" act can be summed up in the exercise of a power that very directly imposes a modifying physical action. The infant is by now only a passive agglomerate of organs, subjected to the adult's imagination.

The desired uprightness should be established in the very first months of life, and the limbs should be able to be strengthened according to a previously set shape. To straighten the body requires an "adroit" manipulation. In these constant and repeated pressures, a pedagogical theory finds the abrupt simplicity of its archeology. Without words, on a body made of malleable materials, the rules are entrusted to the measured strips of the swaddling clothes.

The clothes the child will wear as he grows no longer have such an obvious and exclusive purpose. Before wearing adult clothing the child is dressed, beginning in the sixteenth century, in a long dress, reminiscent of a cassock: "One adds [on children] a camisole, some warm socks, a petticoat and a dress over it that hampers the shoulders and the hips with a great amount of material and folds, and they are led to believe that this gives them a marvelous appearance."[71] Erasmus does not mention the stitched corset[72] which was to guarantee the waist, although it was to become widespread by the following century. Nevertheless, there is no doubt that the bodies of little girls were subjected to pressure whose purpose was corrective. Feminine beauty was to be perfected by a system of bandages about which the written texts are still vague; these practices are very empirical, and are not mentioned by the physicians, although the latter dwell at length on swaddling clothes:

> Worse is done to girls…at times they are made to wear men's hats and collars which hamper their shoulders; over their shirt an underdress which is well doubled over, and over that another dress which hangs to the ground and is large enough that one could make a complete dress just with the excess. It is true that the cloth is folded and cut around the hips, and that the hem, which would drag on the ground, is lifted and attached to the belt in the back, but the child's body is all the more weighed down by it…. I know that it is done with the aim of making their waist thinner, and that nothing is saved for the fit, as if it were a very important matter.[73]

Paré is doubtless referring to the same custom when he mentions a few girls who have become "hunched and deformed from having had their body too tightly bound."[74]

As for the adult corsets and whalebones, which the child very quickly inherits, they do not really serve the straightening function of swaddling clothes. They are mainly meant for women. They are a matter of "dress etiquette" and do not really pertain to a gradual change in morphology. They are involved in the temporary outline of a garment, rather than in a lasting distortion of the anatomy. They define an affected silhouette, rather than attempting to modify some weakness permanently. In the case of a real deformity they are a simple disguise. The advice of Marie de Romieu, in her *Instructions pour les jeunes dames*, a treatise on manners in dialogue form, shows this desire to create an artificial straightness:

> Thus, we must acknowledge that such natural defects and imperfections need to be remedied as soon as possible, whether with cotton to fill out what is too flat, or to make one part the size of the other, or to help in another situation by some indented edges, in another by a higher slipper, a corselet in another and various remedies, as needed.[75]

Such intentions show an empirical knowledge of bodily statistics, with the use of a compensatory thickness in a shoe, but no details of its effectiveness are given. Above all, they show an attempt simply to play with appearances by superimposing volumes and shapes. The "corselet" is here a wrapping that hides rather than strengthens. Straightness, even when illusory, is widely commented upon. Resorting to deception underscores this tendency toward symmetry. But it also points out the extent to which such understanding remains tentative. By filling certain spaces which a malformation might show as unpleasant, manipulation appears to us today to be heavy and imprecise. By accepting such approximate arrangements, the stated need for uprightness appears only relative to modern eyes.

The corrective corset makes its appearance around the middle of the sixteenth century. Paré appears to be the first in France to describe it, with accompanying illustrations. Called a corselet, it was a metal cage intended, for example, for "girls who are hunched over and deformed."[76] It imposes a firmness which is all the more constant since a number of adjustments are offered to make it "bearable," and adapted to the problem or to its improvement:

> In order to correct and to hide such a defect, they will be made to wear iron corsets, which shall be full of holes so that they will not be so heavy, and they will be well fitted and padded so as not to hurt at all, and will be changed often if the patient has not fully achieved the three dimensions, and for those still growing, it will have to be changed every three months.[77]

For the first time the rigidity of steel tries to impose its shape on a deformation of the body. Ambrose Paré also suggests metal boots to straighten a crooked leg, thus confirming the mechanical trend.

The action of iron on vertebrae that have already hardened is doubtless evidence of a new faith in technical power, as well as more frequent use of metal. Iron is invested with powers of transformation. Despite their relative insignificance on the larger scene of technology, corrective practices are nevertheless an indication, among other things, of such new tendencies.

In the sixteenth century two types of corsets appeared: those whose stiffness derived from whalebone stays, acting mainly in feminine aesthetics, and those whose stiffness was due to metal fastenings, for therapeutic purposes. Both show a new sensibility toward physical uprightness, but the former is the creation of a tailor and pertains mainly to fashion in dressing, whereas the latter is the instrument of a surgeon,[78] reserved for pathology. A system of bandages and of dress tightening preserves, at least for girls, those early corrective constraints exercised by swaddling clothes. The first pedagogical "language" of uprightness is composed of manipulations, the effectiveness of which is supposed to be proportional to the strength of the pressure being exerted.

So this is an extreme and revealing picture of childhood, subject throughout to a hand which molds it by kneading it. Its shape is to emerge from that sovereign gesture which can only be exerted by an adult's molding. It exists thanks only to them, and they become symbolic of a theory of education that consists of imposing a model rather than promoting autonomy. It should be added that the same pedagogical approach finds a sort of justification, even complicity, in "physiology." The material weakness attributed to the child's body — which is approached as if wanting in substance — confirms the need for such modeling techniques.

A Code of Elegance

The seventeenth century will see both the systematization of trends that arose in the preceding century and the cautious beginnings of a renewal. Physical uprightness spreads to various segments of pedagogical literature. Courtesy books gradually tie in with thoughts on posture, though they do not increase the precision with which they determine the right position. Even the text by J.B. de La Salle, in 1736, is still very close to that of Erasmus in this respect.[79] In pedagogical treatises of a new type, addressed to parents and encompassing the themes of civility,[80] uprightness is described in the same terms, with insistent precepts which have become somewhat formal. Such a new literature, which addresses the family, warns against forgetting deportment and its implications for posture. At the table "one should always sit straight, without moving the arms and legs and, if possible, without importuning those who are near."[81] The remarks concerning straightness are taken up by a large body of pedagogical literature. Madame de Maintenon, in remarks which are essentially moralizing, does not hesitate to mention them. There is nothing surprising in learning that good manners are part of the education of the young women of Saint-Cyr: "Hold yourselves straight, carry your head high, do not lower your chin; modesty is in your eyes, which you must know how to move in a modest fashion, and not in your chin."[82]

A new emphasis emerges. Good manners are increasingly expressed through self-control and "modesty...the effect of humility."[83] Good bearing relies on measured movements, where physical uprightness and control have moral connotations. Through a bearing that must always be "honest" and unchanging, one is able to disguise the emotions. "Nothing must show on the outside."[84] Good manners are also the rule of "good countenance," which must have a postural equivalent: "Elegance is a pleasant accompaniment to other good qualities."[85] In the classical world, posture had to show the ability to control one's passions. It was to set against them an impassible physical deportment.

Posture is mentioned in many contexts. It appears in the sort of treatises that had ignored it until that time or had at most implied it. Fencing and chivalry manuals of the sixteenth century attempted, not without difficulty, to describe the body's positions and the movements which were considered technical.[86] The halo that was to be added by grace or gracefulness was hard to define. The necessary ease was mentioned alongside "suppleness" and strength, but the positions were not explicitly fixed with a view to correction. During the seventeenth century, "the maximum in such matters consists of a certain natural grace, which in all activities, and down to the slightest actions, must shine like a small ray of divine nature in all who were born to please in the world."[87] However, despite this apparent vagueness, some details emerge that did not appear in technical writings of the preceding century. The discussion of such practices suddenly becomes concerned with the correction of posture and with a more precise definition of elegance. In a very trivial way and in familiar terms, words come to define the place of the torso and the shoulders. An outline takes shape that used to be left almost completely in the dark by the specialized texts. Doubtless this is because positions are now seen as the many elements of a spectacle. In order for the latter to be appreciated, a few rules are imposed. The staging cannot ignore demeanor and posture in situations involving demonstrations, such as fencing and riding. A "defect" in posture is held up to the spectator for ridicule, "its author more mocked than praised in good company."[88] Should one not always be "looked at with approval"?[89] A morality based on civility and propriety establishes sanctions. It is important to "cut a fine figure." The public is to be the judge. The good manners of an actor are appreciated, among other things, through his physical uprightness. Technical fencing treatises now mention posture as a component of proper behavior: "In order for the body to be positioned correctly, one should hold it up straight and free, with bold movements, turn one's face toward one's adversary, and then move the right foot forward with a natural step."[90] The demeanor of a gentleman, in turn, calls for description. Here again, the body undergoes an "inspection" not found in earlier texts of the kind. Such changes underscore the slow invasion of its *habitus* (demeanor) by the new patterns of language. Things are mentioned that had not been mentioned before. Words penetrate a space made of subtleties and details; they design an outline and then prescribe it by setting it down. Such changes, in the end, stress an increased appeal of physical appearance, but also precise specifications, in the pedagogical approach of the ruling classes: "His shoulders should be equally forward, and his stomach well forward, forming a small hollow in the back, at waist level. Both his elbows should be equally and effortlessly held somewhat away from the body."[91] A few comments suggest the opposite of a controlled posture: "And in order not to appear hunchbacked, or stooped, he should hold his stomach somewhat forward, and hold his lower back straight and steady, thighs together and without movement...."[92] The description of deportment in the art of a fencer, just as in that of a gentleman, is first of all one of "appearances." Formalism takes on customs which have become a spectacle. Pluvinel, whose "royal manège" is accepted as an authority, goes so far as to show the shape and size of a hat to be worn by a rider. Fencing instituted a code of compulsory bows and was to be practiced with "a wig, jabot and oversleeves,"[93] where style had become, obviously, more highly valued than strength. The bout was not to begin without a codified greeting, a precaution which was absent in sixteenth-century books:

> After taking one's guard, one must, first of all, remove one's hat with one's left hand, and let it fall onto the left knee while pulling the right foot back behind the left by about an inch's length, while keeping the body straight, then put the left foot back behind the right while putting one's hat back on, and resume guard.[94]

Court society extends its jurisdiction over attitudes and movements, defining elegance and "proper appearance." One must have one's "arms and legs beautifully in hand."[95]

Rules and order direct behavior until it is an art. Manners become a theatrical and showy element which is largely privileged. Prestige is never far from pose. The body is offered as a picture in a place where glances intersect. One must keep one's place. The vagueness surrounding the sovereign's power, and which depends on him, strengthens the importance of appearances, all the more since it is lacking in such power. Court society demands of its actors a constant awareness of their posture, and in such decorum can be read, among other things, the "science of decent people."[96] One must "show." All spontaneity is erased, and thus a secretive and calculated structure of bearing and behavior is encouraged. Etiquette became the ultimate reference organizing the latter. "Carry your body properly"[97] is what stands out in a subtle code of elegance and appearances.[98]

It is clear that uprightness has a distinctly social meaning here. Moreover, there may be a frequent and revealing explanation of the forward projection of the stomach, an immediate and subjective symbol, almost a measure of how the shoulders are played down. An upright position responds here to intuitions based on quick, deceptive, visual or perhaps even confusingly cenesthetic impressions. The temptation to correct the posture by struggling against any collapsing of the torso led to its being reversed backward. The stomach pushed forward and the hollow lower back, in their familiar and nonanalytical definitions, are an oversimplified way of avoiding a stooped back. The shoulders stiffen, the body becomes arched. The perceptible signs are based on an arched outline. The fact that such references, though they were definitely present,[99] were not ubiquitous in seventeenth-century iconography does not at all prevent the ideal of the proper bodily position from being expressed along a convex forward line. Such language, on the other hand, remains allusive: it does not go into anatomical details. In this increased need to formalize the demeanor, it is always easier after all to list the parts of a dress or to describe a ceremonial act than to undertake an abstract analysis of a behavior. Thus, it should not be surprising that Pluvinel dwells on a meticulous description of a costume, or that La Touche[100] lingers on the ritual of bows.

Fencing and riding are "fields" in which the body's uprightness is a sign of good manners. In these "technical" activities the straight body is filled with a self-controlled politeness. The measure is less and less one of strength, and increasingly one of elegance. In the end, it is dance that sets up models aimed at excellence and distinction. It was to be the foundation for an art of controlled, developed and privileged performance. Dance allows people "to be taught how to walk well, to curtsy, to carry their body properly and to loosen their arms and legs."[101] It is an exercise for maintaining and perfecting one's bearing. On the stage of the body, signs of strength are fading further. The creation, in 1661, of the Royal Academy of Dance,

in charge, among other things, of the training of teachers, confirmed the institutionalized prestige of an art "recognized as one of the most decent and most necessary to shape the body and to give it its first and most natural preparation for all sorts of exercises, among which is fencing."[102]

Taken as a whole, the educational theory of deportment gives a larger place to movement. A number of activities are suggested, leading more consciously and precisely to uprightness. Madame de Sévigné recommends to her daughter, whose child seems to have a curvature, a therapy of exercises and the use of a corset: "He should move and loosen up."[103] The latter verb is used more often when the rules for bodily movement are mentioned. To loosen up means to make it "easy to adapt to all sorts of exercise."[104] It is like untying, releasing what limits the range of one's movements, as well as what conflicts with the elongation and straightness of one's shape. To loosen, in the end, means to rectify. The metaphor is a little confused. Attention does not necessarily lead to precision of movement: any activity should force the joints to increase their flexibility, in order to ensure a better posture. The process acts as a succession of "jolts," an action which, paradoxically, is unsystematic, and which points out basic analogies with any objects whose movement increases elasticity and malleability.

However, it appears that at the same time, during the seventeenth century, movement was in an uncomfortable position. It seemed to be rejected just as soon as it had been accepted, or at least very quickly subjected to limitations. Exercise was always to be "modest" and moderate.[105] Strenuous movement "is more appropriate for tumblers."[106] It loses its nobility. It is seen as a danger that risks overstepping what is proper, since aristocracy had a duty to show complete and visible self-control.

Hic púdor, hic morum probitas hic aúlica suada,   Et lepor, & vitæ generosa modestia gliscit.   Qùid mirùm, divas vltrò si diâ sequi

Country dance and city dance, 16th-century France (Paris, Bibliothèque nationale).

Similarly, dancing was to be practiced with a great deal of caution, as it threatened to become "dirty and immodest, and to go beyond all degree of propriety."[107] Dancing must be the bearer of order or, even better, the restrainer of passions: "Dancing is useful in moderating four dangerous passions: fear, melancholia, rage and joy."[108] All abruptness must be banished along with any too perceptible desire. From that point on, dance inevitably appeared full of contradictions: "When the austere Lancelot became the tutor of the Princes of Conti, he forbade them 'figured dancing'." However, a dance teacher was to come every day to "teach them to walk well, to bow, to carry their body properly and to loosen their arms and legs."[109] The teaching of posture had as its goal the control of movement, rather than any benefit from it. It tends to control and contain movement, rather than developing and encouraging it. Its interest supposedly derives from its different activities which allow learning, since dexterity comes from practice: this, however, consists mainly in the repetition of positions, rather than in widely dynamic displacements. What prevails is the body's enactment of conventional images.

The pupil must, before anything else, acquire good manners. And these do not assume any possible benefit to be derived from movement. Rather, they are always an a priori which is taken up again and again for inspection. Ultimately, Lancelot's ban to the young Conti princes agrees with the cautious learning and the codes proposed by the teachers themselves. The dance lesson, an initiation into the rigors of deportment, is punctuated by rituals whose extreme formalism serves a very specific function:

> The pupil should go before the teacher when he arrives; he must receive him very
> politely, with two bows, one very deep, the second less deep. He must then lead him

into the apartment and show him a chair. As soon as the teacher is seated, the pupil (be it a young lady or a young master) will give him both his hands, place himself in first position and then make four bows.... At the end of the lesson, the pupil shall take care to lead the teacher to the door of the apartment, then bow to him twice, the first time deeply, the second less so. He shall thank him politely for the trouble taken and the attention given.[110]

At a time of moral rigidity, full of references to the "bad habits" threatening the body and condemning those pupils who "get into the habit of being so restless, so impatient and so quick that they become incapable of carrying out regular and peaceful activities,"[111] those precepts concerning deportment seem more than ever directed at holding back what are considered to be excesses. Teaching involves setting, blocking. The notion of "deportment" acquires its meaning where poses are fixed and gestures counted. Successful teaching almost depends on subjugating by immobilizing. Such an undertaking was to be denounced by eighteenth-century criticism: "They only exercise when the teacher comes to dance, and he, with a solemn and serious demeanor, has them move their little bodies with a restraint which is even more unbearable than the discomfort in which they had been kept."[112]

During the seventeenth century the essential plan was the achievement of a dominant position by the body. This was the object of exhortations, of better-developed and more pressing commands, but not really of exercises in which movement and its use were central. The insistence on correct position became more widespread, and that is what was new about it. It soon gave rise to injunctions to which even the occasional pedagogue resorted: "I was at my aunt's, one of the chambermaids was taking care of me; she would dress me meticulously, and she constantly told me to stand up straight; otherwise, she let me do as I pleased."[113] Of course, it became common to complain that this was the only thing being learned, and that children, girls in particular, were being entrusted to ignorant chambermaids. "Only do leave them alone as little as possible with the maids, and especially with the footmen."[114] This shows new needs and a new awareness. And, when they concerned the body, these new tendencies resulted in increased monitoring. Uprightness became, even more than before, the object of pedagogical vigilance.

It should be added that uprightness became inscribed in a framework of justifications that had somewhat shifted. Previously it had been based on a mystique of proportion, an ethics of propriety and the threat of a physical evil (a hump). But now, the body was no longer seen as a microcosm, a simple reduplicating of the universe, playing out through its resemblance the whole set of its relations. Uprightness and physical posture no longer had to reflect figures and proportions given elsewhere. Yet, the other two arguments — the formal appeal to the rules of propriety, without a deeper explanation, and the threat of a hunched back — were not abandoned. In particular, the rules of decorum were increasingly presented in the permanent depiction of a severe and critical audience. One must exhibit proper deportment in order to put on a good front and to avoid ridicule. No rationale is offered. The pedagogical word is satisfied through conformity or shame. It seldom gives a justification; it just prescribes and threatens.

However, another argument was to be put forward often in order to persuade the child to adopt a straight and correct bearing. With the growing moral rigidity of the seventeenth century, a sense of the possible contradiction between the goals aspired to was inevitable. Rectitude and an "elegant bearing" were felt by many Christian writers to be necessary to comply with the rules of civil behavior, yet to be dangerous to the child's conscience, which is liable to be trapped by vanity and "self-love." We often find the uneasiness of such a pedagogical approach, which attempts at the same time to protect the fragile child from the world but also to prepare the future courtier for the world. Such an approach is in keeping with a new view of childhood, which is now seen as fragile and constantly threatened by evil, against which it has no defenses: "The devil attacks children, and they cannot fight him."[115] The cult of posture and its inevitable worldly implications thus impose a lasting danger. The pedagogue is afraid of not being able to master the risks inherent in what is required by social observances. We must also watch what arguments he uses to justify the effort required. To stress appearances too much is always a trap. The child should mind his deportment, with its train of rectitude and corrections, without being overly aware of its social purpose. Some authors prefer to discuss it in terms of quasireligious values. The emphasis is not on the eye of the audience but on the eye of God. Worldly preoccupations are made less obvious, though it is not possible to escape them. In short, they are presented in disguise:

That is why, in those things which are necessary to the shaping of the body, you must make sure that the advice you give them does not lead them imperceptibly to love them-selves; give them other reasons than those which the love of the world might inspire in them. Thus, if you demand that your daughters carry themselves straight, tell them that we must take care to keep our figures because God gave them to us and He wants us to always have our eyes raised to Him to bless Him and to beg for grace from Him; because it is for those who have love for nothing but the things of this world to bend their bod-ies toward the ground, and because Jesus Christ broke the chains that were weighing us down, only so that we would walk with our heads raised to heaven.[116]

Physical uprightness is now suggested and imposed on a child in the name of religion.

The Jesuit Theater

The precepts given by the Jesuits are an interesting illustration of seventeenth-cen-tury pedagogical practice concerning physical uprightness and deportment. Since private schools directed their students to important positions in the state hierar-chy, the adoption of "civil and honest" subjects for teaching was bound to receive prominent mention. Refinement through good manners, the study of the sciences and the proper conception of "religious duties"[117] are the three points that Father Croiset dwells on in his rules of study. Good manners, which rule "one's appearance, gestures and countenance,"[118] become omnipresent. They have "rights over every-thing...the number of duties is infinite, everything is a precept."[119] A sequence of details lists the lapses that will draw moral condemnation: "A posture that is a bit soft, a gait that is too hurried, a bow that is too abrupt...an informal step, a melan-choly air or one that is too lively...all are offenses against decorum."[120] This is a fragile balance since the demands have become so heavy. The bearing of the body shows a detailed insistence, so that customs are mentioned that until now have been absent in books on civil behavior: fencing, for example, and dance seem unques-tionably to improve the skills needed for proper deportment. The latter, and the expressive equivalents it presupposes, will be increasingly locked into an art of rep-resentation; such art, in the end, acquires a new dimension by elaborating a theo-rized performance. Learning will tend, in a subtle way, to make posture into a very specific stage.

It is often claimed that the Jesuits were the first to show a new awareness of the physical life of their pupils: "Education was not as scholarly as it had been for us some years before: it granted a rather large place to muscle development."[121] So the Fathers bought houses in the country, where the students could have space and exercise. The Fathers would sometimes join in the sports. But these were simply recesses, and their details are only rarely described.[122] One cannot attribute to them a detailed pedagogical plan for learning and behavior. During the eighteenth century Marmontel still gives the most elaborate examples: "Our recesses were spent in old-fashioned exercise: during the winter, on the ice or in the snow, in good weather, far into the country, in the burning sun, and running, wrestling, boxing, the game of discus and of longshot, the art of swimming, none were foreign to us."[123] But such an evocation, which is by far the most precise, appears literary. Such activities were not directed by special teachers, nor do they appear to have been the object of a "preparation" or of any didactic precaution. Rather, they appear here as an imitation of ancient times (wrestling, discus, boxing) where the dominant feature is that of the games and the historical and literary references; they are recreation rather than technical research with a pedagogical aim.[124]

On the other hand, the teaching of fencing and dancing seemed to be truly organized. They were taught according to a precise point of view. Fencing and dance teachers, "the most skilled, come at a specified time to give you a lesson, and it will be up to you not to need to take other lessons elsewhere."[125] Such subjects are not compulsory, although strongly encouraged. "Young men must be educated well so that they will be able to hold themselves and to walk in a pleasant way."[126] The Jesuits make a compromise with the ways of the world.[127] The emphasis on fencing also shows the desire to compete against the military academies founded by Richelieu,[128] where, during the seventeenth century, part of the French aristocracy, which was destined to a military career, would spend about two years of its adolescence. But "it is not well enough known to what extent such public Academies are harmful to innocence, they are usually the first threat."[129] Classical teaching, which considers itself safe from the influence of the world, taking refuge in Latin culture in order to better secure its boundaries, cannot avoid being tainted by it. However, it faces the world only for the purpose of mastering it: to teach fencing rather than to leave such teaching to other institutions, which might compromise the patient learning of decorum and posture; to make sure that the preparation for the future takes place within the safe walls of a private school. Not that such activities are learned differently there – the place is the only element to be moved, but it is a crucial one: "We want you to have the opportunity to learn the same exercises as in the academies, but without the same dangers."[130]

Dancing, too, encounters an ambivalence, which has already been mentioned. It must be limited to learning proper posture and to acquiring a few assured steps, for civility must impose strict limits to all excess: "Do not believe, however, Sirs, that the indulgence shown to you will tolerate any kind of dance, or even balls, which we condemn strenuously. 'I always considered balls dangerous,' said Monsieur Bussi-Rabutin, the most polite courtier of his century."[131] The reference to a courtier is not incidental. He is the example whose success should make the limitations and demands acceptable. Dancing is a "training," not an amusement.

With the Jesuits, the true learning of deportment takes place, however, through the "address" and the stage. The former is a presentation which concentrates both on words and on deportment. Its purpose is to improve the delivery, but also to impart elegance and ease. Jouvency lists its basic rules:

> The posture should be firm, steady and straight, with the head not leaning sideways or forward, and not moving or raised without reason; the hands should not be brought too far forward, or lifted above shoulder level; they should not hang at the sides as if one were one-armed, nor should they both be placed on the hips in an arched or bowed shape.[132]

It is not simply an exercise in elocution. The effort also aims for an awareness and control of one's bearing. The body is partly the object of a metaphorical description, a sign that it is still difficult to describe it objectively and in detail. The language used is intended to project the strength of a conviction. Positions are fixed with metaphors and everyday terminology (do not "throw your head forward," avoid the arms forming "an arch or a bowed handle"). One must become accustomed to taking one's position and being stared at, while at the same time acting. One must express oneself and be secure in a pose. There is the prestige of words, of course, but also the prestige of the demeanor and of the physical manifestations that express it; and finally there is the prestige of the discipline they presuppose, and the decorum they show. The "address" is already a way of learning a code – the code of a performance.

The stage, after all, even more than an "address," is the place for learning posture and the worldly uses of the body. The Jesuits did not invent the use of theater in the schools, but with them it became an institution and found a real pedagogical role. Plays shown in schools during the sixteenth century presented essentially a joyful character, one of amusement, a break. After the battle of Pavia, the Parliament, which declared a national mourning, advised the rectors and the principals of all private schools "not to let the pupils act in any farce, childishness or foolishness, for the next Feast of the Kings, so that mischievousness will not be able to take advantage of the freedom of such games to plant some words which might have evil consequences."[133] During the sixteenth century, tragic plays made their appearance on school stages.[134] However, their pedagogical aim was not stated and their status kept fluctuating: Father Maggio, in his inspection in 1587, forbade "tragedies, comedies, buffooneries and dances,"[135] while the 1599 Ratio authorized tragedies and comedies again. But strict regulations specified that they be infrequent, be written in Latin, have no female roles and present an edifying goal.[136]

During the seventeenth century, however, their use became systematic, and their educational value was judged to go well beyond the simple interest in the play chosen. A whole pedagogical theory was constructed around them: "Do not regard theatrical games or plays that are shown publicly in the schools as futile exercises that undermine the pupils' studies and dissipate the mind of youth."[137] They strengthen and stretch the memory, while forming the mind, but they also "give [the pupil] a noble boldness."[138] Theater teaches the pupil how to take a position and to keep a better watch over his gestures. It becomes the ideal exercise, for it inculcates the correction and mastery of one's physical bearing. It is a privileged way to prepare for life in the world. In a society of performances, whose roles are played out and positions are juggled for, according to a detailed code of rules, acting in the theater can occupy a fully focused pedagogical place. It is, just like the "real life" to come, a play of positions and roles. It allows one to "give inflection and pleasantness to one's voice, elegance to one's gestures, dignity to one's step and bearing, and decency and grace to one's countenance."[139] Here good speech and proper manners are cultivated par excellence. Jouvency stresses the constant preoccupation with causing "gestures to be free, the step noble, demeanor elegant and distinguished."[140] Court society was trained to learn the actor's play. The culture of the body becomes set as a stage performance: attitudes and glances. The rules governing deportment are more than ever an integral part of a spectacle. Posture is still linked to the control of one's gestures and references to "distinction." The Fathers, on the other hand, tend to play down comedies in relation to other performances, because the demeanor of their characters is not sufficiently noble: "Who would wish to see young people being taught the gestures, the mores and the ineptness of slaves and servants of the lower strata?"[141] In this theater, one must adopt one's positions with care, for they are those of a social group.

Such exercise was bound to be controversial.[142] The controversy even deepened during the seventeenth century, if we consider that "ballet [the first was shown in 1638] is the truly original aspect of Jesuit theatre. Ballet was the main attraction of their productions, and it was there that they displayed all the resources of their imagination."[143] From a pedagogical standpoint, dance was expected to respect the boundaries that a theatrical performance always threatened to overstep. Some condemnations did cause repercussions, underscoring the pitfalls of preparing for a worldly life without being caught up in certain of its aspects. The Bishop of Mandemont, in particular, banned a performance in 1682, and wished to reemphasize the rules as he strengthened them: "We forbid participation in the performance of such tragedies, comedies and operas with dances, which can only sow corruption among young people, who, at this tender age, are very impressionable."[144] The theater, he stressed, is a place for "instruction" and "not an amusement."[145] The discomfort became apparent after the time when an implicit social choice was made, but also when the performance and the audience began to make their own demands.[146]

As for the precise pedagogical approach that governed the play and determined stage behavior, it is difficult to establish its content. At least it did explicitly declare that its aim was to give elegance and decorum. The application of this approach, which has vanished along with the gestures it taught, has left few traces. The "game" was what made the correction of one's demeanor desirable. The goal was, first of all, to assume a position and have an elegant physical demeanor, although the details of the steps to be taken are never fully explicated. But the recourse to the theater means much more. Playing a role involves putting it at a distance in order to dominate it better. Theater is here an exercise in control and vigilance where only noble positions and movements are chosen. It is an educational theory of vigilance. At least, that is the ideal of these stage performances with simplified and conventional gestures. The upright body is the one that mimics and adopts the positions required by decorum. It must offer a performance, and it is shaped through the performance. Court society imposes a code of posture as its very specific pedagogical requirement.

NOTES

1. C.V. Langlois, *La vie en France au Moyen Age de la fin du XIIIème au milieu du XIVème siècle*, 2 vols. (Paris: Hachette, 1924-25), vol. 2, p. 193.

2. Anonymous, *Le roman de Flamenca* (thirteenth century) in *ibid.*, vol. 1, p. 144.

3. Robert de Blois, *Le chastoiement des dames* (late thirteenth century) in *ibid.*, vol. 2, p. 177.

4. "Elegance and strength were the characteristics of an ideal that was not always achieved. But strength was more highly regarded than beauty." Léon Gautier, *Chivalry*, trans. D.C. Dunning (London: Phoenix House, 1965), p. 105.

5. The text of a Dominican writer of legends in J. Le Goff, *La civilisation du Moyen Age* (Paris: Arthaud, 1964), p. 414. For the cult of physical strength and an analysis of Bertrand de Born's verse, see *ibid.*, p. 45ff.

6. R. de Blois, *Le chastoiement des dames*, p. 195.

7. Anonymous, *Le Mesnagier de Paris* (late fourteenth century) (Paris, 1846), vol. 1, p. 15. It can be seen here how straightness is associated, for reasons of decorum and modesty, with the direction of one's gaze, and thus, almost, the very direction of one's step.

8. Frederick J. Furnival, ed., *The Babees Book* (New York: Greenwood Press, 1969), vol. 1, p. 18.

9. Urbain Le Courtois (thirteenth century) in *Romania* (Paris, 1903), p. 71.

10. Rules for all servants in *The Babees Book*, vol. 2, p. 20.

11. *Ibid.*, vol. 1, p. 4.

12. Hugues de Saint Victor, *La règle de Saint Augustin* (twelfth century) (Paris, 1818), p. 206.

13. Erasmus, "On Good Manners for Boys," in *Collected Works*, ed. J.K. Sowards (Toronto: University of Toronto Press, 1985).

14. B. Castiglione, *The Book of the Courtier*, trans. George Bull (New York: Penguin Books, 1967).

15. Norbert Elias discusses this problem in *The Civilizing Process* (New York: Urizen Books, 1978).

16. C. Calviac, *La civile honesteté pour les enfants avec la manière d'apprendre à bien lire, prononcer...* (Paris: R. Breton, 1560), p. 14.

17. *Ibid.*

18. On this subject see below, "The Ambiguities of Physical Exercise."

19. Erasmus, "On Good Manners for Boys," p. 277.

20. Such stigmatization is, obviously, not based, nor could it be, on evidence that might link in strict concatenation the slackening of posture and the resulting hunchback.

21. *Ibid.*

22. Giovanni Della Casa, *Galatée ou la manière dont un gentilhomme se doit gouverner en toute compagnie* (Paris, 1562), pp. 510-12.

23. A. Chastel, *Art et humanisme à Florence au temps de Laurent le Magnifique: Etudes sur la Renaissance et l'humanisme platonicien* (Paris: Presses Universitaires de France, 1961), p. 305.

24. *Ibid.*, p. 299ff.

25. "The more enthusiastic the Renaissance authors wax about the metaphysical significance of human proportions, the less disposed they seem, as a rule, to empirical study and verification." Erwin Panofsky, *Meaning in the Visual Arts* (Chicago: University of Chicago Press, 1955), p. 92.

26. Della Casa, *Galatée*, p.104.

27. *Ibid.*, p. 106.

28. Rabelais, *The Histories of Gargantua and Pantagruel*, trans. J.M. Cohen (Harmondsworth: Penguin Books, 1955), p. 157.

29. Henry Estienne, *Dialogue du nouveau langage français, italianisé* (Paris, 1579), vol. 1, p. 210. The author confirms that these new customs come from Italy. François Boucher, in *Histoire du costume* (Paris: Flammarion, 1965, p. 227ff.), mentions some rigid corsets at the end of the reign of Francis I and points out their Italian and Spanish origin.

30. Montaigne, *The Complete Essays of Montaigne*, trans. Donald Frame (Stanford: Stanford University Press, 1957), p. 41. In the sixteenth century, there was an oppositon to such rigid corsets, to which we shall return, but this does not call into question the passivity of the corrected body. In ancient times, young girls were wrapped, to narrow their shoulders and widen their hips, with cloth strips which even Galen criticized for their tightness.

31. Della Casa, *Galatée*, p. 534.

32. Castiglione, *The Book of the Courtier*, p. 67.

33. *Ibid.*, p. 66.

34. *Ibid.*, p. 68.

35. Arcangelo Tuccaro, *Trois dialogues sur l'exercice de sauter, et de voltiger en l'air* (Paris: Claude de Monstr'oeil, 1599), p. 2.

36. T. Arbot, *Orchésographie* (Paris, 1599), p. 2.

37. Gérard Thibault, *Académie de l'espée* (Paris, 1626).

38. The author augments abstractions and very verbal analogies with the arts of his time: the compass and navigation, fortifications and military sieges, the bar and the art of oratory, etc.

39. *Ibid.*, p. 3. Thibault traces a circle on the ground within which is a grid of lines. Both are inspired by the proportions (very rarely "morphological") taken from a fencer. The gestures of the fencer are to follow such models, which appear to be very sophisticated, but are, in fact, very difficult to apply and are indicated by the above design, resulting in a crisscross of straight and curved lines. Just as the proportions are the result of metaphysics, so the circle reflects the macrocosm. Their relationship with movement is more imaginary than real.

40. *Ibid.*, p. 4.

41. The image of the circle imposes a priori some directional lines that falsify an objective description, also concerning intensities, as it imposes the search for "centers" rather than for lever arms or muscular forces. Finally, muscles are never mentioned in these propositions.

42. *Ibid.*, p. 1.

43. Leonardo Da Vinci, *The Notebooks of Leonardo Da Vinci*, ed. Jean Paul Richter (New York: Dover Publications, 1970), vol. 1, p. 188.

44. Serge Moscovici, *Essai sur l'histoire humaine de la nature* (Paris: Flammarion, 1968), p. 244.

45. Da Vinci, *The Notebooks*, p. 190.

46. *Ibid.*, p. 197.

47. George Sarton, "Léonard de Vinci, ingénieur et savant" in *Léonard de Vinci et l'expérience scientifique au XVIème siècle* (Paris: PNF, 1953), p. 17. Obviously, the image of specific muscular structures and their consequences will be difficult to isolate, as it requires an analogy with a macrocosm of disparate elements, motley and heterogeneous: "his body contains a summary not only of all we see on earth, but as well as that which is in Heaven" (Thibault, *Académie de l'espée*, p. 1).

48. Galen, *De sanitate tuenda*, in *Corpus medicorum graecorum* 5.4.2, ed. Konrad Koch et al. (Berlin, B.G. Teubner, 1923), 2.9.20. Translated by Robert Montraville Green as *Galen's Hygiene* (Springfield, Ill.: Charles C. Thomas, 1951), p. 83.

49. Tuccaro, *Trois dialogues*, p. 184.

50. Ambroise Paré, *Oeuvres* (Paris: Baillère, 1840-41), vol. 2, p. 611.

51. During the eighteenth century, scarcely pronounced deformities and their correction by exercising were highlighted for the first time. It is also during the eighteenth century that the muscles were considered as the very explicit reference for a new pedagogical approach to posture (see Vigarello, *Le corps redressé: Histoire d'un pouvoir pédagogique*, Paris: Editions Delarge, 1978, ch. 3).

52. "The child is a blend of damp and hot elements, as he is composed of them and formed in

them. For what is close to birth is very humid and very warm, and develops the best.... Adult man, after his body has stopped growing, is dry and cold, as the flow of heat no longer dominates but stops, and as the body, having stopped growing, cools off." Hippocrates 1.33.1 and 1.33.23.

53. "Without the return to Greek sources that was characteristic of the sixteenth century, it is impossible to read the Greek physicians; their lessons make up a large part of what Arabic physicians bring us. Hippocratic doctrine was not to affect pediatric medicine in a decisive way until the sixteenth century." J. Ulmann, *Les débuts de la médecine des enfants* (Paris: Palais de la Découverte, 1967), pp. 22-23.

54. *Ibid.*, pp. 15-16.

55. Soranus of Ephesus, *Traité des maladies des femmes* (Sorani Gynaeciorum libri), trans. J. Herrgott (Nancy, 1895).

56. J. Guillemeau, *De la nourriture et gouvernement des enfants* (Paris: N. Buon, 1609), pp. 26-27.

57. S. de Vallembert, *De la manière de nourrir et de gouverner les enfants* (Poitiers, 1565), pp. 49-50. Vallembert's work is the first French work on the subject.

58. O. Farrarius, *De arte medica infantium, libri quatuor, quorum duo priores de tuenda eorum sanitate, posteriores de curandis morbis agunt* (Brixiae, 1577), p. 49.

59. Soranus, *Traité des maladies*, p. 1.

60. *Ibid.*, pp. 115-16.

61. The general meaning of the word "l'apostume" (translated here as "swelling") is abscess. The frequent comparison between a hump and an abscess demonstrates the difficulty of understanding the latter in a precise morphological structure. The image of a sack filled with humors prevails over that of "deviations" related to the bony architecture (see Vigarello, *Le corps redressé*, pp. 40-48, and G. de Chauliac, "Des apostèmes du dos," in *La grande chirurgie*, Lyon: Estienne Michel, 1580, p. 172).

62. Vallembert, *De la manière de nourrir*, p. 45.

63. *Ibid.*, p. 56.

64. Guillemeau, *De la nourriture*, p. 396.

65. Soranus, *Traité des maladies*, p. 91.

66. Galen, *De sanitate tuenda*, p. 43.

67. Soranus, *Traité des maladies*, pp. 91-92.

68. Paré, *Oeuvres*, vol. 2, p. 365.

69. Such an analogy was to play, in particular, an important role in thought on orthopedic devices during the seventeenth and eighteenth centuries. See Vigarello, *D'un corps redressé à un corps qui se redresse: Machines à redresser le corps*, in *Annales de l'ENSEP* (Paris, May 1974).

70. Eucharius Roeslin, *Des divers travaux et enfantements des femmes* (Paris, 1536), p. 95.

71. Erasmus, *Le mariage chrétien* (Institutio Christiani matrimonii) (Paris, 1714), p. 333.

72. A corset made with whalebone stays stitched into the folds of the cloth.

73. *Ibid.*, pp. 333-34.

74. Paré, *Oeuvres*, vol. 2, p. 611.

75. Marie de Romieu, *Instructions pour les jeunes dames* (Paris, 1976), p. 20.

76. Paré, *Oeuvres*, vol. 2, p. 611.

77. *Ibid.*

78. The medical question of straightening belongs to the field of surgery.

79. Jean Baptiste de La Salle, *Les règles de la bienséance et de la civilité chrétienne* (Reims: R. Florentain, 1729).

80. Philippe Ariès, *Centuries of Childhood: A Social History of Family Life*, trans. Robert Baldick (New York: Knopf, 1960), p. 111.

81. Pierre Coustel, *Règles de l'éducation des enfants* (Paris: E. Michallet, 1687), p. 343.

82. Madame de Maintenon, *A la classe verte, juillet 1716*, in *Choix de lettres, entretiens et illustrations* (Paris, 1884), p. 116.

83. Antoine Courtin, *Nouveau traité de la civilité qui se pratique en France* (Paris: H. Iosset, 1671), p. 12.

84. B. Gracian, *Le héros* (Paris: Champs libre, 1973), p. 26.

85. Coustel, *Règles de l'éducation*, p. 341.

86. On this, see above, "The Ambiguities of Physical Exercise."

87. Nicolas Faret, *L'honnête homme ou l'art de plaire à la cour* (Paris, 1630), p. 32.

88. Pierre de la Noue, *La cavalerie française et italienne* (Strasbourg, 1620), p. 32.

89. Faret, *L'honnête homme*, p. 34.

90. P. La Touche, *Les vrais principes de l'épée seule* (Paris, 1670), pp. 6-7.

91. Antoine de Pluvinel, *Le manège royal* (Paris, 1623), pp. 13-14.

92. La Noue, *La cavalerie française*, p. 34.

93. A. Pierlants, *L'escrime et les escrimeurs* (Brussels, 1888), p. 120.

94. J.B. La Touche, *L'exercice des armes ou le maniement du Fleuret* (Paris, 1635), p. 6.

95. *Ibid.*

96. J. Croiset, *Heures et règlements pour messieurs les pensionnaires* (Paris, 1711), p. 100.

97. N. Fontaine, *Mémoire pour servir à l'histoire de Port Royal* (Paris), vol. 2, p. 481.

98. Concerning "court society and theater society," see Norbert Elias, *Court Society* (New York:

Pantheon Books, 1983), pp. 110-12: Drama is "an integral part of social life at court, not a leisure activity. The spectators sit on the stage, filling the background and sides. What is performed shows the same measured deliberation of structure that is characteristic of court life as a whole." The difference from the following is clear: "Bourgeois-industrial rationality is generated by the compulsion of the economic mesh; by it power-opportunities founded on private or public capital are made calculable. Court rationality is generated by the compulsion of the elite social mesh; by it people and prestige are made calculable as instruments of power."

99. They are very clearly defined in the engraving taken from a drawing by J. Rigaud, "Le château de Versailles du côté de la terrasse" (seventeenth century), reproduced in P. Lacroix, *Lettres, sciences et arts* (Paris, 1882), p. 424.

100. P. La Touche, *Les vrais principes*.

101. Fontaine, *Mémoire pour servir à l'histoire*, vol. 2, p. 481.

102. Letters patent . . . for the establishment of the Royal Academy of Dance for the city of Paris, March 1661.

103. Madame de Sévigné, *Lettres* (Paris: Hachette, 1862), vol. 4, p. 434.

104. Faret, *L'honnête homme*, p. 25.

105. J. Defrance, *Transformation des usages sociaux du corps* (Paris, 1974).

106. J. Du Chesné, *Le portrait de la santé où est au vif représenté la règle universelle et particulière de bien sainement et bien longuement vivre* (Paris, 1606), p. 309.

107. *Ibid.*, p. 306.

108. P. Menestrier, *Des ballets anciens et modernes selon les règles du théâtre* (Paris, 1682), p. 311.

109. G. Snyders, *La pédagogie en France aux XVIIème et XVIIIème siècles* (Paris: Presses Universitaires de France, 1965), p. 148.

110. The words of the seventeenth-century dance master Guillemain quoted by Félicien de Menil in *Histoire de la danse à travers les âges* (Paris, 1887), pp. 177-78.

111. P. Nicole, *De l'éducation d'un Prince* (Paris, 1670) in Félix Cadet, *L'éducation à Port-Royal* (Paris, 1887), pp. 206-07.

112. J.C. Desessartz, *Traité de l'éducation corporelle des enfants en bas âge* (Paris, 1760), p. 398.

113. Madame de Maintenon, *Instructions à la classe verte*, in *Choix de lettres*, p. 90.

114. Alexandre Varet, *De l'éducation chrétienne des enfants* (Paris, 1666), p. 115.

115. Fontaine, *Mémoire pour servir à l'histoire*, vol. 1, p. 195: "It is this double theme: detachment from the world and guarding ceaselessly in order to reduce the child to its terrible natural posture which seems to us characteristic of this moment of pedagogical theory."

116. Varet, *De l'éducation chrétienne*, pp. 195-96.

117. Croiset, *Heures et règlements*, p. 2: "There are religious duties to be carried out, proprieties to follow, sciences to learn."

118. *Ibid.*, p. 101.

119. *Ibid.*, p. 104.

120. *Ibid.*, p. 105.

121. André Schimberg, *L'éducation morale dans les collèges de la Compagnie de Jésus en France sous l'Ancien Régime* (Paris, 1913), p. 300.

122. Most often they appear as a simple relaxation upon which dwell neither descriptions nor explanations: "It was customary to take our recess in the courtyard as long as the water in the chapel's font was not frozen." Henri Beaune, *Voltaire au collège* (Paris, 1867), p. 71. Beaune, for example, added nothing further, mentioning only in one word the game of "passe-volant," *ibid.*, p. 73.

123. Jean-François Marmontel, *Mémoires* (Paris, 1804), vol. 1, pp. 20-21.

124. It is interesting to note how Schimberg (*L'éducation morale*, p. 300), whose analysis dates from 1913 and who mentions games without describing them, connects them very briefly and allusively to the sports of his time: "These games from the old days, which we are, happily, returning to...." Such remarks can only create confusion. Recess, for the Jesuits, was not "directed." It did not obey laws of learning or of coaching. Even less did the games that took place obey a specific institutional structure (codification of rules, federation, championship, etc.) as in the case of sports. The Ratio do not, in any case, offer any text in this direction. There are, on the other hand, special teachers for dancing, horseback riding and fencing, the gentleman's exercises.

125. Croiset, *Heures et règlements*, p. 116.

126. *Ibid.*

127. Such a "compromise" is nothing more than a social choice: in the seventeenth century, "the Jesuits give in more and more to the spirit of the world; they acquire the manners of well-bred people, they take on the air of a young and glittering court; they want to please the Master (the King) and they succeed in doing so" (Schimberg, *L'éducation morale*, p. 417). Schimberg's moralizing question, although classical, is worth noting: "One may seriously ask oneself whether the Fathers, precisely by increasing their 'concessions,' are not responsible for the vanity of the ruling classes at the end of the Old Regime" (*ibid.*, pp. 419-20). This debate, which was definitely present in the seventeenth century, was to lead to the introduction of worldly ways and to the "necessary" exclusion of their possible "perversion."

128. Cf. H. Cherot, *Trois éducations princières* (Paris, 1836).

129. Croiset, *Heures et règlements*, p. 115.

130. *Ibid.*, p. 116.

131. *Ibid.*, p. 117.

132. J. Jouvency, *Christianis litterarum magistrid de ratione discendi et docendi* (Paris, 1892), p. 44.

133. Henri Louis Bouchet, *Le collège d'Harcourt Saint-Louis* (Paris, 1891), pp. 179-80.

134. *Ibid.*

135. G. Dupont-Ferrier, *Du collège de Clermont au lycée Louis-le-Grand, la vie quotidienne d'un collège parisien* (Paris, 1921-25), vol. 1, p. 285.

136. *Ibid.*

137. Croiset, *Heures et règlements*, p. 119.

138. *Ibid.*, p. 120.

139. Le P. Ch. Porée in S. de la Servière, *Un professeur d'Ancien Régime* (Paris, 1899), p. 93.

140. Jouvency in Schimberg, *L'éducation morale*, p. 408.

141. *Ibid.*, p. 56.

142. The severe restrictions imposed by the 1599 Ratio were never completely followed. A number of plays had women's roles. Antoine Monaco de Vallentinois played one, for example, in a play performed before Louis-le-Grand in 1672 (Dupont-Ferrier, *Du collège de Clermont*, p. 289).

143. Ernest Boysée, *Le théâtre jésuite* (Paris, 1880), p. 31.

144. Guy de Sève de Rochechouart, Bishop of Mandemont, letter of September 28, 1698, in L.V. Gofflot, *Le théâtre au collège du Moyen Age à nos jours* (Paris: H. Champion, 1907), p. 191.

145. *Ibid.*, p. 192.

146. Snyders, *La pédagogie*, p. 144.

From *Le corps redressé: Histoire d'un pouvoir pédagogique*, Paris, Editions Delarge, 1978.
Translated by Ughetta Lubin.

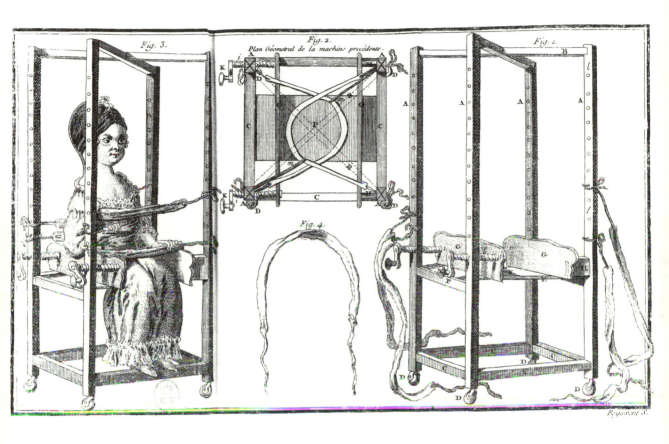

Compression Chair. From M. Levacher de La Feutrie, *Traité du rakitis ou l'art de redresser les enfants contrefaits*, 1772 (Paris, Bibliothèque nationale).

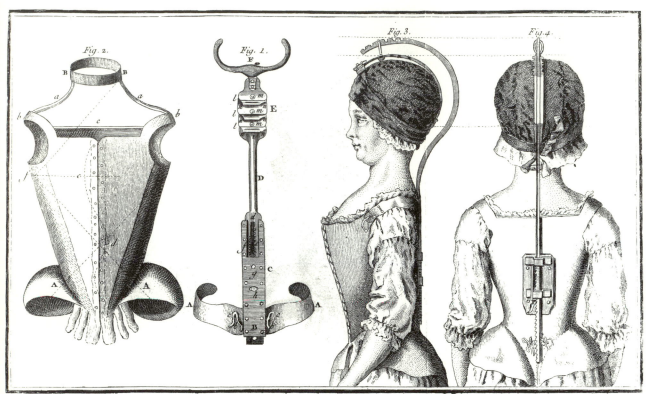

Figure 1: Machine for extending the vertebral column.
Figure 2: Machine for correcting an extremely curved spine.
Figure 3 and 4: Machine for curing rakitis.
From M. Levacher de La Feutrie, *Traité du rakitis ou l'art de redresser les enfants contrefaits*, 1772 (Paris, Bibliothèque nationale).

zone

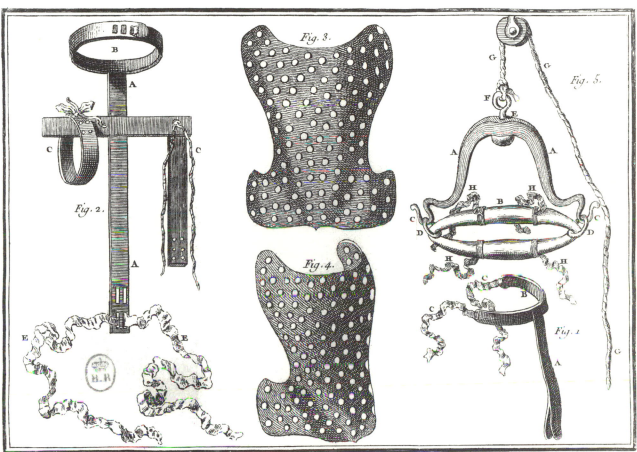

Figure 1: Brace for correcting the neck.
Figure 2: Cross, neck brace and shoulder straps for prevention of gibbosity.
Figure 3: Corselet for prevention of rakitic gibbosity.
Figure 4: Machine for correcting a crooked neck through muscle retraction.
From M. Levacher de La Feutrie, *Traité du rakitis ou l'art de redresser les enfants contrefaits*, 1772 (Paris, Bibliothèque nationale).

Geerewol: The Art of Seduction

Text and photographs by

Carol Beckwith

Once a year, at the end of the rainy season, in the Sahelian steppe of Niger, the Wodaabe nomads* perform a series of dances known as the *Geerewol*.

For seven days, up to one thousand men participate in a dance competition judged solely by women. Two dances — the *Yaake* and the *Geerewol* — dominate the festivities. At these, handsome young men vie for the honor of being chosen the most charming and the most beautiful, thus proving their outstanding ability to attract women. Romance flourishes and many marriages grow out of alliances formed at the *Geerewol*.

The Wodaabe say that the *Geerewol* is an expression of their special birthright of beauty handed down by their ancestors Adam and Adama. To enhance this beauty Wodaabe men use *maagani* — the knowledge of secret potions, both real and magical. The Wodaabe feel that it is this legacy of beauty and their unique ability to express it that forges their true identity among African people.

* On the Wodaabe nomads, see my book: *Nomads of Niger* (Abrams, 1983).

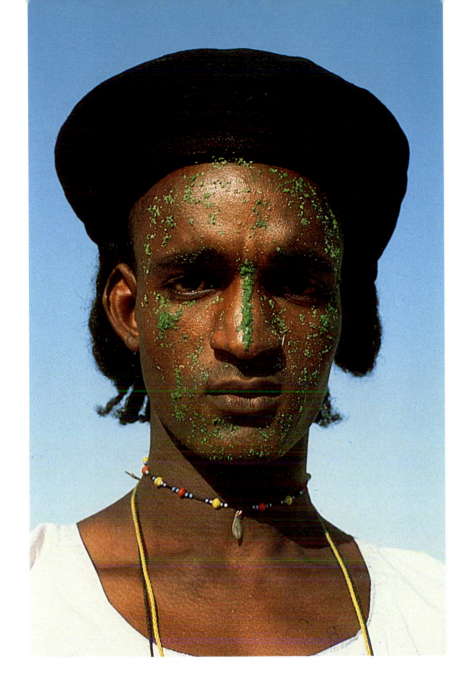

Before the dances begin, young Wodaabe men chase about the Sahel catching chameleons. They dry and pulverize the skin in order to make a green cosmetic make-up which is applied to the face. They believe, rather poetically, that this make-up will transform a man's face the way the chameleon changes color. It will rid a man of the parched, tense look of the dry season and bring out his natural beauty — his ancestral birthright.

Many hours of preparation precede each dance. For the *Yaake* — the charm competition — pale yellow powder is liberally applied to lighten the skin tone; borders of black kohl are painstakingly applied to highlight the whiteness of teeth and eyes. A painted line running from forehead to chin elongates the nose; a shaved hairline heightens the forehead. These are among the physical features the Wodaabe most admire.

Necklaces of talismans containing secret potions are worn by the male dancers both for protection and to increase the power of performance. They contain blessings for charm and beauty, ward off evil words, protect from jealousy, make the wearer irresistible and render him impervious to injury. One, in particular, makes a man invisible at night when he goes off to steal a woman. From each man's necklace hangs a small vial of perfume containing *maagani*. Sensitive to fragrance, the Wodaabe believe that by wearing this perfume infused with secret potions, they will become irresistible to their female judges.

A man indicates his desire for a woman by winking. When a man winks, a woman is required to lower her eyes demurely. She is not allowed to look directly into the eyes of someone she desires. However, if she is interested, she will not lower her eyes all the way, at which point the man then twitches the corner of his mouth, indicating which bush he wants to meet her behind.

Women play the more passive role of observer-judges. They spend less time making themselves up but nonetheless follow certain procedures. After tressing the hair, a woman inserts six to ten lightweight brass earrings into each ear. When possible, she sports a colorful umbrella for protection against the searing Sahelian sun.

Women spend between three and four months hand-embroidering costumes for themselves and their menfolk. Each design has a specific name and story. As a final decorative touch, a young girl adds new sandals to her headdress.

When Wodaabe men sing about the ideal beauty of a woman, they say she must have eyes resembling those of a gazelle, skin as clear as water, teeth as white as milk, and a back as long and straight as a young acacia tree.

The *Yaake* is the dance of charm and personality. The male dancers form a long line in front of a large crowd of women who scrutinize their every move. Shoulder to shoulder they quiver forward on tiptoe to accentuate their height and launch into a series of wildly exaggerated facial expressions on which their charm, magnetism and personality will be judged. Eyes roll; teeth flash; lips purse, part and tremble; and cheeks pout in short puffs of breath.

Elders dash up and down the line of dancers challenging, mocking and criticizing in an effort to incite the contestants to even greater performance. A dancer knows he is receiving favorable attention when an old woman dashes toward him yelling "Yee hoo" and gently butts him in the torso.

If a man can hold one eye still and roll the other in and out, this is considered especially alluring to women. The Wodaabe say that it is through the strength of the eyes that seductions and marriages are made.

Right: several outstanding winners of the *Yaake* charm dance.

The week, as it progresses, becomes an exhausting dance marathon highlighted by afternoon and evening performances of the *Geerewol*. In this dance, the most physically beautiful men are selected.

Uniformly dressed in tight wrappers bound at the knees, strings of white beads crisscrossing bare chests and turbans adorned with ostrich feathers, the men line up before their audiences.

Three unmarried girls chosen for their loveliness are brought out by the elders to serve as judges. Kneeling modestly, they conceal with the left hand their scrutinizing glances. After a period of observation, the girls rise and advance slowly toward the dancers of their choice.

In order to hold their attention, the finalists resort to every facial expression and bodily movement they can muster. The girl-judges indicate their favorites with a graceful swinging of the arm. In this way the most beautiful men are chosen.

Kneeling down, the winners are crowned with horse tail plumes. The winners reap only intangible rewards: increased pride in themselves, the admiration of other men and the ardor of women. In their hearts, these men know that they personify the legacy of beauty handed down by Adam and Adama.

Breviary of Love, 13th-14th century.
From a Provençal codex (Spain, Biblioteca Escorial).

Love's Rewards

René Nelli

Gazing on the Naked Lady

In Provençal erotics, there existed between the kiss and the "act" (the latter was indefinitely deferred) other more secret ways for a lady to reward her lover. Out of discretion, the troubadours spoke of these only hypothetically, but their existence can be taken for granted. These two intimate ceremonies, daring but continent, were early on assimilated into the culture through custom and convention. They were: gazing on the naked lady, and the *asag* — the test of love. Sometimes the lady displayed herself naked only during the *asag*. But at other times, after she had let herself be kissed, either naked or scantily clad, by her clothed lover, she decided that it would not be proper for him to be put to the test, which for him would be the crowning of *Fin'Amors*. Therefore, the two kinds of rewards are not necessarily related and should not be confused.

The high estimation accorded to the lady's beauty in Provençal poetry may be partially explained by the fact that a majority of early masters during the time of Guillaume IX attributed a quasi-miraculous quality to the female body. It was supposed to have almost magical effects on men. It seems possible that the troubadours (after learning about it from Arab poets?) recalled what Mircea Eliade notes was the intrinsic mystical value of female ritual nudity in India, where it was regarded as an incarnation of nature (the *Prakṛti*).[1] The troubadours often emphasized the physical beauty of the lady in question by calling it "the perfect work of God," and consequently viewing it as a kind of summary of nature, which explains its power over the lover's heart and body. This was clearly articulated. For example, Guilhem de Cabestanh writes, "God himself made her faultless out of his own beauty [*quelh eys Dieus senes fallida la fes de sa eyssa beutat*]" (1.5-6), and "Christ never brought a more

219

beautiful woman to life [*tam bella non aspiret Crist*]" (3.17-18). Giraudet le Roux, addressing his lady, declares: "God took affectionate care when he adorned your body with traits that beautify it."[2] The troubadours made female beauty into something touched by the sacred, not in the way the Indians did for the *yogini*, but rather by referring to it as God's creation, and thereby placing it in a purifying context where it could not be confused with the mere promise of carnal pleasure. While it is futile to look for a frank and vibrant celebration of the sexual act in the troubadours' poems, one can find an ardent desire to see the lady naked, a desire that is formulated in several ways. In fact, the contrast between the troubadours' customary timidity and the boldness of this wish is surprising, but it recurs so often in all Provençal poetry and in every period that one is forced to believe that the practice of viewing a lady naked was a legitimate, accepted custom in good society and was one of the rewards a lady had at her disposal to secure the affection of a faithful lover.

This theme appears at the very beginnings of courtly poetry — in the work of Cercamon — and continues without modification through Occitan civilization, during which time love may be said to reside entirely between the imagined image of the lady's body and the lover's memory of her beauty. Often this beauty is only imagined or glimpsed in a dream, especially in the works of such reticent troubadours as Arnaut de Mareuil.[3] Often this beauty is idealized and interiorized to such an extent that when his love is at its peak, the suitor, by identifying perfectly with his lady, is able to evoke it in his heart.[4]

Such absolute idealism, however, did not prevent even the most diffident of troubadours from aspiring to the favor of actually gazing on their ladies' bodies. Undoubtedly, Cercamon was only articulating a wish when he wrote: "I shall pray to God that one day I may touch her [*l'ades*] or see her preparing for bed" (1.23-24). A majority of classical troubadours expressed the same desire. Arnaut de Mareuil shyly admits his hope to be "where the lady undresses, for she would be doing me a great honor" (15.25-30). Clearly, such prayers would have been pointless had there been no hope of their ever being answered. Sometimes they were.

It has to be said that when a lady granted such a reward, she in no way compromised her honor — it contradicted neither the Right of Love nor *Fin'Amors*. It was easy for her to receive her lover "where she undressed" without her virtue being questioned, because she could always summon her attendants, who rarely left her alone, or even her husband. A highly favored lover, one who was in the third or fourth stage of vassalage, was accorded the honor of being present at his mistress's bedside when she was waking or retiring. (According to a *razo*, this is how Bertran de Born was able to gaze on his lady's naked body without ever being granted further favors.) Nevertheless, to keep up appearances, avoid slander and preserve the modesty of these noble ladies, the ceremony was for the most part clandestine. After making an ally of a servant girl, the lover was supposed to spy on the woman without her knowledge as she undressed and got into bed. A passage from the novel *Flamenca* probably refers to this lover's ruse: "You other men," cry the guests of Archambaut, "you are content as long as the lady is pleasant, as long as she welcomes you, but he who sees her *when she is undressing, when she is retiring or rising, will, if he is wise, no longer wish to give such great handsels to the chambermaids*" (570-80). Wiles and amorous strategies of this kind exist in every century (eighteenth-century engravings are particularly apt at illustrating them), but only in Occitan erotics are these strategies made into a rite of pure love, intended to maintain *joi* in the lover's heart and reward his fidelity. The ceremony varied in degree: depending on her whim, the lady could show herself naked or almost completely clothed. The charming scene depicted by Bernart de Ventadour, also in the hypothetical mode, offers us only an image of partial or progressive dishabille:

> It would be a great wrong if she did not call me to her chamber where she is undressing so that at her command [*per sa comanda*] I might be near her, and at the edge of the bed, humbly on my knees [*a genolhs et umilians*] remove her well-fitting shoe if she deigned to offer me her foot. (B. de Ventadour, *Languan vei per mei la landa*, st. 5)

Finding himself in such favorable circumstances, it was very likely that the lover would give or receive a few stealthy caresses. Provided he did not show too much boldness or impatience, he might lightly brush against his lady's skin. Cercamon wanted more than this but only in his imagination: "I cannot go on living unless I can kiss her and hold her [*baizar e tener*] near me [*josta mi*] in a curtained chamber" (2.45-49). Were we to follow him, however, we would leave behind codified love and enter the realm of passion, which follows only its own whim. It has to be made clear that in the Middle Ages the kisses a lady gave were always considered more chaste than those the lover took. A naked woman could kiss her clothed lover, take him in her arms ("*Pros m'es et honors... que m volesetz far de vostres bras sentura*," Guilhem de Cabestanh, 4.28-30), and surprise no one that she had taken the initiative and kissed him, but he did not return the kiss (at least nowhere is it recorded that he did). What often happened, in fact, was that after the lady had received from her admirer these few tokens of friendship, to which she attached little erotic value, she dismissed him. And if he respected the *mezura*, he had to obey. In the event that he was able to gain further favors from her, the encounter took on all the characteristics of the *asag*. The two ceremonies were almost always distinct, separated from one another by a border of patience. Usually, however, the relations between lady and suitor went no further than these few tokens of affection; first, because of the difficulties that could arise and, second, because the lady did not always feel real passion for her faithful suitor. In the *asag*, however, she abandoned herself to real passion.

The *Asag* (or Test of Love)

In the theory of courtly love, the *asag* or the *asais*[5] took the place of the chivalrous "act." In the *asag*, passion was born, exalted and tested, and it usually ended before the lovers reached sexual climax. It had three fundamental meanings that corresponded to quite different goals. (1) In certain respects it resembles the erotic subterfuge used by prudish women in modern society to fend off a man's passion without sacrificing their honor.[6] It was therefore *amor imperfectus*. (2) For the lover who could finally look on and kiss his lady, it was the supreme reward for his fervent loyalty. The *asag* gave merit. (3) Finally and most importantly, it allowed the lady to "put her lover to the test" to see if she really was loved from the heart, *amor corau*, or only desired as a carnal object. The *asag* was a test the woman imposed on the man.

Viewed from this last perspective, one can see how the *asag*, through its ancient roots, escapes the all too narrow definition with which literary studies have usually constricted Provençal love. In fact, modern European myth includes many tests of this kind in which the lover — often the fiancé in traditional Christian societies — puts himself in trying and heroic circumstances to show his young lady that he loves her for herself and not just for his own sensual gratification. Even in the last century, it was common in many Occitan regions for a young man to make a symbolic climb to his beloved's chamber and spend the night beside her in the same bed fully clothed. Were he to show any disrespect, it would be a grave breach of decorum.

The Provençal *asag*, however, is more closely allied to men and women's instincts than it is to these ancient bequests of an archeo-civilization. In effect, it may simply be a law of nature that when men are genuinely in love, they find it easy to remain chaste, but when they are not in love, they are impatient. In contrast, women have more desire when they feel truly loved and are reticent when they fear they are not loved enough. Fabre d'Olivet expressed this when he said, "Pleasure before possession — that is the instinct of man; possession before pleasure — that is the instinct of woman."[7] It should also be noted that the *asag* is perfectly attuned to the feminine sensibility, which is more slowly aroused than its masculine counterpart. Furthermore, when physical harmony is the result of spiritual harmony, the lover's restraint, his consideration for his mistress's feelings, becomes in itself a proof of love.

Finally, let me say that because true love cannot be fully satisfied through the physical act, because the act cannot in itself guarantee a union of hearts and only takes on its full value as an expression of reciprocal passion, women quite naturally interpreted a certain physical coolness on the part of their lovers as a sign that they were loved sincerely and lastingly, as long as this coolness was accompanied by protestations of great feeling. The reason for the *asag*, therefore, was less a test of male willpower and stoicism than it was a way of showing *in re* that love originates naturally and spontaneously in chastity. Some Catalan *coblas* still attest to these ideas and practices, which at first glance may appear to be essentially chivalric or "precious" in nature, but which are really primitive and popular. The following *cobla* suggests that such behavior, which may be virtuous and heroic in a saint, is, in a lover, only a direct expression of a feeling so profound it temporarily transcends corporeal union:

Even the Holy Father of Rome
Would not do what I have done:
Sleep with you the whole night through
And never touch your body.

Therefore, one should not confuse these tests of love, of which the Provençal *asag* is the most perfect, with other probative rites that may resemble it superficially but do not have the same meaning. Resisting sexual temptation and temporarily refusing the physical act were often part of young mens' ceremonial obligations during initiation. Although the circumstances in these two ceremonies may be similar, the woman's role in an initiation rite is completely different from her role in the *asag*: in the former, she is to excite the boy's lust, and the boy must vigorously reject this sensuality, not welcome purified love into his heart. He has to prepare himself for an anti-erotic test. Similarly, in the fourteenth century, a number of St. Francis's Beguines maintained that it was worthy for a man and woman to sleep together in the same bed as long as they displayed a mutual scorn for the flesh. This is another version of the example cited above with a single difference: the woman shares the rite's mystical benefit with the man. They lay in bed together not to establish a platonic love between them, but to prove to themselves that their thoughts were occupied solely with the divine. This, too, then was an anti-erotic spiritual exercise.

A similar lovers' test is found in neo-Celtic traditions: the lovers lay in the same bed, separated by a sword or a child. Insofar as they forced themselves to remain chaste out of obedience to God, the bishop or religious morality, this test resembles the two described above. But it is like the Provençal *asag* in that the young lovers are passionately in love. Nevertheless, it should not be confused with the *asag*. In the neo-Celtic test, the lovers generally succumbed to temptation, because *they loved each other too much*. In the courtly *asag*, however, if the troubadour fell prey to his instincts and broke the vow he had made to his lady, it was because *he did not love her enough*.

Finally, it should be pointed out that, according to certain Eastern ideas — specifically Buddhist and Yogico-Tantric — *amor imperfectus* (semen is not emitted), when practiced ritually, is supposed to ensure the adherent's spiritual salvation. This erotic ceremony also superficially resembles the Provençal *asag*. But apart from the fact that the real woman, although she was supposed to incarnate divinity, served only as an object or symbol (this certainly was not the case with the troubadour's lady), it would be unwise to attribute the same principle of sexual magic to the courtly *asag*. In the *asag*, the lover and his lady proposed to each other that they experience mentally — and in a sense magically, but a different kind of magic — a purely spiritual feeling of love.

The *asag* (and its various popular forms) remains absolutely distinct from all the erotico-spiritual exercises with which one might be tempted to ally it. It is located within the context of heterosexual love, which it defines through temporary continence. It assures the testing of the man by the woman and, consequently, the symbolic dominance of the female sex.

In the oldest poetic texts — as early as the work of Guillaume IX, it is always the lady who tries, tests (*assaia, prueva*) her lover. But this does not mean that the *asag* existed in the same form at that time as it did in the late twelfth and the thirteenth centuries. Without returning to the time when the only trials knights had to undergo in order to earn the favors of their ladies were of an athletic or military character, and thus had no direct relation to love, the tests given knights at the end of the eleventh century (although less far removed from this passion) were still governed entirely by external regulation. Because they did not want to appear to give in too easily to their lovers' advances and invite ridicule, the ladies "tried" their lovers' patience, courtesy and attentiveness before they surrendered. Or one might say that the *asag* was then merely an ensemble of conventional delaying tactics that ladies observed out of a fear for their reputations. In a late thirteenth-century allegorical poem, *Chastel d'amors*,[8] one can still find an allusion to such tests of love, more chivalric than courtly: "At first," says the poet, "the dwelling's 'walls' are disappointing. The ladies make them of pain and torment so that their lovers suffer until they reveal their true feelings. For one does not welcome them until they have been well tested [*recognogud*]." As far as one can tell from the allegory, if the ladies of the castle tormented their lovers initially, it was so that they might refuse them nothing in the end. This example proves that such precourtly tests long survived and coexisted with the *asag*. In fact, they outlived it: the performance of heroic deeds for the love of a woman existed in some form until the French Revolution. And from a woman's point of view, long delays followed by surrender, pure and simple, lasted until about 1926. But these tests really have nothing in common with the classic *asag*, which, in addition to the long period of preliminary patience that it required of the courtly lover, comprised more subtle rules that applied even to the *jazer* and to those moments when love ordinarily heeds no laws.

The troubadours rarely used the word *asag* (or *assais*), or described what it was. Undoubtedly this was because few were deemed worthy of such an honor, and because if they were granted it, they had to be discreet. Furthermore, they were supposed to celebrate only unrequited love and *joi* in their *cansos*. The *trobairitz* (female poets), however, were far less reserved. Because it was the ladies who proposed the *asag* as a privilege of their sex and an expression of their moral superiority, some of them spoke of it quite naturally as a final ceremony that conformed to convention. One of the most charming of them, the Countess of Dia, has, it seems, been slandered on account of several misunderstandings about her. She was called the Provençal Sappho. Raynouard attributed to her "a purely worldly sensuality," Jules Véran added further "a sensuality she sometimes displayed crudely," and André Berry noted "her exceptional lack of virtue." Yet there is nothing in her poems that does not precisely reflect the commonplaces of her era's purified eroticism and that peculiar blend of sensual glorification and chastity that characterized Provençal love in general and the *asag* in particular. In fact, what does her "lewdest" song (*Estat ai en gran cossirier*) say that does not conform perfectly to convention?

> For the love of a knight, I have suffered great pain. I want the intemperate passion I have had for him to be known in all times. And here I am abandoned [*trahida*] *under the pretext that I did not give him my love*. Yet how I have strayed in bed or dressed. Oh how I long to hold my knight in my bare arms for a night, *as long as he is contented with my just making a cushion of my breasts for him*. I am more taken with him than Flore was with Blanchefleur. I give him my heart and my love, my spirit, my eyes and my life.
>
> Beautiful friend, gracious and kind [*avinens e bos*], if ever I held you in my power [*en mon poder*], may I lie next to you for a night [*jagues ab vos*] and give you the kiss of love [*un bais amoros*]. You know, it would give me great pleasure to hold you in my arms instead of my husband [*en luoc del marit*], as long as you first promise [*ab so que m'aguessetz plevit*] to do everything I wish (that is to say, *to do no more than what I ask*).[9]

Let us look closely at this poem. It is obvious that the woman has not given herself completely to her knight. She makes this quite clear, and that is why he has abandoned or left her. Evidently he did not feel sufficiently rewarded by her strayings, "in bed or dressed," which were most likely those permitted by the least daring of the *domnei*. The second word "dressed" weakens considerably the phrase "in bed" that precedes it. We do know that young women of society did not hesitate to ask their male friends to lie in bed with them. The Countess of Dia's only liberty (one more apparent than real) is that she invites her knight to the test (or perhaps to a new test). He is to undergo the *asag*, but he must not surrender to temptation unless she also wishes to succumb, and then after he has sworn to accept only what she offers him. (This may be seen as a common feminine response to the brutal and loveless rights of a husband in the thirteenth century: the lady wants to hold her lover *en son poder*.) Therefore, the lover has to be content with resting on the cushion of his lady's naked arms, with lying beside her (*jazer*), with gazing on her (*remirar*), and finally with *tener, abrassar, baizar* and *manejar*. These are the liberties allowed by courtly love: both substantial and continent, and all formulated in the same conventional way. The most chaste of troubadours used these "clichéd" terms without any roguish intent: Arnaut de Mareuil, for example, and even Matfre Ermengaut,[10] who quotes a *canso* by Daude de Pradas on the subject. Although the lovers did not want the *domnei* to "go too far," they nevertheless wanted the encounter to be physical — *tener, abrassar, manejar*. It is unnecessary to reemphasize the "courtly" aspects of the settings in which these three words occur. They constitute the very definition of the *domnei* as it develops into the *asag*. Even in chivalric erotics, they are a part of courtship — when it is still chaste: "*Ab vostra dona domnejar/e lieys tener e abrassar*" (*Nouvelle du Perroquet*, 151-52). In the novel *Jaufre*, Brunissen desires from the hero she fancies only *baizar, abrassar, tener*.

The Countess of Dia does not refer directly to these courtly caresses in her poem. Rather, she sums them up by saying, "You know it would give me great pleasure to hold you in my arms [*que-us tengues*]...as long as you first promise to do everything I wish...." When interpreted in the Gallic spirit (which is far removed from the Occitan), these last words seem humorous and libidinous. But is this possible? A warped imagination is required to read these words as the lady's request for erotic refinements. Would the knight have to be sworn to these? Let's examine the evidence. What the Countess displays is virtue — either relative or absolute, sincere or hypocritical. In other words, she displays a modesty that must be treated with delicacy. This means that there are certain "realities" to which the lover may not aspire. She says it categorically, "Oh how I long to hold my knight in my bare arms for a night, as long as he is contented with my just making a cushion of my breasts for him."

The ladies of the thirteenth century were not stingy with these rewards, which were regarded simply as signs of courtesy hardly more significant than others. The Countess of Dia had only to remember what she had been taught as a girl to know what was permissible and what was not. She had most likely read "lessons" very similar in content to the *Cour d'amour*,[11] a somewhat late Art of Love (that nevertheless predates the *Roman de la rose*), in which young girls are given instructions on how to behave in the world. Baillive d'Amour says to them, "Do you know what a maiden should do when her dear friend is near her and when *Fin'Amors* has granted her the great honor of lying next to him [*qu'ab son bon amic l'a colgada*]? She should *at once* present him with a kiss, and then with a smile and sweet words, she should make a cushion with one of her arms [*que-l fassa coissin de son braz*], and with the other pull him towards her and embrace him, saying, 'May great honor and fortune be yours. You can see my handsome friend that I am here for your pleasure. I am not protecting myself from you. You are so gracious and good [*tan bels et tan bos*] that you will not harm your beautiful friend. I abandon myself to your discretion [*cauzimen*]. And you know there is no honor in deceiving [*abetar*] a young girl' " (1159-84).

Here the *Cour d'amour* describes a test, because the young girl relies on her lover's discretion and she permits everything (*tener, abrassar, baizar, manejar*) as long as she is not "dishonored." The test is rather chivalric in character because it is directed at young girls, not married women. But this is of little importance; both girls and married women must have the same confidence in the virtue of gentlemen and accept the same convention, which dictates that certain caresses — particularly those they offer — are proper or in "good form." As I have often pointed out, Provençal love is above all an expression of woman's desire to escape the tyranny of man. In modern times, young women have had boyfriends or fiancés who, out of a sense of ethics, respected their honor, or if they didn't, then they married them out of duty. In the courtly *asag*, however, the lover's loyalty consists of his respecting the married woman's modesty. Were he to trespass beyond the specified boundary, he would show that he did not love her. The liberties taken by girls and women are of exactly the same kind. It is clear from their words that *colgar ab si, josta si* or *ab si* mean nothing more than "to sit near one," despite the Gallic echoes that these words have now — *colcar, baizar*. The young woman is the one who invites the man to the intimate tête-à-tête, who draws him to her, kisses, embraces him and bids him lie near her. This is courtly love. If, however, the man were to force himself on the woman — push her down beside him, kiss and embrace her without her encouragement, he would violate *mesura*; it would be *leujaria*. Such distinctions in behavior always correspond to semantic nuances in the vocabulary. The heroine of *Flamenca* invites Guillaume to come to her, and she is the one who kisses him. It is the same in other novels of the period, and is particularly noteworthy because it is unlike real courtship where the woman is reserved, haughty and never makes advances.

Therefore, the Countess of Dia (to return at last to her) behaved just as all "well-brought-up" ladies of her century, and had just as many scruples. She gives her lover her "heart," "love," "spirit," "eyes" and "life," but nothing more – or at least she does not promise him anything more. And as for the "kiss of love," it is difficult to understand how it acquired a bad reputation, because if it is to be maligned then courtly love itself must be maligned. This lovers' kiss, the *bais amoros*, is opposed to the conjugal kiss. Thirteenth-century ladies distinguished the two just as women do today: the first is given by choice, the second out of duty. Ostensibly, courtly love placed the lover in the husband's position, but this is true only up to a point, as the *trobairitz* make clear. In the *asag*, the lover did not have all the rights of a husband; he had to swear to obey his mistress and not act as husbands usually do – as master.

Although the Countess of Dia does not call it by name, she is proposing the classic *asag* to her knight. Anyone who still doubts that the *asag* existed in the thirteenth century need only reread the poem *Ar em al freg temps vegut* by Azalaïs de Porcairargues.[12] The *assais* is described in detail and even named. The fourth and fifth stanzas, the only ones applicable to this subject, appear below:

I have a very valiant friend
Who is better than all the others.
His heart bears me no evil
for it grants me his love.
I confess that mine belongs to him
And God should grant an evil fate
To anyone who contradicts this.
For of this I am well assured.

Handsome friend, of my own will
I have pledged myself to you forever
You, who are courteous and well-mannered
　　[*cortez e de bel semblan*];
Ask nothing dishonest of me
　　[*sol no-m demandes outratge*]
Soon we will come to the test
　　[*tost en venrem a l'assai*]

And I will place myself at your mercy.
You have sworn to me that you
Will not ask me to give in [*fail*].
   [*Vos m'avetz la fe plevida*
   que no-m demandes faillida].

Here the same probative rites are described, and Azalaïs de Porcairargues uses them with her lover in the same way that the Countess of Dia does with hers. She asks him before the *assai* to swear that he will not attempt to gain anything from her that would dishonor her (*outratge*), and then she puts herself at his mercy (*merce*; cf. *Cour d'amour*: "*cauzimen*"). The word *falhida* cannot be interpreted in the Gallic sense, because such an interpretation would be contrary to the morality of the period. We do know that *falhir* means (in *Flamenca*, for example) that "a woman commits a sin by refusing to reward a good knight who deserves her love." But this is not the case here. If the lady were to give herself entirely to her lover, she would transgress both her own honor and that of her husband.[13] As it figures in Azalaïs de Porcairargues' *canso*, the *asag* verifies what we already know from the Countess of Dia, and what additional evidence will confirm.

It is undeniable that the *asag* was often hypocritical and made it possible for chivalric tendencies to prevail over courtly ones. A *tenson* written by an unknown lady, Lady H., with Rofin (Rofin, *Digatz m'ades de cors*),[14] seems to show that when regarded in a chivalric spirit, the *asag* appeared rather ridiculous, but this fact only further establishes – indirectly – its social existence.

In the *tenson*, a lady has two lovers. (This is hardly in keeping with courtly teaching, but the debate, which in this case is entirely theoretical, is presented in order to contrast two types of lovers.) According to convention, she wants each lover to promise to do nothing more than hold her and give her a kiss before she will let him near her (*enanz que-ls voil ab si colgar*): *Que plus mas tener e baizar/no-lh faran* (6-7). (Always the same legitimate liberties.) Lady H. asks Rofin which lover behaved more correctly, the one who hastened toward the "deed," or the other who respected his vow. The arguments of Lady H. are chivalric and "Gallic"; it is the lady in this case who is less idealistic. She says that the nature of the bold lover is to show his worth (*sa valor enansar*), to take all that is within his reach and generally to scorn women who, in fact, enjoy being forced. Furthermore, she argues, he who is not daring in love will not be daring in combat, etc. In short, according to Lady H., he who respects the vow he made to his mistress is something less than virile.

Rofin, however, categorically takes the opposing point of view: that of the ideal of courtly love. The lover who has "taken" his pleasure has forfeited the "high jewel" (*la joia autiva*), the merit associated with loving purely. "A lover who is truly in love [*d'amor coral*] must not seek a pleasure that is contrary to his lady's honor [*qu'a sa donna non s'onors*]," a pleasure gained against her will. He must not break his word to her. He must not violate her morally.

The *asag* required of the lover at least such temporary restraint and moderation — *mezura*. Obviously, completing the act of love was left to the lover's discretion, but for him, if he was sincere, the rules of the game consisted in his not wanting anything but *tener, baizar, abrassar* and *manejar* from his lady. And even if he were not sincere, out of consideration for the lady, he had to show that he was able to respect her until the next encounter. If he suffered too much, he could (in fact, he had to) hope for her mercy (*esperar de si dons socors*). This helped considerably to mitigate the hardships of the test.

Flamenca is the only novel in which a true *asag* appears, and in which a theory of the *asag* is explicated.[15] In this novel, chivalric and courtly adventures are juxtaposed. In the first part of the poem, a purely courtly atmosphere is predominant, and in the second, a chivalric one. The first part (which occurs entirely within the framework of a *castia-gilos*) ends in a great love scene which takes place in an underground passage, or rather, in the secret chamber to which it leads (5896-97).[16] This scene describes the *asag* in detail. Nothing is missing, neither the carnal atmosphere nor *mezura*. The poet tells us that "eyes, mouths, hands are not lazy, the two lovers kiss and embrace each other [*l'us autre bais e s'estrein*]" (5957), and that love tells them to do everything they please (5949-50). As for the *mezura*, these are perfect lovers and therefore they desire everything except the "act." This purity takes on further significance in that the novel is on the whole rather libidinous and immoral, at least in terms of Christian morality. If the lovers do not complete the act of love, it is because they do not want to; their love is spiritual (*amoretas son corals*: 6011). Even though in accordance with the rules, Flamenca may "hang about Guillaume's neck, embrace him tightly, welcome him and do all that love desires," Guillaume may ask nothing of her. "He satisfies himself with what the lady offers him, and she is not slow to give him pleasure" (5962-66). Love brings them so many pleasures, in fact, and the poet emphasizes this — "that there was no question that day of their sleeping together [*jassers*]."[17] "At this first meeting, love satisfied them simply through kisses, hugs, caresses [*embrassar, estreiner, manejar*] and through those games [*jocs*] with which love rewards those in whom there is true feeling [*amistat fina*]" (5968-74).

What the novelist evokes here is completely consistent with his theory of courtly love. I have shown this elsewhere and will simply note here that, for him, *Fin'Amors* is found in the *joi* created when the lovers' gazes meet, and that legitimate and illegitimate caresses alike have value only insofar as they are a part of this purified *joi*. True lovers are those who, without making the least effort, show, through this interlude of restraint and relative continence, that pure love exists prior to and triumphs over its physical fulfillment.

The text of *Flamenca* is so clear, so explicit, that it seems unnecessary to provide further proof of the *asag*'s existence as a social reality. A *tenson* composed by Mir Bernat with Sifre serves to reconfirm my thesis by supplying some additional details. Following a theme already used by André le Chapelain, the game proposed in this *tenson* is that a lady has promised half of herself (the top half) to one lover and the other half (the bottom half) to another. Her top half (face and breasts) obviously symbolizes courtly love, and her bottom half symbolizes chivalric or natural love. Sifre chooses the top half, Mir Bernat the bottom. (The latter celebrates his choice in the most crude terms, which have, for the scholar at least, the merit of being precise.) How does Sifre justify his choice? He glorifies the "assay" — "*us gens assays*" — during which one embraces, kisses and caresses (*embratz, manei e bays*). "It is better," he says, "to embrace, caress and kiss the mouth, eyes, face and forehead." (One may recall that this is just about what the Countess of Dia offers her knight.) In a few words, he defines *Fin'Amors*. True love has undoubtedly been more robust at times, but for Sifre it necessarily excludes the act of love itself, which took on real significance in the Middle Ages, because virtues and vices were believed to be hereditary. When perceived in a chivalric spirit, however, kisses and caresses mattered little. Mir Bernat observes with humor that he "embraces and kisses his brothers, his first and second cousins every day," pretending that lovers' kisses and those of family members are hardly different. This is why husbands, at least in theory — in reality, they were often very jealous — allowed their wives to take part in the courtly test. Sifre says, "for I, with the husband's authorization [*Car yeu ab cosselh del marit*]," will go peacefully through the gentle "test."

Mir Bernat, on the other hand, defends the chivalric position very much in the same terms and with the same arguments as Lady H. He establishes the same equivalence between love and war. How can someone who is afraid of a jealous husband possibly defeat an enemy? He believes that the true lover, the *drut*, is he who tries to possess his lady carnally. Thus Sifre and Mir Bernat inform us about what courtly love was and what it wasn't, and they demonstrate the true nature of the *asag* — one by the value he assigns it, and the other by the contempt he has for it.

The examination of these various texts, showing the agreement between the events and the vocabulary used to describe them — always the same — establishes that in the thirteenth century there existed, as the ultimate end of courtly love, an essentially continent but at the same time physical process that followed a conventional scenario and was more or less determined by custom. The lady invited her friend to join her in a secret place where she abandoned herself to his discretion. They were both undressed, but before allowing him to lie beside her, she made him swear (this was the ritual aspect of the ceremony) that he would not take any other liberties than those in keeping with *mezura* and the Right of Love (those always designated by *tener, abrassar, baizar* and *manejar*). He had to swear that he would not take any initiative, that he would abstain from the "act" and would obey his mistress in all things. If she wished she could extend her favors, but for either him or her to show too much impatience would have been dishonest. The fall, if it were to happen, should occur later.

No matter how one views the *asag* — as the natural expression of passionate love between a man and a woman, as a lover's hypocritical ruse (despite the fact that he was forced to exercise self-control), or even as an expression of feminine wiles — one cannot dispute the fact that, beyond its function as a kind of regulator of desire that tended to keep outright libertinism at bay, it was also an homage to spiritual love. It was an homage founded on the idea that lovers have a need for a communion of pure feeling, and that without this communion, their physical coupling is nothing more than lewdness.

Notes

1. Mircea Eliade writes, "If before a naked woman, you do not find in the deepest part of your being the same terrifying emotion that you experience before the revelation of a cosmic mystery, then there is no rite but only a profane act." "Note sur l'érotique mystique indienne," *La Table Ronde* 97 (January 1956), p. 28. Ancient Manichaeans revered beauty; they did not see it as a reflection of the Good imprisoned in matter. For the Cathars, women were angels from the second sky. Their bodies were demonic but wasn't their beauty heavenly?

2. Quoted by F. Diez, in *La Poésie des troubadours*, French trans. by Roizin, Paris, p. 163.

3. "At night, when I am in bed, my desire to hold you in my arms is stronger than my desire to be the lover of another" (11.53-55). "He kisses his lady in a dream and wants to sleep all year" (9.34-35; 10.18-21).

4. "Often when I pray, I see you before me" (Guilhem de Cabestanh, 2.47-48). "In my thoughts, I gaze on your gracious and beautiful body" (5.5-6). A. de Mareuil sees his lady in his heart (8.28-32); the heart is a mirror where he sees his lady (4.43-45); he always looks at her in his heart (4.23). "My lady," says Raimbaut d'Orange, "I gaze upon you without a veil in my heart" (Diez, *La Poésie des troubadours*, p. 158).

5. *Asajar* means "try, test, seek to know," and not always, of course, in an erotic sense. In *The School of the Jealous*, by R. Vidal de Besalú, the lady, hearing her disguised husband knock on the door, says to her maid: "It is my lord who wants to know the truth about my (supposed) carnal dealings with Bascol" (*Que m'asage ma drudaria*, l. 215).

Asag or *assays* sometimes means "undertaking": *Bel senher dos, tan fol assay — co vos auzes anc enardir?* (Irenée Cluzel ed., 342-43). Most often, however, and always in the work of the *trobairitz*, *asag* is taken to mean "test" of love. In another story by R. Vidal de Besalú (*En aquel temps c'om era jais*), one reads: "Through a test she wanted to know his heart better (soft and uncertain or hard and constant). But such a test (too severe or too unjust) is not wisdom, but folly, here among us [*Non es sabers aitals assays — Mas folia, say, entre nos*]" (Mahn, *Gedichte*, vol. 2, p. 35).

6. Petting, for example.

7. *Histoire philosophique du genre humain*, vol. 1, p. 74.

8. A. Thomas, "Chastel d'amors, fragment d'un ancien poème provençal," *Annales du Midi* 2 (April 1889), p. 193.

9. Jules Véran, *Les poétesses provençales du Moyen Age et de nos jours* (Paris: Quillet, 1946), p. 163.

10. *Pensan vos bais e-us manei e-us embratz*

   Aquest dompnei m'es doutz e cars e bos. (A. de Mareuil, 8.38-39)

E si per mai d'entresenha
Si dons embrassan l'estrenha
o-lh baiza la boca e-l mento
o-lh dona anel d'aur o cordo
Non deu despueis per ren pessar
Que lh'o pogues gazardonar
E deu mai voler attendre
L'autre major do que penre;
Car assatz lh'es gazardonat.... (*Breviari d'amor*, 32355-63)

11. L. Constans, "La Cour d'amour," *Revue des L. Romanes* 20 (1881), pp. 219-20.

12. Jules Véran, *Les poétesses provençales*, pp. 116-20.

13. In certain cases, the husband was aware of his wife's relations with the courtly lover. Another *trobairitz*, Castelloza, consoles herself over her lover's infidelity by confiding her pain to her husband: "*mout avetz faich long estatge*" (st. 5).

14. Jules Véran, *Les poétesses provençales*, pp. 101-06.

15. Was it during an *asag* that Jaufré Rudel, naked under the covers, was attacked by his rivals? and that the Marquis de Montferra surprised his sister in the company of Raimbaut de Vaqueiras?

16. After this *asag*, the lady, having regained her freedom, gives the knight his freedom, so that he may have chivalric adventures.

17. Obviously used here in the "chivalric" sense.

From *L'érotique des Troubadours*, Paris, Privat, 1963.
Translated by Alyson Waters.

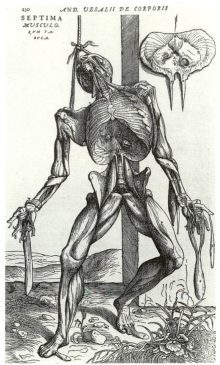

THE TRUTH ABOVE ALL

Left: Matthias Grünewald, The Small Crucifixion,
ca. 1511/1520 (Washington, National Gallery
of Art).

Right: Vesalius, De fabrica, 16th century (Paris,
Bibliothèque de l'Ancienne Faculté de Médecine).

236

Between Clothing and Nudity

Mario Perniola

The Glorious Garment and the Naked Truth

In the figurative arts, eroticism appears as a relationship between clothing and nudity. Therefore, it is conditional on the possibility of movement – transit – from one state to the other. If either of these poles takes on a primary or essential significance to the exclusion of the other, then the possibility for this transit is sacrificed, and with it the conditions for eroticism. In such cases, either clothing or nudity becomes an absolute value.

Clothing prevails as an absolute whenever or wherever the human figure is assumed to be essentially dressed, when there is the belief that human beings are human, that is, distinct from animals, by virtue of the fact that they wear clothes. Clothing gives human beings their anthropological, social and religious identity, in a word – their being. From this perspective, nudity is a negative state, a privation, loss, dispossession. The adjectives denuded, stripped and divested describe a person who is deprived of something he or she ought to have. Within the sphere of this concept – which extended broadly through the Near Eastern populations (Egyptian, Babylonian and Hebrew) – being unclothed meant finding oneself in a degraded and shamed position, typical of prisoners, slaves or prostitutes, of those who are demented, cursed or profaned.

In ancient Israel, the primacy of clothing acquired a metaphysical significance associated with the notion of *chabod*, which means splendor, glory and honor, and which refers etymologically to that which is weighty, grave or important. The "glorious garment" (*beged chabod*) mentioned in Sirach 45.9 refers to the priestly robes of Aaron (to whom the biblical tradition attributes the institution of the priesthood), and to the solemn ornaments of the high priest Simon (who "when he put on his glorious robe and clothed himself with superb perfection and went up to the holy altar, he made the court of the sanctuary glorious" (Sirach 50.11-12). The connection between robe and priesthood, between clothing and the service of God, is rooted in the fact that God Himself "clothed" the earth in the process of Creation and that He manifests Himself "clothed with honor and majesty,/ who coverest thyself with light as with a garment" (Psalm 104.1-2). The glory of the priestly robe is nothing but a reflection of the glory of Yahweh's *chabod*.[1] Its character can be represented only by reference to the transcendent, which is essentially "clothed," which in all its relations with human beings always veils, covers or clothes its power, because they cannot bear the direct sight of God. God said to Moses, "you cannot see my face: for man shall not see me and live" (Exodus 33.20). Closely connected with God's raiment is His dwelling place, His habitation — the Ark of the Tabernacle that Moses founded with Aaron's priesthood. The ark was built at the same time as the priestly robes were made (Exodus 39). Solomon's construction of the Temple represented the crowning achievement of this outlook: the House of God was associated with his *chabod*, with his glory.[2]

The Greek experience of nudity stands in opposition to the metaphysical preeminence the Hebrews gave to clothing. Even before its manifestation in art, the Greek position was expressed in the Panhellenic games through the ethical and aesthetic ideal of *kalokagathia*. Here, the ideal human figure was presented as essentially nude. In their celebration of nudity, the Greeks distinguished themselves from all other peoples. For them, nudity was not a matter of shame, ridicule or dishonor. Rather, nudity assumed a paradigmatic significance that involved clarity of vision (an aspect of Greek religious experience) with an athletic perspective (aristocratic in origin) that viewed victory and its glorious celebration as an end to be most energetically pursued.

With Plato, clarity of vision acquired metaphysical significance. In the myth of the cave, the path that leads to truth moves progressively from a vision of shadows and specular images to the contemplation of ideas. The metaphor of the "*naked*" *truth* comes from a conflation of the concept of truth as visual precision and the idea that eternal forms are the ultimate objects of intellectual vision. From this foundation, the entire process of knowledge becomes an unveiling of the object, a laying it entirely bare and an illumination of all its parts.[3] The body itself then came to be considered an obstacle, a tomb of the soul. Only when the soul is naked — *psuchē gumnē tou sōmatos*, the soul stripped of the body (*Cratylus* 403b) — does it acquire complete freedom. The very notion of *theōria*, which carries such great importance in Greek thought,[4] is connected to the primacy of seeing. According to one etymological hypothesis, the word *theōria*, which is derived from a fusion of *thea* (seeing) and *hōra* (care, solicitude, urgency) implies careful or exact seeing, that is, the metaphysical ability to see beyond all robes, veils and coverings through to the thing itself in its exact particulars.[5] The representation of the nude in classical Greek statuary rests on these metaphysical premises. It was conceived as the ideal form of the human figure, of which our phenomenal bodies are the replicas.[6]

Neither of these conceptions of the human figure, the one rooted in the Greek tradition and the other in Judaic culture, has anything to do with eroticism, precisely because neither allows for any transit between clothing and nudity. Rather, they fix one of the two extremes as a metaphysical absolute that excludes the other. The metaphysics of clothing and of nudity have had a continual influence on Western culture into our own times. They return wherever the conflict between the body's dignity and its freedom is posed in absolute terms.

However, the Judaic tradition cannot be reduced to a metaphysics of clothing, and the Greek tradition cannot be reduced to a metaphysics of nudity. Even in Antiquity, Jewish thinkers such as Philo of Alexandria interpreted the Old Testament from a Greek mentality, giving nakedness at least the possibility of a positive meaning. Philo wrote:

> The High Priest shall not enter the Holy of Holies in his robe, but laying aside the garment of opinions and impressions of the soul, and leaving it behind for those that love outward things and value semblance, shall enter naked with no colored borders or sound of bells. . . .[7]

In addition, the original nudity of Adam and Eve provided a point of departure for whomever wanted to graft Platonism onto the Bible, such as the medieval Adamite sects, the Brothers and Sisters of the Free Spirit who sought to imitate Adam's nakedness and who inspired Hieronymus Bosch.[8] But this grafting remained superficial and did not succeed in going beyond the limits of a metaphysics of naked truth. On the other hand, the literature of Gnostic and Neopythagorean hermeticism rethought Hellenic philosophy and its cultural tradition in terms of a concept of "clothed"

ICONOCLASM DEFEATED

Left: Albrecht Dürer, Lucretia's Suicide
(Munich, Staatsgemäldesammlungen).

Right: Lorenzo Bernini, Truth Unveiled
(Rome, Galleria Borghese).

SIMVLACRVM·VERITATIS·TEMPORE·DETEGENDAE
QVOD·LAVRENTIVS·BERNINIVS·EQVES
OLIM·CALVMNIA·ADPETITVS
IN·SOLATIVM·DOLORIS·INSCVLPSIT

truth, visible in its ineffable glory only to a few initiates. Truth is clothed not only to the profane who have no access to knowledge, but in the end to the elect as well. Truth reveals itself to the elect not in its theoretical nakedness, but in its glory, in its *doxa*. "When you can no longer say anything about the beauty of the Good, then alone will you behold it," says the Corpus Hermiticum (10.5-6), "because supreme knowledge is divine silence and all the senses at rest." Souls, ideas, Gnostic aeons, are all free from the impure nudity of the flesh and are considered endowments of a spiritual garment: "And they shall put on royal robes/And be arrayed in splendid raiment," says a Gnostic hymn quoted in the *Acts of Thomas* (7).[9] To whatever extent the practice of unlimited sexual license may be attributed to the Gnostic sects (attributions which have inspired writers of our century such as Lawrence Durrell), the erotic dimension seems excluded in *gnōsis* precisely by a rigorous dualism between the naked body, destined for perdition, and the clothed spirit, destined for salvation. This dualism impedes any thought of an intermediate state, of transit.

The discovery of the possibility for such transit within Hebrew and Greek culture belongs to contemporary thought, particularly to the work of Hans Uns Von Balthasar and Martin Heidegger. The metaphysics of clothing and the metaphysics of nudity correspond to each other by assigning an absolute value to visibility, but in opposite ways. In fact, Von Balthasar demonstrates how the Hebrew notion of *chabod* not only implies visible glory, but also refers to something else, to something invisible. According to his interpretation, *chabod* is not a static notion but a dynamic one that occupies the tension between a "formless" glory and an image invested with form.[10] This implies a seeing that is not seeing, a figure that is not a figure; a blend of dazzling light and profound darkness. The meaning of *chabod* therefore goes beyond its liturgical and cultural contexts and extends to everything created, above all to man, who was created in the image and likeness of God. Therefore, a transit does exist between the visible and the invisible, between clothing and what it covers. Von Balthasar argues for the possibility of a biblical eroticism independent of Platonism. He affirms a literal, profane interpretation of the *Song of Songs*. Here, Eros is not a symbol or an allegory. It represents nothing but itself and displays itself "in dressing up the boy and girl as king and queen" in "the game of naming in a veiled way that which ought not to be named and nevertheless must be absolutely indicated."[11]

Similarly, Heidegger demonstrates how the Greek notion of *alētheia* has an original meaning that goes beyond the theoretical idea of exact vision. According to Heidegger, the word *alētheia* implies hiddenness no less than uncovering. In fact, the term *alētheia* is characterized by an alpha privative modifying something that is concealed, enclosed, placed under guard, masked, covered up, veiled, falsified. Heidegger proposes its translation with the word *unverborgenheit*, unhiddenness, precisely because the dimension of hiddenness is an essential component of its meaning. This dimension, "understood as a hiddenness, reigns throughout the essence of Being as a quality that hides itself and thereby defines even beings in their presence and accessibility."[12] The Greek *alētheia* then would not imply the primacy of nudity at all, but, rather, a transit between hiddenness and uncovering, irreducible to the Platonic concept of pure and complete clarification and illumination. Similarly, Marcel Detienne maintains that in the archaic period, the religious notions of *alētheia* and *lēthe* form a composed, antithetical and complementary couple.[13] In effect the *korai*, the young girls of archaic Greek sculpture, with their *draperie mouillée* (wet drapery) and their ambiguous and cryptic smiles, open up an erotic space incomparably wider and more profound than the callipygian nudity of classical Aphrodite. *Déhanchement*, the turn of the hips, the basis for the classical female nude's "sex appeal," and the *cuirasse esthétique* (aesthetic cuirass), the basis for the classical male nude's sex appeal, are as apparent as Platonic ideas. According to Heidegger, "In Greek 'outward appearance' is *eidos*, or *idea*."[14] But this very outward appearance, that is, the fact that one's gaze is free to see male and female nudity in their ideal and eternal aspects, renders the experience static and precludes forever erotic transit.

The Erotics of Undressing: Nude and Veil

Christianity made the consummate representation of eroticism possible in the figurative arts because it introduced a dynamic that was insufficiently developed in biblical and classical Antiquity. The force of this dynamic could be directed toward taking clothes off or putting them on. In fact, Saint Paul says, "you have put off the old nature with its practices and you have put on the new nature, which is being renewed in knowledge after the image of its creator" (Colossians 3.9-10). From the first action — undressing — came the erotics of the Reformation and Mannerism; from the second — dressing — the erotics of the Counter-Reformation and the

ICONOCLASM IN SUSPENSION

Left: Parmigianino, Madonna della Rosa,
Dresden.

Right: Boucher, Vénus désarme l'Amour, 1749
(Paris, Louvre).

244

Baroque. Georges Bataille was the most acute contemporary interpreter of the erotics of undressing. In his work, erotic desire and the drive to undress oneself and others, to transgress the taboo of nakedness are inseparably fused. He wrote:

> Stripping naked is the decisive action. Nakedness offers a contrast to self-possession, to discontinuous existence, in other words. It is a state of communication.... Obscenity is our name for the uneasiness which upsets the physical state associated with self-possession, with the possession of a recognized and stable individuality.[15]

Bataille worked within a tradition that assigns great spiritual value to undressing. After Saint Paul, this spiritual value found an important expression in Saint Jerome's proposition, *nudus nudum Christum sequi* (to follow the naked Christ naked), which became a highly developed idea in the Middle Ages. In the Reformation, it was understood in an even more radical sense: the Cross, the punishment and agony of Jesus, was considered the pinnacle, the ultimate point, of Christian experience. From this, it follows that perdition, torture, annihilation, the abyss, confusion, disorder, fear, trembling and death present themselves as models of erotic experience.[16]

For Bataille, the fundamental affinity between the sexual drive and death resides in the iconoclastic tendency that animates both of them. Both tend to dissolve form, destroy the image and violate beautiful appearances in search of a more essential truth, a more radical purity, an absolute. This tendency, therefore, does not stop at nudity; it goes further. The naked surfaces of the body are still only a shadow, an image, a mask. For Bataille, sexuality and death carry the process of denudation to its most extreme consequences. To be wounded, exposed, opened or flayed, on the one hand, or to wound, expose, open or flay on the other, means to lose oneself in an abyss that ruptures the body's deceptive continuum.

This experience reaches a point that can no longer be considered transit, and it is doubtful whether it can truly be defined as erotic. As described by Bataille, denudation taken to the extreme does not allow for a return to clothes. Clothing is held in categorical opposition to nudity. The process of denudation seeks rest, peace and repose in conjunction with a totality of being, in the unlimited fusion of the orgy, in a new metaphysical unity. It precludes the very possibility of representation, because above all its iconoclasm turns against images, against any representation of nakedness. Bataille himself, however, did not adhere to this metaphysical extremism. In his book *Les larmes d'Eros* (The Tears of Eros), he reproduced the world's greatest masterpieces of erotic painting and commented on them with extraordinary acumen.[17] How can this paradox be resolved?

In reality, the process of undressing has limits. Beyond these limits, all erotic tension is lost and it falls into a metaphysical stasis. The most eloquent proof of this is demonstrated in those sixteenth-century paintings by Lucas Cranach the Elder, Hans Baldung Grien and the Mannerists to whom Bataille assigned such importance in his history of eroticism. These paintings are erotic not only because they make the iconoclastic tendency their own, but also because they pose a limit to iconoclasm.

It has been observed that at the end of the Middle Ages, a new image of the female nude spread through the Northern countries, with characteristics profoundly different from the Greek nude. While the dominant rhythm of the classical nude came from the curve of the hips, in the Northern nude this fundamental rhythm came from the curve of the belly.[18] It has also been said that this Northern nude should be associated with the Christian tendency to find spiritual meaning in ugliness, representing bodies in their "naked" reality rather than their ideal nudity. However, the true innovation of Christianity did not consist so much in having reevaluated ugliness, or in having introduced the exemplary image of the wounded, naked crucifix, so much as in having kept the possibility of the image alive after having questioned it. It took painting many centuries to arrive at the figure of a naked Christ, wounded and dead on the Cross. Only in the immediate wake of the Reformation with Grünewald and Holbein did painting dare to represent Christ as a decaying corpse.[19] The fact is that only with the Reformation did the problem of the image of Christ's death present itself as a solution to the problem of the death of the image. Meanwhile, Christ could be represented naked, crucified, dead and decaying, to the extent that the image was only a veil through which His divine and unrepresentable nature could show through. To depict Christ as an Apollo, as the Renaissance proposed, meant to fall into idolatry, paganism. Not to represent him at all would have meant supposing that the human figure assumed by Christ could identify itself metaphysically, through iconoclastic asceticism, with a God that remains, as Luther taught, essentially other. Finally, it meant to aspire to a holiness that by definition is denied to man.[20] The Reformation painters resolved these problems by assigning to the veil an importance equal to that of the nude and establishing a transit between nude and veil of the greatest erotic significance. The veil was not a mere obstacle to seeing

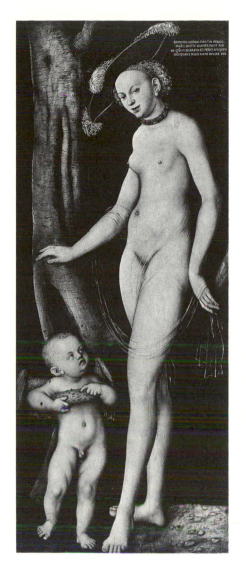

NUDITY AS VEIL AND CLOTHING AS NUDITY

Left: Lucas Cranach, Venus and Cupid
(Rome, Galleria Borghese).

Right: Gianlorenzo Bernini, The Ecstasy of
St. Theresa, 1645-52
(Rome, Santa Maria della Vittoria).

247

with the naked eye, but actually the condition that makes vision possible. The expression that typifies the theology of the Lutheran cross, *Deus absconditus*, means that God manifests himself, reveals himself in a veiled form. To lift off those veils means to preclude the possibility of revelation itself.

There were two dangers in Reformation painting: the iconophilia of the classical nude and the iconoclasm of metaphysical mysticism.[21] An intermediate space had to be created, within which a few dozen sixteeenth-century paintings, masterpieces of the Western erotics of disrobing, were born. The numerous versions of *Lucretia* by Cranach, Dürer (Melanchthon considered Dürer and Grünewald to be *the* painters of the Reformation), Baldung Grien and others, have a double meaning. Caught in the act of lacerating the nude and the canvas together, both the flesh and the painting are saved from destruction. Both are preserved as indispensable veils over a truth that in its nudity remains unrepresentable and other. Their eroticism consists in their being undressed, in their posing no obstacles to undressing, in their self-contradiction as images, in their posing no obstacles to their own destruction; and no less in that they still present their own nudity as a veil that cannot be lifted and iconoclasm as an action that cannot be finished. The impulse toward denudation and truth should be followed without reservation because only in this way can the intimate connection that binds nude and veil be discovered — the truth as well as its concealment. In the painting *Venus and Cupid* by Lucas Cranach the Elder, at the Galleria Borghese in Rome, the erotics of undressing reaches its peak. With her gaze, this Venus creates and follows a series of continuous transits, at once endlessly granted and destroyed, in which the spectator is lost. From her body, which repeats the cliché of the Northern nude with extraordinary grace, the viewer's attention is displaced to the tree that she touches so sweetly. This tree is without doubt the crucifix tree, the *xulon*, the wooden rood where Christ's naked body was hanged, the foundation of Reformation eroticism. However, it is this that opens up, splitting toward the base of the trunk, while Venus's body has an organic suppleness that evokes the *stauros*, the stake planted upright — the Cross. Penetrated and penetrator have switched places: what ought to open up is closed and veiled, and what ought to remain compact shows a cleft and is delicately caressed. The nude Venus veils the Cross. One must see what cannot exactly be seen: that here the Redeemer's body is hidden, and vice versa for the tree. The Cross veils the nude Venus: one must see what one does not suspect is visible; here the naked Venus is hidden.

The transit established by Cranach between the mythological and the religious was developed in a different way by Parmigianino in the *Madonna della rosa*. With Cranach, we saw a Venus that resembles Christ; here we have a Madonna that resembles Venus. Such an exchange, however, has a completely different significance from the one developed by Neoplatonic humanism in the Renaissance, for which, as Edmund Spenser puts it in *An Hymne in Honour of Beautie*, "soule is forme, and doth the bodie make." Parmigianino's canvas is based on the experience of iconoclasm that he knew from the terrible sack of Rome in 1527 and from which he emerged miraculously unharmed.[22] In Renaissance painting, Venuses and Madonnas resembled each other because both participated in the metaphysical idea of beauty. The new iconoclasm, which pushed the divine beyond form toward an unrepresentable otherness, made possible the motion, the passage, the transit from one form to the other. Nothing remains stable in its metaphysical identity. Everything circulates and changes. Mannerism is precisely the artistic experience of this circulation joined to the awareness that any form can veil otherness. The extraordinary eroticism of Parmigianino's canvases does not consist simply in the veil that covers the Madonna's lovely breasts, nor in the lascivious charm of the child, but in the transit that it creates between the rose and Christ's genitals. The first inspired motion is iconoclastic: her grabbing hold of and violating the rose with one hand, and taking the little rosebud of flesh with the other. But the impulse is held back. The act is left incomplete. The Madonna's gaze does not fall exclusively upon one object but takes in both. Her hands, in hesitant pose, seem incapable of taking what has been offered. The incompleted act functions in the same way as the veil over the pubic area of Bronzino's Venus or the nudes of the School of Fontainebleau. There is a threshold to undressing, and once it is passed all motion stops. Like the veil, the incompleted act opens and maintains the intermediate space between clothing and nudity, between Hebrew and Greek culture that the Cross, the point of encounter between opposing metaphysics, opened up.

The Erotics of Dressing: Clothes and Body

Along with an erotics of undressing, there is in Christian culture an erotics of dressing that offers no less charm and wealth of articulation. It is founded on the bibli-

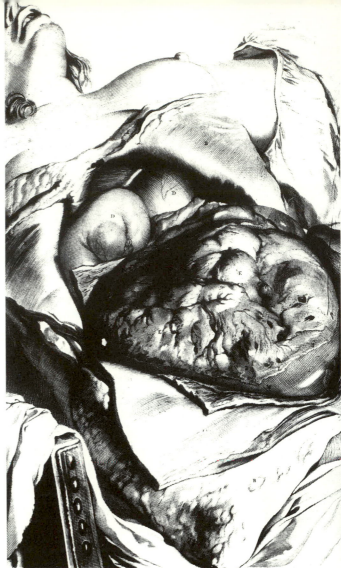

BEYOND THE VEIL, BEYOND THE BODY

Left: Agnolo Bronzino, Venus, Cupid, Folly and Time (London, National Gallery).

Right: G. de Lairesse after Bidloo, *Anatomia humani corporis*, 1685. Private Collection.

cal comparison between the body and the robe, and between these two extremes it creates a transit that makes possible a number of different results.

The most acute contemporary interpreter of the erotics of dressing is Pierre Klossowski, for whom eroticism is inseparable from the experience of incarnation. From the experience of incarnation he draws the notion that the nudity of bodies is not the point of arrival of a process of undressing, of violation, but on the contrary it is the consequence of a process of enclothing, materialization, personification. The notion of nudity itself makes no sense, neither in its classical Greek meaning of ideal model, nor in its Christian Reform meaning of naked body. What counts is not being nude, but being a body, physical and material flesh. The origin of this concept may be found in the patristic writings of the first centuries of Christianity. Tertullian sustained categorically that "everything that exists is body of a determined sort; nothing is incorporeal except what does not exist."[23] The fundamental point of reference is not therefore Christ's suffering, the naked and wounded body nailed to the Cross, but rather His Incarnation, the spirit become flesh, and the glorious Resurrection in flesh and blood. The demonic, says Klossowski, is not carnal but spiritual.[24] The modern world's sickness does not consist in the prevalence of the external over the internal, of false clothes over naked truth, but rather in the fact that the spiritual can no longer be incarnated, in the failed possibility of possession.[25] The phenomenon of possession is not therefore a manifestation of the demonic, but rather its very exorcism. Because of the simple fact that it is incarnate, the demonic ceases to be demonic.

From this comes the liberating force shared by both art and eroticism. Both furnish an exterior covering, an image, a simulacrum to that which otherwise lacks reality. They make present what is absent. They make visible what is merely spiritual. Bodies and art participate in the same work of salvation. They confer form and they redeem what in itself is only nonbeing, negation and contradiction. Both are the actualization of something incommunicable and unrepresentable. This something, which Klossowski defines as "demonic," does not come from within, from subjectivity, from the self. Rather, it comes from outside the self. Thus, it is not expression but *resemblance*. Both eroticism and art move in a sphere of mimesis. The imitation, however, can never be verified, because the original, the phantasm, the demon, can never appear as such.

In the eroticism of dressing, the body is considered a garment: "It inhabits other bodies as if they were its own and in the same way it applies its own to others."[26] The essence of eroticism is thus *hospitality*, that is, dressing what is foreign as if it were familiar and what is familiar as if it were strange. The corporeal transitivity reveals itself in Klossowski's narrative trilogy *Les lois de l'hospitalité* in the act of giving one's own spouse to one's guest. Such an act, which is as irreducible to common adultery as it is to libertine prostitution, emphasizes in the extreme the idea of body as garment. Only by allowing others to take on a body that belongs to us can we continue to see it in its exteriority, as clothing.

The concept of the body as *resemblance* prompts Klossowski to reevaluate nude statuary in traditional and academic painting, the nude as pictorial object of the old masters. In fact, he criticizes the avant-garde, which from Klee onward opposes the body's anatomy to "the anatomy of the painting itself" and thus emancipates itself from any model — any exterior original. In this way, Klossowski says, the "graceful nude" becomes gradually disarticulated and dissolved by the imposition of painting's autonomous laws.[27] According to him, the nude's decadence from the beginning of the twentieth century on is a manifestation of modern iconoclasm that leads to arbitrary production in which possession no longer operates. It is nevertheless legitimate to ask whether the nineteenth-century academic nude could be defined as truly erotic. In the final analysis, the process of dressing that Klossowski defends results in an ultraformalism and neoclassicism based on the contemplation of pleasing surfaces without the possibility of activating a transit between clothing and nudity.

There is, therefore, a limit to dressing, beyond which the notion of clothing makes no sense and gets stuck in a sepulchral immobility. The courtesans of ancient Rome, described by Klossowski in his book *Origines culturelles et mythiques d'un certain comportement des dames romaines*, do not have statuesque bodies, but simulacra of flesh that are rocking and shaking between the arms of the spectators. In another very fine text, *La monnaie vivante*, Klossowski mentions industrial slaves, referring to fashion models, pinup girls and film stars, whose bodies are rescued from their status as merchandise to the extent that they are transformed into the general equivalent of exchange value — into living, circulating coinage.

That is why the great interpreters of the erotics of dressing should not be sought in nineteenth-century academic painting, but rather in Baroque art, where movement was considered essential. The transit it established between clothing and nudity shows up in two fundamental ways: in the use of the erotics of drapery or attire, as we see in Bernini, and in the depiction of the body as a living garment, as we see in anatomical illustrations.

Drapery acquired autonomy very slowly in the history of painting. In the first half of the fifteenth century, in his treatise *De pictura*, Leon Battista Alberti proclaimed that drapery is dependent on what it covers: "Folds act in the same way, emerging like branches from the trunk of a tree. In this way they adhere to all the movements so that no part of the cloth is bare of movement."[28] In Verrocchio's school between 1470 and 1480, drapery achieved independent representation, and later, primarily because of Leonardo's work, it became a determining element in figurative representation. Nevertheless, in his *Trattato della pittura* (Treatise on Painting), Leonardo himself recommended not encumbering cloth with "a confusion of too many folds," but rather letting it fall simply and plainly.[29]

In the second half of the sixteenth century, under the influence of the Council of Trent, the premises for a new view of drapery that would free it of preoccupations with realism were accepted. Representations of the Resurrection and even more significantly of the Ascension of Christ and the Assumption of the Virgin played a determining role in this process.[30] The place once occupied by the naked, crucified body in Reformation spirituality was now taken by the clothed body of the triumphant Resurrection. Thus, a new erotic sensibility was born, one that saw clothing in the light of a new body redeemed from sin and innocent at last. Religious orders played a role in this process, promoting the iconographic celebration of their saints and imposing a model human figure entirely wrapped and clothed in a tunic.

It is necessary to keep these premises in mind in order to fully understand the extraordinary erotic magic of Bernini's masterpiece, the *Ecstasy of Saint Theresa*, made for the Cornaro chapel in the Church of Santa Maria della Vittoria in Rome. Its magic does not depend simply upon the angel's splendor, the evident sexual symbolism of the arrow, or upon the expression that crosses the saint's lovely face, clearly indicating that she is about to faint, but mostly on the fact that Saint Theresa's body disappears in the drapery of her tunic. It has undergone a transformation that has emancipated it from human form, while it still projects all the impetuous and vibrant shuddering of a body in ecstasy. This is why the damaged terracotta model for the

THE BODY AS THING

Left: Hans von Aachen, Bacchus, Ceres and
Cupid (Vienna, Kunsthistorisches Museum).

Right: P.P. Rubens, Venus in Furs
(Vienna, Kunsthistorisches Museum).

254

work preserved in the Hermitage in Leningrad seems even more significant than the finished marble.[31] By conceding less to the formal unity of the work, it accentuates the essential: the transit between body and clothes, the displacement of what lies beneath the drapery.

The deep cavities formed in the cloth of the tunic repeat the folds of a body that continually offers itself, that invites stimulation, arousal, penetration. In the finished work, the angel has the arrow in one hand and with the other he prepares to uncover the saint's breasts. But his pose, much more static than in the terracotta version, demonstrates the incongruity of the act that he is about to perform. In fact, transit has completely engulfed the form of her body and transformed it into fabric.

The passage of Saint Theresa's natural body into the glorious body of her tunic is a transit from same to same that recalls the transubstantiation of the Eucharist. In Catholicism the experience par excellence of Christ's body and blood does not occur in the contemplation of the Cross, but in Holy Communion. Christ is present in the Host, just as Saint Theresa's body is present in her tunic. It makes no sense to seek anything beneath the fabric: "Theresa lives essentially in her tunic."[32] Here, triumphantly innocent in her material covering, in her autonomous and self-sufficient clothing, everything is given. Nevertheless, this new body of hers is not an immobile form. The sacramental presence is a living presence; it is "an ever-renewed motion...that sees clearly how form is only one aspect of what exists."[33] It does not find peace, rest or repose in a pleasing surface, nor in a spiritual marriage nor in theatricality as an end in itself.[34] Rather, it tirelessly and continually flows, ebbs, moves and shifts.

Baroque erotics, however, were not exhausted in the tunic of Saint Theresa. They continued on the path that leads from clothing to body. Baroque nudity is not an end to a process of disrobing. It is a resplendent "tunic of flesh" that in no way differs from the "tunics of light" spoken of by the Church Fathers. This was already evident in Bernini's nudes, in the *Apollo and Daphne* marble or in *Truth Unveiled*, in which nudity and drapery are placed side by side in complete and surprising autonomy. The body as a garment celebrated its triumphs with those great painters who were the most exceptional interpreters of the erotics of dressing. It is enough to mention Rubens, who exalted the texture of skin with incomparable effect and who set up erotic transits between skin and fur, as in the famous *Het pelsken*; or Poussin,

THE THING REFLECTED

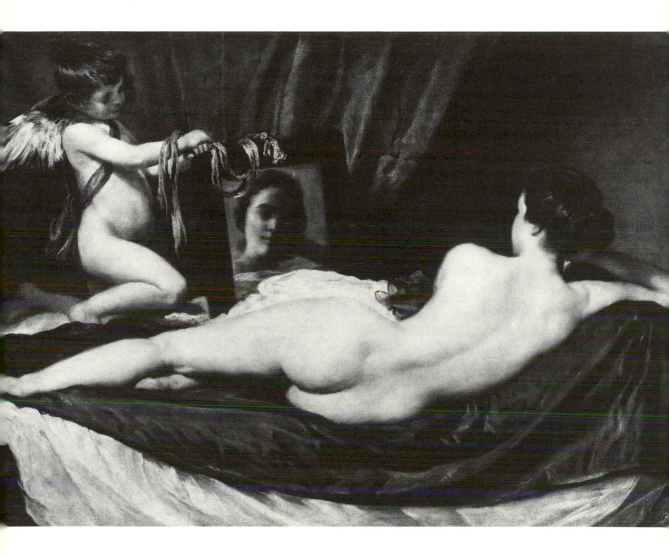

Left: Atelier of Memling, Polyptych: Vanity
(Strasbourg, Musée des Beaux Arts).

Right: Velasquez, The Toilet of Venus
(London, National Gallery).

257

who orchestrated vast compositions in which nudity and drapery are treated with the same indifferent detachment; or Velasquez, painter of glorious garments and of a silken *Venus at Her Mirror*. The high point of this way of understanding the body occurred in Boucher, who painted "tunics of flesh" that do not even seem naked, and who did a canvas that shows Venus disarming Cupid, a symbolic representation of the suspension of the iconoclastic impulse.

The impulse is suspended, not by being postponed, nor by being held behind a veil, but by being rendered useless through the awareness that bodies are garments, not statues, clothing, not substantial forms. From this awareness came Baroque anatomical drawings that pass a surgical blade, the razor's edge, through Poussin's pretty "tunics of flesh," open them up and pull the layers back to show the pleasing surfaces of the muscles and internal organs, celebrating to the utmost their erotic charm. The most significant work conceived from this perspective is probably the treatise by Goffredo Bidloo, *Anatomia humani corporis* (The Anatomy of the Human Body), published in Amsterdam in 1685 and illustrated with stupendous drawings by Gérard de Lairesse, an artist of Poussinian taste and sensibility. Medical doctors as well as artists considered it useless.[35] But it constitutes one of the high points of Baroque eroticism, and it furnishes an extraordinary counterpart to Bernini's "Saint Theresa." In the latter, clothing was as vibrant and lively as a body, and, in the former, the body was as external and glorious as a garment. In both cases the subject is annihilated, one in ecstasy, the other in death.

The representation of the body as garment was certainly not a Baroque novelty. It occurred in fifteenth-century anatomical drawing. Beginning with Vesalius's *Fabrica*, published in 1543, there was a whole series of anatomical works, initially made for medical doctors, and later expressly for artists, that represented skinned bodies with flesh left on the hands.[36] While these clearly bore a relationship to the paintings of the period (especially to Titian and Michelangelo), for the most part they never rose above the aesthetic category of the horrible.[37] A transit between life and death is established, because the cadavers are represented as objects of dissection that are indiscernible from objects of erotic attention. This is precisely the transit created in the illustrations to Bidloo's treatise, which represent the skinned, lifeless bodies of a young man and woman. In these illustrations there is no hint of decomposition, nothing to remind us of slaughterhouses or dismemberment. The internal organs are as pretty as curving breasts, buttocks or vulva. The erotics of dressing go beyond the skin and dress the insides of the body. Even the underside of the skin, delicately folded back to face outward, remains clean and bloodless. It resembles suede or velvet, a nicer fabric than the funeral shroud that wraps the body or the cloth that ties hair, but not essentially different from them.

At first glance, nothing distinguishes these cadavers, drawn, as the frontispiece says, *ad vivum*, from living bodies in a moment of careless abandon, stretched out as if asleep. In an extremely pleasant gesture, the dead woman's hands cunningly follow the opened flap of her skin. The hands seem almost to come forward on their own in order to offer a view of something not internal, but of a finer and more praiseworthy fabric. The illustrations represent a complete dissection in progressive sequence without ever exposing anything intimate or secret. From the sound and healthy corpse shown in the first illustration to the skeleton drawn in the last, there are 105 drawings full of transits from the same to the same. His curls, her pubic hair, the wings of the fly that accidentally lights on his belly, her turgid nipples, his skinned penis that stands up majestically while little nails tack down the scrotum onto the table... it is all clothing, covering, fabric. The tendons resemble the cord's fibers that hold the corpse up by the throat or the straps that bind the wrists together. Even the bones are presented as fabric, albeit somewhat threadbare. Everything is reduced to its minimal terms, cut to pieces and drawn from every angle, such as the tiny footbone illustrated in the final drawing. Everything is fabric, clothing to the very end. Everything turns to dust, but dust is still an extreme covering; it envelops everything.

The Electronic Nude and the Fleshly Garment

In our century, the erotics of dressing and the erotics of undressing appear in porno theaters and striptease acts, but only very rarely do they achieve an effective erotic transit. This happens in striptease when, through an intense look at her audience, the stripper succeeds in inverting a relationship that is usually one-way. From the moment the spectator feels himself watched, it is as if the stripper's nudity functions like a mirror: he has to confront himself and his own potential nudity. Peep shows allow the spectator to watch without being seen, and therefore reinstate

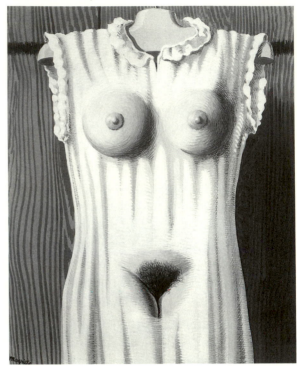

NUDITY AS IDEA AND NUDITY AS CLOTHING

Left: Henri Matisse, Nu Bleu III, 1952.
Private Collection.

Right: René Magritte, Philosophy in the Boudoir.
Private Collection.

the Greek metaphysical perspective, the rights of pure theory, cutting off all possibility of transit.

In porno shows where actors couple on stage, a transit can be created only when the threshold of touch is crossed. The woman who sits on a spectator's lap, or asks him to hold her wrists while her partner possesses her can occasionally be perceived as garment, covering, clothing. But this transit cannot last. In fact, in Western culture, touching is a prelude to full possession that leads to orgasm as its natural conclusion.[38] So the tension built up in the porno show remains inconclusive and quietly relaxes back to normal.

In reality, the erotics of our own times are moving toward much newer and more disquieting prospects than striptease acts and porno shows. These include the electronic nude in computer graphics and the fleshly garment in Afro-American religious possession rituals. Computer graphics seem to be able to generate an absolutely realistic image of a body that does not exist in reality. In contrast to a photograph, which refers to a living model, a computer-generated image is independent of the existence of an original. The electronically realized nude has nothing at all to do with the body. In a positive way it has carried to the extreme the Reformation and Mannerist impulse to undress. In theory, nothing prevents the electronic realization of perfectly realistic images of wooden, iron or glass nudes. So the body can be stripped even of the appearance of flesh. This subversion of the world of forms is accompanied by a potentially unlimited production of images.

At the opposite pole, the phenomenon of the *trance*, the basis of Afro-American religious rituals (candomblé, macumba, voodoo...), offers the image of bodies possessed, inhabited and placed at the disposition of divinity. The Counter-Reformation and Baroque impulse to dress the body becomes radicalized in these rituals. We do not see statues, paintings or drawings, but actual bodies dispossessed of their subjectivity, animated by a force that manifests itself in them. Possession cannot be reduced either to mere iconophilia or to iconoclasm. The possessed body is there in flesh and blood, but it no longer signifies itself. It counts for nothing except as a vehicle that provides an image to a divinity who will not tolerate being painted or represented theatrically in a mask. The divinity needs to don a face, a body.

The electronic nude made of light and the fleshly garment of the Afro-American religions seem to pave new ways toward erotic transit. But even in these areas, there

Idea as Nudity and Clothing as Nudity

Left: Marcel Duchamp, The Bride Stripped
Bare by Her Bachelors Even (Second State).
From *The Large Glass and Related Works*,
vol. 2 (Philadelphia Museum of Art).

Right: Balthus, The Golden Days, 1944-1945
(Washington, D.C., The Hirshhorn Museum and
Sculpture Garden, Smithsonian Institution,
Gift of J.H. Hirschhorn 1966).

remains a present danger of falling back into metaphysics. We have not left Plato's world of metaphysics as long as the products of computer graphics can pass as super-forms whose meaning ends in their visibility. It is not by accident that one of the first proposals for using the new technology explored the possibility of drawing in a single composite image the best features of various actresses, Greta Garbo's eyes with Brigitte Bardot's mouth and Raquel Welch's breasts, for example. This reenacts the neoclassical ideal of beauty achieved by assembling the prettiest attributes of various bodies. But eroticism has nothing to do with such collages.

Likewise, we have not left the world of metaphysical thought when we think of the trance as a mystical unity of man and god, finally reconciled to each other in an environment of spiritual superelevation. On the contrary, the fleshly garment associates itself with the body's otherness. Under these circumstances, the body is not a mere instrument of the subjective will; it becomes an element of ceremonial ritual which is finally free from subordination to myth. The trance never rises to theophany, nor falls into the delirium of pathology. It is "an admirably regulated corporeal liturgy,"[39] often indistinguishable from conventional dancing.

NOTES

1. E. Haulotte, *Symbolique du vêtement selon la Bible* (Paris: Aubier, 1966).

2. M.-J. Congar, *Le mystère du temple*, 3d ed. (Paris: Cerf, 1963), p. 115ff.

3. H. Blumberg, "La metaforica della 'nuda' verità," in *Paradigmi di una metaforologia*, Italian trans. M.V. Serra Hansberg (Bologna: Il Mulino, 1969), p. 57ff.

4. J. Ritter, "Origine e senso della 'theoria,'" in *Metafisica e politica*, Italian trans. R. Garaventa and C. Cunico (Casal Monferrato: Marietti, 1983), p. 3ff.

5. Compare G. Delling's entry, "hōra," in G. Kittel and Gerhard Friedrich, *Theological Dictionary of the New Testament* (Grand Rapids, Mich.: Eerdmans, 1964-76), 10 vols.

6. K. Clark, *The Nude: A Study in Ideal Form*, Bollingen Series 35 (Princeton: Princeton University Press, 1972).

7. Philo of Alexandria, *Legum allegoria* 2.56, trans. F.H. Colson and G.H. Whitaker (Cambridge, Mass.: Loeb Classical Library, 1929), p. 259.

8. W. Fraenger, *Il regno millenario di Hieronymous Bosch*, Italian trans. R. Bigatti (Milan: Rusconi, 1978), p. 229.

9. Quoted in H. Leisegang, *La gnose*, French trans. J. Gouillard (Paris: Payot, 1951), p. 29.

10. H.U. Von Balthasar, *Gloria: Un'estetica teologica* (The Glory of the Lord: A Theological Aesthetics), vol. 6, *L'antico patto*, Italian trans. M. Fiorillo and U.C. Derungs (Milan: Jaca Book, 1980), p. 20.

11. *Ibid.*, p. 116

12. M. Heidegger, "*Plato's Doctrine of Truth*," trans. John Barlow, in *Philosophy in the Twentieth Century*, vol. 3, ed. W. Barrett and H.D. Aiken (New York: Random House, 1962).

13. M. Detienne, *I maestri di verità nella Grecia archaica* (Les maîtres de vérité dans la Grèce antique), Italian trans. A. Fraschetti (Bari: Laterza, 1977), p. 112.

14. M. Heidegger, *Plato's Doctrine of Truth*, p. 260.

15. G. Bataille, *Erotism: Death and Sensuality*, trans. Mary Dalwood (San Francisco: City Lights Books, 1986), p. 17.

16. On this argument, see M. Perniola "Bataille e l'Italia," in *L'erba voglio* (1977), pp. 29-30.

17. G. Bataille, *Les larmes d'Eros* (Paris: Pauvert, 1961). The Italian translation (Roma: Arcana, 1979) includes my essay, "L'iconoclasma erotico di Bataille."

18. K. Clark, *The Nude*.

19. L. Reau, *Iconographie de l'art chrétien* (Paris: Presses Universitaires de France, 1957), vol. 2.2, p. 462ff.

20. Luther's position on this argument is completely different from that of Meister Eckhart or of mystics like Suso and John Tauler. While the mystics look toward a union of the completely naked soul with a God whose essence is denied image or form, Luther excludes this possibility. See the entry for "Dépouillement" in the *Dictionnaire de spiritualité, ascetique et mystique* (Paris: Beauchesne, 1937), and G. Miegge, *Luterno giovane* (Milan: Feltrinelli, 1977), p. 105, n.37.

21. On the relationships between the Reformation and art see C.C. Christensen, *Art and Reformation in Germany* (Athens: Ohio University Press, 1959), and M. Pianzola, *Peintres et vilains: Les artistes de la Renaissance et la grande guerre des paysans de 1525* (Paris: Cercle d'Art, 1962).

22. See A. Chastel, *The Sack of Rome*, trans. Beth Archer (Princeton: Princeton University Press, 1983).

23. Tertullian, *De carne Christi* 11.4.

24. P. Klossowski, *Un si funeste désir* (Paris: Gallimard, 1963), p. 41.

25. P. Klossowski, *La rassemblance* (Marseilles: Ryôan-ji, 1984), p. 107.

26. P. Klossowski, "La moneta vivente" (La monnaie vivante), Italian trans. C. Morena, *Il piccolo Hans* 13 (1977), p. 83.

27. P. Klossowski, *La rassemblance*, p. 83.

28. L.B. Alberti, "De pictura," bk. 2, pt. 45, in *Opere volgari*, ed. Cecil Grayson (Bari: Laterza, 1973), vol. 3, p. 78; *On Painting*, trans. John R. Spencer, rev. ed. (New Haven: Yale University Press, 1966), p. 81.

29. Quoted in G. Dalli Regoli, "Il 'piegar dei panni,' " *Critica d'arte* 21.150 (1976), p. 35.

30. E. Mâle, *L'art religieux après le Concile de Trente* (Paris: Colin, 1932).

31. G. Matzulevitsch, "Tre bozzetti di G. L. Bernini all'Ermitage di Leningrado," *Bollettino d'arte* (1963), p. 67ff.

32. R. Kuhn, "Die Unio mystica der Hl. Therese von Avila von Lorenzo Bernini in der Cornaroka-pelle in Rom," *Alte und moderne Kunst* 12.94 (1967), p. 5.

33. This is what Yves Bonnefoy wrote about Bernini in *Roma, 1630*, Italian trans. D. Grange Fiori (Rome: Istituto Editoriale Italiano, 1970), p. 18.

34. Rudolph Wittkower observes correctly that Bernini's work cannot be reduced to empty the-atricality: see *G.L. Bernini: The Sculptor of the Roman Baroque* (London: Phaidon Press, 1955), p. 35.

35. L. Choulant, *Geschichte und Bibliographie des anatomischen Abbildung* (Lipsia: Weigel, 1852), p. 93.

36. L. Premuda, *Storia dell'iconografia anatomica* (Milan: Martello, 1957); also M. Duval and E. Cuyer, *Histoire de l'anatomie plastique* (Paris: Societé française d'édition d'art, 1898).

37. J. Guillerme, "Sur l'esthétique du décharnement," in *Revue d'esthétique* (1969), p. 139ff.

38. This is not so in Oriental culture. See R. Van Gulik, *La vie sexuelle dans la Chine ancienne* (Paris: Gallimard, 1961).

39. R. Bastide, *Le rêve, la transe et la folie* (Paris: Flammarion, 1972), p. 56.

From *Transiti — come si va pallo stesso allo stesso*, Bologna, Cappelli, 1985.
Translated by Roger Friedman.

"The Face of Compassion," Late Mirng dynasty. From *ACW*. Note how the boddhisattva's lower body has been absorbed into the abstract expressiveness of her swirling clothes.

Tales of *Shen* and *Xin*:

Body-Person and Heart-Mind in China

during the Last 150 Years

Mark Elvin

The human body in traditional China was not seen as having its own intrinsic physical glory. One will look in vain in the Chinese arts for anything remotely approaching classical Greek statues of young unclothed male athletes. Even less can anything be found comparable to the complex interfusion of sexuality, maternity and spirituality that one glimpses in the face of a Bellini madonna. Chinese pictures of the human body, clothed or semi-clothed (in a furtive pornography),[1] are — to Western eyes — meager, schematic and inadequate. Considered from the outside,[2] the Chinese body (*shen**) is a peg-doll whose role is to be a carrier of corporeal and/or sartorial attributes. The corporeal attributes may be the expression of the heart-mind or *xin*, a concept that can be interpreted as the psychological field of force that is attempting to control the body,[3] and which reveals itself in physical structure and posture, or they may be more superficial properties like beauty in the sense of "prettiness." The sartorial attributes are clothes, and items like clothes, such as auras. They basically express social and, to some extent, moral status. Traditional artists often also used them, as it were, in their own right, for what might be termed the parasomatic expression of affect. Thus, the twisted ferocity of a general's armor might be used to convey his martial rage and inner tensions.

Note that before the twentieth century, the Chinese had almost nothing corre-

---

*I have used the pinyin system to transcribe Chinese words and names, but with three modifications to show the tones. Post-vocalic *r* marks the rising tone, a doubled main vowel the low dipping tone, and a post-vocalic *h* the falling tone. These extra letters are *not* sounded, and the standard forms can be recovered simply by omitting them. Their main use for the non-sinological reader is to stop all Chinese names from "looking alike." Those not familiar with pinyin should note that *c* is sounded like *ts*, *q* like *ch*, *x* like *sh*, and *zh* like *j*.

sponding to "fashion." Fashion, which seems to be of late-medieval European origin, has had complex functions (including social intimidation) and complex effects (such as the inculcation of a conscious taste for novelty — though this last, it is true, can be found in a nonsystematic manner in China in the upper-class "crazes" for such rarities as out-of-season flowers and the like). Its appearance also presupposes a particular social milieu, with legitimate fora for the public display of persons of both sexes — social settings which on the whole did not exist in China. Clearly, too, it also critically requires the acceptance of a significant *individual* component, expressive of a particular personality, if it is to come into being. It was primarily for this reason that it did not exist in more than a fleeting form (chiefly hairdo and makeup, it seems) in Chinese society before its partial Westernization early this century. One cause and effect of this overall Chinese syndrome (since the feedback was self-reinforcing) was the depth of the gulf between the morally proper and the morally improper in the traditional conception of the world. There was no accepted dialogue, either philosophical or artistic, between the correct-upright (*zhehng*) and the depraved-oblique (*xier*), or between the public-impartial (*gong*) and the private-personally-biased (*si*). Thus, "virtue" remained uncompromising, unrealistic and sterile, and "vice" remained human and vital but irredeemable, instead of enriching each other by their interaction, as seems to have happened in the classical, medieval and early-modern West.[4] The intrusion of this dialogue, in a crude form, into China in the early twentieth century was felt by most Chinese to be a deadly allurement (especially when it took the form of a high moral value placed on "romantic" or "free" love, disrupting the stereotyped certainties and obligations of conventional family structure), and also a source of general social anomia, precisely because it weakened the barriers between the "correct" and the "depraved" aspects of life. They lacked the cultural resources needed for the easy handling of this powerful, if peculiar, Western aberration, and the Chinese Communist Party, with its savagely puritanical morality (functionally linked to its quest for an emotional monopoly in Chinese society), has tried since 1949 to restore the barriers in even stronger form than before. In all the societies of the Chinese world, whether on the Mainland, in Taiwan, in Hong Kong or overseas, the long-term question — acceptance or decisive rejection of this complex Western mode of perception — remains unresolved.

Let me try to illustrate some of these Chinese attitudes, though it will have to be in a sketchy fashion. Most of the general propositions just put forward, and most of those offered in the pages that follow, will not be more than superficially intelligible, or believable, to readers who do not have their own inner repertoire of experience or of past reading in Chinese sources to draw upon for examples and points of reference. In order, therefore, to make them fully conceptually accessible to those who are not specialists in Chinese culture — and this also means accessible to well-grounded criticism — I have done what I can to furnish the basic elements of such a repertoire more or less in parallel with the theoretical discussion. This has meant adopting a somewhat unusual format. In particular, I have limited myself to a mere three Chinese works, albeit unusually rich and revealing ones in terms of their representative qualities, *not* their literary merits, and I have quoted from them at much greater length than is usual. The reason for both procedures — the restriction on the range of sources and the expansion of the length of citations (all of which are, needless to say, my own translations) — is the same, namely to provide control of context. The contextual determination of the meaning of a given expression of an attitude usually extends beyond the sentence or paragraph in which it is embedded, and requires some sense of the chapter or episode where it occurs, and — often — of the structure and tonality of the book as a whole. Some further remarks on this methodology and its implications are to be found at the end, when readers may judge it after having seen it in action. It can only be hoped, at this point, that the mental switching involved in moving in and out of these imagined worlds, while at the same time following an analytical argument, will not prove too disconcerting.

* * *

My first source is a novel, *The Destinies of the Flowers in the Mirror*, written by Lii Rurzhen in the first decades of the nineteenth century.[5] It is a complex mixture of fantasy and social satire, and needs to be treated with caution, especially as the author enjoys presenting conflicting points of view on most of the subjects with which his characters become concerned. It is, however, just for this reason that the book is a useful guide to areas of problematization in social attitudes, and religious and philosophical beliefs, among the educated members of late-traditional Chinese society.

衛尉安成兵銚期

A General, 1846. From *ACW*. Formidable somatic power comes
through the beetling brows, the hoisted shoulders and the protruded
belly. To a great extent, though, the effect is of head, hands and
animated clothes and accoutrements rather than an authentic bodily
presence. Note how the epaulettes, the belt-buckle and the ankle-
guards all have eyes.

Tarng the Roamer, the hero of the first half of the novel, visits the land of the learned Black Teeth, by whom he is much impressed. Their "refined air...with its atmosphere of Confucian elegance," he says, "seems to come right through the blackness." The inner propriety of the heart-mind transforms the outward ugliness, to the point where he and his fellow travelers find their own inadequacy a source of both shame and discomfort:

> Suffering from the comparison, they found that neither walking nor standing seemed right. Moving along quickly was no good. Going slowly was just as bad. They didn't know what to do! The only way seemed to be to gather their mental resolve, steady their stride, tuck in their waists, thrust their chests forward, straighten their necks and take each pace looking to the front. With some difficulty they made their way outside the city walls, where they were happy not to find many people about. They allowed their stomachs to expand again here, let out a puff of air, and more or less relaxed....
>
> "In normal times," said Seafarer Lirn, "I am used to behaving in a disorderly way. Having been grabbed hold of by you two gentlemen, I have been obliged on this occasion to assume a scholarly air, and make a pretense of Confucian elegance. Who would have thought that merely trying to put on airs would have given me backache, blurred vision, a sore neck, a dizzy head, a parched tongue and a dried-out mouth?"

The moral qualities of the heart-mind had physical correlates, and these were hard — perhaps impossible — to counterfeit.

Conversely, defects of character could lead to bodily deformity. Lii Rurzhen illustrates this in several of his fables about the strange Lands Beyond the Seas. One people are too lazy to do anything but eat and drink. We are told that they are "unable to digest what they consume, and this gradually turns into a constipated accumulation, so a large lump swells out in front of their breasts. With the passing of time, this has become a chronic complaint, causing generation after generation to be like this." The same Lamarckian "evolution" affects the greedy fisherfolk who develop preternaturally long arms, and the winged people who grow swollen heads "from their love of compliments and flattery."

The conviction that moral worth should be visible is most fully developed in the fable of the Country of the Great. People here ride on clouds whose color corresponds to their inner nature:

Brine-lake Salterns, 1249. From *ACW*. The degree of nudity varies
inversely with social status. Workers are stripped except for breech-
clouts; muleteers and weighers mostly wear three-fifths-length
tunics and leggings, and merchants and overseers have full-length
robes and caps.

zone

The color comes entirely from the heart-mind. In general it depends on whether a person's actions are good or evil, not on whether he has riches or rank, or is poor or of mean status. If the conscience in the breast is clear and correct, a rainbow-colored cloud will appear of its own accord below his feet. If...the breast is full of villainy and darkness, then a black cloud will form there spontaneously. The color of the cloud below the feet changes as the heart-mind changes. It cannot be forced in the slightest degree.

In China, we are told, although there are no clouds of this sort, a black vapor rises from the heads of the evil and "goes up to heaven," which is an even more serious matter.

In the Country of the Two-Faced, Seafarer Lirn is thoughtless enough to go out in a tattered cotton gown. Tarng the Roamer, in contrast, wears a silk gown and a Confucian head-scarf. Tarng reports on their outing:

Our original intention was to have a look at what form their two faces took. To our surprise, every single one of them was wearing the sort of head-scarf...that covers the back of the head. Only the front one could be seen. The other face was concealed.

The two-faced people are so charming to Tarng that, as he says, "one instinctively liked them." But they snub the shabby Lirn. When the two companions exchange clothes as an experiment, the treatment they receive is reversed. Tarng, now scruffy and ignored, creeps up behind one of them and lifts the scarf from the second, concealed countenance:

Hidden inside was an evil face. The eyes were rat-like, the nose like a hawk's beak, and the expression surly. When it saw me, it wrinkled its eyebrows into a frown. The mouth opened wide, like a basin of blood. It stuck out a long tongue and spat forth a gust of foul vapor.

The hatefulness hidden behind the veneer of politesse still takes a physical expression.

The ideal form of dress was a system of social labeling. In the so-called Land of Pure Scholars, Tarng finds that all respectable citizens have passed at least one public examination and dress like men of letters. This prompts him to ask an old man if this uniformity of clothing means that "no distinction is made between honorable and mean status?" The old gentleman answers him as follows:

Though the system of dress is the same for all, the color of the cloth is different. Yellow is the most honorable. Red-purple is the next, blue after that, and green the humblest. Farmers, artisans and merchants also wear the clothes of the literati because...any

Kuafuh Chasing the Sun, 1597. From *ACW*. Kuafuh is a complex figure, supernatural but sometimes assigned human ancestry, and also given theriomorphic characteristics, hinted at here by the snake and scorpion he is carrying. He is said to have died of thirst even after drinking the Yellow and Weih rivers and the Great Marsh. Violent physical activity of the sort shown here is not often portrayed in traditional Chinese pictures except for such demonic beings.

> commoners who have not yet taken an examination are termed "vagrants." This sort of
> person performs menial tasks.... Even if there were one or two of them who made farm-
> ing or a craft their profession, everyone would laugh them to shame. Were a "vagrant" to
> manage affairs of state, everyone would shun him.

This place is, of course, a Chinese Land of Barataria ("With this conclusion you'll
agree, / When everyone is somebody, / Then no one's anybody"). What is significant is that both the visitor and the local take it as a matter of course that clothing
should be imposed by society.

We have described the Chinese "body," seen from the outside, as a peg-doll, a carrier of attributes. Seen from the inside, however, it was felt to be almost incomparably precious. We might feel inclined to say "felt by its owner," but this would be
to fall into a characteristically Western way of thinking. From a linguistic point of
view, we can note that in most Chinese phrases that translate into English phrases
where the ideas of "person," "self," "life," or "lifetime" are used or implied, the
word *shen* appears. Some examples will make this clear:

an shen = make peaceful one's body = "settle down in life"

chu shen = put forth one's body = "start one's career"

shen fen = one's body's allocation = "personal status"

shen shih = body's world = "one's lifetime's experience"

zhong shen = to body's end = "to the end of one's life"

been shen = basic body = "oneself"

suir shen = following the body = "on one's person"

It is for this reason that *shen* is translated as "body-person" in the title. From a philosophical and religious point of view, we can further note that Confucianism regarded
the son's body as a gift from his parents, and one that it was his filial duty to preserve safe from harm and reproduce, while Daohism (i.e., Taoism) fostered the search
for a literally physical immortality through the accumulation of virtuous deeds and
the consumption of magical macrobiotic foods. From the perspective of everyday
life, longevity was regarded as the foremost of the five kinds of good fortune (according to one of the traditional rankings), and it was assimilated to the status of a virtue recorded in the local histories alongside exemplary cases of filial piety and of
the faithful chastity of widows. Perhaps the presumption was that heaven gave long

Detail from an illustration to the *Lotus Sutra*, Sohng dynasty. From
ACW. Note how karmic destiny is issuing from the Buddha's mind
in the form of a thought-streamer. The left-hand branch appears to
show devils with a fiery cauldron. Observe also the mirror at the
extreme left.

zone

life to those of whom it approved, though skeptics (of whom Lii Rurzhen was one) noted that many virtuous people had died young.

Late-traditional Chinese were hypochondriacs, obsessed with diets, medicines and health generally. Lii's *Flowers* even contains an attack on tea, which is said to be a slow-acting poison, and he lists many herbal remedies, with full details of their ingredients and preparation, which would be somewhat unusual in a Western novel. Physical exercise was also a matter for concern. When the young lady Purple Mushroom wins an archery contest, she complains:

> People tell me that one does this to relax one's muscles, but I feel pains in my arms after I've been shooting. They say one does it to strengthen one's constitution, but after I've been shooting all I feel is my heart jumping about.

Her friend Second Orchid then explains to her how to shoot with the correct posture, adding that if one can achieve this then "all one's life one will be without illnesses." She goes on to observe:

> People frequently shoot arrows for recreation. They intend to relax and invigorate their bodies, and stimulate the flow of the blood. It is possible by these means to dispel chronic indispositions and increase the appetite.... But if you do not pay attention to proper style and — for example — drag the bow open rather than drawing it, which was what Purple Mushroom did just now, then — although no harm is done in the short run — if you go on dragging for several days one after the other, both your shoulders and elbows will ache. If you don't lower your waist and your vital energy, all your forces will accumulate at the front of your chest. In the long run, you will be out of breath and your heart will pound, but what is more, you will feel pain in the front of your chest and may even develop symptoms of debilitation.

There has been a belief from time to time among Western scholars[6] that educated Chinese of the late-traditional age had no appreciation of the value of physical exercise. This view is evidently a misapprehension.

The effects of mental attitudes on bodily well-being were well understood. The helmsman of Lirn's ship, Duo the Ninth, gives this description of burnout in the Land of the Intelligent:

> They are addicted to astrology, divination, trigonometrical calculations, all sorts of ingenuity and every kind of mechanical art. They compete against each other and take risks to come off best. They use all their mental powers in their determination to surpass

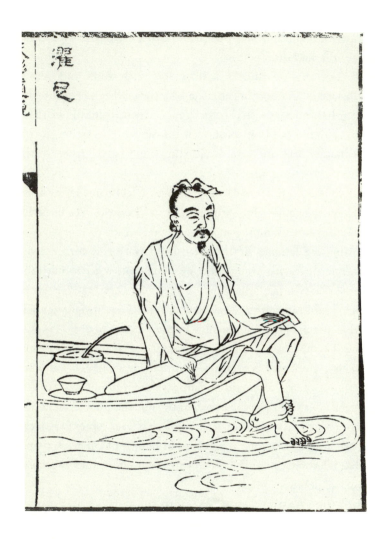

Daohist Sage Relaxing on the Stern of a Boat, late Mirng. From *ACW*.
It is rare to find so frank a depiction of physical pleasure as shown
here in this trailing of feet in water. Significantly, the context is
not Confucian.

others, with anxious thoughts and ill-intentioned cogitations, which are more and more ingenious.... From the beginning of the day to its end, they are only concerned with scheming, until eventually the forces of their minds are worn out. Before they are thirty years old, the hair on their temples is as white as frost. By the time they reach forty, they are farther gone than a seventy-year-old. For this reason none of them reaches a great age.

Another such cautionary tale tells of the Land of the Worried:

Throughout their lives, what they most dread is falling asleep. They fear that if they do once go to sleep, they may never wake up again, and so perish. There are no coverlets or pillows here. Beds there are, and mosquito nets, but they are for the purpose of resting.... All through the year they are in a state of mental confusion. They force themselves to keep going until their nervous energy is exhausted and they cannot even be propped up.... Often there are people who do not wake up after falling asleep.... Since they do not sleep all year long, but keep themselves awake until their heads swim, their vision is blurred and their limbs without strength, while day and night they burn with anxiety, their chests full of depression. If they do once fall asleep, then their nervous energy has been dissipated. They are like lamps that have used up their oil.

Tarng the Roamer comments that "being too anxious is clearly not the way to nourish one's life." He vows that he will "banish all care from this time forth, and, with the relaxed attitude that comes from contentment, live for many more years." Though these exercises in imaginary anthropology may be jeux d'esprit, they had to relate to matters of common and accepted concern among Lii Rurzhen's readers in order to work. For this reason, we can see them as illustrations of a Chinese preoccupation with looking after themselves physically, with feeding, exercising, medicating and resting their bodies.

The Destinies of the Flowers in the Mirror is famous for those passages in which women are shown as successfully playing the social gender roles of males. This was not a notion that originated with Lii — there is, for example, a "Country of Women" in *The Record of a Journey to the West*, though it is omitted from Waley's charming partial translation of this work, entitled *Monkey*[7] — but his exploration of the idea is not only unique in the precision and conviction of its imagined details, but also for showing men playing the roles of women. It is worth quoting some of the key passages describing events in the Land of Women for the insights they afford into a number of different psychological domains: the Chinese idea of physical attractiveness,

Female Acrobat on a Tightrope, 1609. From *ACW*. This shows how
the Chinese delighted in physical dexterity but not in gymnastics in
its strict etymological sense of exercises of the unclothed body.

including the obsession with small feet, which seemed to them as alluring as, let us say, female breasts to men in the West; the way in which the heart-mind could be reconditioned by the breaking-in and domesticating of the body, especially in the case of women; and the uneasy sense that was abroad during this period, at least among the more perceptive members of society (for Lii was not alone in this), that the roles assigned by social convention on the basis of bodily differences were, to a large extent, arbitrary.

When the travelers arrive, dressed in the male clothing that is normally worn here only by women, they see a middle-aged "woman" (in other words, a man) sitting at "her" doorway sewing shoes:

> Her [i.e., his] blue-tinted black hair was rubbed with oil to a gleaming luster. It was so smooth that, in truth, a fly would have slipped and fallen over on it. It was combed into a coiling-dragon top-knot on her head. The garments at her temples dazzled the eyes. Sevenfold precious rings of gold dangled from her earlobes. She wore a gown of rose-purple silk and, underneath it, a leek-green petticoat. Tiny golden-lotus feet peeked out below, fitted with embroidered crimson slippers scarcely three inches long. Her jade-like hands, with tapering fingers, were engaged in stitching flowers. Eyebrows like a moth's two antennae arched above her lovely eyes. Cosmetics lay thick upon her face. A second look at her lips showed she had a beard in the form of a mustache that joined with the hair on her jaws. When they saw her, they could not repress a burst of mocking laughter. The woman stopped her needlework. She glared across at Tarng and yelled:
>
> "Hussy! How dare you laugh at me!"
>
> Her voice had a well-seasoned quality, and sounded like a cracked gong.
>
> "You have beards on your faces," she continued, shouting. "You are clearly women. Yet you're wearing hats and clothes to play the part of men. This is improper. You show no concern about causing confusion between the sexes. You're making a show of peeking at the women [i.e., men like "herself"], but what you're really after is sneaking a glimpse of the men [i.e., the women]! You stinking baggage! Go and look at yourselves in a mirror! You've forgotten what you really look like! Look at your hooves of feet — how utterly shameless! It's lucky for you that you only met *me* today. If you'd met the others, and they'd taken you for men sneaking glances at women, I'm afraid they'd have flogged you half to death!"

Children Playing, Mirng dynasty. From *ACW*. These youngsters' head-
to-body proportions are closer to those of babies than to those of
seven- or eight-year-olds, and remind one of the strong and con-
tinuing Chinese taste for pictures of plump, well-nourished infants,
most commonly shown on traditional New Year's posters.

The inspiration for such scenes was probably the theater where, at this time, male actors normally impersonated females. Off the stage, however, transvestism was a serious offense.

Lii also shows — by reversing in the imagination the real-life roles of the two genders — how women were turned into sex objects, without a full social personality or control over what happened to their bodies. The "King" of the Land of Women has Seafarer Lirn seized for her (male) harem. He is dressed up as a woman, his ears are pierced, and "maids" with mustaches bind his feet with bandages so tightly that the circulation stops, and he is in agony:

Suddenly he felt the need to urinate. He said to the ladies-in-waiting:

"I have to have a piss. May I trouble you, elder brothers, to lead me downstairs, so that I can 'take a stroll'?"

The palace maids' response was to bring a purity-bucket. When Lirn saw this he realized he would be obliged to use it. He tried to stand up. Alas! His feet were bound so tightly he could not move. All he could manage was to get off the bed, supported by the maids, and sit on the bucket.

After he had pissed, he washed his hands. The maids then brought him a basin of hot water and said:

"We would ask Madam to use the water."

"I've just washed my hands," said Lirn. "Why do you want me to use the water again?"

"It's not a question of washing your hands," said the ladies-in-waiting, "but of washing down below."

"What do you mean," said Lirn, "by 'washing down below'? I don't understand."

"That place from which Madam has just relieved herself," replied the ladies-in-waiting, "is the place she should now wash. Since she is afraid to set her hands to the task, let the servant-girls do it for her."

Two fat ladies-in-waiting came forward. One unloosed Lirn's undergarments. The other soaked a crimson silk handkerchief in water and rubbed his private parts. Lirn shouted at her:

"This is a nasty sort of playing about! This gentleman should not make improper use of his hands! I'm a man. It makes my private parts tickle. It's not nice. Not nice at all! The more he rubs, the more it tickles."

When the palace maid heard this, she muttered under her breath:

兩關鎮打拳轄提魯

Luu Tirxiar Gives a Fatal Beating to the Bully Butcher Zhehn, Mirng dynasty. From *ACW*. A scene from the novel *The Water Margin* by Shi Nai'an.

> "You say the more I rub, the more it tickles. In my case, the more it tickles, the
> more I rub!"
>
> When the washing was finished, his feet hurt unbearably.... All he could do was col-
> lapse on the bed and lie there with his clothes on.

The process of breaking him in goes on. When he tears off his footbindings, he is
flogged. He promises to behave and is given a special soup to ease the pain, but his
feet are rebound. He feels that "the dauntless spirit with which he had once braved
the lakes and seas had become like soft chopped tripe." He rebels a second time,
and is hung upside down by his feet. His efforts to commit suicide are thwarted.
Lirn has become just a pretty object:

> The rotting flesh and blood of his feet had little by little turned to pus and been drained
> away.... His body had been cleansed with daily baths of perfumed water. His bushy eye-
> brows had been pared away to arcs like newly risen moons. Bloodred lipstick had been
> applied to his vermilion lips, and they shone in his powdered face.... When the King
> came upstairs to take a look in person...he [i.e., she] gazed with attentive pleasure at
> the golden-lotus feet, smelled him all over his head and body, and fondled him in every
> possible sort of way.... This made Lirn blush all over his face...He was so ashamed he
> wanted to die.

Lirn interests the female King purely as a body.

It is necessary to be cautious in making generalized remarks about the somatic pre-
dispositions of an entire culture, but a number of scholars have remarked that the
Chinese seem to have a relatively strong consciousness of their oral and digestive
systems, and a relatively weak consciousness of their genital systems.[8] Sex is frequently metaphorically assimilated to eating: examples being the comparison of
intercourse with a woman to eating a plucked chicken, and the Shahnghaai term
for the virile member, "the eating finger" (shir-zhii). I am inclined to agree with this
assessment — it is probably part of the explanation for the absence of that perceived
physical glory in the body on which I remarked in my opening sentence. The ideals of female beauty that emerge from the passages quoted above concentrate on
the superficial (perfume, makeup and hairdo), the artificial (eyebrows and bound
feet), the peripheral (fingers and feet) and the sartorial. Sexuality will be discussed
a little further on, in the context of the problems presented by the modern West.

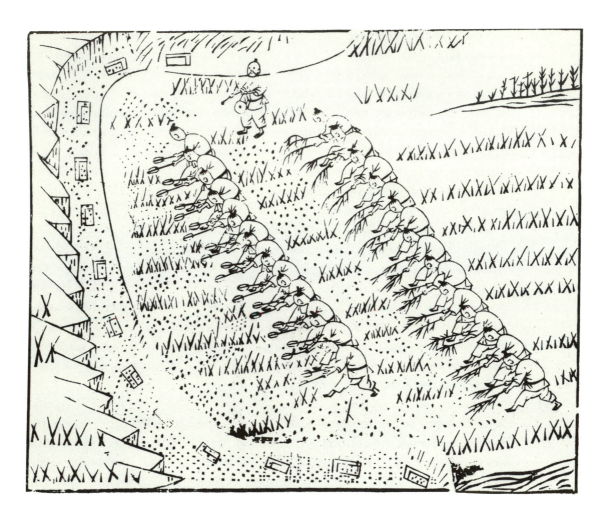

Beating Locust Larvae, Late Qing dynasty. From *ACW*. The larvae were driven against screens and into pits where they were destroyed. This shows that the Chinese sense of the distinctive powers of a collectivity of bodies working together predates the Communist era in which it became so important.

Here, let us conclude our survey of late-traditional attitudes to the body as shown in *The Destinies of the Flowers in the Mirror* with two passages that illustrate something of the oral–alimentary obsession.

Tarng the Roamer, who is searching for the physical immortality promised by Daohism, has just eaten a magical red herb and is delighted to find that, all of a sudden, he can remember everything he has ever written. It does not last:

"I feel a pain in my stomach now," said Tarng. "I don't know why."

Before he had finished speaking there was a noise inside his belly, followed by a down-draft of foul vapors and a slight sound.

"...Can you still remember the poems and essays you wrote in the past?"

Tarng hung his head and thought a moment.

"...I can't call to mind more than a tenth of them," he confessed.

"The nine-tenths you can't remember," said Seafarer Lirn, "are that blast of foul air to which you gave vent just now. The red herb disliked their smell and expelled them. They have already revealed their true nature and penetrated into my nose.... If in the future you want to have your student writings printed...there's no need to entrust some-one else with the job of making the selection. Just cut out the nine-tenths you cannot remember today, and only have the printing blocks cut for the tenth you can remem-ber. I will bet you that those are the good ones!... It's a pity this herb is so rare. If we took some home and gave it to people to eat, think how much work could be saved for the cutters of printing blocks!"

It is doubtful if any other culture would have attributed powers of literary criticism to flatulence, even in jest.

Scatological humor is probably found in some form in most cultures, but the Chi-nese variety could focus on the digestive process as such in a way that was some-what distinctive. Here is a dialogue from the *Flowers* about the Land of the People Without Intestines:

Duo: Before they eat something, they first find a place where they can excrete. Once they eat, they have to shit. It's like when you've drunk too much wine and have to "give a return banquet" with your lower parts at once.... Once something's been consumed, it goes straight through them. That's why, whenever they eat, they...skulk off and do it out of sight of others.... They spend huge sums on food and drink every day. You'll laugh when I tell you how rich families make economies in their budgets. Because the food

"The Face of Compassion," Late Mirng dynasty. From *ACW*. The boddhisattva's body is mainly expressed in terms of her clothes, which mimic the fractured planes of the rocks and have their own life, as do the crumpled rags of the wretch prostrated before her.

they eat passes straight through their stomachs, it may be called "shit," but since it isn't retained in the stomach it doesn't get putrid and smelly. That's why they carefully store this sort of "shit," and keep it for feeding to their servants....

Lirn: Do they eat it themselves?

Duo: This nice stuff doesn't cost them a penny. How could they not be willing to do so?

Tarng: ...It's going too far to make their servants of both sexes devour such muck.

Duo: ...They not only make the servants put up with being poorly fed, they make them eat *and then re-eat* shit that has gone through three or four times. Only when it hurts the servants to the point that they vomit it up, and food and shit can't be told apart, do they start the process over again from the beginning.

A minor but significant aspect of the humor here is the depiction of eating as a solitary vice, since, for the Chinese, meals taken together were — and are — the supreme social activity.

★   ★   ★

A different perspective on Chinese attitudes to the human body can be found in the literature describing the demimonde and the flesh trade. The lower Yarngzii valley, often known as "Wur," was historically the area best known for its refinement and heartlessness in this line of business,[9] though no doubt comparable tastes and practices could have been found in the great cities in other parts of China.

From the later nineteenth century until at least the middle of the present century, these old attitudes developed a new complexity as a crude and oversimplified form of the Western idea of "freedom" in the choice of sexual partners, especially for women, became interwoven with feelings about what was and what was not permissible. Such "freedom" was experienced, on the one hand, as alluring, modern and an impulse that should not be wholly repressed lest a crushed spiritlessness or a self-destructive perversity result, and, on the other hand, as a poisonous solvent of familial duty, social stability and personal integrity. As an illustration of this complex of emotions (which was, of course, essentially an urban one), let us look at a novel called *Shahnghaai: The Living Hell*, written by Leir Zhusheng in 1929.[10]

The *Living Hell* is what the Chinese of that time called a "social novel." This term had a sense rather different from what the words would imply to us today. From a superficial point of view, this genre was sometimes seen as a form of soft pornography masked as aversion therapy, with a flourish of Buddhist apologetics at the beginning and end of the volume, and from time to time in the colophonic couplets with which the chapters opened and concluded. The prefaces contributed by the author's friends to the *Living Hell* give the flavor of this aspect:

> Shahnghaai is the Fairy Capital of the World of Desires [writes Zhaoh Huahntirng], and the Voluptuous Swamp of External Appearances. It is in truth the place where one is "dazzled by gold and drunk on the light from paper windows," where one selects beauties and appraises songs. Why then is it called a "Hell"? Because there are manifold pitfalls. Machinations lie in wait on all sides. If one does not take care not to lose one's footing, one is certain to fall straightaway into the muddy blackness. Powder and eyepencil on a skull! — A beautiful woman is a man-devouring devil. For those who fall into her toils, it is as if they slept before the demonic portals of the Nine Hells.

He expresses his hope that Leir's book will help its readers "to vanquish this Demon of Lust, and escape from the Sea of Desires." Zhang Xiuhnzii, another preface-writer, expresses the same moralist's disgust at the city's society:

> When men are in a ceremonial social situation, they all adopt a compassionate appearance toward others. But — if ever a moment comes when their power and profit are at stake, they bare their arms and look like a pack of dogs fighting for a bone, with loathsome expressions on their faces.... For some thirty years now, I have passed through this world, and whether I have looked up at the gentry or down at peddlers and herdboys, every last one of them has conformed to this pattern. How dignified they are by day, with their tall hats and their broad belts! But once the night has fallen, they are as restless as flies, as slovenly as dogs, in their cravings. Thus, they are devils. Their conflicts are sharpest over money and sex. The Buddha said that when men reincarnate they either go up to the Nine Heavens or sink into the Nine Gulfs. My view is that this world of sufferings belongs to these hells. Those who in former times spoke so loudly about "virtue" and "conscience" to the multitudes were, if one looks into their real nature, merely messengers from Hell and man-eating devils who devoured people, consuming even hair and bones....

A truer idea of what Leir Zhusheng was up to was given by a third friend, Xuu Jiinfuh. It was the tension between the prudence of the controlling heart-mind and the demands of the body:

> "Heaven" and "Hell" originally belonged to the Buddhists' discussions of karma. They

were within each person's heart-mind. One could regard avoiding the fiery pit and living in this world unstained as being, in effect, what common opinion saw as escaping from "Hell" and being able to go up to "Heaven." But how many living creatures are there, among the multitudes that exist in this dissolute world, who can really slough off all bitterness? Leir Zhusheng's new work — *Shahnghaai: The Living Hell* — is full of sadness for this corner by the sea...where good and evil are so mixed. He is not concerned only with the Hells of which the Buddhists speak. He is also concerned with how the young people of Shahnghaai enter into this Hell and often drown, how they are unable to find their way back, and sometimes ruin their families and squander their substance, or else lose their jobs and even their lives. With this in mind, he has grasped the brush of Goong Guu [an ancient annalist famed for his plain speaking] and, lit by the horn of Wen Chiaoh [who used it to light his path in the underworld], has detailed the warped and weird nature of our present-day society.

When we turn to the author's own preface we see that it is, in fact, the problems of human life that absorb him, rather than the titillation tricked up in the cosmetics of Buddhist piety:

> The culture [of Shahnghaai] is our most developed. There is not its equal anywhere else in the country. Most of the young people born here are imbued with the spirit of the times. For the most part, they love freedom and talk in an exaggerated fashion about "liberation." If, by some misfortune, they are born into a conservative home, where the father and mother are despotic and unable to make allowances for the aspirations of their sons and daughters, then a tragedy is played out.

Nonetheless, on the last page of his four volumes, he boasts that he has seen to it that his evil characters have all received, in karmic terms, their just deserts. Thus, the once-lovely Jade Elegance, who has coldly prostituted her body to a sequence of higher bidders in order to rig her own election to the position of "Dance Empress" of Shahnghaai, makes her last appearance as a disfigured and almost unrecognizable beggar-woman on the city's streets.

Leir's underlying, though unavowed, philosophy of *shen* and *xin* is that they are both allies and enemies. The body-person is driven by powerful urges, especially for sex, but also for money, gourmet food, fame, power and security. *Emotions are experienced and described as somatic.* Misery is a physical thing, with a taste in one's mouth and a presence twisting one's guts. Anger is *pneuma* rising in one's body like

"Promising to give up smoking opium, but not till tomorrow," 1927.
From *AS*. For the Chinese world, there is a new and direct physicality about the young lady's posture, in the sense that the viewer
is immediately conscious of a real body beneath the clothing.

steam. The task of the individual heart-mind is to maneuver its body-person with a skillfully devised strategy of interpersonal relations in such a way that these urges are satisfied in a guise that meets society's acceptance, and is physically and medically safe and also long-lasting. The ever-present danger is that the demands of the body-person will overpower the heart-mind. Impulsive action will result, and the consequence will be some form of self-destruction: the loss of inner self-esteem or external reputation, or of fortune or health, or of the body-person itself. Thus, after the petty gangster, gambling addict and ne'er-do-well Jinsheng has failed in his attempt to terrify his former wealthy mistress into leaving a new and more pleasant lover, partly by means of an intimidation campaign that includes having his hoodlums throw excrement wrapped in lotus leaves at the young man, he kidnaps her uncle and guardian, hoping to block the marriage, murder him in revenge and make some money. He bungles the collection of the ransom and ends up in front of a police firing squad:

> It was too late for him to repent, so all he could do was "look on death as going home." Along the road to the execution ground he rasped out arias from Beeijing operas, and then, as the shots rang out, his life returned to the shadows. That these are the consequences for evil men is a glorious display of the Principles of Heaven. His mother bought a coffin for his corpse and buried it in an unmarked grave.

Jinsheng had been a man without compassion. Having caused a street accident in which someone had been badly injured, his only comment had been that "the lives of those who die under motor cars are not worth anything." His nature was that of a man at the mercy of his desires. Leir describes him as "one who, if he has wine in the morning, is drunk that same morning, and if he is without wine the next day, contrives something else." Given to grand gestures toward his cronies when he had done well at gambling, and a bossy exuberance, his compulsion would drive him back to the tables where he would ruin himself again, "with a feeling in his heart like Beeijing cuisine frying food in bubbling oil." He would become listless, and then do something despicable or desperate to recover his fortunes. In the end it killed him.

Sincerity is a peril of a different kind. It is a sort of hypertrophy of the heart-mind, or at least of its moral part, which blots out sharp perception and coldhearted calculation. Its end is almost invariably misery. The heart-mind's job is to serve the body-person, to see that it is serviced and pacified. The heart-mind may ride it, like a horseman, but it cannot wholly subdue it. If the heart-mind of the individual tries to do so, usually by joining forces with the heart-minds of superiors and equals, so forming a collective field of psychological force, the result is a virtuous listlessness at best, a vicious and self-damaging retaliation by the body at worst. The traditional moral standards thus take on an inherently ambiguous quality. They must be observed for a sustainable human existence, at least to the extent required for social approbation and support. But, equally, they are fetters that restrain the fulfillment of the body-person (and of the heart-mind). One will usually be destroyed if one rebels against them. One will also be destroyed, though in a different sense, if one does not rebel against them. This is the knife's edge with which Leir's story cuts.

The fate of an individual lies in the interplay of circumstances over which he or she has virtually no control and the ingenuity of maneuver that he or she can contrive within these circumstances. Those who can maneuver most adroitly are the most admired. Resourceful lying is a social skill appraised with the taste of a connoisseur, and it draws no censure, rather the reverse, if done with inventiveness and poise for the sake of a good cause. The novel's drama thus lies in the tensions between the body's desire and the mind's calculation. The characters live in an undeclared war of almost all against almost all, where everything turns on the success or failure of stratagems to motivate, manipulate and deceive parents, lovers and friends in the pursuit of some gratification. Friendship is to help another with his or her maneuver. Its most refined art is to assist two or more friends who are scheming against each other in such a way as to give both of them most of what they want, and still retain the goodwill of both. The grand master of this skill is a young Shahnghaai stockbroker, called Hua Yurnsheng. He is so finely versed in the intrigues of the demimonde, and at manipulating both courtesans and customers to their mutual benefit, that his acquaintances call him by an honorary title, "The Doctor of Danglies." But even Hua goes wrong on one occasion and has to flee Shahnghaai from an enemy that his impulsive temper has made him in the underworld. The causes are intricately complex, but stem from a dance-hall girl who has deceived him — by being sincere in her devotion, something neither predictable nor comprehensible.

The body-person is also the heart-mind's most important single resource. It is (obviously) the carrier of physical beauty, both female and male. It is the repository of "face," both in the all-or-nothing sense of social credit-worthiness and in the incremental/decremental sense of prestige. Even its wealth seems to stick to it like a physical characteristic, and affects how it is perceived by others. The expected dowries and inheritances of the sons and daughters of the rich are discussed in the same breath as their appearance and their behavior. Female bodies have a precise market value. It goes without saying that this is so for the young ladies — far from the most unfortunate in this society — who are purchased as investments when young by the madames who run the houses of pleasure, and sell them off later as secondary wives to rich businessmen in whom a besotted lust has been artfully induced. Even respectable parents, if poor, may rely critically on the betrothal money they can obtain for their daughters. So when Grace is pursued by a young teacher of literature who makes her heart "turn over like a pulley," her mother cautions her not to be swept away by the lusts of the flesh, and goes on:

> You are my only living treasure. I shall have to rely on you to survive during the second half of my life. You must not study the current fashion and become enamored of freedom, going first one way and then another. Although I have cared for your body, I have not cared for your mind, but I cannot nail you up for the whole of your life. Only — if you are to marry someone, my minimum limit for the betrothal presents coming into my hands is two thousand ounces of silver. One ounce less than this is not acceptable.... Choose someone with a pigtail and from a rich family. Then you will have more than enough to eat all your life! Only — since this is the Republican era, there are very few men with pigtails. But there are any number of tricksters and good-for-nothings in Shahnghaai. If you are off your guard, even for an instant, you will fall into their devilish paths. They will push you into a living Hell. Then you will have regrets!... These words of mine are truly of priceless value.

The less respectable, such as dance-hall hostesses, usually demand a large deposit in the bank and control of the bank book as the condition for giving up their earnings and living with a man. Premature loss of virginity devalues the goods, and so girls talk about it as "losing one's body" or "sacrificing one's body."

Some of these themes may be illustrated by the episode of Jade Semblant. She is a "young lady of the reformist type, with her hair put up in the current fashion." She spends "the whole day ordering the servants and the maids about, and enjoying to the full the good fortune given her by her parents." The author continues:

> It is the nature of humankind that "when one is well-fed and warm, one's thoughts turn

上海春秋　第十六回

今日卻他見亂頭粗服

"Today, however, he saw her with her hair dishevelled and her clothes
in a mess," 1927. From *AS*. The depiction of physical discomfort
and awkwardness is new at this time in a Chinese context.

to sex." Jade Semblant was just at that delicate age when the reproductive organs have completed their development, and which biologists call the most dangerous period, that of "green spring." We may add that she had been born in Shahnghaai, this extravagant place, where she regularly paid visits to the theater and watched dancing, and where every place could stimulate her sexual inclinations. When she was engaged in recreation, it was still easy to dispel them. The hardest moments to endure were when she slept alone under her lonely coverlets, and her sexual feelings surged forth, her pink neck flushed red, and she had wild and disordered thoughts that made it difficult for her to sleep. Sometimes in her dreams she would embrace and kiss a young man until she woke with surprise to find it an empty happiness. Her desirous thoughts grew more and more unrestrained until you could have described her as being permanently in this state. How could she endure it? The biological changes of this age affect all young women. When the menstrual periods begin, and the "milk-mountains" stick proudly out, they all have this sort of sexual inclination.... When young men reach the point where their bodies develop, they too undergo this sort of change, but they can relieve their sexual tensions by going to "steal perfume and thieve jades," and "sleep among flowers and lodge amidst willows" [or, in plain language, frequent houses of pleasure]. Jade Semblant was a young lady from an important family. Such matters were related to family prestige. She could not go out without good cause, and increasingly felt she had no way of easing her tensions.

She therefore starts to flirt with Genluh, a good-looking male servant, who is forever reading pornographic ballads, and is "a hungry ghost ravening for sex." This dalliance, as the Chinese law then stood, was a criminal activity on his part, whereas the plans being made at this time by Jade Semblant's brother, Rurxiarn, to set up his mistress in a house of her own were perfectly proper. When Jade Semblant says to Genluh that she is going to tell her mother that he has been making advances, he is so scared he farts and wets himself. She laughs and says it's only a tease, after which he recovers his self-confidence and slips his head up her trouser leg. They are discovered in this misbehavior by his aunt, old Nanny Rorngma, but she promises not to tell on them, mainly out of fear that she may be punished too. The young servant then induces Jade Semblant to tell some lies to her grandmother, in whose room she sleeps, so that she can be given a bedroom of her own, and he can visit her privily at night. He tells her to be certain that the legs of her new bed are steady, or they may make a noise when he comes to see her. For the next six months "they were mistress and servant by day, but husband and wife by night." Disaster strikes when Jade Semblant is told that she has been betrothed to the son of a rich merchant from Suzhou. She realizes she is pregnant and becomes bad-tempered toward everyone. Nanny Rorngma, confident that her knowledge of Jade Semblant's crime protects her, grows lazier and more insolent every day. She is sacked, and — to her surprise — the young lady does not spring to her defense. So she plots revenge. Disguising herself as a flower-seller, she goes to the fiancé's house. There she strikes up a casual conversation with his younger sister and mentions her previous employment. Jade Semblant, she observes, has "an uncommonly vile temper, and is filthy as a high-street whore." The sister blushes, being at the age "when her conduits of sensuality were just opened," but she tells her brother, whose teeth chatter with rage as he declares that he doesn't want to be a "black turtle," and demands the match be broken off. His go-between, a pompous elderly bigot called Wur Jinfarn, goes to see Jade Semblant's uncle and makes a rambling speech full of remarks like the following:

> When young men and women live in Shahnghaai, it is simply as if they were in a Living Hell. If they make the slightest slip as regards careful behavior, they lose their footing. Their reputations are broken. They are rejected by society. The more advanced a place is in civilization, the more illicit sex affairs there are. This is a general law of evolution!

The uncle finally gets the old go-between to explain what is really on his mind, and he goes back to Shahnghaai to persuade her brother to spy on her, to see if there is any truth in the allegations. Rurxiarn manages to catch Genluh one night fleeing from Jade Semblant's bedroom, but just as he is drawing off his leather shoe to give him a beating, Genluh wriggles free and bolts out the front door "like a dog that has lost its home." He takes refuge with an innkeeper he knows, and makes use of the innkeeper's daughter to keep in touch with Jade Semblant. The innkeeper suggests the best plan would be to persuade her to lend him some money to start a shop, and when the servant expresses doubt as to whether she would be willing to do such a thing, his friend observes:

> She's still willing to have her body messed about by you. Money's something external to the body-person. How could she possibly be unwilling to make the loan?

Genluh slips back to see her, tells her — untruthfully, as it later turns out — that he is not married, and she promises to marry him and be faithful in life and death. In any case, no one else will want her now. She gives him a small amount of money and jewels, and says she will run away the following evening. The innkeeper becomes alarmed at giving shelter to a man who is both a sex criminal and, he thinks, a receiver of stolen goods, so he urges Genluh to move off somewhere else, adding:

> I can foresee that this will certainly not be a peaceful business. The only good course of action is for you to make a pact with Miss Jade that, whether or not there is a lawsuit, she will stick to her oath that she agreed to have intercourse with you, and that in this life she definitely wants to be given in marriage to you. And that if she isn't, she is prepared to commit suicide and is not willing to go back home. In this way you can make sure of being free of blame.

In the meantime, Jade Semblant's brother is fanning his mother's suspicions. Since she doesn't look as if she is in the mood to commit suicide, he says, she is probably planning to run away. It would be a wise idea to check through her jewelry, to see if any is missing. Her mother searches the next morning and demands to know why a box is no longer there. Jade Semblant answers:

> It's mine. Some of the pieces of jewelry are presents given to me by members of the older generation when visiting. Others I bought myself. They are all my property. There is no need for you to check them off.

Her mother flies into a rage and says:

> *Your body and your life both belong to me.* How can you say that I can't check on your jewelry?

She starts to slap Jade Semblant, something she has never done before in her life, and is only stopped by the girl's grandmother. As her mother leaves, Jade Semblant lies crying on her bed and "resolves that this evening she will escape far away with Genluh, and remain no longer in this Living Hell to be the butt of accusations." This exchange encapsulates the clash between the generations that Leir Zhusheng saw as one of the causes of the disintegration of families in modern times. It does not make sense to Jade Semblant that her body-person might in some way belong to her parents.

She had previously been of two minds about whether or not actually to abscond. Now she is decided. She takes a modest quantity of the family's money from the strong room, and some securities from an unlocked chest — not too great a quantity, in the forlorn hope that her brother will not become her "mortal enemy" — and flees. The lovers set up house in Suzhou in rooms rented from a friend of the inn-

The Cold, 1927. From *AS*. The pictorial rendering of everyday pain
is new in the Chinese tradition, though traditional woodcuts of
tortures in Hell were perhaps — to a limited extent — precursors.

keeper. This gentleman, a certain Xuu Wuucherng, has enough local prestige to protect them from blackmail by the local ruffians, who can spot without difficulty that it is a case of free love, or in the vulgar phrase, "a free meal." For a few weeks they live in "the land of warmth and softness" and "enjoy their voluptuous good fortune."

Back in Shahnghaai, her brother observes: "Our reputation already stinks. We might just as well report the case and have the evil servant caught and dealt with severely." His mother sighs and replies:

> How unlucky our family is to have produced this degenerate daughter! Once we report the case and everyone gets to know about it, you and I will have no face with which to meet other people.

Brother and uncle therefore track Genluh in secret, but once they have found him and seized him, they take him before a court. He is sentenced to a year in jail for being "a servant who has enticed a woman into having intercourse." Jade Semblant has evaded capture by her family, and uses what little money she has left to hire a lawyer to appeal against the sentence. To her horror, the appeal court doubles it. She goes to see Genluh in jail and asks him if he holds a grudge against her. He replies: "Your intentions were good. How could I hold it against you?" He then asks if she intends to go back to Shahnghaai. She responds:

> In this life I do not wish ever to return, nor do I want to see my brother's or my mother's face again. It is not a viable plan to live in Suzhou on my own. I want, while I am alive, to be yours in person *and, when dead, to be yours as a ghost*. [This was a traditional belief: the marital bond perdured into postmortem existence.] Leaves fall, and return to the root. Eventually I must go to your home. I should like to go at once to your place in Wurtaa, and wait out there these twenty-four months in bitterness, and then be reunited with you as before.

Then, and only then, does the ex-servant reveal that he already has a wife, though he had been intending to divorce her. Can Jade Semblant forgive even that? What choice does she have, she replies, having left her family for him? He declares that after his release he will do anything, even be a beggar, to support her, and she says she believes he has a good heart.

Chinese novels have a habit of suddenly dropping characters in midstream, which is disconcerting but oddly true to life. Jade Semblant and Genluh disappear from Leir's pages at this point as people, but make a final appearance as fictions. Their

z o n e

Shahnghaai Robbers Administering a Beating-up, 1927. From *AS*.

story has become the sensation of Shahnghaai. Dramatic reconstructions based on information wormed from the family's servants are running in several theaters, and plans are afoot to shoot films of their adventures. At the first night at the Little Theater, we are told, the audience includes "all the madames and the girls from the brothels, all the famous beauties and seductresses from the houses of ill fame, all the movie stars, the men-about-town and their ladies." The miseries of flesh-and-blood people have become the pabulum on which the demimonde amuses itself.

Leir Zhusheng does not take sides in this story, merely commenting:

The guilt of enticing intercourse is heavy as the hills,
The manifold feelings of passion run deep as the sea.

It is clear, though, from many small comments, here and elsewhere, that he has no taste for the class discrimination embedded in the law and in society, and that he sees the illogicality of the double standard for men and women, without really approving an equal freedom. What comes through most clearly, though, is his sense of the war of the bodily impulses against the constraints of convention, and the destruction caused by an insufficiently expert handling of their requirements.

The story of the dance hostess Little Phoenix illustrates not only the perils of sincerity, but also several other themes: how an awkwardness in body language reflects an underlying wrongness in the feelings between two people, Leir's belief that psychic shock could cause severe or even fatal illness and his underlying ambivalence about what he calls "the arena of the emotions." When we first meet her, Little Phoenix is fending off the advances of Hua Yurnsheng, promising to "open a room with him" (as the phrase goes in the Chinese of that time), and then postponing matters. He rebukes her:

You've already failed to turn up on three occasions. I've treated you with the purest loving sentiments. All you've done to me is put me off with flashy talk. I'm also well aware that in the days to come, once this year has passed, next year will arrive. I don't have that sort of time to spare!

Little Phoenix looks at him and says: "If you've such an ardent character, I'm afraid you'll get angry. We'd better keep our date." Once they've settled in a room, she makes the following naive declaration:

The ordinary run of good-time gentlemen regard us dancing girls as playthings. They disport themselves happily with us, affectionately intimate to the point of calling us "my

Intoxicated with Dancing, 1927. From *AS*. By traditional standards, this degree of physical intimacy in public was shocking.

dear," as if we were newlywed husband and wife. When they have wearied of playing with us, they cast us away like worn-out slippers with no heels. Although I'm only seventeen, I've heard and seen a lot about the inclinations of these good-time friends who fall in love with a dancing girl. Eight or nine times out of ten they begin in reckless ardor, but end by abandoning her. Few affairs continue to the conclusion of marriage. That's how I've been a dance hostess for three months, but I've never gone to bed with a dance-hall guest. All the other dance hostesses have their "pulled carriages" [in other words, lovers attached to them as if to a locomotive]. Only I don't. I'm not deceiving you. The reason I twice missed a date with you was because I was wary about starting anything. Now I've "pushed the cart against the wall" [as the saying goes], and have no choice but to sacrifice my body-person. Yet I come from a good family background. I've been to school to study. The only reason I was forced to become a dance hostess was that my father and mother died early, and our family was poor, cleaned out by the way my elder brother spent without restraint. But a person may be poor without being poor in ambition. I've never valued myself at a low worth. When you poured out your heart to me, and said I was a lotus rising from a filthy pool...I looked on you as the foremost friend in my life. I want to entrust myself to you till the end of my days. I do not, as it happens, aspire to the status of a dance hostess. If you regard me as no more than a willow by the wayside, or a flower beside the wall, and your intent is to begin in eagerness but to end by throwing me away, then I swear that's not what I want. Today is "the night when affections are settled [for life]." Please make clear your intentions toward me. If you are driven by sexual desires into dragging me into sleeping with you, then I don't want to share your company. Tell the waiter Ahgui to call in someone else to be your whore.

Yurnsheng observes that he is already married, and suggests he set her up in an independent house in Shahnghaai. How much betrothal money does she want? Little Phoenix answers:

My body-person's free. I'm not asking you for any betrothal money. I only want you to pay over five thousand dollars as guarantee money, and deposit it in a bank.

This will let her maintain herself if he later leaves her. He replies:

One word settles it! Let's neither of us have any regrets! Now I must ask you to sacrifice your body.

She tells him he's a "sex fiend," the "time's much too early" and the money must be paid a day in advance. He pleads that it will take him two months to assemble such a sum in ready cash — a mere pretext, we learn later, since he has absolutely no intention of paying so much — and urges her to make love to him at once. She is foolish enough to trust him.

From the start, their body language is not in good rapport. When she offers him a cup of tea, he says, "I don't want to drink tea. I want to drink your milk." There is a tussle as he tries to undo some of her many buttons, and she gets covered with tea dregs. Later on he pushes her over. Fortunately she falls onto a pillow. "Thank you very much!" she says. "There's no need for you to manhandle me!" Then he finds she is covered with layer after layer of protective clothing: an outer robe and trousers, a close-fitting skirt, under-trousers and a sleeveless waistcoat. She explains why she is dressed like this:

> Dance hostesses have to do so. The usual run of slippery rogues who pay to dance with me think they can have a bit of something from me, once they've paid their thirty cash. They take advantage of the electric lights going out to stretch their hands out in utterly shameless fashion to my breasts, and feel about. To begin with, I wore a double-thickness hygienic slip, but they actually undid the buttons so their ice-cold demonic hands could pierce their way to my breasts. I could not keep to the dance hall rules, but wildly pushed them off, fleeing like a puff of smoke to my original seat. These dance customers fled abashed, and did not dare to dance with me again. So I decided to make this waistcoat and short skirt to wear under my dancing clothes.

Yurnsheng says to her, with a smile: "I've undone your buttons. Don't you want to run away once more like a puff of smoke?" She tells him: "My body is already promised to you. Where should I run to?" "Since that's how things stand," he replies, "undo your waistcoat and let me see your Himalaya Mountains, and look your virginal beauty over." The author then comments: "Half refusing and half consenting, she fulfilled what Yurnsheng had long desired, but since this was a filthy matter, it is not appropriate to describe it."

After they have had intercourse, Little Phoenix asks him: "Why refer to women's breasts as 'Himalayas'? They only stick up 'the most trifling amount.' " Yurnsheng replies with a preposterous pun, showing that the phonetic transcription of "Himalaya" into Chinese points to the following underlying meaning: "When a sex addict sees a lady's breasts, he is as happy as anything.... When he suddenly 'pulls the milk,' she is sure to curse him roundly. When the sex addict forcibly fondles them, she makes an effort to pull free, and as she does so, her shirt is torn." Little Phoenix thinks this is clever, and asks why he has compared her to "the flesh of a newly plucked chicken?" He replies that this was an allusion to the famous but ill-fated Tarng dynasty concubine, Yarng Guifei, whose beauty was said to have started a rebellion by a general thwarted in his lust for her. This seems an ill-omened remark to Little Phoenix. Why, she says, has he chosen the night when "feelings are settled for a lifetime" to compare her to "this doomed demoness?" Yurnsheng answers:

> Who told you to subject me to the process of "cutting down the tree and asking about the roots"? [i.e., asking too probing questions] Times have changed. Emperors and imperial concubines have been done away with.... There are no more taboos of any kind now. Why stir up such useless worries?

But a lurking premonition of disaster has been effectively planted in the reader's mind, as well as a wariness toward the over-presumptuous attitudes of "modernity."

In the morning, Little Phoenix irritates Yurnsheng by the adroit way she manages to wash without letting him see her undressed. He smokes a cigarette to pass the time, and when she emerges from the bathroom, stubs it out on her forehead. Fortunately, she is wet with perspiration and no blister is caused. When she tells him he is "bothersome," and had seen enough the evening before, he tells her she is "a slovenly devil." By putting on underclothes beneath her bathrobe, she has been making fun of him. "But," he adds, "Heaven had eyes, and so the cigarette scalded your forehead." There follows a tense series of exchanges in which she tries to persuade him to agree to act "courteously" in future, but he retorts: "Where's the fun in that?" The relationship, expressed in this mixture of body language and abuse, is breaking up almost before it has begun.

That very afternoon, Yurnsheng engages in some lewd horseplay with two other dance hostesses, Grace and Pearl, in front of Little Phoenix, and she throws him out. Feeling so angry her "stomach could split open," she goes to see a film with a young man called Zhu Chunsheng — a corrupt, charming dandy from a former official family and with close links to the city's underworld. Later, during her working hours at the Soul-melt Dance Hall, this leads to a quarrel between Hua Yurnsheng and Zhu. Hua has come to make up with Little Phoenix and bought her a bottle of champagne. By dance hall rules, this gives him the exclusive right to dance with her. When Zhu tries to claim a dance, he hits him. Zhu rushes off in a rage to find

zone

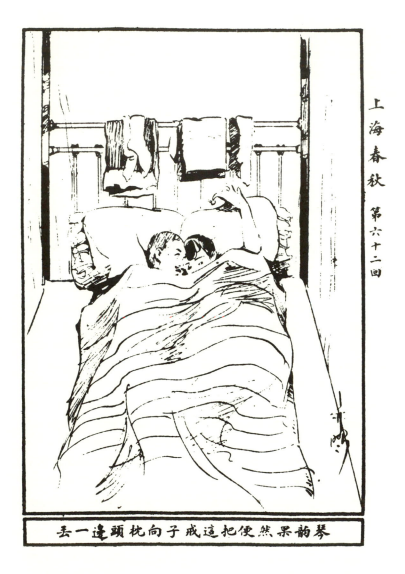

上海春秋 第六十二回

丟一邊頭枕向子戒這把便然果韻琴

The Affair, 1927. From *AS*. The young lady is removing her wedding
ring to show her emancipation.

some fellow mobsters and take his revenge for this insult. When Yurnsheng learns whom he has offended, he is terrified and blames Little Phoenix as the cause of the trouble. She cries and protests: "It was your own fiery nature that was too strong." He snaps back: "You deliberately teased me, and provoked me into striking someone with my hand." He strides off into the night. Little Phoenix calls after him: "If you go to the horizon, I will go to the horizon [i.e., anywhere]." He looks at her "swallowing her sobs and drinking her tears," thinks of the previous night and agrees to forget his grudge. At this moment they run into Zhu Chunsheng with a number of his cronies. Yurnsheng flees headlong and finds a hiding place under a ragged quilt in the shack of a hot-water vendor. Little Phoenix, lying with brilliant resourcefulness and charm, placates Zhu and agrees to make atonement by letting off some firecrackers and lighting some candles at the dance hall. But the unnerved Yurnsheng takes a train out of the city and vanishes. The author continues:

> To speak candidly, Little Phoenix may be thought to have shown the greatest sympathetic concern and dutifulness toward Yurnsheng. Unexpectedly...he was like a kite with a broken string. No news came from him. Phoenix's hopeful eyes became as narrow as gimlets.

She writes him a letter, but it is "like casting a stone into the water." Yurnsheng had not expected her to pledge herself to him like this, and the five thousand dollar deal had never been a reality in his eyes. The dance hostesses he had known before had cared only for immediate money.

Little Phoenix falls into a depression that makes her ill. "For a day she neither ate nor drank, and in the evening suffered from cold and hot spells. Her soul, in its dreaming, turned topsy-turvy." She thinks of Yurnsheng all the time: "What love there had been! And now her young man had already become a stranger. When her thoughts reached this point, love welled up from within her and she wanted to kill herself." The author observes: "Defeats on the field of the affections are the bitterest thing in the world. Men can pursue pleasure forcibly in order to drive away their grief. Women have a softer nature. When they meet with disappointment, they think about it and think about it without ever forgetting it. Thus, only women commit suicide because of defeats on the field of love." Little Phoenix survives thanks to the care of devoted friends. This influence of the mind on the health of the body is a frequent theme with Leir, though he also mentions sudden exposure to cold and sexual exhaustion as common causes of illness.

While she is convalescing, Little Phoenix is paid a visit by a young man called Zhu Jiehrur. The following conversation takes place:

Zhu: I know you've been suffering from lovesickness. I wanted to come and see you, but was afraid I'd stir up your wounded heart-mind. So — I both wanted to come and to stay put. Now, Heaven and Earth be thanked, they predict you'll get better without any need for medicine...ever more graceful, like a willow tree in the wind, or plum flowers laden with the rain, calling forth the pitying love of others.

Phoenix: Who should feel pitying love for me? I loathe my unfortunate life. There's no savor in going on living. I'm only looking for a quick death. The doctor, I'm sorry to say, did nothing splendid. He pulled me back from the devils' gate so I could be a plaything, and give others their stupid amusement.

Zhu: ...It is commonly said that it is better to hate life than to love death. You're in Shahnghaai, what's more. You eat. You're clothed. In both respects you're better off than those in the interior. You've grown to be like a flower in bloom.... Don't you want to change those thoughts of revulsion with the world, and quickly?

Phoenix: I knew that love was pure, that it came from the heart-mind. What I did not expect was that, at the present time, people's heart-minds would have changed so much that faithless young men would put on false masks and trifle with the women in their hands, that with oaths of everlasting devotion on their lips they would draw forth these women's love, besmirch their bodies, play with them until they were bored, and — then — toss them aside like worn-out shoes. What happiness is there in being a woman?

Zhu: There's only one Yurnsheng in the world. You mustn't wipe out two hundred million other men with one phrase! Be optimistic, I beg you. Look on everything that's happened as if you'd died yesterday, and on everything that is to happen as if you'd been born today. If you chance to meet Yurnsheng, plan to act as if you don't know who he is.... Preserve both your body and your mind in good shape....

Phoenix: Don't tell me to lead a romantic style of life! If you think of what's happened to the beauties of former times, the future will most likely lead me to a condition in which I can neither die nor live. My desire is to become a Buddhist nun, and so cut off the three thousand shocks of vexed anxiety, and make the six "roots" pure [i.e., the eyes, the ears, the nose, the tongue, the body and the mind]. Then, to the end of my days, I will not make a cocoon within which I bind myself fast.

Here, briefly, is the authentic mood of disgust at the servitude of the soul to the demands of the body-person. It does not last. Zhu persuades her to join his new film company as an actress, this having been the motive behind his visit, and behind his kindly words of philosophical encouragement. Little Phoenix starts a new life and soon becomes a star, but she carries the karmic scars of the past, especially a deep fearfulness of trusting herself to men.

Thus, sex is a delicious food (and, at one point, Leir makes a character discuss the "flavors" of the different orifices), but it is also demonic, dirty and enslaving. Nor is the female body intrinsically particularly attractive. According to Leir, "the fact is that in this world only men are beautiful with a natural beauty unadorned by decoration. The beautiful faces of women are thirty percent natural and seventy percent pretense, relying entirely on cosmetics, clothes and accessories to create an artificial loveliness."

Success in the battles of *shen* and *xin* goes to those who are able to master their own bodily impulses and play skillfully upon the impulses of others. This is the way in which Red Jade captures Little Hamlet, an amiable, handsome young man who has a certain rather passive susceptibility to emotional pressures, though he can be physically vigorous when roused in an emergency. His most alluring asset is his father's enormous wealth. Of Red Jade we are told that "when she turned her eyes, from one smile a hundred winsome charms were born," so lovely they could "cause a man's soul to become disordered and melt away." When Little Hamlet first meets her at a party where she has been hired as a singing girl, he indeed "loses his soul." She flirts with him, and when he speaks of her beauty, replies in assumed self-deprecation: "My face is like a foot-binding cloth, and my throat sounds like the splitting of a large bamboo. If you go on praising me to my face in this shameless way, I shall die of creepy-crawly feelings." Hua Yurnsheng, whose practiced eye has already spotted "the spring light leaking out" of Little Hamlet, murmurs to Red Jade: "Don't let go of him. Bind him fast with the threads of affection." If she can manage this, and can have him set her up in a "secondary house" (since he is already married), she will have "fortune and happiness" all her life.

Red Jade at seventeen was still "a pure geisha," but only

because her own mother had been treating her as "goods kept back to increase the price," and her director of operations was her maternal aunt, who saw her as "a cash tree" and was not willing to sell her cheaply.

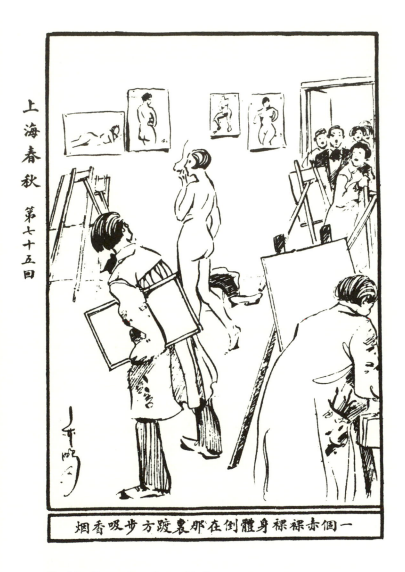

上海春秋　第七十五回

一個赤裸裸身體倒在那裏跛方步吸香烟

The Life-Class, 1927. From *AS*. Though the art students take the nude model, who is smoking a cigarette, as a matter of course, the general public at the door find her quite startling. The unclothed human body was not seen as an aesthetic object in China before Chinese taste was — in the largest cities — influenced by Western ideas on this subject.

zone

One would-be purchaser, a silk-cocoon merchant, has already turned her down as being too expensive. We are told that sexual urges are bubbling up in the young lady, and she thinks sourly to herself: "the truth of the matter is that Auntie plans to rely on me to amass money. It's too bad I have to be paired up with her, and can't meet a passionate gentleman to my taste." So when Little Hamlet informs her that he feels lonely, she at once lets him know her status:

> I'm a person with a free body. Although I'm not my own director of operations, I'm not a chattel servant. I work on a split-account basis. My director of operations cannot interfere with my freedom. I have only to ask you if you want to or not. If you do, then I'll keep you company to the end of your days. It's as easy as turning your hand over.

So when, a little later, she gets an assignation card summoning her to meet him in a hotel, "the blossoms in her heart-mind open forth." Auntie, the practiced professional, scolds her and says that a hotel room assignation is not a good way of proceeding. She should take a companion as a chaperone. Red Jade replies that Little Hamlet is a rich young man "just out of a thatched hut" – he comes from Saigon – and "someone who will not dare to get lubricated." She plays on Auntie's greed, adding: "If I can get a firm hold on this customer, you can expect to get rich." Auntie consents, but warns her: "Don't stay too long, or he'll treat you as a 'geisha chasing after people.' " When Little Hamlet asks her why her aunt has agreed to her coming alone, Red Jade tells him: "I fooled her into thinking that if I could hook you as a customer, she could expect to get rich. I buttered her up a little and she let me come alone. What she's in fact afraid of is that you'll get yourself lubricated." Little Hamlet smiles and says: "Since you have come alone, you certainly will let me get lubricated." She rebukes him. He is a self-controlled person, she says. Why does he have to act like a sex fiend? She is a virgin, even if she does live in a geisha house. "If you don't believe it," she says, "you've only to test it." Little Hamlet replies: "You won't let me get lubricated but tell me to test your virginity experimentally. Let me ask you, if I don't get lubricated, how can I test whether you are a virgin or not?" "Think about it again – carefully," says Red Jade. "When they test for virginity in the law courts, you can hardly mean to imply the inspecting officials test on the spot for themselves?" He persists, and she protests: "If I'm tested by you in person now, my red warrant of chastity will be gone, and even if I have guarded my body like jade, you won't be able to believe it. So please restrain your desires and guarantee the preservation of my purity." Little Hamlet gives verbal assent, but his fingers continue to unbutton her clothes. So she plays the trick she has been planning all along. Just as he is "about to begin dishonest activities," she pushes him away and scatters a handful of coins from her pocketbook onto the floor with a ringing sound:

> She had guessed in advance that he would be unable to suppress his desires, and had turned her bag upside down on purpose, so her money spilled all over the floor. "Pick up my precious things!" she cried at once to him. "I'm relying on you!" Little Hamlet hurriedly let her go and bent down to gather them up. Red Jade took advantage of this breathing space to button up her dress...and push the electric button to call the waiter. Little Hamlet stamped his foot and said: "Who told you to press the button?" Red Jade laughed and said: "I told you to pick up those things to help you extinguish the fires of your lust."

They continue to talk and she lays down her terms for marriage: ten thousand dollars. He agrees and asks her where she learned the coin trick. She explains:

> When my mother and I lived in Wurxir, there was a little tobacconist's shop next door, in which there lived a father-in-law, his widowed daughter-in-law and a student. One night lust rose up unexpectedly in the old man, and he broke into his daughter-in-law's room intending to "crawl in the ashes" [in other words, commit incest]. His daughter-in-law realized that if she complied with his wishes she would lose her fidelity to her dead husband, but that if she resisted she would be unfilial. If she called out in a loud voice and the neighbors heard her, her father-in-law would be both very ashamed and extremely angry. Luckily she was quick-witted and thought of a plan for quelling his lust. She pretended to be careless and scattered several tens of copper coins from her bag onto the floor, crying to her father-in-law, "Help me pick them up!" All the old man could do was to squat down and gather them up. She rushed in the meantime to call the student to come up, and — pretending she was hungry — asked him to cook her some rice gruel. By now the fires of lust had long since gone out in the father-in-law. He reflected that he had offended against his dead son and had no further wish to commit incest. I heard about this when the student inadvertently mentioned the matter to my mother later. When, to my surprise, I subsequently found myself having to make my living in a geisha house, it proved an effective emergency method of dealing abruptly with sex fiends who wanted to get lubricated.

This is far from the end of the story — there is a great deal of unpleasant haggling about the "body-price," which needs arbitration by Hua Yurnsheng — but this episode illustrates well enough the manipulative artistry of the emotions by which the successful in life were thought to have to live.

⋆　⋆　⋆

We approach the present, which in some ways is as strange as the past.

The concept of the body in the literature of the high tide of Chinese Communist emotional extremism, and especially the "Great Proletarian Cultural Revolution" (1966-76), is a polyphony of old themes modulated and transformed and new motifs that self-consciously clash with older sensibilities. The body becomes idealized as the transfer mechanism between generations and the source from which the brighter future will flow. The Confucian insistence on the son's reverence for his own body as a gift from his parents is realigned to accord with this Communist worship of the future. It is used — in a way that echoes, even as it alters, the Confucian vision of woman's duty as providing for the continuation of her husband's family line, stockpiling blessings for her descendants through her own devotion and goodness — to raise the symbolic value of women, who must give physical birth to this future if it is to exist at all. The old ideal of nourishing the body reappears in the form, for example, of the exaltation of the mother's milk that gives the baby life and makes her strong. At the same time, the traditional Chinese tendency to make a "mother" out of Nature is linked in a kind of umbilical patriotism to the concept of the "Ancestral Land," the modern Chinese term for what Westerners would call a "fatherland" or a "motherland." The Chinese conceive of the body as being nourished by this land, and hence they owe it a debt of quasi-filial obligation, and their being is imagined as geospiritually remerged with it after death.

Sexual attractiveness virtually disappears, except for a slightly furtive strain of what may be called "kiddy prettiness." Tourists used to see this in shows by the so-called "Little Red Soldiers," rouge-cheeked boys in shortish trousers and girls in skirts (both unusual forms of dress at this time), doing "progressive" song-and-dance routines. A puritanical internalized sexual self-control allows (in principle) young men and women to walk out alone together at night without impropriety or the suspicion of impropriety. Instead of sexuality, there is an emphasis on health and

"Converting Hydraulic Catastrophes Into Hydraulic Benefits," by
Zhang Xueefuh, 1954. From *Contemporary Chinese Paintings*
(Oxford, 1964). The individual workers are dwarfed by the immen-
sity of the dam that rises from their collective endeavors. Their
bodies are the component parts of a super-organism.

316

vitality as positive physical attributes. Class enemies and national enemies almost always appear as grotesquely ugly and ludicrous, stage villains without that element of remaining humanity which (in Western eyes) makes evil tragic. Obviously, this conception derives from the old notion of the transformation of the outer appearance by the inner moral state. The corpse of an evil person who has been killed is viewed with an excited and satisfied relish.

There is a powerful mystique of the heroic revolutionary body driven by a *xin* that is now a will immune to physical weaknesses, such as pain, hunger, fatigue, disease and fear. This body is a remarkable all-purpose tool and weapon, hardened in a training that removes the old supportive physical affection and toughened by constant tests. Illuminated by Communist and patriotic religious faith, it can overcome firearms with its bare hands, keep back the rising sea when joined with others into a human tide-wall or substitute for broken machinery on a warship. In production, it is capable of a superperformance that, for example, compresses two days work into that of one. Faced with torture, it rises above its suffering in implacable heroic defiance. Where women are concerned, it no longer preserves its virginal purity or marital integrity by preemptive suicide when threatened with dishonor, but by struggle, to death if need be. In war and revolution, its sacrifice becomes a magical flesh-and-blood offering that guarantees ultimate victory.

What is being described here is, of course, the new and distinctive elements contributed by Chinese Communism, not the totality of Chinese attitudes toward their bodies in these decades.

As an illustration of these themes, let us look at Haoh Rarn's novel *The Children of the Western Sands*, published in 1974.[11] It is an inspirational work, awash with revolutionary romanticism, and compared to the best non-Chinese examples of this genre — for example, the Albanian writer Dritero Agolli's *The Bronze Bust* — it appears as something of a wish-fulfilling fantasy. But Haoh Rarn is a master of pace, suspense and highly colored description. He sets in motion a narrative that carries the reader along like a canoeist over a series of rapids without his always having time to be fully aware of the ideological scenery through which he is being taken: the joy and duty of morally justified hatred; the never-ending nature of the revolutionary struggle against class enemies, national enemies and backward thought; the inevitable victory of those with superior moral power; and the inspiration of building at break-

Warng Jihnxii, the "iron man" of the oilfields at Dahqihng, leads his
team in hauling a sixty-ton drill into position. From *SCSD*. This
picture shows the painful but necessary symbiosis of the human
body and man-made machinery, which is both its merciless master
and obedient servant.

neck speed a technically advanced society based on self-sacrifice and a rejection of any ambitions for oneself or for one's family.

The Children of the Western Sands is set in the Paracel Islands, the "Western Sands" of the title. This is an archipelago between Vietnam and the Philippines, and claimed by several countries besides China, because of the oil there. Part one, entitled "Correct Attitudes," describes the period of the war with the Japanese. The struggle of the fishing people against their boss, whose soubriquet is "Shark's Teeth," is interwoven with the Communist-led partisans' fight against the invaders. Part two, called "Exceptional Ambitions," describes the Western Sands under Communism. The first subsection tells of the Great Leap Forward in 1958, and the second tells of the later part of the Cultural Revolution, around 1972. The underlying structure is the sequence of social developments, and it is set up to show how human character changes in a fashion that reflects, in one way or another, these circumstances.

The opening chapter evokes the romance of birth. It is a dark night and a storm is raging. On a fishing boat, a woman is in danger as she labors in the last moments of pregnancy. The midwife, old Mrs. Fur, tells the woman's husband, Cherng Liahng, that she can save mother or child, but not both. He pleads with her to save both, and launches into an impassioned speech:

> Her mother fell ill, and there was no cash for a doctor.... Her father did not have the money to pay the rent for his boat. He was beaten by the Boss of the Fishermen until he spat fresh blood from his mouth. As he was about to breathe his last, he drew my father by the hand and...gave his daughter in betrothal to me.... For fifteen years now, among the births and deaths in the winds and waves of these Western Sands in the southern seas, she has not enjoyed one day of happiness with me. How could I toss her away like this? We have had two girls.... The eldest died of hunger. The second fell into the sea and was drowned.... How can I not want this baby? Midwife Fur...think of something for me!

But the midwife is helpless. Standing on his boat, facing the sea and the sky, Cherng Liahng bursts into a rhetorical address to the unborn child:

> Baby! Little baby! Why won't you be born? Do you look with distaste on our poverty? Yes, we are poor, with no patch of heaven above our heads, no board beneath our feet. Our ragged clothes do not cover our bodies. But child! Your father is strong. Your mother works perseveringly. The great sea is kind to us. The Western Sands give us their hidden treasures. We shall hazard our own lives to bring you up.... Do you fear

the darkness of the world? Yes, it *is* dark. There are sharks in the sea, plunging through the evil surges. There are wolves on the land, doing cruel and wicked things. Poor people are in deep water and blazing fire. But the present time is not the same as your grandfather's day. The risen tide is reaching the point of return. When the dark night is past, the daylight comes. Poor people will lift their heads then, and straighten their backs. The ways of the world will be greatly changed. *Baby, little baby, you are the root of the generations of us fisherfolk to come.* The more the rich cheat us and oppress us, the more we shall live with our chests thrust proudly forward...and continue for generation after generation!

Ideology works its magic on nature:

This voice sounded like thunder. It flashed like lightning. It shook the fishing boat. It pierced the great ocean.

Fierce winds, you have lost heart!

Huge waves, you have lowered your heads!

Wild rains, you have drawn back!

People in the boat, brush your tears way and lift your heads!

Was it in answer to the father's call, or the urging of kinsmen? As the sun broke through the mists, and cleared away the dark rains, at that instant when the wind-beaten waves rested a brief space for breath, the Cherng family's baby cried *wa-la* — the birth had taken place!

These passages should not be read casually. They express the Maoist vision with exemplary clarity: a secular Zoroastrianism illumined by the hope of a secular redemption. The human drama is a never-ending war between the evil, those people who devour others, and the good, those who assist others to have life and to have it more abundantly. Outside this drama, Nature has no meaning, coming into human consciousness only as an expressive background, a contrastive counterpoint or an appropriate response, just as in the oldest Chinese poetry, *The Book of Songs*, now almost three millennia old.

We return now to the sharpening conflict. When Shark's Teeth hears of the birth, he interrogates his sidekick, One-Eyed Crab, about it:

"Dead baby or live one?"

"Alive...."

"Fuck it, man! Didn't I tell you no live ones were to be allowed?"

"Big crowd at the boat just then, Sir. The midwife was one of their lot, too. There was no way I could easily interfere...."

"There will be difficulties — for us — if it stays alive."

"No, Sir. Not a chance. It's a girl."

"A *girl*! They drowned her?"

"They're too poor. I don't think they'll be able to keep a girl alive."

Shark's Teeth, it appears, needs to find a wet nurse for a Japanese army interpreter, which is why he does not want any live births in his workforce just at present. One-Eyed Crab goes to see Cherng and offers him some "gifts from the boss": a sack of rice and two chickens. His wife, he adds, is to "come up to the mansion" in three days. Cherng rejects this bribery and drives the Crab off his boat. His friends criticize him. Such bravery might have been worth risking for a boy, but it's foolish to pick a quarrel like this just over a girl. He disagrees:

The greatest of all losses is to abandon future generations.... Why have so many people despised girls since ancient times right down to the present? Moneylenders and depraved bosses think like this. Should we poor people, with our darkened understanding, think the same way?... We cannot go on like this! From this generation onward we must change this Heaven and this Earth around, smash this tradition! The sons of poor fishing folk are jewels. The daughters of poor fishing folk are jewels, too. We rely on them to carry on our people. We rely on their spirit of struggle to bury this man-eating world!

And he names his daughter Ah-baao, "Jewel." As Haoh Rarn develops his story, he evokes in her, toward her and around her a new complex of somatic stereotypes: kiddy-directed sentimentality, the toughening of physical solitude, antisensual healthiness, revolutionary asceticism....

Some time after her birth, we see the idyll of parenthood, gently but firmly tempered with the Communist work ethic. The family is out at sea:

Ah-baao was placed in the cabin, next to the doorway. Her cushion was ragged fishing nets. Her head was pillowed on her father's torn cotton shirt. How sweetly she slept!

The sea wind blended the strong smell of the fish with the pure cool of the sea, and blew gently through the inside of the cabin. Shining on the thousand layers of the jade-blue waves, the sun lit up ten thousand flecks of silver light whose reflections flashed inside the cabin.

The heavy white sails, the grumbling surges, the rhythmic sound of the fishtail oar,

向沟要地战「三九」，三战猿窝掌大仗打起来。条条石坝映红心，世代红心永不改。

Levering Boulders. From the comic strip story *The Road of Dahzhaih* in *SCSD*. The Dahzhaih Commune was built up, for propaganda purposes, as a model of what could be achieved by heroic self-help. This romanticized, and in places revealingly posturally implausible, picture shows bodies contending with hard, refractory nature.

322

the irregular tread of busy feet as people hauled in the nets — to their accompaniment Ah-baao dreamed dreams of honeyed sweetness.

When her mother went to the cabin to look at Ah-baao, she could not stop herself from clapping her hands softly and calling to her husband: "Ah-liahng! Come quickly and have a look. Ah-baao has smiled!"

Cherng Liahng did not so much as glance over his shoulder but called the woman impatiently: "Hurry! Hurry up and help me haul the nets on board!"

Concerting their strengths, man and wife together dragged the heavy, fine-meshed nets onto their boat. Each netful of fish, flashing blue-silver, crowding thickly against each other, leaping and jumping, was piled into the fish hold. One little saffron-colored fish leapt into the cabin and — with a flick of its tail — sent a droplet of water to splash like a pearl on Ah-baao's plump and rosy cheeks.

Ah-baao's spirits stirred a moment. She opened a pair of dark and shining eyes, and looked in surprise all about her. When she saw her father and mother, she smiled again. She unclenched two little roly-poly hands and, looking toward her parents, began to say *Ah! Ah! Ah!* ...

Her father smiled and rubbed the drops of sweat from her brow.

Her mother smiled and stuffed a nipple between Ah-baao's lips.

Today was a prosperous day.... Just after noon, the boat was already laden full ... and it was time to put the helm about and sail home with the wind astern.

"Today," said Cherng Liahng, "the great sea has given its rewards to our Ah-baao."

This is an evocation, in more modern terms, and with a transposition to the sea, of the traditional delight in the plump babies and bulging ears of grain that used to feature in the colored posters pasted up at the New Year in almost every Chinese peasant home, and delight in human multiplication and the abundant provision of nourishment.

The minions of the fishing boss now kidnap Cherng's wife and try to kill Ah-baao by setting fire to the fishing boat while she is sleeping in it. Her father hears the baby's screams and rescues her just in time. Meanwhile, her mother is lying bound, gagged and hooded in Shark's Teeth's private jail. His plan is simple. He wants to persuade her or force her to act as a wet nurse for the child of his Japanese friend, the army interpreter. This will repay a favor he owes the man and have the additional advantage of discrediting Cherng Liahng in the eyes of the fishermen, among

Little Red and her younger brother, Little Tiger, help the Liberation Army track enemy special agents by finding cigarette butts, cigarette papers and tobacco on the seashore. From the comic strip story *Little Sentries of the Eastern Sea* in *SCSD*. These children are no longer at play, but have become absorbed into the purposiveness of an adventure with adult overtones. The pictorial style, though directly derived from Russian "socialist realism," has echoes of the illustrations of Western children's adventure literature of the period after the Second World War.

whom he has been spreading pro-Communist propaganda. The theft of a mother's body's milk is the ultimate form of exploitation, being the theft of life itself.

The boss begins by having Mrs. Cherng unbound and trying bribery. She contemptuously retorts that "neither gold nor silver can be turned into mother's milk." Then he says he will release her if she suckles the Japanese baby for four days. She snaps back:

> Shameless, shameless man! This milk of mine is to feed the future generations of the poor. Not one drop is for running-dogs or traitors, still less for the wolves come from abroad. If you think you can force me, you are dreaming.

At this point Shark's Teeth ceases to be amiable: "If you don't do what I tell you," he says, "you will never escape from this house, and neither your husband nor your baby will survive." Mrs. Cherng knocks the tray of jewels, used to tempt her, out of the hands of the serving woman holding it, and attacks the fishing boss with a stool. He runs from the room in terror, yelling at his servants to tie her up again. Ritual convention requires that evil be shown as gutless when faced with a principled resolve.

The boss then has her given to a junior Japanese officer to take to the interpreter. On the way there, by boat, she leaps overboard and begins to swim for the shore. The Japanese soldiers kill her in the water with a hail of bullets. The author comments:

> This resolutely pure woman from a southern seas fishing family, unwilling to enter the foreign-style house of the Japanese devils, sank with her heart at ease to the depths of the seas of the Ancestral Land, *becoming one with its rocks and shoals*!

The literal meaning of the phrase he uses in the last clause is "to coexist with."

Mrs. Cherng's determination to risk death rather than defilement puts her in the tradition of the "heroic women" whom late-traditional Confucian piety celebrated with countless memorial arches in the countryside and hagiographical biographies in the local gazetteers.[12] But there are also differences. She does not deliberately seek suicide, which was the time-honored course when rape was threatened. Nor is her motive the preservation of her own bodily "purity." It is a patriotic concern for the next generation. Nor is she going to an afterworld. The most common view in late-traditional China was that wives and their husbands were reunited after death "under the ground," but there were a number of alternative scenarios. One of these, though it was not taken as being the norm, was that the virtuous dead continued to dwell in the groves and rivers around their homes as a sort of benevo-

Woman worker Tiarn Huihzhen on the power lines. From the comic
strip story *The Sparkling Arc-Lights* in *SCSD*. It is interesting to
contrast this picture with the traditional woodcut of a girl performing on the tightrope (see the previous illustration of 1609 entitled
"Female Acrobat on a Tightrope"). Tiarn is said to be thinking, as
she works her way along, that "in order that the lamp of Socialism
shall shine out brightly above, we really must pull out the teeth in
the jaws of Old Tiger Electricity!" She seems, at first glance, more
solid and more real than her sister of 1609, but at a second glance
one wonders: she appears in contrast almost too free of gravity,
too unaware of her precarious position and of the danger of falling.

lent *genii loci*. It is from this earlier idea of postmortem geospiritual absorption that Hoah Rarn has drawn his solution to the problem of finding a meaningful fate for the individual after death that meets the requirements of being both patriotic and free from "superstition."

Cherng himself now flees with Ah-baao to a small island called Gold-and-Silver Island and joins the Communist guerrillas there, who are led by an old man known as Grandpa Weih (a name that, incidentally, means "guardian"). This island also serves as a symbolic parent, and parental body, because it is a source of nourishment:

When his mother was pregnant with him, they had come to catch fish in the Western Sands Isles.

His father had planted in the ground a coconut he had brought from Haainarn.

Amid eager expectations, Cherng Liahng had been born on the little island, and here the coconut had put forth its sprouts.

Thereafter, fishing folk traveling north and south could touch the shore and taste the fresh nuts, whose fame spread far and wide....

Cherng also went to see the well of fresh-tasting water [dug by his great-grandfather].

The well was like a mirror full of light, firmly inset in the soil of the little island. It supported the blue sky and the white clouds. It reflected the green branches and their red blossoms. *It kept within itself the kindly mirrored faces of generation after generation of the sons and daughters of China.*

This well is a symbol of Chinese culture, an ever-renewed source of sustenance, drawn up from unseen depths. Like the Western Sands, it inspires in Cherng a sort of territorial filial piety, because it feeds him in this parental way:

For more than thirty years, Cherng Liahng had...constantly been eating the fruits from its trees and drinking from the springs below its soils. This had enabled him, his body brimming with strength, to go down to the sea to catch turtles, sea slugs and fish....

How could he not be grateful to the Western Sands? How could he not be grateful to the spring of fresh water?

The island responds like a living being to the events of the human world. Thus, when Grandpa Weih goes down to confront the Japanese, planning to fool them into thinking there is no drinkable water on the island:

The rolling breakers on the great sea sounded like drums booming!

The shaking of the tips of the island's trees seemed like flags being hauled up!

From the beach came the wolf-like and dog-like cries of the invaders!

Eventually, suspected by the Japanese of misleading them, Weih is shot and left:

The clouds did not move. The birds did not fly. No tree stirred. Stillness was complete.

Dying, Weih gasps his last injunctions. The coming generations must do all that he has been unable to do. And then, only then:

The wind came up.

The tide swelled.

The disordered clouds rolled along.

The seabirds soared.

The thickets shook.

The southern seas of our Ancestral Land, the Western Sands of the southern seas, the mighty tumbling breakers, lifted up their dirge of heroic grief!

Ah-baao and a friend ask what has happened to Weih, and her father answers:

He has kept safe for us this rich and lovely island.... *He will be with us forever. Remember! Grandpa lives where you planted your coconut trees* [at his graveside]....

The light from the clouds burned and flamed. Brighter it burned, and redder.

The impetuous sea, the stern islands, the raging forests, all that was hidden beneath the waters, perched on the land or flying through the air, all — all — seemed to be covered by one immense red banner.

In this magical world, the human being and his fate are sensed as being mystically interwoven with their environment. When Weih protects the well, he is protecting China, both actually and symbolically. Traitors, who are in league with outsiders, are described as having "no predestined affinity" with it. One would be startled, though, in the context of this way of thinking, to meet with some line like Burns's, "How can ye chant, ye little birds, And I sae weary, fu' of care?" some presentiment of Nature's ultimate indifference.

The partisans have an orphan in their charge, a boy called Ah-haai, who is as sturdy as "the iron anchor from a great ship." His first encounter with Ah-baao, by now perhaps seven, is the nearest the first part of the book comes to even a hint of sexuality. She is having a nap in a grass hut when he arrives:

Ah-haai entered the hut, swallowing down the words that rose to his lips.

A mosquito net hung over the bed, and a plump child was asleep there, with a little pigtail bound on her head.

Ah-haai came up softly and pushed his head in through the curtain. . . .

Little Ah-baao slept sweetly, unaware that someone was looking at her.

Little Ah-baao slept on one side, her plump little cheek pressed against the pillow. Her little lips hung awry, with a single drop of saliva on them.

She had fallen asleep while playing. A bunch of wild flowers was placed at one side, and a branch of red coral was still gripped in her hand.

When Ah-haai saw her, he thought to himself: What a fine little sister. Why doesn't she get up and play with me? 'I've come to play with you!' Shall I wake her? No, I can't. . . .

Ah-haai . . . sat at her side, waiting. He waited for a while. Then for a bit longer. But Ah-baao didn't wake up, which he found too vexing.

He took a small bag from his back, opened it, and out of a pile of much-loved playthings selected two tiger-striped shells and put them before Ah-baao's eyes. . . . He further drew out his little wooden pistol, played with it for a moment, then pulled out the red coral from Ah-baao's hand and pushed the little pistol in its place. Last of all, he thought of the sweets in his pocket. He was just about to take them out when he heard a sound of movement inside the curtain, so he stopped.

Little Ah-baao was startled awake. Her two large black eyes flashed all of a sudden.

She saw the shells by her pillow . . . and the little pistol in her hand.

She also saw a head sticking in from the outside that was not the old man's, nor an "uncle's," nor her father's. . . .

She scrambled fiercely into an upright position . . . and asked in amazement!

"Who are you, who've come to our island?"

The scene is done with restraint, in spite of its sentimentality, but the Freudian symbolism is evident: the moist, half-open lips, the torn-out red coral, and the thrust-in pistol. Perhaps this sort of kiddy romance was to some extent a substitute for the adult sexuality that was taboo during this period. Children's bodies were the only bodies in which adult eyes could take a public and permissible pleasure.

When we meet Ah-baao in the first section of part two, almost grown up, the author's emphasis is on a healthy attractiveness:

Her jet-black hair was worn in a long, coarse plait. Her round face was of a ruddy, youthful delicacy, her large eyes bright and vivacious. She wore a flower-patterned shirt with short sleeves, and loose-fitting dark blue trousers. On her lapel was the badge of the Communist Youth League.

Battling the Waves. From the comic strip *The Surging Waves of the Haaiher River* in *SCSD*. Visually, this has much in common with the earlier picture of Kuafuh chasing the sun. Violent physical activity of this sort is now no longer demonic, but, even so, there is something unreasonable and requiring quasi-supernatural powers in the attempt to deal, in this way, with a breach in a dike.

The nearest Haoh Rarn comes to a hint of sexuality here is in the following episode, which ends with a brisk return to ideological propriety. Ah-baao is poling her
sampan along the shore one day when she finds a crowd waiting anxiously by a reef.
They tell her "a naval comrade" has dived in to find the cause of a recent wreck,
but he has been under the water worryingly long:

> Ah-baao took off the bamboo hat from her head, removed the singlet that covered
> her chest, curved her body with her legs together and plunged into the water with a
> neat sound.
>
> A flower-like whirlpool appeared on the clear blue surface of the sea, then swiftly
> subsided, leaving the ripples floating like veins in marble.
>
> Her empty sampan tossed about uncontrolled. In the waves, the shaft of the oar stirred
> time and again, and banged against the gunwales. . . .
>
> Ah-baao sank down to the sea floor and swam this way and that, groping.
>
> A large, fat fish brushed across her back, then fled, startled.
>
> A bunch of long, soft seaweed floated past, rubbing against her chest.
>
> Suddenly her hand encountered a sturdy, pillar-like arm, and at the same time her
> own arm was grasped by a firm hand.
>
> Pulled by that hand, her head broke clear of the surface. . . .
>
> Following the sailor, who had risen through the water at the same time as she had,
> she scrambled back onto the little tossing sampan.
>
> She took a breath of air, wiped the water from her face with her hands, looked up,
> and was all at once struck dumb.
>
> "It's you, Ah-baao!" cried the sailor.
>
> "Elder brother Haailorng [Ah-haai's real name]!" Ah-baao could not prevent herself
> from exclaiming. . . .
>
> "What have you come to do?"
>
> "Build up the Western Sands," she said. "And you?"
>
> "Defend them!"

On the surface the episode is wholly proper. But it seems unlikely that it is only
the European mind that finds the undressing, the dive, the whirlpool, the jerk-
ing oar and the underwater caressing as suggesting rather more than they speak
of openly. The old Shahnghaai slang for sexual penetration was "entering the
fish pool."

zone

331

On another occasion, Haailorng and Ah-baao stroll together through a moonlit night – talking about the problem of imperialism and on their way to a Party meeting. Some time later, when Ah-baao's closest female friend, Yahjuan, says that young men and women should not sing together, because her mother has told her to keep men at a certain distance, Ah-baao disagrees:

That's a remnant of old feudal thought. We can't bring it into our pure Western Sands.

We mustn't follow their way of thinking or acting. We must do the opposite!

Internal restraints are now assumed to be so effective that traditional external caution appears – through what it implies about human impulses – to be provocatively dirty. Physical proximity between those of the opposite sex becomes permissible in proportion to the establishment of a kind of inner psychological distance.

Except for a few crafty exceptions who manage to conceal their true nature, class enemies and national enemies appear physically repulsive. They are frequently described as devils or animals. The morality play of Communist existence is, to a considerable extent, acted out in terms of a body language in which appearance, expressing an inward power of character, has an immediate effect on the course of events. Westerners who were astonished to read press reports of Chinese soldiers taking down their trousers and presenting their buttocks to Soviet Russian soldiers during the quarrel between the PRC and the USSR over Zhenbaao/Damianskii Island in the Amur River, mostly failed to realize that this was a form of morale-vaunting insult deeply rooted in Chinese Communist culture. Haoh Rarn gives a number of illustrations of this which are particularly clear-cut because they are fictional. Here is how a Chinese fishing boat, steered and inspired by Ah-baao, cows a South Vietnamese frigate:

The enemy vessel seemed like a wild beast. It loomed up, clearer and clearer, rushing with a grunting-chugging sound toward the fishing boat from the [Chinese] Sunwards Brigade.

Its large guns stuck out their necks.

Its signal lights winked unceasingly.

Scrawny soldiers of different sizes stood about limply, or sat dejectedly on the deck.

There were a few officers, with their caps set awry, and with evil glances, holding rifles in their hands, while cigarettes dangled from their mouths. . . .

An officer on the enemy vessel, who was wearing a hat that did not fully cover his scabby head, was somewhat surprised when he saw the fishing boat did not give way. He blinked his eyes and gave the order:

"Let them begin by feeling our authority. Straight ahead! Straight ahead!"...

The enemy vessel and the fishing boat came closer and closer together. They were about to collide.

The soldiers dodged backward in panic.

The officers hid themselves — even more quickly and further away.

"Captain! Captain!" said a little officer, almost unable to speak, "This won't do, won't do! We're going to meet head on!"

Without any concern for doing it in the proper form, or putting on a proper act, Scabby-Head pettishly gave the hand signal to go astern....

The fishing-boat forged past, straight ahead.

Its motor sounded *putt-putt*.

The water shouted as it swashed past.

The red flag made a brisk flapping sound.

Some of the Commune members even laughed at the enemy derisively.

Ah-baao stood, as tall as tall could be, in the wheelhouse, staring angrily at the foe....

To us, this is a literary comic strip. People's physical attributes, and the way they move, express their simple inner characteristics with a brutal unsubtlety. But the element of theatricality inherent in the Chinese conception of the conduct of life probably makes the passage seem less overdone to them than it appears to the European or North American. The roles have their own power, but only if they are played with conviction.

Some days later, the battle resumes. This time there are two South Vietnamese warships:

The scabby-headed officer, who was in a rage from his shame, stood at the prow of one ship and purposely stuck out his stomach and blew up his cheeks, with his two hands placed on his hips.

The soldiers who had turned tail, with their heads reeling, had all revived their spirits and, with beetling eyebrows and wide-open eyes, assumed an appearance of ferocity....

Several large guns rotated swiftly and trained their barrels on the Sunwards boat.

Several tens of rifles rose and together took aim at the fisherfolk in the Sunwards boat.

The fisherfolk scowled and faced them with cold disdain....

The Face of Compassion — Socialist Style. From the comic strip
story *Cliffs of the Flying Eagles* in *SCSD*. Little Xiuh Liipirng, shown
kneeling here, has suffered tortures at the hands of an evil land-
lord, and here her rescuers, stars on their caps, and pity mingling
with grim resolution on their faces, gently console her. She is crying,
but the tears are wholesome.

Scabby-head wiped away the beads of sweat dribbling down his face and stamped his foot, shouting: "Be quick and leave the seas around the Western Sands Islands. If you don't, we shall not treat you kindly!"

Uncle Lii put his fingers to his nose and replied:

"The seas around the Western Sands are China's. Bastards are not allowed to boss us around. Hurry up and beat it!"

Scabby-head went brown with anger, and suddenly pulled a pistol from his waist.... The soldiers...pressed in cartridges and pushed down the bolts on their rifles.

Ah-baao, in the wheelhouse, had already seen that the enemy were outwardly strong but inwardly feeble.... She at once resolved to crush the morale of the foe....

Just at this instant Uncle Lii, who was at the prow, gave a glare and took a pace fiercely forward. With a ripping sound, he pulled open his clothes and stuck out his broad chest at the enemy.

With a swishing sound, Yahjuan and the other Commune members surged forward and all did the same as Uncle Lii, facing the bayonets and rifles with no sign of weakness.

Scabby-head could not help himself. He took a gulp of cold air. He brandished his pistol.

"If you don't retreat, we'll fire!"

Uncle Lii slapped his chest with a large hand: "Fire, you bastards! If any of you have the guts to do so, fire here!"

Scabby-head's hand holding the revolver wobbled....

Ah-baao gave a faint smile...: "If you are blinded by lust for gain and dare to disturb even one of our hairs, the entire Chinese people, the people of the entire world, will not forgive you! Not one of you need think of reaching old age!"

Cold sweat covered Scabby-head's brow. His hands could not move. His lips could not speak. They had this final ace to play and would not throw in their hands....

The muted playacting of everyday Chinese life, which is often conducted with a considerable finesse, has become easily visible here because of literary exaggeration.

When, later, there is a real naval battle between South Vietnamese warships and a Chinese frigate captained by Haailorng, the vanquished Vietnamese are depicted as grotesque:

The enemy ship broke out everywhere in flames.

The enemy on the decks either died or crawled away.

Chagrin at Having Been Tricked. From the comic strip story *Flames of War Beside the Furnaces* in *SCSD*. Little Mirng (seated left) has been tricked by a class enemy into causing a steel-furnace to explode. He is overcome with remorse, but the Party Secretary (center) simply smiles and tells him never to forget the lessons of this experience.

The junior officers expired on the spot.

Scabby-head hung over the rails like a dried fish....

The enemy soldiers still alive leapt into the sea at random like terrified, itchy frogs.

There are no honorable foes — a concept probably requiring a feudal background, something absent in clear form from China for about two-and-one-half thousand years. Killing class enemies and traitors is experienced as a moral and physical pleasure. When Ah-baao discovers One-Eyed Crab making his getaway one night in a sampan, carrying military intelligence to the South Vietnamese, she leaps fully clothed into the sea to swim after him. By a feat of remarkable strength, she carries her militia rifle above her head to keep it dry. Revolutionary superperformance is a routine payoff of advanced ideological dedication. In a symbolic reversal of her mother's death in the waves, she rise out of the sea to take her revenge. She scrambles on board the little boat. The terrified One-Eyed Crab argues with her that he is guiltless. She is not convinced. He leaps into the water. When his head breaks the surface to breathe, she shoots him:

> The corpse of One-Eyed Crab was turned over again by the sea. Then it sank once more.
>
> Ah-baao felt her heart give a jump at this moment, a tremendous jump.
>
> It was a jump of excitement, a jump of joy.
>
> She pressed her young face, her slightly flushed face, lovingly against the chamber of the rifle that was grasped in her hand.
>
> The chamber of the rifle was warm too.
>
> The waves leapt happily at her side. Was it because they wished to come on board the sampan to hug her or to hold her hand affectionately?

Haoh Rarn has the sinister gift of making violence beautiful.

The Communist's body is thus the servant of a revolutionary and patriotic will. Even as a toddler on Gold-and-Silver Island, Ah-baao is already teaching this lesson to adults. On one such occasion, the guerrillas have to lie in wait to ambush a Japanese munitions ship. This means no fires, and hence no cooking of food. (Chinese regard raw food, apart from fruits, as barely being edible.) Days go by, and those waiting get hungry.

> One of the soldiers said: "We grown-ups can bear it, but what about the little one?"...
>
> Grandpa Weih wanted to say something, but he swallowed down his words and looked at Cherng Liahng.

On Duty. From *HDF*. How insignia transform the meaning of a person — here just the red cross on the armband, and the star upon the satchel. The humble becomes heroic.

Cherng Liahng gritted his teeth and said: "No. No. Don't cook even a little food. The orders of higher levels — discipline — must be obeyed."

"What are we to do," said a solider, "if the little one starves?"...

Cherng Liahng gave a dismissive wave of his hand: "No cooking of rice even if she is starving...."

Grandpa Weih nodded.

"Ah-baao," he said, "if we're going to give the wolves a thrashing, thrash the Japanese devils, we've got to take a bit of suffering, bear a bit of hunger. Can you manage?"

Ah-baao turned her jet-black eyes first on one person, then on another.

"I'm not in the least bit hungry," she said crisply. "Even if I am, still don't cook rice!"

No one laughed when they heard this sincere and moving answer. They all nodded gravely in her direction.

By afternoon even the grown-ups' stomachs were rumbling with hunger.

Little Ah-baao snuggled in her father's arms, blinking her eyes but not uttering a sound.

None of the soldiers could bear to look at the child....

This physical self-discipline is reinforced by a new style of child-rearing. Although Cherng Liahng is a devoted single parent, he believes that his daughter "will rely on all of us to be brought up, and when she is grown-up will belong to all of us." "Ah-baao," he tells Grandpa Weih, "is everybody's. Everyone will be concerned with Ah-baao." By slowly withdrawing from his earlier physical closeness to her, he produces a more independent and self-sufficient character. She is trained for an inner solitude:

In the past, Ah-baao had been Cherng Liahng's shadow. Wherever he went, she went. If he didn't see her for a moment, he would call her anxiously and search busily, not relaxing until she was in his arms. But now, when Ah-baao followed him, he would say: "Go and play by yourself!"

Once they went out to sea to catch fish. As soon as Grandpa Weih noticed that Ah-baao was not in the boat, he wanted to go back onto the shore and call her.

Cherng Liahng blocked him: "Let her stay on the island and wait for us."

"Leaving her all by herself —" said Weih, "is that right?"

"It's testing her!" said Cherng....

There came a day when, around noon, Grandpa Weih saw Cherng Liahng take a torn mosquito net out of a bundle, patch it up and then hang it in a separate place in his grass hut. He asked him what he was doing.

"*Letting Ah-baao sleep by herself*," was the answer.

"If she wakes up, won't she be unable to find you?" asked Weih.

"It's testing her!" said Cherng....

This change in Cherng Liahng produced many changes in Ah-baao.

Chinese parents always used to have their small children sleep in the same bed beside them, and many still do.

The motive for Cherng's new physical remoteness is soon explained. He has been steeling her so she will not miss him when he leaves to fight the Japanese. He tells Weih:

Ever since I resolved to enter the Party, I gave myself and my descendants to the Party. What's more, the child can't be forever sticking to my side. We are fighting for our land on their behalf. We must make sure that they grow up able to fight for it. In this way I can fulfill my duty as a father and will not have toiled bitterly in vain.

So the older Ah-baao approaches life as an endless moral obstacle course, whose purpose is continuous self-toughening. She decides, for example, to go out in a small boat with some other girls, *because* a storm is coming up. When the some-what weak-natured Brigade Leader tries to stop her, she retorts that if courage is to be developed, the danger has to be real. Of course, the author sees to it that they return safely.

The age-old Chinese love of food is scorned by the true revolutionary. "Eating," says Ah-baao, "is a minor matter." In her mature years, when there is a water short-age during a battle, she commands others to drink while refusing to do so herself. Cherng Liahng, bringing relief supplies, puts his daughter last on the list for help, knowing that she will hold out where others cannot. She does — even as she faints and begins to spit blood. Haailorng, who is now her husband, later sees the condi-tion that she is in and reminds her gently:

Your body is an important prerequisite for the struggle. You must get it strong and powerful!

She goes one better:

For victory in this struggle, I am prepared to give my body and my life.

The revolutionary's body is a component in a collective structure or a collective machine. When an exceptionally high tide threatens to engulf most of Gold-and-Silver Island, there is a desperate race against time to shift the cement needed for a new pier onto the only piece of high ground. As "collective property" it has to be defended at all costs, but other valuables need to be rescued too. (I have italicized the key phrases, here and later.)

Ah-baao stood in the wind and rain beside the pile of cement bags. Her heart seemed to be burning....

"Armed People's Militia!" she cried. "Follow me!"

As she shouted, she rushed into the angry tide.

With a cry, the crowd of people followed her....

The tide was already up to their waists.

With difficulty they moved forward.

The tide was already up to their chests....

"Let's go to their aid!" said Haailorng to his sailors....

The surging waves knocked a militiaman over.

Ah-baao pulled him up.

The roaring wind blew another militiaman over.

Again, Ah-baao pulled him up.

The two lines met.

The tide tumbled over their shoulders, trying to drown them and roll them away....

The foam leapt over their heads.

"Comrades!" yelled Ah-baao, "*link arms*!"...

Commune members and sailors joined arms, one to the next, forming a line in which everyone helped everyone else push forward....

At last they reached the high ground....

Ah-baao wiped the sweat from her face and urged the others on: "Comrades, we now face a severe test, which is also a precious opportunity for steeling ourselves. True gold does not fear the refining fire!..."

She made all the comrades *link their arms* and confront the still mounting winds, the still heavier rains, the still rising waves and tide, and the still greater test!

What is expressed here in Communist terms is the traditional Chinese yearning for

341

Title page of *The Great Way*, by Fang Zengxian. From *HDF*. A youth, looking up hopefully to the future, is watched over by age and experience, looking down with concern and responsibility.

physical togetherness, and also that exhilaration felt at the increase in power that results from the combination of relatively weak individuals into a collectivity equal to the challenge facing it.

In the final encounter between Scabby-head and Haailorng's ship, *Sturdy Pine*, the human body becomes an all-purpose mechanism that both serves machinery and transcends it, because of the will holding it in mastery. Both the electric steering/ signal system and the main and auxiliary steering on *Sturdy Pine* have been disabled by enemy fire:

"Captain," said Chief Helmsman Liarng Juhnfeng, "please order us to operate *a human-powered rudder!*"

He shouted this, then raced toward the afterdeck....

He took off the hatchcover, and leapt into the aft steering cabin.

He grabbed the clutch and gave it a powerful pull.

The clutch had been smashed by a piece of shell, and could not be pulled by hand.

Two sailors leapt in after him and pulled with him.

The clutch seemed as if it were cast solid into what was above it, and could not be budged by pulling.

Liarng Juhnfeng grabbed an iron hammer, swung it round, and struck fiercely.

The clutch was finally knocked free.

He gave a great shout: "Operate man-powered steering!"

Six sturdy young hands together held the wheel firm....

Seawater like torrential rain poured in uncontrollably through the hatchway and into the man-powered steering cabin.

A band of sailors followed Liarng Juhnfeng's plan and stood one next to the other along the deck, relaying orders from the bridge to the afterdeck.

"Increase speed!" commanded Haailorng.

The chief navigator passed on this command to the first sailor below the bridge, who passed it on in turn.

This was using human beings to form a transmission line, swiftly and accurately passing on commands....

The bandit sailors [i.e., the South Vietnamese] were scared out of their wits....

The enemy ship shuddered and swayed. Slowly, and as if it were reluctant to do so, yet helpless to resist, it sank to the bottom of the sea!...

343

Young Intellectual, by Warng Xijing. From *HDF*. The young lady is, to all appearances, refreshingly *un*intellectual and is very possibly one of those "sent down to the countryside" to learn from the rural masses, since she has a straw hat across her shoulders. We may therefore suspect a complex message: she has the traditional glamour (in Chinese eyes) of an educated person, but the ideological healthiness of someone who has gone back to the "people."

> In the thick billowing smoke of the aft engine room, a strange and magnificent scene unrolled before people's eyes:
>
> The three sailors operating the man-powered steering were standing submerged to their waists in water, water that was awash with fresh blood.
>
> Liarng Juhnfeng, that man usually of so few words, crouched in a daze over the wheel, crying out without stopping: "Follow the orders! Operate the wheel! Don't pay attention to me!..."

Only the collectivity of bodies, to which each individual body is consciously dedicated by its mind, can accomplish such feats, and the glory of the revolutionary human being is to become the ultimate interchangeable part, both superior to and subordinate to the unthinking machine it serves.

Last of all, the sacrifice of the revolutionary's body is seen as having magical powers. As children, Ah-baao and Haailorng planted coconuts at the grave of the martyred Grandpa Weih. When later they celebrate the destruction of the fishing boss, Shark's Teeth, at the end of the first volume, Ah-baao asks her father:

"Will the coconut trees we planted bear fruit?"

And her father answers:

> "Don't worry, Ah-baao. *They are cared for and cultivated by life and fresh blood. They are certain to bear fruit!*"

This is the guarantee conferred by sacrifice. The martyrs of the revolution assure its eventual triumph.

*   *   *

The passages quoted in the foregoing pages are both illustrations and more than illustrations. Illustrations because, obviously, they are not exhaustive. The Chinese repertoire of somatic conceptions is richer than it has been possible to show here, though I have tried to select points of view that are, as far as possible, contrasting extrema without losing their representative quality. More than illustrations because I have tried to place all of them in a well-defined context and so avoid the style of citation of "this, that and the other morsel en brochette" that makes so much writing on the history of ideas and emotions difficult to digest, however initially appetizing.

The illustrations further serve to give an idea of the nature of the process of intuitive induction, so far from hard science, by which the general formulations presented here have been derived from the primary materials on which they are based. Such induction is not capricious, but it is hazardous and subject to the perpetual danger that a researcher tends to perceive what he or she is looking for, and the more ambiguous the data, the more easily this is done. It is important that the reader and critic be obliged to be respectful of the evidence, such as it is, on the one hand, and not be lightly dismissive, while on the other hand keeping a wary reserve toward the theory and not accepting it in more than a provisional fashion, at best.

Lastly, to use extensive quotations, as I have presented here, helps in some degree to make unfamiliar attitudes and emotions credible. To the extent that the reader can be drawn for a moment into a story and see them at work in an otherwise comprehensible framework of narrative or conversation, the more easily he or she can at least entertain the notion that it might be possible to feel the same way. In other words, it offers, in however fleeting a fashion, the experience of fieldwork in the armchair.

To some extent the three works analyzed define a chronological sequence, but I doubt if the older attitudes have wholly disappeared. China is also changing so rapidly at present that even the most recent of them, Haoh Rarn's world of the early 1970s, already seems remote. If there is a constant theme, and one that will presumably continue to be central in the future, it lies in the multidimensional tensions between *xin*, the heart-mind that is both in the individual and, simultaneously, part of a collective social heart-mind, and *shen*, the demanding, egotistic body-person, or — with some Joycean shuffling about of sounds and categories — the Chinese proxies for Shem and Shaun: that is, God and Everyman.

NOTES

1. R.H. van Gulik, *Erotic Colour Prints of the Ming Period, with an Essay on Chinese Sex Life from the Han to the Ch'ing Dynasty, B.C. 206-1644* (privately printed, 1951, and distributed to the libraries listed in R.H. van Gulik, *Sexual Life in Ancient China*, Leiden, Brill, 1961 and 1974, p. 360).

2. The view from the inside is brilliantly described by Kristopher Schipper in *Le corps taoïste* (Paris: Fayard, 1982), especially ch. 6, "Le paysage intérieur," which takes as its theme the old tag "Le corps de l'homme est à l'image d'un pays."

3. Interesting remarks on the concepts of *shen* and *xin* may be found in Sun Lorngji, *Zhongguor wernhuah de "shencerng jiergouh"* (The "Deep Structure" of Chinese Culture) (Hong Kong: Jirxiarnsheh, 1983).

4. L. Guillerm, J.-P. Guillerm, L. Hordoir and M.-F. Piéjus, *Le miroir des femmes*, vol. 1: *Moralistes et polémistes au XVIe siècle* (Lille: Presses Universitaires, 1983); and M. Elvin, "Female Virtue and the State in China," *Past and Present* 104 (August 1984).

5. Lii Rurzhen, *Jihng hua yuarn* (Destinies of the Flowers in the Mirror) (Hong Kong: Zhonghuar shujur, 1958). For a list of the main sources of Lii's fantasies, see Tamori Noboru, *Kyoo ka en* (Destinies of the Flowers in the Mirror), 2d ed. (Tokyo: Heibonsha, 1961).

6. A sophisticated and qualified example of this trend of thought may be found in Mao Ze-dong, *Une étude de l'éducation physique*, trans. and intro. by S. Schram (Paris: Mouton, 1962), esp. p. 31ff.

7. Wur Cherng'en, trans. A. Waley, *Monkey* (New York: Evergreen, 1943). Complete translations are now available by W.F. Jenner, *Journey to the West* (Beeijing: Foreign Languages Publishing House, 1982), and by Antony (Kuo-fan) Yu, *The Journey to the West* (Chicago: University of Chicago Press, 1978-83).

8. For example, Sun Lorngji, *Zhongguor wernhuah*, who develops the insights of earlier observers and scholars such as Arthur Smith, Max Weber and H. Münsterberg, and combines them with his own observations and quotes from the Confucian scriptures and other old literature in an intriguing if somewhat unqualified and unhistorical fashion.

9. This is illustrated in Shaoh Charngherng's poem, "Selling a Daughter" (from the *Qing Bell of Poesy*, an anthology of verses about everyday life compiled by Zhang Yihngchang between 1856 and 1869):

Wur folk fuss a lot about the birth of a daughter,
But it's *not* because they hope that she'll run a family house,
They wash her young complexion in peach-flower water,
And pray at her young movements men's lust will be aroused.

She's only aged eleven when she puts on rouge and powder,
While at twelve she's coaxing tunes from silken strings.
At fourteen her hair's tumbling down upon her shoulders,
And her moth's-antennae eyebrows can bewitch.

Mommy permits herself a smile of satisfaction:
She'll fetch a thousand — silver — to the ounce,
When the best class of customers come seeking matrimony
And do not spare expenses buying beauties from the South.

Just let one of them hear word of this darling's reputation,
And he'll be outside the door, pleased to offer his respects.
She'll come out to meet him, and will kneel in obeisance,
Gently steadied by the go-between as she sinks to genuflect.

She'll sweep back her skirts to reveal her dainty feet,
While circlets on her wrists will set off ice-cool flesh.
He'll ask then, "Does she know how to strike the strings sweetly?"
When she'll tune the zither's bridges, and play Lii Bor's "Crows at Rest."

He'll ask, "Has she been trained to use the brush and inkstone?"
Like breakers overflowing are the verses she'll invent.
"Any good with the pieces?" is the next thing he'll think of,
And facing one another, they'll try a game of chess.

The client is delighted. He observes to the mother,
"In no way is a thousand too much!"
Let tonight become the night that decides a lifetime's love,
How he piles the golden hairpins and the bangles up and up!

They interlock ecstatically beneath the red silk canopy,
And at all four corners how the tassels swing like pendula,
The scent wafting off her has the odor of marsh-orchids,
And she twines herself around him like the dodder-plant's tendrils.

So the master and his girl pass the nighttime with each other,
Next morning comes the moment when she bids her Mom goodbye.

There's no feeling of affection in the daughter for her mother,
And the mother's just the same — *she's* not inclined to cry.

Off they go, then, unconcerned, with no feelings for their kin,
Once a chick's become a grown-up, well — she makes her own way.
Money is what matters. Flesh and blood mean nothing.
For you, me, and all of us, just the thought of this is hateful.

10. Leir Zhusheng, *Haaishahng huor-dihyuh* (Shahnghaai: The Living Hell), 4 vols. (Shahnghaai: Huarcherng shujur, 1929). I have the second impression, which appeared in 1930, and which I bought in Hong Kong in 1965. To date, I have not yet come across another copy of this work, though it is hard to believe that it can have disappeared entirely.

11. Haoh Rarn, *Xisha err-nüü* (Children of the Western Sands) (Beeijing: Rernmirn Chubaansheh, 1974). The make-believe dramatics and stage-lighting of this propaganda masterpiece conceal the often grim realities of everyday life. For an account of the desensualization and denaturalization of the body, which is illuminating precisely because it is about another extreme, namely life in the labor camps of the People's Republic of China, see Zhang Xianliang, *Half of Man is Woman*, trans. M. Avery (London: Viking, 1987).

12. For the late-traditional background, see M. Elvin, "Female Virtue."

A NOTE ON THE ILLUSTRATIONS
Illustrations for the Imperial period are from Zhehng Zhehnduo, *Zhongguor guudaih muhkeh-huah xuaanjir* (A Selected Collection of Ancient Chinese Woodcuts: ACW) (Beeijing, 1974). Those for the Republican period are from Bao Tianxiaoh, *Shahnghaai chunqu* (Annals of Shahnghaai: AS) (Shahnghaai: Dahdong shujur, 1927). Sources for Communist-period illustrations are: Liarnhuarn-huah xuaanjir (A Selection of Comic Strip Illustrations: SCD) (Beeijing: Rernmirn meeishuh chubaansheh, 1973); *Contemporary Chinese Paintings* (Oxford, 1964); Warng Chorngrern, Rernwuh-huah jihfaa (How to Draw Figures: HDF) (Tianjin: Rernmirn meeishuh chubaansheh, 1974); and *Contemporary Chinese Painting Today: An Exhibition from the People's Republic of China* (Birmingham: Chinese Culture Center, 1983); and *Xianndaih zhonghuar huahxuaan* (A Selection of Contemporary Chinese Paintings) (Beeijing: Zhongguor guorjih shudiahn, 1977).

Courbet, Despair. Private Collection.

The Natural and Literary History of Bodily Sensation

Jean Starobinski

The following essays are part of a larger study currently under preparation. It will examine, on the one hand, that particular register of the body's life which consists of somatic sensations, and, on the other hand, the literary use of the images and modes of expression pertaining to that register. Also under investigation will be several of the main variations that have occurred in history, both in the area of medical and psychological theory, and in the most prominent literary works. In the first instance, such a study allows for a broad comparative exercise in which the field observed will include both the most highly developed objective thought and testimonies relating to the most "immediate" subjective experience. Further, beyond any thematic restriction, these essays will also focus on the notion of person, or, if you like, the individual; in other words, the way sensory experience (and, more particularly, the organic and locomotive elements) contributes to the formation — or the decomposition — of the subject or the self, and on the several literary representatives of this kind of bodily message.

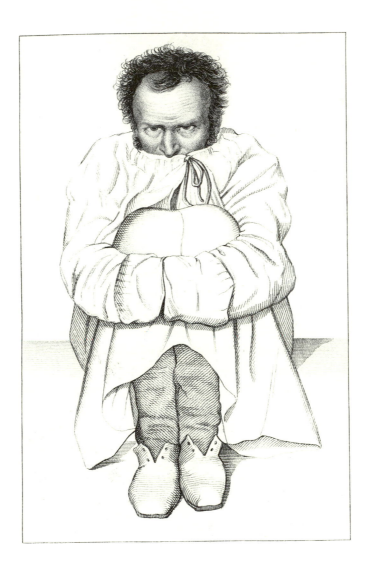

Esquirol, Dementia, 1838.

A Short History of Bodily Sensation

In one of his *Cahiers*, Paul Valéry has the note:

> Somatism (heresy of the end of time),
>
> Adoration, cult of the machine for living.[1]

Have we come to the end of time? The heresy anticipated by Valéry has almost become the official religion. Everything is related to the body, as if it had just been rediscovered after being long forgotten; body image, body language, body consciousness, liberation of the body are the passwords. Historians, prey to the same infection, have begun inquiring into what previous cultures have done with the body, in the way of tattooing, mutilation, celebration and all the rituals related to the various bodily functions.[2] Past writers from Rabelais to Flaubert are ransacked for evidence, and immediately it becomes apparent that we are far from being the first discoverers of bodily reality. That reality was the first knowledge to enter human understanding: "They knew that they were naked" (Genesis 3.7). From then on, it has been impossible to ignore the body.

Nevertheless, body consciousness, as it is practiced and spoken of in our society, does have certain new and original aspects that it is important to bring out and whose antecedents it would be useful to set in order in sound genetic fashion. But so as not to let myself be led astray (and because I believe that the most fruitful generalizations are those arising from fairly precise studies of limited topics), I will confine myself to a somewhat circumscribed area: the internal perception of our own bodies — *cenesthesia* — which is undeniably a component of our contemporary "sensibility," whether among philosophers or writers, or in certain psychotherapeutic practices (e.g., Schulz's "autogenic training," relaxation, "body contacts"), or, finally, in psychoanalytic thinking.

We shall not dwell on the theories developed by the ancients, however fascinating they might be; but let us recall a few stages of earlier thinking, before pausing a little longer over the discussions that prevailed at the end of the nineteenth century and Freud's response to them.

In Antiquity, the disciples of Aristippus of Cyrene spoke of an "internal contact" — *tactus intimus* in Cicero's translation.[3] Montaigne, quoting Cicero, reminds us that "the Cyrenaics...maintain that nothing external to themselves is perceptible, and that the only things that they do perceive are the sensations due to internal contact, for example, pain and pleasure."[4]

For a long while, pain and pleasure were not attributed to a specific sensory system; they were called "bodily passions," whereas the traditional term, *internal sense* (*sensus internus*), referred to the conscious activities that the mind developed in and of itself (reason, memory and imagination) on the basis of information provided by the *external senses* (sight, hearing, taste, touch and smell). According to Aristotelian doctrine, the information provided by the external senses reached the internal sense only after having been unified by the *common sense* (*sensorium commune, koinon aistheterion*).[5] The body was in no way forgetten; but as long as Galenic medicine prevailed, it was principally by way of the humors, and not through nervous information, that the body was capable of modifying the activity of the soul and, in turn, of being modified by the soul.

In his treatise *The Passions of the Soul*, Descartes put forward a clear distinction between three different categories of perception: "that which relates to objects external to us" (art. 23), "that which refers to our body" (art. 24), and "that which refers to our soul" (art. 25). Bodily sensations were of many kinds:

> The cognizings we refer to our body, or to certain of its parts, are those we have of hunger, thirst and of our other natural appetites — to which may be added pain, heat and the other affections which we sense as in our limbs, not as in external objects.[6]

Descartes thus analyzes and classes sensory activities as belonging to three specific areas — the body, the world and the consciousness — daily experience of which leads us to an awareness of how they coincide and are superimposed one upon the other. But Descartes's influence in this regard was not particularly great among eighteenth-century doctors. Some of them, particularly in Montpellier, were more taken by Stahl's ideas, which conferred on the viscera a sort of relative autonomy and independent sensibility. Nonetheless, some philosophers, such as Lignac, Turgot or d'Alembert, spoke with precision of a "sense of coexistence with our bodies," of an "internal touch" and so on.[7] Some of them (for instance, Bordeu, Lacaze and Diderot) came to pick out a phrenic or diaphragmatic center, whose role merged with that of the splanchnic nexus of the sympathetic nerve. Cabanis, in 1800, attributed great importance to the "organic sensations" that ended in certain centers of reaction, the most important of which was, obviously, the brain. Thus, the instincts were the transformation, at the level of behavior, of the most long-standing and most persistent of organic sensations. Instinct, thus, could be seen as the motor branch of a sensorimotor connection, the sensory branch of which was made up of "organic sensations."

It was in 1794, in Halle, in the title of a doctoral thesis at which Johann Christian Reil presided and of which he was the inspiration, that the word *coenesthesis* was used for the first time. The term was equivalent to the German *Gemeingefühl*, for which the French equivalent subsequently became on some occasions *sensibilité générale* (general sensibility) and on others *cénesthésie* (cenesthesia).[8]

Reil (through the medium of his disciple Hübner) returned, without mentioning Descartes, to the tripartite division that we have already seen in *The Passions of the Soul*:

We encounter in the soul three sorts of representations, which differ in relation to the objects represented:

1) Its own intellectual state, its powers, its actions, its representations and concepts; it distinguishes these things itself, and in this way becomes conscious of itself.

2) It represents to itself its external state or the relations of the whole man to the world.

3) Finally, it represents to itself its own bodily state.

Each of these sorts of ideas, by which man is represented according to the three different types of state, is sited in the body in its own particular organic apparatus:

1) *Cenesthesia*, by means of which the soul is informed of the state of its body, which occurs by means of the nerves generally distributed throughout the body.

2) Sensation (sensatio externa). This is excited by the senses and represents the world to the soul.

3) Finally, the activities which originate and are carried out integrally within the organ of the soul. [*Organ der Seele* is the term Reil uses to designate the brain.] By means of these (that is to say, by the *internal sense*) imagination and judgment are formed; the soul receives the representation of its powers, its ideas and its concepts, and is thus rendered conscious of itself.[9]

This distinction between three specific organic apparatuses can be found again, at the beginning of our own century, but without any direct reference to Reil, in

Carl Wernicke. He proposed, as is well known, a model of psychic life that involved collaboration between an *allopsyche* (in relation to external objects), a *somatopsyche* (in relation to corporeal existence) and an *autopsyche* (in relation to its own system of representations).[10] In Reil (as in Wernicke), this functional distinction formed the basis for a pathogenic classification. Reil not only envisaged changes in cenesthesia due to general disorders, but he allowed there to be idiopathic disorders of the cenesthesia: there were in fact cases in which the disease was limited to the nervous apparatus involved in transmitting the somatic information — in the absence of any real lesion in the visceral organs or in the brain itself. A distortion (the anatomo-pathological substratum of which Reil was entirely incapable of indicating) then sent a misleading message to the brain about the body's condition. A bodily illusion occurred — giving rise to a belief in a tumor or an abdominal parasite, despite the lack of any objective evidence. Up to a certain point, judgment could correct this false impression. But when the impression managed to take hold, it created a state of madness. A good hundred years before the concept of *cenestopathy* appeared in France (with Dupré and Camus), Reil included in his psychiatric nosology a class of ailments characterized by a primary disturbance of bodily representations. This very extensive class contained the classic examples that had occurred for the previous two or three centuries in chapters on melancholia or hypochondria: people who believed themselves to be made of glass and liable to shatter at the slightest blow or who had lost the feeling of being present within their actual bodies. Reil had no difficulty adding affective disorders or derangement of the instincts or the appetites, such as pica, bulimia and polydipsia on the one hand, and nymphomania and lubricity on the other.

"Romantic" thought readily welcomed the concept of cenesthesia. From a genetic point of view, Reil had already accorded it priority in the order of sensory activities: it was the first that appeared in the fetus. Evolutionist speculation, right up to physiologists like Purkinje, could propose the notion of a primarily bodily sense from which all the other sensory activities could be seen as being differentiated developments. As the first vital sensation, cenesthesia could be considered, by some, to be the source of all psychic life, insofar as that life was made up of sensory differences. What came to prevail, among scholars or philosophers claiming to be determinists or monists, was a "sensualist" conception of mental life, which opened the way for a sort of imperialism of cenesthesia. If mental life was determined by sensory activity, and if all sensory activity was made up of derivatives of cenesthesia, then one could finish by asserting, as Ribot did in 1884, in *The Diseases of the Personality*, that our personality resided entirely in the messages, partially unconscious, that derived from bodily life.

The fifteen French editions of Ribot's *The Diseases of the Personality* (published between 1883 and 1914) bear witness to the immense influence exerted by this book and justify a fairly close examination of the theories propounded in it.

A first assertion was based on physiology: "Its [consciousness's] production is always associated with some activity of the nervous system."[11] In accord with the physiologists, however, Ribot allowed that a significant part of nervous activity might remain unconscious: "All nervous activity does by no means imply psychic activity — nervous activity being far more extended than psychic activity. Consciousness, accordingly, is something superadded."[12] It was, but it was doomed to *intermission*. (Ribot underlines the term, a term to which, as is well known, Proust was to attach great importance.) The personality was thus a variable kaleidoscopic phenomenon, by very reason of the incessant fluctuation of bodily states:

> If, accordingly, we admit that the organic sensations proceeding from all the tissues, organs and movements produced — in a word, from all the states of the body — are in some degree and form represented in the *sensorium*; and if the physical personality be only their sum total, it follows that personality must vary as they vary, and that these variations admit of all possible degrees, from simple distemper to the total metamorphosis of the individual. Instances of "double personality"... are but an extreme case.... We should find in mental pathology enough observations to establish a progression, or rather a continuous regression from the most transient change to the most complete alteration of the ego.... The ego exists only on the condition of continually changing.[13]

Following Ribot, Sollier proposed an interpretation of hysteria as the result of changes in cenesthesia: Séglas attributed to this same "peripheral" mechanism states of depersonalization and melancholic deliria of negation.

One would have no difficulty in demonstrating that what one is dealing with here is an entirely theoretical construction, supported in large part by an entirely *metaphorical* method of argumentation. The fundamental assumption is of a causality that operates on the basis of elementary materials, in which complex phenomena are *built up* from simple units. Ribot refers to Taine, who himself refers to Dr. Krishaber to maintain: "The Ego, the moral person, is a product of which sensations are the prime factors."[14] To this neosensualism are added curious political metaphors, which could have flowed only from the pen of a convinced democrat. Thus, after having declared that "in every animal the basis of its psychic individuality is the organic sense," he adds:

> But, in man and with the higher animals, the turbulent world of desires, passions, perceptions, images and ideas covers up this silent background. Except at given intervals, it is forgotten, from the fact that it is not known. Here the same takes place as in the order of social facts. The millions of human beings, making up a large nation, as regards itself and others, are reduced to a few thousand men, who constitute its clear consciousness, and who represent its social activity in all its aspects, its politics, its industry, its commerce and its intellectual culture. And yet these millions of unknown human beings — limited as to manner and place of existence, quietly living and quietly passing away — make up all the rest; without them there would be nothing[15]

Ribot, in the closing sentences of the book, introduces terms like *consensus* and *solidarity*, which have an equally clear social resonance:

> The unity of the ego, in a psychological sense, is, therefore, the cohesion, during a given time, of a certain number of clear states of consciousness, accompanied by others less clear, and by a multitude of physiological states which without being accompanied by consciousness like the others, yet operate as much and even more than the former. Unity, in fact, means coordination. The conclusion to be drawn from the above remarks is namely this, that the consensus of consciousness being subordinate to the consensus of the organism, the problem of the unity of the ego is, in its ultimate form, a biological problem. To biology pertains the task of explaining, if it can, the genesis of organisms and the solidarity of their component parts. Psychological interpretation can only follow in its wake.[16]

What this radical biologism lacked, without yet having at its disposal the more recent concept of the genome, was any apparatus of clinical experiments and proofs. It was hardly surprising, then, that after a brief moment of glory this "peripheral" theory of the constitution of the ego, and above all the interpretation it suggested of disturbances of the personality, became the object of lively criticism. Ribot was the first to admit its shortcomings[17] and recognized later that in attributing so great an importance to somatic sensory information, he had neglected the motor components of psychic activity. Pierre Janet[18] observed that in all the cases of depersonalization he had examined, he had never been able to demonstrate any kind of peripheral sensory disturbance and, as a corollary, that when dealing with tabetics whose bodily perceptions were seriously upset, he had not noted any psychic disturbances. To allege a disturbance in "corporeal sensoriality" was, according to him, to remain trapped in a "metaphysical" hypothesis. Psychopathological phenomena, such as depersonalization or a sense of emptiness, should be considered as a lack of action (or lack of the psychic energy available for action) and not as a disturbance in sensory receptivity. "Scientific psychology must consider psychological facts as actions and express them in terms of action. A sense of emptiness is a disturbance of action and not of the sensibility nor of a poorly understood consciousness."[19] This led Janet to introduce a distinction between what he called "primary actions" and "secondary actions." Primary action takes its cue from sensory stimuli, whether internal or external, and reacts directly to them; secondary action brings to primary action the reinforcement of a *belief*, an integrating device effective in the circumstances experienced. Pathological disturbance, in depersonalization, affects the secondary action, which can break down without the primary action showing the slightest anomaly. It is in the "relation to the real" that the real disturbance is to be found.

The affirmation of the primacy of the *active* response over somatic information was also characteristic of Freud's thinking. But before lingering more closely over a few significant pages of Freud, it would be appropriate to devote a moment to the theory put forward by Charles Blondel in *La conscience morbide* (1914). (Both a doctor and a philosopher, Blondel began as a careful follower of the teachings of Durkheim and Bergson; after the war, he wrote one of the first important studies of Proust and composed a hasty and disappointing work on psychoanalysis.) In *La conscience morbide*, Blondel opposed to the "peripheral theory" an active force – and this active force was language. It was not that the cenesthetic message was nonexistent, but it was not its supposed disruption that explained the disturbances of the sick mind. According to Blondel, a purely physiological theory was incapable of explaining the phenomena observed by the clinician. The "cenesthetic masses" (which he also called "pure psychology") did not by themselves determine mental illness: the "morbid" factor lay entirely in the insufficiency of the verbal response to the bodily perceptions — a response worked out by the individual in the act of thinking according to the linguistic tools he has received from society. Noting, as Dupré had done in his studies on cenestopaths, that the mentally ill had recourse to a wealth of metaphorical formulas with which to describe their symptoms,[20] Blondel sited the anomaly not in the (supposedly neutral) bodily nervous information but in a fault in the "eliminatory action" that should have resulted from a successful intervention of language. The normal mind, according to Blondel, eliminates the idiosyncratically individual, the "pure psychology," by putting into effect the interpretive tools and concepts provided by the system of collective representations. The law of language, which is the result of social training, has as its function the *depersonalization* of the expression that we give to our individual states. Blondel quoted in this respect a revealing passage from Durkheim:

> There really is a part of ourselves which is not placed in immediate dependence upon the organic factor: this is all that which represents society in us. The general ideas which religion or science fix in our minds, the mental operations which these ideas suppose, the beliefs and sentiments which are at the basis of our moral life, and all these superior forms of psychic activity which society awakens in us, these do not follow in the trail of our bodily states, as our sensations and our general bodily consciousness do.... This is because the world of representations in which social life passes is superimposed upon its material substratum, far from arising from it.[21]

Blondel concluded from this that the normal mind was a mind in which the cenesthetic factor was dominated and controlled by the impersonal system of socialized discourse. While believing himself to be asserting his *ego*, the rational individual was in fact affirming the triumph of collective norms. The disturbed mind, incapable of manipulating language according to these collective dictates, was a mind embroiled in the individual cenesthetic experience — in the nonverbal or the preverbal, which even the most daring play of metaphor was incapable of expressing. Blondel did not fail to remark the poetic nature of these attempts, which tended to imply that poetry was deviant from the social norms, that it was sited on the side of "pure psychology," that it had something in common with the "sick mind."

It was thus not the body that imposed its law on the mind. It was society that, through the intermediacy of language, took the commands of the mind and imposed its law on the body. Blondel's theory tended to dispose of the body as cause in order to return to it later as the agent of the *expressive* intentions that the individual imposed on it under the dictates of the collective consciousness. Thus, we can see interest shifting from the body as physiological object (primarily the producer of internal information destined to be filtered by language) to the body according to society (primarily carrying out messages bearing *meaning*, according to the collective codes and rules). Social prescriptions dictated not only language, but also nonverbal bodily manifestations; there is nothing, in the passage that follows, that could not be quoted with approval by any of the sociologists or "paralinguists" of today who talk to us of "the body as a medium of expression":[22]

> In order to find the motor or vasomotor expression of our states of mind, we are dumbly preoccupied in seeking the right note, of finding the mime, regulated and defined by custom and propriety, corresponding to the emotion standard to which our own emotion refers. From this point of view mime seems, so to speak, to have received its morphology and its syntax from the collective.... If one thinks about it hard, it becomes apparent that there is not a single one of our motor manifestations which is not thus more or less stringently defined and with regard to which there does not exist a collective model, that is to say, a motor concept, to which it has to conform.[23]

In writing the *Traumdeutung*, Freud began by running up against the generally held late-nineteenth-century theories which assumed that dream activity derives from peripheral or visceral sensory excitation. Ribot, in *The Diseases of the Personality*, had formulated in passing a theory of the dream that was in perfect accord with the rest of his theory of the primacy of cenesthesia:

> Constantly active, they [the physical bases of the personality] make up by their continuity for their weakness as psychic elements. Hence, as soon as the higher forms of mental life disappear, they pass to the front rank. A clear example of this exists in dreams (whether pleasant or painful) aroused by organic sensations, like nightmares, erotic dreams, etc. In these dreams, even with a certain degree of precision, we may assign to each organ the part that belongs to it.[24]

Freud, well aware of the vast body of literature that, even before Ribot, tended in the same direction, devoted several pages of his historic Introduction to *Leibreiztheorie* (he used the term *Gemeingefühl* more rarely) and concluded that "the theory of somatic stimulation has not succeeded in completely doing away with the apparent absence of determination in the choice of what dream-images are to be produced."[25]

He returned to the question again in Chapter 5 ("The Material and Sources of Dreams"), section C ("The Somatic Sources of Dreams").

Freud did not deny that "organic impressions" played their part in the production of dreams. But he did not allow that they could be a sufficient condition and the only cause: it was not enough to invoke them to be free of the need to provide any other explanation. Like Janet, Freud was opposed to a purely physiological theory, the more so to one that might be unifactorial or unicausal, according to which dreams were seen as being merely the cerebral propagation, through loose associations, of visceral sensory stimuli. He noted that these stimuli were not always efficient; organic sensations, by definition, are never interrupted, whereas dreams are intermittent: "These stimuli are present at all times, and...it is difficult to understand, then, why the mind does not dream continuously all through the night."[26] In a number of cases, a dream may derive solely from psychic sources. And even when the presence of somatic sensations can be admitted with a certain degree of probability, they can be seen as being simply the *material* to which *work* is then applied from quite another quarter, and that alone gives it meaning. In relation to its somatic sources, the dream is a "reaction," an interpretive working out, and our scientific attention should be directed to that reaction; our interpretation should be of the act of interpretation carried out by the dreamer:

> There can be no doubt that physical cenesthesia...is among the internal somatic stimuli which can dictate the content of dreams. It can do so not in the sense that it can provide the dream's content, but in the sense that it can force upon the dream-thoughts a choice of the material to be represented.... The cenesthetic feelings left over from the preceding day link themselves up, no doubt, with the psychical residues which have such an important influence on dreams. This general mood may persist unchanged in the dream or it may be mastered, and thus, if it is unpleasurable, may be changed into its opposite.
>
> Thus, in my opinion, somatic sources of stimulation during sleep (that is to say, sensations during sleep), unless they are of unusual intensity, play a similar part in the formation of dreams to that played by recent but indifferent impressions left over from the previous day. I believe, that is, that they are brought in to help in the formation of a dream if they fit in appropriately with the ideational content derived from the dream's psychical sources, but otherwise not. They are treated like some cheap material always ready to hand, which is employed whenever it is needed, in contrast to a precious mate-

rial which prescribes the way in which it is to be employed. If, to take a simile, a patron of the arts brings an artist some rare stone, such as a piece of onyx, and asks him to create a work of art from it, then the size of the stone, its color and markings, help to decide what head or what scene shall be represented in it. Whereas in the case of a uniform and plentiful material such as marble or sandstone, the artist merely follows some idea that is present in his own mind.[27]

All that the somatic sources do, then, is provide one of the most common materials, of which the mind of the dreamer, working from other sources, will make something of its own. Freud, in his turn, has recourse to metaphors; the image of the sculptor brings us back to Aristotelian notions of causality. In Aristotelian terms, the somatic source is, in the best sense, the material cause of the dream. But the neurophysiological is not simply a neutral and anonymous substratum. The dream has meaning because of the *form* imposed on this substratum. This setting into form is the result of an intention, of which the active agent is called the "spirit," the "wish," "dream-work." Freud assigned a double aim to the dream: to protect sleep and to fulfill a wish. In both cases, the dream works according to its own ends, *against* the somatic sensation — either to neutralize it or to transform it. Accepting these postulates entails an important consequence for anyone wishing to achieve an adequate understanding of dreams. It is vain to trace dreams back to their physiological source and to invoke a particular visceral disturbance, which could be measured in terms of the strength of the painful stimuli or in variations in the cardiac rate. What one now has to understand is the new language, the original form in which this material — in itself unimportant — has been interpreted and recast by the dream. Analysis is an exegesis of the final cause of the dream: it seeks to understand what the wish is aiming for, and why.

In other words, dream analysis can be seen as the "informed" interpretation of a "naive" interpretation, which has itself been reworked at the moment of narrating the dream. But this formula is still too simple; for the somatic stimulus is the starting point for a double translation. First, it gives rise to the deployment of *latent thoughts*, in which the wish can express itself without reserve; then it transports itself — through the distortions and puzzles of which Freud so carefully established the vocabulary — in the *manifest* dream. The "somatic source," the material cause, was in addition only an occasional cause, a pretext. Freud did not fail to recognize this, but he felt it unnecessary to reiterate it. This meant in effect reworking the definition of the unconscious. Despite what is fairly widely believed today, it was quite usual to speak of the unconscious before Freud's time, but it was an unconscious associated with the obscure murmurings of visceral functions, from which would emerge, intermittently, conscious acts. For Freud, the unconscious was the first interpretation of visceral stimuli, it was the *latent thoughts of the dream* and the process that gave form to the manifest dream. Freud's original contribution was not to have spoken first of the unconscious but to have, so to speak, lifted the monopoly held on it by organic life and to have installed it within the psychic apparatus itself. It was thus at the price of abandoning the body (in which it was definable only in terms of weakness or strength, whether organic or "nervous") that the unconscious became the custodian of a language and the producer of palimpsests or puzzles that were then open to being deciphered. Having ceased to have the life of the body as its exclusive source, the unconscious then escaped from the exclusive competence of a medical approach and became dependent on hermeneutics.

Thus, before Durkheim and Blondel opposed to cenesthesia the conceptual categories of language set up by the collective consciousness, Freud, in 1900, opposed to cenesthesia, to "organic stimuli," the operation of language, but a language in which the social norms were only partially represented — by censorship and interdictions. Another similarity — apart from any questions of priority — is worth noting: though the body might see itself being refused any sort of importance as a causal source of psychic disturbance, it found a crucial role for itself as the *place* or *scene* in which this disturbance manifested itself. In a vision that placed in the background the sensory information being provided by the body, and that emphasized the reaction manifested in the psychic act and in language, the body came to appear as the primary target of the act and as the primary signification worked out in the language. Just as Durkheim and Blondel, after having rejected the hypothesis of a cenesthetic source of psychosis, reestablished the importance of the body as bearer or enactor of manifestations of a gestural code of social origin, so Freud equally returned to the body, no longer considering it as explanatory *source* but as the place in which were carried out the expressive *aims* of the wish. Breuer and Freud had already taken this direction in their studies of hysteria. The case of the dream was equally clear; and among the different types of dream, the nightmare provided a typical example.[28]

Received medical opinion held that nightmares were the representational trans-position of a purely somatic oppression. According to Freud, such a case was the exception; the greatest number of somatic sufferings felt in dreams were, on the contrary, the representation of a censored wish loaded with suffering: what could not be denied was that the suffering then *expressed* itself in the language of the body, though the "source" should be sought in the psyche. The inquiry should turn from the disturbed body to the affect that was at once revealed and hidden in the somatic register. The body was the wrong turn, the dead end taken by energy originating from the psyche, and to which the term *intention* was more appropriate than *excitation*.

At this point, it seems that in marking a radical difference between psychological explanation and physiological explanation, in "dephysiologizing" psychology, Freud was "desomatizing" the causal system commonly accepted by his predecessors. There is, in Freud's explanations, less body and more language than in the majority of his contemporaries; this explains the dissension that was to grow, at least for a while, between psychoanalysts and neurophysiologists. Freud took care never to sever the links with biology (which is far from being the case with some of those who subsequently claimed to be his followers). To be sure, what Freud retained of biology did not consist of experimentally measurable mechanisms but, rather, of general schemes and of supposedly permanent laws of the nervous system and living matter. If Freudian psychology became detached, to some extent, from the physiological body, *metapsychology*, in compensation, showed itself to be a return to physiology and to the body in an intuitive and imaginative manner, but guided by phenomena that had been established sufficiently securely by experimental physiology to serve as *models*. One of the most illuminating texts in this regard is the 1915 study entitled *Instincts and Their Vicissitudes*. The physiological model on which Freud's thinking was based was that of stimulus and response, the sensorimotor reflex arc. To this was added another physiological assumption: "The nervous system is an apparatus which has the function of getting rid of the stimuli that reach it, or of reducing them to the lowest possible level; or which, if it were feasible, would maintain itself in an altogether unstimulated condition."[29]

On the basis of these assumptions, Freud established a distinction (a distinction already largely foreshadowed in the writings of nineteenth-century physiologists on instincts and passions) between external excitation, which is usually unique and momentary, and internal excitation, of somatic origin, which acts "as a constant force," whose effect is translated as "need," and whose satisfaction, whose "mastery," cannot be carried out according to a single muscular response, such as flight, which would constitute the adequate response to the external excitation. Not only does the instinct derive from a somatic source, but its satisfaction can be obtained only by a set of actions directed *toward* the exterior. The individual must bring into play a series of complex behavior patterns, the aim of which is to modify (to reduce) "the internal source of excitation."

Where the dream was concerned, the "somatic source" was optional. Where instincts were concerned, there was no question of its central role. But Freud, while conceding it precedence by right, by the status of a necessary condition and a material cause, in fact declared it to be irrelevant to the psychological investigation. At this level, physiology would have been in command had it not been (provisionally? definitively?) disarmed; as for psychology, it cannot say much:

> By the source of an instinct is meant the somatic process which occurs in an organ or part of the body and whose stimulus is represented in mental life by an instinct. We do not know whether this process is invariably of a chemical nature or whether it may also correspond to the release of other, e.g., mechanical, forces. The study of the sources of instincts lies outside the scope of psychology. Although instincts are wholly determined by their origin in a somatic source, in mental life we know them only by their aims. An exact knowledge of the sources of an instinct is not invariably necessary for purposes of psychological investigation; sometimes its source may be inferred from its aim.[30]

First remark: The transition from somatic to psychic, in the case of the instinct, is not the perceptive order; the instinct is not simply the cry of the organ echoed and recorded. At least Freud does not lay any emphasis on this element, which would immediately raise the question of its more or less conscious character. The concept he used was that of *representation* (*repräsentieren*), which implies an operation of a "semiotic" nature. This foreshadows the "second topic," in which the id can be seen to take on a good part of this representative function.

Second remark: Contrary to what happened with the dream, the somatic source is regained at the end of the instinctual activity, since the *aim* of the instinct is a modification in the source of excitation. But this aim, at first held to be invariable, can have others substituted for it. Thus the "physiological" return to the somatic source does not take place. That phenomenon, displacing the *site* of satisfaction, creates to some extent an illusory body which has nothing to do with the true (organic) body:

> The aim of an instinct is in every instance satisfaction, which can only be obtained by removing the state of stimulation at the source of the instinct. But although the ultimate aim of each instinct remains unchangeable, there may yet be different paths leading to the same ultimate aim; so that an instinct may be found to have various nearer or intermediate aims, which are combined or interchanged with one another. Experience permits us also to speak of instincts which are "inhibited in their aim," in the case of processes which are allowed to make some advance toward instinctual satisfaction but are then inhibited or deflected. We may suppose that even processes of this kind involve a partial satisfaction.[31]

If "inhibition in their aim" implies a relative avoidance of the normal bodily satisfaction, a sidetracking or diversion in relation to the necessary "modification of the source," consideration of the *object* of the instinct brings up a number of substitute possibilities, among which our "own body" is called upon to play a major role:

> The object of an instinct is the thing in regard to which or through which the instinct is able to achieve its aim. It is what is most variable about an instinct and is not originally connected with it, but becomes assigned to it only in consequence of being peculiarly fitted to make satisfaction possible. The object is not necessarily something extraneous: it may equally well be a part of the subject's own body. It may be changed any number of times in the course of the vicissitudes which the instinct undergoes during its existence; and highly important parts are played by this displacement of instinct.[32]

Our "own body" thus reappears, in the wide-open repertoire of places (that *in which*) or of means (that *by means of which*) that the instinct can choose in order to obtain its aim and on which it can on occasion become *fixated*. That is the case when there occurs — as in narcissism or masochism — a "turning around of an instinct upon the subject's own self."

Thus there appears a new role for the body; I was about to say a new body — the body as support for fixation or investment. And there is nothing to stop a new representation, prolonging or transforming that in which the somatic excitation has already been prolonged or transformed. We have not left the body. But if it is true that there persisted, for Freud, a distant analogy between the simple reflex arc and the way in which instincts work, then one could say that the body-object, the body of investment, corresponds to a *motor* performance, which seeks immediate confirmation in the order of perceptions, without being able to avoid getting mixed up in a whole imaginary or symbolic projection. When Schilder[33] came to study the image of the body, he paid very little attention to the primary bodily schema, as derives from the different kinesthetic or somesthetic apparatuses; he was much more concerned with the image, in part fantasized, that accompanies the different types of libidinal investment. What Freud established, through a system of representations taking over one from the other, was a circuit that could renew itself virtually infinitely: from the body as the source of the instinct to the body as aim, site or means of "satisfaction."

All that I have done here is to recall, in a very simplified form, the essential characteristics that make it possible to place Freud's thinking in the history of ideas about cenesthesia and bodily sensations. His contribution was considerable: before him, cenesthesia was the first stage of a system of sensory information, from which sprang the personality, fully armed. Whether conscious or unconscious, these physiological data exercised their full power straightaway. All that remained to the higher centers was to submit to their law, or to respond as best they could; the traditional model included two terms, in relation to reciprocity. Traditional medical thinking used to be able to make only this simple account, reiterated in innumerable nineteenth-century works, which started in visceral irritation and ended in, for instance, mania (or vice versa), or started in a break in the apparatus of the somatic sensibilities and ended in depersonalization. In Freud, instincts had a goal and gave rise to much longer and more circumstantial accounts, as he pursued their migrations, their substitutions and the meshing of different aims or objects. It was now a complex circuit that had to be considered, and no longer a simple short shuttling between "action" and "reaction." The feeling of depersonalization, for instance, is a loss that occurs at the end of a long process; *Mourning and Melancholia* traces the various stages, in which the first false step is the choice of a narcissistic object. It has no relation to the primary organic and sensory dysfunction that Ribot thought to discern.

At the beginning of this essay, I almost suggested a synonymity between *cenesthesia* and *awareness of the body*. But after our rapid rereading of Freud, and recalling what he said about the "turning around of an instinct upon the subject's own self" in narcissism and masochism, there is a question that cannot be avoided: Where do we draw the line between cenesthesia, which must be a basic assumption of every human existence, and *body awareness*, which would be the hypochondriacal or perverse consequence of a narcissistic or autoerotic investment?

Sartre (who is, through Dumas, so close to Ribot's ideas) would answer without a moment's hesitation that the manner in which we "exist our contingency" reveals itself to us in cenesthesia:

> When no pain, no specific satisfaction or dissatisfaction is "existed" by consciousness, the for-itself does not thereby cease to project itself beyond a contingency which is pure and so to speak unqualified. Consciousness does not cease "to have" a body. Cenesthetic affectivity is, then, a pure, nonpositional apprehension of a contingency without color, a pure apprehension of the self as a factual existence. This perpetual apprehension on the part of my for-itself of an *insipid* taste which I cannot place, which accompanies me even in my efforts to get away from it, and which is *my* taste — this is what we have described elsewhere under the name of Nausea. A dull and inescapable nausea reveals my body to my consciousness.[34]

As for Merleau-Ponty, the discussion of the notion of the bodily schema leads him to assert that "one's own body is the third term, always tacitly understood, in the figure–background structure, and every figure stands out against the double horizon of external and bodily space."[35] But if to this inevitable and naive presence of the body — a "nonpositional" (Sartre), "tacit" (Merleau-Ponty) presence — is added an intentional *awareness*, it is then appropriate to ask, with Freud, whether this interest presupposes a regressive or narcissistic libidinal investment. What I devote to an awareness of the body, I subtract from my presence in the world, from my investments in the *other*. In a conscious awareness of the body, the *aesthetic* element of cenesthesia is in the nature of an instinctual satisfaction undeniably confused with primary physiological information. It is a variation on "turning around upon the subject's own self." There is nothing very bold in drawing the only superficially banal conclusion that the present infatuation with the different modes of body consciousness is a symptom of the considerable narcissistic component characteristic of contemporary Western culture. I am, I know, far from being the first to say so. The so-called Chicago school, Richard Sennett,[36] and a variety of others have made such a declaration, based on other premises, a recurrent motif in their critical thought.

Perhaps one could also enter a plea on behalf of Narcissus (or at least invoke extenuating circumstances in his favor). In a world in which technological mastery has made such rapid strides, can one not understand that the desire to feel — and to feel *oneself* — should arise as a compensation, necessary, even in its excesses, to our psychic survival?

From *Humanities in Review*, vol. 1, New York, The New York Institute for the Humanities, 1982.
Translated by Sarah Matthews.

Monsieur Teste Confronting Pain

Adverse Body and Compliant Body

Close to the beginning of his first Notebook, which he calls his *Logbook*, Valéry writes the following lines in a hand which is rapid and at times hard to read:

> Isn't it true that each person will leave behind him a formless mass of perceived fragments, pains broken against the world, years lived in a minute, unfinished and chilly constructions, immense labors embraced in a single glance and dead.
>
> But all these ruins have a certain rose.[1]

We recognize this "glance" as the phenomenon which was called, at that time, the "panoramic vision of the dying."[2] We come upon the moment of dying, a few pages farther on, in the first Notebook:

> He dies, his mouth emptying of a taste which goes off to join the other things standing around.[3]

While the rest of the world remains vertical, the dying man, on his back, loses his last bodily sensation, which joins the last sight of the outside world.

Everything seems to indicate that the young Valéry wanted to put the material for a deathbed scene down on paper, while waiting for a way to "use" it. Was he already dreaming of his hero, whose name would eventually be Edmond Teste, spiritual descendant of Edgar Allan Poe's Chevalier Dupin? We know that "remnants"[4] of numerous entries from the first Notebooks will appear in the composition of *An Evening with Monsieur Teste* (La Soirée avec Monsieur Teste). The original nebula could include the idea of an intellectual hero put to the test of sleep and death. In a letter of 1927, Valéry declares that the death of Teste "was the first idea that came."[5] In "End of Monsieur Teste" ("Fin de Monsieur Teste," which came out in 1946, after Valéry's death), we find this wonderful synthesis of the "panoramic vision," in which the "glance" of what was almost the first entry in the *Notebooks* reappears: "Perhaps I will hold myself entirely in a terrible glance." The pronominal verb *to hold oneself* (se tenir) is perfectly bivalent here. It can be understood to mean *appear*, but also *seize oneself*. It is the last self-image which *is offered* to the dying gaze; it is the dying man who grasps his entire life in a death-bearing gaze....

The early notes we have just read are astonishing, especially the first: in them,

we see that Valéry is already posing the problem of fragmentariness, of incomplete-
ness, which will crop up again and again in the *Notebooks*, right up to the end. In
them, we also see an early, still quite spontaneous version of the three-term relationship which Valéry will conceptualize in the Body–Mind–World (Corps–Esprit–
Monde [CEM]) triad, to which he will devote a constantly revived attention in his
Notebooks.[6] The "pains broken against the world" express the body–world relationship in terms of a conflict. The "unfinished…constructions," the "glance," are acts
of the mind, which is dedicated to superiority, but also to imperfection. Generally
speaking, the question posed is that of remainder (what a man "leaves") and of sum
(the "rose" that is supposedly made up of all these scraps).

In this quick sketch of a mental theater, objects and actors cannot immediately
be distinguished, because the objects still bear the mark of the agents that constituted them. The agents, nevertheless, allow themselves to be defined: the perceiver
(or the "glance"), the laborer creating and building, the sufferer. The gaze, the acts
of the mind and the pain are put on an equal footing. This confers an importance
that is rather surprising, compared to the active faculties, on what, according to the
intellectual tradition, belongs to the domain of passivity, even if, in the present case,
the "pains broken against the world" make us think of an assault led by an individual, and not an aggression coming from outside.

Among many texts, let us cite this praise of the body in the *Notebooks*:

Limiting object, slave and master of knowledge. Site of happiness and unhappiness, of
the present, past and future, site of space. – All this has meaning only through it.[7]

Or this statement, which will find its illustration in *Alphabet*:

The Day and the Body, two great powers.[8]

It is not completely irrelevant to note that at the time of keeping the *Logbook*
and writing *An Evening with Monsieur Teste*, Valéry was suffering from persistent attacks
of neuralgia, and sometimes complained of it in letters to his friend André Gide.[9]
He was prepared to fear them, accept them and measure himself by them. The pain-
material was there.

But during this period, he also wrote: "Words are more a part of us than our
nerves. We only know our brains by hearsay."[10] His attention to pain could also have
originated in "words," in books. His passionate reading and rereading of *Against the
Grain* (A Rebours) could have had a great deal to do with it. Des Esseintes, the dandy

Huysmans creates as his amazing and pitiful hero, takes refuge, out of exhaustion, in solitude: here, far from the world of men, he leads a life devoted to cultivating the rare sensation, to the luxury of the artificial. Hence, his project of making a stage production of his own life, in a setting where each detail will have been chosen with the most anxious exactitude. But he will not be able to exercise complete domination over the "refined hermitage" he has arranged, any more than he was able to control the pleasures of his worldly life. Yet, he has not lacked the desire to be both the sole provider and sole receiver of tangible pleasures. For every natural object, Des Esseintes has substituted a second object, dependent on himself alone, which theoretically does not carry the potential for hostility with which every external object, every strange person, may be charged. It seems that one need fear no adversity when, in the absence of any material concerns, one surrounds oneself with objects which replace the world. Whether the substitute be mimetic, metaphoric or imaginary; whether it be poems, paintings, locomotives, candies with special flavors (which replace women by a fragrant "essence"); whether, at a height of artificiality, it be "natural flowers imitating imitation flowers": everything falls within the province of art, everything has had to be approved by the most exacting "taste." This perverse criticism and this imperious classification, all through the celebrated chapters devoted to the works collected by Des Esseintes, construct a bizarre world, which is, nevertheless, a mirror world in which each of the individual's desires should find the object that appeases or exacerbates it. In this uneventful story, in which the hero encounters no adversaries except in his dreams, we nevertheless witness the appearance of a major "opponent": the pain, the nausea, inflicted by "gastric neurosis." One begins to believe that the aesthetic life, dominated by a permanent will-to-feel, will-to-enjoy, in the end abandons the feeling apparatus, too broadly deployed, to the possibility-limit it contains within itself, which is pain. Hyperaesthesia, incapable of maintaining a sufficient distance from the object of pleasure, blinds itself in the painful excess in which it no longer knows anything but itself, in the prison it is for itself. Pain marks the triumphant return of nature in its primitive form, after all the efforts to have nothing more in common with it. The dandy is taken from behind, in his body, by the adversary whom he thought he had subdued.

La bêtise n'est pas mon fort. J'ai vu beaucoup d'individus ; j'ai visité quelques nations ; j'ai pris ma part d'entreprises diverses sans les aimer ; j'ai mangé presque tous les jours ; j'ai touché à des femmes. Je revois maintenant quelques centaines de visages, deux ou trois grands spectacles, et peut-être la substance de vingt livres. Je n'ai pas retenu le meilleur ni le pire de ces choses : est resté ce qui l'a pu.

Paul Valéry, etched engraving. From Paul Valéry, *Album de Monsieur Teste* (Paris, Bibliothèque nationale).

zone

"Literature Lacks a Bedside Scene"

Teste's "very small furnished apartment" with its "gloomy, abstract furniture"[11] is the exact opposite of the villa Des Esseintes has decorated so delicately. This difference is emblematic of the entire distance separating the two characters. There remains, as a common denominator, one schematic element: a hero whose only story is to have striven for a form of total domination and who suffers, through an adversity issuing from his own body, the complete reversal of the relationship of superiority he believed he had established to his advantage. Teste, if one is determined to compare him with Huysmans' character, is a Des Esseintes who has been dried up, intellectualized, made manly.

Almost everything that has been written on *Monsieur Teste* concerns the first two parts of the work in which, under the gaze of the "reciter," Teste appears to be the absolute intellectual hero. Of the two-point program formulated by Balzac's Louis Lambert — to become famous, to become a "chemist of the will"[12] — Teste (and his witness) have resolutely sacrificed the first point, because fame is a form of submission in which the individual leaves himself open to the discretion of others. Through pitiless discipline, Teste has set out to overcome inner chance, to do away with the original automatisms, social in origin ("to kill the puppet"[13]), and to create others through voluntary exercises ("I sought a mechanical sieve"[14]). What has fascinated readers is the radical nature of the plan for mastery, which culminates in the scene at the opera where Teste, at the height of his power as spectator, dominates the sum of the groups formed by the place, the performance and the subjugated audience: and how, as readers and critics, can we fail to be sensitive to this scene, in which Teste adopts the attitude of a hyperbolic reader or critic, confronting the text offered him by the ritual of the theater? Here he takes cognizance of the interplay of all the tangible exchanges, all the vulgar weaknesses, all the easy magic — with the exception of himself. He reveals himself to be a virtuoso in high irony, pushing reflection and negativity to their limits. Is his face "inflamed" by the lights and the heat of the spectacle, or by the ecstasy of understanding everything without being caught in the trap of participation? He retreats into the singular gaze, the *glance* that embraces everything above the other gazes, which are captive to a partial magic. His mental art reduces the total work of art — the opera — to no more than a system of easily effective stimulants. (The reciter/narrator, Teste's witness, nevertheless takes the time to paint, in the manner of Degas, the brilliant or muted lights, the half shadows, the bejeweled flesh of a theater interior.)

The third part of *An Evening with Monsieur Teste* — Monsieur Teste's retiring to bed — will form the exact reverse of this state of glory. It is now that fatigue sets in, then pain, then drowsiness under the effect of the contents of a "medicine bottle."[15] Let us say that this reversal constitutes the veritable, and unique, peripeteia in the story. The intellectual powers that make Teste so singular are put to the test by an opponent worthy of him: himself, his own body. Just as his achievement had consisted in disciplining himself, without external effect or consequence, the danger comes to him from himself, and the response to the challenge is perception, awaiting, inner "listening," monologue — until the moment when the response is exhausted. Valéry had noted, before writing *Teste*: "Literature lacks a bedside scene. No one has ever done that."[16] As for pain, he will return to it more than once in his *Notebooks*:

> The strongest thing there is in the world
> — pain.[17]
> Man has only himself to fear —
> his capacity for pain.[18]

And in 1923, the subject still seems to him to deserve to be noted among projects to consider:

> Struggle between the intellect and sharp pain.
> The most surprising *subject*.[19]

On this last page of *An Evening with Monsieur Teste*, then, we are certainly in the presence of a question which will not cease to occupy Valéry's thoughts. Rather than citing the abundant collection of *Notebooks*, I need only refer to the texts belonging to the Teste "cycle," to clarify laterally the development of the words of the hero, who is falling asleep.

Such is actually the meaning that Valéry himself seems to have given his story (allowing for the offhandedness with which Valéry answered the questions he was asked, in order to be done with it all as quickly as possible). To Frédéric Lefèvre, he states:

> Teste...is a character obtained by splitting up a real person whose most intellectual moments could be extracted to compose the whole of the life of an imaginary character; but however specialized he may be, however detached from common modes of being,

there comes a moment when physical pain is stronger than he is, and I wanted to show in M. Teste what the sensation of sharp pain is like when it invades and traverses the field of an intelligence that is itself always irritated.[20]

At the theater, Teste and the reciter had noted the power of the musical ritual, which caused the extinction of the other consciousnesses, their fusion in passivity. At the height of vigilance, these "superior" minds had discerned in the others a twilight of thought. But Teste has only deferred his own twilight. In the very first part of the story, his witness had, in advance, asked the question that was the condition of the experiment: "What becomes of M. Teste in pain?" To which the reciter answered himself, as though anticipating the bedtime scene: "He loves. He suffers. He grows bored. Everyone imitates everyone else. But I want him to bring the rules and forms of his whole mind into his sigh, his elemental groan."[21] This is what will happen.

Leaving the theater, this "broad-shouldered" man, whose entire appearance had until this moment signaled his strength, suddenly allows an unsuspected fragility to appear. It is an abrupt change of "level," unforeseen, irrevocable:

M. Teste complained slightly of the midnight coolness. He alluded to old pains.[22] While his "step" remains "military," the habitual neatness of his remarks momentarily blurs: they seem "incoherent" to his hearer. But the law of parataxis, the discontinuity which confers on each moment the aspect of a new beginning, favors the return of full lucidity as well as the sudden intrusion of disease or disturbance. (Valéry, writing to Gide on October 5, 1896, spoke of a book made up "of rather sieved…elements," and of "notes joined together."[23]) The text must be read with full awareness of the value of its staccato. This type of writing, though threatened by indifference, since each distinct occurrence is equal in value to the next, nevertheless successfully escapes it: each recommencing of the statement introduces a gradient of negation or "surpassing" with respect to the element that immediately precedes it. As we shall see, distancing and contradiction will prevail in Teste's monologue as he falls asleep. But already, in the preceding story, the abrupt nature of the interval between the sentences is noteworthy. From the very beginning, Valéry, more than any other writer, works with interruption, making it the theme of a reflection that is itself interrupted.

Let us listen to this, for instance:

> He coughed. He said to himself: "What can a man do?... What can a man do?"
>
> ...He said to me: "Here you have a man who knows that he does not know what he is saying!"

The cough, sign of a disease, of an unspecified "attack," enters punctually to give way immediately, without transition, to the main question, uttered twice: "What can a man do?"

A question in which Valéry invites us to read Teste's motto: "He is none other than the very demon of possibility. Concern for the sum total of what he can do dominates him."[24] Thus, after the intrusion of the cough, the expression of the dominant intellectual concern is literally juxtaposed with the signal of bodily suffering.

This juxtaposition occurs again at the close of the monologue, preceding the moment of going to bed. Teste, overcome by fatigue, has expatiated at length on money; he has cited "very large numbers":

> He conveyed the fever of the *Bourse* [stock market] to me, and the long successions of names of numbers gripped me like poetry. He correlated news events, industrial phenomena, public taste, and the passions, and numbers again. He said: "Gold is in some sense the mind of society."

This sentence is the most succinct formulation of an overall socioeconomic view. Then, one goes to the next line and reads, in three groups of three syllables that scan as anapests, the very formula of interruption, and the isolated, intransitive, undeniable fact of suffering: "Suddenly, he was still. He felt pain [*Tout à coup, il se tut. Il souffrit*]." The arrangement of the text, with its elliptical parsimony, is responsible for the non sequitur which substitutes a passive "phase" for an active "phase." Teste's activity had consisted in *correlating* "news events, industrial phenomena, public taste," etc.... But then comes silence, which separates, and pain, which moves the witness to look away: "Once again I examined the cold room, the nullity of the furniture, in order not to look at him."

The juxtaposition of opposites which I have just pointed out will be seen again in Teste's monologue in bed, at the moment the emblematic formula issues from his mouth again: "What can a man do? I fight everything – except for the suffering of my body, beyond a certain intensity." Teste has interpreted *to be able to do* to mean *to fight*, and he himself has perceived the point where a certain adversary, which he calls the "suffering of my body," refuses to allow itself to be subdued. What was at first told by the witness, as though objectively, in two brief sequences, reappears within the hero's speech; the juxtaposition of inner power, and the pain that is eluding him, is now the object of a considered statement, in a "discourse on himself" which recognizes a limit that can be quantitatively evaluated. Pain forms the exception to the omnipotence of Teste as *gladiator* or *agonistes*. An exception that undermines the affirmation of omnipotence: as soon as it is submitted by the consciousness, the *everything* so proudly proclaimed in "I fight everything" is no longer really everything. This person *can* no longer match his own strength to that of the world opposing him — within his own body. The self — the "I" — and the pain are two, *outside* each other, and the domination of the *individual* ends at the point where the enterprises of his faceless adversary begin, the adversary who imposes on him a *division* in his innermost being. Valéry will keep returning to this experience of the limit: thus, in *Note and Digression*, he writes: "Our knowledge, I feel, is limited by the consciousness we may have of our being — and perhaps of our bodies."[25] And Valéry knows very well that this limit imposed on knowledge forms at the point where consciousness originates: the ultimate point beyond which knowledge will not progress coincides strangely with the source from which consciousness itself proceeds:

> [Consciousness] naively reminds one of an invisible audience sitting in the darkness of a theater. A presence which cannot contemplate itself, condemned to the spectacle opposite, and which nevertheless feels it, composes this whole breathless night, so invincibly oriented. A complete night, a very avid night, a night which is secretly organized, all built of organisms that limit and include one another; a compact night, its shadows stuffed with organs, each of which beats, blows, heats up and defends, according to its own nature, its placement and function....[26]

More concisely, in his "For a Portrait of Monsieur Teste," Valéry posits the following formula: "At the end of the mind, the body. But at the end of the body, the mind."[27] This double abutment is equivalent to a circularity. For the body is not only what the act of thinking proceeds from; it is what accompanies it and proposes itself to thought as an object.

We can understand better why *An Evening with Monsieur Teste*, that "story of a good fellow who thinks," that "vivisection," ends with the epiphany of a body, and with the outbreak of pain: thus the entire extent of the activities of thought will have been traveled to the limits:

> He undressed peacefully. His dry body immersed itself in the sheets and played dead. Then he turned over and buried himself deeper in the bed which was too short.

The "bed which was too short" is here related proportionately to the entire physical structure of the room, ascetically planed down by ellipsis. In their very poverty, the bed, the "commonplace" room, leave the field open for the mind. And on this empty stage, Teste maintains perfect control over his one-character drama. To turn over,* to bury *himself* mark the ever preponderant share of the reflexive, of the action of self on self. Teste has assigned the spectator his place, foretold events, given his orders:

> "Don't leave," he said to me, "you're not bored. I'm going to bed. In a few moments, I will be asleep. You will take the candle to light your way down."

Sleep, and the luminous *departure of the witness* — the candle — will, in fact, form the conclusion of the story: "I took the candle, I crept out." In a few sentences, Teste imposed on his companion all that he expected of him: to stay there, to listen, to slip away. Of course he will now and then address a questioning "*You*" to him, but without expecting any answer. There is an imperceptible transition from the tone of addressed speech to "interior" monologue.

"Smiling, he said to me: 'I'm doing the back float. I'm floating!' " Teste smiles: he mimics an expression opposite to that called for by the pain, which he is beginning to feel, though intermittently. In fact, throughout the monologue, the register of pain coexists with that of euphoria. In the text, one can trace certain rapid substitutions, incessant variations, which express in an already perfectly perceptible way what Valéry will say about the "instability" and "change" required by the "life of the mind." Teste's monologue interweaves hedonistic kinesthetic themes and reactions to pain. The whole metaphoric series of swimming, of navigation, of the "flow of sleep and linen" is marked by pleasure to serve as background and foil to the stabs of pain. The parataxis, the ellipses, mark the interruptions, the resumptions.

"I'm doing the back float. I'm floating!" After "sinking" into the bed, Teste feels that he has become lighter, and he expresses and interprets this immediately. He recaptures the sensation in a metaphorical statement. It is an active response that transforms the surface of the sheet into the surface of the sea. The active nature

---

*To turn over (*se tourner*) is a reflexive word in French.

of the response is reinforced by the verb *faire* (to do), which implies the production of something: in this case, the production of a lightened immobility. To float, which is intransitive, appears to be the result of "doing the back float (*faire la planche*)," a deliberate behavior that implies a *postural* positioning of the recumbent body.

"I feel an almost imperceptible roll under me – an immense movement?" From *doing* (the back float) to *feeling* (a roll) there is a transition to perception, but always in the same marine element, in the same metaphorizing tension. No doubt the roll thus felt is merely an illusion – the projection, onto an imaginary surrounding, of the internal oscillation felt by a tired body (in which a drug is beginning to take effect). One will have noticed that the question mark signals a change of voice: the voice becomes interrogative, after a hexasyllable that rings like a hemistich, "an im*mense* move*ment* (*un mouve*ment *immense*)," amplified by the nasals. But the change of voice causes the final interrogation to point to a term – "immense" – which marks the extreme opposite of the "imperceptible" uttered earlier. The prefix of negation (*im-*) is present in both, but the reversal is staggering: it has occurred with an extraordinary rapidity, as though the bodily message had changed its nature from one moment to the next. In a *Notebook* kept at more or less the same time as "Teste" was being written, one reads this entry: "Sensation is that which is susceptible to many interpretations – of *n* adjacent mental ph(enomena)?"[28]

"I sleep an hour or two at the very most." Teste's less than normal sleep corresponds perfectly to the vocation assigned him by his name ("Conscious – Teste, testis").[29] His brief sleep in a narrow bed causes his state of vigil to persist to the point that thought does not succeed in discovering at what point it has broken off: "Often I can no longer distinguish my thought from before sleep. I do not know if I have slept." Not that he has not wished for sleep. But by calling it, in his outburst of marine metaphors, "the navigation of the night," Teste again makes it into a directed activity: there can be no navigation without piloting, without attention to direction, without the risk of losing sleep.

We read, in the *Logbook*:

Sleep and Memory
other worlds.
blink the eyes, widen them slowly

catch the right foot in the left

hand, squeeze it.[30]

What follows in Teste's monologue is like an explication of this note. Teste will try to prove, "show," that he feels himself to be old. Here again, a statement — "I am old" — is paired with a voluntary act, an affirmed power: "I *can* show you that I feel myself to be old." The demonstration depends on a reflexive perception: "I feel *myself*...." In a later text, Valéry has Teste say: "Proof is the elementary politeness one owes oneself."[31] And, at the end of his monologue, on the edge of sleep, Teste will declare: "If the person speaking to me doesn't prove what he is saying — he's an enemy." How does he go about proving his age? He no longer has recourse, as he did before, to the memory of "what had pleased [him], forms, things, minutes," in order to drift off to sleep. This possibility — of calling up soothing images — seems to have been exhausted. More than anything else, the feeling of being old is the disappearance of the need to explore one's body, a need which characterized childhood, with its areas of ignorance and its sensori-motor conquests. In days gone by, the body was a storehouse of unknown postures; it was an *object* of surprise for the hand:

> When we are children, we *discover* ourselves, we slowly discover the extent of our bodies, we express the particularity of our body through a series of efforts, I suppose? We twist ourselves around and we find ourselves or rediscover ourselves, and we are surprised! We touch a heel, grasp the right foot in the left hand, hold that cold foot in that warm palm!... Now I know myself by heart. My heart too. Bah! The whole earth is marked off....

The child's act of discovery, as described by Teste, is tireless and discontinuous: it implies not only the sense of touch, the crossed *grasp* which objectifies differences in temperature, but also the proprioceptive sensation that accompanies efforts and torsion. And one will inevitably make the powerful accusation of narcissism which goes along with multiplying the resources activated in order to perceive *oneself* (the gaze being temporarily excluded). There is a progression here, in the use of reflexive verbs: *one twists oneself* (*on se tord*) marks an overall movement of the body; *one finds oneself* (*on se trouve*) marks an appropriation of oneself as object of the verb; *one rediscovers oneself* (*on se retrouve*), presumably after an interval, adds the repetition of the act of appropriation. The series of propositions moves toward an increasing control, a growing success in the finality of the gesture.

Every activity, as Valéry acknowledges, comes up against a limit. The exploration of oneself ceases when the body no longer offers any terra incognita. To know oneself "by heart" is to have learned the whole text. And in a literal sense, the heart itself is part of the known text. Teste has metaphorized the exhaustion of knowledge of one's "own body" in two areas: the first deploys the spatial image of the conquered globe (implicitly: the old age of civilization); the second plays with the idea of a text, the whole of which can be repeated from memory. (We know to what extent the thing that can be repeated — notably in *The Solitary* — will become a reason for exasperation, for negating fury, itself repetitive, in Valéry's later texts.)

Pain Enters

The body's old age seems to exclude the invasion of anything new. That invasion will take place, however, in the guise of pain. In order to give more force and more contrast to this invasion, Valéry precedes it by a period of euphoria: "I love this flow of sleep and linen: this linen which stretches and wrinkles or rumples — which comes down on me like sand when I play dead, which curdles around me in sleep." The "flow of sleep and linen" obliterates the limits between interior and exterior, between Body and World. The attention stops at the thin part of the world that enters into contact with the body and merges with it: linen — immediately metaphorized into sand and milk, that is, into a delicate caress, either inorganic (sand) or organic (milk) on the skin of a subject who, by playing "dead," regresses pleasantly to a primitive life (to a "primary narcissisim"). Teste, having compared linen to sand, to curdling milk, does not stop at these natural substances. Linen is also the product of an artifice, an artifact: annexed by the enveloped body, it confers on it its character of "quite a complex mechanism." Flesh, too, is a *tissue*. And the interrupted sentence, which heralds the pain, begins by defining it as an infinitesimal disorder that alters the regularity of the tissue (in a technical sense): "In the direction of the warp or the woof, a very small deformation...Ah!" The origin of the pain has been metaphorically objectified as a displacement of materials; it has therefore been held at bay, up to the breaking point, where the cry ("Ah!") signals the fact that a limit has been crossed. But as we shall see, the *cry*, signal of the unbearable, will itself be taken up in the reflexive speech.

Pain comes on stage: until then, the monologue on the recumbent body, on what

383

changes in one's perception of oneself from childhood to old age, had constituted no more than a prelude, a setting for the intrusion of the brutal actor:

> He was in pain.
>
> "What's wrong?" I asked him, "I can..."
>
> "I..." he said. "It's not important. I...a tenth of a second is appearing...Wait...There are moments when my body is illuminated...."

The narrator has heard the cry, noted the suffering, asked a question, proposed his services — immediately ignored. At first, Teste's speech remains attached to objects which it *minimizes*: from a "very small deformation" to "not important," then to the "tenth of a second" and to the "moments," it determines or notes an order of size that limits, to the extreme, the space–time of pain. In addition, pain is immediately *transformed* into something visible. First, it is time (a tenth of a second) made visible; time, therefore an independent parameter. A *variation* intervenes when this visible thing, intensified, can be said: *my body*. Illumination transfers a property to the body, a privilege that mystical tradition attributed to the mind. The body is the site of a revelation — but a revelation for which it is itself the source. (As we shall see, the question of the similarity with the mystical "states" will be posed again more explicitly.) The expectancy of the gaze, the desire to *see* will find employment:

> It is very strange. I suddenly see it in me.... I distinguish the depths of the layers of my flesh; and I feel areas of pain, rings, poles, plumes of pain. Do you see these living figures? This geometry of my suffering? There are flashes of lightning that completely resemble ideas. They make me understand — from here to there.

The immediate presence of this to the suffering self ("*my* flesh," "*my* suffering") is not canceled out. Nevertheless, Teste's speech builds a structured space, from which an observing gaze is distinct. And under this gaze, endowed with a remarkable power of resolution, objects become more and more tenuous and differentiated. There is a gradation, on a visual level, from the more massive to the more tenuous, in the order in which the following succeed one another: *layers, zones, rings, poles, plumes*. The transition is a sort of progressive drying out, from the physiological (layers of flesh) to the electric (rings, poles, plumes). The effect of this is to detail, amplify, renew the banal metaphor of the *fulgurating* nature of pain. A little farther on, there will be a mention of *flashes of lightning*, but with an immediate passage to the abstract, that is, to *figures* and to *geometry*, then to *ideas*. The space thus invaded by legible signs is finite; it extends *from here to there*. Teste invites his witness to *see* this, as though there could be a meeting of gazes on one and the same external object. We are witnessing the process by which pain becomes an object for the mind: it is the reverse of the hysterical process, as understood by Freud and Breuer, which postulates the transformation of the idea into an unconscious symptom. (*An Evening with Monsieur Teste* and the *Studien über Hysterie*, 1895, appeared within a few months of each other!) Up to a certain limit, Teste creates consciousness, creates something that can be visualized using somatic events; Freud and Breuer's hysterics, on the contrary, create something somatic using thought subjected to hypnosis (Breuer) or repression (Freud).

Suddenly everything changes, through a substitution, or "self-variance," which causes the domination of distinct pain to be succeeded by the domination of the indistinct (of which Teste retains the power to speak distinctly, by watching his words):

> And yet they leave me *uncertain*. Uncertain is not the word.... When *it* is about to appear, I find in myself something confused or diffused. Areas that are...hazy occur in my being, expanses of space appear. Then I take a question from my memory, any problem at all...I plunge into it. I count grains of sand...and, as long as I see them.... My increasing pain forces me to observe it. I think about it! I await only my cry...and as soon as I hear it – the *object*, the terrible *object*, getting smaller, and still smaller, steals away from my inner sight.

Another state is temporarily established: it is no longer that of manifest pain, but that of expectation, an expectation directed first toward a neutral and undetermined "*it*" destined soon to be transformed into a "*terrible object*." The end of the text quoted concludes a cycle: the "Ah!" we had *heard* before the succession of illuminating images becomes the cry ("my cry") which Teste does not utter, but of which he speaks in full knowledge: after the cry has been heard comes the reduction in dimension, the "*smaller*" which connects back with the "not important" and "tenth of a second" with which the description of the spectacle of pain began.

The hazy inner space, the indeterminate expanses, metaphorize the imminence of the pain, of which at first we know only the discharge. Teste speaks of the preceding moments, when the "increasing" pain and the mind are as close as possible to each other. The mind's resource is diversion. (A method recommended by Montaigne, whom Valéry did not esteem at all, as we know, because of his trivial confidences.) The diversion summons what is more abstract; number, numeration, "any problem at all." Calculation, this time bearing on *something else*, intervenes so that the field of consciousness may not belong only to the thought of pain. Thought goes to the extreme of abstraction, beyond any form (except the arid form of the grains of sand). But it is the pain that will inevitably win out, during the entire time when, because of its increasing dimensions, it forces attention and binds thought. At least this is what Teste declares, describing from memory the imminence of suffering. For the suffering does not return. The analgesic drug has taken effect, but it has respected the power of opposition that allows the mind to recall everything it has witnessed or to foresee what might be repeated.

All these episodes take place in the domain of the visible, of the visual. Nothing else is involved but seeing, or foreseeing or observing what "appears," what comes into view, what is inscribed in a field or on the "expanses." The acoustic domain is present only in the *cry*, and in the listening which has the power to reduce the hostile object. But what we have here is only one of several possible systems of metaphorization. There are others. Valéry, in *A Few of Monsieur Teste's Thoughts*, introduces musical equivalences:

> Pain is due to the resistance of the consciousness to a local arrangement of the body. — A pain which we could consider clearly, and in some way circumscribe, would become sensation without suffering — and perhaps in this way we would succeed in knowing something directly about our deeper body — knowledge of the sort we find in music. Pain is a very musical thing, one can almost speak of it in terms of music. There are deep and high-pitched pains, andantes and furiosos, prolonged notes, fermatas and arpeggios, progressions — abrupt silences, etc. . . . [32]

Here again, the metaphorization is closely connected to a plan for control. Because every metaphorization implies an interpretation, and every interpretation involves a distance between an interpreting power and an object interpreted — even if that object is an event taking place in "my body" (or, as Valéry will say in a phrase that accentuates the objectification even more: "the my-body"). For Valéry, "pain has no meaning,"[33] hence its indefinitely interpretable nature. We have cited the following from one of the first Notebooks: "Sensation is that which is susceptible to many interpretations — of *n* adjacent mental ph(enomena)." And immediately afterward comes the following rapid note, which schematizes Teste's monologue as he confronts pain: "What causes pain is that one moves away from the disgusting image — and that one comes back to it. That oscillation."[34]

When subjected to that oscillation, control cannot be continuously achieved. Among the thoughts attributed to Teste is this one: "I am what is unstable."[35] To become aware of instability appears to be an attempt, on the part of reflection, to regain stability. Nevertheless, one must take note of an interruption which has not left intact the very faculty that is taking note. Thus, a web is created of a combination of breaks suffered, of deliberate new beginnings which the mind, in its pride, would like to see not as repetitions but as higher stages of reflection.

Thus, when we go on with our perusal, we read of a plan (or rather, a hypothetical wish) to begin:

> What can a man do? I fight everything — except the suffering of my body, beyond a certain intensity. It is there, however, that I ought to begin. For to suffer is to give supreme attention to something, and I am somewhat a man of attention.

But one has only to read what follows to see that the *beginning* which has just been discussed is only the repetition of a deliberate *foreseeing* which occurred long ago. Surprising "variability": the man who had spoken as though *having to begin* eventually speaks of himself as *having already foreseen*:

> You know, I had foreseen my future illness. I had visualized precisely what everyone now knows. I believe this vision of a manifest portion of the future ought to be part of our education. Yes, I had foreseen what is beginning now....

Pain yields to sleep, under the more pronounced effect of the drug, through an induced variation or a change of "phase." This is signaled by the witness's brief note: "He became calm." Yet the voice persists ("a murmur in the pillow"), while on the periphery "his hand was already asleep":

> He went on: "I think, and that does not disturb anything. I am alone. How comfortable solitude is! Nothing sweet weighs on me.... The same reverie, here, as in the ship's cabin, the same at the Café Lambert.... If the arms of a Berthe become important, I am robbed — as though by pain.... If anyone says something and does not prove it — he is an enemy. I prefer the brilliance of the least event that occurs. I am being, and seeing myself; seeing myself see myself, and so forth.... Let us think very closely. Bah! One can doze off over any subject.... Sleep can continue any idea...."

In their paratactic discontinuity, each phrase seems to exist for itself, briefly. Nevertheless, they are headed in a general direction from "I think" to "sleep"; but their motion is circular, since sleep is still thought (according to another system of organization), and since it can continue any "*idea*." This is precisely the circle described, in one of the secondary texts which we have already read, by the chiasmatic formula: "At the end of the mind, the body. But at the end of the body, the mind."[36]

The Ghosts of Descartes and Pascal

It is not difficult to read, in the phrases spoken by Teste before he sleeps, the *transformed*, *deformed* echo of several famous texts. Although we cannot positively demonstrate that this reference was intentional, it is, at least, real, perceptible. When a brief statement begins with an absolutized "I think," what reader would not perceive the shadow of Descartes? But here, instead of "therefore I am," we encounter: "and that does not disturb anything." In place of the fullness of being, a double negation, in which the subject and complement are neutral, colorless, elusive: *that*, *anything*, as though the "I think" were preserved from all contact, from all exterior friction. True, just afterward and a few lines down, as though it is playing with our disappointed expectation, we will find: *I am alone*, then *I am being*. But this latter proposition is not conclusive; it does not result from a *therefore*. On the contrary, it is initial, the first term in a series of increasingly reflexive statements.... In the same way, "I am alone" is only an initial assertion which will be reinforced by a euphoric acquiescence ("How comfortable solitude is!"), then by an ambiguous phrase, in which the double negative ("*Nothing* sweet weighs on me [*rien* de doux *ne* me pèse])" either affirms or denies the sweetness, depending on how one reads it: what is sweet, like solitude, does not weigh on one; or, no importunate sweetness comes to weigh one down. The sentence is anamorphic. In any case, the solitary *I* excludes everything that is not it. The phrase that follows establishes a constancy ("the *same* reverie"): identity with itself is demanded by reverie. The value of this identity is heightened by its contrast to a succession of different places. The isomorphism of the reverie resists heterotopy. More simply, let us say that the places ("here," "the ship's cabin," "Café Lambert") are reduced to equivalence: they become indifferent, interchangeable. The solitary individual appropriates for himself the right to variation, from *thought* to *reverie*, but he is constantly referred back to himself. He wants to be the exclusive possessor of himself. Hence, another series of equivalences,

Une prière de M. Teste : Seigneur, j'étais dans le néant, infiniment nul et tranquille. J'ai été dérangé de cet état pour être jeté dans le carnaval étrange... et fus par vos soins doué de tout ce qu'il faut pour pâtir, jouir, comprendre et me tromper ; mais ces dons inégaux.

Je vous considère comme le maître de ce noir

Paul Valéry, etched engraving. From Paul Valéry, *Album de Monsieur Teste* (Paris, Bibliothèque nationale).

which place on an equal footing (with what scorn for women!) "the arms of a Berthe," "pain" and a third enemy: "anyone who does not prove it." These are three homologous forms of the adversary. Woman, reduced and simplified by synecdoche to her arms alone, then to the metonymic indeterminacy that makes her *a* Berthe of all possible Berthes and all possible women, is a danger to this treasure — the self — which Teste wants jealously, greedily, to preserve. (Teste would provide arguments for those who see a relation between capitalism — he lives "off paltry weekly transactions at the *Bourse*" — excessive individualism and the venality of love — one encounters him "in a sort of b....") This is how Teste has answered two questions which the reciter had asked at the beginning: "What happens to M. Teste when he is suffering? — In love, how does he reason?" With all that training has made "mechanical" in him, he functions like a "bachelor machine." Indifference dissipates love, as the anesthetic has dissipated the pain. Any dialogue is doomed. If all those who talk to him without proving what they say are enemies, who will not be an enemy, since language (unless it has recourse to "more subtle numbers") never allows one to prove anything? No one is left. What does Teste's consciousness still allow in the face of this? Pure contingency, "the least event that occurs," and which the factual evidence adorns with a brilliance. "The least event" is a minimalized demand. But for someone who experiences such voluptuous pleasure in finding himself alone again, the world can just as well disappear, replaced by the self which has become object. Here, now, is the complement of "I think": "I am being, and seeing myself; seeing myself see myself, and so forth." The field of consciousness is occupied by the participial redoubling of the *I am*, which becomes fixed for an instant in a *being*, to be succeeded by another momentary state, *seeing myself*: the *I* of "I am" is no longer more than *myself* as object of the act of *seeing*, itself supplanted by a new act of seeing, which, in turn, makes it an object. The infinite reflexivity thus initiated liberates a series of visions, each of which reduces the preceding vision to the state of an object. "And so forth": this is the *formula* for a series, and it is enough to have stated it, as mathematicians do, to be excused from carrying it out. For by letting go of itself in order to objectify itself, *seeing* is condemned to an indefinite distancing, without any increase in power. What remains is to experience the inverse direction: "Let us think very closely." That is to say, think at a diminishing distance. The diminution, the spatial narrowing, are such that thinking no longer has an object; thinking no longer has more than an adverbial complement of distance.

One other reference appears here: and that is Pascal! In his *Logbook*, Valéry notes: "Think more closely," and just below, "Pascal 59."[37] Farther on, one will read the sentences or phrases that will be used in *An Evening with Monsieur Teste*: "One can doze off over any subject." Then: "He saw things very closely" (*Logbook*). Fragment 59 of the Havet edition corresponds to fragment 139 of the Brunschvicg: "But *when I have thought more closely*, and when, after having found the cause of all our ills, I have tried to discover the reason for it, I have found that there is one very effective one, which consists of the unhappiness of our weak and mortal condition, so miserable that nothing can console us for it *if we think about it closely*." For Valéry, to think very closely is to think in the immanence of thought itself, without any distance. This is the path of sleep, but conceived as another system of organizing thought — one that will be explored by the text of *Agathe* (which had originally been imagined as a "Night of Monsieur Teste"). But in the extreme proximity of thought, Valéry, unlike Pascal, does not find "the unhappiness of our condition," but what the mystics called God; in "For a Portrait of Monsieur Teste" we read:

> Pain sought the apparatus which would convert pain into knowledge — what the mystics have glimpsed, dimly seen. But the reverse was the beginning of this experiment.
>
> God is not far. He is *what is closest*.[38]

Only Teste's last words before sleeping do not speak of any god, unless it is of *one or another* (*quelconque*), of *any one at all* (*n'importe quoi*): "Bah! One can doze off over any subject... Sleep can continue any idea...." In absolute proximity, the consciousness speaking this monologue gives up pursuing its choices. It chooses not to choose objects and ideas any longer. The very close god is none other than what this renunciation allows to happen. Indifference, "disinterest" abandons thought to its own mobility. The mind, having subjugated the body's message and lost the world, spends all the energy it has within itself. Elsewhere, Valéry will write:

> As the great steamship plunges down and sinks slowly, with all its resources, its machines, its lights, its instruments....
>
> Thus in the night and in the nether part of oneself, the mind descends to sleep with all its equipment and its possibilities.[39]

Engulfment in sleep, transcribed here as a great navigation metaphor, akin to those of which Teste is fond, ends in a situation of "sensory isolation" which abandons the mind, not to total night (the steamship keeps *its* lights), but to functioning *in a closed system*. The triangular complex Body–Mind–World is reduced to an undifferentiated point; all relation with the World is extinguished, and the presence of the body is confined almost to brushing against what is impalpable: the mind, stuck fast inside the body, and incapable of reducing the body to an object, works in its own "milieu." It loses its masculinity, its reasons for fighting. It becomes a sleeping woman. This is when Agathe's monologue could begin: "The more I think, the more I think."[40] Continuation can take place without any hindrance, leaving the field clear for pure variation, infinite substitutions, which follow one another without discrimination, in the most complete lack of determination:

> I am changing in the shadow, in a bed. An idea, having now no beginning, becomes clear, but false, but pure, then empty or immense or old: it even becomes nil, to rise to the unexpected, and it leads my whole mind.
>
> My body hardly knows that the tranquil masses of my bed lift it up: on it, my reigning flesh watches and mixes the darkness....[41]

Here the "pure self" is called upon to speak, the incorruptible witness of all that is change, variation, ignorance in the individual.... As Valéry has repeated so often, it is a nonperson which keeps watch in the person. ("The pure and simple consciousness whose single characteristic is to *be*...is perfectly *impersonal*."[42]) At the last extremity of the life of the mind, and through attention to the individual, an "unaltered," anonymous power, "in the most abstract state," triumphs. But the same is true at the last extremity of the life of the body. What is most singular, most singularizing about pain, also takes on the aspect of the most complete strangeness: the attention which, narcissistically absorbed in the individual experience, observes the appearance of the painful event, sees it take on the aspect of the nonself, what cannot be appropriated: among the "Thoughts of M. Teste," we read:

> [We are sources] of pain or voluptuous pleasure. We feel "coming from us..." (I don't know how to say it) – modifications – values – greatnesses, "sensations" – "accelerations" which are at once most *ours* and most alien, our masters, our *we* of the moment, and of the *coming-moment*.
>
> How to describe this depth, so variable, so without reference – which has the most important, but the most unstable, relations with "thought."[43]

At this point, everything can be reversed. The person, the individual, recompose themselves *a contrario* through all that they have discovered which is impersonal at the end of the mind, at the end of the body. Out of the *stranger*, which they see appear at the extreme limit, they form the very constituent part of the being itself. Teste inscribes in his *Logbook*: "It is the unknown that I carry in myself that makes me myself."[44] The unknown is *carried* by an *I*. Therefore, there is a reappropriation: but it is the appropriation of something that cannot be possessed, of something that cannot be known. Such is pain — mine and not-mine, at the same time. And what happens if knowledge gets the upper hand? If the force of the gaze opposes "weakness" and "fragility"? This force, in its excess, opposes the self, overflows it.... It is not equivalent, for Teste, to a liberation of the person through the exercise of consciousness. It is another *strange* power, contained *in* the self, but "distinct" from it:

There is in me some faculty more or less practiced in considering — and even in having to consider — my tastes and my distastes as purely accidental.

If I knew more about it, perhaps I would see a necessity — instead of this chance. But seeing this necessity is still distinct.... What constrains me is not me.[45]

Between tastes, distastes, pains — all reducible to the accidental, to the inessential — and this pure faculty of seeing, the individual, tributary of his sources, is encircled by impersonality. To it, he owes his sudden firmness, perpetually destroying, perpetually rebuilding.

Translated by Lydia Davis.

In addition to these two essays, I have published the following related texts: "L'échelle des températures. Une lecture du corps dans *Madame Bovary*" (*Le temps de la réflexion*, vol. 1, Paris, Gallimard, 1980, pp. 145-83); "L'immortalité mélancolique" (*Le temps de la réflexion*, vol. 3, Paris, Gallimard, 1982, pp. 231-51); "Rêve et immortalité chez Baudelaire" (*Corps écrit*, vol. 7, Paris, 1983, pp. 45-56); and "Propositions de l'immortalité" (*I linguaggi del sogno*, edited by V. Branca, C. Ossola and S. Resnik, Florence, Sansoni, 1984, pp. 235-49). Most of these studies have appeared in German translation, with an introduction by H.R. Jauss, under the title *Kleine Geschichte des Körpergefühl* (Universitätsverlag Konstanz GMBH, Constance, 1987). This volume represents a provisional stage of the work which was first delivered, in its earliest form, for the Noguchi Lectures at Johns Hopkins University in October, 1978. Another part of this book, corresponding to the first of the two essays included here, was the subject of a James Lecture at New York University in June, 1979.

Paul Valéry, etched engraving. From Paul Valéry, *Album de Monsieur Teste* (Paris, Bibliothèque nationale).

APPENDIX

Some Simple Reflections on the Body

Paul Valéry

On the Blood and Us

1. How we can kill the living creature by giving it *gratis* (and in the best quality) what is ordinarily supplied by its organism and by its own acts in its environment.

2. When I look at a living thing, what I see and what first occupies my attention is this mass, all of a piece, which moves, bends, runs, jumps, flies or swims; which howls, speaks, sings, performs its many acts, takes on many appearances, assumes a multiplicity of selves, wreaks its havoc, does its work, in an environment which accepts it and from which it is inseparable.

This thing, with its discontinuous activity, its spontaneous movements springing suddenly from a state of immobility to which they always return, is curiously contrived: we note that the visible organs of propulsion, legs, feet, wings, occupy a considerable part of the creature's total bulk; and we discover later on that the rest of its volume is made up of organs of internal work, some of whose outward effects we have witnessed. It would seem as though the creature's whole life span were the effect of this work, as though its entire production, visible or not, were expended in feeding the insatiable consumer of matter that the creature itself is.

3. But I also know that what the system of implements which is almost the whole animal is continuously looking for or manufacturing might be provided by other means than his own. If his blood were supplied directly, from the outside, with the substances whose preparation now requires so many coordinated industries and so elaborate a directing apparatus, if all this equipment and its functioning, now useless, were eliminated, it seems likely that life might still be sustained, perhaps more efficiently and reliably than it is by the natural mechanisms. An artificial mode of

conversation would first do away with the organs of relation: the senses, the muscles, the instincts, the "psyche"; and then with the grinders, mixers, conveyors, filters, tubes, burners and radiators, in short, the whole production line that is put to work when the senses give the signal.

4. The whole organism has no other function than the renewal of its blood — except perhaps the maintenance and service of the reproductive equipment, a very special, almost lateral function, which is often suppressed without vital damage.

But the blood itself has no other use than to restore to the apparatus which regenerates it what that apparatus needs in order to function. *The body makes blood that makes body that makes blood....* Actually all the body's acts are cyclic in relation to the body itself, for they break down into comings and goings, contractions and decontractions, while the blood itself pursues its cyclic journey around its world of flesh, the continuous circumnavigation wherein life consists.

5. There is something absurd about this monotonous system of mutual conservation. It shocks the mind, which abhors repetition and even ceases to understand or to pay attention once it has grasped what it calls a "law"; for a *law* is what does away with "eternal returns."...

6. Yet we observe two escapes from the body's life cycle: on the one hand, the body inevitably *wears out*; on the other hand, *it reproduces itself*.

7. To go back for a moment: if we suppose that the blood is regenerated directly from the outside, that the creature is preserved as today we preserve bits of tissue in an appropriate medium and temperature, in this case the animal will be reduced to nothing, or perhaps to a single "cell" endowed with some sort of elementary life. Once what we call sensibility and action have been done away with, the mind must disappear along with what permits and compels it to emerge, for it has no other function indispensable to life than to cope with the variety, uncertainty, unexpectedness of circumstances. It devises actions which respond to the formless or the multiform. But where unconscious operations or reflex (that is, uniform)

responses suffice, the mind is superfluous. At most it will disturb or prevent the proper functioning of the organism. This it does not fail to do, and there are famous examples to show that it is sometimes quite proud of the fact.

8. Accordingly, such products of life as memory, thought, feeling, invention, etc., with all the quality of the marvelous we attribute to them, are inevitably reduced to the rank of accessories. All our intellectual passions, our superfluous actions, our strivings to know or to create, amount to developments, *impossible to calculate in advance*, of a function that tended originally to do no more than compensate for the inadequacy or ambiguity of our immediate perceptions and to relieve the resulting indeterminateness.

The great variety of species, the amazing diversity of the forms and instruments they manifest, their resources, their many different solutions to the problem of living, suggest that sensibility and conscious thought might have been replaced by entirely different properties rendering the same services.

What one species obtains by trial and error, by a kind of statistical method, another achieves with the help of a *sense* that the first does not possess; or else ... by some internal process akin to "reasoning."

9. I note that our senses provide us with only a bare minimum of hints, which transpose into forms of sensibility only an infinitesimal part of the probable variety and variations of a "world" we can neither conceive nor imagine.

10. To sum up what I have said above: if we divest what we call *our life* of everything we have considered as replaceable — if its organs, forms, functions are replaced by artificial devices and so relegated to the rank of useless accessories (we are reminded of the cases of atrophy that have occurred in the course of evolution) — life is reduced to nothing or next to nothing; then sensation, feeling, thought, are not essential to it, but mere accidents.

There is an example of this: life reduced to nothing but life gives us the embryo, such a paltry thing at the beginning of its career, and sprung from next to nothing — from a germ.

11. And now one last reflection in the form of a question: In what way is the mind's peculiar activity indispensable to the preservation of life, under circumstances that offer a man the possibility of action? I think it would be interesting to look into this. We should be led no doubt to define the mind as the "power of transforming" its own formations, a power such that, in the face of a situation that cannot be met by simple automatisms and reflexes and therefore calls for the exercise of that power, it seeks to provide the corresponding idea and impulses to action which will ultimately restore the living system to a state in which its resources are again available to it — the state one might call "freedom." Whatever internal combinations, creations, modifications have occurred — the process as a whole will always tend to restore the system to a state of free possibility.

The Problem of the Three Bodies

In common usage the word "body" responds to several very different needs of expression. One might say that each of us in his thought has *Three Bodies* — *at least*. Let me explain.

The first is the privileged object of which, at each instant, we find ourselves in possession, although our knowledge of it — like everything that is inseparable from the instant — may be extremely variable and subject to illusions. Each of us calls this object *My Body*; but we give it no name *in ourselves*, that is to say, *in it*. We speak of it to others as of a thing that belongs to us; but for us it is not entirely a thing; and it belongs to us a little less than we belong to it. . . .

It is for each of us, in essence, the most important object in the world, standing in opposition to the world, on which, however, it knows itself to be closely dependent. We can say that the world is based on it and exists in reference to it; or just as accurately, with a simple change in the *adjustment* of our intellectual vision, that the selfsame body is only an infinitely negligible, unstable event in the world.

But neither the word "object" that I have just used nor the word "event" is appropriate. There is no name to designate our sense of the substance of our presence, our actions and feelings, not only in their actuality, but also in an imminent, deferred or purely potential state — something more remote and yet less intimate than our secret thoughts: we find in ourselves a capacity for modifications almost as varied as the circumstances surrounding us. This *My Body* obeys or disobeys, favors or obstructs our designs; it engenders surprising strengths and weaknesses connected wholly or in part with its perceptible mass, which at times takes on a sudden charge of impulsive energies that make it "act" in response to some interior mystery, and at other times seems to become the most crushing and immovable weight....

The thing itself is formless: all we know of it by sight is the few mobile parts that are capable of coming within the conspicuous zone of the space which makes up this *My Body*, a strange, asymmetrical space in which distances are exceptional relations. I have no idea of the spatial relations between "My Forehead" and "My Foot," between "My Knee" and "My Back."... This gives rise to strange discoveries. My right hand is generally unaware of my left. To take one hand in the other is to take hold of an object that is *not-I*. These oddities must play a part in sleep and, *if such things as dreams exist*, must provide them with infinite combinations.

This thing that is so much mine and yet so mysteriously and sometimes — always, in the end — our most redoubtable antagonist, is the most urgent, the most constant and the most variable thing imaginable: for it carries within it all constancy and all variation. Nothing moves before us unless this *My Body* traces a corresponding modification that follows or imitates the movement perceived; and nothing ceases to move unless some part of it is immobilized.

It has no past. The word "past" has no meaning for this *My Body* which is the present itself, wholly made up of events and impending events. Sometimes certain of its parts or regions make themselves felt, light up, take on an importance before which everything else ceases to be; they dominate the moment with their incomparable pleasure or pain.

Our *Second Body* is the one which others see, and an approximation of which confronts us in the mirror or in portraits. It is the body which has a form and is apprehended by the arts, the body on which materials, ornaments, armor sit, which love sees or wants to see, and yearns to touch. It knows no pain, for it reduces pain to a mere grimace.

This is the body that was so dear to Narcissus, but that drives many to despair, and is a source of gloom to almost all of us once the time comes when we cannot help admitting that the aged creature in the glass, whom we do not accept, stands in some terribly close though incomprehensible relation to ourselves. How can we admit that we are that wreck of a man?...

But our knowledge of our *Second Body* goes little farther than the view of a surface. One can live without ever having seen oneself, without knowing the color of one's skin; that is the fate of the blind. But life compels none of us to know what is under the relatively unbroken skin of our *Second Body*. It is worthy of note that the living, thinking, acting man is without knowledge of his inner organization. He is not equipped to know it. Nothing leads him to suspect that he has a liver, a brain, kidneys and the rest: in any event such information would be useless, for under normal conditions he has no means of acting on these organs. All his faculties of action are turned toward the "outside world," so much so that the "outside world" might be defined as what can be affected by our means of action. Everything I *see*, for example, can be transformed by *my movement*; I act upon my environment, but by what mechanisms I do not know.

Thus there is a Third Body. But it has unity only in our thought, since we know it only for having dissected and dismembered it. To know it is to have reduced it to parts and pieces. It gives off scarlet or whitish liquids, or hyalines, some of them quite viscous. We remove elements of varying sizes, fashioned so as to fit quite exactly in place: sponges, vessels, tubes, fibers, articulated rods.... Reduced to thin slices or tiny drops, our specimens reveal under the microscope corpuscular shapes that resemble nothing at all. We try to decipher these histological cryptograms. We wonder how this fiber produced motive force? And in what way these little asterisms with their fine radicles could have been related to sensation and thought? But what would a Descartes, a Newton, ignorant as they would be of our electromagnetism, make of induction and all the other phenomena discovered since their day, if without explanation we gave them a dynamo to examine, merely describing its effects? They would proceed as we do with a brain: they would take the machine apart, unroll the spools, note the presence of copper, carbons, steel, and in the end admit defeat, acknowledging their inability to guess the workings of this machine which, we have told them, effects the transformations familiar to us all.

These *Three Bodies* which I have just claimed for us are necessarily related in a number of ways that it would be highly interesting, though rather arduous, to explore. I prefer at this point to resort to a kind of fantasy.

I suggest that each of us has a *Fourth Body* which I might call the *Real Body* or equally well the *Imaginary Body*.

Let us consider this body as indivisible from the unknown and unknowable medium intimated by the physicists when they torture the perceptible world and, proceeding by the indirect means of *relays within relays*, disclose phenomena whose origin they situate far below or above the scope of our senses, our imagination and ultimately of our intellection itself.

From this inconceivable medium my *Fourth Body* is neither more nor less distinct than is a whirlpool from the liquid in which it is formed. (I am entitled, it seems to me, to dispose of the inconceivable as I please.)

It is not one of the Three other Bodies, for it is not the *My Body*, nor the *Third* which is that of the scientists, since it is made of what they know nothing about.... And moreover, the mind's knowledge is a product of what this *Fourth Body is not*. Necessarily and irrevocably *everything that is* masks for us *something that might be*....

But why bring up this utterly fruitless notion here? Simply because an idea, even if thoroughly absurd, is never entirely without value; and an expression, an empty sign, never fails to goad the mind in some way. Where did I get this idea of a *Fourth Body*?

As I was reflecting on the notion of "body" in general, and on my *Three Bodies* that we have just been discussing, the famous problems that have been raised by these themes arose dimly in the half-darkness of my thoughts. I own that I ordinarily banish them from the most sensitive and urgent point of my attention. I seldom speculate on the origin of life and the species; I seldom ask myself whether death is a simple change of climate, costume and habits, whether or not the mind is a by-product of the organism; whether our acts can ever be what we call *free* (though no one has ever managed to say exactly what we mean by that); and so on.

It was against this background of timeworn difficulties that my absurd and luminous idea emerged: "I give the name of *Fourth Body*," I said to myself, "to the unknowable object, *knowledge of which would solve all these problems at one stroke, for it is what they imply*."

And as a protest arose within me, the Voice of the Absurd added: "Think carefully: Where do you expect to find answers to these philosophical questions? Your images, your abstractions, derive only from the properties and experiences of your *Three Bodies*. But the first offers you nothing but moments; the second a few visions; and the third, at the cost of ruthless dissections and complicated preparations, a mass of figures more indecipherable than Etruscan texts. Your mind, with its language, pulverizes, mixes and rearranges all this and from it, by the abuse, if you will, of its habitual questionnaire, evolves its notorious problems; but it can give them a shadow of meaning only by tacitly presupposing a certain Nonexistence — of which my *Fourth Body* is a kind of incarnation."

From "Aesthetics," in *The Collected Works in English*, vol. 13, Bollingen Series 45, Princeton, Princeton University Press, 1964.
Translated by Ralph Manheim.

NOTES TO A SHORT HISTORY OF BODILY SENSATION

1. Paul Valéry, *Cahiers* (Paris: Pléiade, 1973), vol. 1, p. 1126.

2. Cf. Robert Brain, *The Decorated Body* (New York: Harper & Row, 1979); Victoria Ebin, *The Body Decorated* (Thames and Hudson, 1979).

3. Cicero, *Academia* 2.24.

4. Montaigne, *Essais* (Paris: Presses Universitaires de France, 1965), p. 587.

5. Aristotle, *De anima* 3.2.

6. Descartes, *Traité des passions de l'âme*, in *Descartes' Philosophical Writings*, trans. Norman Kemp Smith (London: Macmillan, 1953), p. 290.

7. Cf. Georges Gusdorf, *Naissance de la conscience romantique au siècle des lumières* (Paris, 1976), pp. 285-316.

8. "Coenaesthesis, dissertatio [...] quam praeside J.C. Reil, pro gradu doctoris defendit Chr. Friedr. Hübner" (Halle, 1974).

9. On the history of the concept of cenesthesia in the nineteenth century, cf. Jean Starobinski,

"Le Concept de cénesthésie et les idées neuropsychologiques de Moritz Schiff," *Genserus* 34 (1977), fasc. 1/2, pp. 2-20.

10. Carl Wernicke, *Grundriss der Psychiatrie*, 2d ed. (Leipzig, 1906).

11. Ribot, *The Diseases of the Personality* (Chicago, 1891), p. 5.

12. *Ibid.*, pp. 5-6.

13. *Ibid.*, p. 30.

14. Hippolyte Taine, *De l'intelligence*, 12th ed. (Paris, 1911), vol. 2, p. 474.

15. Ribot, *Diseases of the Personality*, pp. 19-20.

16. *Ibid.*, p. 157.

17. Notably in *Problèmes de psychologie affective* (Paris, 1906), p. 26.

18. Pierre Janet, *De l'angoisse à l'extase*, 2 vols. (1926; new ed. Paris, 1975), vol. 2, chs. 1 and 2.

19. Janet, *De l'angoisse à l'extase*, vol. 2, ch. 2, sec. 8, p. 71.

20. Ernest Dupré, *Pathologie de l'imagination et de l'émotivité* (Paris, 1925), pp. 289-304.

21. Charles Blondel, *La conscience morbide* (Paris, 1914), p. 264. The quotation refers back to Durkheim, *The Elementary Forms of the Religious Life*, trans. J.W. Swain (London, 1915), p. 271.

22. See, among others, Ted Polhemus, ed., *Social Aspects of the Human Body* (London: Penguin, 1978); Jonathan Benthall and Ted Polhemus, eds., *The Body as a Medium of Expression* (London: Allen Lane/Penguin Books, 1975).

23. Blondel, *La conscience morbide*, pp. 259-60.

24. Ribot, *Diseases of the Personality*, p. 25.

25. Sigmund Freud, *The Interpretation of Dreams*, trans. J. Strachey (London, 1955), p. 39.

26. *Ibid.*, p. 226.

27. *Ibid.*, p. 237.

28. *Ibid.*, p. 236.

29. Sigmund Freud, *Instincts and Their Vicissitudes*, in *The Standard Edition of the Complete Psychological Works of Sigmund Freud*, trans. J. Strachey (London, 1964), vol. 15, p. 120.

30. *Ibid.*, p. 123.

31. *Ibid.*, p. 122.

32. *Ibid.*, pp. 122-3.

33. Paul Schilder, *L'Image du corps*, trans. F. Gantheret and P. Truffert (Paris: Gallimard, 1968).

34. Jean-Paul Sartre, *Being and Nothingness*, trans. Hazel E. Barnes (London: Methuen, 1967), p. 338.

35. Maurice Merleau-Ponty, *Phenomenology of Perception*, trans. Colin Smith (London: Routledge,

Kegan & Paul, 1962), p. 101.

36. Richard Sennett, "Le narcissisme et la culture moderne," in *Former l'homme*, Rencontres Internationales de Genève (Neuchâtel, La Baconnière, 1979), pp. 187-203.

NOTES TO MONSIEUR TESTE CONFRONTING PAIN

1. Paul Valéry, *Les Cahiers*, facsimile ed. (Paris: CNRS, 1957), vol. 1, p. 4.

2. On the philosophers' and psychologists' interest in this problem, see Georges Poulet, "Bergson: Le thème de la vision panoramique des mourants et la juxtaposition," in *L'espace proustien* (Paris: Gallimard, 1963), pp. 139-77.

3. Valéry, *Les Cahiers*, vol. 1, p. 11.

4. Paul Valéry to Albert Thibaudet, 1912, *Oeuvres*, ed. Jean Hytier, 2 vols. (Paris: Pléiade, 1957-60), vol. 2, p. 1383.

5. *Ibid.*, vol. 2, p. 1394.

6. Valéry, *Cahiers*, definitive ed., introduced and annotated by Judith Robinson (Paris: Pléiade, 1973-74). A selection of notes, entitled "Soma at CEM," can be found in vol. 1, pp. 1119-49.

7. *Ibid.*, vol. 2, p. 1322.

8. Valéry, *Oeuvres*, vol. 2, p. 810.

9. Paul Valéry to André Gide, *Correspondance: 1890-1942* (Paris: Gallimard, 1955), pp. 272, 275, etc.

10. Valéry, *Les Cahiers*, vol. 1, p. 175.

11. Translator's note: In quoting from *An Evening with Monsieur Teste*, I have used Jackson Mathews's English translation (New York: Knopf, 1947), adapting it as necessary.

12. Henri Balzac, *Louis Lambert*, eds. Marcel Bouteron and Jean Pommier (Paris: Corti, 1954), p. 82. Valéry was very familiar with this work by Balzac, but found some "cheating" in it (Valéry to Gide, *Correspondance*, p. 213). The "Café Lambert" mentioned in the last sentence of Teste's monologue is perhaps an allusion to the book!

13. Valéry, "Monsieur Teste," in *Oeuvres*, vol. 2, p. 17.

14. *Ibid.*

15. *Ibid.*, p. 23.

16. Valéry, *Les Cahiers*, vol. 1, p. 176.

17. Valéry, *ibid.*, vol. 2, p. 364.

18. *Ibid.*, p. 372.

19. *Ibid.*, p. 1324.

20. Valéry, *Oeuvres*, vol. 2, p. 1381.

21. *Ibid.*, p. 20.

22. *Ibid.*, p. 22.

23. Valéry to Gide, *Correspondance*, p. 281.

24. *Ibid.*, p. 14.

25. Valéry, *Oeuvres*, vol. 1, p. 1233. Cf. *Cahiers*, vol. 2, p. 1350: "What I can do is of the same weariness or strength as my body. My 'soul' begins at the very point where I can't see any more, where I can't do anything more...."

26. Valéry, *Oeuvres*, vol. 1, p. 1224.

27. *Ibid.*, vol. 2, p. 65.

28. Valéry, *Les Cahiers*, vol. 1, p. 208.

29. Valéry, *Oeuvres*, vol. 2, p. 64.

30. Valéry, *Les Cahiers*, vol. 1, p. 33.

31. Valéry, *Oeuvres*, vol. 2, p. 61.

32. *Ibid.*, pp. 72-73.

33. Valéry, *Cahiers*, vol. 2, p. 1392.

34. Valéry, *Les Cahiers*, vol. 2, p. 208.

35. Valéry, *Oeuvres*, vol. 2, p. 69.

36. *Ibid.*, p. 65.

37. Valéry, *Les Cahiers*, vol. 1, p. 59.

38. Valéry, *Oeuvres*, vol. 2, p. 65. Valéry was to write: "Teste is a mystic and a physicist of the *self-conscience* — pure and applied" (*Les Cahiers*, vol. 1, p. 263).

39. Valéry, *Oeuvres*, vol. 1, pp. 354-55.

40. The complete text can be found in Paul Valéry, *La jeune parque et poèmes en prose*, ed. Jean Levaillant (Paris: Gallimard, 1974), pp. 45-53, review and note pp. 165-75. Jean Levaillant offers a suggestive reading of "Teste" in *Les critiques de notre temps et Valéry*, intro. J. Bellemin-Noël (Paris, 1971), pp. 88-95.

41. Valéry, "Agathe," in *Oeuvres*, vol. 2, p. 45.

42. Valéry, *Oeuvres*, vol. 1, p. 1227.

43. *Ibid.*, vol. 2, p. 70.

44. *Ibid.*, p. 40.

45. *Ibid.*

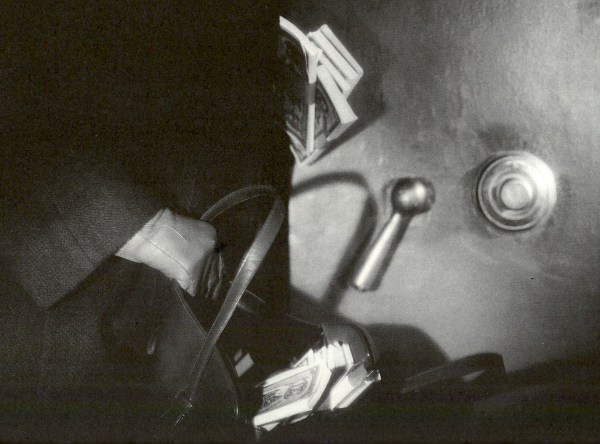

The Three-Body Problem and
the End of the World

Hillel Schwartz

At Clerkenwell Sessions, the wealthy American belle, Ella Castle,
was convicted of shoplifting by a London court and sentenced to
three months in jail. Mrs. Castle became hysterical, began to moan
piteously, finally to scream and struggle violently. "What does it
mean?" she cried. "My God! what does it mean?"

— *New York Times*, November 7, 1896

Attention. Readers eager for a chance at the Three-Body Problem must first pass a
simple quiz.

Please complete the following quotation from a well-known English essayist of
this century:

"Imprisoned in every fat man..."

Twenty seconds.

Ten seconds.

Close enough. As Cyril Connolly wrote during the Second World War, "Imprisoned in every fat man a thin one is wildly signalling to be let out."

A disturbing sentence to be so familiar, to stand as the most frequently quoted,
misquoted, paraphrased and parodied aphorism about obesity. A sentence enjoin-
ing comment, entering as it does by way of prison, yet endowed with the prospect
of freedom, enjambing fat and thin, entailing furious gestures just before the end.

How did this thin Western man come to be in prison, how did his prison come to
be a fat Western man, and why, if he is so desperate, why oh why is the thin man mute?

I shall not answer these questions head-on. In the age-old manner of the histo-
rian who has a story for every reason and a reason for every story, I begin by retreat-

ing: *reculer pour mieux sauter*. The retreat takes us from Connolly's wartime essays, *The Unquiet Grave*, to a prewar novel with the epigraph, "He's dead, but he won't lie down." One of Connolly's St. Wulfric schoolmates is at work here, in *Coming Up for Air* (1939), where we find a likely locus classicus for the disturbing aphorism. "I'm fat," admits George Orwell's George Bowling, "but I'm thin inside. Has it ever struck you that there's a thin man inside every fat man, just as they say there's a statue inside every block of stone?"

Bowling is fat and forty-five but not quite fair. He is troubled by new false teeth, a soapy neck, bombers flying low overhead. He makes five to ten quid a week selling Flying Salamander insurance and lives out along "a line of semi-detached torture chambers," part of the suburban Hesperides Estate. In his garden golden apples do not grow. Fear grows there, on the bare patch where his two brats play. Fear grows as well in the eyes of his jealous wife, "one of those people who get their main kick in life out of foreseeing disasters. Only petty disasters, of course."

Beyond, in the somewhat larger world, the great news is about legs, a pair of woman's legs discovered at a railway waiting room, done up in a brown paper parcel. The legs themselves seem untraceable ("They're all the bleeding same, aren't they?" says one vulgar commercial bloke), but the brown paper could be the real clue (says another). George is sitting opposite the blokes on the train into London, thinking about bombs, musing about fat. "Mind you, I haven't always been fat. I've been fat for eight or nine years, and I suppose I've developed most of the characteristics. But it's also a fact that internally, mentally, I'm not altogether fat.... I've got something else inside me, chiefly a hangover from the past. I'll tell you about that later. I'm fat, but I'm thin inside. Has it ever struck you that there's a thin man inside every fat man, just as they say there's a statue inside every block of stone?"

Straightaway, three lines down, to the case of the woman's legs, but George is staring over miles of London houses. "Christ! how can the bombers miss us when they come? We're just one great big bull's eye." He sees "houses going up into the air, bloomers soaked with blood, canary singing on above the corpses."

What a foul mess. Already the food has become foul. At a cheap London milk bar two paragraphs beyond the singing canary, Bowling is dismayed that everything is "slick and shiny and streamlined.... Everything spent on the decorations and nothing on the food. No real food at all. Just lists of stuff with American names, sort of phantom stuff you can't taste and can hardly believe in the existence of. Everything comes out of a carton or a tin, or it's hauled out of a refrigerator or squirted out of a tap or squeezed out of a tube.... Everything's streamlined nowadays, even the bullet Hitler's keeping for you."

George orders a pair of frankfurters while a newsboy outside cries, "Legs! 'Orrible revelations! All the winners! Legs! Legs!" The frankfurters are not what George supposes them to be – the meat is fish. Ersatz frankfurters. "It gave me the feeling that I'd bitten into the modern world and discovered what it was really made of. That's the way we're going nowadays. Everything slick and streamlined, everything made out of something else.... Rotten fish in a rubber skin. Bombs of filth bursting inside your mouth."

Consoled by a cigar, pure Havana leaf, he walks up the Strand "as if I was the only person awake in a city of sleepwalkers." He waxes philosophical, prophetic. "And this kind of prophetic feeling that keeps coming over me nowadays, the feeling that war's just round the corner and that war's the end of all things, isn't peculiar to me. We've all got it, more or less."

George, to be sure, has more of it. Newsboys shout the late headlines: LEGS. FAMOUS SURGEON'S STATEMENT. But other news draws notice: KING ZOG'S WEDDING POSTPONED. Zog is Ahmed Bey Zogu, Albanian freedom-fighter-turned-king. He is also Og, King of Bashan, and George is a kid in church singing Psalm 135, imagining kings Sihon and Og ("whom ye utterly destroyed") as great Egyptian statues, "a faint mysterious smile on their faces."

We are on our way back to 1900, to another body, when George was thin and seven. George's hangover from the past is at work again despite the intrusive presence, and presentness, of his bothersome bulk, as if only his fourteen stone anchored him to a fateful 1938. After 50,000 words of reminiscence, he decides to return for a week to his birthplace, Lower Binfield, presenting himself as a solid businessman in a new blue flannel suit with the "reducing effect" of a thin white stripe.

But "you can't put Jonah back into the whale," now can you? Lower Binfield in '38 is a manufacturing town: gramophones, Truefitt stockings, bombs. No one recognizes George Bowling, son of Samuel. He is "only a fat tripper in a blue suit doing a bit of sightseeing," just a stranger, "a bit fat, no doubt, but distingué." He goes a-hunting in this place now more bin than field, tracking childhood village buried within adult town. "And all that time I never ran across a soul that knew me. I was a ghost, and if I wasn't actually invisible, I felt like it.

"It was queer, queerer than I can tell you. Did you ever read a story of H.G. Wells's about a chap who was in two places at once — that's to say, he was really in his own home, but he had a kind of hallucination that he was at the bottom of the sea?"

Nonetheless, George is substantial and he knows a way to center himself. He steps onto a penny scale. Too much to drink these past three days, and too much food: he has gained four pounds. A printed fortune on the automatic ticket reassures him: "You are the possessor of exceptional gifts but owing to excessive modesty you have never received your due reward.... You are too fond of standing aside and allowing others to take the credit for what you have done yourself."

One paragraph later he catches sight of a vaguely familiar woman. His first love. "No chance of mistake. Elsie! That fat hag!" Elsie had been something else a quarter-century ago, but now she has turned into "this great round-shouldered hag, shambling along on twisted heels." George shadows her, enters her confectionery shop, becomes her customer, unrecognized for who he once was, "just a customer, a stranger, an uninteresting fat man. It's queer what an inch or two of fat can do."

His last day, George is caught on the outskirts of an explosion. A bomber on routine practice has accidentally dropped one of its bombs just off High Street. The bomb has blown up a greengrocer's shop, blood is mixing with marmalade, and a crowd is staring at a leg. "Just a leg, with the trouser still on it and a black boot with a Wood-Milne rubber heel."

George clears out, certain that "the old life's finished," and what is coming, like the mistaken bomb, is going to come regardless, like it or not. "The bad times are coming, and the streamlined men are coming too. What's coming afterwards I don't know, it hardly even interests me. I only know that if there's anything you care a curse about, better say good-bye to it now, because everything you've ever known is going down into the muck, with the machine guns rattling all the time."

Where George is going is home, to face a jealous wife convinced that he has been unfaithful. What to do? He might tell the truth, explain that he has revisited his old haunting grounds. He might lie, confess to an affair, and take his medicine without the rattle of an argument. Or he might "pull the old gag about losing my memory."

I have quoted so liberally from *Coming Up for Air* because I need to make clear at the outset the strength and persistence of certain webs of association whose origins I shall be at pains to examine further on. I need also to plant certain mines in this unquiet graveyard, and play off certain ghostly echoes — the somnambulism, the wrappings and casings, the invisibility, the standing to one side, the amnesia. Each will come into its own down the line.

For the nonce, we have before us the Three Bodies. The first is the substantial body of middle age: fat and present. The second is the sweet body of youth: thin and past. The third is the phantom body of death: streamlined and futuristic. They are the three kings Og, Zog and Gog (of Gog and Magog, or, as Orwell might prefer, of the Russian Ogpu, who makes a fleeting appearance in one of Bowling's meditations). They are the three industries of Lower Binfield: Truefitt hosiery, shaping the present; gramophones, recording what has passed; bombs, preparing for the future. They are anxiety, nostalgia, nightmare — the active modes of consciousness, memory, fantasy.

We have also before us the end of the world, not as an afterthought, not as a subplot, but as part and parcel of the Three Bodies. The world as George Bowling knows it in all his heft is about to end, the world he knew in Lower Binfield is gone, and whatever new world there may be hardly interests him.

The Three-Body Problem is the problem of being at home in one's body through time. It is a problem posed in the modern West as a problem of fatness, thinness, streamlining. That the end of the world and the contours of the body should be so closely configured, that a machine that weighs us should also be the machine that tells our fortunes, that we should so consistently confuse pounds (or stones) with the passage of time, such must give us pause. And cause. Cause enough for a cultural history of the thin body inside the fat body, and of a third body beyond, dangerous, and possibly explosive.

The moment has come for a full retreat.

Hesperidean Estates

Our first haven is the department store. There, during the last half of the nineteenth century, just as "overnutrition" ballooned into a significant disorder, another disorder was making a name for itself. The two disorders had more than a little in common. They were remarkably easy to detect, remarkably difficult to control. They were both caught up in the perplexing folds of an industrial abundance. They were diseases of desire and consumption, of impulse and will.[1]

The department store was a feast for the eyes and the hands. Most things lay open to view and to touch. Mirrors and cornucopia moldings on walls and ceilings did not so much deceive the senses as expand the horizons of desire. With this bazaar of riches clearly marked at fixed prices, the shopper was disengaged from the rawness of the open market and the pressures of the attentive small retailer. She was left to flow through aisles toward the finer things in life, or she was lifted from beneath by elevators rising toward the higher goods.[2]

So seductive that "even the hand of the strong-minded instinctively grasps her pocket-book before the bewitching array," department-store counters became the site for a new class of shoplifting where the taking, not the owning, seemed paramount. By the 1870s, this impulsive theft, this taking-without-needing, had a popular name, "kleptomania," which referred in particular to that department-store syndrome of stereotypically well-to-do middle-aged women who stole trivial items they could easily afford. Kleptomania was as clear a case of overnutrition as contemporaries could wish for, outside the dining room. It was not simply coincident with concerns about obesity; it was a cultural correlate.[3]

Baptized *klopémanie* in 1816, renamed in successive decades "cleptomania," *kleptomanie* and "kleptomania," the disorder saw light of day as one of a new category of "chronic cerebral affections" known as monomanias and characterized by "a partial lesion of the intelligence, affections or will." Like pyromania, kleptomania was a lesion of the will, therefore an *instinctive monomania*, according to the French physician Jean Etienne Esquirol, who described such a monomaniac as the sort of patient "who is drawn away from his accustomed course to commit acts... which conscience rebukes and which the will has no longer the power to control. The actions are involuntary, instinctive, irresistible."[4]

Critical to the diagnosis of this monomania was the prevailing assumption that a monomaniac aside from his (or her) single mania was not only physically healthy but discernibly righteous. "I know an instance of a woman, who was exemplary in her obedience to every command of the moral law, except one," wrote American physician Benjamin Rush in 1786. "She could not refrain from stealing. What made this vice the more remarkable was that she was in easy circumstances, and not addicted to extravagance in any thing." Rush had not at hand (of course) the later terms, but this hardly meant that monomaniacs in general, or kleptomaniacs more specifically, had held their manias at bay until the turn of the century. As with the new designation of any disease, there was much retrospective diagnosis of klepto-mania when the monomanias became certifiable between 1825 and 1860.[5]

"Certifiable" — because monomania, or partial insanity, had legal implications. Partial insanity had been used as a defense in a case of repeated petty theft as early as 1815. Beau-Conseil (!), ex-commissioner of police in Toulouse, argued that he should not be held responsible for his admitted crimes because he was a virtuous man suffering from an indomitable propensity to steal. Subsequent cases would follow this line of reasoning, which was legally curious, since the defense would be engaged in highlighting a characterological inconsistency such that the crime(s) became proof of the disease. The sentence against a French woman convicted in 1844 of three petty thefts was overturned when a physician showed that the wom-an's entire character changed while she was stealing gloves, ribbons, cloth, brooches: normally she was a calm, reasonable, economical housewife and mother, but when she was in the kleptomaniac state, she was agitated, bitter, profligate and a lover of vegetable soups.[6]

The point was that the crimes — the thefts — were committed despite oneself, and apparently with no other motive than, ultimately, to spite oneself. The pur-loining was neither polished nor profitable; the loot was either hoarded or given away most innocently as gifts, and in either case immediately forgotten. Kleptoma-niacs were fiendishly but randomly furtive, hence easily exposed, as if compelled to draw public shame upon their otherwise upstanding lives. It was, if not absolute insanity, a kind of moral insanity.

This was the term implied in the first important case of kleptomania cited in American medical jurisprudence.[7] Charles Sprague, twenty-five, at eight in the morning of an August day in 1848 in Brooklyn, had run up behind Sarah Watson, thrown her down, wrestled a shoe off one of her feet, and run away. The shoe was found dangling from Sprague's coat pocket the next morning at the printing office where he worked as a journeyman. Charles made no effort to conceal the shoe or explain its presence.

In court, his father, the Congregationalist minister Isaac N. Sprague, testified that Charles had been acting strangely for some ten years, ever since he had fallen from a second-story balcony. Women in the family had begun to miss some of their shoes (always singletons), and these were usually to be found under his son's pillow, between the layers of his bed or in his pocket. Charles would deny the thefts, would be punished, but "he seemed not to have a memory of the fact," and, the Reverend added, his son's "moral sense seemed to be somewhat blunted," though only in respect to these crimes. After testimony from two physicians who defended the concept and relevance of monomania or partial insanity in the case of Charles Sprague, the judge told the jury that "the peculiarity of his insanity consisted in what appears to the sane mind an objectless desire to possess himself of the shoes of females, and to hide and spoil them." The jury soon returned a verdict of "Not Guilty."

This case deserves an essay of its own, but whether we might now put forward other diagnoses, for English-speaking courts in the mid-nineteenth century, *People v. Sprague* began to shape the legal and cultural perceptions of kleptomania. Even in its youth kleptomania was far more than the propensity for inconsequential thefts by well-heeled individuals. It entailed also a "vacancy of the eye," a hint of fetishism, a selective amnesia, an erratic furtiveness, all indicative of a dramatic if temporary change of character.

Medical historians may here accuse me of willfully and woefully confusing partial insanity with monomania, monomania with moral insanity, moral insanity with fetishism and so on. The confusions, however, were endemic to Victorian psychiatry, especially with regard to kleptomania, since petty theft itself, unattended by other evidence of mental or physical disorder, was often acknowledged as the first and premonitory symptom of full-fledged mania or, worse yet, something called general paralysis.[8] The confusions were also popular confusions, for as kleptomania moved in its maturity to the Hesperidean Estates, inexplicable petty thefts could appear as "the impulse of a diseased imagination,"[9] a transient failure of will or an abrupt and fugitive moral delinquency — each in its turn subtly promoted by department-store designers.

Indeed, before and beyond the end of the century, it was common for critics to blame department stores for the concurrent epidemics of shoplifting and kleptomania. These large stores with their novelties, open counters, bargain sales and lavish appointments, encouraged the sudden impulse, exploited the confusion of need and desire, sapped the will, wore probity down to its white knuckle. The stores were worlds apart, "dream worlds," where shoppers with vacant eyes might fall in love with things, where time might be forgotten, where a woman of means might find sanctuary in changing rooms, restrooms, tearooms. And the stores made every effort to obscure the boundaries between the utilitarian and the luxurious, the vital and the trivial.[10]

No wonder women stole. Men too, but mostly women, and not simply because women did the shopping. Department stores played on women's innate weaknesses: their delight in the senses, their daydreaminess, their somehow-glandular cravings for the exotic, most obvious during their monthly periods and their pregnancies. Women had been known to steal at such times, usually shiny things, baubles, trinkets, notions. If the department stores were suffused with a certain sensuality, as most meant to be, then they were affording women a larger arena of expression for their natural propinquities toward a trancelike theft.[11]

Trance. During an epoch when spirit mediums and somnambulists toured Europe and North America giving lectures and demonstrations, when séances were parlor games and animal magnetism was giving way to hypnotism, when photographers managed convincing pictures of floating apparitions and invalids spent long afternoons in semidarkness, trance was clearly in the air.[12] Shoplifters were distinguished from kleptomaniacs by purposiveness, directedness, the absence of trance. They were purposive, of course, because they were poor, and whatever temptations they succumbed to were by virtue of neediness rational temptations, therefore culpable. That shoplifting and kleptomania were differentiated less by the theft than by the social circumstances of the thief was noted early on, and is still to this day being pointed up.[13] I need not detail further such injustice; rather, I need to insist that shoplifting and kleptomania were also differentiated by the quality of the thieving act. If it seemed calculated, if it was a collaboration, if it had been repeated exactly in other stores, if the escape route demanded forethought, then the theft was shoplifting; if it seemed impulsive, if it was solitary, if it followed no plan, if the woman continued aimlessly about the store, then the theft was kleptomania. Shoplifters in their poverty (or their greed, or their criminal slyness) were always clearheaded; innocent kleptomaniacs were momentarily in a trance.[14]

Impulse and trance rarely go together, one would think, but from the start klep-tomania had been fixed by paradox: the person of means who steals trifles — the king who takes spoons, the chevalier who takes napkins, the philanthropist who takes candy. It occurred to some observers around the turn of the century that a third paradox might also be at work: the housewife educated to domestic thrift who steals patently impractical kickshaws. Such women, wrote the superintendent of a large department store in 1915, were made thieves by their husbands, who granted them little spending money of their own. After arguments over household budgets, after pleas for pin money, such a woman would come to the department store feeling guilty, resentful, overwrought. Then, seeing this gewgaw, that bright bagatelle, she became "like the child who wished for the moon — and almost instinctively — she reached for it."[15]

More radical observers put this reaching for the moon within the context of the capitalist drive to acquire, the industrialist pattern of personal thrift and economic expansion — avenues open to women only by proxy in the midst of the commercial splendor of the department store. "It seemed to me as if everything belonged to me," the kleptomaniac was supposed to confess; "I might have taken all." Recently historians have emphasized that the theories of scientific management that under-lay the Second Industrial Revolution had their repercussions in terms of domestic economy, and that well-off women imbued with the modern scientific spirit were as likely to have put themselves on severe budgets as factory girls or immigrant wives. Inside that infinitely blessed world of the department store, what they could least justify as a purchase — the fanciful, the frivolous, the evanescent — was what they were most prone to take. Their thefts were at once an unconscious protest against the tyrannies of a male, industrial thrift, and an instant claim to the rightness of their own desires for what was beautiful and phenomenal.[16]

The department store itself profited from paradox, despite the thefts. The large stores operated on the contradictory axioms that no desire is unfulfillable and that no desire can be fully satisfied. Store managers were reconciled to a degree of theft, especially by "respectable" women; shoplifting had to be as chronic as shopping. Kleptomania was the faithful if furtive handmaiden of abundance.[17]

By the 1880s, kleptomania was a disorder popular enough to be used as a defense in a case of horse-stealing in Texas, familiar enough to be the pivot in an English

Illustration by Joseph Franké

Flossie looks around furtively and then opens her handbag

Kleptomania, a play by E. Carty Ranck. From *Theatre Magazine* 32, 1920.

three-act comedy, prevalent enough that a lady's maid could hand calling cards to Boston shopkeepers from whom her mistress had just stolen. People in the year 2000, looking back to 1887, would recall the handling of kleptomaniacs as the sole parallel to their own handling of criminals, since in Edward Bellamy's utopia, crime would lack any rational motive.[18]

By the year 1905 there had been a Minnesota suit asking for divorce on grounds of a wife's kleptomania; a transoceanic ruckus over the trial of a wealthy San Francisco belle caught red-handed with eighteen tortoiseshell combs, seventeen fans, sixteen brooches, seven ivory-framed hand mirrors, as well as sable and chinchilla furs all stolen from London shops; cross-channel speculation about the identity of the English duchess arrested for shoplifting in Paris; secondhand news of German and Russian princesses forced to pay heavy fines for their own thievery; vaudeville skits and songs, including "Mamie (Don't You Feel Ashamie)," in which Mamie was "a kleptomamie, kleptomamiac"; and a quite significant film in the history of cinema, Edwin S. Porter's *The Kleptomaniac*.[19]

So much publicity meant that the criteria for a legal and medical judgment of kleptomania were common knowledge in higher social circles and among professional thieves and their respective lawyers. In fact, anyone caught stealing — above all, from department stores — might hope to beg off as a kleptomaniac, unless obvi-

Music for "Mamie (Don't You Feel Ashamie)"
in P. Charosh and R.A. Fremont, eds.,
Song Hits from the Turn of the Century
(New York, 1975).

ously indigent or disreputable. How a culprit reacted when caught was itself telling evidence for or against a presumption of kleptomania.

There were virtues and advantages, then, to knowing exactly how a kleptomaniac should react. Respectable, moneyed women who failed to respond in a kleptomaniacal manner might well be prosecuted as ordinary thieves. Mary Plunkett, store detective for Macy's in Manhattan, felt compelled to call the law down upon one respectable woman, "as she was rebellious, reticent about herself, and disposed to be defiant." Another woman was also respectable, "but had to be made to feel the weight of the law, because she pleaded innocence and protested and threatened." The criminal type was brazen, vehement, hard to crack.[20]

The true kleptomaniac, on the other hand, was shocked and penitent. When accosted just outside the store, she began with an indignant denial born of amnesia and surprise, in this format: "How dare you accuse me of such a thing! I would never do such a thing! Why would I of all people do such a thing?" But soon, back in the privacy of the manager's office, there would be a naive, tearful confession and a fearful shame: "I have no recollection of taking the articles, I did not mean to take the articles, I had no intention to steal anything, I was in a daze, I did not know what I was doing, an irresistible power prompted me, a sudden impulse, I was not myself, I couldn't help myself, I'll pay for the articles, please do not expose me, my name would be ruined, I could never live it down."[21]

We may appreciate the popularity of the kleptomaniac confession and the notoriety of the shoplifting shame by glancing at two articles across the front page from each other in the *New York Times* for December 11, 1897. On the right, in column six, "She Stole to Live," a homeless woman, neither so young nor so pretty as a morning paper had led the *Times* reporter to believe, confessed to stealing four bottles of whiskey and a jar of olives from S.S. Pierce Company of Boston. In her testimony Marie Wilkins claimed to be dazed by her arrest, so dazed that she gave two different addresses and said, "I have forgotten everything." No, she had never stolen before, and she did not know why she had taken the whiskey, as she never drank. Guilty or not, dazed or not, here was a woman desperately trying to lay claim at once to poverty and kleptomania, a heroic and nearly impossible task.

On the left, in column two, "Rush to See Shoplifters," was a crowd overflowing from the spectator seats into the dock of the court where four quite respectable women of Lynn, Massachusetts, were to appear on counts of petty theft. Hours before the court opened, some of the most well-known women in town had lined up to catch a glimpse of the accused, who arrived veiled and would shortly be driven away in a closed carriage to the judge's private office.

Given such contexts, we may appreciate as well the thrust of the kleptomaniac confession, which reclaimed innocence by taking the theft first through the daze of shopping, then through the haze of a temporary amnesia, offering it up at last before the altar of an irresistible power. This ritual did not merely purify the sinner, who had taken without needing to take; the ritual shifted responsibility onto something, someone else. It was not, after all, I who did that. So women in their confessions and court cases often gave false names, due in part to fears of a husband's wrath or social disgrace, but also and equally due to a belief that someone else really was the thief.[22]

Who? Wasn't it, really, another self, active, dexterous, emotionally labile, needy and not to be denied? Wasn't it, really, a self without the moral, social and economic restraints of a sober married woman? Wasn't it, really, a younger self, childish, perhaps adolescent, open to the sensual prospects of the department-store world and given to an impulsive grabbing? Wasn't it a rapscallion self, rebellious, theatrical, like the vaudeville Mamie:

> She took things so easy, she took things so nice,
> People always wondered, she never took advice.
> She became an actress, but the show could never start.
> For Mamie took a fancy, she took a leading part.[23]

Wasn't it a daring, even arrogant self, one likely to risk total ruin?

Og/Zog

Wasn't it, to tell the truth, a second self?

Between 1860 and 1912, another strange disorder made an apt, abrupt public appearance: multiple personality. And in nearly every famous case, the second self to surface was more athletic, demanding, outgoing, irresponsible, juvenile, sensual, spontaneous, defiant, dramatic and reckless than the woman in her first person.[24]

Mary Reynolds (1811 onset; reported obscurely in 1816, 1830, 1843; published prominently in 1860 and 1888; cited widely as the seminal case) was sedate, melan-

MOLLIE FANCHER AND HER AUNT, MISS SUSAN E. CROSBY, TAKEN IN 1886.

From Abram H. Dailey, *Mollie Fancher: The Brooklyn Enigma*
(Brooklyn, 1894).

choly, bookish, reserved; her alternate personality grinned down a bear, seized rattlesnakes by the tail, ran through the woods, and played inventive, embarrassing tricks on her stick-in-the-mud other self.[25] Félida X (1858 onset; reported incessantly from 1860) was depressed, morose, uncommunicative; in her alternate personality she was lively, gay, confident and chatty.[26] Mollie Fancher, "The Psychical Marvel of the Nineteenth Century," achieved notoriety first as a fasting girl, then in 1875 began to manifest several alternate personalities – Idol, Rosebud, Pearl, Ruby – who were (in turn) more mischievous, more spiritual, more childish and more vivacious than Mollie in her invalid bed.[27] Anna O. (1881-82; reported by Breuer and Freud in 1893-95, and cited ever after as a critical case in the history of psychoanalysis) was brilliant but melancholy; in her alternate personality she was naughty, abusive and spoke often like a polyglot toddler.[28] Alma Z. (1883-84; reported 1893) was dignified, literate, thoughtful, bedridden; as "Twoey" she was childish, with a limited vocabulary spoken as if in an Indian dialect, and she was free from pain.[29] Léonie (reported in the 1880s by the Janets) was herself sad, calm, slow, gentle, timid; as Léontine she was gay, noisy, pert, restless and vivacious.[30] Miss Beauchamp (1898-1904; described with panache in 1905; played in the theater in 1912) was reserved, morbidly conscientious, serious, dignified. She was hounded by several alternate personalities, the most resilient of whom was wickedly adventurous, witty, sociable, flippant and prone to

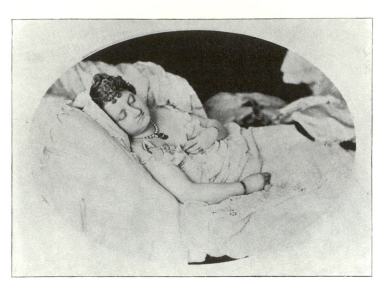

AS MOLLIE FANCHER APPEARED IN 1887, IN A TRANCE.

MOLLIE FANCHER AS SHE APPEARED FIVE MONTHS AFTER
THE ACCIDENT.

harsh pranks that forced her more saintly self into compromising situations. "And, curiously enough," wrote the reviewer of Frances Starr's performance in David Belasco's production of *The Case of Becky* in 1912, "such is the emotional effectiveness of the roles as Miss Starr acts them, that one is as deeply moved to see 'wicked little Becky' going back into the darkness from whence she came as one is happy in seeing 'sweet Dorothy' relieved of her fears."[31]

Not all famous cases involved women. When men took on other selves, however, they tended to go to extremes – beyond childhood to earliest infancy,[32] beyond pranks to criminal lives, assault, murder.[33] Or they disappeared, amnesiac, to turn up weeks, months, years later in another city, another country.[34] The reading public in Europe and America knew of them from romantic novels beset by doppelgängers, from newspaper and magazine stories of befuddling disappearances, above all from Stevenson's *Dr. Jekyll and Mr. Hyde*, first published in 1886 and immediately popular.[35]

The flurry of medical cases, the force of the fiction and drama, the philosophical intrigue with the related phenomena of hypnosis, the growing notoriety of mediums claiming to contact themselves in earlier lives, all this led to speculation that each of us might well be host to one or more other selves. Wrote psychologist and philosopher William James, tentatively: "The same brain may subserve many conscious selves, either alternate or coexisting." At the same time, his friend Morton

z o n e

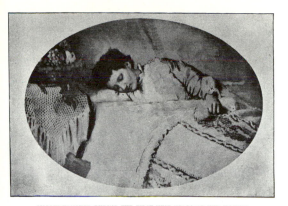

MOLLIE FANCHER DURING THE FIRST NINE YEARS OF HER ILLNESS.

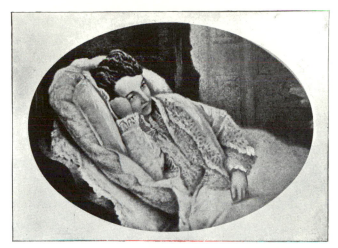

MOLLIE FANCHER AS SHE APPEARED AT THE EXPIRATION OF NINE YEARS AFTER HER INJURY.

Prince, eventual therapist to Miss Beauchamp, was asking, "Have we all within us such a second personality...which observes, remembers and governs our actions more than we dream of?" British physiologists were studying the two halves of the brain, wondering if each might hold a separate personality. Emile Durkheim in 1893 was granting each of us *deux consciences*, one selfish, the other oriented toward community. By 1897 the New York physician R. Osgood Mason was willing to dare the blatant question, "Is it not quite possible, then, that other normal, ordinary people, possess a second personality, deep-down beneath their ordinary, everyday self, and that under conditions which favor a readjustment, this hidden subliminal self may emerge...?"[36]

I mean to suggest, of course, that this second self, culturally present and available in the late nineteenth century on both sides of the Atlantic, was the second self to which kleptomaniac confessions were pointing. It was, as we have just seen it in female cases of multiple personality, a younger, less constrained, more lively, more mischievous, more erratic self. Already, on occasion, it had been caught stealing.[37] It assumed or was given another name. It could take over the body, move the hands toward all that glittered, compromise the integrity of the first person. Irresistibly.

Guilt by dissociation, yes, but hardly mistaken identity. The kleptomaniac's thief and the first person's trickster were more than look-alikes. They had the same

Scenes from *The Case of Becky* (*New York Times*, October 20, 1912).

method of operation. They materialized during twilight states while the first person was knitting or sewing, waking from a nap, entering a hypnotic trance, shopping in the "dream worlds" of department stores. They were otherwise oblivious to time, losing track of it, unable to read it off watches or clocks. They freed the body from pain and paralysis, from tightly laced budgets and repressed desires, granting a temporary right to the joyful and frivolous. Gone, they had vanished like a thief in the night: out of sight, out of mind, out of memory. They left behind, from time to time, certain mementos so that the first person might have clues as to where they had been, what they had been doing. Miss Beauchamp learned of social engagements made by her second self only upon discovering messages scribbled by that messy, uninhibited alter ego. Kleptomaniacs learned of new acquisitions made by their second selves only upon searches that turned up scarves, ribbons, rings secreted on their first persons.[38]

The second self was the second of the Three Bodies, the sweet body of youth. She was the body of the past, with a child's disregard for time and property. "*Hysterics*," wrote Breuer and Freud in italics about Anna O., "*suffer mainly from reminiscences*," so hypnotism might effect its cures by taking patients back to a pivotal trauma — but whatever the therapy (mesmeric, Proustian, spiritualist, theosophical, Freudian), it seemed agreed that the second self lay fixed in a Binfield past, the Og of Zog.[39]

Phantom Stuff

The second self was the sweet body of youth: *thin* and past. She was lighter on her feet, more buoyant, more energetic. She was virgin and dynamo, at once naive and powerful. She embodied those sensations we now associate with a dynamic leanness and which were a feature of yet another phenomenon characteristic of the late nineteenth century. This too had at its hidden center a second self.

Fasting has been bound up with the spiritual and the visionary from time immemorial. It may serve as the shaman's avenue to trance or the ascetic's path to clear-mindedness. It may express private repentance or public atonement, private resolve or public determination. In the Christian world it has had as its foil the Eucharist and notions of the transubstantial or consubstantial, an especially complex Three-Body Problem looming just beyond.[40]

For some children and young women known as "fasting girls," fasting led past piety to new powers. Since at least the thirteenth century,[41] these new powers had regularly been thaumaturgic and prophetic, but in the later nineteenth century fasting girls were engaged with a transparent present and an invisible past. For Louise Lateau of Belgium, fasting accompanied ecstasy and stigmata, her body erupting in 1864 with the bloody wounds of an earlier crucifixion.[42] For Sarah Jacob in Wales, the fasting was rather a spiritual marriage, her parents dressing her in 1867 at the age of ten as the bride of Christ, wreaths of flowers about her bed.[43] For Mollie Fancher in Brooklyn in 1865, fasting was the first step toward clairvoyance, a gift that did not leave her once she began again to eat sometime in the 1880s. She could see through envelopes enclosed within envelopes, could tell colors by touch, knew exactly what a man was doing at a certain hour more than a thousand miles distant, and she met up with people who had passed away.[44]

The fasting was not directed toward achieving a coveted thinness; a thin body was not itself the virtue. Indeed, Sarah Jacob grew plumper in her bed, and Mollie Fancher was "every inch a woman." Rather, fasting gave access to an interior self and another world in which contacts with the spiritual, the ethereal, the transcendental were so much easier. Fasting laid open the inner person and the stuff the world was really made of. Mollie Fancher's clairvoyance was possible because her fasting had made the world itself thinner, easier to see through, such that "no retirement, however secluded, but yields to her penetrating gaze."[45]

For contemporary health reformers who advocated fasting as a kind of active homeopathy, fasting invigorated the body by removing poisons from the system and bringing one back to the vital nub of oneself, to "natural hunger." Long fasts were at one and the same time proof of the enormous spiritual resources of the inner person and the wastrel's way back to them. After the forty-day fast of Henry S. Tanner in New York in 1880, the Reverend C.S. Williams of the Seventh Street Methodist Episcopal Church lectured confidently on the superiority of the immaterial over the material and the sanctity of self-control. Tanner himself declared that "I wanted to show the power of the human will, and to prove to materialists that there is something beside oxygen, hydrogen, and carbon in the brain."[46]

If prolonged fasts were theological statements and physiological propaganda, they were also news, reported in the style of serial fiction, and they were very popular entertainment. Famous hunger artists made their livelihoods from fasting in public for thirty or forty days or more. Giovanni Succi, Stefano Merlatti, Clare de Serval attracted paying crowds large enough to finance tours of Europe and the United States between 1880 and 1912. The crowds came not to gawk at walking skeletons such as those customarily exhibited by P.T. Barnum, but to gape at the stamina of Kozawa, Cetti, Beauté, Tosca, Cavanagh (the Irish imposter), who could summon a power from within themselves to stave off death.[47]

Fasting then was drama, a drama women suffragists in England in 1909 would exploit with some of the first political hunger strikes.[48] Fasting exposed the material world for what it was, invoked a second and vehement self, drew back the veil from the spiritual realm. It was a means of restoration – of justice, of health, of clarity. It led back to harmony, the "natural hunger" of the infant, the acuity of the child, the inner radiance of the pristine spirit. Back to that sweet body of youth, thinner and past.

It led also to a change of character. Mollie Fancher was first a fasting girl, then a multiple personality. Mrs. H. in England in 1824 (reported 1879) went through a fasting sleep for months immediately upon her marriage, waking with no memory for anyone but livelier, hungrier and more childlike than her first, disconsolate person. Anna O. ate extremely little and for a period "refused nourishment altogether" unless fed like an infant by Breuer. Marceline R., treated in 1886, could not eat at all in her first person, but the hypnotically induced secondary self regained her spirits, her appetite and her weight under Jules Janet's supervision. B.C.A., one of Morton Prince's patients, went into shock upon the death of one dear to her, could neither eat nor sleep for months, suffered a second shock, and recovered as B, lighthearted, informal, happy, a walker in woods. Shocked once again, she became A, a neurasthenic, and lost her appetite. In the case of Doris, severely abused as a young child, the first person ("Real Doris") lost most of her sense of taste between 1892 and 1911, and "never ate anything because she liked it." As the young tomboy Margaret, who appeared around 1909, she could taste her food and was fond of eating.[49]

So, like the kleptomaniac's thief, the appetite of the second self was unrestrained. But it was an appetite out of the past, a child's hunger, feeding a body out of the past that was active and inspirited, athletic and light of foot, free from anxiety and indigestion. It could be, therefore, as Orwell's George Bowling remembers himself to have been, much thinner, yet capable of handling with grace enormous meals, "boiled beef and dumplings, roast beef and Yorkshire, boiled mutton and capers, pig's head, apple pie, spotted dog and jam roly-poly." No wonder Bowling's appetite improves as he leaves the ersatz frankfurters of the present for meals out of the past at the George, Lower Binfield's grandest hotel, whose old signboard had revealed St. George "on a very thin horse trampling on a very fat dragon."

There in Binfield, Bowling becomes curiously invisible and double-sighted. He talks with people from his childhood who do not recognize him; he feels himself to be in two places at once; he has visions of the turn of the century behind the cheap new facades of 1938. By recourse to his second self, it seems that he has acquired special powers, like those of the fasting girls and those frequently attributed to multiple personalities. Alma Z.'s "Twoey" had a preternatural sagacity. Reverend Thomas Carson Hanna, who had to be taught hunger in his fully regressed second state, developed into a clairvoyant, a finder of hidden objects. Anna Winsor, who took only liquids and small pieces of cracker in her first person, could see through her forehead as her second self. Mary Lurancy Vennum, "The Watseka Wonder," lying as if dead, saw a brother and sister who had died, and then, taken over by the personality of her dead neighbor Mary Roff, she displayed convincing knowledge of the intimate details of Roff's life.[50]

Well, there we have it: the somnambulism, the invisibility, the wrappings and casings, the amnesia. I have sought to show how the shared fiction of one person inside another, one body inside another, might have taken on such strength during the last half of the nineteenth century. I have sought to show how, in so many arenas — the department store, the invalid parlor, the consulting room, the mental hospital, the courtroom, the newspaper column, the exhibition hall — that second self came to be identifiable with the sweet body of youth, thin and past, restless, mischievous and needy. I have tried to show how deeply sunk were the roots of the Orwell–Connolly aphorism in European and American culture of the last half of the nineteenth century. The fiction of one body within another was shared by thieves, lawyers, judges, genteel women, medical men, spiritualists, hypnotists and playwrights, vaudevillians and moviemakers. We might have looked beyond kleptomaniac confessions, multiple personalities, fasting girls, to other phenomena: the enthusiastic reception of George du Maurier's Trilby and the image of Svengali; the use of double exposure in the new art of photography; the developments in internal medicine due to antisepsis, anesthesia, bacteriology, cell biology and X rays....

But we do not need more evidence for this shared fiction of the second self inside the first person. What we need now are some answers to some very bothersome questions. How did the second body come to be *imprisoned* within the first? Wherefore the desperation? And whence the muteness?

'Orrible Revelations!

In Edwin S. Porter's film, *The Kleptomaniac*, a poor, starving woman steals a loaf of bread for her sick child. Caught, she is dragged off to jail. Meanwhile, a wealthy woman shoplifts some trinkets. Apprehended by a store detective, she goes to court in her own car. The poor woman is humiliated and sentenced as a thief. The wealthy woman is excused as a kleptomaniac. Epilogue: the figure of Justice, blindfolded, holds a scale balancing a bag of gold against a loaf of bread. The scales tip in favor of the gold, and the blindfold slips from Justice, who has only one eye, focused on the gold.[51]

Porter's use of parallel sequences in 1905 was an innovation of almost as much consequence as his invention of the close-up and dramatic editing. The moral of his story, however, was not so new, and in fact his film was one good sign that Justice had begun to look askance at kleptomania.

There had always been doubting Thomases, among them the French cartoonist Honoré Daumier, who as early as 1846 had a client complaining to his lawyer, "Ce qui m'chiffonne, c'est que j'suis accusé de douze vols!" "Il y en a douze?" says the lawyer. "Tant mieux. Je plaiderai la monomanie!"[52] Kleptomania (the monomania for theft) did seem too convenient an excuse to Alfred Swain Taylor at mid-century, who wrote in his *Medical Jurisprudence*, "The evidence of a disordered state of the mind should not here be allowed to depend on the nature of the act, or every morally depraved person might bring forward a plea of insanity for any crime or offence." Johann Ludwig Casper turned a skeptical eye upon a number of such pleas and found most of them wanting. A physician at the University of Berlin, he argued in his 1860 handbook on forensic medicine that few thieves actually did steal out of need; that the instinct for possession was a deeply human trait which had to be mastered by rich and poor alike; and that theft alone, without concomitant evidence of epilepsy,

429

H. Daumier, from *Les gens de justice*, 1846 (Paris, Bibliothèque nationale).

imbecility or dementia, could be no proof of mania and was subject to legal punishment like any other crime.[53]

But kleptomaniacs, with their confessions of amnesia and irresistible impulse,
with their allusions to a second self, could hide behind the still-opaque folds of the
1843 McNaughton case, which warranted leniency where the accused could show
that he (or she) did not know right from wrong at the time the crime was committed. It was not until the abuses foreseen by Taylor came to public attention that
kleptomania began to lose its legal footing. In 1893, for example, one "Mary Smith"
was charged with stealing a piece of silk and two pairs of gloves. In court she carried a silver-handled umbrella and claimed to have stolen "unconsciously." "Yes,"
replied the Justice, "I suppose this is another one of those respectable family cases,"
and he fixed bail at $300. When Mrs. S. Solomon (Mrs. D. Landberg, a wealthy
widow) was arrested in 1899 for secreting articles in the lining of her sealskin coat,
her lawyer said that "he thinks that she is suffering from kleptomania." By 1906, lawyer Mark Alter claimed to have defended over five hundred such cases in New York
City. He estimated that four thousand shoplifters were arrested each year and no
more than fifty convicted.[54]

At about this time, nonetheless, courts elsewhere[55] had become extremely suspicious of the defense of theft by "an irresistible impulse to steal," and criminolo-
gists would soon rename kleptomania "pathological stealing." Akin to pathological
lying, pathological stealing bore the fingerprints of fraud; people pleading kleptomania were portrayed as con artists or criminal lowlifes. In a 1920 one-act play, a
scheming couple convinces the "portly, puffy and pompous" Dr. Dabney Wilshire
that the wife Flossie is a kleptomaniac. Flossie, acting very nervous, drops the doctor's pocketbooks, watches, surgical instruments and silver picture frames into her
handbag as her husband promises to pay for the losses and return the goods at a din-
ner that night. Of course, the couple does not appear. In *What No Man Knows*, a 1921
six-reeler, a lawyer who tries to cover up his wife's kleptomania by bribing a witness is exposed and disbarred, forced into the slums, only to find out later that his
wife is a dissolute thief. By 1925 the president of the propaganda section of the
Mental Hygiene League in France was campaigning flat out against the notion of
kleptomania, which he maintained was neither a legitimate clinical entity nor a legitimate legal defense. He proposed that department stores station ornately uniformed

"inspecteurs de prophylaxie mentale" at conspicuous junctions, to intimidate prospective shoplifters who might otherwise surrender to "irresistible impulses," and perhaps to administer spankings to those who persisted and were caught.[56]

Renamed, repudiated, intimidated, spanked or imprisoned, kleptomaniacs did not vanish overnight. If the cultural attitude toward them was less conciliatory, the idea and image of a kleptomaniac remained. The war wounds and shell shock of World War I brought into the public forum a certain acutely male nervousness which would allow for kleptomania to resurface as a man's malady, or at least a man's delusion.[57]

Moreover, the pathology of "pathological" stealing had still to be explained. In the shift from kleptomania to pathological stealing, explanations shifted from the commercial and social to the sexual and private. The disorder was less the result of a diffuse desire for possessions in a society of Veblenesque conspicuous consumption, and more the manifestation of a sexual neurosis, repressed desires displaced onto seemingly trivial objects. Such a theory had begun outside the psychoanalytic world, first with reference to the obsessions of collectors, then to fetishism, but the theory was given its greatest momentum by the members of the Vienna Psychoanalytic Society, who discussed the problem of kleptomania in 1908 and 1909. Wilhelm Stekel, citing as evidence Emile Zola's novel about department-store passions, *Au Bonheur des Dames* (1883), insisted on the sexual genesis of kleptomania, which he associated with masturbation, or "secretly doing something forbidden." The logic was powerful because it was reversible. A female who masturbated often in early life was less likely to be sexually satisfied as a woman, so she would turn in frustration to the symbolic theft of phallic objects. Reversed, theft could be a defense against actual masturbation by women who repressed their insatiable sexual desires. Otto Rank went one step further, equating pathological stealing with pathological lying: "Just as the pathological lie serves to conceal masturbation (defense), so, on the other hand, the symptomatic act of kleptomania betrays the fact that the person is still masturbating – that is, that she is 'doing the forbidden thing in secret.' "[58]

Although Freud objected to Rank's paper, articles and textbooks on the psychology of crime would repeat these sexual wisdoms over the course of the next half-century.[59] Since the old connections between theft, pregnancy and menstrual periods were strengthened by psychoanalytic talk, pathological stealing came also to be explained as the theft of a child or the theft of love itself.[60]

What had happened to the second self of the kleptomaniac confession? Where in all this was the sweet body of youth, thin and past? Had it been exiled? evacuated? wiped out?

It was still there, though farther from the surface and less articulate. It had been culturally transformed from a *co*consciousness to a *sub*consciousness, from a secret sharer to a guarded secret. It was still childish in its masturbatory play, its wayward fetishism, but no longer was it engaging. It was still a figure out of the past, but no longer was it a free spirit; it was stuck in time, "fixated." And it was still needy, but no longer could it declare itself directly; it had to make its desires known by tortuously symbolic acts.

A slower yet coincident and identical transformation of the second self took place with regard to fasting. As kleptomaniacs became pathological thieves during the first decades of this century, fasting girls became anorexics. Given the recent visibility of anorexia nervosa, there has been much retrospective diagnosis, but few people in 1900 saw any equivalence between extraordinary fasting and psychological disorder. Called "hysteric apepsia" by English physician Willian W. Gull in 1868, described in its exasperating complexity as "hysterical anorexia" by French physician Ernst C. Lasèque in 1873, renamed "anorexia nervosa" by Gull in 1874, the willful starvation of some adolescent girls was scrutinized by such as Pierre Janet and Freud but not formally classed as an independent syndrome until 1909.[61]

Unlike the clairvoyant second self of the fasting girl, the anorexic's second self saw the world from behind the bars of melancholy. If the first person became furiously energetic, it was because the second self was furiously sad. That sadness often remained mysterious, for anorexics were notoriously uncooperative with family, friends, physicians and therapists. What was clear was that the second self was drawing the body of the first person back to childhood thinness, away from sexuality and maturation. Freud wrote in 1895, "The famous *anorexia nervosa* of young girls seems to me (on careful observation) to be a melancholia where sexuality is undeveloped. The patient asserted that she had not eaten, simply because she had *no appetite*, and for no other reason. Loss of appetite — in sexual terms, loss of libido." Nadia confessed to Pierre Janet that she was terrified of pubic hair and her developing breasts, and that she did not want to be attractive to men, so she would keep herself extremely thin. Janet had to resort to forced feeding — the final

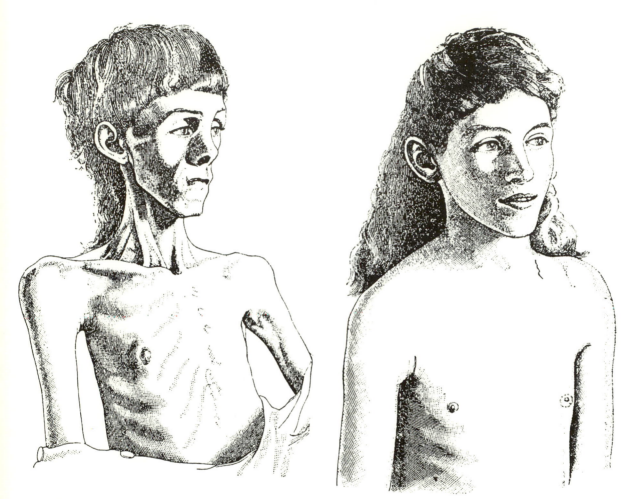

FIG. 1.—April 21st, 1887.   **FIG. 2.—June 14th, 1887.**

William W. Gull, "Anorexia Nervosa," *Transactions of the Clinical
Society of London*, 1874. Reprint in *Lancet* 2, 1936.

recommendation of most authorities of his era – in order to keep her alive.[62]

Although few cases resulted in death,[63] anorexia was a vexing, frightening disorder which provoked the use of force in a far more elemental way than "pathological stealing" invoked criminal punishment. The second self of the anorexic was so childish as to be extravagantly, dangerously regressive; so much a figure of the past as to be defiantly inaccessible; so thin a figure as to threaten a fat invisibility.

And still needy. During World War I, anorexia was confused with Simmonds' disease, the atrophy of the anterior lobe of the pituitary gland, and anorexics were considered hormonally deficient, in need of endocrine treatment. This physiological approach was shaken off during the Depression, by which time there had been 117 cases of anorexia recorded at the Mayo Clinic and hundreds of other cases reported worldwide, as well as occasional articles in the semipopular press. The Depression literature viewed obesity and anorexia as mirror images, gluttony and starvation as equivalently extreme responses to fantasies of oral impregnation in the midst of a subtly confining family. Where earlier physicians had been quick to insist on isolating the anorexic patient from her family, psychologists during the Depression began to look to family dynamics for the origin of the syndrome itself: anorexics were born into what later would be called a "golden cage," a family whose implicit demands made them feel inadequate if less than perfect. The girl – and sometimes the boy – resorted in effect to a second self whose asexual, incredibly thin body was at once a powerful demonstration of perfection and an unspoken protest against imprisonment. That second self was terribly hungry but terribly stubborn, a political prisoner on a hunger strike, absent the manifesto.[64]

With the juxtaposition of kleptomania and anorexia, we are well on our way to explaining how the second self came to be imprisoned within the first person, desperate and mute. This juxtaposition does not arrive by fiat. Kleptomaniacs have had a historical penchant for stealing food, anorexics a penchant for shoplifting. Benjamin Rush's exemplary woman of 1786, like kleptomaniacs before and since, "when she could lay her hands upon nothing more valuable she would often, at the table of a friend, fill her pockets secretly with bread." Such thefts of food were the least remarkable of compulsive crimes, for kleptomania was perpetually linked to pregnant women by analogy to their notorious and overwhelming desires for peculiar foods.[65]

Turn and turn about, those who obdurately denied their physical hunger were often found to be compulsive thieves, as if one way or another that needy second self had to take what it could – if not food, then luscious silk, if not love, then shining jewels. When Dr. William Hammond, former United States Surgeon General, turned from his book on *Fasting Girls* (1879) to "A Problem for Sociologists" (1882), or kleptomania, he was moving no great distance; the fasting girls were clearly hysterical, kleptomaniacs the all-too-willing victims of "emotional insanity," and both were deserving of punishment for letting their impulses take over. At the same time, Dr. Lasègue in Paris was suggesting that anorexia might be the origin of kleptomania, at least in the case of one woman caught stealing stockings, perfume and a cravat while in a state of self-induced semistarvation. Either anorexics were denying themselves so strictly at the table that they had to take at the department-store counter, or their powers of resistance had been so weakened by their inanition that they could not but help themselves to alluring goods. Forty-five years later, psychoanalyst Mary Chadwick wove all the prominent strands together in her compassionate discussion of "A Case of Kleptomania in a Girl of Ten Years." The girl, who "used to be afraid if I ate too much I'd bust," was a chronic petty thief obsessed by images of oral impregnation and the fantasy of a baby being made from food. The pins, pencils and pennies she stole were "the theft of the baby she wanted so much."[66]

The weave between anorexia and kleptomania could be just as fine for boys as for girls, especially when the child was beset by an "overprotective" or demanding mother. A 1939 study of a boy's "neurotic stealing" revealed that he had always been a feeding problem, detested fatness and hated his mother as a depriving, castrating woman. "The stealing," decided psychiatrist Esther Menaker, "represents an attempt to retrieve from the mother those objects – breast, feces, penis – and the satisfactions which they represent, which he feared she had the power to deprive him of, and which he wants to steal back."[67]

"Starved for affection," anorexics might take what they could, when they could, impulsively. The anorexic predilection for shoplifting would still call for comment in 1979, 1984, 19....[68] But we have some work yet to do back near the turn of the century, for as kleptomaniacs became pathological thieves and fasting girls became anorexics, multiple personalities became schizophrenics.

Legs

Protest though one may that multiple personality and schizophrenia are discrete disorders, in common parlance they have been mightily confused, and in medical practice they have frequently been the flip sides of the same record. The truth is that shortly after schizophrenia was fully designated and described by Eugen Bleuler in 1911, reports of multiple-personality diagnoses tailed off. In the fifteen years previous to Bleuler's *Dementia Praecox oder Gruppe der Schizophrenien*, four dozen cases of multiple personality were published. In the next fifteen years, there were two dozen such cases and one hundred of schizophrenia. Between 1927 and 1939 there were a dozen cases of multiple personality and 3,500 cases of schizophrenia. When Thigpen and Cleckley wrote up their famous case in 1954, and again, more dramatically, as *The Three Faces of Eve* in 1957, they believed that they were dealing with the only multiple personality alive, while schizophrenics occupied the majority of beds in mental hospitals in Europe and North America.[69]

"Schizophrenia," as Bleuler himself acknowledged, was a misnomer, leading understandably to the confusion of split personality with multiple personality. However, the unfortunate name was not solely to blame for the confusion. Schizophrenia itself presented a problem. Wrote Bleuler: "Personality anomalies, indifference, anergia, querulousness, obstinacy, moodiness, and what Goethe could describe only with the English *whimsicality*, hypochondria, etc. need not be symptoms of a mental disease; but only too often they are the only visible signs of schizophrenia. Because of this, the diagnostic threshold is in no other illness as low, and the latent cases so common." Despite years of refinement and debate, that threshold has barely risen; the American Psychiatric Association's review in 1981 held that "the limits of the concept of schizophrenia are unclear."[70]

"Schizophrenia" was a misnomer meant to fend off yet another misnomer, *démence précoce*, assigned in 1852 by Benedict Morel to the case of a fourteen-year-old boy who had become withdrawn and parricidal. Dementia implied mental degeneration, progressive and irreversible. When Emil Kraepelin in the 1890s brought together catatonia, hebephrenia and paranoia under the black umbrella of dementia praecox, he was searching for an anatomical lesion at the base of the deterioration common to most (but not all) cases. Bleuler, more interested in the psyche, hoped to dissuade physicians from using the generally poor prognosis of the disease as the main criterion for its diagnosis. Accepting an unknown organic default as the origin for the primary symptom of schizophrenia — disintegration, or "the 'splitting' of the different psychic functions" — Bleuler was less the physiologist than the psychologist, focusing less on decay than on disjointedness.[71]

"Schizophrenia" referred not to an evenly divided consciousness, not to intact selves doing battle with each other, but to fragments of personality flying out like shrapnel in the first heat of explosion, then lodging helter-skelter in the shell-shocked body. Schizophrenia was characterized by blunted affect, a disorderly, tumbling flow of associations in thought and language, a tremendous ambivalence or drifting indecisiveness, and an eventually autistic withdrawal. These were attended by stereotyped movements, by language that was coded, collapsed, condensed or self-contained, by visual or auditory hallucinations, and by delusions, sometimes paranoid.[72]

Schizophrenics, unlike multiple personalities, did not have the solace of amnesia, even when they suffered delusions of grandeur and confusions of personas. "I am Noah's ark, the life boat and the esteem, Maria Stuart, Empress Alexander," announced a seamstress in hospital in 1887, but she and other schizophrenics always remained in part alien to the delusion, condemned to stand by and watch while "the ego loses all power of resistance against the inimical onslaught of an apparently more powerful unconscious." So wrote Carl Jung, Bleuler's student and research associate, in a later article, 1939, on the psychogenesis of schizophrenia. Jung there contrasted multiple personalities, remarkable for a "smooth, even a tactful cooperation between the different persons," with schizophrenics whose split-off figures "break in and make a disturbance at any time." Multiple personalities suggested "the presence of an invisible *spiritus rector*, or a central manager, who arranges the stage for the different figures in an almost rational way, often in the form of a more or less sentimental drama." That *spiritus rector* was absent in schizophrenics, who experienced instead "an apparent chaos of inconsistent visions, voices and characters.... If there is a drama at all, it is certainly far beyond the patient's understanding."[73]

Indeed, it was a cosmic drama, a Big Dream, for Jung saw the schizophrenic as a person overtaken by dreams: not the personal dreams analyzed by Freud but dream material from the collective unconscious in all of its mythological, legendary, archaic glory. While Freud was continually frustrated by schizophrenics because, in the depth of their narcissistic withdrawal of libido from the world, they were unhappily immune to transference, Jung was impressed and more hopeful. He knew that there were ways to work with the collective, primitive, archetypal powers.[74]

Cosmogonic dreamer or paraphrenic narcissist, the schizophrenic inhabited much the same world as the multiple personality. It was a world beset by voices, bespeaking usurpers, bewildered by time. For schizophrenics, voices might shriek more often from the outside, but they could also call across the body[75] or shout from within. The usurpers might be described more often as invaders, but they could also be traitors, parasites, fifth columnists. Time might never be lost to schizophrenics, but there was dislocation, apocalypticism, discontinuity.[76] If schizophrenic delusional characters took over at random, cruel and hurly-burly, they were just a degree or two more abrasive and obscene than some multiple personalities. If schizophrenics yielded to no trances, fugues or hypnotic dazes, Jung dwelt upon their ultimate dreaminess, Freud upon their retreat to inviolately personal fantasies, Bleuler upon their twilight states and the fact that "only in this disease is it possible for patients to knit a stocking without making a single mistake although otherwise their actions are entirely irrational."[77]

We have met this knitter before as the first person of the multiple personality about to make the transition to the second self. What I mean to show here is that the new disorder of "schizophrenia" took that second self to its extremes — a bittersweet body of youth that was not only childish but narcissistic as an infant, not only past but archaic and phylogenetically primitive. And not only thin but weightless.

Bleuler had noticed that among schizophrenics anorexia and bulimia were frequent symptoms. Unlike others of the insane, their body weights bore no relation to changes in mental condition. Ninteenth-century alienists and asylum directors had been accustomed to making prognoses according to the weight gains of their patients. If weight returned as mania subsided, the prognosis was good; if weight grew and the mania grew with it, prognosis was bad. Such a formula seemed futile with schizophrenics, whose weights fluctuated widely and irregularly, and who felt themselves to be at once larger and lighter than they actually were.[78]

On June 1, 1885, the day of his discharge from the University Clinic for Nervous Diseases in Leipzig, Daniel Paul Schreber imagined that he had lost thirty or forty pounds, but the scales showed that he had gained some four pounds. Aside from this distorted body image, he seemed to have recuperated from his nervous breakdown and severe hypochondria. He enjoyed eight years of good health and good times before returning to Dr. Paul Emil Flechsig's clinic with the first symptoms of paranoid schizophrenia (paranoid dementia). In 1903 he published his extraordinary memoirs, which Freud read and analyzed in 1911, the same year as Schreber's death.[79]

In the years leading up to his death, Schreber had had to be force-fed. He believed that he no longer had a stomach and that his bowels had disappeared; he refused to eat, swallowing masses of air so that his belly was always fully extended but empty, large and light. He may well have shared with other paranoid schizophrenics a fear of being poisoned. He may well have been on a messianic fast. He was also, clearly, reenacting in extremis the famous system of therapeutic gymnastics devised by his father, a physician and physical culturist who had trained his son most rigorously to restrict the appetite, restrain the bowels, hold the body together and the stomach in. Under the care of Dr. Flechsig (=Dr. Sinewy, whom he called a "soul-murderer"), Schreber seemed to relive his father's regimen; "miracles" (oxymoronic) were "in preference directed against my stomach, partly because the souls begrudged me the sensual pleasure connected with the taking of food, partly because they considered themselves superior to human beings who require earthly nourishment; they therefore tended to look down on all eating and drinking with disdain." The father's imperial drive toward physical perfection had become in the son a calisthenics of the disembodied.[80]

If anorexics, initially overactive and overambitious, were almost olympically engaged with the world in order to prove that they were healthy despite their loss of weight, schizophrenics like Schreber were disengaged, and their olympiads were hollow. With the second self fragmented, the body of the first person could fall away, fly apart, disappear into thin air. The schizophrenic catastrophe of the self was also a catastrophe of the sinews.

Later, in the 1930s and 1940s, the same family constellations held responsible for obesity and anorexia would be suspected as schizophrenogenic families. The "bad me" which American psychologist Harry Stack Sullivan found to dominate the schizophrenic was a second self shaped by an anxious, overprotective mother and a weak or distant father. Sullivan had worked with a patient to whom "it seemed...as if I were losing all my weight," and he sympathized with the schizophrenic's horror "that he lives in a collapsed world." The "bad me" slowly became "not me" and disincarnation began.[81]

Disincarnation was a wonderful release for spiritualists and mediums, but for the schizophrenic it was a terrifying terminus, a final thinness, a fade-out. At the climax of his memoirs, Schreber "became convinced of the imminence of a great catastrophe, of the end of the world." Freud, who read the case as one of repressed homosexuality, had little trouble explaining the cataclysmic feelings: Schreber had withdrawn libidinal cathexis from the external world, so for him the world had come to an end.[82]

Though the most celebrated case, Schreber was neither the first nor the last schizophrenic to be convinced of the coming End. Such a sense of impending world destruction, such a *Weltuntergangserlebnis*, was indeed regarded as an earmark of schizophrenia, especially in the years between the World Wars and during the first Cold War. The German *Weltuntergangserlebnis* had its roots in the French *délire des négations* detailed in 1882 by Jules Cotard. A patient with Cotard's Syndrome would complain of having lost everything – possessions, strength, appetite, parts of the body or the entire body. The world itself was being lost, and the patient was responsible: a world destroyer, an antichrist. This was solitude most supreme; Cotard thought it a chronic melancholy. Séglas in 1887 argued that the *délire des négations* was common to many disorders and that patients with Cotard's Syndrome were in effect denying any continuity between themselves and the world, themselves and their bodies, themselves and time. Their blanket denials were a form of mutism in the midst of despair: "I no longer have a heart: true, I have something that beats in its place, but it's not my heart, it doesn't beat as it used to. I no longer have any stomach, I never feel hungry. When I eat, I do taste the food, but once it's down my throat, I no longer feel anything, it seems as if the food has fallen into a hole."[83]

After the trenches, gaping wounds and shell shock of the Great War, schizophrenics seemed to take upon themselves those cosmic negations to which the war had alluded. In their acute stages the *Weltuntergangserlebnis* put them in the raging middle of a collapsing world where they were the last linchpins. Wrote the German physician Wetzel in 1922: "The end of the world is experienced as a transition to something new, vaster, and is felt as a terrible annihilation. Despairing agony and blissful revelation occur in one and the same patient. At first everything seems queer, uncanny and significant. Catastrophe is impending; the deluge is here.... Patients are exposed to all these terrifying and magnificent experiences without showing them to anyone. The feeling of being quite alone is unspeakably frightening and patients implore not to be left to themselves." The universe is about to fall to pieces, and they are the universe. A man lets himself fall from bed in a peculiar way "in order to make the world turn round, so that the wheels keep on moving." There is estrangement and panic, since the schizophrenic in this context is the world, the world assassin and possibly the world redeemer. Another man in 1939 has been listening to episodes of Buck Rogers on the radio: "Prepare for world destruction," a mad professor keeps repeating, and the man worries that he is the one responsible, fearing his own suicide as the world's self-destruction. He cannot afford to stand to one side, can he? Mustn't a man with exceptional gifts make use of them to save the world?[84]

By the 1930s, the *Weltuntergangserlebnis* of the schizophrenic, with its experience of chaos and its sense of a new order, had become something of a cultural metaphor. "Schitz," "schiz," "schitzo," "schizo," "skitz" and "skiz" had already become part of the slang for people of two minds or contradictory wishes or discordant careers. Well-adjusted but sensitive persons might under stress become "schizoaffective" if not schizophrenic, "schizoid" if not "schizophreniform." Samuel Beckett wrote in *Murphy* of "an emaciated schizoid," and sociologist Robert E.L. Faris asserted, in the *American Journal of Sociology*, that schizophrenia derived less from pathology than from social isolation. The schizophrenic was not an extraordinary and extreme person, but an ordinary person forced by economic, aesthetic or cultural circumstances toward an extreme reclusiveness. He compared schizophrenics to long-term prisoners who, when their sentences finally expired, desired to return to their cells.[85]

It was, according to an essayist in *Harper's Magazine* in 1937, "The Age of Schizophrenia." Leslie C. Barber, believing that "the coming of the next cataclysm appears to be only a question of time," reframed the *Weltuntergangserlebnis* as a cultural crisis. While schizophrenics in the news were receiving insulin shock therapy, Barber was proposing that Western civilization was mired in its own sort of schizophrenia and needed to be shocked into a more capable state. The problem was that our emotions were still unavailingly primitive, while our intellects were as modern as our industry. If schizophrenia was the splitting apart of the archaic and emotional from the intellectual (and *au courant*), then this was the great problem of the world today — "to bring the emotional life of its citizens to some agreement with the intellectual and industrial achievements of the period" — lest everyone "wind up in a half-hearted compromise between Dr. Jekyll and Mr. Hyde."[86]

Still the confusion with multiple personality, but now schizophrenia was fraught with the shadows of world war and, as Barber warned, despotism. It was fraught also with feelings of utter loneliness, impossible guilt, imminent peril. In the shift from multiple personality to schizophrenia, we can see how the second self, that bittersweet body of youth, came to be imagined as an inaccessible prisoner in a collapsing cell; as a desperate prisoner, desperately thin; as a mute whose signals were archaic, primitive, increasingly wild.

What then of the other sides of schizophrenia — the fragments and the flying apart? the body lost and then reconstituted amid delusions of grandeur? the messianic talk of the world reborn, of death and resurrection?

Bombs

The *délire de négation*, the *Weltuntergangserlebnis*, the delusions of grandeur, the messianic talk of the schizophrenic have brought us to the third of the Three Bodies, the phantom body of death, streamlined and futuristic. If the schizophrenic has been the cultural refuge of the archetypal past, the infant, the primitive, that same schizophrenic has been haunted by a future, dangerous, explosive.

It is a slick, efficient future, whose language is newspeak, neologism, headlines and slogans. Such, often, has been the language of the schizophrenic, a language of abbreviations and codes and parataxis which may seem like autism or derailment but may also be a genus of economy.[87]

It is a streamlined future whose invasive forces are the characteristic rays, radio waves, telephone lines, television cameras of the schizophrenic's more paranoid experiences. The schizophrenic imagination has been particularly affected by science and science fictions and is peculiarly up-to-date on technology.[88]

It is an ersatz, mechanical future engineered for automata and substitutions. Early on, schizophrenics appeared as either machines with stereotyped movements or the creatures of "influencing-machines" whose operations controlled their own.[89]

It is an immediate future, not so much a "when" as a "where." It lies just beyond the first person, volatile, immensely powerful.[90]

And it is metamorphic — not so much unstable as transformative. Your friends today may be your enemies tomorrow.

Yes: it is the future as represented in *1984*. When Orwell published *Coming Up for Air* in 1939, Egas Moniz in Lisbon had less than four years of experience performing prefrontal lobotomies on psychiatric patients. When Orwell published *1984* in 1949, more than 20,000 lobotomies had been performed and Moniz received the Nobel Prize in medicine.[91]

The majority of lobotomies during the 1940s were performed, of course, on schizophrenics, who were the majority of mental patients in hospitals. There arose at that time a new word in the English language, "zombie," for which the London *Daily Express* in 1943 gave this derivation: "After the voodoo cult which insists that dead men can be made to walk and act as if they were alive." Lobotomized people were placid, unambitious, unimaginative, sometimes uncaring. They were soon called zombies, the living dead.[92]

More than any other cultural construct, the schizophrenic has posed the problem of the Three Bodies, of being at home in one's body through time. Phenomenologists working with schizophrenia, and particularly with the schizophrenic *Weltuntergangserlebnis*, have caught wind of this, depicting the schizophrenic as a person who has lost all space to live in, who has no home body. A patient claims to have been carbonized by a holocaust long ago; now she is a burnt star, a tongue of fire.[93]

Some have made schizophrenia out to be the human condition: "Schizophrenia is nothing less than the predicament of each one of us." Some have made schizophrenics into paradigmatic artists, or heroes and heroines.[94] These temptations to exalt schizophrenia have been strongest and most predictable in industrialized societies, where the Three Bodies have been most problematic because most at odds.[95] George Bowling is uncomfortable with each of his bodies — the fat present, the thin past, the streamlined future. He can find no point of equilibrium, no place to rest. When he returns to Lower Binfield, imagined as "a sort of quiet corner that I could step back into when I felt like it," he discovers industry and noise, "and lest there should be any mistake the Royal Air Force had followed up with five hundred pounds of T.N.T."

That thin man inside the fat man was not so quiet a statue with so mysterious a smile on his face. Connolly during the war had got it right: the thin man was signaling wildly, threatened by explosion and implosion. But where, in all this, had the fat man come from? How had the first person put on so much weight?

Shadow and Substance

I have intended from the start to explain how the thin past became imprisoned in the first person's *fat* body. I had first to show how it could seem culturally reasonable that one body might be inside another, and how that inner body might be accepted as a thinner body. I had next to show how the inner body became a captive, how certain cultural constructs of repression might promote images of imprisonment and terror. I had occasion along the way to trace some critical lines of filiation between thinness and the past, streamlining and the future. As one might expect of a man nearing forty, I have left the present to the last.

I will be brief about it. Obesity came on the scene as a commonly recognized *disease* at the same time as kleptomania and multiple personality, but there was no culture of slimming until the traditional bodies of prosperous adults began to seem fat and heavy rather than aptly substantial. The middle-aging body became a fat, heavy body just as kleptomania became pathological stealing, multiple personality became schizophrenia, and fasting became anorexia nervosa. In the United States, the chronological conjunction just before the Great War was especially nice.

The catalytic question was fraud. For kleptomania: Were society ladies, professional thieves, common criminals hiding behind the false front of "overwhelming impulse"? For multiple personality: Were the other selves artifacts of hypnosis, triumphs of drawing-room theatrics, or perhaps a somewhat more innocent collusion between therapist and patient? For fasting: Were the girls and the hunger artists eating nothing at all, or were they mistresses and masters of sleight of hand, and were the girls' visions simply hysterical or dramatically planned? For obesity: Were fat people as healthy as they claimed to be, and were they eating as little as they claimed to eat, or were they cheating, sneaking food on the side?

If the issue was fraud, the agency was the detective. A romantic but shady character in Eugène-François Vidocq's *Mémoires* (1828-29), the detective was launched more honorably by Edgar Allan Poe's *Murders in the Rue Morgue* (1841) and given professional compass by Allan Pinkerton in Chicago in 1850. Promoted by Charles Dickens and volumes of Pinkerton stories, the detective in the last half of the nineteenth century was no longer a rogue or a spy but a solid citizen. By the time Sherlock Holmes made his appearance in 1887, the figure of the detective was so attractive and respectable that Pinkerton himself had constantly to deny that detectives had supernatural powers: "Many unthinking people have come to believe that there is something mysterious, wonderful, and awful about the detective. All my life, and in every manner in my power, I have endeavored to break down this popular superstition," he wrote in 1879, "but it would seem that it could not be done." The superstition, he suggested, accounted for the success of bogus detectives pretending to be his agents, and for the legion of "would-be detectives" who offered their services to him in the mail every day.[96]

Yet there *was* something mysterious, wonderful and awful about the detective. He was from 1859 a "shadow," one who "possesses naturally the power...to follow his quarry." He was at once a dogged shadow self and a stranger who could see through to the inner self. It was a detective, Professor Craig Kennedy, whose machine for reading the thoughts of a helpless kleptomaniac solved the department-store thefts by that queen of the rogues, Annie Grayson, in a 1912 story in *Hearst's International Magazine*.[97]

That fictitious machine was a slight anticipation of the polygraph put to use in the 1920s, but it was an immediate reflection of the extraordinary gifts attributed to the detective, who was simultaneously a clairvoyant and a scientist, a ghost and a student of human character, a master of disguises and the ultimately honest man. He made use of Alphonse Bertillon's anthropometric method of classifying criminals, designed in 1879, and then of Sir Edward Richard Henry's fingerprinting system completed in 1901, and yet there was something more than patience and order to his nature: "Good detectives are born not appointed. God makes them, not a boss. If a man hasn't the detective instinct he can't be inoculated with it."[98]

Such a figure, divinely inspired, nattily attired, toured department stores watching for thefts and frauds. By the 1880s the Pinkerton National Detective Agency had numerous records of the scams and confidence games played in the name of kleptomania, and in 1895, asked if she believed in kleptomania, store detective Mary Plunkett answered, "Hardly." She thought some people absentminded, some

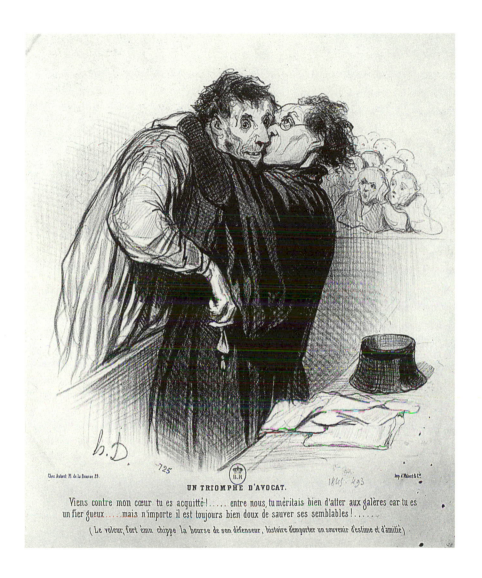

H. Daumier, A Lawyer's Triumph.
From *Les beaux jours de la vie*, 1845 (Paris, Bibliothèque nationale).

budget-stricken, some plainly dishonest, but no one kleptomaniac.[99]

Psychologists and physicians, enthralled by the theoretical implications of multiple personality, were easy marks for impostors. Or so some began to think as they realized the vulnerable position they had put themselves in. An English doctor explained in 1903: "When I heard that the question of double consciousness was to come on for discussion I was afraid that a new terror was to be added to life. We have kleptomania and all the other manias, and alcoholism, and degeneracy.... And I can imagine that if we are to go before a sceptical judge and an enlightened British jury and plead that a person should not be held responsible because his consciousness was in a Jekyll-Hyde condition, in a state of mental *alibi*, we would find our position a difficult one to establish." Hypnotism, responsible for perhaps the majority of cases of multliple personality, began to seem malign: it did not merely allow the other personas to come forward; it created and then controlled them. There was the evil Svengali; there was the medical villain in *The White Cat* (1907), who hypnotized the heroine in order to summon up her evil alter ego; there was Professor Balzamo in *The Case of Becky*, who had lured away the good Dr. Emerson's wife to share the life of a traveling hypnotist and must, at the climax of the play, do battle with Emerson for the life of the child. Once gullible, physicians and psychologists began to act like detectives, suspicious of mental alibis.[100]

Physiologists too became detectives, shadowing hunger artists. They were concerned, like Dr. Willian Hammond, with fraud, but much more interested in what *did* happen to the body when a person starved. They distrusted the plumpness of fasting girls, looked for the secrets of nutrition, the basic daily requirements, the essential foods. Physiologist Francis G. Benedict at Harvard studied the Italian hunger artist Agostino Levanzin, devising first a foolproof chamber to prevent cheating, then examining the bodily changes in the proud artist, who was upset when commanded to end his fast after less than thirty-two days.[101]

From physiological detective work, more painstaking than divinely inspired, came the notion of the nutritional calorie and the first thorough diets-by-numbers: from Vienna, Gustav Gaertner's *Reducing Weight Comfortably* (1914); from New York and Hollywood, Vance Thompson's *Eat and Grow Thin: The Mahdah Diets* (also 1914). The diets were popular in part because of the prevalence of another detective stationed on subway platforms, in movie houses, in front of pharmacies, in the forecourts of banks and city halls: the public penny scale, introduced in the 1880s and widespread by the turn of the century. The scales promised true weight and, most of them, a mirror image. They advertised themselves with slogans and banners as monitors of health, accurate and indefatigable. And soon, as people grew embarrassed by the big clock faces of the original penny scales, other, less public scales were designed — scales that dispensed printed tickets through small slots, so that the report was confidential; bathroom scales that gave personal weight a naked intimacy. Most well known of the American bathroom scales was — it would follow — the Detecto.[102]

Calorie-counting diets became popular because people were becoming accustomed to considering their bodies in measured, arithmetic modes, like detectives applying the Bertillon and Henry methods of criminal identification. Adults with pennies to spare knew their weights day by day and had in mind some standard weights for their height and age. Between 1912 and 1914, the insurance companies and actuaries who prepared these charts of standard weights changed their minds about weight and longevity. The Actuarial Society of America and the Association of Life Insurance Medical Directors produced statistics and graphs to show that the healthiest weight was not the average weight. Indeed, the longest-lived bodies in general were those that clung to the thinness of their twenties.[103]

From 1914 on, the middle-aging body became progressively fatter and heavier as the culture of slimming insisted on an "ideal" weight rather than an average weight, and as heaviness became equated with fatness, fatness with heart disease, heart attacks, diabetes, gallstones, ugliness. As for those who claimed that they were not overeating, that it was just their metabolism, by the 1930s physiologists and physicians preferred to consult the scales. Scales told no lies: if you gained weight on a diet, you were cheating. Scales, like detectives, could see behind pantry doors, penetrate darkness, read the conscience. No wonder they might also tell your fortune.[104]

Down into the Muck

Men's fortunes as well as women's. In fact, the base data on morbidity and mortality came from studies of lives of insured men, not women, and conclusions drawn from the heights, weights and deaths of adult males were typically extrapolated (with bias) to adult females. Readers may already have noticed the pattern: with the shift from kleptomania to pathological stealing, from multiple personality to schizophrenia, even from fasting girls to anorexia nervosa, and certainly from middle-aged substance to chronic obesity, there was a slight but perceptible shift of cultural focus from women to the generic "man."

It could well be, then, that "imprisoned in every fat *man* a thin one is wildly signalling to be let out." Imprisoned by the detectives and Detectos, by physicians and statisticians, the thin one was young, energetic and healthy, a reminder of the past. He was subject to the life sentence of arteriosclerosis and the capital punishment of strokes. That wild signaling was his heart.

Men's hearts, more than women's. Whatever evidence there was (or is) linking fat to heart disease, that evidence pertained (and pertains) to men, not to women.[105] The thin man and the fat man were, for Connolly and Orwell, *men*, neither neutered nor generic. When George Bowling sees Elsie, that fat hag, he invokes a categorical distinction between his (male) fat and her (female) fat: "No man ever goes to pieces quite so completely as that. I'm fat, I grant you. I'm the wrong shape, if you like. But at least I'm *a* shape. Elsie wasn't even particularly fat, she was merely shapeless. Ghastly things had happened to her hips. As for her waist, it had vanished. She was just a kind of soft lumpy cylinder, like a bag of meal."

Bowling was resuming a turn-of-the-century distinction between the exogenous fat of fat men and the endogenous fat of fat women. Fat men were fat on the outside, thin enough on the inside. They had ruddy complexions and strong, cheerful constitutions and had only to exercise their wills in order to release the inner self. Fat women were fat through and through, their muscles flab, their complexions pasty, their constitutions sad and weak. They could not help themselves, had to rely on reducing drugs, medical regimen.[106]

The fat man had within him an intact thin man who was the guarantor of shape. The fat woman could "go to pieces" because her second self was not intact. Remember those legs discovered in the shapeless brown bag? They were women's legs. Remember that leg in a black boot with a Wood-Milne rubber heel? That was a man's leg. Neither private nor public violence could undo the categorical distinction between a man's intrinsically shaped body and a woman's ultimately shapeless body.

If the fat man kept his shape, he kept his power and his not-so-generic humanity. The fat woman, going to pieces, lost her power and her humanity. She could resemble the food she had taken in, an impossibly vague geometry, half bomb ("cylinder") and half bag of meal. The man remains to the end an individual with a Wood-Milne rubber heel, while the woman's legs become anonymous ("They're all the bleeding same, aren't they?").

We must therefore read the Orwell and Connolly aphorisms in two different contexts. Directed at men, the aphorisms present slimming as an act of liberation, releasing the thinner form within – a form that has been there since youth, patient as Og or anxious as the Thin One. Directed at women, the aphorisms in their more generic sense present slimming as an act of creation – a figure *taking shape* from a matrix of stone, a svelte child being born and "wildly signalling to be let out."

For men, slimming promises reformation; for women, transformation. Herein lies one good reason for the culture of slimming as a women's culture.[107]

From the Bottom of the Sea to the Flying Salamander

In the culture of slimming, the loss of weight, the exile of fat, the erosion of bulk are but preludes to a change of personality. Either the dieter will develop a personal confidence, retrieve a dynamic youth or discover a vital new self. Diets (and exercises) fail when the personality does not change, or does not change radically enough, or does not change quickly enough.

Slimming has become the primary Western solution to the Three-Body Problem. Reducing schemes offer more than techniques and moral encouragement; they present compelling visions of being at home in one's body through time. They promise the first person the gift of agelessness, of not looking one's age. The fat body of the mature present, once reduced, is no longer a prison. They promise the second self rejuvenation. The sweet body of youth can escape, take command. They promise the total transformation necessary to embrace the third self, streamlined and futuristic.

These promises are so appealing, so reassuring, precisely because they rest on an elaborate cultural web spun over the last century. When the promises fail, illusive as they are, we do not abandon them. Like those anticipating the End and the New World, we have also made preparations for the Delay and for a World Not-So-New. We were at fault – we cheated on the diet, we did not persevere, we misunderstood the directions, sensual holidays intervened and we were weak of will. Or this diet was a hoax, I was not transformed, but that one is the truth, it will reveal the true me. Or somewhere there is the diet meant for my body, and I must expect dark nights of the kitchen table before I reach the grail.

Slimming is an alarming solution to the Three-Body Problem not because it is selfish but because it leads to an obsessive, delusive search for the Other. It is not about becoming ourselves but becoming Other.

The culture of slimming is hazardous, for it offers to put us at home in our bodies only in exchange for a denial of the passage of time. Such bodies may be houses but they are not homes.

NOTES

1. On "overnutrition" or obesity, see my book, *Never Satisfied: A Cultural History of Diets, Fantasies and Fat* (New York, 1986). Compare also an article that appeared after my book was completed: Keith Walden, "The Road to Fat City: An Interpretation of the Development of Weight Consciousness in Western Society," *Historical Reflections* 12 (Fall 1985), pp. 331-73.

2. Rosalind H. Williams, *Dream Worlds: Mass Consumption in Late Nineteenth-Century France* (Berkeley, 1982), pp. 66-71 passim; William R. Leach, "Transformation in a Culture of Consumption: Women and Department Stores, 1890-1925," *Journal of American History* 71 (1984), pp. 319-42; Susan Benson, *Counter Cultures: Saleswomen, Managers and Customers in American Department Stores 1890-1940* (Urbana, 1986).

3. William R. Leach, *True Love and Perfect Union* (New York, 1980), p. 253, quoting an 1876 article from *New Century*; Elaine Susan Abelson, " 'When Ladies Go A-Thieving': The Department Store, Shoplifting and the Contradictions of Consumerism, 1870-1914," Ph.D. thesis, New York University, 1986.

4. Patricia O'Brien, "The Kleptomania Diagnosis: Bourgeois Women and Theft in Late Nineteenth-Century France," *Journal of Social History* 17 (Fall 1983), pp. 65-78; Raymond de Saussure, "The Influence of the Concept of Monomania on French Medico-Legal Psychiatry (from 1825 to 1840)," *Journal of the History of Medicine and the Allied Sciences* 1 (1946), pp. 365-97, quoting Esquirol's *De la monomanie* (Paris, 1838).

5. Benjamin Rush, "An Inquiry into the Influence of Physical Causes upon the Moral Faculty (1786)," in his *Medical Inquiries and Observations upon the Diseases of the Mind*, 4th ed. (Philadelphia, 1815), vol. 1, pp. 101-02; Franz Josef Gall, *Sur les fonctions du cerveau* (Paris, 1825), vol. 4, pp. 206-22.

6. *Journal de Paris*, March 29, 1816, summarized in an important early work, Isaac Ray, *A Treatise on the Medical Jurisprudence of Insanity*, ed. Winfred Overholser (1838. Reprint: Cambridge, Mass., 1962), p. 142; M.H. Girard, "Kleptomanie," *Gazette médicale de Paris* 2ᵉ sér., 13 (1845), pp. 735-37.

7. *People v. Sprague* (1849), in Amasa J. Parker, *Reports of Decisions in Criminal Cases...in the Courts of Oyer and Terminer of the State of New York* 2 (New York, 1869), pp. 43-48.

8. See Francis Wharton, *A Monograph on Mental Unsoundness* (Philadelphia, 1855), p. 155; John C. Bucknill and Daniel H. Tuke, *A Manual of Psychological Medicine* (Philadelphia, 1858), pp. 208-11; W. Julius Mickle, "General Paralysis," in *A Dictionary of Psychological Medicine*, ed. Daniel H. Tuke (London, 1892), vol. 1, p. 521.

9. Wharton, *Mental Unsoundness*, p. 157, citing the *Times* (London) of April 1855.

10. Abelson, " 'When Ladies Go A-Thieving,' " pp. 62-65; Williams, *Dream Worlds*, esp. pp. 64-66; Michael B. Miller, *The Bon Marché: Bourgeois Culture and the Department Store 1869-1920* (Princeton, 1981), esp. pp. 197-206; "Kleptomania," *Medico-Legal Journal* 14 (1896), pp. 231-32, extracting a paper by Alexandre Lacassagne; Paul Dubuisson, "Les Voleurs des grands magasins," *Archives de l'anthropologie criminelle* 16 (1901), pp. 1-20, 341-70.

11. Alfred Swain Taylor, *Medical Jurisprudence*, 2d American ed., from 3d London ed. (Philadelphia, 1850), p. 653; Thomas Byrnes, *Professional Criminals of America* (New York, 1886), p. 32; "Nervous Disorders (Especially Kleptomania) in Women and Pelvic Disease," *American Journal of Insanity* 53 (1897), pp. 605-06; O'Brien, "The Kleptomania Diagnosis," pp. 68, 75 n.13; Arthur B. Reeve, "The Kleptomaniac," *Hearst's International Magazine* 22 (December 1912), p. 67.

12. See esp. Logie Barrow, "Anti-establishment Healing: Spiritualism in Britain," in *The Church and Healing*, ed. W.J. Sheils (Oxford, 1982), pp. 225-48; Edward M. Brown, "Neurology and Spiritualism in the 1870s," *Bulletin of the History of Medicine* 57 (1983), pp. 563-77; Howard Kerr, *Mediums, and Spirit-Rappers, and Roaring Radicals: Spiritualism in American Literature, 1850-1900* (Urbana, Ill., 1972); R. Lawrence Moore, *In Search of White Crows: Spiritualism, Parapsychology and American Culture* (New York, 1977); Janet Oppenheim, *The Other World: Spiritualism and Psychical Research in England, 1850-1914* (Cambridge, 1985).

13. Bucknill and Tuke, *Manual*, p. 324; Juanita A.N. Dobmeyer, "The Sociology of Shoplifting," Ph. D. thesis, University of Minnesota, 1971; Meda Chesney-Lind, "Women and Crime: The Female Offender," *Signs* 12 (Autumn 1986), pp. 78-96.

14. See esp. J. Baker, "Kleptomania," in *A Dictionary of Psychological Medicine*, ed. Daniel H. Tuke (London, 1892), vol. 2, pp. 726-29.

15. "The Husband Who Makes His Wife a Thief: The True But Little-Known Reason Behind Many

a Shoplifting Incident," *Ladies' Home Journal* 32 (March 1915), p. 16; and cf. John C. Bucknill, "Kleptomania," *Journal of Mental Science* 8 (1862), p. 265.

16. "Kleptomania," *Progressive Review (London)* 2 (1897), pp. 311-15; "Kleptomania," *Medico-Legal Journal* 14 (1896), p. 232, citing the French criminologist Motet on kleptomaniac confessions; Abelson, " 'When Ladies Go A-Thieving,' " ch. 1; Mary Owen Cameron, "An Interpretation of Shoplifting," in *The Criminology of Deviant Women*, eds. Freda Adler and Rita J. Simon (Boston, 1979), pp. 161-62.

17. On the reluctance to prosecute, see "With a Mania for Stealing," *New York Times*, July 1, 1883, p. 12, col. 3; "Shoplifting in New York," *New York Times*, January 2, 1906, p. 15, col. 1; Abelson, " 'When Ladies Go A-Thieving,' " pp. 208-09.

18. *H.H. Harris v. The State* (1885), *18 Texas Court of Appeals*, pp. 287-95; and cf. *Alfred Lowe v. The State* (1902), *44 Texas Criminal Reports*, pp. 224-26; Mark Melford, "Kleptomania: A Farcical Comedy in Three Acts," *French's Acting Edition* 138 (London, 1888), produced in 1888, 1890 and 1908; "She Cannot Help Stealing," *New York Times*, December 22, 1888, p. 2, col. 5; Edward Bellamy, *Looking Backward 2000-1887* (1888. Reprint: New York, 1951), p. 164.

19. *Lewis v. Lewis* (1890), *44 Minnesota Reports*, pp. 124-26; *New York Times*, articles on Mrs. Castle, the San Francisco belle, from October 8 through December 31, 1896, esp. October 14, p. 9, col. 1, and October 18, p. 1, col. 6; "Kleptomania as a Disease and a Defense," *American Lawyer* 4 (1896), p. 533; "Kleptomania," *Law Times* 102, November 14, 1896, p. 28; "Mrs. Castle's Case," *Medical Magazine (London)* 5 (1896), pp. 1211-13; Shobal V. Clevinger, *Medical Jurisprudence of Insanity* (Rochester, N.Y., 1898), vol. 2, pp. 848-49, citing the *Chicago Record*, September 26, 1895, on the English duchess, with references also to Germans and Russians; Abelson, " 'When Ladies Go A-Thieving,' " p. 317 n.39; Gus Edwards and Will D. Cobb, "Mamie (Don't You Feel Ashamie)," in *Song Hits from the Turn of the Century*, eds. Paul Charosh and Robert A. Fremont (New York, 1975), pp. 162-66. More on Porter's "The Kleptomaniac" in note 51 below.

20. "Mrs. Martin's Dual Role," *New York Times*, April 11, 1895, p. 8, col. 1.

21. *Ibid.*; M. Motet, "French Retrospect: Shoplifting," *Journal of Mental Science* 26 (1880), pp. 625-29, reviewing the work of Lasègue; Dubuisson, "Les voleurs des grands magasins," p. 348; Abelson, " 'When Ladies Go A-Thieving,' " pp. 265, 268, 269, 270, 271, 94; and cf. "A Self-Accused Thief," *New York Times*, May 9, 1877, p. 8, col. 3.

22. On false names, see Abelson, " 'When Ladies Go A-Thieving,' " pp. 265-68.

23. Edwards and Cobb, in *Song Hits*, p. 166.

24. I cannot give a full history of multiple personality here. See H.F. Ellenberger, *The Discovery of the Unconscious* (New York, 1970), pp. 126-41; Eric T. Carlson, "The History of Multiple Person-

ality Disorder in the United States," *American Journal of Psychiatry* 138 (1981), pp. 666-68; George B. Greaves, "Multiple Personality: 165 Years After Mary Reynolds," *Journal of Nervous and Mental Disease* 168 (1980), pp. 577-96; W.S. Taylor and Mabel F. Martin, "Multiple Personality," *Journal of Abnormal and Social Psychology* 39 (1944), pp. 281-300. Good early surveys include Charles L. Dana, "Consciousness, Disorders of," in *A Reference Handbook of the Medical Sciences*, ed. Albert H. Buck (New York, 1886), vol. 2, pp. 277-79; F.W.H. Myers, *Human Personality and Its Survival of Bodily Death* (New York, 1903), vol. 1, pp. 34-70, 298-368; Boris Sidis and Simon P. Goodhart, *Multiple Personality* (New York, 1905).

25. Eric T. Carlson, "The History of Multiple Personality in the United States: Mary Reynolds and Her Subsequent Reputation," *Bulletin of the History of Medicine* 58 (1984), pp. 72-82; Michael G. Kenny, *The Passion of Ansel Bourne: Multiple Personality in American Culture* (Washington, 1986), esp. pp. 28-63; William S. Plumer, "Mary Reynolds: Case of Double Consciousness," *Harper's New Monthly Magazine* 20 (1859-60), pp. 807-12; Silas Weir Mitchell, "Mary Reynolds: A Case of Double Consciousness," *Transactions of the College of Physicians of Philadelphia* 3d ser., 10 (1888), pp. 366-89.

26. See the full retrospective of this case in Etienne Eugene Azam, "Double Consciousness," in *A Dictionary of Psychological Medicine*, ed. Daniel H. Tuke (London, 1892), vol. 1, pp. 401-06; and also Sidis and Goodhart, *Multiple Personality*, pp. 381-86.

27. Abram H. Dailey, *Mollie Fancher: The Brooklyn Enigma* (Brooklyn, 1894), which reproduces many of the newspaper articles as well; on her personalities, see pp. 74-107 passim.

28. Josef Breuer and Sigmund Freud, *Studies on Hysteria* (1895), trans. James Strachey et al. (New York, 1957), pp. 3-17.

29. R. Osgood Mason, "Duplex Personality," *Journal of Nervous and Mental Disease* 18 (1893), pp. 593-98.

30. Pierre Janet, "Les actes inconscients et la mémoire pendant le somnambulisme," *Revue philosophique* 25 (1888), pp. 238-79; Morton Prince, "Some of the Revelations of Hypnotism," *Boston Medical and Surgical Journal* 122 (1890), pp. 493-95.

31. Morton Prince, "An Experimental Study of Visions," *Brain* 21 (1898), pp. 528-46; *idem*, *The Dissociation of a Personality*, 2d ed. (New York, 1908); " 'The Case of Becky': A Remarkable Play," *New York Times*, October 2, 1912, p. 13, col. 3; Adolph Klauber, " 'The Case of Becky' and the Real Case," *New York Times*, October 6, 1912, Part 9, p. 2, col. 1-2. Alma Z., Léonie and Miss Beauchamp all had more than one other personality, but the one I have described here was in each case the most prominent, prevalent and troublesome.

32. Carlson, "History of Multiple Personality Disorder" (1981), on the case of William Tennent

cited by Rush; Dana, "Consciousness, Disorders of," pp. 277-79, on the Scull case; *idem*, "The Study of a Case of Amnesia or 'Double Consciousness,' " *Psychological Review* 1 (1894), pp. 574-75, on Mr. S.; Sidis and Goodhart, *Multiple Personality*, Part 2, on the most remarkable of these male cases of regression to infancy, the Reverend Hanna.

33. Anselm R. von Feuerbach, *Narratives of Remarkable Criminal Trials*, trans. Lady Duff Gordon, from 3d German ed. (New York, 1846), pp. 212-28, on the Sörgel case; L. Camuset, "Un Cas de dédoublement de la personnalité," *Annales médico-psychologiques* 7 (1882), pp. 75-86, on Louis Vivé; as also A.T. Myers, "The Life History of a Case of Double or Multiple Personality," *Journal of Mental Science* 31 (1886), pp. 596-605; Lewis C. Bruce, "Notes of a Case of Dual Brain Action," *Brain* 18 (1895), pp. 54-65, case of H.P.

34. Kenny, *The Passion of Ansel Bourne*, pp. 64ff.; Azam, "Double Consciousness," vol. 1, p. 402, case of Albert D.; A.E. Osborne, "People Who Drop Out of Sight," *Medico-Legal Journal* 12 (1894), pp. 22-41; J. Milne Bramwell, "Hypnotic and Posthypnotic Appreciation of Time: Secondary and Multiplex Personalities," *Brain* 23 (1900), p. 202, case of George Ridderband; Edward E. Mayer, "A Case of Localized Amnesia," *Journal of American Medical Association* 37 (1901), pp. 1601-05; Sidis and Goodhart, *Multiple Personality*, pp. 404-19, case of Dr. Gilbert; Edward B. Angell, "A Case of Double Consciousness," *Journal of Abnormal Psychology* 1 (1906), pp. 155-69, case of Mr. Robbins; Earl E. Gaver, "A Case of Alternating Personality," *Journal of the American Medical Association* 51 (1908), pp. 9-13.

35. Clifford Hallam, "The Double as Incomplete Self: Toward a Definition of Doppelgänger," in *Fearful Symmetry*, ed. Eugene J. Crook (Tallahassee, 1981), pp. 1-31; Claire Rosenfield, "The Shadow Within: The Conscious and Unconscious Use of the Double," in *Stories of the Double*, ed. Albert J. Guerard (Philadelphia, 1967), pp. 311-31; Jeremy Hawthorn, *Multiple Personality and the Disintegration of Literary Character* (London, 1983); Myers, *Human Personality*, pp. 300-03, on Robert Louis Stevenson's own experience of "a supraliminal duality"; and see an intriguing story about disappearances, T.C. Crawford, "The Disappearance Syndicate," *Cosmopolitan* 17 (February 1894), pp. 483-98, 589-608.

36. See the bold speculations by J.H. van den Berg, *Divided Existence and Complex Society: An Historical Approach* (1963. Reprint: Pittsburgh, 1974), on the underlying reasons for this interest in double selves; for the dual-brain theory, see Anne Harrington, *Medicine, Mind, and the Double Brain: A Study in Nineteenth-Century Thought* (Princeton, 1987). Quotations here from William James, *The Principles of Psychology* (New York, 1890), p. 401; Prince, "Some of the Revelations of Hypnotism," p. 464; R. Osgood Mason, *Telepathy and the Subliminal Self*, 2d ed. (New York, 1897), p. 141.

37. As in E. Mesnet's case of "F.," pleasant and honest in the first person but "a kleptomaniac" in the second, summarized by Taylor and Martin, "Multiple Personality," p. 289.

38. On the instrumental role of needlework, see William Sharpey, "The Re-education of the Adult Brain," *Brain* 2 (1879), pp. 1-9, case of Mrs. H.; Myers, "Life History," pp. 596-97, case of Vivé; Azam, "Double Consciousness," p. 405, case of Félida X.; Dailey, *Mollie Fancher*, pp. 65, 74-79. On the reading of time, see H. Dewar, "Report on a Communication from Dr. Dyce of Aberdeen," *Transactions of the Royal Society of Edinburgh* 9 (1823), p. 369, case of Mrs. L.'s servant; Jules Janet, "L'Hystérie et l'hypnotisme d'après le théorie de la double personnalité," *Revue scientifique* 41 (1888), p. 617, case of Blanche Wittman; Breuer and Freud, *Studies on Hysteria*, pp. 39-40, case of Anna O.; Sidis and Goodhart, *Multiple Personality*, p. 393, case of Mary Vaughn; Prince, *Dissociation of a Personality*, p. 153, case of Miss Beauchamp.

39. Breuer and Freud, *Studies on Hysteria*, p. 7. Cf. Stephen J. Kern, *The Culture of Time and Space, 1880-1918* (Cambridge, Mass., 1983), ch. 2, on the past.

40. P.M.J. Clancy, "Fast and Abstinence," *New Catholic Encyclopedia* (New York, 1967), vol. 5, pp. 847-50.

41. See esp. Caroline Walker Bynum, *Holy Feast and Holy Fast: The Religious Significance of Food to Medieval Women* (Berkeley, 1987).

42. H. Graef, "Lateau, Louise," *New Catholic Encyclopedia* (Washington, 1967), vol. 8, p. 403; "Hysteria and Its Causes," *New York Times*, December 15, 1878, p. 5, col. 1.

43. William H. Hammond, *Fasting Girls* (New York, 1879), pp. 13-28; John Cule, *Wreath on the Crown: The Story of Sarah Jacob, the Welsh Fasting Girl* (Llandyswl, 1967).

44. Dailey, *Mollie Fancher*, pp. 28, 44, 66-68, 102 passim; Schwartz, *Never Satisfied*, pp. 115-19.

45. Dailey, *Mollie Fancher*, pp. 173, 242. Joan Jacobs Brumberg, *Fasting Girls: The Emergence of Anorexia Nervosa as a Modern Disease* (Cambridge, Mass., 1988) ch. 3.

46. Schwartz, *Never Satisfied*, pp. 119-24; *New York Times*, August 9, 1880 p. 5, col. 1 and September 10, 1880, p. 2, col. 4; *New York Daily Tribune*, August 9, 1880, p. 5, col. 1.

47. Schwartz, *Never Satisfied*, p.122; Sergius Morgulis, *Fasting and Undernutrition* (New York, 1923) pp. 142-72; and cf., of course, Franz Kafka, "A Hunger Artist," in *The Penal Colony*, trans. Willa and Edwin Muir (New York, 1976), pp. 243-56.

48. E. Sylvia Pankhurst, *The Suffragette* (London, 1911), pp. 431-35, 440-43, 482-86. The earliest political hunger strikes took place in Russian prisons; see Vera Figner, *Memoirs of a Revolutionist* (New York, 1968 [1927]) ch. 7.

49. Sharpey, "Re-education of the Adult Brain," on Mrs. H.; Breuer and Freud, *Studies on Hysteria*, p. 26, on Anna O.; Myers, *Human Personality*, pp. 331-32; and Pierre Janet, *The Major Symptoms of Hysteria* (1907), 2d ed. (New York, 1927), pp. 86-87, on Marceline R.; B.C.A., "My Life as a Dissoci-

ated Personality," *Journal of Abnormal Psychology* 3 (1908), pp. 240-60; Walter F. Prince, "The Doris Case of Quintuple Personality," *ibid*. 11 (1916), pp. 73-122.

50. Azam, "Double Consciousness," vol. 1, p. 405; Mason, "Duplex Personality," and cf. his "Duplex Personality — Its Relation to Hypnotism and to Lucidity," *Journal of the American Medical Association* 25 (1895), pp. 928-33; Sidis and Goodhart, *Multiple Personality*, p. 424, on "Twoey," and p. 173 on Hanna; Myers, *Human Personality*, pp. 354-56, on Winsor, pp. 360-61, on Vennum.

51. Kemp R. Niver, *Early Motion Pictures* (Washington, D.C., 1985), pp. 176-77; Lewis Jacobs, *The Rise of the American Film* (New York, 1939), ch. 3.

52. Recently translated as "What gets me is being accused of twelve robberies." "There were twelve? Good! I'll plead kleptomania." See Bruce Harris and Seena Harris, *Honoré Daumier: Selected Works* (New York, 1969), p. 117.

53. Taylor, *Medical Jurisprudence*, p. 653; Johann Ludwig Casper, *A Handbook of the Practice of Forensic Medicine* (1860), trans. G.W. Balfour, from 3d German ed. (London, 1865), vol. 4, pp. 292-311. Cf. also Orpheus Everts, "Are Dipsomania, Kleptomania, Pyromania, etc., Valid Forms of Mental Disease?" *American Journal of Insanity* 44 (July 1887), pp. 52-59.

54. "She Stole 'Unconsciously,' " *New York Times*, February 18, 1893, p. 8, col. 6; "Alleged Thief Worth $175,000," *New York Times*, January 14, 1899, p. 1, col. 4; "Shoplifting in New York," *New York Times*, January 2, 1906, p. 15, col. 1. See also Charles Rosenberg, The *Trial of the Assassin Guiteau: Psychiatry and the Law in the Gilded Age* (Chicago, 1968).

55. Francis Wharton and Moreton Stillé, *Medical Jurisprudence*, 5th ed., rewritten by James Hendrie Lloyd (Rochester, N.Y., 1905) p. 613; and, for American cases, *John Henslie v. The State* (1871), *50 Tennessee Reports, Supreme Court*, p. 202; *J.R. Looney v. The State* (1881), *10 Texas Court of Appeals*, pp. 520-26; *Commonwealth v. Fritch* (1890), *9 Pennsylvania County Court Reports*, pp. 164-70; *Alfred Lowe v. The State* (1902), *44 Texas Criminal Reports*, pp. 224-26.

56. William Healy, *The Individual Delinquent* (Boston, 1915), p. 771; Key L. Barkley, "A Case Illustrating Probable Sublimation through Pathological Stealing," *Journal of Abnormal and Social Psychology* 31 (1936-37), p. 208; L. Pierce Clark, "A Psychologic Study of Stealing in Juvenile Delinquency," *Archives of Neurology and Psychiatry* 1 (1919), pp. 535-46; Ralph Hamill, "Amnesia and Pathological Stealing," *ibid*. 12 (1924), pp. 124-26; Edwin C. Ranck, "Kleptomania," *Theatre Magazine* 32 (July-August 1920), pp. 10-12, 65, 68; American Film Institute, *Catalog of Motion Pictures...Feature Films 1921-30*, ed. Kenneth W. Munden (New York, 1971), vol. 2, p. 881; A. Antheaume, "La Légende de la kleptomanie," *Encéphale* 20 (1925), pp. 368-88; Norman R. Phillips, "Review of A. Antheaume's *Le Roman d'une épidémie parisienne: La Kleptomanie?*" *Journal of Mental Science* 72 (1926), pp. 393-95.

57. American Film Institute, *Catalog*, vol. 1, p. 604; Norman Fenton, *Shell Shock and Its Aftermath* (St. Louis, 1926), pp. 86-87.

58. On collectors, see esp. James G. Kiernan, "Kleptomania and Collectivism," *Alienist and Neurologist* 23 (1902), pp. 449-55; R. Dupouy, "De la kleptomanie," *Journal de psychologie normale et pathologique* (Sept.-Oct. 1905), pp. 406-26. On the sexual theories, see Vienna Psychoanalytic Society, *Minutes*, eds. Herman Nunberg and Ernst Federn, trans. M. Nunberg (New York, 1975), vol. 2, pp. 39-40, 200-02; Wilhelm Stekel, "The Sexual Root of Kleptomania," *Journal of the American Institute of Criminal Law and Criminology* 2 (July 1911), pp. 239-46.

59. See, e.g., Maurice P. Fryefield, *Girl Gangs* (New York, 1952), ch. 4; "Kleptomania," *Encyclopedia of Aberrations*, ed. Edward Podolsky (New York, 1953), p. 285; David Abrahamsen, *The Psychology of Crime* (New York, 1960), pp. 128-29; M. Aggernaes, "A Study of Kleptomania with Illustrative Cases," *Acta Psychiatrica et Neurologica Scandinavica* 36 (1961), pp. 1-46; C. Franchini and A.M. Ferutta, "Aspetti medico-legali et clinici di un caso di cleptomania," *Lavoro neuropsichiatrico* 34 (1964), pp. 547-56.

60. August Wimmer, "De la kleptomanie du point de vue médico-légal," *Annales médico-psychologiques* 11ᵉ sér., 1 (1921), pp. 211-33; Mary Chadwick, "A Case of Kleptomania in a Girl of Ten Years," *International Journal of Psycho-Analysis* 6 (1925), pp. 300-12; Franz Alexander and Hugo Staub, *The Criminal, the Judge, and the Public* (1929), trans. Gregory Zilboorg (New York, 1931), pp. 90ff.; Max Friedemann, "Cleptomania: The Analytic and Forensic Aspects," *Psychoanalytic Review* 17 (1930), pp. 452-70.

61. William W. Gull, "Summary of Oxford address," *Lancet*, August 8, 1868, pp. 171-76; E.C. Lasègue, "On Hysterical Anorexia," *Medical Times and Gazette* (1873), pp. 265-66, 367-69, trans. from the *Archives générales de médecine*, April 1873; *idem*, "Anorexia Nervosa," *Transactions of the Clinical Society of London* 7 (1874), pp. 22-26; Breuer and Freud, *Studies on Hysteria*, cases of Anna O. and Frau Emma von N.; Pierre Janet, *Les obsessions et la psychasthénie* (Paris, 1903), vol. 2, pp. 368-70. On the historical diagnosis of anorexia nervosa, see Petr Skrabanek, "Notes Toward the History of Anorexia Nervosa," *Janus* 70 (1983), pp. 109-28; John A. Sours, *Starving to Death in a Sea of Objects* (New York, 1980) ch. 3; Joan Jacobs Brumberg, " 'Fasting Girls': Reflections on Writing the History of Anorexia Nervosa," in *History and Research in Child Development*, eds. Alice B. Smuts and John W. Hagen (Chicago, 1986), pp. 93-104. Edward Shorter, "The First Great Increase in Anorexia Nervosa," *Journal of Social History* 21 (1987), pp. 69-96, puts the change in the 1870s but I am still skeptical.

62. Lasègue, "On Hysterical Anorexia," p. 367, cautions that the anorexic's fasting does not resemble the refusal of food in melancholia; H.H. Donkin, "Hysteria," in *A Dictionary of Psychological Medi-*

cine, ed. Daniel H. Tuke (London, 1892), vol. 1, p. 626, and cf., vol. 1, p. 94; "Anorexia Hysterica," Sigmund Freud, *The Complete Letters…to Wilhelm Fliess, 1887-1904*, trans. and ed. Jeffrey M. Masson (Cambridge, Mass., 1985), p. 99; Janet, *Les Obsessions*, vol. 2, pp. 368-70.

63. See John A. Ryle, "Anorexia Nervosa," *Lancet* 2 (1936), pp. 893-99, for a review of deaths.

64. Mara Selvini Palazzoli, *Self-Starvation* (1963), trans. Arnold Pomerans (New York, 1978), pp. 4-8; John M. Berkman, "Functional Anorexia and Functional Vomiting Relative to Anorexia Nervosa," *Medical Clinics of North America* 23.4 (1939), pp. 901-12, for Mayo Clinic cases; R.S. Allison and R. Picton Davies, "The Treatment of Functional Anorexia," *Lancet* 1 (1931), pp. 902-07, survey of cases; Ryle, "Anorexia Nervosa," fifty-one cases; Craig Johnson et al., "Anorexia Nervosa and Obesity: An Overview," in *Progress in Pediatric Psychology*, eds. W.J. Burns and J.V. Lavigne (Orlando, 1984), pp. 163-200, esp. p. 166, on number of cases. On family dynamics, Lincoln Rahman et al., "Anorexia Nervosa with Psychiatric Observations," *Psychosomatic Medicine* 1 (1939), pp. 335-65; John V. Waller et al., "Anorexia Nervosa and Psychosomatic Entity," *Psychosomatic Medicine* 2.1 (1940), pp. 3-16; Jules H. Masserman, "An Analysis of a Neurotic Character with Psychodynamisms of Vomiting and Anorexia Nervosa," *Psychoanalytic Quarterly* 10 (1941), pp. 211-42; Hilde Bruch, *The Golden Cage*: The Enigma of Anorexia Nervosa (New York, 1978). Contrast Brumberg, *Fasting Girls*, ch. 8.

65. Rush, *Medical Inquiries and Observations*, vol. 1, p. 102; Wharton, *Mental Unsoundness*, pp. 155-57, and linking this also to the first recorded theft in history, Eve's taking of the apple; "Kleptomania," *Chamber's Journal* 57 (1880), pp. 637-38.

66. William Hammond, "A Problem for Sociologists," *North American Review* 135 (1882), pp. 422-32; Motet, "French Retrospect," p. 627, on Lasègue's case; Chadwick, "A Case of Kleptomania," pp. 300, 305; and see also Alexander and Staub, *The Criminal, The Judge, and the Public*, pp. 90ff.

67. Esther Menaker, "A Contribution to the Study of the Neurotic Stealing Symptom," *American Journal of Orthopsychiatry* 9 (1939), pp. 368-78; and see also Sandor Lorand, "Compulsive Stealing: Contribution to the Psychopathology of Kleptomania," *Journal of Criminal Psychopathology* 1 (1940), pp. 247-53.

68. Peter J. Dally and Joan Gomez, *Anorexia Nervosa* (London, 1979), pp. 65-66; A.H. Crisp, "The Psychopathology of Anorexia Nervosa," in *Eating and Its Disorders*, eds. A.J. Stunkard and Eliot Stellar (New York, 1984), p. 211.

69. Milton Rosenbaum, "The Role of the Term Schizophrenia in the Decline of Diagnoses of Multiple Personality," *Archives of General Psychiatry* 37 (1980), pp. 1383-85, though I have corrected his numbers on multiple-personality cases, for which see also Greaves, "Multiple Personality"; Taylor and Martin, "Multiple Personality"; Myron Boor and Philip M. Coons, "A Comprehensive Bibli-

ography of Literature Pertaining to Multiple Personality," *Psychological Reports* 53 (1983), pp. 295-310. See also, Corbett H. Thigpen and Hervey M. Cleckley, "On the Incidence of Multiple Personality Disorder," *International Journal of Clinical and Experimental Hypnosis* 32 (1984), pp. 63-66; and on the incidence of schizophrenia in hospitals, "Schizophrenia: Diabetics' Insulin Shock Relieves Insane," *Newsweek* 9 (January 23, 1937), p. 38; Danielle F. Turns, "Epidémiologie des schizophrénies," *Annales médico-psychologiques* 138 (1980), pp. 637-46.

70. J. Hoenig, "The Concept of Schizophrenia," *British Journal of Psychiatry* 142 (1983), p. 551, quoting Bleuler's *Dementia Praecox oder Gruppe des Schizophrenien* (Leipzig, 1911), p. 239, trans. Joseph Zinkin as *Dementia Praecox, or the Group of Schizophrenias* (New York, 1950) (hereafter Bleuler/Zinkin *Dementia Praecox*); American Psychiatric Association, *Diagnostic and Statistical Manual of Mental Disorders*, 3d ed. (Washington, D.C., 1981), p. 181.

71. R.D. Chandrasena, "Phenomenology and Nosology of Schizophrenia: Historical Review," *Psychiatric Journal of the University of Ottawa* 8.2 (June 1983), pp. 17-24; Anthony Clare, *Psychiatry in Dissent* (London, 1976), pp. 116-19; P. van Meerbeeck, "D'où nous viennent la démence précoce et la schizophrénie?" *Acta Psychiatrica Belgica* 82.3 (1982), pp. 243-76; World Health Organization, *Report of the International Pilot Study of Schizophrenia* (Geneva, 1973), vol. 1, pp. 14-15; Bleuler/Zinkin, *Dementia Praecox*, p. 8; Ellenberger, *Discovery of the Unconscious*, pp. 286-88.

72. In addition to Bleuler and WHO, see on symptomatology, Sue A. Shapiro, *Contemporary Theories of Schizophrenia* (New York, 1981).

73. Bleuler/Zinkin, *Dementia Praecox*, pp. 59, 127; Carl Gustav Jung, *Psychology of Dementia Praecox* (1906), trans. A.A. Brill (New York, 1936), p. 91; *idem*, "On the Psychogenesis of Schizophrenia" (1939), in *The Basic Writings of C.G. Jung*, ed. Violet Staub de Laszlo (New York, 1959), pp. 382-86.

74. Jung, "On the Psychogenesis of Schizophrenia," pp. 388-91, 395; Sigmund Freud, "On Narcissism" (1914) and "The Unconscious" (1915), trans. James Strachey et al., *Standard Edition*, vol. 15, pp. 74, 197.

75. Jung, "On the Psychogenesis of Schizophrenia," p. 396.

76. Bleuler/Zinkin, *Dementia Praecox*, pp. 32, 37, 55-56.

77. *Ibid.*, pp. 62n. and 307-08. Americans in particular conflated schizophrenia and multiple personality; see S.P. Fullinwider, *Technicians of the Finite: The Rise and Decline of the Schizophrenic in American Thought, 1840-1960* (Westport and London, 1982), pp. 39-51, 106-07, passim.

78. Bleuler/Zinkin, *Dementia Praecox*, pp. 161-62; Adolf Meyer, "The Dynamic Interpretation of Dementia Praecox," *American Journal of Psychology* 21 (1910), pp. 385-403; Schwartz, *Never Satisfied*, p. 152. For later reports of an assumed connection between schizophrenia and anorexia, see A.A. Brill,

"Comment," *Journal of Nervous and Mental Disease* 89 (1939), p. 74; Rahman, "Anorexia Nervosa," pp. 336-37, 343, 346, 354-55, 364; J.M.C. Holden and U.P. Holden, "Weight Changes with Schizophrenic Psychosis and Psychotropic Drug Therapy," in *The Psychology of Obesity*, ed. Norman Kiell (Springfield, Ill., 1973), pp. 379-91. Manfred Bleuler, son of Eugen, found that pyknic or round bodies were rare among schizophrenics, who themselves tend to overestimate their body size. See Chandrasena, "Phenomenology and Nosology of Schizophrenia," p. 18; Seymour Fisher and Sidney E. Cleveland, "Personality, Body Perception, and Body Image Boundary," in *The Body Percept*, eds. Seymour Wapner and Heinz Werner (New York, 1965), p. 63.

79. Franz Baumeyer, "The Schreber Case," *International Journal of Psychoanalysis* 37 (1956), pp. 61-74; Sigmund Freud, "Psychoanalytic Notes upon an Autobiographical Account of a Case of Paranoia (Dementia Paranoides)" (1911), in *Three Case Histories*, ed. Philip Rieff (New York, 1963), pp. 103-86 (or vol. 12, *Standard Edition*).

80. Baumeyer, "The Schreber Case," pp. 65-67; William G. Niederland, *The Schreber Case* (New York, 1974), a book popularized by Morton Schatzman, *Soul Murder* (New York, 1974), whose quotation from Schreber's *Memoirs* (p. 133) occurs on p. 59. For less famous cases of schizophrenic delusions of abstinence and horrors of food, see Bleuler/Zinkin, *Dementia Praecox*, pp. 117, 144; Clifford W. Beers, *A Mind that Found Itself* (1907), 5th ed. (New York, 1921), p. 39; Mark Vonnegut, *Eden Express* (New York, 1975), p. 109; and see Palazzoli, *Self-Starvation*, p.29, contrasting anorexic and schizophrenic approaches to food.

81. Fullinwider, *Technicians of the Finite*, pp. 131-45; Harry Stack Sullivan, *Schizophrenia as a Human Process*, ed. Helen S. Perry (New York, 1962), p. 136.

82. Freud, "Psychoanalytic Notes" (1911), pp. 171-73.

83. Jules Cotard, "Du délire des négations," *Archives internationales de neurologie* 4 (1882), pp. 152-282, further elaborated in his *Etudes sur les maladies cérébrales et mentales* (Paris, 1891), pp. 314-44; Henri Ey, "Délire des négations," *Etudes psychiatriques* (Paris, 1948-54), vol. 2, pp. 428-52, quoting J. Séglas, *Le Délire des négations* (Paris, 1897), pp. 14-15, on p. 429 (author's transl.); Dario de Martis, "Réflections [*sic*] sur les délires de négation et de fin du monde," *L'Evolution psychiatrique* 30.1 (1965), pp. 111-21; M. Bourgeois, "Jules Cotard et son syndrome cent ans après," *Annales médico-psychologiques* 138 (1980), pp. 1165-80.

84. Elmer E. Southard, *Shell-Shock and Other Psychiatric Problems* (Boston, 1919), pp. 200-21; Peter Barham, *Schizophrenia and Human Value* (Oxford, 1984), pp. 42-43; Albrecht Wetzel, "Der Weltuntergangserlebnis in der Schizophrenie," *Zeitschrift für die gesamte Neurologie und Psychiatrie* 78 (1922), pp. 403-28, quotation trans. in Karl Jaspers, *General Psychopathology* (1913), 7th ed., trans. J. Hoenig

and Marion W. Hamilton (Chicago, 1963), p. 295; Alfred Storch, *The Primitive Archaic Forms of Inner Experiences and Thought in Schizophrenia* (1922), trans. Clara Willard (New York, 1924), p. 4; Anton Boisen, *The Exploration of the Inner World: A Study of Mental Disorder and Religious Experience* (1936), (New York, 1962), pp. 33, 34, 43; William J. Spring, "Observations on World Destruction Fantasies," *Psychoanalytic Quarterly* 8 (1939), pp. 48-56, and cf. Milton S. Gurvitz, "World Destruction Fantasies in Early Schizophrenia: A Rorschach Study," *Journal of the Hillside Hospital* 1 (1952), pp. 7-20.

85. Eric Partridge, *A Dictionary of Slang and Unconventional English*, ed. Paul Beale, 8th ed. (London, 1984), p. 1018; *Oxford English Dictionary*, Supplement, vol. 3, p. 1526; Theo C. Manschreck and Michelle Petri, "The Atypical Psychoses," *Culture, Medicine and Psychiatry* 2 (1978), pp. 238-41; Robert E.L. Faris, "Cultural Isolation and the Schizophrenic Personality," *American Journal of Sociology* 40 (1934), pp. 155-64. On schizophrenia itself as metaphor, see Thomas Szasz, *Schizophrenia: The Sacred Symbol of Psychiatry* (New York, 1976).

86. Leslie C. Barber, "The Age of Schizophrenia," *Harper's Magazine* 176 (December 1937), pp. 71, 72, 75. Popular attention to schizophrenia was primed by news of insulin-shock therapy brought to the United States by Dr. Manfred Sakel, a Viennese psychiatrist, in late 1936.

87. See *Language and Thought in Schizophrenia*, ed. Jacob Kasanin (Berkeley, 1944), papers delivered in 1939. Cf. *Language and Cognition in Schizophrenia*, ed. Steven Schwartz (Hillsdale, N.J., 1978).

88. Jaspers, *General Psychopathology*, p. 733, notes the changes in delusions according to historical epoch, so that electronic technology plays a greater part in modern schizophrenic paranoia.

89. See Louis A. Sass, "Introspection, Schizophrenia, and the Fragmentation of Self," *Representations* 19 (Summer 1987), pp. 1-34, discussing Victor Tausk, "On the Origin of the 'Influencing Machine' in Schizophrenia," *Psychoanalytic Quarterly* 2 (1933), pp. 519-56.

90. Eugene Minkowski, *Lived Time* (1968), trans. Nancy Metzel (Evanston, Ill., 1970), p. 275.

91. Franz G. Alexander and Sheldon T. Selesnick, *The History of Psychiatry* (New York, 1966), pp. 352-53; Fullinwider, *Technicians of the Finite*, pp. 158ff.; Szasz, *Schizophrenia*, pp. 90-92.

92. Partridge, *Dictionary of Slang*, p. 1527; Alexander and Selesnick, *History of Psychiatry*, p. 353.

93. Alfred Storch and Caspar Kulenkampff, "Zum Verständnis der Weltuntergangs bei den Schizophrenien," *Der Nervenarzt* 21 (1950), p. 104; Bruno Callieri and Aldo Semerari, "Alcuni aspetti metodoligici e critici dell'esperienza schizofrenica di fine del mondo," *Rassegna di studi psichiatrici* 43 (1954), pp. 55-77, esp. p. 59; de Martis, "Réflections," p. 114.

94. See, for example, David Cooper, *Psychiatry and Anti-Psychiatry* (London, 1967), quotation on p. 45; Martti Siirala, "Psychotherapy of Schizophrenia as a Basic Human Experience, as a Ferment for a Metamorphosis in the Conception of Knowledge and the Image of Man," in *Psychotherapy of*

Schizophrenia, eds. David Rubinstein and Yrjo O. Alanen (Amsterdam, 1972), pp. 130-55; Brian W. Grant, *Schizophrenia: A Source of Social Insight* (Philadelphia, 1975). For a critique of this hero-making, see Sass, "Introspection, Schizophrenia, and the Fragmentation of Self," but Sass too succumbs to the temptation to identify schizophrenic experience with the modern condition.

95. Gilles Deleuze and Félix Guattari, *Capitalism and Schizophrenia*, 2 vols., trans. Hurley, Seem, Lane (vol. 1); Massumi (vol. 2) (Minneapolis: University of Minnesota, 1983-1987), push furthest the argument that schizophrenia, with its invariable contradictions between desire and repression, is the paradigmatic disease of capitalism, with its inevitable contradictions. I am not making such an argument here, in great measure because the history of the body deserves a richer, less schematic approach. For other cultural-historical analyses of schizophrenia, see esp. Jane M. Murphy, "Psychiatric Labeling in Cross-Cultural Perspective," *Science* 191 (1976), pp. 1019-28; E. Fuller Torrey, *Schizophrenia and Civilization* (New York, 1980); Horacio Fabrega, Jr., "Culture and Psychiatric Illness," in *Cultural Conceptions of Mental Health and Therapy*, eds. Anthony J. Marsella and Geoffrey M. White (Dordrecht, 1982), pp. 39-68; Barham, *Schizophrenia and Human Value*.

96. Allan Pinkerton, *Criminal Reminiscences and Detective Sketches* (New York, 1879), ch. 20, quotations on pp. 282, 290; Ian Ousby, *Bloodhounds of Heaven: The Detective in English Fiction from Godwin to Doyle* (Cambridge, Mass., 1976), esp. ch. 2.

97. *Oxford English Dictionary*, vol. 9, p. 591; Eric Partridge, *A Dictionary of the Underworld*, new ed. (New York, 1961), p. 611; "Detectives' Methods," *New York Times*, May 22, 1869, p. 2, col. 1; Arthur B. Reeve, "The Kleptomaniac," *Hearst's International Magazine* 22 (December 1912), pp. 54-67.

98. *Dry Goods Economist*, November 23, 1901, p. 21, cited by Abelson, " 'When Ladies Go A-Thieving,' " p. 195, and see her ch. 4. On lie detectors, see Schwartz, *Never Satisfied*, pp. 149-53.

99. Abelson, " 'When Ladies Go A-Thieving,' " pp. 285 n.44; "Mrs. Martin's Dual Role," *New York Times*, April 11, 1895, p. 8, col. 1; Allan Pinkerton, *Thirty Years a Detective* (New York, 1886), pp. 236-55.

100. A certain Dr. Scott, commenting on Albert Wilson, "A Case of Double Consciousness," *Journal of Mental Science* 49 (1903), p. 655; Frank Gelett Burgess, *The White Cat* (Indianapolis, 1907); " 'The Case of Becky,' " *New York Times* (October 2, 1912, p. 13, col. 3; and cf. the reexamination of nineteenth-century cases by Philip M. Coons, "The Differential Diagnosis of Multiple Personality," *Psychiatric Clinics of North America* 7 (1984), pp. 51-67.

101. Francis G. Benedict, *A Study of Prolonged Fasting* (Washington, D.C., 1915); Irving J. Eales, *Healthology* (London, 1913), pp. 211-20.

102. Schwartz, *Never Satisfied*, pp. 86-88, 131-34, 164-68.

103. *Ibid.*, pp. 153-59.

104. *Ibid.*, pp. 135-40, 192-93.

105. *Ibid.*, pp. 213-21, 321.

106. *Ibid.*, pp. 135-38.

107. I hasten to note that the culture of slimming has itself been shaped by men and women, together and apart, and that it is a women's culture only insofar as in this century it has appealed primarily to women. I do not, however, subscribe to the theory that the culture of slimming has been imposed lock, stock and sliced carrots by men upon women. Such a theory makes women out to be, if not shapeless, then spineless.

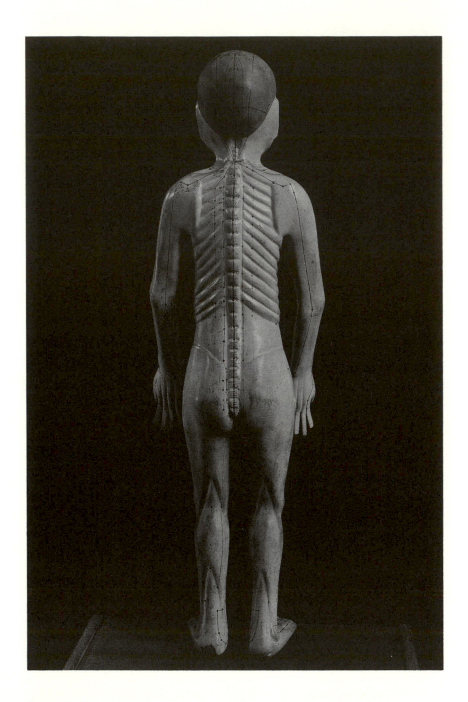

Japanese ivory statuette showing the meridians and acupuncture points.

The Ghost in the Machine:

Religious Healing and Representations

of the Body in Japan

Mary Picone

In 1774 a Japanese practitioner of Chinese medicine carried out the first dissection of a corpse ever to be performed in the archipelago. He compared the inside of the body thus disclosed with the diagrams in the medical books of the Red Hairs (the Dutch).[1] To his great astonishment, the ancient Chinese classics appeared to be far less accurate than the new science of the barbarians (Keene 1969). About one hundred years later, Western biomedicine was officially adopted by the Meiji government, and earlier systems of therapy were condemned. As is often the case, however, changes in Japanese representations of the body were far from simple or unequivocal. Today Chinese medicine (*kanpō*) has been partially reinstated, and thirty-seven percent of Japanese biomedical physicians sometimes prescribe herbal or acupuncture treatments (Lock 1980:VII).

The two main religious and philosophical systems that gave rise to Japanese ideas of the body are Mahayana Buddhism and Chinese medicine. Historically, the first served, in spite of great conceptual differences, as a vehicle for the transmission of the second. But as Paul Unschuld (1987:1025) reminds us, Chinese medicine is itself a combination of several systems of therapy, and the "systematic correspondences" described below were a theory propagated by a learned minority. Other important trends (shamanism, exorcism of demons and so on) were more widespread, particularly among the people, at least until very recently. This is still the case in expatriate Chinese communities today (Goschecheck 1987). Contemporary practice in the People's Republic and in Japan also emphasizes particular elements within a complex system, and several types of syncretism with biomedicine have been attempted. Although I shall briefly summarize several principles of Chinese and Buddhist medicine — at the risk of misleading the nonspecialist and disappointing the

467

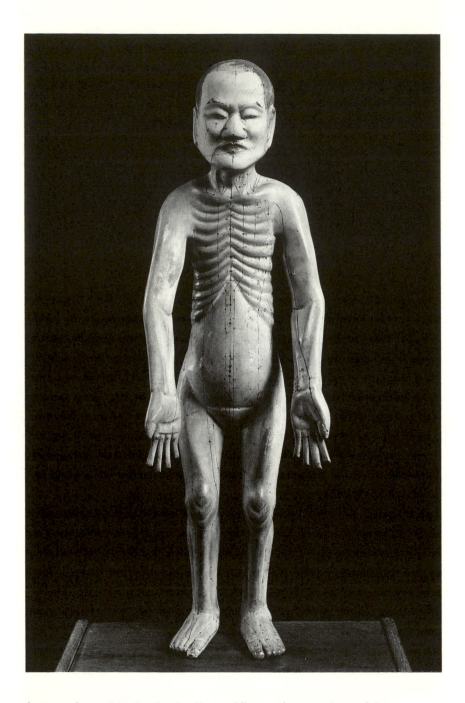

Japanese ivory statuette showing the meridians and acupuncture points.

zone

Orientalist — I am primarily interested in the representations of the body deriving from those systems as expressed by laymen or popular healers. The latter, along with the leaders of Japan's many new sects, seem to me the best source of "authentically Japanese" representations.[2]

The nonspecialist Western reader will have heard that East Asian concepts of the body are "holistic" and should be compared favorably with the "objectification" of the body resulting from Western biomedical ideals and practice. In this line of argument, mind/body dualism is said to be characteristic of Western thought and to lead to purely physiological views of illness. Yet this is not precisely accurate, for until fairly recently this opposition was expressed as that between soul and body or, in Descartes's formula, between ghost and machine.

A mechanistic view seems to be appropriate only to ideas current in this century. For most of us today, the "soul" has become more and more precisely localized in the functions of the brain, and mind itself, since Turing's famous test, which has been objectified to the point where it has been artificially recreated outside the body by means of a computer.[3] Nevertheless, the success of psychoanalysis and religious healing (from Western movements like Christian Science or Scientology to imported therapies like yoga) shows that the psychological and moral determination of bodily states is a human need, and medical pluralism a necessity.

It is often suggested that in East Asia the body is not treated separately from the mind and that health is a spiritual as well as an organic condition. But if we look more closely at Chinese medicine, or at *kanpō*, its Japanese form, holism assumes a different meaning: all aspects or parts of a person's body are thought to be interrelated, and the body in turn is itself only one element in a universe of interrelated entities. Illness, in this ordering of things, does not exist as a separate nameable condition deriving from a cause, nor can it be diagnosed objectively in different individuals and cured in each one in approximately the same way. A *kanpō* physician will recognize a unique pattern of imbalance (*fuchō*) in each patient, although the general components of his or her body and their relationships reflect those of the universe (Porkert 1974). It is somewhat misleading to state that, in Chinese medicine, the body is "made of" certain substances, because basic terms like yin and yang, or *ch'i*, are closer to what in various translations are rendered respectively as complementary classes of "attributes" or "emblems" (cf. Schipper 1982:37-39), or as "energy," "fluid," "finest matter vapours" (Lock 1980:35; Unschuld 1987: 102-05), rather than organic or chemical constituents of matter. So each part of the body, for instance, can be defined as yin or yang. Medical and other classifications are relational; for example, the upper part of the body is more yang than the lower, but the intestine is one of the yang organs, whereas the lungs are yin. All things, moreover, have yin and yang aspects: time, for instance, is divided into night and day, animals and mankind into females and males and so on (Schipper 1982:37-39). Medicine intervenes to restore harmony between yin and yang components at whatever level an imbalance has occurred. Preventive therapy is the ideal, and whenever possible the most natural methods are preferred. Thus, yin or yang foods are often prescribed, since food is also considered medicinal. Herbal medicines, massage and acupuncture are used in more evident cases of imbalance. "Cold" medicines, for example, are prescribed when the patient manifests an excess of yang (a fever, for example). Biomedical discoveries are sometimes integrated into this pattern: vitamin B is considered yang and penicillin yin (Kaptchuk 1983:26).

By the early Han Dynasty the Chinese had developed another system of classification in addition to yin/yang: the five-phases theory. In this system all phenomena are thought to belong to five "phases," represented by wood, fire, earth, metal and water. It has been suggested that these phases are elements because of their similarity to the constituents of matter identified by the Greeks. In fact, as Porkert (1974: 43-45) explains, the five phases instead "typify qualities of energy" and serve as a very extensive system of correspondences. Moreover, they are not limited to physiological processes or to bodily parts but extend to directions, seasons, colors, weather, planets, styles of government, emotions, tastes, animals and so on. (A shortened list under "wood" gives: east, spring, blue-green, wind, the planet Jupiter, liberal government, sour, chicken, anger, acid, etc., which are related to liver, gallbladder, eyes, tendons, etc. See Lock 1980:32 and Needham 1954:2.262-63.) Obviously, medical applications were primarily limited to correspondences in the body, but practitioners who wished to have a full grasp of the scientific thought of their time could turn to related disciplines like geomancy or astrology. Present-day *kanpō* physicians, according to Margaret Lock (1980:203-07), dismiss much of this background as irrelevant. It seems that only popular religious healers, who possess disparate fragments of the knowledge contained in these vast interrelated categories, still attempt to

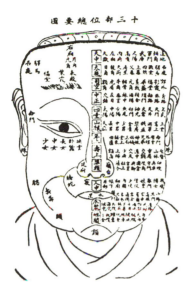
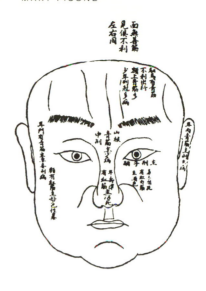

Physiognomic chart from a modern
almanac published in Hong Kong.
Private Collection.

cure clients by relating spatial orientation (geomancy) or time and the heavenly bodies (astrology) to physical states. Some religious specialists claim that an examination of the lineaments of a client's face (physiognomy, *ninsō*) or of his or her bodily
proportions is a clue to inner physical states or reveals the patient's future. Body
divination of this sort is rarely used for diagnosis even though the system of correspondences described above is a part of the theoretical background of most schools.
During a consultation the face is scrutinized minutely and, as in a drawing, divided
into sections, each of which gives indications concerning the client's future pros-
perity, health or lifespan. Moreover, to the expert, the body's shape reveals a person's
character and abilities, which, in Confucian morality, were thought to determine
his future social status.

As exemplified by ancient techniques like physiognomy, Chinese and Sino-
Japanese holism, then, is a correspondence between the physical universe, the social
order and the microcosm of the human body. According to Joseph Needham (1975:
491), Chinese scientific thought "saw related phenomena as synchronous or emblem-
atically paired, and emphasized lineal relations of cause and effect far less than Western thought." The Western ideal of holism, in contrast, implies a search for the causes
of bodily states in external factors, rather than a "contextualization" of the body in
the Chinese sense.[4] Instead there is an attempt to focus on and at the same time to

zone

relativize the individuality of the patient. First, a sufferer's state of mind and representations of his or her illness are identified and discussed with the therapist. Then, with his or her aid, these data are related to a particular familial and social environment. Even in long-established relationships between *kanpō* practitioners and patients, there is virtually no discussion of psychological problems. Yet both patients and healers fully admit that difficult interpersonal relations or work conditions are an important cause of illness. Nevertheless, patients will not discuss these problems spontaneously and, even when chemically diagnosed as depressed or neurasthenic, will describe their condition in purely somatic terms (Lock 1980:221; Kleinman 1976). Thus, the functioning of the body is explained in relation to the physical world, however extensively conceived. Of course, many European or American patients will not expect help from a general practitioner and may consult an analyst and a physiotherapist, describing different aspects of their problems to each one. Japanese patients today have an even greater choice of specialized practitioners, including *kanpō* physicians (although the latter's prescriptions are often more time-consuming and expensive). Psychologists and psychoanalysts, however, are very rare. The spread of religious healers is most probably a consequence of this lack.[5] Yet, like *kanpō* practitioners, the religious healers often do not accept patients they consider insane (*kichigai*). In premodern Chinese medicine there is no recognition of the nervous system. However, a strong imbalance of one of the substances composing the human body — *shen* — is thought to result in madness. *Shen* has a far broader connotation than human body or even mind and vitality (as implied by modern medical usage); it also means "deity" or "spirit." To complicate matters further, there are other characters for the several types of soul. In Japan, even orthodox institutionalized medicine, notwithstanding the efforts of literati influenced by Confucianism, was connected with religious healing until the nineteenth century (Briot 1979).

Present-day religious therapies also use other basic concepts and methods derived from Chinese medicine. One of the most widespread of these, employed by both traditional and "scientistic" healers, is *ki* (Chinese *ch'i*). Sometimes "scientistic" healers also use the English loan word *enerugi* as an equivalent. Several *kanpō* physicians associate *ki* with electromagnetic and thermal energy (Lock 1980:204), and a number of innovative acupuncturists measure electrical changes on the skin as an aid to diagnosis. Any single translation, however, is bound to be somewhat misleading.

Porkert (1974:168) has suggested that there are thirty-two different types or meanings of *ch'i* in the Chinese medical classics. Over time, from the most ancient texts to the elaborations of the medicine of systematic correspondences, a number of gradually more inclusive and intangible meanings have been attributed to this term: from "wind" or environmental "influence" to "finest component of matter." *Ch'i* is thought to flow through the earth (e.g., the veins of *ch'i* tapped by geomancers) and in the body. The body includes an "original" or innate *ch'i*, and various sorts of *ch'i* produced by the organism (e.g., protective *ch'i*) (Unschuld 1985:72-78) that are derived from the assimilation of food and from the air we breathe. Stagnant *ch'i*, considered the cause of imbalance and hence of ill health, is stimulated by acupuncture. *Ch'i* flows to the various parts of the body through pathways known as meridians (*keiraku*), which do not have an objective existence recognized by biomedicine. Hundreds of points (*tsubo*) can be stimulated by needles or other means in order to affect the substances flowing through the meridians. An imbalance in an organ may manifest itself in the corresponding meridian. Kaptchuk (1983:78) cites a simple example of this process: "an excess of fire in the liver may follow the meridian and generate redness in the eyes." As we shall see, in Buddhist medicine these correspondences were often used to express different meanings, and a symptom may be the occasion for a causal investigation. In five-phases theory the liver (said to be a yin organ) corresponds to the emotion of anger. So in the moral aetiology Buddhism imposed on the earlier therapeutic system, crimes dictated by anger, such as murder, are believed to cause eye diseases (Demiéville 1929:235).

Most of the modern *kanpō* physicians studied by Lock (1980:203-07) continue to believe in the usefulness of *ki* as a therapeutic concept, but there is no real consensus regarding its nature and functions. In contemporary usage, *ki*, at least vestigially, is still considered to determine health. Thus, illness is *byōki*, "sick *ki*," and the common term for madness is *kichigai*, "different *ki*," or "*ki* that has changed." This alteration is often thought to be irreversible (Picone, forthcoming), and the insane are often thought to be beyond medical aid (Lock 1980:85). Among the healers I met, this was always the case, although their definitions of *kichigai* could not have been made according to psychiatric criteria and may have been formulated a posteriori to justify their refusal to accept certain clients. If investigations of this sort are made in a different perspective – that of the psychiatrist – the conclusions appear to be radically different. Eighty percent of the mental patients in a public general hospital in the Tohoku area (Nishimura 1987:61) had consulted shamans before starting their medical treatment and had subsequently continued these consultations.

Ki has been integrated into religious therapy in a particular form by a modern healer called Osumi Itsuko.[6] Like all the healers I have met, she is extremely eclectic and refers to virtually all the traditional aetiologies known to the Japanese. Osumi, however, tends to theorize less than most and seems to have evolved her methods by a sort of physical gnosis. As she puts it, "A therapist's body can create an almost endless variety of techniques depending on the patient's condition" (Osumi 1987:59). Other healers tend to limit themselves to diagnosis and to leave the client to "cure" himself by performing rituals to appease the angry spiritual entity causing the condition.

Osumi's therapy is essentially a transfer of the *seiki* (literally "living *ki*") concentrated in her own body to that of the patient. She does not claim to have discovered her therapeutic principles but only, like most healers, to continue an ancient tradition that was in danger of being lost.[7] In concrete terms, her techniques include various types of massage. Sometimes she presses *tsubo* points with her fingernails or blows hot air on affected parts. Before studying anatomy at the age of fifty in order to earn her certificate as a masseuse, she had already spent years learning all about her body by introspection, in the most literal sense:

> I learned how the body works in relation to its surroundings. How certain movements relate to certain organs and nerves and the relationship between all of these things; if some part of my body felt painful it called on some other part of my body to heal it.... I could concentrate on my body until it became as though it were made of glass and I could see all its functioning. At these times I became totally unaware of any of the sounds of the world around me.... Sitting taught me the reasons why I had become ill. How everything that had happened to me in my past and present had causes and how whatever I was doing now affected the future. (*Ibid.*:53-54)

Studies of Buddhist techniques of meditation as well as shamanic experiences (Eliade 1951) describe self-induced hallucinations of a similar type, in which the organs and the skeleton are visualized one by one. Osumi's introspection also corresponds to a moral anatomy recreated by seeking the karmic causes of illness in the past and projected toward the future determination of bodily states. Osumi is not a *kanpō* practitioner, but, drawing on Chinese elements that have entered popular medical knowledge, she refers to acupuncture points in an idiosyncratic way, stating:

> The whole body is a *tsubo*, [and] the points are constantly changing position [according to] the presence of excessive tension or the lack of natural tension in nerves, muscles and veins.... In some patients the change may be only a hair's breadth. Nothing is fixed in the human body. The body is alive. (Osumi 1987:60)

As in *kanpō*, the patient's *ki* is said to stagnate or to be in excess in certain areas, and must be redirected. A patient describes this experience as follows:

> Okajima [Osumi's main disciple] began working on my spine, neck and shoulders, at first lightly, then with increasing pressure. Now and then he slapped my back all over and gently hit my spine.... Behind me, periodically, someone would hit the wall with what sounded like the palm of the hand and scream or shout.... They were breathing very deeply...and hissing, screaming, clapping their hands, working themselves up to a state of excited concentrated tension.... They did this in order to attract *seiki*, and while they did so it was essential to maintain a condition of emptiness or no-thought. Suddenly the sounds and movements reached a...climax and I felt a hand or hands on top of my head. The room seemed filled by a mighty wind. Then "Hudtss!" I hear Osumi give a loud *kiai* and felt her hand gently rocking my head back and forth. (*Ibid.*:116)

The *ki* transmitted in this manner is said to be in Osumi, but it must be localized and tapped in the surrounding space. In *kanpō*, meridians lie within the body and, as Osumi explains, enlarging the concept of flow of energy by geomantic metaphor, the path of *seiki* is related to an invisible topography that transcends the individual:

> I can see where a *seiki* line is on the drawing of a plan of a home. And I can feel what the energy is like underneath the land in an area and whether it is stable or unstable. (*Ibid.*:60)

Contemporary *kanpō* physicians concentrate on the flow of *ki* in a patient's body and completely disregard the premodern vision of the world, of which medicine was only one aspect, encompassing geomancy and astronomy. In the early Chinese ordering of things there were three "powers" — heaven, earth and man. Now this grandiose synthesis is only transmitted by popular healers, and in simplified form. Another example of the orientation of buildings influencing the human body is the relatively recent (in Japan) practice of "tomb-divination" (*bōsōgaku*). Self-appointed specialists, who say they derive their "science" from Chinese geomancy, claim to be able to trace the causes of a family's illnesses and other problems to the location, shape and construction materials of the family grave. If the ancestors are uncomfortable, they write, "there will be ninety-nine percent rate of cancer" among surviving kin (Sugiura 1980:233-38).

Two of the religious therapists I consulted also claimed to be able to "read" places by means of their effects on clients' bodies (cf. Matsuno 1981). A transcription of most consultations, however, shows that several explanatory principles are juxtaposed, and the client's choice of the determinants of his own state is left open. The shamaness Mrs. Mori (a *burakumin*[8] woman in her sixties) had been consulted by a young couple. The husband complained of inexplicable pains in his legs:

"Where do you live?" the healer asked. "Near Takadanobaba [a section of Tokyo]. Very near it? To the east? Once there was a well over there. You are bothered by the Well-God [*ijinsama*]. You live on the second floor, don't you? You are sick, you quarrel a lot. Ah, it's the man who starts it! It is really stupid to have rows with such a pretty little wife." The telephone rang. After a short conversation the shamaness immediately resumed her trance where she left off. "I can see six of your husband's past lives. He suffers, *kaminarisama* [thunder god]! Wake up early in the morning, pray and make offerings to the Well-God.... Who bought the house, the man or the woman? Make an offering on the feast day of the earth god. My last piece of advice is: leave that house, it is badly oriented, too narrow!"

It is very likely that the shamaness was trying to discover whether the husband's physical problem was the main reason for the consultation. After all, in many cases, clients have already been treated unsuccessfully by Western medicine, and their afflictions are therefore probably more susceptible to alternative therapies and explanations. Mrs. Mori suspected marital problems, perhaps because both husband and wife were present. The reactions she observed in the wife persuaded her that she was right. Different levels of interpretation surfaced in her "trance" revelations. First, external factors were evoked, that is, an inauspicious orientation combined with the ancient idea of "disturbing the Well-God." Then, deftly shifting from the spatial to the economic and psychological aspects of the house (which in Japanese also means "lineage"), she made an attempt to confirm her suspicions and to discover what we might consider the real causes of the husband's illness and of the family conflict. She hinted at lack of living space and at money problems, but it seemed to me that Mrs. Mori did not favor any particular level or consider one explanation to contradict another.

The young couple were occasional clients who visited a shamaness for a single consultation. Others, however, are converted by the experience of being healed and become disciples of the healer or adherents of a sect for the rest of their lives. In this case, the reformation of the body and the mind undertaken at the time of the first consultation continues until death. Disciples and adherents are said to derive a variety of physical benefits from the correct practice of different disciplines. For some sects (for example, Tenrikyō), the ideal is longevity, a lifespan of 115 years, which all should attain if a proper mental attitude is achieved. Others, like Shinreikyō and Joreikyō (1985:6), transcend this claim by promising an ideal death in which the body does not stiffen into rigor mortis, decays slowly or not at all and exhales fragrance. In these and other new religions, it is also possible to improve the living form. Prayers and discipline will "make the skull round," as a branch leader told me proudly, guiding my fingers to his head. "Before," he confessed, "my cranial flatness showed that I had not fully developed my psychic potential." Still other modifications of physical form, relating especially to sensory perception, are limited to a few exceptional individuals, those with *chōnōryoku* (extraordinary psychic power): clairvoyance, levitation, fire walking, control of the autonomous nervous system and so on (Oishi 1982). A return to premodern ideas of the superhuman powers to be acquired by asceticism (traces of Tantric and Daoist influences) is combined with parapsychology, considered by many healers to be a new science.

But for most people the religious therapies are a means of solving problems or healing illnesses which they cannot deal with by "this-worldly" means. Biomedicine is still incapable of treating a large number of diseases or conditions causing chronic pain. Besides serious illnesses, these include common, relatively minor psychosomatic complaints like headaches, back pain and asthma. The new sects, which enjoin a change of attitude or of heart (*kokoro*), are often particularly effective in mitigating those conditions (Hardacre 1982). It is mainly in Mahayana Buddhist doctrines, which predate the new religions in Japan by more than a millennium, that the most radical and, potentially, the most coherent form of mental change is considered equivalent to a cure.

In the teachings of Shakyamuni, the historical Buddha, illness (along with birth, old age and death) is but one aspect of suffering, that is, of the condition of those who have not attained enlightenment. Illness, which makes us aware of suffering, should be borne with patience. Yet the doctrines promise healing, if only in a particular sense. The "four sacred truths" described in the earliest texts (suffering must be known, the origin of suffering must be destroyed, its destruction must be realized [nirvana], the path to nirvana must be followed) correspond to the ways in which we in the West deal with illness — diagnosis, aetiology, healing and therapeutics (Demiéville 1929:225); and it is difficult to distinguish purely religious therapy (good works, performance of rituals, contrition, meditation) from magical therapy (recitation of formulas, or *daharani*, etc.) and medical therapy proper (diet, the administration of drugs, etc.). Sutra recitations, for example, have practical efficacy because illness can be the consequence of acts performed in a previous existence. The medical aspects of Buddhism were emphasized in Japan at the time of the first importation of the doctrines, and in one of the first temples erected, Buddha was venerated as King of medicine (Yakushi). Several schools among the Mahayana sects adopted by the Japanese elaborated different interpretations of the nature of matter. All schools agreed, however, that beings are in constant flux. Thus, no bodily state, whether painful or pleasurable, is thought to last. A clear exposition of these ideas can be found in the chapter on disease in the Vimalakirti sutra, translated into Chinese and known in Japan as *Yuimagyō*. The saintly layman Vimalakirti is ill and explains the nature of illness to his fellow citizens: "Friends, the body is made of four great elements, it is transient and fragile, untrustworthy and weak, it is without constancy, short lived, the site of suffering, filled with disease and subject to changes" (Lamotte 1962:132). These elements are the solid element or earth (e.g., bones, organs), the humid element or water (e.g., blood), the hot element or fire (e.g., the process of digestion), the mobile element or wind (sometimes rendered as *ki*). As in Chinese medicine, an imbalance of these elements leads to illness, and at death the body dissolves into them once again. Later texts refer to the elements as "the four poisonous snakes," in part because of a disbelief in the reality of matter but also because, over time, these elements came to be considered pathogens. Thus, there are exactly 404 diseases, 101 for each element (Demiéville 1929:224-65). The nonexistence of matter in Absolute Truth — as opposed to the relativity of sense perception taught by schools such as Mahadhmika — is already present in the Vimalakirti sutra. Detachment from the body, as Vimalakirti explains through metaphors, will result in deliverance from suffering: "It is by not taking anything that one must take food, one must see color like a person blind at birth, hear sounds as one hears as echo" (Lamotte 1962:152).

At the highest level of understanding (Absolute Truth), illness, which is an affliction of an illusory entity, is itself illusory, and healing consists in the realization of this illusion. The chapter on illness in this sutra, from which the above passages were taken, was read as part of the healing rites at the sickbeds of members of the aristocracy and in an annual ritual continued until the nineteenth century (Demiéville 1929: 260). In modern Japan, the Heart sutra (Hannya Shingyō), which a large number of laymen can recite from memory, fulfills a similar purpose. Its message is the same: the nonexistence (emptiness) of the body, and of death, mind and consciousness. Yet, though the sutra is supposed to recall doctrinal truths, very few of those who recite it or hear it understand its meaning. In diametrical opposition to its original intent, the efficacy of the ritual today is thought by many to depend on the correct renderings of each sound: ancient Japanese renderings of the original Sanskrit. Instead of inducing the realization of the meaninglessness of phenomena, the Hannya Shingyō has itself become meaningless to its lay hearers.

Aetiology in Buddhist medicine also admits natural causes. A classification compiled by the monk Chiki at the end of the sixth century lists six causes of illness: unbalanced diet, cold, two sorts of demonic influence, incorrect practice of meditation and karmic retribution for acts committed in a previous existence or in this life. Chiki suggests several types of remedies: drugs, spells to repel demons and, for illnesses derived from karma, "internal treatments" (contrition, confession and so on. See Demiéville 1929:257). In modern Japan, a patient can still use all of these remedies but would obtain them from different sources: *kanpō* physicians prescribe medicine, but only Buddhist priests of certain sects can provide charms or perform exorcisms.

It would be misleading to suggest that most Japanese today are consistently interested in Buddhism. Elements of these doctrines, which I have simplified enormously here, are often rediscovered only in time of need, for example, by entering a new religion in which they have been syncretized, or at the suggestion of an individual healer. Once a patient has recovered his or her health or a family member has been cured, religious ideas are often set aside. Yet, if the illness recurs, such neglect often becomes an aetiological factor.

Karma, however, remains the most important cause of illness in popular therapy. This form of moral causation is more extensive in practice than orthodox formulations. Originally, karmic ties (*innen*) meant that all a being's intentions, words or acts in this existence determine those in a future life or lives, and that all experiences (thoughts, words or deeds) in this life are a consequence of those in earlier existences. Moreover, and this aspect has been stressed in Japanese Buddhist texts since the *Nihonryōiki*,[9] karma is also thought to act in the short range (*genpō*): that is, one's conduct can influence events or bodily states in one's present life. In the most literal sense karmic causation implies that the mind constantly creates the body. And the positive karma allowing for rebirth in human form (which is only one of six possible forms of reincarnation) also determines what sort of body one is born with: thus a meager share of merit will result in the misery of congenital deformity, in subsequent chronic illness or, in being born female or, at best, into a very poor family. *Genpō* allows the mitigation of these initial misfortunes, and, in popular belief, karmic determination is further modified by related forms of causation. The ritual severing of karmic ties (for example, by sutra recitations) is said to be accomplished in various ways: the merit is transferred directly to the sufferer or his family members, or is transferred to other beings, such as neglected ancestors, whose own negative karma influences that of the afflicted person in various ways. In the teaching of some sects, sutra readings are thought to exorcise the malevolent entities (such as fox spirits) who possess the sick person. In this case, the possession is a "disease," a discrete bodily state in itself and not a cause of illness.

A healer's diagnosis generally follows one of several patterns. For example, a sterile woman whose condition has been confirmed by biomedicine, will be told by a healer that her problem is due to the spirits of former family members or of beings connected with her family in the past who have not been worshiped at the domestic altar (*butsudan*). In villages where a person's kin and family connections (for example, the father of a husband's divorced wife, a family servant dismissed because of illness) are part of local collective memory, the spirits considered responsible for illness or other problems, who are sometimes said to have been wronged by kin or by the individual himself in a previous existence, will be found in the comparatively recent past.

Even in this case, however, retribution is often indirect. A new wife, for example, who is not "connected by blood" to her husband's family, will be afflicted in place of a direct descendant of the supposed wrongdoer. In cities, where the client is most frequently a stranger to the therapist and verification by means of local memory is impossible, the chain of causation is followed back to the remote past. Since few Japanese, even if they preserve ancestral mortuary tablets, remember more than three or four generations of their ancestors (cf. Smith 1974:113), proof of these spirit connections can only be found by supernatural means. However, the more remote an event, the greater the psychic ability attributed to the person discovering the connection. An example of this deductive process was the diagnosis I was given by Mrs. Hirose, a self-proclaimed medium, whom I consulted in Tokyo:

> "I see a grave of cherry trees in bloom near Yoshino," she chanted, recalling my past lives. "You were the wife of a samurai who was killed in battle two centuries ago, and you entered a Buddhist convent there."

In a few phrases she had explained several apparently puzzling facts to her satisfaction. Why was I, a European, in Japan, and how could I speak her language? (Many Japanese consider this an impossible feat for a foreigner.) Why was I, a woman of marriageable age, alone and not at home with my children? Her reading of my past implied two forms of karmic retribution. First, my samurai husband had been killed and could not attain Buddhahood because of his violent death. The problems that had supposedly brought me to consult the medium were not due to retribution for my own actions in a past life, but the result of a transfer of karma from my "husband" to myself. In Japan, intentionality is not always individualized. A person may suffer if he or she is too passionate, too attached to this world or if he or she involuntarily inspires excessive passion in others. Second, although I could not know of the existence of this spirit, I had neglected a ritual duty. Now that the "real" cause of my affliction was known, the correct rites could be performed (*kuyō*, memorial services), and my problems would be solved.[10] The social class of the unaffiliated spirit was another important element in her diagnosis. Like many other clients, I was said to be married to or descended from samurai. Japanese attitudes toward the old warrior class are ambivalent. On the one hand, I was told that samurai are thought to have very bad karma because they killed and "oppressed the common people," but on the other hand, aristocratic connections give prestige.

The interpretation of many of the consultations I have recorded presupposes an understanding of complex problems in Japanese religion.[11] It is important to stress, however, that therapists or the leaders of new sects generally impose conformity to a "traditional" ethos (cf. Hardacre 1984). A young wife, for example, is said to be responsible for her husband's illness or business problems because she disobeyed her mother-in-law in this life or in a previous existence; or a woman who has had an abortion — other means of contraception being difficult to obtain — is considered the cause of all family troubles.[12]

At present, there is a tendency to widen the sphere of an individual's responsibility beyond traditional social or ethical transgressions and, as in the case of abortion, to induce guilt for actions that had not previously been widely condemned by village communities (Picone 1986). Patterns of this sort are also common to *kanpō* practitioners and biomedical physicians (cf. Lock 1980:210), and mothers are widely thought to be totally responsible for their children's health.

Even the most recently discovered diseases, or those caused by contemporary events like nuclear fallout, are logically integrated into karmic aetiology. Thus, a physician, author of a recent popular book on AIDS (Ōshima 1986), tells his readers that immune deficiencies are not the result of bad karma or of spirit retribution. Today, Western influences have been integrated into popular representations of the body. A healer who specialized in extracting "insects" (*mushi*), said to be the cause of disease, from the fingers of his clients told me that after years of pondering, he had realized that the *mushi* were a visible form of cholesterol. Scientific discoveries and techniques are used to prove the efficacy of traditional concepts and methods. For a number of Japanese today, the "ghost in the machine" does not refer to a duality between soul and body. The concepts underlying karmic causation and *kanpō*, as we have seen, give a very different sense to these entities and effectively dissolve the individual, both as a body and as the source of intention. For some Japanese, however, the ghost is literally placed in a machine or at least identified by means of a mechanical apparatus. There are several variations on this leitmotiv. Plots in popular literature, notably in science fiction or in the omnipresent comic books read by children and adults, often feature a mad scientist who removes a person's brain and replaces it with a computer terminal. The body continues to live and to carry out its appointed tasks, but consciousness is manipulated by an external agency. In real-life experiments, which might seem to some as implausible as these fictions, healers use machines to trace or prove the existence of "spirit influence" (such as by measuring auras or photographing the ghosts of ancestors: Picone 1986). Other healers combine the use of machines with acupuncture and intensify the stimulation of the pressure points by electricity. This is a common practice in China and in a number of Japanese *kanpō* clinics. Religious therapists, however, carry syncretism much further by attempting to harmonize *kanpō* techniques with popular aetiologies of Buddhist derivation. The acupuncturist Motoyama Hiroshi, a scientific healer claiming to have doctorates in psychology and philosophy, is a representative example of this trend. Motoyama has invented a "*chakra* machine" to measure the eponymous centers of energy described by *yogin*. The role of *chakras* in determining the functioning of the body is explained as follows:

> In each human being one *chakra* is naturally more active than the others, but it is not the same for each person; according to the nature and the karma of the individual the *chakra* that will be most early awakened by the practice of yoga also depends on the karma and the nature of each being. (Motoyama 1985:82)

Mechanical means are also used to project the influence of a healer's body and mind onto distant clients, who can be cured by telephone and receive prerecorded therapeutic prayers in answer. A number of temples have also adopted similar practices enabling devotees to send in requests for rituals by telefax. Although I believe clients' personal contacts with healers do facilitate the therapeutic process and may be compared favorably with the objectivity of biomedicine, the magical power attributed to words seems to remain important for the Japanese. If the realization of the nonexistence of the self is one of the main aims of Buddhism, prerecorded sutra readings ordered by remote control may be a useful theological device.

In conclusion, I would like to suggest that the most interesting and distinctive element in Japanese popular representations of the body is the persistence of karmic aetiology — the conviction that the mind has potentially absolute power over the body. The Japanese have the choice between several forms of healing: biomedicine, in which the malfunctioning of the body is attributed to morally neutral factors like microbial infection, and to which certain individuals are susceptible by chance; or

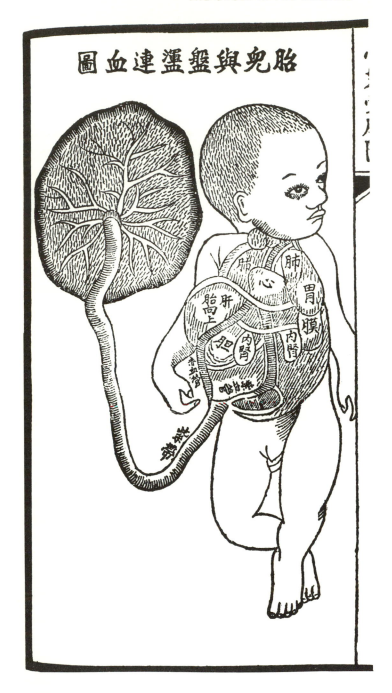

Drawing of a fetus from a modern almanac published
in Hong Kong. Private Collection.

kanpō, in which causation is not stressed and the search for a pathogen is rarely attempted. Yet, the many Japanese who join new sects or consult religious therapists are searching for a moral cause for bodily ills or death, and they choose to reassume responsibility or even guilt for illnesses or "accidents" that in other systems are value-free. The formation of the body, and its subsequent preservation and nurture, is seen in religious therapy as a constantly renewed result of an individual intention instead of a random product of undirected entropy. A person's intentions, moreover, are thought to influence the bodies of others; thus, a mother would be understood as continuously recreating or preserving her children beyond the nine months of gestation.

Before we judge these representations as entirely alien, let us turn to a recent historical and literary study, *Illness as Metaphor*. By comparing Western representations of tuberculosis and cancer over the past century, Susan Sontag (1977:59-61) has shown that a similar process is at work, at least selectively, in European and American society. Cancer, in particular, the most common of the fatal diseases that have an unknown cause, is often "explained" as resulting from a "cancer-prone character." Psychologists, physicians, even the sufferers themselves are ready to categorize victims of this disease condescendingly as "low gear persons, seldom prey to outbursts of emotion," with "a memory of emotional deprivation in childhood," who are "empty of feeling and devoid of self." A comparative perspective is extraordinarily interesting here because, for the Japanese, precisely the opposite personality is thought to be prone to disease. Excessive emotion and its expression, as we have seen, creates bad karma in traditional aetiologies, and, for modern social theorists or the psychotherapists of autochthonous schools, it is the direct cause of social problems or mental illness (for example, *shinkeishitsu*) as defined by Japanese psychotherapists.

Sontag argues further that secular interpretations of certain illnesses, which in our society are expressed in psychological terms, imply that "people get sick because they (unconsciously) want to and they can cure themselves by a mobilization of the will." Even if these theories give patients some hope, though it is often illusory, it is at the price of instituting an unjustified personal responsibility for becoming well. Japanese medical doctors, as a rule, do not make these inferences, which are instead the point of departure of religious therapies. Few societies, in short, whatever the aetiologies invoked, refrain from blaming a sufferer for his or her afflictions. The healer Georges Ōsawa (1967:142), best known as the inventor of the macrobiotic diet, carries this process to its logical conclusion when, misunderstanding the irony in Butler's *Erewhon* (a utopia in which the sick are punished as criminals), he praises the novel as an example of the social ordering of the body.

My research on Japanese medicine has been funded by grants from the Fyssen Foundation, the Collège de France and the Singer-Polignac Foundation.

NOTES

1. From 1600 on, the Tokugawa shōgunate forbade foreigners to set foot on Japanese soil, with the exception of a few Dutch traders. Western science, therefore, entered the archipelago through Dutch books or translations into that language.

2. It is very difficult to estimate correctly the number of healers active in Japan and, even more so, the number of their clients. My main sources are two dozen of the medico-religious manuals I have collected and Ōishi's compendium, which lists nineteen practitioners. The sales figures of these manuals, as revealed by their publishers, average 30,000 copies, but not all buyers may have consulted the authors. It is also possible that satisfied customers have directed friends or family members to the healers they patronize. When engaged in field work in various parts of Japan, I found that some areas had one or two healers of various types in each large village, whereas inhabitants of other regions went to the nearest city. Urban areas seem to have higher percentages of healers. This is certainly the case in Tokyo, and M. Lock (1980:99) discovered that forty-three out of fifty Kyoto families had visited shrines or temples in search of healing and that forty-five out of fifty had performed rituals at home (see also Nishimura's figures cited in the text). People joining the new religions (approximately thirty percent of the population, according to the Ministry of Education, Tokyo: Shūkyō Nenkan, 1982) are also often motivated by physical or mental illness.

3. Recent cognitivist approaches to the mind/body problem are collected in D.R. Hofstadter and D.C. Dennett's source book, *The Mind's I* (New York: Basic Books, 1981).

4. For Unschuld (1987:1025) the "individualistic" concept of medicine described above is only one of the main Chinese trends. There is also a "pragmatic" approach (such as pharmaceutics and massage) and an "ontological" approach, in which illness is "a being in itself" or represented by a "definable pathological event." Specialized practitioners or influential theorists propagated these approaches in Japan, where a number of indigenous schools were founded.

486

5. There are about 8,000 psychiatrists in Japan, the same number as those practicing in France, but Japan has twice the population of France. Moreover, most psychiatrists are less specialized than their Western counterparts. I have not been able to find statistics on the number of psychoanalysts of the various schools, but all sources confirm that they are a fraction of those in Western countries (*Impact Médecin*, Jan. 23, 1988).

6. Osumi has written an account of her life and methods of therapy in collaboration with her disciple Malcolm Ritchie, who has also described his experiences in the book (Osami and Ritchie, 1987). Ritchie is not an anthropologist and writes from the perspective of a patient. His reactions are, of course, particular to him but they do not seem to differ profoundly from those of educated Japanese clients, even if his life and problems are unique.

7. To my knowledge, religious healers today do not commonly use the term *seiki*. Osumi mentions receiving *seiki* from an aunt, but does not connect this form of therapy with a particular tradition. However, *shen ch'i*, "living *ch'i*," is a concept of Daoist origin, associated among other things with the early hours of the day or with specific breathing techniques.

8. The *burakumin*, who until fairly recently practised "polluting" trades, are a separate ethnic group in Japan. They have been compared to the untouchables in India, even though the discrimination to which they are subjected is now much less severe.

9. The *Nihonryōiki* is a collection of exemplary stories, compiled at the end of the eighth century, showing the workings of karma (see also the later *Konjaku monogatari shū*, B. Frank 1968). Contemporary manuals (see n. 2) follow a similar pattern.

10. It might seem that I am deducing too much from the medium's explanation, but I am only placing it in the context of the many other roughly similar narratives that I have heard (cf. Picone 1984).

11. For reasons of space, I have not described the representations of the body and of illness which derive from the complex of autochthonous beliefs known as *Shinto*. Their main concern is with states of purity and impurity (see Onuki-Tierney 1984).

12. Up to the Meiji period, infant mortality was very high, and infanticide was practiced in certain regions, but successive governments imposed legislative control on natality, forbidding abortion. After the war, abortion was legalized and, in the past fifteen years, a cult of the spirits of aborted fetuses (*mizukorei*) has become widespread (see Picone 1984). It is thought that the would-be mothers who created these malevolent spirits are responsible for all the illnesses and other misfortunes that afflict family members.

BIBLIOGRAPHY

Briot, Alain, "La médecine dans le Japon ancien," in *Encyclopédie permanente Japon*, 1979.

Demiéville, Paul, *"Byō" Hobogirin*. Paris: Maison Franco-Japonaise, 1929.

Eliade, Mircea, *Le chamanisme et les techniques archaïques de l'extase*. Paris: Payot, 1951.

Frank, Bernard, trans. *Histoires qui sont maintenant du passé* (*Konjaku monogatari shu*). Paris: Gallimard, 1968.

Goschecheck, Norbert, "Médiums chinois," *Nouvelle revue de psychanalyse* (1987).

Hardacre, Helen, "The Transformation of Healing in the Japanese New Religions," *Journal of the History of Religions* 20 (1982).

———, *Lay Buddhism in Contemporary Japan: Reiyukai Kyōdan*. Princeton: Princeton University Press, 1984.

Huard, P., and M. Wong, *La médecine des Chinois*. Paris: Hachette, 1967.

Jorei Igakujutsu Fukyu Kai, *Goshin-i igaku kakumei* (The Divine Mind Revolution in Medicine). Society for the Diffusion of Pure Spirit Medical Techniques, 1985.

Kaptchuk, Ted, *Chinese Medicine*. London: Rider, 1983.

Keene, Donald, *The Japanese Discovery of Europe, 1720-1830*. Stanford: Stanford University Press, 1969.

Kleinman, Arthur, "Depression, Somatization and the 'New-Cross-Cultural Psychiatry,' " *Social Science and Medicine* 10 (1976).

Lamotte, Etienne, trans. *L'enseignement de Vimilakirti*. Louvain: Bibliothèque du Muséon, 1962.

Lock, Margaret, *East Asian Medicine in Urban Japan*. Berkeley: University of California Press, 1980.

Matsuno, Seizan, *Kasō no kikkyō* (Good and Bad Luck in House Divination). Tokyo: Manbow Books, 1981.

Motoyama, Hiroshi, *Rinne tensei no himitsu* (The Secrets of Reincarnation). Tokyo: Shukyō Shinri Shuppan, 1981.

———, *Chakra no riron* (Theory of the *Chakras*). Tokyo: Shukyō Shinri Shuppan, 1985.

Needham, Joseph, *Science and Civilisation in China*, vol. 2. Cambridge: Cambridge University Press, 1954.

———, "Chinese thought," *Annals of Science* 32 (1975).

Namihira, Emiko, *Byōki to chiryō no bunka jinruigaku* (The Anthropology of Illness and Healing). Tokyo: Kaimeisha, 1984.

Nishimura, Kho, "Shamanism and Medical Cures," *Current Anthropology* 28.4 (1987).

Ōishi, Ryuichi, *Nihon no reinōryokusha* (Psychic Specialists). Tokyo: Nihon Bungeisha, 1982.

Onuki-Tierney, Emiko, *Illness and Culture in Contemporary Japan*. Cambridge: Cambridge University Press, 1984.

Ōsawa, Georges, *La philosophie orientale et la médecine*. Paris: Librairie Philosophique J. Vrin, 1967.

Ōshima, Kyoshi, *Sekaimatsu no yamai* (Illnesses of the End of the Century). Tokyo: Kōbunsha, 1986.

Osumi, I., and M. Ritchie, *The Shamanic Healer*. London: Century, 1987.

Picone, Mary, "Rites and Symbols of Death in Japan." Ph.D. dissertation, Oxford University, 1984.

———, "Buddhist Popular Manuals and the Contemporary Religions in Japan," in *Interpreting Japanese Society*. Edited by J. Hendry and J. Webber. *Journal of the Anthropological Society of Oxford, Occasional Papers* 5 (1986).

———, "La communication de la causalité: Etiologie et téléologie dans les thérapies religieuses," in *La Maladie au Japon*, edited by G. Siary. Paris: Privat (forthcoming).

Porkert, Manfred, *The Theoretical Foundations of Chinese Medicine*. Cambridge: MIT Press, 1974.

Schipper, Kristopher, *Le corps Taoïste*. Paris: Fayard, 1982.

Smith, Robert J., *Ancestor Worship in Contemporary Japan*. Stanford: Stanford University Press, 1974.

Sontag, Susan, *Illness as Metaphor*. New York: Penguin Books, 1977.

Sugiura, Kōshō, *Mizukorei kuyō* (Memorial Rites for Mizuko Spirits). Tokyo: Take Shōbō, 1980.

Unschuld, Paul, *Medicine in China: A History of Ideas*. Berkeley: University of California Press, 1985.

———, "Traditional Chinese Medicine: Some Historical and Epistemological Reflections," *Social Science and Medicine* 24.12 (1987).

Bodybuilders on the *ghāts*.

The End of the Body

Jonathan Parry

The Corpse and the Bodybuilder

Death and its transcendence are the hallmarks of the religious identity of the major north Indian pilgrimage city of Benares, which is sacred to Śiva — the Lord of the Cremation Ground and the Destroyer of the Universe. Many pious Hindus go there to die; thousands of corpses are carried there each year for cremation, and the ashes of thousands more are brought for immersion in the Ganges (Parry 1980, 1982a).

The funeral pyres burn day and night on Manikarnika *ghāṭ*, the city's main cremation ground — on average about sixty-two in any twenty-four-hour period. Midway through its combustion, the corpse's skull is violently broken open with a bamboo staff by the chief mourner; toward the end, a lump of the remaining carcass may be unceremoniously poled into the river "to feed the fishes" — sizzling fiercely as it hits the water and spurting a residue of blood that flecks the muddy brown current with translucent streaks of scarlet. More usually, however, the corpse is thoroughly reduced to ash, and the ash flushed into the river. Two or three Aghori ascetics are normally resident on the *ghāṭ*, and even a casual Western tourist may see one of them smearing his body with such ash, or pilfering the pyres of charcoal and fragments of wood on which to cook the food he eats out of the human skull which is his constant companion and alms bowl. Such practices, the tourist is liable to be told, represent an ascetic contemplation on the transience of all bodily existence (Parry 1982b).

What our tourist will probably find just as disconcerting, however, is the vibrant life that, seemingly impervious, goes on all about: boys flying kites, the pious performing their daily ablutions in the river, hawkers calling their wares and muscular men and youths devotedly perfecting their bodies in one of the two wrestling schools

491

(*akhāṛās*) that are located not a hundred paces away from the burning corpses. One is single-mindedly engaged in countless push-ups and sit-ups; another effortlessly swings a stout wooden club with a solid head of rounded stone the size of a football (*gadā*) from shoulder to shoulder – as though he were himself the god Hanuman limbering up to dispose of the demon army of Ravana. A third achieves yoga positions that seem to defy all physical possibility, while others – their daily regimen fulfilled – lounge in the shade of a tree, being massaged, preparing a concoction of the narcotic *bhāng* or parting their hair and curling their moustaches in front of a broken fragment of mirror.

It is this ostensibly paradoxical and incongruous juxtaposition of the corpse and the bodybuilder which is one of my most dominant visual memories of Benares, and in what follows I want to reflect on it. How can an almost narcissistic cultivation of the body apparently cohabit so cosily with a set of ascetic practices which unflinchingly contemplates its inevitable end, and with a set of mortuary practices devoted to its radical – even violent – destruction?

The Body and the Caste Order

At least since Mauss (1936) so engagingly insisted that the ways in which men walk, swim, sleep or copulate are to a significant degree culturally determined – illustrating his point with the claim that he could generally recognize a girl who had been raised in a convent by the fact that she will walk with her fists closed – attitudes to the body have been recognized as a central object of anthropological inquiry. Whether implicitly or explicitly, the two most ambitious of our current anthropological models of Indian social order firmly return us to this central concern.

As is well known, Dumont (1970) argues that the crucial morphological characteristics of the regime of castes – hierarchy, separation and the division of labor – all have an intellectual basis in the opposition between purity and pollution. Castes are held to be ranked according to the relative degree of purity inherent in their bodily constitutions; and this purity is constantly threatened by involvement with biological processes, and by contact with those of inferior substance. If they are to maintain their purity, the high castes require the services of others to remove the bodily pollution they inevitably incur in the normal course of life. Implicit in this scheme, then, is a supposition that the body is central to Hindu thinking about the social order — or, perhaps more accurately, that Hindu society is organized on a war footing *against* the body and its natural processes.

More explicitly, the body is also accorded a pivotal position in the ethnosociological model of the Chicago Indianists who drew their original inspiration from Schneider's (1968) cultural account of American kinship. This viewed the domain of kinship as being organized around a fundamental division between those related by "blood" or shared bodily substance, and those related only "in law" — by moral code alone. A blood relationship is a blood relationship — which is to say, immutable. Changes in code do not produce changes in substance. We inhabit a dualistic universe where natural substance is one thing and cultural code another. For Marriott and his Indianist colleagues, the contrast was striking for they had to do, they believed, with a world in which

> the assumption of the easy, proper separability of action from actor, of code from substance (similar to the assumption of the separability of law from nature, norm from behaviour, mind from body, spirit or energy from matter), that pervades both Western philosophy and Western common sense...is generally absent: code and substance... cannot have separate existences in this world of constituted things as conceived by most South Asians.... (Marriott 1976:110)

Conduct alters substance, and to a greater or lesser extent any transaction involves an exchange of bio-moral qualities and consequently transforms the substance-code of the parties to it (as is well illustrated by *dāna*, gifts offered to the priest, which embody the sins of the donor and which, as a result, are held almost inevitably to result in a quite literal corruption of the priest's body and his subsequent commitment to hell: Parry 1980, 1986, 1989). Two corollaries follow. The first is that body and soul are not radically dichotomized. Unlike — it is claimed — the Christian sacraments, ritual actions are directed at the whole person and not just at his "spiritual" aspect (Inden and Nicholas 1977:91).[1] Indeed, there is no such thing as a purely "spiritual" aspect — e.g., a soul without a body — for "even the utterly subtle [*suksma*] vehicle of the self [*atma*] that escapes from the dead body is itself a body [*sarira*]" (Nicholas 1982:375). The second corollary is that Indian thought is not only "emphatically monistic and dynamic" but also "highly particularistic" (Marriott 1976:112). By contrast with the Western concept of the individual as an autonomous, indivisible, bounded unit with an immutable bio-genetic makeup, South

Asians represent the person as "divisible" and, as it were, constitutionally volatile "since circulations and combinations of particles of substance-code are continually occurring" (*ibid.*). Not only is "each actor and action unique," but the "unique essence" of each is *constantly* changing (cf. Daniel 1984:72).

Though there is much in this picture that I find persuasive and immediately recognizable, I suspect that it is also somewhat overdrawn. It is, no doubt, difficult for us to think ourselves into a world in which persons conceive of themselves as protean entities ready to be shaped anew by every chance encounter, or to imagine a social world in which my intimate associate of today may be a *substantially* different person tomorrow. But certainly such a conception does not altogether accord with the quite robust and stable sense of self that many of my Indian friends seem to project. Nor, to put the problem slightly differently, is it altogether clear how this construct of the person as composed of highly fluid substance squares with Marriott's earlier writings on caste ranking, which were premised on the assumption of an equivalence between all members of the same caste such that each caste could be assigned to a single cell in the matrix of food transactions (e.g., Marriott 1968). How, one wonders, could such equivalence be sustained in a world in which *each* actor's substance–code is endlessly modified and transformed by the myriad exchanges in which he is *uniquely* involved? How, indeed, could anybody ever decide with whom, and on what terms, to interact?

Yet there is surely something in both of these – on the face of it mutually inconsistent – formulations that rings true to the ethnographer's experience. At least for certain purposes, castes *are* regarded as units of equivalence composed of people of the same general kind; and persons *are* seen as having a transformable bio-moral substance which is continually modified by the transactions in which they engage. How can this be? Unlike either Dumont or Marriott, I am prepared to entertain the possibility of a contradiction here, for I am not persuaded that Hindus – or others – really think quite so systematically as these authors imply. What I propose to argue, however, is that there is a sense in which these two strands in the ideology fit together, and that the protean representation of the person sustains and reinforces the static ideology of caste. We will return to this later.

A second source of discomfort with the ethnosociological model is that it replaces Dumont's radical contrast between *homo hierarchicus* and *homo aequalis* with an *even*

494

One section of the cremation ground at Manikarnika *ghāt*.

more radical contrast between the dualistic conceptual world we inhabit and the monistic conceptual world of South Asians: more radical because it makes no explicit place, even at a secondary or "encompassed" level, for any ideological recognition of the contrary value scheme. This contrast is partly premised on the assumption that the way in which white, middle-class Middle Americans of the second half of the twentieth century supposedly think about kinship may be taken as standing for Western thought in general. But while it is easy to appreciate that this is a tempting assumption if you come from Chicago, I am not sure that it is entirely safe. It is after all but a hundred years, and not so very many miles, that separate Schneider's *American Kinship* from Morgan's *Systems of Consanguinity*, in which Morgan suggested that a classificatory kinship terminology, and even such practices as wearing the breechcloth and sleeping naked at night, could be somatically stored and transmitted "in the streams of the blood" (Trautmann 1987:29). Nor am I sure that the rigorous monism held to characterize the Hindu worldview is quite so rigorous as these writers suggest. But again this argument is best left to the end.

The Body and Its Refinement

Though my main focus will be on "the end of the body" — a literal rendering of *dehānt*, meaning "death" — I need to begin at the beginning. In the beginning — according to the male Brahmans who were my main informants on the matters discussed here — was Brahma, which cannot be apprehended by the mind or described by speech, and which is without shape, name, color or any physical attribute (cf. Parry 1982a). The world was created out of this unitary primeval protoplasm by a process of progressive differentiation which was triggered by a disruption of the precarious equilibrium that exists within each material entity.

Differentiation implies degradation — movement away from the original ineffable wholeness of Brahma. The universe is steadily running down toward cosmic dissolution, and we now live in the basest and most degenerate of the four epochs of the world cycle. The human body is equally subject to this law of time. In the *Satya Yuga* — the Golden Age of original time — a man's vital breath (*prāna*) resided in his bones; he subsisted on air alone, enjoyed a lifespan of 100,000 years and reproduced asexually. In *Tretā* the vital breath was situated in his bone marrow, and he lived for 10,000 years; in *Dvārpara* it was in the blood, and life expectancy was reduced to a thousand years. But now in the *Kali Yuga* the vital breath resides in the grains we eat, we live to a maximum age of 125, and few are virtuous enough to attain even this modest target. The objective of much indigenous medical practice (cf. Egnor 1983) and of many of the rules and practices to which the ordinary householder subjects himself (cf. Daniel 1984), is to arrest this disequilibrating flow within his own body; or even to swim against the stream and refine it — the project of the ascetic being to get all the way back to the source and realize his identity with Brahma (Eliade 1969; Parry 1982b).

There are conventionally said to be 840,000 kinds of life forms (*yonis*) arranged in an elaborate hierarchy with crawling and slithering creatures at the bottom and men at the top. Every soul (*ātmā*) moves up this ladder (passing through each one of the 840,000 life forms) until it is incarnated in a human body. Some say that such a body is envied even by the gods, for only human beings are capable of pursuing the path of salvation — or "liberation" from the endless cycle of rebirths (*mokṣa, mukti*) — though few will actually attain this goal. While the most heinous sinners fall back to the bottom of the ladder and must begin their ascent all over again, ordinary people are expected to return as a human being in a station and with a fate appropriate to their karmic balance.

The body they assume begins to take shape when the father's semen is "caught" by the menstrual blood (*raj, māsik dharam*) of the mother. Such "bad blood" is then retained throughout the period of gestation to form the flesh of the embryo. The hard parts of the child's body, especially the bones, are the product of the father's semen; and — as is consistent with the predominantly patrilineal ideology of caste — this is considered the more significant and enduring contribution. Pure descent is expressed idiomatically as having "clean bones," on which an inferiority in the mother may produce a "blemish" (*khot, dāg*), though this does not disqualify her children from membership in their father's caste.

With the mixing of semen and menstrual blood, a *piṇḍa* is formed — a term that can denote any rounded mass, and which here signifies an embryo, but which most commonly refers to a riceball offered to the ancestors. The *piṇḍa* is matured — I am tempted to say "cooked" — in the woman's stomach by her "digestive fire" (*jaṭharāgni*). By the end of the first month the head has been formed; and by the end of the fifth month the body is complete. Up to this point it appears to be regarded as pure matter, as body without soul. The soul or "vital breath" (*prāṇa*) — my informants do not discriminate — which will now enter it has meanwhile been wandering in the atmosphere (*vāyumandal*) in search of a new "house," having left its previous one five months before. But it is only at this point that its quest can succeed. Entry is gained through the suture at the top of the skull.

The material body is now quickened by consciousness (*chetnā*), and spends its last five months in the womb in a state of acute mental and physical torment. While we tend to vaguely picture the fetus as luxuriously floating in the secure and balmy bliss of its own custom-built swimming pool, my informants see things differently. Bound in an excruciatingly constricting confinement, suspended in filth and pollution where every minute is as a year, it serves its time contemplating the sins of its previous life — the knowledge of which it loses at parturition. When I asked people why liberation from the cycle of rebirths should have any appeal, they would often explain that having attained it you no longer "have to bear the pain of the womb" (*garbha-kasht*).

At the end of the ten-lunar-month period of gestation, the baby negotiates a river of blood, mucus, excrement and other foul substances to emerge from this "hell" — headfirst. Its first act is to yell from the pangs of hunger. All human beings are born through the same vagina (*bhag*), all emerge from "the place of urination," and consequently all are equally Shudras by birth. Brahmans are not born, but made by the life-cycle rituals through which they pass. Only the product of Brahman seed has the capacity for such transformation, however. Only one whose father and father's father were Brahmans can learn to pronounce Sanskrit with the inflection necessary to please the gods and ancestors.

A person's disposition, however, is almost as likely to be explained by what his mother happened to eat before, or see immediately after, conception as it is by genetic inheritance. "What did your mother eat before she gave birth to you?" one might reprovingly ask. The raja's son behaves like a washerman, the washerman's son like a raja, because these were the first persons their mother happened to see after intercourse. Even more important is the time at which conception takes place and the parents' thoughts at that moment. "If you think, 'Oh god, this is good,' then the child will be like that. He will say, 'While you two were enjoying yourselves I just happened to drop by in the middle.' " Intercourse for a man is a dangerous squandering of vital fluids; its only proper justification is the conception of a dutiful son, and this requires scrupulous scheduling. Conceived at the wrong moment a Brahman child will be like a demon (*rākshas*); while even an obliviously improvident Shudra who by chance ejaculates at the right moment will sire a paragon. Intercourse should therefore be regulated by the almanac: certain days (e.g., *pūranmāsī*, fast days), certain parts of the night (the first) and certain times in a woman's monthly cycle (the first seven nights after the onset of menstruation) should be avoided; odd nights for a girl, even for a boy; the most dutiful son is conceived on the fourteenth night and so on.[2] Family planning is a precise and ancient art, and was a subject on which I received much unsolicited advice.

Not only is the Brahman a Shudra by birth and his flesh formed out of the "bad blood" of a woman's menses, but this blood is the precipitate of sin. "A woman's pollution," my informants say, "is the pollution of murder [*hatyā*]." What is invoked here is the well-known story of the god Indra's brahmanicide, the sin of which could only be eliminated by dividing it up and passing it on to others. From women — who received a quarter share — it emerges in the form of menstrual blood. In passing I note that each year the *men* perform the ritual of *Shrāvanī*, at which they purify themselves of the sins of the previous twelve months, and that my informants endlessly emphasize the expiation of sins connected with the improper circulation of gifts. The female equivalent is *Rishī Panchamī*, but, in their case, the preeminent stress is explicitly on sins concerned with the improper circulation of food during their periods. This is emphasized by the story (*kathā*) to which they must listen on that day, and by the fact that girls only start to participate when they are about to attain puberty, while women who have reached menopause terminate their observance with a closing ceremony (*uddyāpan*). The main point that I want to stress here, however, is that the body is not only made out of a polluting substance but that the substance is the product of the most horrific of crimes. The claim that any equivalent of the notion of original sin is entirely absent from the Hindu universe is therefore exaggerated.

Sudhir Kakar (1982:236-37) draws a sharp contrast between "the legacy of rejection of the body in the West [which] persists in the unconscious fantasy of the body as a dirt-producing factory," and the positive attitude to the body which is characteristic of Indian culture. It is certainly the case that my informants are unashamedly explicit about their bodily functions, and are in general unconcerned to eliminate waste products under the conditions of Fort Knox–like security on which we are apt to insist – as if truly depositing gold. Benarasi Brahmans are, however, nonetheless liable to represent the body as a sack of impurities. A consistent pre-occupation is with the idea of food lying rotting in the stomach, and with the need to evacuate it speedily (Parry 1985). The body, moreover, is both the cause and agent of lust (*kāma*), anger (*krodha*), greed (*lobh*) and infatuation (*moh*). Each of the five material elements of which it is composed is associated with one of the senses (earth with smell, water with taste, wind with touch, fire with sight and sky with sound) – any of which is sufficient for damnation, inexorably lethal in combination.

The body's equilibrium is subject to constant disturbance, the strategy of Ayur-veda – "the science of long life" – being to correct such imbalances between, above all, its three humors: phlegm (*kaph*), bile (*pitta*) and wind (*vāyu*). But good health depends on a thermal as well as humoral equilibrium. Colloquially, one whose "blood has frozen," or who has "become cold," is a corpse; while a woman whose periods are long-delayed, or whose sexual desire is deprived of all outlet, becomes danger-ously overheated and is likely to go mad. Again medicines – the thermal properties of which depend on climate and season – are prescribed to restore the balance.

In order to preserve the body, a stringent self-discipline involving a strict regimen is required. We have already encountered the dangers of sex, but what is even more elaborated are the dangers of irregular dietary practices – the wrong kind of food, prepared and served by the wrong person, eaten at the wrong time or place. Both one's bodily substance and one's moral disposition are created out of food. "As the grains you eat, so will be the mind." "By eating the grains of expiation [gifted in *dāna*] the intellect [*buddhi*] is corrupted." Not only sex and food, but sleeping – even breathing – seem to represent a health hazard. Great stress is placed on the impor-tance of early rising. Sleep (*Nidra Devi*) is the younger sister of Death (*Mrityu*). The scriptures are said to recommend a maximum of three hours per night, and it is widely held that the less you sleep the longer you live. The explanation for this is that each of us is granted a finite number of breaths, and that in the waking state one breathes predominantly through one nostril only, which uses up a smaller proportion of one's quota. By the control of breath (*prāṇāyāma*), the adept yogi can enormously prolong his life – by up to a thousand years according to one confident estimate.

At bottom, sin and pollution are the really life-threatening conditions. Bodily pollution is not only the ultimate cause of much organic illness, but it lays one open to ghostly affliction and cuts one off from the protection of the gods. "Man dies from sin" which manifests itself in emaciation, illness and decay. It grows out of our bodies in the hair (which must therefore be shaved off at the time of important rituals of expiation). Consistent with this, the term *dosha* refers both to "a moral fault" and to "a disorder of the humors of the body." The state of the body thus provides an index of the state of the soul. Put in Marriott's terms, we might alternatively say that in this monistic worldview it is hard to distinguish the two. No less than in many of the cultures of Highland New Guinea, the external body reveals the inner self; the moral condition of the person shows on the skin (O'Hanlon 1983; Strathern 1979). The sinner rots with leprosy; the face of the priest who accepts the gifts of the pilgrims and mourners rapidly loses its "luster."

So far I have stressed the dark side of the picture; but to leave it at that would be to distort a far more complex and paradoxical reality.[3] We have already seen that even the gods may envy the human body, and it is well known that Hindu thought regularly postulates a homology between body and cosmos. The *Garuda Purana* (part 15) — the authority of which my informants repeatedly invoke — describes the "transcendental body" (*pārmarthik sharīra*) as containing the fourteen "worlds" (*bhuvan*), the seven island-continents (*duīp*), the nine planets (*grah*), all the gods and so on. The temple, too, is constructed on the plan of a human body (Beck 1976), and the sacred space of Benares itself is represented as a body — with the Manikarnika cremation ground as its navel (Parry 1982a). It is by an absolute mastery of his own body that the ascetic attains salvation. "The wealth of the yogi is his body. There is nothing more precious than this."

I will have more to say about the ascetic later; but what this already suggests is the body's capacity for transformation, refinement and even perfection. Many myths suggest that even gender is not immutable. The preeminent agent of all such transformation is heat, which matures the embryo, which distills semen out of blood, and which can be generated by an ascetic austerity which burns up the sins of the body. Both symbolically and in terms of the etymology of the word itself (*tapasyā*), such austerities are a process of heating the body; and it was through the heat of the austerities he performed at Manikarnika *ghāṭ* that Vishnu created the world at the beginning of time. Austerities, like pilgrimage, undertaken by the householder are not only directed at saving the soul but also at saving the body. There are sixteen *samskaras* — or "sacraments" — through which the twice-born should theoretically pass between conception and death, of which the most important are birth, initiation, marriage and death itself. The term *samskara* has the connotation of "purification," "refinement" or even "rendering perfect" (Inden and Nicholas 1977:37). Those who fulfill them are "rendered perfect."

A whole and perfect body is both a sign of one's moral state and a prerequisite for making sacrificial offerings to the gods and ancestors. A one-eyed man or a hunchback has no right to perform "the work of the gods." A Brahman who has black teeth, bad nails or is excessively corpulent should be excluded from the feast for Brahmans held on the thirteenth day after death; and nobody with an open wound should act as chief mourner. In animal sacrifice the victim's body should be without blemish; and it is a sin to worship an image of a deity that is broken or cracked. Consistent with this premium on physical perfection, I would argue, is a certain predilection for forms of violence aimed at disfiguring one's enemies — for example, in the internecine competition between the powerful Pilgrimage Priests for control over what is an extremely lucrative trade, the throwing of sulphuric acid.

This quest for bodily perfection brings me back to the wrestlers and bodybuilders with whom I began. It is perfectly true that the violent competition to which I have just alluded partly explains this commitment, and that those who regularly exercise often attribute their devotion to a desire that people should know that "someone is coming" when they walk down the street. But what I would like to emphasize is that such activity is also given a religious cast, and is to be conducted in a state of purity, having *first* bathed and evacuated the bowels (Kumar 1984:159-60). A wrestling school is an *akhāṛā*, a term that also refers to an ascetic community — recalling that our own word "asceticism" derives from the Greek for "gymnastic practice." Many are held to have been founded by religious leaders, some are attached to a temple and most contain a shrine to the god Hanuman who is famed for his prodigious strength. This is closely associated with his celibacy, as is any real prowess as a wrestler. Wrestling, then, is a pastime particularly appropriate to the first of the four stages of life — the stage of *brahmācarya*, before one becomes a householder. Its object, however, is a more enduring refinement of the body.

New Bodies for Old

Refinement to what end? Not only does such bodily perfection set one up for life, but more importantly, I believe, it also sets one up for death. To show this I must go back over ground I have covered in detail elsewhere (Parry 1982a, 1982b, 1985).

Death, and more especially cremation, are symbolically constructed as a sacrificial offering of the self to the gods. Sacrifice is a preeminently creative act which not only results in the rebirth of the sacrificer on a new and higher plane, but also renews the cosmos by reenacting the primal sacrifice of Prajapāti, who created the world through the sacrificial dismemberment of his own body. Since the human body contains the cosmos, its destruction through fire and water is both a repetition of the conflagration and inundation of the cosmos at the end of time, and a prelude to its regeneration. For our purposes, the essential point is that to serve as a means to such momentous ends, both the offering itself — the sacrificer's own body — and its renunciation must be perfect.

Death must therefore be a *voluntary* renunciation of life, a *controlled* evacuation of the body. It should happen at the right place (ideally in Benares on the banks of the Ganges with the lower limbs in the water), and at the right time (ideally in "the fortnight of the ancestors [*pitri paksa*]"). In the paradigmatic case, the dying man forgoes all food for some days before death, and consumes only Ganges water and the mixture in which an image of a deity has been bathed (*charan-amrit*), in order to weaken his body so that the vital breath may leave it more easily, and in order to make himself a worthy sacrificial object free of foul fecal matter. He should die to the sound of the chanting of the names of god, for his thoughts at that moment may determine his subsequent fate (as his disposition in life was determined by the thoughts of his parents at the moment of his conception); and he should be empty of all desire for the things of this world, for those who remain in bondage to it are condemned to wander in misery for a thousand years as malevolent ghosts. Moreover, those who obstinately cling to life when their time has come imperil others. If an old person refuses to heed its summons, death will carry off a younger member of the family as a surrogate. A "good death" occurs after a full and complete life: having lived to see the marriages of one's sons' sons, when one is still in full command of all one's faculties and in the presence of all one's close family. Having previously predicted the time of his going, the dying man gathers his sons about

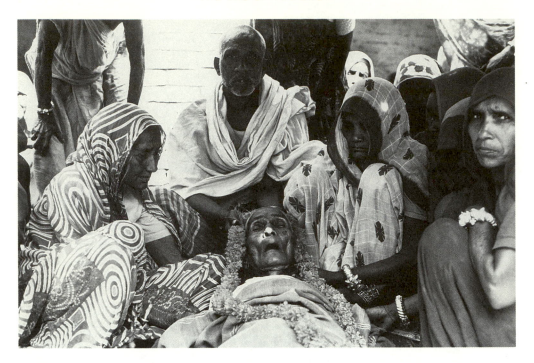

The corpse of an elderly woman of the Butcher caste with her son
(the chief mourner) and female kin. The body has been washed
and dressed for cremation and is about to be taken to the cremation ground in a joyful all-male procession on an elaborately decorated bier preceded by two bands.

him and — by an effort of concentrated will — abandons life. He is not said to die,
but to relinquish his body.

Generally speaking, those whom the gods detest die young — an early death being
the fruit of the sins of this and previous lives. The quality of life determines its dura-
tion. A good death is the product of a good life (Parry 1982b; Madan 1987:122) and
promises a good state after death (*sadgati*). It is hardly surprising, then, that — in
the recounting — the actual death of a loved one is rather rapidly mythologized and
sanitized. Conversely, there is a marked tendency to dwell on the agonizing end of
an enemy — a body wracked by pain and rotted by leprosy, bowels over which all
control had been lost. What this last detail evokes is the notion that the soul's route
of exit from the body through one of its seven orifices is a measure of the life it has
led. That of a just and pious man emerges through the suture at the top of the skull;
that of an abject sinner through the anus with excrement.

A "bad death" (*akāl mrityu* — literally "untimely death"), by contast, is one in which the deceased had shown no intention of renouncing the body — the extreme example being a sudden death as a result of an accident or violence.[4] Alternatively, it is that of a person whose body does not constitute a fit sacrificial object — the extreme case here being the leper, though this also applies to the one-eyed and para-lyzed, the goitrous, hunchbacked and lame. A perfect body is a prerequisite for a perfect death; and — in theory at least — imperfect bodies such as these must not be cremated but rather immersed in the Ganges. Indeed, it is almost as if the fire itself would reject an offering so unworthy. Hence, for example, the peculiarly incombustible nature of the corpse of a prominent minister in the government of Bihar. Despite the size of the pyre and the liberality of the *ghee* and resin applied to it, the body would only burn with the greatest difficulty on account — said my friends — of the enormous burden of sin accumulated with his corrupt earnings. Con-versely, the cremation pyre of the "true wife" (the *sati*), who voluntarily joins her husband in death, is commonly represented as igniting spontaneously.[5]

The "gross" outer body is said to have three possible fates: it is eaten as carrion and turns to excrement; it is buried and turns to maggots; or it is burnt and turns to ash. The rotting or putrescence of the body is viewed with particular repugnance, and the last of these is consequently the least unpalatable and is seen as the swift-est way of recycling the five elements (*panch tattva, panch bhūt*) from which the body is constituted.

There is, as this suggests, a sense in which nothing is totally lost at death: the five elements return to the common pool for reuse; the soul is immortal and is reborn; the body particles a person shares with his kinsmen endure in their bodies.[6] The person is never entirely new when born, never entirely gone when dead. Both his body and soul extend into past and future persons, and to a signifi-cant degree his biological substance is shared in the present with kin who have the same body particles.

Cremation not only recycles the five elements, but it also continues and elabo-rates on the symbolic theme of sacrifice. It is known as *antyeṣti* — "the last sac-rifice"; and the purification of the site, the preparation of the corpse, the ten substances offered into the pyre and the type of wood from which it should be con-structed, all directly echo the rules laid down for the conduct of a sacrifice. Like the sacrificial victim, the corpse is itself treated as a being of great sacredness, even as a deity. It must be guarded against pollution, is circumambulated with the auspicious right hand toward it, and the funeral pyre is ignited by the chief mourner only after he has passed through an elaborate series of purifications (cf. Stevenson 1920:144-48) and with his sacred thread worn in the manner appropriate for offerings to the gods (as opposed to that appropriate for offerings to a ghost or ancestor).

Indeed, much in the mortuary rites and their exegesis suggests that the sacrificial victim is not really a corpse at all, but an animate oblation to the fire. The coup de grace is delivered by the chief mourner at the rite of *kapāl kriyā*, midway through the cremation, when he cracks open the skull with a staff. It is only at this point that one can begin to refer to the deceased as a ghost (*preta*); and many people say that it is only then that death pollution begins. Cremation, then, is an act of violence perpetrated by one's own son, whose subsequent isolation and purification is undertaken in atonement. The victim "does not die but is killed," I was told. "He dies on the pyre."

That in one form or another life remains in the corpse is clear; and it is consistently spoken of as though it were a sentient being. "If you burn your finger," I was invited to reflect, "think how much you suffer. What then of the whole body?" Less clear, however, is exactly *what* remains to be released by *kapāl kriyā*. The general answer is the "vital breath" (*prāṇa*), which most people see as synonymous with the soul (*ātmā*). Some speak as though cremation itself ensures a proper evacuation of the body, for it is the heat of the pyre that "causes the 'vital breath' to climb into the *brahmānd*" at the top of the skull. A handful of informants, however, know that the textual authorities postulate five or even ten types of "breath" (*prāṇa*) or "wind" (*vāyu*), which are located in different parts of the body and perform different functions associated with the circulation of blood, the digestion of food and the elimination of waste products.[7] One of these — the *dhananjay vāyu* — pervades the whole body, and it is this, they say, which remains in the corpse to be liberated by *kapāl kriyā*.

Given that cremation is a creative act of sacrifice, it is only to be expected that "the last sacrifice" should be pervaded by the symbolism of birth and parturition. The body is taken to the cremation ground head first because that is the way a baby is born; while the corpse of a man should theoretically be laid facedown on the pyre and the corpse of a woman faceup, for this is the position in which the two sexes enter the world. During the fifth month of pregnancy, the vital breath enters the embryo through the suture at the top of the skull, and it is from there that it is released during cremation. Throughout the pregnancy the body is sustained by the digestive fire that resides in the mother's belly, and at death it returns to the fire from which it came and is thus reborn. At both parturitions an Untouchable specialist acts the indispensable role of midwife — cutting the umbilical cord at birth and providing the sacred fire and superintending the pyre at death.

How, then, are those with bodies unworthy of the cremation pyre to be reborn? The answer is by making them worthy through "the method of the effigy" (*putlā vidhān*). The corpse itself is immersed in the river, and the funeral priest, the Mahabrahman, or the barber in the case of a low-caste death, constructs an elaborate and anatomically detailed effigy of the deceased out of fifty-six ingredients: red beads for nipples, white wool for the hair of an old person or black for that of a young one, aubergine for the penis, honey for blood and so on. The deceased's spirit is then invoked into the effigy (*prāṇa kā āvāhan karnā*) by lighting camphor in the navel. While it burns the mourners are instructed to chant the names of god, and when it is extinguished the person is said to have expired. The effigy is then covered with a shroud and cremated in *exactly* the same way as an ordinary corpse. The unworthy body of the deceased is replaced by a worthy offering to the fire; a "bad" death is rerun as a properly controlled release of life.

Though death is *dehānt*, "the end of the body," it is by no means the end of the soul's embodiment. Initially the deceased exists in the invisible form of a "microscopic" (*sūkṣam*) or "airy" (*vāyumay, vāyavya*) body the size of a thumb, which is often represented as being a precise miniature replica of the "gross" body it has left behind. Though those who are fortunate and deserving enough to die in Benares are promised a privileged fate after death, it is said that even they must suffer for their sins. Their punishment is infinitely quicker but much more intense than that which awaits the rest of us; it is exacted on the microscopic body, and is described as preparing the soul for Śiva's gift of salvation by "burning up" its sins "as gold is purified by fire."

Even in Benares, however, everything proceeds as if salvation was still rather remote. The whole sequence of mortuary rites must therefore be followed. These are conventionally held to involve the offering of three sets of sixteen *piṇḍas*, or rice ball offerings. The number sixteen denotes totality or completeness (Malamoud 1982), and we have already seen that the "gross" body is completed by the performance of sixteen life-cycle rituals.

By the same token, the purpose of the first set of sixteen *piṇḍas* is to complete a new body for the deceased with which he can journey to "the abode of the ancestors" (*pitṛ loka*). Until this has been accomplished, he remains in his ethereal thumb-sized casing, which is given a "house" in a pitcher that is hung in the branches of a *peepal* tree. The pitcher is known as "the body pot" (*gath kumbh*) and is smashed by the funeral priest on the eleventh day after death when the deceased enters the new body that has been created over the previous ten days, explicitly paralleling the ten (lunar) month period of gestation.

Of the first set of sixteen offerings, ten are specifically known as "the ten body *piṇḍas*" (*dasgāttra piṇḍa*) — a term that, as we have seen, also applies to an embryo. They must be round "like a womb," or like the ball that forms "when the father's semen and the mother's menstrual blood mix," and a number of the substances used to construct the surrogate corpse I referred to above are either mixed with, or offered to, these body *piṇḍas*. Each one builds specific limbs or organs of the body. That of the first day constructs the head — as the head of a fetus is formed in the womb by the end of the first month. Completed on the tenth day, this body is the size of the distance between the elbow and the tips of the fingers (*hastmāttrā*).

The second set of sixteen *piṇḍas* are conventionally offered on the eleventh day. In the ideal sequence they are preceded by the ritual of *Vrishotsarga* (literally "bull sacrifice"), the crucial part of which relates to the journey to "the abode of the ancestors." Halfway along his road, the deceased — driven forward with unremitting cruelty by the messengers of death — must cross the terrifying Vaiturni River, which is flowing with pus and blood, has banks of unscalable bone, mud of flesh and gore and entrances congested with hair. The calf given at *Vrishotsarga* helps the soul across, and this scene is acted out in the course of the ritual. At first sight, this might seem out of sequence, for what follows clearly suggests that the journey is yet to begin. Its appositeness here, however, becomes plain when we remember that on the eleventh day the deceased is born into the new body that has been prepared over the preceding days — the Vaiturni River being a clear metaphor for the birth passage of a child. Moreover, the only one of these sixteen *pinḍas* which is held to be absolutely indispensable is now offered, and this is food. As a baby yells from pangs of hunger as soon as it is born, so the newly created body of the deceased must first be comforted with food.

The third and final set of sixteen *pinḍas* now follow. These are for the sustenance of the deceased on his yearlong journey to "the abode of the ancestors," and should in theory be offered at various intervals throughout this period. In fact, however, the whole lot are generally given on the twelfth day as a preliminary to the rites of *sapinḍīkārana*, which should actually be performed at the end of the twelfth month, for the rite itself represents the deceased's arrival at his destination and his union with his ancestors. The *preta*-ghost becomes an ancestral *pitṛ*.

This is effected by *pitṛ miloni* ("the mixing with the ancestors"), when an elongated *pinḍa* that represents the body of the *preta* is cut up by the chief mourner into three equal parts; these are then merged with three rounded *pinḍas* which represent the deceased's father, the father's father and *his* father. My informants insist that these are the actual bodies of the deceased and his ancestors, though they are somewhat reluctant to admit that the rite therefore amounts to an act of literal butchery. This implication is, however, unflinchingly acknowledged elsewhere in north India (Stevenson 1920:185-86), and I believe I am justified in concluding that just as cremation is an act of sacrificial violence directed against the "gross" body, so *sapinḍīkārana* is an act of sacrificial violence directed against the intermediate *preta*-body of the deceased.

What happens next is explained in terms of two different and rather contradictory theories. The commonest formulation of the first vaguely pictures the deceased as residing "in the abode of the ancestors" in an "airy" body. The *ritual* sequence is more precise in that it locates each of the three ascending generations in a different cosmic layer: the father on earth, the father's father in the atmosphere and the great-grandfather in heaven (Knipe 1977:117ff.). Each is steadily progressing toward a more etherealized state of being, and with the death of a direct lineal descendant, the one who stood on the highest rung of the ladder is, as it were, promoted off the edge into the unknown world beyond. Now admittedly, this relates to a rather esoteric level of ritual discourse; but the general idea is very much part of popular consciousness. Every two or three generations the ancestors should be collectively taken to the holy city of Gaya, where — by the offering of *piṇḍas* — they are finally liberated from their bodies, and their souls merge back into the primeval protoplasm of the Universal Spirit. Either way, the body is progressively refined, until it is more or less refined out of existence.

The second theory is that at *sapiṇḍīkāraṇa* the deceased sloughs off his arm-long *preta*-body, and assumes a new body — known as the "punishment" or "experience" body (*yātnā-deh*, *bhoga-deh*) — through which he suffers the torments of hell, or the joys of heaven. Having thus expiated his sins or exhausted his merit, he is reincarnated on earth. The essential point here is that by his ritual endeavors, the chief mourner enhances the deceased's prospects of a more desirable rebirth. In short, the goal is again a progressive refinement of bodily being.

An additional strand in the symbolism is of some relevance here. As I have documented in detail elsewhere (Parry 1985), a recurrent theme in the symbolism of the mortuary rites is that of eating the deceased. The "gross" outer body is consumed by the fires of cremation; on the eleventh day the impure funeral priests eat an offering which represents the substance of the deceased, while the pure Brahmans who attend the feast which follows *sapiṇḍīkāraṇa* on the twelfth day are again said to partake of the dead man. Finally, some of the textual sources relate how the body through which he experienced the joys of heaven or the torments of hell is eaten by deformed and hideous demons before his soul is reincarnated on earth (O'Flaherty 1980:17). In short, it would seem that each time the soul acquires a new body, the old one is "eaten" — which is to say that it is consumed by the fires of digestion. Digestion is seen as a process of distilling the good and nourishing part of food from the bad waste products, and it provides a metaphor for talking about many other activities. By ingesting and digesting the deceased, his pure essence is distilled and refined, while his impure sins are eliminated. Once more, then, the same message is repeated: the soul is engaged in an endless quest for refinement and perfection. It passes through a whole sequence of bodies which are constantly purified and transformed by being subjected to the cleansing fires of the cremation pyre and the Brahman's stomach, until eventually the body can be transcended altogether.

But the ascetic, of course, has a shortcut — the theoretical objective of his austerities being to "burn up" all bodily desire in preparation for a more immediate union of his soul with the Universal Spirit. In practice, however, what my informants endlessly stress is not the ascetic's rejection of the body, but his absolute mastery over it. By his austerities he acquires the powers (*siddhis*) to expand or contract it to any size or weight, fly through the air, appear in two places at once or leave his body and assume another. Entering into a cataleptic state of deep meditation he "takes *samādhi*," which is to say that he is entombed, and thereby escapes the normal consequences of death: the severance of the connection between body and soul, the corruption of the body and the transmigration of the soul. His body is immune to putrescence and decay, and is still the occasional habitation of his soul which wanders the three worlds (*lokas*) assuming any bodily form it chooses and changing from one to another at will. It is his ability (known as *parkāya pravesh*) to switch bodies as he pleases which is seen as the hallmark of an "arrived" ascetic and as his most enviable accomplishment.

The general scenario, then, is one in which the human body exists in a state of precarious and constantly threatened equilibrium. It is nevertheless capable of transformation and refinement; and it is to be perfected by a good life in preparation for a good death, which is in turn a precondition for a more refined state of embodiment – until at last a real "end of the body" is achieved.

The Body, the Soul and the Protean Person

Rather than elaborate further on this theme, which is, I hope, already plain enough, I want in conclusion to return to the two questions prompted by the Chicago ethnosociologists with which I began: How does the construct of the person as made up of almost infinitely malleable bio-moral substance fit with the static ideology of caste? And to what extent is the radical contrast between the monism of South Asian thought and the dualism of the West justified?

To take the second of these questions first, it is undeniable that much of the data I have presented is entirely in line with an essentially monistic worldview. Bio-moral substance is constituted and altered by the properties of the food one consumes; thoughts have the power to determine future states of bodily being; the condition of the body reflects that of the soul; sin renders the corpse incombustible; and so on. But it is also true that by emphasizing a different strand in my ethnography I could equally argue that my informants inhabit a markedly dualistic universe. The body is the "house" of the soul which it leaves behind like "old clothes," and until the end of the fifth month of pregnancy, it is merely matter without spirit. "It is not by coloring our bodies but by coloring our minds that we obtain salvation." "His body was impure," I heard it said of an Untouchable friend, "but his mind was pure." Moreover, a ghost or an ancestor might assume the form of a monkey, a crow or a spider to drop in on the mortuary rituals, but there is no implication that these temporary bodily forms reflect their nature. A degree of dualism is again surely implied by my informants' insistence that each person possesses a unique soul which is entirely particular to him or her alone, while their bodily substance is composed of particles shared with a diffuse set of bilateral kin (the *sapiṇḍa* relatives of the legal treatises).

Nor is the inseparability of code and substance apparent in the much-repeated stories of ascetics who took refuge in an alien body — like that, for example, of the original Shankaracharya's debate (*shāstrārth*) with the learned Benares pandit, Mandan Misra. When the Sankaracharya claimed victory, Mandan Misra's wife objected that a woman is "the half-body" of her husband and that she was yet to be defeated. When she then posed a series of searching questions about the sex life of the householder, the Sankaracharya — an ascetic — had to beg a six-month adjournment, during which he borrowed the corpse of a lustful prince. The suggestion that when he came back and defeated the pandit's wife, his soul had been transformed by residence in a different body, or that his body was transformed by the vicarious experience of his soul, would, I think, be regarded as absurd. By the same token, the concept of spirit possession seems to suggest a quite radical duality between the flesh and the spirit. Though it is this or that ghost, this or that deity, who speaks to us, its "vehicle" is indisputably the body of our neighbor Ramji Yadav, the milkman.[8]

Nor, I would argue, is the pervasive dualism of Western ideology really quite so pervasive as Marriott and his colleagues would have us believe. It is, of course, true that Christianity has often represented the body as the prison of the soul; but it is worth remembering that Saint Paul described the body as "a temple of the Holy Spirit, within you, which you have from God" (1 Corinthians 6.19), and that the central orthodoxy of the Catholic church views the body in a positive — though also rather contradictory — light. On the one hand, the body is a mirror of the soul, and suffering the consequence of sin (original or otherwise); while, on the other hand, the suppurating, tortured body is a mark of election, a privileged opportunity for identification with the Cross (cf. Stirrat; Turner 1984:67). But either way, it is accorded a profound significance (Dahlberg 1987), and in neither discourse is it rejected or straightforwardly opposed to the soul (cf. Bottomley 1979).

This last point is brought out with admirable clarity in Bynum's (1987) recent study of religious women in the late Middle Ages. While a thoroughgoing dualism was characteristic of groups like the Cathars, the late medieval Church was explicitly concerned to counteract such heresy. It was God made *flesh* that redeemed mankind; it is His suffering body that becomes incarnate in the Eucharist and that holds out to us the promise of a resurrection *of the body*. A tradition that so emphatically stresses the immanence of divinity in the human body surely cannot be said to reject it, or to see it as radically opposed to the soul (Dahlberg 1987). Indeed, if one focused on the fact that a good Catholic can expect to retain his body for eternity, while a good Hindu must continually trade his in for a better one until he can do without it entirely, one might even perhaps perversely conclude that we are heirs to a conceptual monism *more marked* than that of South Asians.

At any rate, the emphatic contrast between their monism and our dualism certainly does little justice to the real complexities of either conceptual world, and one cannot help wondering if Inden's (1986) recent critique of the "Orientalism" implied in attempts to portray "the essence of Indian civilization [as] just the opposite of the West's" might not have been best stated as a repudiation of his own "ethnosociological" past — a case perhaps of motes and beams? More importantly, one of the effects of insisting on a contrast of this kind is to ignore the way in which ideas in *both* worlds act as ideologies; and this brings me back to my first question about the relationship between caste and the construct of the person.

What I believe my own data, as well as much else in the ethnographic record, would suggest is that Hindu society has often seen itself as engaged in an endless battle against impending chaos and disintegration, of which the ever-present danger of a disintegration and degeneration of the actor's own person is the most immediate and apprehensible manifestation. Constant vigilance is required to hold the balance of the body; decay and death result from involvement in disequilibriating transactions. The impact of this menacing vision can surely only be a message of strict obedience to the rigid order of caste. What, in other words, the ideology of fluid substance implies is nothing less than that the disintegration of the self results from stepping off the tried and tested tracks of the established pattern of caste inter-actions. Since, moreover, one's bio-moral substance extends into other persons — both through one's transactions with them and through the body particles shared with kin — any irregular exchange in which one engages also represents a direct threat to these other selves. In such a world nobody can be allowed to act as an autono-mous individual, and all with whom one associates have a directly *personal* interest in monitoring one's conduct. The point that Marriott and his colleagues miss, then, is that the protean construct of the person, which they have rightly identified as at least one important aspect of the Hindu worldview, acts as an "ideology" in the clas-sic Marxist sense. As with "the law of the fishes," according to which the big ones eat the little ones unless there is a raja to restrain them, it is the symbolic elabora-tion of louring disorder which creates and sustains the world of order and regulation.[9]

This paper is based on fieldwork in the north Indian city of Benares carried out between September 1976 and November 1977 (supported by the Social Science Research Council) and in August 1978, August–September 1981 and March–April 1983 (supported by the London School of Economics and Political Science). I am deeply obliged to Virendra Singh for his language instruction, and to him and Om Prakash Sharma for their research assistance. The paper itself was written in the congenial surroundings of the Netherlands Institute for Advanced Study, and I am grateful to my colleagues in the "Working Group on Ritual" for their constructive criticisms of a preliminary version. Maurice Bloch, Andrea Dahlberg and Peter van der Veer also generously responded to my importunate demand for immediate comment with some characteristically acute suggestions.

NOTES

   1. But compare Bottomley (1979:158) who argues that in many respects the early Christian church had valorized the body, and that this was "expressed through material rites and sacraments applied to the *whole* man" (emphasis added). According to Tertullian, it is by washing the flesh in baptism that the soul is cleansed (*ibid.*, p. 45); while the sacrament of extreme unction has certainly been widely represented as *both* a means of purifying the soul and of relieving bodily suffering.

   2. Cf. Das's (1985) interesting discussion of the way in which ritual discourse transforms the sex-ual act into "a supreme religious duty on the model of sacrifice."

   3. Again Das (1985:188-89) notes the ambivalence: sometimes the body is likened to a temple,

at others it is seen as an ephemeral object of disgust. She associates this with the distinction between the body as "a system of moral relations" and the body as "biological substance" — ritual striving to substitute the first definition for the second.

4. Over the soldier or hero who dies violently in a just cause there is much ambivalence. Such a death would still generally be rated as an "untimely" one, and the spirit of such a person is generally said to remain an unincorporated ghost (*preta*) as opposed to an incorporated ancestor (*pitṛ*). But those fallen on the battlefield often figure as powerful territorial guardians with jurisdiction over lesser spirits, and are not normally credited with the blind malevolence and utter lack of self-control characteristic of the ghosts of most others who have died a sudden death.

5. Similarly, people sometimes talk as though the difficulty the "digestive fire" of the Brahman's stomach has in assimilating the gifts of the donor is roughly proportionate to the latter's moral state. I return briefly to the idiom of the Brahman's digestive fire below. See also Parry 1985.

6. According to the legal treatises, traced through the father, one has common body particles with those with whom one shares an ancestor not more than seven generations removed, and traced through the mother not more than five generations removed.

7. Despite my informants' refusal to distinguish between *prāna* and *ātmā*, they invariably speak of the latter in the singular — one "person" (*vyakti*), one "soul."

8. It is perfectly true that there must be a basic compatibility between the nature of the spirit and the body it possesses. Thus, the body that acts as host to a powerful goddess like Durga or Sitala must be pure; evil and malevolent ghosts can only successfully appropriate the bodies of the impure. But this requirement that body and spirit must be matched or compatible certainly does not imply an identity between them — even at the time of possession itself.

9. As I have argued elsewhere (Parry n.d.), not only protean persons and cannibalistic fishes, but also the chaotic and disorderly world of spirit possession, serve to reproduce the hierarchical world of caste.

BIBLIOGRAPHY

Beck, B.E.F., "The Symbolic Merger of Body, Space and Cosmos in Hindu Tamil Nadu," *Contributions to Indian Sociology* n.s. 10 (1976), pp. 213-43.

Bottomley, F., *Attitudes to the Body in Western Christendom*. London: Lepus Books, 1979.

Bynum, C.W., *Holy Feast and Holy Fast: The Religious Significance of Food to Medieval Women*. Berkeley: University of California Press, 1987.

Dahlberg, A.L.G., *Transcendence of Bodily Suffering: An Anthropological Study of English Catholics at*

Lourdes. Unpublished Ph.D. dissertation at the University of London, 1987.

Daniel, E.V., *Fluid Signs: Being a Person the Tamil Way*. Berkeley: University of California Press, 1984.

Das, Veena, "Paradigms of Body Symbolism: An Analysis of Selected Themes in Hindu Culture," in *Indian Religion*. Edited by R. Burghart and A. Cantlie, pp. 180-207. London: Curzon Press, 1985.

Dumont, L., *Homo Hierarchicus: The Caste System and Its Implications*. London: Weidenfeld and Nicholson, 1970.

Egnor, M.T., "Death and Nurturance in Indian Systems of Healing." *Soc. Sci. Med.* 17.14 (1983), pp. 935-45.

Eliade, M., *Yoga: Immortality and Freedom*. Princeton, N.J.: Princeton University Press (Bollingen Series 61), 1969.

Garuda Purana. With Hindi commentary by Sudama Misra Shastri. Varanasi: Bombay Pushtak Bhandar, n.d.

Inden, R., "Orientalist Constructions of India," *Modern Asian Studies* 20.3 (1986), pp. 401-46.

Inden, R. and R. Nicholas, *Kinship in Bengali Culture*. Chicago: Chicago University Press, 1977.

Kakar, Sudhir, *Shamans, Mystics and Doctors: A Psychological Enquiry into India and Its Healing Traditions*. Boston: Beacon Press, 1982.

Knipe, D.M., "*Sapiṇḍīkāraṇa*: The Hindu Rite of Entry into Heaven," in *Religious Encounters with Death: Insights from the History and Anthropology of Religions*. Edited by E. Reynolds and E.H. Waugh, pp. 111-24. University Park, Pa. and London: Pennsylvania State University Press, 1977.

Kumar, Nita, *Popular Culture in Urban India: The Artisans of Banaras, c. 1884–1984*. Unpublished Ph.D. dissertation at the University of Chicago, 1984.

Madan, T.N., *Non-renunciation: Themes and Interpretations of Hindu Culture*. Delhi: Oxford University Press, 1987.

Malamoud, C., "On Rhetoric and Semantics of *Purusartha*," in *Way of Life: King, Householder and Renouncer (Essays in Honour of Louis Dumont)*. Edited by T.N. Madan, pp. 33-54. New Delhi: Vikas, 1982.

Marriott, McKim, "Caste Ranking and Food Transactions: A Matrix Analysis," in *Structure and Change in Indian Society*. Edited by M. Singer and B.S. Cohn, pp. 133-72. Chicago: Aldine, 1968.

————, "Hindu Transactions: Diversity without Dualism," in *Transaction and Meaning*. Edited by B. Kapferer. Philadelphia: Institute for the Study of Human Issues, 1976.

Mauss, M., "Les techniques du corps," in Marcel Mauss, *Sociologie et anthropologie* (1936). Paris: Presses Universitaires de France, 1960.

Nicholas, R., "*Sraddha*, Impurity and Relations between the Living and the Dead," in *Way of Life:*

King, Householder and Renouncer (Essays in Honour of Louis Dumont). Edited by T.N. Madan, pp. 367-79. New Delhi: Vikas, 1982.

O'Flaherty, W.D., "*Karma* and Rebirth in the *Vedas* and *Puranas*," in *Karma and Rebirth in Indian Classical Traditions*. Edited by W.D. O'Flaherty, pp. 3-37. Berkeley: University of California Press, 1980.

O'Hanlon, M., "Handsome Is as Handsome Does: Display and Betrayal in the Wahgi," *Oceania* 53.4 (1983), pp. 317-33.

Parry, J.P., "Ghosts, Greed and Sin: The Occupational Identity of the Benares Funeral Priests," *Man* n.s. 15 (1980), pp. 88-111.

————, "Death and Cosmogony in Kashi," in *Way of Life: King, Householder and Renouncer (Essays in Honour of Louis Dumont)*. Edited by T.N. Madan, pp. 337-65. New Delhi: Vikas, 1982a.

————, "Sacrificial Death and the Necrophagous Ascetic," in *Death and the Regeneration of Life*. Edited by M. Bloch and J. Parry, pp. 74-110. Cambridge: Cambridge University Press, 1982b.

————, "Death and Digestion: The Symbolism of Food and Eating in North Indian Mortuary Rites," *Man* n.s. 20 (1985), pp. 612-30.

————, "*The Gift*, the Indian Gift and the 'Indian Gift,' " *Man* n.s. 21 (1986), pp. 453-73.

————, "On the Moral Perils of Exchange," in *Money and the Morality of Exchange*. Edited by M. Bloch and J. Parry. Cambridge: Cambridge University Press, 1989.

————, "Spirit Possession as 'Superstition.' " Forthcoming.

Schneider, D.M., *American Kinship: A Cultural Account*. Englewood Cliffs, N.J.: Prentice-Hall, 1968.

Stevenson, S., *The Rites of the Twice-born*. London: Oxford University Press, 1920.

Stirrat, R.L., "Suffering and Salvation in Sinhala Catholicism." Forthcoming.

Strathern, M., "The Self in Self-decoration." *Oceania* 44.4 (1979), pp. 241-57.

Trautmann, T., *Lewis Henry Morgan and the Invention of Kinship*. Berkeley: University of California Press, 1987.

Turner, B.S., *The Body and Society: Explorations in Social Theory*. London: Oxford University Press, 1984.

Jacob's Ladder, ca. 1490 (Avignon, Musée du Petit-Palais).

Celestial Bodies:

A Few Stops on the Way to Heaven

Nadia Tazi

Heaven cannot be expressed or represented: the mind can grasp it only by recognizing its own limitations and the necessity of coming to terms with it. Whether it is called the Kingdom of God, the Homeland or the Crown of Justice or Glory, the Christian Heaven is an abstraction or, as Plato would put it, the object of "bastardly reasoning."[1] Plato himself projected first causes and finalities into a mythical anteriority; in the *Parmenides* he questioned the very possibility of a theology by appealing to the ancient Greek wisdom of limits: man must not try to comprehend what lies beyond his understanding. But all this does not apply to Christ, the God-man who promised the Kingdom of Heaven to all his followers and reconciled opposite worlds and conditions. At the heart of faith is enclosed a mystery, verified as such. Moreover, Heaven is represented not only as a state of original perfection nor as the abode of eternity out of which God's voice is heard. It is also known as the Kingdom of Ends, which in its double meaning refers both to a messianic advent depending on God's will and to the objective all believers must attain. Eschatological expectation must be based on a spiritual process, undergone by the Spirit, in the Spirit and toward the Spirit. In short, Heaven is the reward of a life of exile, a life wherein all that is right and redemptive is lacking in the world and comes only from above.

Heaven is, then, ideality at its fullest, at once reality and virtuality. It joins absolute transcendence to the immanence of spiritual progress; it looms beyond death, first to give it limit and then to abolish it forever. Any representation of this end can only be an approximation, but not all approximations are of the same order, nor are they achieved in the same way. Nothing can prevent faith from feeding on hope, or expectation from thriving on Edenic images: within the very speculations that attempt to turn Heaven into a pure ideal, there are warnings, resistances, tales. Inspired speech, whether caught in the evocation of hyperbolic and redundant images or overly cautious, expresses hope through aporia. Christians had to be careful neither to lend Heaven a materiality it does not have, nor to deprive it of its reality and consistency.

While seers, mystics and the first followers of Christ were often carried away by this other world, the first theologians were often confused by it. Forced to define its location, its setting or the state of bliss and eternal life implied in its promise, they resorted either to the opposition Heaven/Earth or to a "logic" whose premises led them back to the threshold of the ineffable, to the brink of total blankness. In the end, they surmised, all one can do is believe. And those who decide to believe must give up all desire to know and to see. The martyr who asked to glimpse the Good to come before his final trial was chided: "Where is your faith?"

But confronted with waiting, a waiting exacerbated by asceticism, sacrificial enthusiasm and the presumed imminence of the End, how could one explain such an *absence*? How could one resist the temptation of exchanging, as if before a significant departure, a token of what was to come? How could one refuse fables and their soothing powers? As Emile Benvéniste has noted, belief always involves the relinquishing of something on the condition of getting it back later, the replacing of a present good with a future advantage.[2] In this case, those "who believe in Him do not die" (John). But what sort of contract is this if, in the absence of any guarantee, nothing is made explicit by the law, whether that of priests or that of theologians? The moment the Kingdom of Heaven is designated as the inheritance and reward of the Just, the least Christian teachers can do is to paint this paradise for us, to fence in this Garden. And, indeed, some of them do give some substance to this reward by picturing it as a verdant meadow endowed with fruits and perfumes, the abode of prophets, patriarchs and angels. By virtue of an old visionary tradition, Heaven is thus sensualized, "orientalized": "And God showed us a vast region, away from this world, dazzling with light, the air flooded by the rays of the sun, the earth blooming with flowers which do not fade, and full of spices and plants which blossom gloriously.... So great was the fragrance of the flowers that it was borne unto us" (Apocalypse of Peter).[3] This luminous and impenetrable realm lavishes endless joy and grace on the creature who reflects it in his newly recovered original condition. This is as close as one can get to fiction, to fantasies of orphic inspiration and other liberating wanderings. Augustine, on the other hand, refuses to offer us even a glimpse of the future feast, to anticipate in any way the final victory. "You would like to know," he says, "where is the peaceful abode where God will show himself directly to you? Once this life is over, God will himself be the abode of our souls."[4] It is better to reformulate the question and to pose it in an absolute sense than to resort to the vulgarity of anthropomorphism. There is no other place for the soul than in its Creator: to believe is to acknowledge actively the presence of Christ, who established his Kingdom on earth.

Thus, the theologian's task was to specify what links man to God, to define Heaven as a normative space of intelligibility that would, first, establish a hierarchy among beings, according to their degree of similarity with spiritual models; second, validate the processes of the elevation of soul, that is, specify the points of contact between the earthly and the divine. Heaven would then appear as a horizon where all ways to salvation converge or, alternatively, as a center diffusing, by analogy or existential anticipation, its harmony, its ideal virtues, the purity of its bodies and its affections throughout the community that identifies with it. While waiting for the end of time, this community was to build the City of God by trying to live supernaturally on earth.

In the first four centuries after Christ progress was made: a new doctrine provided the believer with a number of fixed points of reference and hierarchical relationships derived from the notion of this intensely significant Beyond, from this reality whose very distance evidences the limitations of a fallen humanity. Heaven was no longer comprehended in terms of divination; it was also dissociated, with greater difficulty, from a philosophy based on the distinction between the intelligible and sensible, a philosophy that sought the image of being in the heavenly vault and there found its object of contemplation, even adoration.[5] Nor did the concept of Heaven in the early Church conform strictly to the notion of a forever deferred messianic advent as proposed by the prophets. Heaven does, however, retain its sacred height which, bordering on the invisible, lends eminence and radiance to its populations; but it also now combines, with this absolute alterity, a degree of spiritual similarity with the earthly world.

While pagan dualism saw Heaven as the place of eternity that only the soul recovers after the death of the body, Christian thought opened it up to resurrected man in his entirety. Yet how could theologians negate the philosophers' drastic separation of body and soul without hypostasizing a simple anthropological continuity? How could they conceive a dualism between the sensible and the intelligible, or outline an absolute difference between the earthly and the heavenly, without pure contradiction? Such is the problem that confronted those who attempted to put reason in the service of faith, and who recognized a rupture only between the believer and the disbeliever, the chosen and the reprobate.

The transition from one realm to the next, the notion of "trespass" (as opposed to death), evoked images of steep paths and ladders, a lengthy corporeal progression that was no longer seen to lead to a totally disincarnated, stellar world. For the body was now also invited to meet with God — a body that was at once its former self and newly glorious like the place that welcomed it. To understand the difference between pagan salvation and Christian promise, it is necessary to explore the fundamental contradictions implied in this concept of the celestial body. Indeed, the presence of the body in such an ethereal region is more puzzling than the nature or location of Heaven. Such a presence suggests the possibility of corruption, deceit and dissolution, and the flesh retains its natural tendency to err.

In this formulation certain propositions remain in place: the body's total subordination to the spirit, its perfect agreement with the soul, and its affinity with the milieu that envelops it. This paradoxically open enclosure (*hortus conclusus*) contains creatures of light whose remoteness can be measured in terms both of space-time and of dematerialization — because the higher one rises (both physically and spiritually), the less substantial the body becomes, the closer it gets to its shadow and soul: cosmic breaths and flashes, diaphanous shells, angelic figures — winged things, difficult to identify, that encompass physical quintessence and blissful sublimity. The essential nature of these creatures can only be approximately defined as a systematic inversion of all that is earthly — even though, for the sake of mystery, there is much more to it than this. With the help of both science and visionary experience, this particular nature comes to be compared to that of other celestial bodies, such as angels and stars; but its definition is constantly emptied by redundancy and rhetorical excess. There is something flimsy in the Kingdom of God: it lacks both the carnivorous opulence of Hell and the sumptuous density of its Oriental versions. In fact, it operates mainly as a model for, and a support of, *this* world — the world over which the theologians of late Antiquity quarrel, a world rife with oracles and revelations, with urgent questions, fears and doubts.

However, all this lies somewhat beyond the scope of this study whose intent is to sketch the main theological obsession of those times: the will to repeal or to absolve matter, to alleviate the weight of the world. This concern explains the vehemence of the debate concerning resurrection, a theme of Judaic origin (and a focus and cause of its opposition to Hellenistic thought) which we shall follow through the writings of Origen, Augustine and Tertullian, each of whom deals in his own way with the ambivalent status of the body. Then we shall move on to representations of the glorious body, with its celestial properties and the homologies that they evoke. Finally, we shall examine the experience of martyrdom, which anchors the doctrine of resurrection in the actual presence of a body glorified, sanctified by the most extreme of deaths.

Resurrections

Addressing the "dreamers" who clung to the sensible world and considered their body a reality, Plotinus wrote, "The true awakening of the soul is a real resurrection, not with the body but rather starting from the body."[6] He probably also had in mind those Christians who, through their faith in a God "who gives life to the dead" (Romans 4.17), uttered a Credo that proclaimed their belief in the resurrection of the dead or of the flesh. The misunderstanding of the word "resurrection" here turned into a contradiction which defined Christianity for what it was: a religion of salvation that, born out of an initial loss (that of Christ's body), expressed its hatred of death with uncommon purity and violence. Although this belief in the immortality of the soul was general to the Greco-Roman world, the return of the body after death was contrary to the most steadfast assumption of the times (including both philosophical knowledge and popular doxa): that the sensible realm was a place of exile and error. In this way, the Christian notion of resurrection confirmed the pagans' suspicion of a return of obscurantism (along with other tendencies from the Orient) that was not to be tolerated, for fear of intellectual indignity, if nothing else.

In fact, this intellectually archaic notion of resurrection, which was of Judaic origin and, it is suspected, of Iranian inspiration, had managed to make its way into the apocalyptic domain. It was already clearly sketched in the prophet Ezekiel's fantastic description of the Valley of the Dead, where scattered bones, nerves and flesh recompose themselves and where the divine breath wakes up the dead multitude which then transforms itself into a gigantic army. Enoch, Baruch, Isaiah and others state that in the final hour of prodigies the earth will give back the dead "as it received them." But, aside from the fact that, in the Judaic perspective, there is no radical separation between body and soul, the idea of individual resurrection is still overshadowed by the promise of the day when all the Jews, dead or alive, will achieve national restoration.

"But if there is no resurrection of the dead, then Christ has not been raised. And if Christ has not been raised, then our preaching is in vain, and your faith is in vain" (1 Corinthians 15.13-14). That resurrection was a source of hope is one thing; that this belief originated in Christ's Resurrection – as the Apostles testified – is another. Nothing can challenge this certainty; it has become the backbone of the new faith. The language of messianic narrative is not drastically modified, however; at the moment when Christ expires, the earth quakes, graves open up and the veil of the sanctuary is torn. Nonetheless, such language no longer refers to an ideality nor functions symbolically: a unique, insurmountable and unrepeatable event now anchors it outside myth and beyond the intelligible, both in the establishment of a new history and in the wonder of a mystery.

John insists on the continuity inherent in true faith: to believe is already to possess eternal life. Paul goes even further in his defiance of death, and in the articulation of the doctrine that such a defiance generates. Not only does death become a reward for all those who want to rejoin Christ – the Head whose mystical body is the Church – but it is also a general advantage since man cannot possibly escape his fallen condition on his own. The initial equation (original sin=flesh=death) could only be solved by He who suffered and bore death without being annihilated; by He who, born of a virgin and begotten by God's Spirit, sacrificed Himself to redeem the flesh and atone for sin. The second Adam restores the ruins caused by the first Adam and ushers in a new humanity – which, at the end of time, will witness the ultimate restoration: Christ's definitive victory over death.

A moral alternative is drawn out of this: "for if you live according to the flesh, you will die, but if by the Spirit you put to death the deeds of the body you will live" (Romans 8.13). The hatred of death must be entirely transferred onto its cause: this flesh fraught with guilt. Thus man, after having been divided by the flesh and handed over to the caducity of the old order, rises in his totality. "[L]et those who have wives live as though they had none," and "those who have dealings with this world as though they had no dealings with it" (1 Corinthians 7.29b, 31). The terms of the exchange are clear: in Heaven, mankind will be "like God's angels, who do not marry." Virginity and corporeal asceticism anticipate the future life by sketching it out on earth. The heavenly destiny is, at first, achieved negatively, through the renunciation of what, in the body and in a world that is already obsolete, is synonymous with nonbeing, loss, evil.

This is the outline of a difficult concept that imposes itself only gradually. It is a concept, moreover, whose basic principle can be questioned from the very start: if the flesh, in its animality and mortality, is antinomic to the Spirit, then why should it be accepted into the Kingdom? Or, alternatively, why bother to rescue the argumentation of Greek philosophers concerning the body when its premises and conclusions are radically opposed to a Christian perspective? Even among those Corinthians who were evangelized, Paul's words are not heard: "[F]lesh and blood cannot inherit the Kingdom of God, nor does the perishable inherit the imperishable.... For this perishable nature must put on the imperishable, and this mortal nature must put on immortality" (1 Corinthians 15.50, 53). The notion of immortality, perfectly comprehensible to the Greeks, no longer refers to a substantial attribute of the soul, but rather to a gift of God to man, created in his image but marked by impotence. One should understand resurrection here not as the soul's resumption of its body, but rather as a true creation in its own right, a transformation that cannot be explained as a simple reanimation. "What is sown is perishable, what is raised is imperishable. It is sown in dishonor, it is raised in glory. It is sown in weakness, it is raised in power. It is sown a physical body, there is also a spiritual body" (1 Corinthians 15.42-44).

Opposed by the Sadducean Jews, the dogma of resurrection primarily develops from the encounter with Hellenistic and Roman thought, according to which, since Socrates, death had come to represent a willed separation between body and soul, a separation synonymous with philosophical choice. At this time, to philosophize meant to "attain heights," in other words, "to think with the Thought that encompasses all things" (Marcus Aurelius), "to be one with the One, like the center of a circle coinciding with another circle," or, more mythically, "to join the procession of the gods to contemplate an intelligible Heaven" (Plotinus), or else, "seized by sober exhilaration, to climb atop the vault of the Intelligible and thus come into the presence of the divinity" (Philo of Alexandria).

The control of passion and pleasure is only part of a much larger endeavor: an *apatheia*, or a folding back upon oneself leading to both a broadening of the mind toward the cosmic horizon and a concentration of the soul upon itself until it attains full fusion with the Divine. It is, once again, the theme of the bird-soul, introduced in the *Phaedrus*, and of its flight toward its land of origin, "the valley of truth." It is the figure of the "divine man," or the "true man," who, in the process of purification, manages to rediscover the pulsations of eternal life within himself. Even though Paul decides to contrast the true folly of the Cross with the Gentiles' vain wisdom, all these worn-out formulas are deliberately reactivated by some Fathers to convince "those who wish to obtain faith by demonstration." "Come, I shall show you the Logos and the mystery of the Logos with the help of your own imagery," says Clement of Alexandria, explicitly recognizing philosophy as a preparation for Christian truth. But independently from these various forms of persuasion and other strategies of power, it is most often spontaneously and at the risk of distortion that those common opinions are reinvested. Thus, what is culled from the Platonic inheritance is the dualist side of the *Phaedrus* and the *Phaedo* and not the cosmological optimism of the *Timaeus* or the *Laws*. The delphic maxim, "Know thyself," becomes the recognition of sin and the elaboration of all that is in the image of God: Plato's intellect is fused with the Logos of John's Gospel, the fall of the soul as it appears in astral theologies is interwoven with the Biblical story. The arms of the Crucified represent the bird with outspread wings (Saint Ambrose), and virtue (virginity) allows one to fly like a cloud (Gregory of Nyssa) and leads up to ethereal summits (Methodus of Olympia). It is impossible to keep track of all the "feathered" ones — the term Plato applies to *Eros* — now "feathered by Christ's Spirit," the doves of the Holy Spirit. Just as it is hard to account for all the references to the Pythagorean pun condemning the body, this shameful body which "nails" or "limes" the soul.

In such driftings, however, the question of resurrection always returns. Very much debated, it is always approached from a dual perspective — theoretically as well as strategically. How can one reconcile the moral dualism of man with his unity after death? How can one go beyond philosophy, the science that molded the Church Fathers? Once again, asceticism, made strict and systematic for everyone, becomes a distinctive pillar of the Christian community. But how can one conceive resurrection? How can one accept the notion that the body, essentially corruptible, has the right to survive death in and through Christ? Indeed, what similarity is there between the body redeemed by Christ's Incarnation or Resurrection and the body that ultimately is supposed to be devoid of any reality? It is not surprising that pagan philosophers would consider the dogma of the Resurrection a misunderstanding, a misinterpretation of the old Pythagorean idea of the transmigration of the soul that is the lot of all sinners, or of the Stoics' idea of the eternal return.[7]

The depth of the mystery, as well as the fervor and intensity it released, had a double effect on Christian thought: on the one hand, these qualities restrained it; on the other hand, they animated it, forced it into action, made it claim a different kind of truth, another sort of method. The fact that resurrection finds no support either in myth or in common experience demands rather than invalidates speculative effort. But this effort is governed by the religious dimension of the question, its character both as a theoretical issue (to be interpreted, elaborated and inscribed within a general economy) and as a cause to divulge and defend against unbelievers and heretics. By insisting on "the simplicity of the heart,"[8] by resorting to magic rites such as baptism and the Eucharist, and by embodying aristocratic virtues such as virginity and abstinence, Christian teachers disclosed notions concerning the status of the body that were previously confined to an intimate group of followers. But from the very start, resurrection was the touchstone of belief, the test of its real strengths, the topos where its system of thought had to gain its autonomy; at the same time it was precisely where theology most often faltered, exposing its limitations, contradictions and shortcomings.

Thus, when Clement of Alexandria[9] or Tertullian argued that Greek philosophy is merely an incomplete faith, distorted and misled by demons, they not only behaved like sophists in order to gain political authority, but they also mixed two irreconcilable approaches to truth. This discrepancy became obvious when Origen, revealing himself as the heir of the philosophical tradition, concocted the first Christian system worthy of the name. In his theology, the repudiation of the body and the flesh reaches as far as the resurrection. For his part, however, Augustine has difficulty finding a stance: he is caught among his will to give new meaning to the idea of immortality, his mistrust of the body (acquired during his contact with both Manichaeanism and Platonism) and his role as both an evangelist and a defender of the faith. The address of the old Bishop of Hippo to his congregation is pertinent here: "I know you want to go on living. You do not want to die. You want to pass directly from this life into the next so that you will never have to wake up dead but rather fully alive and transformed. This is what you want. This is the deepest human feeling. Mysteriously enough, even the soul instinctively wishes and hopes for the same thing."[10] Augustine's great power is his rhetorical capacity to touch all bases, to accommodate his audience and still not compromise himself by mentioning the body directly. It is difficult here to distinguish between a theoretical discourse aimed at elaborating a dogma and a rhetorical discourse responding to particular circumstances. They tend to overlap in the course of an intellectual growth which, once it touches the question of the resurrection, leaps ahead, overlooking secondary causes.

And, indeed, the question of the Resurrection is dodged for quite a while. Augustine is repeatedly embarrassed by "the limbs" of the resurrected Christ; and when he speaks of the "Word become flesh," the term seems to assume pejorative connotations the moment it is related to the Resurrection (*De fide et symbolo*). Moreover, he will always insist on the need for asceticism, the purity that honors the Christian as it had honored philosophy "in its chaste embrace of truth." Despite his quarrel with Pelagius (who rejects original sin in order to be even more severe with the flesh),[11] and despite his past Manichaean inclinations, Augustine does not give an inch when it comes to the moral dualism that lends even greater emphasis to sin. "On earth we must walk as the dead so as to be dead while living, and not so as to be dead above while living below." But the moment he broaches the question of resurrection and the doubts expressed by the Manichaeans, things change. His argument grows blurred, his voice breaks with anguish as he evokes the "hard face of death," or in the middle of lyrical exaltation as he evokes the beauty and purity of the redeemed bodies in Heaven. For even if, in the end, resurrection itself remains unthought in the City of God, it is important that the body be rehabilitated and allowed the possibility of being without sin. After all, how could it be considered bad in itself when Christ himself deigned to wear it? How could it be held responsible, when it is never anything more than a mere instrument of the soul, its vital principle? It is the soul that, in the beginning and of its own free will, altered and alienated the body by imbuing it with mortality, that is to say, by a principle of mutability that manifests itself from birth, in the process of aging.

But if the body is secondary to the soul, the soul, far from being immortal in its essence, depends entirely on God (in whose image it was created) and on its love for God. Thus, it follows that man also depends on God by virtue of his mortality, whose meaning takes on double implications. Physical death is not minimized, far from it: death existed even before sin and has been, since the Fall, an ordeal that can only be conceived of as a passage toward resurrection and the regaining of Paradise. But there are two kinds of death, one of which, strictly physical, is contained in the other, which explains the first as sin. Death seen as punishment is an effect and not a necessity; and there is another, absolute death, a true and irrevocable nothingness for the soul that turns away from God, His goodness and His justice: "let us concentrate on the death that strikes the soul that has lost God, its own life."[12] The duality of soul and body is the result of this essential separation of God and man's soul that entails temporality and exile, and is each time reenacted by a moribund life — a life controlled by the body, whose precariousness is made more poignant in view of the eternity to which it aspires.

In the beginning, Augustine explains, Adam had total freedom and a body which, though animal and mortal, was kept powerful by the tree of life. He could have — and this is the main point — avoided sin, and thus avoided death: in this case his end would have been only a caesura that would not have entailed the destruction of the human compound. Evil is not the lot of the body since it is not even consubstantial with the soul: it is the result of a wrong choice, an accident characteristic of being-in-the-world — a world where, however, there is still the possibility of relegating evil to its contingency and thereby of being saved.

The Immaterial Body

To grasp the difference between Augustine and Origen it is necessary to look at their respective representations of Paradise. For Augustine, as long as Adam is faultless, harmony reigns in the garden, and an a priori perfect relationship joins both body to soul and man to his other half (indeed, there is no reason to believe they did not have children). Following the example of Philo, Origen, on the other hand, gives the biblical story an allegorical dimension. Not without a certain complicity with Celsus, his Platonic and pagan adversary, he barely conceals his spite for the simpletons who "believe that God has planted his garden in the west like a simple gardener,"[13] and that Adam has eaten the fruit of the tree "with real teeth" — in other words, for all those who go no further than the surface of the text, "the body of the Scriptures," without trying to attain "the mysterious truths," the hidden meaning of its figures. He shows no mercy for either the golden age of the chiliasts or the verdant prairies vividly depicted by the sermons: although he expects a direct, intuitive grasp of intelligible reality, Origen intellectualizes everything.

In his history of the succession of the worlds, there was (and again will be) a time when God's creature knew an angelic condition, a time when we wore a spiritual body endowed with all the qualities characteristic of such a state of bliss and glory. This body methodically displays all the qualities it shares with Heaven and the soul, as if aspiring to an absence of figuration, an invisible and intelligible reality, luminous, subtle, light and incorruptible in nature, nourished solely on the contemplation of God. This entity made of fire and pure air, whose quasi-immateriality reflects moral perfection, is nevertheless a body, as implied by two premises according to which only the Trinity is incorporeal, while the soul, though incorruptible and impassive, requires a body to exist and subsist. One thing is certain: this pure medium, whose only function is to envelop and convey the soul or the spirit (its upper part), is not carnal.

Since Paul, it was necessary to distinguish between the body-temple of God, the sanctuary of the image, and the flesh, here understood as an ontological leap into a mortal condition: the "becoming animal" to which Origen applies the usual metaphors of the carnal body as a grave, a net or a weight bearing man down, chaining him to the process of corruption. How could this flesh rise again, Origen asks, when it partakes only in what is mutable, heavy, dense — in short, what is earthly? And what if it were only an addition made to man after his Fall? This Fall must be understood symbolically, according to the Pythagorean image adopted by the Neoplatonists: a descent through various spheres, from eternity to the rivers of fire and the waters that mark the edge of time and of the sensible, on toward the firmament and the sky; a descent that is accompanied by a progressive thickening of the soul, entailing forgetfulness and blindness as it gets closer and closer to the earth — this planet which, because of its weight and density, has fallen to the center of the universe. Layers upon layers of matter have gathered upon the soul or, rather, upon its spiritual body. They are given a new name and their interpretations change: they are the well-known "coats of skin" that Adam wears after the Fall, as mentioned in the Bible. For Origen, they symbolize sexuality and the mortality of the flesh, but they also happen to designate the carnal body itself, "the wordly habitation." This interpretation is responsible for a number of ambiguities found among the commentaries on Origen and, above all, for the condemnation of a theology that leans dangerously in the direction of metaphysical dualism.

Origen's theology, however, is quite different from the Gnosticism which it sometimes resembles, at least in one important aspect: it is not the body that is the source of sin, but rather the soul, which the Stoics saw as the abode of free will. It is the soul which, through self-satiation, turns toward the sensible, perceptible dimension and, in its exile, finds a collaborator and zealous accomplice in the body. This emphasis on the preeminence of the soul does not prevent Origen from being concerned with the body, its nature as well as its possibilities: the body-river, which changes according to the process of generation and corruption, as well as the permanent body, which keeps its identity beyond death itself. In order to reconcile these opposites, Origen does not simply introduce a principle of hierarchy into his anthropology and specify the union of body and soul. He also proposes a new concept, that of corporeal form (*eidōs, logos spermatikos*), which permits him to preserve both aspects (the corporeal and the spiritual) and to introduce in the body a principle of continuity that allows it to remain quite independent of both the states and the stages it goes through. The cohesion endangered by death and other-worldly fluctuations does not stem from the soul: as the *pneuma* of Stoic philosophy (but without sharing in its materiality), the corporeal form keeps all the elements of the body together. As in Aristotle, it informs matter and mixes with it without being altered by it (following the stoic principle of total copenetration). The most essential feature of this corporeal form remains its immutability, which guarantees the preservation of individuality throughout its various evolutions in time and space. Without being an abstract idea or an external figure, it manifests itself at once as invisible and corporeal: it cannot be apprehended by the sensory organs even though it is connected to the material substratum. This is why it is said to be mortal, but, Origen adds, it can become "better," more beautiful, that is to say, it can be glorified by the Spirit. In the moment of resurrection, this corporeal form abandons the matter dissolved by death and clings to the soul or to the ethereal body that coexists with it.

As always, the question of the body's identity is the center of the problem of resurrection. What indeed is this body that endures as a whole, having never ceased dying, this body whose reversibility — from dust to dust — is negated by resurrection, this body which, while keeping its own individual attributes, must also don qualities that are the opposite of those it possessed on earth, a surplus of glory that confers its true reality or perfection? And what about its identity which, though it does not deny the rupture caused by death or resurrection, is not a mere perpetuation? One can always invoke the mystery before which everything else must give way, and which, preexisting all things, gives them a basis and unites them absolutely. Without downplaying mystery, Origen discovers in the body itself the principle of a permanence and a union that involves at once the intelligible and the sensible. But Origen attains such a result only by stripping the body of its flesh, its death (which Augustine considers an essential feature of humanity), and by rarefying it enough to bring it as close to absence as possible.

Methodius of Olympus's refutations concern precisely this point: as Origen's main Christian opponent, he criticizes his attempts to eliminate the flesh and thereby to reduce the difference between the body and the spirit. If the flesh alone dies and its form survives, this might mean not only that form cannot rise again, since it has never died to begin with, but also that it must exist as a separate personal entity, similar to the platonic *eidōlon*,[14] which survives death and preserves its distinctive features. On the other hand, if form is mortal (which amounts to saying that it does not exist on its own), then there is resurrection. This, however, raises again the question of the resurrected body's identity: it cannot possibly be the same body — it must be another body, totally disincarnated, a body to which Christ has given new life and new attributes. According to Methodius, these distinctions stem from a mysterious difference, resurrection itself, while the identity of the glorious body implies at once wholeness and individuality. For Origen, on the contrary, immortal qualities are quite independent of matter, owing to a principle of preservation (*logos spermatikos*) which removes the question of individual permanence or dissolution by transferring mutability onto the flesh. But here the problem of Christ's Resurrection in His flesh arises. To ward off the return of the flesh, Origen deploys a wealth of diversely valid arguments, most of them gleaned from Scripture and relying heavily on the notion of Christ's Transfiguration. It is Christ's form, he argues, and not His flesh that was transfigured; the form which, inaccessible to the senses of the apostles, was confused with His external figure. Nothing could disprove that "flesh and blood cannot inherit the Kingdom of God." This is the Gnostics' war-horse, the weapon they employ to counter the resurrection, a weapon Origen himself relies on whenever he has to defend his notion of the spiritual body. And when Paul says God "will give life to your mortal bodies" (Romans 8.11), he is referring to their form and only to their form. As for Ezekiel's vision, it should be understood as an allegory, while the parable of Lazarus and the rich man[15] proves the soul's need of a body. But since Origen also doubts there is any need for limbs in Heaven, and asserts that angels have no flesh, the tenuousness of his spiritual body is again confirmed.

The Resurrection is a "difficult" matter, in the scrutiny of which "one must try to remain faithful to the traditions of Antiquity and beware of falling prey to the weakness of the senses by daring things that are impossible and unworthy of God's majesty."[16] It would be impossible to speak more clearly and go any further in the spiritualization of matter — or any closer to the Greek Empyrean and its celestial bodies. The Church will not forgive Origen his theory of the soul's preexistence, nor his notions of original sin, of universal salvation and of the glorious body it believed to be spheroid. How could such viewpoints be reconciled with the concept of Incarnation? Or with the Eucharist? Or with corporeal penance, or the imitation of Christ? The share of negativity borne and abolished by the Crucified, as well as Christianity's peculiar relationship to death, loses all meaning in this beautiful harmony where syncretism triumphs.

But this sort of condemnation does not help the elucidation of the system, and even less an understanding of Origen's notion of the ethereal body, which both preexists the body and replaces it at the moment of resurrection. There is reason to believe that, like Plotinus dealing with the same subject, Origen prefers to indicate a direction rather than to theorize on a seldom mentioned object, the *ochēma*, the envelope and vehicle of the soul.[17] It was easy to regard it as a fiction that dodged a question and preserved the autonomy of the soul in relation to the earth. The celestial bodies swarming through the heavens of late Antiquity, these membranes appearing and disappearing like halos, these pneumatic particles allowed to float at the edge of the intelligible, beyond the field of gravity by the Neoplatonists contemporary or posterior to Origen[18] (but also by the Gnostics, the Hermetists and the Theosophists) – these "beings" are, for the most, nothing more than a speculative compromise. Their only philosophical value resides in their ability to bring together the most diverse, not to say the most antinomic, principles: to bridge the gap between the mortal and the immortal, the human and the divine, the body and the spirit – without undermining the intelligible realm. It is a characteristic of such intermediaries never to achieve autonomy, never to come into their own; they never become pure difference, they only allow for it. In fact, in *De principiis*, Origen does not deny the possibility that the ethereal body will disappear at the end of the *apocatastasis*, the final restoration of all sinful beings to God and to the state of blessedness.

A Material Soul

Origen introduces the notion of *ochēma* both to explain resurrection and to establish a distinction between man and his Creator. Augustine is also careful to set himself apart from the philosophers on this subject: the soul certainly contains more reality than the world, and its supremacy over the body vouches for its moral resemblance to God. But it is not "divine"; it needs grace, and its mutability is enough to prove its distance from God. One of the shortcomings of patristic thought is that it attempts to organize substances into a hierarchy, with prominence given to what is made in the image of God, without compromising the principle of transcendence.[19] In other words, the Church Fathers had to see to it that God would not be postulated in the image of man.

Spirituality is God's essence. Thus, certain Church Fathers privilege the spirit over the soul; at the same time, by relying on the Stoic doctrine of the *pneuma*[20] – a doctrine which allowed the Stoics to rid themselves of metaphysical dualism through materialism – they argue against those who hold the soul immortal and incorporeal. Up until Plotinus's time, and mostly in the realm of myth, the soul, though invisible, was not considered immaterial: spatially determined, it inhabits a place and travels across the universe. The Stoics gave a philosophical foundation to the materiality of the soul which appeared as a divine particle of the Creative Fire that breathes life into the Cosmos and maintains the cohesion of all living things. This breath is so ethereal that it does not modify in the least either the volume or the weight of the body and dissolves after death to return to its source, the Soul of the World.

Obviously, this divine immanentism cannot be accepted by the Christians. Neither can the dry and clear exhalation of blood be in any way confused with the *pneuma*, that is, the Spirit, which since Paul was considered the work of grace — to "bestow perfection" and to be granted only to those "who have God as their hope." "We know two different kinds of Spirit," Tatian says, "one is known as the soul and the other, superior to it, is made in the image of God. Both were present in the first man, part of him above and beyond his material being."[21] The soul inhabits the body and can, in turn, be inhabited by the Spirit which, like the Stoics' *hegemonikon*, controls and unifies psychic life by relating it to the divinity.

Tertullian is the one who, in his stubborn fight against the Gnostics and the Platonists, will inherit the Stoic doctrine, without, however, acknowledging it. "Nihil enim si non corpus," nothing is more absurd than an incorporeal substance. Neither God nor the soul is an abstract entity despite their invisibility — which is explained by the weakness of the human eye, like the eyes of an owl that the slightest light can blind. God's body is simple (that is, indivisible) and incommensurable, and its eternity is evidence of its transcendence. His senses are the same (*eosdem*) as those of His creatures, without being similar (*tales*) to them. And to judge from His anger, as depicted in the Old Testament, He is far from impassive, as the Gnostics maintain. As for the soul, it is enough to turn to the Scriptures and to the parables of Lazarus and the rich man to understand that it is a *flatus*, a breath that survives death and shares in the properties commonly attributed to the body. The *habitus* (disposition), the *terminum* (limit) and the three dimensions compose a sexed figure which grows and decreases in the course of old age, until it becomes an exiguous thing. But its cohesion is such that it remains simple, even though it is endowed with sensory limbs and organs that manifest themselves constantly in its thoughts and dreams. Tertullian adduces as evidence the vision of a Montanist prophetess who described the soul as a delicate figure having the color of air and the form of the human body, though smaller in size.

The fact that the soul comes into existence at the same time as the body (thereby acquiring sensibility and mutability) does not exclude its immortality: the soul is an immortal body within a mortal body. The soul does not juxtapose itself to the body, but rather appears as a kind of double that adapts itself to its container and retains its qualities in every part of the body it occupies. This physical model — inspired by that of the Incarnation — is the basis of a coexistence, intended since the origin of time, that is guaranteed by the promise of resurrection. "So intimate is their union that one could ask whether it is the flesh that envelops the soul or the soul that envelops the flesh, and whether it is the flesh that obeys the soul or the soul that obeys the flesh."[22] They cannot be distinguished; they are united both in their moral responsibility and in their fate after death. They share in everything they do, including thought: the soul can only be understood in and by the flesh, which in Heaven will gain recognition and magnificence and become even more glorious than the angels themselves. The flesh does not resurrect in the garb of some moral weakness that needs to be redeemed, but rather as a substance that plays a central role in God's design, whose main stages are Creation, Incarnation and Resurrection. The first and the second Adam are not set apart by their offspring, as Paul maintains; Tertullian insists on the identity between Jesus' flesh and that of man.

How should one, then, interpret those texts in which the flesh is condemned? Neither flesh nor blood is exiled from God's Kingdom, Tertullian responds; rather, "their works" are all the sins that mar our part of promised glory. Indeed, in his eyes, to exalt the flesh amounts to sacralizing it, to protecting it incessantly against all forms of impurity and compromise likely to shield it from the Spirit. Everything falls back onto a pugnacious asceticism, a Montanist rigor that sees concupiscence as more than a sin, a true betrayal, a violation of the betrothal made by Christ in person, acting here as a mediator between God and man. If soul and flesh are united, then a similar union exists also between the rule of faith and the rule of morality. If the flesh is in Christ, it is necessary to insist on virginity even in marriage and not to give an inch to men's laws. Tertullian stresses the importance of obedience and the probatory value of deeds while at the same time inveighing against the presumptions of philosophy. His profession of faith drives beyond the prescription of obedi-

Adam, Eve and Original Sin. Roman fresco from the 12th century
(Austria, Cathedral of Gurk).

ence to the solicitation of martyrdom — which, according to him, is man's only chance to know redemption in this world and to have access to Paradise.

The Physical Dimension

In the third and fourth centuries there is a proliferation of treatises on the Resurrection, with numerous interpretations and approaches. Such urgency denotes the Church's uneasy realization that it can no longer rely solely on the pledge made by Christ on Mount Tabor — His face shining as bright as the sun, His clothes drenched in light and sparkling white, His body in full possession of its graces (such as He could have been always, Augustine points out, had He not chosen to offer Himself to us in His wounded humanity). The Christian masters will return to this overwhelming vision, just as they will come back to the imminence of a return that is constantly delayed, while they try to structure some form of universality to ward off the arguments of their opponents. (In Celsus and Porphyry, in particular, the Christians find two formidable opponents whose doctrine, strong in its universality and its spiritual demands,[23] presupposes the eternity of the world and the immortality of all the heroes, demons and souls who will sooner or later be rescued from metempsychosis.)

As if it were not enough to jab at the heart of Platonic metaphysics, the notion of resurrection will also attack the cosmology that sustains it. For the very name of Heaven implies a celebration of the great order (the cosmos) where everything is rigorously arranged and organized in accordance with divine harmony and measure. Wisdom conforms to cosmic reason, and Heaven encompasses an entire series of physical determinations, such as the balance and order of the elements or the regularity of movement. Therefore, to assert that the physical body resurrects is to grant it a sidereal nature which belongs only to the soul. It further challenges the theory of balance expressed in the *Timaeus*, according to which the elements composing the world are justly apportioned in terms of their weight, with the heaviest (earth) and the lightest (fire) located at each end and separated by water and air. "It is most ridiculous to assert that living beings, weighed down by their body, may borrow the nature of winged birds."[24] Augustine tackles the subject more than once in his *City of God* (birds are airborne; lead, an earthly body, may float on water when shaped in a particular way). Nor does he fail to recall that the stars worshiped by the pagans are, like the gods of the *Timaeus*, graced with a body in their eternal abode.[25]

Just as God cannot descend into the world without disturbing the cosmic order (Celsus),[26] so the terrestrial bodies cannot bring their imperfect nature along with them into Heaven. The biblical argument concerning divine omnipotence (systematically reiterated in relation to the Resurrection) is no more than an "absurd way out," since God, who has excluded all flaws from his ordering action, cannot allow for anything that goes against nature and reason. In fact, since the Psalms and Paul, there was a Christian tradition that echoed, in its commentaries on Genesis, this reverence for a universal harmony supposed to fill the worshiper with veneration and piety for his Creator — this "deft artisan," sometimes represented as the Platonic demiurge, who in his industrious wisdom arranged all his creatures according to an exact order. Similarly, the early apologists tended to represent resurrection as a natural phenomenon and, therefore, to attenuate the dramatic character as well as the mysteries of eschatology.

God, Clement of Rome explains, placed signs of his saving will in nature, in all those phenomena that show kinship with resurrection: in the succession of days and nights (an image often employed by the Stoics to indicate the periodic rebirth of the world, the mark of its permanence), the cycles of the moon, the rotation of the seasons, the regeneration of the phoenix from its ashes ("even in a bird has he shown the magnitude of his promise").[27] These are the canonical metaphors that will follow those of the seed and the grain already used by Paul.[28] But whereas for the Apostle, this image is anchored in the theme of the two Adams, the metaphors used by Clement, or by Theophilus of Antioch, often lead to confusion when interpreted as examples of metempsychosis, that is to say, within the context of a cosmic continuum that will go on until the end of time, thus foreclosing the notion of transformation related to the *parousia*, Christ's return. At the opposite extreme of the apocalyptic vision, Stoic immanentism gives rise to an optimistic and not very Christological point of view according to which the proximity of God and the perfection of His design would be enough in themselves to guarantee and explain the Resurrection.

Historically, what is most interesting here is not the scholarly debate concerning the physical aspects of the question, but the actual identity of the resurrected body. How can we picture, Porphyry wonders, the reconstitution of bodily organs?

It is readily assumed that God would never let what He has edified fall to ruin, and that there is nothing useless in His creation (Anathagoras); that He would not reject what He has Himself created and doom it to nothingness (Justin); that the judgment would not be perfect unless it concerned man such as he was in life, and that the body must be rewarded for its services along with the soul (Tertullian). But what about the corpse, or the dispersing power of death? Christ, Gregory of Nyssa answers, has rejoined all the separated parts in His own person: He is the principle of the reunion brought about by the soul through death, for the soul is present in every element, whether united or dispersed. Essentially unextended, it eludes both space and time, and is able to encompass the cosmos within its amplitude, without eroding its contemplative faculty. Through its organ of knowledge, the soul stays in contact with what is its own and, at the right moment, pulls all its elements back into place.

Before Gregory, the question of the fate of the body, scattered in ashes, gnawed by worms, devoured by beasts, fish or cannibals, was extensively debated. It is not difficult to detect, lurking behind all the fantasies it evoked, a presence mankind wants to exorcise and obliterate through the perpetuation of identity promised by resurrection: the anguish and fear of death. This death is neither the daily occurrence Augustine perceives in an everchanging life, nor the annihilation brought about by the forces of evil on all that is affected by its baseness, but rather the sudden blast of the moment when the soul leaves the body, the horror of what has neither a form nor a name, the terror of an absence of unity that can only be pictured as the abject disintegration of the body, the dissolution and engulfment of the self into the dark and bottomless realm of the undifferentiated and the amorphous. For, in the end, what lies behind all these seemingly naive questions is the fear of one's own death, the fear of losing an identity that one feels is connected to the body.

Obviously, the Church Fathers could not tackle the question of resurrection without being confronted with the imaginary or without dealing with individual cases: aborted fetuses, organisms maimed, mangled and mutilated by illness or, more often than not, by old age. To this, Augustine answers that God reassembles and renews all the different parts, whatever they are and whatever their condition: as in the instance of a metal statue that is remodeled after being fused, it is not so important that each part recovers its original form and place, provided the whole achieves its purpose. But no sooner is the question of integrality answered and its promise renewed than the otherwise embarrassing question of the flesh arises – the very flesh Christ assumed and kept pure. What is the purpose of ascetic anticipation if the flesh is allowed to find permanence in the other world? And how can one envisage its integration in a place of perfection where there is no need of it, and where it has no purpose? If Origen refuses such a possibility, Tertullian, on the contrary, believes that our sexual organs may be preserved, though their function would, of course, be different. As he puts it, "the body is an old ship that can no longer float, but that deserves to be renovated out of consideration for its past services."[29] As for Augustine, one senses his impatience with such vain curiosity: "Who cares whether the hair will again be hair and the nails nails, or whether the elements that constitute them will be changed into flesh or other things, as long as the Artist's providence sees to it that nothing indecent will occur."[30]

Between the "ability not to sin and not to die of Adam" before the Fall and the abolition of mortality there is more than a difference of degree. The mystery surrounding the difference between the lost Paradise and the one to regain provokes approximations that reveal the impotence of language. For it should not be forgotten that all these evocations of the perpetual youth of a body that has recovered its original strength and harmony, of the beauty of the two sexes finally unhampered by lust, of a general lightness and agility that can no longer be thwarted (since a relentless energy is constantly filling the body which no longer needs either sleep, food or any of the things that make it a slave to nature), of the radiance emanating from a holy assembly that has been blessed with a vision of God's face ("We shall see God and we shall love, we shall love and we shall praise"),[31] that all these evocations are only simple translations of the desire for a continuity that is belied by everything else.

Generally speaking, both the hegemony of mystery and the repudiation of the world have kept the imagination in check and limited thought to the rigid confines of dualism. But the separation between this and the other world inevitably entailed a number of cosmological implications. Indeed, to insist on the similarity between the glorious body and Heaven implied not only a union in and through God, but also an endorsement of certain cosmological premises – that is, the premises that led to an eclectic science whose prestige (thanks to its involvement with soteriology) increased in inverse proportion to its rigor. Rejected by the Christians as a theological framework, dubbed by Paul's followers as "the mad wisdom of the world," cosmology nevertheless underlies all representations of the body in Heaven. Although Heaven is seen above all to signify the recovery of the lost bond with God, it is also a harmonious, resplendent place whose qualities, though only expressive of the divine, subsume the qualities of the bodies it has gathered. These bodies necessarily resemble one another in that they have all crossed the same boundary and share the same site, where, at a higher level of reality, the physical and the spiritual are one. Obviously their nature is enfolded in grace, but this does not prevent it from being viewed in conformity with the laws of the cosmos and its most dominant representations. In other words, the nature of the body in Heaven is akin to that of a star, that intelligible and intelligent body whose splendor, impassivity and perfect revolutions are hailed by Philo of Alexandria — while Origen attributes to it a morality and the capacity to pray.

One of the ways of approaching the glorious body was to mix it with other celestial bodies, within that sphere of light and purity that combines the rational, the sublime and the sacred in the same opposition to the earthly. The condition here was that they were all to be seen as part of the design of creation and, therefore, to correspond to principles and spiritual hierarchies other than those determining pagan science. Although the analogy between the glorious body and the astral body was not authorized, there is hardly any doubt that the star played a heuristic role in the series of celestial congruences, and that it facilitated, both at the level of imagination and belief and at that of theoretical implication, the crystallization of the notion of the glorious body. On the one hand, when Basilius of Caesarea praises the sun for its beauty and the precision of its course, he is in fact referring to the "Sun of Justice" yet to come;[32] it is only thanks to anagogy that the star can keep its own splendor and glory. On the other hand, the insistence and rigor with which the astral cult is forbidden are in themselves revealing of the tenacity of the cosmological model. Indeed, the fineness, brilliance, lightness, mobility and impassivity of the glorious body are all traits corresponding to those of celestial mechanics, such as they are celebrated in astral theology. Furthermore, all these qualities are, of course, also present in the angel, a creature who, according to Clement of Alexandria, is corporeal only when compared with God, but quite incorporeal when compared with man. Angels appear luminous and ethereal (Philo, Origen, Augustine) — while demons are only aerial — since angels are made up of the purest air and fire (Methodius of Olympus) and have a nature at once very refined and tenuous, unlike that of any other element (Gregory of Nyssa). Jean Pépin has pointed out the strange coincidence between these properties and those of the fifth element, ether, introduced by the young Aristotle to explain the eternity of celestial movements. Neither weight nor lightness, neither alteration nor determination can affect its quintessential nature, a nature that is almost immaterial and unlike that of any other element.

This generic integration of celestial bodies also finds its roots in the Judaic tradition. Jerome contemplates a milky way of saints, but there is reason to believe that his vision was already literally part of the collective imagination when Daniel affirmed that "those who are wise shall shine as the brightness of the firmament" (Daniel 12.3). Two centuries later, the Essenes will maintain that the names of the Just have been inscribed in the book since the origins and that their light shines in Heaven: on the last day, the spirit will wear its gown of glory while uniting with the star that has awaited it.[33] As for the apocalypses, if we ignore both hierarchical attributions and their functions, nothing distinguishes the saint from the guardian angel or the angel itself. All too often confused with heavenly light, angels are in charge of, or associated with, the spirits or the crowd of spirits emanating from the divine breath and represented, in turn, as meteors, the instruments that regulate the voice of thunder, the movements of the solar wheel or the cycles of the seasons.

Whether stars or angels, celestial bodies always find their unity of expression and movement in light seen as pure power and act, identical to the spirit that governs both the nature and the relationships between bodies.

The Existential Dimension

The oxymoron of martyrdom we encounter in so many visions before death is the culmination of the systematic inversion of values we have already come across in several religious texts: death — the *summum malum*, the ultimate evil — finds its purification in the arena where the forces of evil confront those of salvation. The invisible manifests itself in the most convincing way possible; belief is rewarded with immediate ascension; the body is rid of both its flesh and the suffering it entails. Floating in its charisma and basking in light, it becomes the symbol of the other

Saint John Climacus, Ladder of Paradise.
From a 12th-century Greek manuscript
(Vatican City, Biblioteca Apostolica).

world, a glaring proof of God's love for his martyrs. If suffering does not weaken this witness, then it means that it no longer has any reason to be: the fire that was supposed to burn him does more than spare him, it puts itself between him and his torturers; it purifies like the fire on sacrificial altars, and, blown by the wind, it carries the victim away. An angel may also intervene and pour cold water on Theodorus's mutilated body or place a blinding barrier between Agnes, the virgin who is awaiting her mystical wedding in her prison, and her attacker. At times, it is Christ Himself who succors His champion by addressing him directly and providing him with the gift of perseverance.

"To the blood!" Such is the devise of God's soldier ready to undergo a second christening in the packed antechambers of the Kingdom, spurred on by Tertullian. But when the faith remains intact, the body is flooded with grace; spurts of blood, like purple flares yet more blinding than those of the sun, wash off sin, drowning horror in the miracle and the promise of appeasement, Paradise and its eternal peace. "Spectacle full of graces," the corpse that comes out of this trial looks more beautiful and younger, having acquired the smile, the pink complexion and the lily-like purity of angels. For martyrdom anticipates resurrection and authenticates it at those crucial moments when anteriority and retrospectivity become confused in one's vision – these are the moments hagiographies are made of. There is hardly any trace of eschatology, no anthropological reflection on the eve of death in the letters Ignatius of Antioch wrote as he prepared for his final combat: "near the sword means near to God. To be with wild beasts means to be with God."[34] The only things that matter to him are sharing in Christ's pain and the imitation of Him in an experience that his torturers see as a "setting," an end, but that he sees as the "dawning" of a new age that will free him from his worldly shackles.

"I am going through the pangs of being born. Sympathize with me, my brothers! Do not stand in the way of my coming back to life – do not wish death on me. Do not give back to the world one who wants to be God's; do not trick him with material things. Let me get into the clear light and manhood will be mine."[35] This is the supreme test that the Church Fathers are called upon to consider. If, fearing for faith, they delayed while dealing with themes that "battered reason," the experience of martyrdom spurs them to talk. As for those who had done their best to obliterate death – the inevitable black passageway toward resurrection and the Kingdom — they will no longer be able to do so now that it has come to coincide with ascension. For how else but with the help of visionary anticipation could one confront those shattering instants in which it is so hard to reconcile the agony of matter and its assimilation to the spirit? The mind reels before such an alliance of horror and desire. This is the cause of the definitive rupture with the pagans who condemn such a barbarity: death cherished and coveted as a sign of election, the infamy of adoring a God who has agonized and died on a cross, the paradox of a body debased and transfigured by the most abominable ecstasy, the vanity of mocking at the order of the world and the laws of the city — all this in the name of mere fables. This is enough to explain, for instance, the emperor Julian's repulsion for "those paroxysms of madness that make them wish for death and give them the idea that the moment they succeed in yanking themselves away from life they will fly up to the sky,"[36] as well as for "the cult of death," or its outcrop, the cult of martrydom — a practice whose novelty as well as plurality of effects Peter Brown has shown.[37] Here again, by following the usual logic of reversal, the Christian bishops are able to conceal what cannot be named and to draw the best advantage from the continuity between Earth and Heaven.

The body of the victim vanishes into thin air; it loses all traces of dereliction and all forms of debasement that branded it, thereby fueling the uncertainty of the believers. Death is obliterated, and time and history are suspended, as the grave of a marvelously restored body exuding the radiance of eternal life becomes an altar. The process of elevation is facilitated thanks to the patronage and personal intercessions of "God's friend," this "Holy Martyr," who is rendered so convincingly by his very proximity to man. Through him, the ideal mediation between the visible and the invisible worlds, two different spheres of being, can be safely located in the human condition. He becomes the manifestation of a presence that only a dead man, and a particular one at that, could restore. Evidence of both the Resurrection and the Kingdom, this fragrant, soothing corpse withstands the most atrocious death — thereby removing it from mankind's horizon — while endowing the mystical body with the power of redemption. From now on, everybody can identify in something tangible, while mystery persists in miracles (exorcisms, healing and so on) wrought in front of the community's eyes. If there is a perceptible point of convergence between the two worlds, then this is it, this buffer zone out of which spring the supernatural and renewal, this field where everything becomes immediate, where the spiritual bond can manifest itself in repeated acts of grace and vibrate with particular intensity, far more substantial than that of creatures of a different kind.

"As they rest their eyes on the relics of the saints, they actually embrace the live body in its prime: they use their eyes, their mouths, their ears and all their senses, and crying tears of respect and passion, they address their prayers to the martyr as if he were present" (Gregory of Nyssa).[38] The body is recovered because that of a dead man has gotten rid of death; time has opened up onto eternity; the forces of Heaven have seeped into the earth and caused the trees of Heaven to bloom there. Thanks to the Holy Martyr, the believer manages to get rid of his anxiety and his frustrations so completely that both Ambrose and Augustine begin to take offense at such an ostentatious and superstitious piety. However, they soon realize what advantages such a stream of *potentia*, duly channeled, can bring. In book ten of the *City of God*, the saint — that is, he whose sacrifice has washed off original sin — is ahead of the angel in the chain of intermediaries leading to God.

Heaven is not a circle but an infinity of circles that can change, move and intersect since they coincide in their centers, that is, in God, and since they are the place of the soul, the intensive space of a spiritual continuity sponsored by the One and the Same. It does not really matter whether the beyond appears as a reality peopled with immortal creatures steeped in goodness, or whether it is conceived as a constantly moving inner limit that can be approached through ecstasy. Whether within or without, transcendent or immanent, potential or actual, Heaven is an openness that excludes evil and death. In every anthropological doctrine, the body (in itself as well as in its effects) is always the "other" that must submit to the "same," a temporary, secondary part which, in order to complete the whole, must be dominated, vanquished or at least neutralized so as not to be in the soul's way. It never exists on its own, neither in the process of elevation nor in Heaven; it is never an agent nor a free principle of life. Its virtues lie elsewhere, *in alio*: it is created, it is taken on by Christ, it serves and supports all that is in the image of God, it is united with the soul and is introduced into the ethereal regions and so on. The soul can anticipate future life only through the continuous *askesis* of the body. The bond with Heaven may manifest itself in a supernaturally preserved corpse, but only a body endowed with a particularly rarefied texture can earn the Kingdom of God. Even there, in its fullest reality, at the top of power and glory, this body is only a correlative of the soul, which it reflects and duplicates in both its movements and its affections. But the soul cannot be dissociated from the body, and its spirituality does not imply real immateriality: whether on its own or through the addition of a pneumatic envelope, the soul partakes of that ethereal nature, that evanescence which denotes, at once, a distance from the earthly (or a proximity to the heavenly) and the impossibility of ever being fully assimilated into God.

A representation of the chosen one must take into account this double inequality (between the soul and the body, the soul and God). It must posit the tension between two poles (the immaterial and the material) in terms of height, and locate it at the outermost edge of a near immateriality, of a maximal degree of spiritualization — maximal but not total — where soul and body coexist in full solidarity and complementarity. In fact, the body and the soul (or its upper part, the spirit) are set in opposition only at the level of morality. Having broken away from Hellenistic harmony and wrapped itself in mystery, the definition of the glorious body had to give in to practical necessities that have stressed contradiction over difference: it is only the process of spiritual elevation that is defined by degrees, mediations, anticipations. Without associating evil and matter, or violating the hierarchy of principles, patristics has tried to conceive of a very particular differential space between the same and the other, so as to define a celestial identity that finds a firm basis only in the exclusion of sin and death, or in the union with God. The paradox of resurrection stems from the fact that it renders immortality at once more sensible or perceptible *and* more mysterious. Whereas the heavenly future of the soul lends itself to all sorts of evaluations, the glorious body truly possesses the dimension of a miracle.

NOTES

1. Plato, *Timaeus* 51c-52c.

2. Emile Benvéniste, *Vocabulaire des institutions Indo-Européennes*, vol. 1, ch. 15. See also Michel de Certeau's article, "Une pratique sociale de la différence, croire," in *Faire croire* (Actes du colloque de l'Ecole Française de Rome, 1979-80).

3. Translation based on C. Maurer, from E. Hennecke and W. Schneelmelcher, eds., *New Testament Apocrypha*, English trans. and ed. R. McL. Wilson (Philadelphia: Westminster Press, 1964), vol. 2, pp. 681-82. *Les plus beaux textes sur l'au-delà*, trans. J. Goubert and L. Cristiani (Paris, 1950). See also J. Ntedika, *L'Evocation de l'au-delà dans la prière pour les morts* (Paris: Louvain, 1971).

4. St. Augustine, *Enarrat in Ps XXX*, sermon 1118. God does not inhabit a place: He is not contained but container; that is to say, He is the place of all things and His own place. This idea, expounded by Philo of Alexandria, was repeated by Tertullian to explain that if God were in a space, this space would necessarily be superior to God and eternal like Him.

5. Heaven is a field of eclectic investigations in which various knowledges and powers compete, where ancient traditions accumulate, where sources, types of logics and levels of analysis blend in a patient research of signs and divine states of being. For the pagans, knowledge of celestial phenomena is "the activity that affords the most serenity in life" and has "no end but ataraxia and confident certainty, which is also the aim of all quests" (Epicurus, *Epistle to Pytocles* 85) — ataraxia achieved through the contemplation of "nature once the veils that conceal it are removed" (Lucretius), an "immersion in the wholeness of the world" (Seneca) and an understanding of the eternal and primary principles governing the universe; a feeling of confidence derived from the contemplation of the soul's blessed impassivity when, after shedding its body, it returns to the heavenly summits. Whichever the school of thought, the contemplation of the celestial bodies is a form of wisdom considered as a spiritual progress, an exercise of pure thought extending beyond the limits of the sensible and the self. Contemplation honors the divine harmony in which nothing is divided or hidden, and the realm of necessity where the mind finds its true objects. The stars are considered divine because they link rationality to splendor and are evidence of the ideal matching of the intelligence that regulates their flawless motion and a luminous body that diffuses light. The hymns devoted to them (and whose formal expression, according to Porphyry, partakes of the sublime) reflect the same *divina voluptas* which can be found in philosophical texts of all tendencies. Cf. P. Hadot, *Exercices spirituels et philosophies antiques* (Paris, 1987), and F. Cumont, *Astrology and Religion among the Greeks and Romans* (London, 1912).

6. *Enneads* 3.6.6.

7. According to Celsus, the Resurrection should remind some of the story of Aristaeus of Proconnesus who, if we are to believe Pindar and Herodotus, was ravished by death and then seen in many points of the world as a herald of God's will. See Origen, *Contra Celsum* 3.26.

8. See Peter Brown, "Late Antiquity," in *History of Private Life* (Cambridge, 1987), vol. 1, pp. 235-313.

9. "Philosophy either came to us in disguise or was given us by a thief" (Clement of Alexandria,

Stromata 1.17.81.4), quoted by J. Pépin, "Christianisme et mythologie," in *Dictionnaire des mytholo-gies*, Y. Bonnefoy, ed. (Paris, 1981). See also P. Courcelle, "Connais-toi toi-même. De Socrate à St. Bernard" (Paris, 1975).

10. Sermon 344.4.

11. Sin, according to Pelagius, is not intrinsic to human nature, and its diffusion is mostly due to imitation and habit. He stresses the power of free will, as the source of both merit and faith.

12. *City of God* 8.15. Cf. J.-L. Chrétien: "Pouvoir mourir et devoir mourir selon la théologie chrétienne" in *Le temps de la réflexion*, vol. 3 (Paris, 1982).

13. *De principiis* 4.3.1.

14. According to the Pythagorean notion of origin, after death the soul assumes an ethereal body that retains the *eidōs*, the form of the body.

15. This evangelical episode fueled the debate on resurrection: from the bottom of Hades the rich man cries and asks Abraham to send him Lazarus, that he may dip his fingertip in water and cool the rich man's tongue (Luke 16.24). The presence of these organs after death has been variously inter-preted, by Origen and Tertullian for example.

16. *Commentary on the Psalms* 1.5.

17. See H. Crouzel, "Le thème platonicien du véhicule de l'âme chez Origène," in *Didaskalia* 7 (1977); A.J. Festugière, "De la doctrine 'origéniste' du corps glorieux sphéroïde," in *Revue de philosophie et théologie* 43 (1959); A.V. Ofm, *Identidad entre el cuerpo muerto y resucitado en Origena segun el "De Resurrectione" de Methodio de Olympio* (Jerusalem, 1981); E.R. Dodds, *The Elements of Theology*, appen-dix 2 (Cambridge, 1963); E.H. Pagels, "The Mystery of the Resurrection: A Gnostic Reading of 1 Cor 15," in *Journal of Biblical Literature* 93 (1974); J. Laporte, "La Chute chez Philon et Origène," *Kyrakion: Festschift J. Quasten* (Münster, 1970), vol. 1; H. Cornelis, "Les fondements cosmologiques de l'eschatologie d'Origène," in *Revue de philosophie et théologie* 43 (1959).

18. According to Plotinus, the soul that is not entirely involved in the material world is surrounded by a pneumatic body which it dons before descending into the body, and which it is allowed to shed after death, provided it (the soul) has remained pure and detached from the world of the senses. For Porphyry, the world's soul possesses an *ochēma*, indistinguishable from the light which preexists being. The halo that surrounds the soul, though less ethereal, is similar in nature. Iamblichus and Proclus also insist on the necessity to purify this protective envelope (which dulls the senses) through knowledge, theurgy and the practice of virtue. This notion (so widespread at the time that one encoun-ters it also in hermetic literature) also involved postmortem apparitions, and all the specters with a human form who sneak in among the living and into their dreams.

19. E.L. Fortin, *La querelle de l'âme en Occident* (Paris, 1959).

20. See M. Spanneut, *Le Stoïcisme des Pères de l'Eglise: De Clément de Rome à Clément d'Alexandrie* (Paris, 1957); G. Verbeke, *L'évolution de la doctrine du pneuma des Stoïciens à Saint Augustin* (Paris, 1945).

21. *Oratio* XV (Paris: A. Puech, 1903).

22. Tertullian, *De carnis resurrectione* 7.

23. "In man, there is something higher than the earthly elements. Those whose soul is what it should be, firmly turn to God who is so close to them, and always desire to hear and think about Him," says Celsus (*Contra Celsum* 1.8). "Faith, truth, love and hope are religion's four foundations. One has to believe for there is no salvation for the man who does not turn to God; one must take great care and pains in learning the truth about God. Once one knows Him, one has to love Him." Porphyry, *Epistle to Marcella* 7.12.13.

24. Cf. De Labriolle, *La réaction païenne* (Paris, 1950), pp. 260-61; and J. Pépin, *Théologie cosmique et théologie chrétienne* (*Ambrose Ex 111-14*) (Paris, 1964).

25. See *City of God* 13 and 22; Sermon 242.

26. *Contra Celsum* 4.5.

27. 1 *Clement* 26.1. Cf. Ton H.C. Van Eijk, *La résurrection des morts chez les Pères Apostoliques* (Paris, 1974).

28. "And what you saw is not the body which is to be, but a bare kernel, perhaps of wheat or corn or some other grain" (1 Cor. 15.37).

29. See A. Michel, "Résurrection des morts," in *Dictionnaire de théologie Catholique* 49-62, col. 881-85.

30. *Enchiridion* 89, col. 273. Cf. A. Chollet, "Corps glorieux," in *Dictionnare de théologie Catholique*.

31. "What the movements of such bodies will be like, I dare not say, for I cannot imagine them. But their movements and their states as well as their external aspects, everything will be what it must be, since nothing unsuitable will be allowed to exist any longer. Naturally, where the spirit will go, there the body will be, and the spirit won't be able to aspire to anything unsuitable to either the spirit or the body.... It will be in itself the end of our desires, for it will be seen forever, insatiably loved, indefatigably praised...." *Enchiridion* 1786-88.

32. *Homilies on Hexameron* 7.1.

33. Cf. B. Teysseydre, *Anges, astres et cieux* (Paris, 1986), p. 187; F. Cumont, "Les anges du paganisme," *Revue d'histoire et des religions* 72 (1915); and A.J. Festugière, *La révélation d'Hermès Trismégiste* (Paris: 1944), 1.4.

34. *Letter to the Smyrnaeans* 4.2, trans. Cyril Richardson, *Early Christian Fathers* (New York: Macmillan: Collier Books, 1970).

35. Ignatius, *Letter to the Romans* 6.2 (trans. Richardson).

36. Quoted by De Labriolle, *La réaction païenne*, p. 419.

37. Peter Brown, *The Cult of the Saints: Its Rise and Function in Latin Christianity* (Chicago: University of Chicago Press, 1981).

38. *Encomium of Saint Theodore* 46.740b.

Translated by Anna Cancogni.

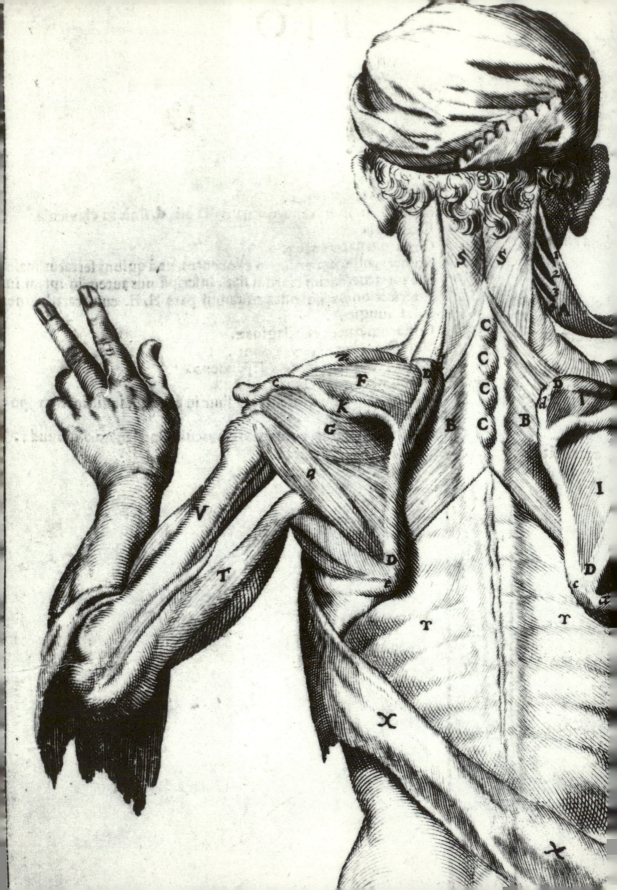

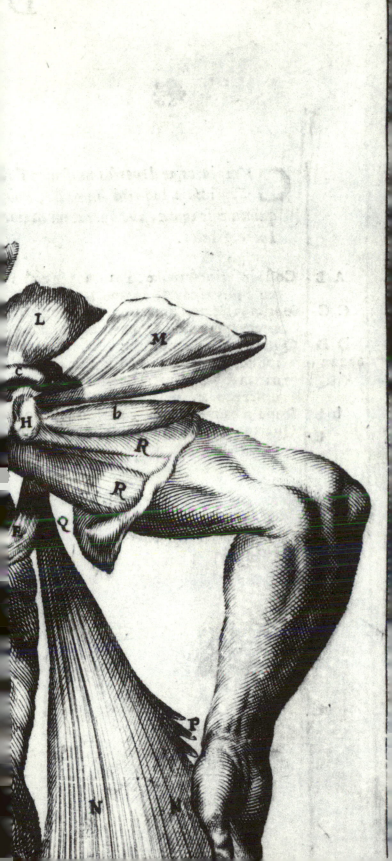